D1069073

The Innovation Decision in Soviet Industry

The Innovation Decision in Soviet Industry

Joseph S. Berliner

The MIT Press
Cambridge, Massachusetts, and London, England

Copyright © 1976
The Massachusetts Institute of Technology

This book was set in IBM Composer Press Roman by Techdata Associates Incorporated, and printed and bound by The Colonial Press Inc. in the United States of America.

Library of Congress Cataloging in Publication Data

Berliner, Joseph S.
    The innovation decision in Soviet industry.

    Includes bibliographical references and index.
    1. Russian—Industries. 2. Industrial organization—Russia. 3. New products. 4. Incentives in industry—Russia. I. Title.
HC336.24.B48   338'.0947   76-2390
ISBN 0-262-02118-8

Contents

Item one on the agenda was the question of whether socialism could work at all. It was not an unreasonable question in the nineteenth century. Private property was the foundation on which the modern industrial societies had been built, and one might well have doubted that a society could survive if that pillar of social organization were removed. The Bolshevik Revolution provided the first great test of the question. It took perhaps a quarter of a century of Soviet history to convince the doubters, but by the mid-thirties the point was largely conceded.

Item two on the agenda was the question of whether a socialist economy could work efficiently. The theoretical groundwork was laid in the famous essay by Oskar Lange[1] and by the outbreak of World War II it was widely conceded that in theory a socialist economy could solve the complex problems of allocating a nation's resources in a reasonably efficient manner. One could nevertheless continue to doubt that it could be done in practice. The question dominated postwar research on the Soviet economy and the main work is now largely done. The principles and practices by which resources are allocated in the USSR are now fairly well understood, and the extent to which they conform to the theoretical requirements of efficient allocation have been studied at length. The evidence suggests that the efficiency with which the Soviet economy converts its inputs of labor and capital into useful output is rather lower than that of developed capitalist systems.[2] But while the Soviet system of economic organization is not distinguished by its efficiency, it is nevertheless a thoroughly viable system of at least adequate efficiency.[3]

The third item on the agenda was the question of how rapidly the socialist economy could grow. It is an important question, for even if an economy is not particularly distinguished by the (static) efficiency with which it organizes itself, its proponents may nevertheless consider it to have succeeded in a significant sense if it demonstrated the capacity of rapid growth. Indeed, the goal of rapid growth must surely be considered among the most important objectives of the Soviet leaders; and not simply rapid growth, but a more rapid rate than that of the leading capitalist countries, if the long held goal of "overtaking and surpassing" the leading capitalist countries is to be taken seriously, as it surely must. The great volume of research that has been devoted to the measurement of Soviet growth has demonstrated that official Soviet claims about their growth rate have been greatly exaggerated. Nevertheless, the statistical record is fairly clear that Soviet growth exceeded that of the United States and most of the advanced capitalist countries before World War II. Since the war the Soviet growth rate has declined, but it remains comparable to that of such leading European countries as France and West Germany. Analysis of the sources of growth, however, has shown that Soviet growth has benefited to an unusual extent from very large increases in the amounts of capital and labor employed.[4] So prominent has this pattern of growth been that it is often described as the Soviet growth "strategy"; that is, growth due to very large rates of investment and of absorption of new labor. In the case of the advanced capitalist countries, however, attention has been turned in recent years to a rather different pattern of growth. In those countries it has been found that the rate of growth of output has been much larger than the growth rates of labor and capital. In the seminal paper by Robert Solow, for example, it was found that of the total increase in output per worker in the United States in the period 1909-1949, only about 10 percent can be ascribed to the increase in capital per worker. The other 90 percent is due to a variety of factors, prominent among which is technological change.[5] It has become clear in a rather dramatic way that the capacity to generate technological change is a most important property of an economy that has economic growth as one of its goals. These research findings about the growth pattern of the capitalist countries have had a marked influence in the agenda of debate on the Soviet economy. Interest has shifted away from item three—the capacity of the economy to grow—and item four of the agenda now holds the center of the stage.

Item four is the question of the capacity of the Soviet economy to generate technological change. It is a commonplace that the modern capitalist economy is characterized by a rapid rate of technological change. New consumer goods, new materials, new types of equipment, new production processes have created a world in which the expectation of change is part of the environment in which people live and work. It is evident that there is something about the structure of the capitalist economic system that promotes the constant innovation of new technology. Technological change is not universally regarded as a good thing, and there are serious questions about whether the rate of change is not too slow in some spheres of socioeconomic life and too rapid in others. But few would deny that on balance the growth of output has contributed to an increase in the national welfare and that the capacity to generate technological progress is a valuable property of an economic system. It is the innovative vitality of the modern capitalist economies that has placed the subject on the agenda of the analysis of the Soviet brand of socialism. It is not so much that questions of efficiency have lost their salience but rather that a new prominence has been given to a new question about the economy—its capacity to promote technological innovation.

The study of innovation has not been neglected in the past, but it has not been the main focus of interest of economists. It is now the main item on the agenda, and the purpose of this study is to contribute to the new effort to evaluate the Soviet economy with respect to its capacity to generate technological innovation.

The major portion of this study was supported by the National Science Foundation. Part of the work was carried out under a fellowship awarded by the John Simon Guggenheim Memorial Foundation. The Social Science Research Council also helped support part of the study. I wish to express my appreciation for their assistance.

The work was conducted at the Russian Research Center of Harvard University, which generously provided the office and library services and above all the invaluable collegiality of its staff. A number of the ideas presented here were launched at the luncheon-seminar program of the Center, conducted by Abram Bergson. I am grateful to him for those opportunities, as well as for his counsel on portions of the manuscript. I have benefited also from the advice of other people who were good enough to read varying portions of the manuscript: Janucz Zielinski, F. Trenery Dolbear, Jr., and Martin L. Weitzman. I wish to thank them, and also Jill Lion, who provided yeoperson research assistance in the early stages.

Just about everybody in the Center's office staff gave a hand in typing some part of this manuscript at some time. To Mary Towle, Rose DiBenedetto, Christine Balm, and Elizabeth Mead, my thanks.

Chapter 10 was published earlier, with a few changes, in the article, "Flexible Pricing and New Products in the USSR," in *Soviet Studies*, Vol. 27:4, October 1975, pp. 525-544. The editors of that journal kindly gave permission to use that material here.

Joseph S. Berliner

Notes

1. Oskar Lange and Fred M. Taylor, *On the Economic Theory of Socialism* (Minneapolis: University of Minnesota Press, 1938).

2. We shall use the term "capitalist" rather than "market" economies in order to exclude such socialist "market" economies as Yugoslavia from the category.

3. The most systematic treatment of the subject is by Abram Bergson, *The Economics of Soviet Planning* (New Haven: Yale University Press, 1964).

4. For an authoritative study, see Abram Bergson and Simon Kuznets, eds., *Economic Trends in the Soviet Union* (Cambridge: Harvard University Press, 1963), particularly Chaps. 1 and 8. For the postwar period, see also Abram Bergson, *Soviet Post-War Economic Development*, Wicksell Lectures 1974 (Stockholm: Almqvist & Wiksell, 1974).

5. Robert Solow, "Technical Change and the Aggregate Production Function," *Review of Economics and Statistics*, Vol. 39, August 1957, pp. 312-320. For the review of the quantitative evidence, see Edwin Mansfield, *The Economics of Technological Change* (New York: Norton, 1968), Chap. 2.

Chapter 1

Introduction

A technique is a method or procedure for accomplishing some desired end. A recipe is a description of a technique for baking a cake or cooking a stew. There are techniques of playing the violin, making love and making war, teaching children to behave, weaving cloth, and driving automobiles. The activities of all social institutions are conducted by means of techniques. Our study is concerned with the techniques employed in the economic institutions of the USSR for the production of goods and services.

A set of techniques is known as a technology. Steelmaking technology consists of all techniques for producing steel, and the society's technology, in general, consists of all the technologies for the production of goods and services. Technological progress may be said to occur when a new technique is added to the set. The notion may refer either to the advance of the technological knowledge contained in the society or to the improvement of the technology actually employed in production. Since the focus of our study is the process of the incorporation of technological knowledge into production, we shall employ the latter meaning of the notion of technological progress. Technological progress will be said to occur only when the technology employed in production may be said to have improved. Advances in technical knowledge that have not yet been incorporated into production will not be regarded as instances of technological progress.

A full description of a technology consists of artifacts and procedures. The artifacts of steel technology are the ores, blast furnaces, rolling mills, and foundries that are employed in the production process, and the various types of steel shapes and products that comprise the outputs. The procedures are the ways in which the equipment and materials are used in the production of the outputs. In the common usage, however, the term technology is reserved for the artifacts alone, and this is the usage that will be employed here. Technological progress will be said to have occurred only when the artifacts employed in production may be said to have improved or when a new or improved product is introduced. Increases in output per unit of input that may be due to new procedures such as improved management techniques, methods of economic planning, practices of production organization, quality control, and so forth, will not be regarded as instances of technological progress.[1] The subject of the study is therefore such things as machinery and materials and the products they produce.[2]

1.1. The Scope of the Study

The capacity of an economy to generate technological progress is a vast inquiry and we do not presume to undertake a study of that magnitude here. The scope of the study is limited in three ways: it deals not with the total Soviet economy but with one of its major sectors; it deals not with the total process of technological progress but with one major portion of it; and it deals not with all the factors that influence technological progress but with one major group of them.

The Focus on Industry

The study deals primarily with the civilian industrial sector of the economy. Innovation takes place of course in all sectors: agriculture, construction, transportation and communications, and so forth. Some of the same principles apply in all sectors, but each sector has special characteristics, and the larger the sectoral scope of the study the greater number of special considerations we should need to introduce. Industry, moreover, is the chief locus of innovative activity in a modern economy, for much of the innovation in the other sectors is based upon new products developed in the industrial sector, such as chemical fertilizers, construction and transportation equipment, and so forth.

There are of course differences within industry; among different branches of industry; between high priority and low priority industry; between producer goods and consumer goods industry; between large and small enterprises. Where the differences in innovational experience are substantial, account will be taken of them in the text. But on the level of the generalizations developed later, it is possible to regard all of industry as a reasonably homogeneous sector. The differences among groups within the industry sector may be regarded as variations around the central themes.

The Focus on Innovation

An instance of technological progress is a long chain of activities beginning with a new idea in the mind of man, proceeding through a variety of stages of research, experiment, development, design, production start-up, redesign, reengineering, and concluding with the attainment of the designed capacity of the new product or process. Our study deals only with those last links in the chain that are referred to as innovation. The identification of innovation as a distinct process is an established tradition in the analysis of capitalist economies, and it occupies the central place in Joseph Schumpeter's influential theory of capitalist development.[3] In that context innovation is distinguished from such other activities as invention and the ordinary management of enterprises; the power of the distinction is that it enables us to explain the troublesome notion of "profit" in a way that is more satisfactory than in the absence of the distinction.

It is not always the case that a category that has proved useful for the study of capitalist economies is also useful in the study of socialist economies, but this is such a case. The reason, however, is not because of any light it sheds on the notion of profit but because Soviet economic arrangements are such that the set of factors influencing the process of putting new products and processes into production are different from those that influence the earlier stages of the technological progress chain. The eminent physicist Professor Kapitsa has called attention to the use of the Russian word *vnedrenie*[4] to refer to the process of transferring technological knowledge from the laboratory into production. The word "*vnedrenie*", he writes, "carries the meaning in Russian that a forward motion encounters resistance in the surrounding medium. We have become so used to the fact that every achievement of science and technology meets with resistance in the process of adoption that we have for a long time employed the word "*vnedrenie*," hardly noticing that with this word we are describing conditions that are not normal in the adoption of new technology."[5] Nor are the problems associated with innovation a new thing; they are so deeply embedded in the structure of the economic system that scholars with long memories like Professor Kachalov recall *vnedrenie* as having been an issue in the early 1930s, when the basic economic arrangements of the Soviet economy were just taking form.[6] And indeed the whole tenor of Soviet discussion of technological progress treats the process of innovation as involving a different set of considerations from those that characterize the earlier stages of the chain. Because the innovation process is governed by a set of factors that are to some extent unique to that process, it makes for a manageable subject of investigation. And because the innovation process is an important—one might say crucial—portion of the chain, an understanding of that process is a contribution to the understanding of the total process of technological change.

The term "technological innovation" is sometimes used to refer only to the first appearance of a new product or process in the world. But it may also be used to refer to the first appearance of the new product or process in a country or in any enterprise in the country. We shall employ the last usage, for the interesting question is not merely the capacity of the system to introduce new products and processes for the first time in the world but also its capacity to promote the diffusion of innovations throughout the enterprises of the system. An act of innovation will be said to have occurred, then, whenever any enterprise introduces a product or process that it has never employed before. The term "innovation," unqualified, will refer to both products and processes; when the two need to be distinguished, they will be referred to as process innovation or product innovation.

One may imagine an economy in which innovation occurs rarely or not at all. The same products are produced year after year, although their quantities may increase and they may be produced in different proportions. And the same production processes are used, although they may be used in different combinations. One may imagine at the other extreme an economy in which innovation occurs at a very high rate. A large number of new and improved products pour forth year after year, and new and improved production processes are introduced with great frequency. The two economies differ with respect to what may be called their rates of innovation. It is the rate of innovation in Soviet industry that we wish to explain.

A satisfactory unit of measurement of innovation has not yet been devised. This unfortunately limits the possibility of testing quantitatively the propositions we shall offer in explanation of the Soviet rate of innovation, a matter to be discussed in Section 1.3. But for the main purpose of our study we do not require a precise quantitative unit. That purpose is to explain the ways in which certain properties of the economic system affect the innovation decision.

One such property, for example, is the price structure. Consider a group of enterprise directors faced with a choice between producing an established product next year or replacing it by a new one; assume for the moment that profit is a significant factor in making the choice. Then the decision to innovate will depend on the prices at which new products can be sold relative to the prices of the older ones. If the pricing system generates high new-product prices relative to old, one would expect a larger proportion of the directors to innovate than will be the case if the pricing system generates low new-product prices relative to old. It is in this sense that we may say the rate of innovation depends on the price structure. For propositions of this form one does not require a precise measure of that rate. One needs only to demonstrate that the rate of innovation will be greater or less according to whether the economy exhibits one or another property.

The properties of the economic system affect not only the frequency with which innovations are introduced but also the distribution of innovations among industries, between consumers and producers goods, between processes and products, between small scale and large scale, between labor-saving and capital-saving advances, and so forth. From time to time we shall have occasion to take note of these distinctions, and we may therefore regard the object of study as both the direction and the rate of innovation. But for our main purpose the notion of "innovativeness" is sufficiently expressed in the broad sense of a rate of innovation.

The Focus on the Social Structure of the Economy

A very large number of factors would have to be taken into account in a full explanation of the rate of innovation in an economy. Our study is limited, finally, in that it deals with only one group of such factors. Our interest is confined to the "working arrangements for resource use"—to use Abram Bergson's felicitous expression—that constitute the "system" part of an economic system.[7] It is the effects of the social structure of the economic system on the rate of innovation with which we shall be primarily concerned.

In limiting the study to economic structure, we must ignore the great many other factors that also influence the rate of innovation. Three groups of such nonstructural factors may be distinguished. One is the historical and cultural traditions of the society. Given the economic structure, a society with a long and honored tradition in science, technology, and enterprise may be expected to generate a higher rate of innovation than a society whose genius lay in other domains of human endeavor. Hence the innovative performance of the Soviet, or any, economy is no definitive test of the quality of the economic arrangements employed for allocating resources. The same economic structure employed in different societies would generate better or worse outcomes.

A second group of factors consists of various technical properties of the society and its economy: the tastes and values that influence the structure of demand, the distribution of factor endowments, the age structure of the capital stock, the interindustry structure of the economy, and so forth. If the capital stock in a certain industry is of recent vintage and highly durable, for example, one would expect a lower rate of innovation of new processes than if the capital stock were older and approaching replacement. Again, therefore, the innovativeness of the economy reflects not only the quality of its social structure but also the nature of its various technical characteristics.[8]

A third group of factors consists of the policies employed in governing the economy. The performance of any system—social, biological, mechanical—depends not only on how it is built but also on how it is run. The poor performance of an automobile may be due not to a defect in its structure but to the ineptness of its chauffeur. In the case of the Soviet economy, for example, it has been shown that a great many of its unsatisfactory outcomes may be ascribed to the policy of excessive "tautness" in economic planning.[9] With no change in the structure of the system, the economy would generate better outcomes if the governors did not strive to squeeze a greater output from it than it was capable of producing. Similarly, policies regarding the rate and direction of investment or expenditures on science and education affect the innovative performance of the economy.

The distinction between structure and policy is of crucial importance. "Down with the system" is the slogan of radicals, who believe that with the existing structure no policy changes could produce outcomes they would regard as satisfactory. To liberals, there is nothing wrong with the structure; it is because of inept or misguided policies that the outcomes are regarded as unsatisfactory. To conservatives, the outcomes are the best that can realistically be expected; neither policy changes nor structural changes are likely to make a better world. Differences in political positions reflect, to some extent, differences in values, in the degree to which a given set of outcomes is perceived as satisfactory or unsatisfactory. But they also reflect differences in beliefs about the nature of a social system—in the analytic "models" employed to explain and predict the changes in outcomes that may be associated with changes in structure and policies. Political positions are not easily influenced by the results of social analysis. But to the extent that they are, there are few contributions that social analysis can make that are more important than the clarification of the nature of the dependence of social outcomes on the social structure and on the social policy of a society.

The distinction we have drawn between the structural and nonstructural determinants of innovation is merely heuristic. No strict lines are intended to be drawn, and whether one regards a particular feature of the economy as structural or nonstructural depends on one's analytic objective. In the next section we shall define in some detail what we will regard as the fundamental elements of economic structure. They are the independent variables, so to speak. The nonstructural factors are the parameters of our inquiry. The analytic problem may then be formulated as follows: *given* the kinds of people who manage the scientific, technological, and industrial establishments of the USSR; and *given* the age structure of the capital stock; and *given* the level of expenditures on science and technology; what are the effects of the structural properties of the economy on the rate of innovation? Or in a different but closely related formulation, how does the rate of innovation vary with changes in the structural properties of the economy? While the nonstructural factors are not the focus of our inquiry, from time to time they will be drawn into the discussion. In those instances we are fortunate to be able to draw on a variety of published research, particularly the authoritative OECD study on Soviet science policy.[10]

A full explanation of the rate of innovation in Soviet industry would require analysis of the influence of all factors just discussed: cultural and historical factors, technical characteristics, governing policies, and economic structure. In limiting this study to economic structure alone, we must renounce any claim to having explained *the* rate of innovation in Soviet industry. The study is intended rather as a contribution to that explanation by the light it sheds on one part of it: on the relationship between the structure of the economy and its innovative performance.

How much of the innovative performance of the Soviet economy is left unexplained by a study the scope of which is limited to the effects of the economy's structure alone? Were the microeconomic data freely available, we might design a statistical model with which to seek a quantitative answer. Having no such data, no quantitative answer can be offered. All that can be said, on the basis of the qualitative evidence presented throughout this study, is that the decision to innovate or not is heavily influenced by the structure of the economic arrangements within which such decisions are made. The influence is clearly sufficiently great to warrant study.

1.2. Economic Structure and Innovation

The rate of technological innovation depends in part on the nature of the social arrangements by which economic decisions are made. The set of arrangements may be thought of as the structure of the economy. One may imagine a set of structural arrangements that so encourages new products and processes as to generate a very high rate of innovation. At the other extreme one may imagine a structure that so inhibits technological change as to lead to a very low rate of innovation. The question is, what are the properties of economic structure that may cause such variations in the rate of innovation? The question is equivalent to asking what are the fundamental properties of an economic system.

If it were a capitalist economy with which we were concerned, we would know at the outset what structural property to look for in seeking to explain the rate of innovation. The two-hundred-year history of economic analysis has taught us to look at the structure of markets for the explanation of a great many outcomes. If the market structure is monopolistic, we expect a rate of output less than optimal and an inefficient allocation of resources; and if the market structure is perfectly competitive, we expect optimal levels of output and efficient allocation. If the market is oligopolistic, we expect a high rate of innovation, but if it is perfectly competitive, we expect a very low rate. The structure of the economy's markets is the fundamental structural property in the explanation of decision making and resource allocation in capitalist economies.

In approaching the analysis of socialist economies, it is often the practice to take as the point of departure the more highly developed theory of decision making in capitalist economies. It is a fruitful approach, because many of the categories of analysis of capitalist economies are sufficiently abstract (abstracted, that is, from the specific institutional arrangements of capitalism) to be readily adaptable to the analysis of socialist economies. Where this has been the case, the analysis of Soviet economic processes and performance falls readily into the mainstream of general economic analysis. The measurement of Soviet national income and product, the analysis of its structure and its rate of growth, the estimation of the parameters of Soviet production functions, the measurement of aggregate factor productivity, the analysis of the input-output structure of the economy—in all these lines of research, the study of the Soviet economy is conducted in terms that differ little from the corresponding research on other economic systems.

But the concept of market structure is too specific to the institutions of capitalism to be readily adaptable to the analysis of the decision-making process under Soviet socialism. Hence in this central area of economic analysis, research on the Soviet economy has had to develop its own categories which, unfortunately, are rather specific to the institutions of Soviet-type economies. The result is an unhappy bifurcation in the field of economic analysis. One might have hoped that the understanding of economic systems in general would have been extended by the study of the Soviet species of economic system. But this has occurred to only a limited extent. The general economist continues to regard the Soviet economy as an aberrant case, perhaps a source of amusing anecdotes illustrating the surprising emergence of familiar economic principles here and there in that unexpected context but offering little instruction on ways of thinking about economic systems in general. Much research on the Soviet economy remains in a compartment by itself, containing its own language and its own categories.

We should like to show now that this unfortunate bifurcation is not necessary. It is possible to identify a set of structural properties that are common to all systems of economic decision making and that explain the outcomes of those systems. What distinguishes different economic systems is not that certain structural properties are present in some and not in others but that the precise form of those properties varies from system to system. Or in other words, all economic systems may be regarded as variations of the same set of fundamental structural properties, and variations in the outcomes of any economic system may be explained in terms of variations in those same structural properties. Those are the structural properties on which we shall draw in explaining the innovative process in the Soviet economy.

Prices and Decision Rules

The point of departure is the aforementioned seminal essay by Oskar Lange. The paper was a response to the argument that socialist societies could not allocate resources efficiently because they do not possess markets. Lange's contribution was to demonstrate that the question of whether or not the economic structure is based on markets is not fundamental in evaluating its outcomes. The fundamental properties are rather the nature of (1) the set of prices that express "the terms on which alternatives are offered," and (2) the set of rules that guide decision makers in choosing among alternatives. The markets of a private-property economy happen to be one type of social mechanism for generating prices, and the profit-maximizing objective of capitalists generates a set of rules for choosing among alternatives. But a system of markets is only one of many other possible ways of establishing prices and rules. If the socialist economy can establish the proper prices and decision rules, it has no need of the markets which are an element of economic structure unique to the historical stage of capitalism. Do not look for markets, says Lange, but look instead for the kinds of prices and rules that govern decisions in order to study the outcomes of economic activity. Following Lange, we shall regard the prices and the decision rules as the basic structural properties in our inquiry into the factors that determine the rate of innovation in the USSR.

Incentives

Lange was aware that prices and rules do not exhaust the explanation of the outcomes of a socialist economy. One may design an ideal price-setting mechanism and a perfect set of decision rules, and yet the socialist economy may fail to function in an optimal manner. But he did not pursue the search for the identification of those other structural properties that would explain the residual variation in the outcomes of economic activity. He limited his remarks to an expression of concern about the need to avoid somehow what he called "the bureaucratization of economic life," but he did not expand on the structural properties implied in that notion.

On the basis of knowledge developed since his time on the ways in which real socialist societies function, it is now possible to give formal expression to the properties of socialist economies that he may have had in mind. One is the set of incentives. In a capitalist system, profit maximization provides both the rules for decision making, and the incentive to make economic decisions. In the absence of the profit-maximizing objective, the designers of a socialist society must take care to establish incentives that would elicit the desired effort on the part of workers and managers and would motivate them to attend to the prices and follow the established decision-making rules. A poorly designed set of incentives may cause the economy to generate unsatisfactory outcomes, however well designed are its prices and decision rules. Incentives, then, are the third structural property to be studied in the search for the explanation of the rate of innovation.

Incentives must be distinguished from decision rules. A decision rule instructs the decision maker on the proper choice to make when confronted with a variety of possibilities. It may simply specify the objective to be pursued, leaving it to the decision maker to determine which possibility best attains that objective. Examples of such a rule would be "always make that decision that maximizes net profit," or "always choose that alternative that leads to the greatest percentage overfulfillment of the output plan." In other instances, the rule may be more specific, such as "choose that output at which marginal cost equals price," or "replace an obsolete machine by a new one when marginal cost on the old machine exceeds average cost on the new machine." A full set of decision rules is like a guidebook that contains an entry for every possible kind of decision that an enterprise may be expected to make, along with the recommended choice to be made in each case. The incentives may be thought of as another guidebook that lists all possible sets of results that an enterprise may attain and the rewards that the enterprise is entitled to claim for any listed set of results.

It is important to note that the rules and incentives are independent properties of the structure of an economic system. It is entirely possible to change the rules without changing the incentives, and vice versa. The rewards for certain results may be doubled, for example, without changing any of the decision rules. Or the rule may be changed from "maximize gross output" to "maximize profits," without changing the rewards available for all attained levels of output and profit. Thus a great many sets of incentives may be employed in conjunction with a great many sets of decision rules.

However, the design of a joint set of incentives and decision rules requires some careful attention. For they must articulate and be consistent with each other, else they will not lead to the desired kind of behavior. If the decision rule requires that a certain decision be made, but the incentives provide the major rewards for making some other kind of decision, the decision maker will be placed in an awkward position. As we shall see, the integration of decision rules with incentives is one of the most difficult problems faced by the designers of the Soviet economy.[11]

Prices, rules, and incentives may be regarded as three fundamental and independent properties of economic structure. But each of them is a complex set of relationships, and each may therefore be regarded as having its own structure. That is, when the relative prices of products change, we may regard it as a change in the structure of prices. Similarly, when some or all of the decision rules have changed, the structure of rules may be said to have changed. And when the relative amounts of the rewards for particular results have changed, the structure of incentives may be said to have changed. The structure of the economic system may be said to have changed whenever there has been a change in the structures of its prices, rules, and incentives.

Organization

The adequacy of incentives was part of Oskar Lange's concern about the danger of "bureaucratization" of a socialist system. But there was more to his concern than incentives alone. Empirical research on Soviet-type economies has devoted a great deal of attention to a set of problems that are clearly of central importance in understanding economic behavior in such systems but which have not yet been given adequate theoretical formulation.[12] They are the problems associated with the great complexity of the system of economic planning as it affects the enterprise, with the difficulties enterprises face in the purchase of inputs from other enterprises, with the pressures on enterprises to violate rules, falsify reports, neglect the quality of output, conceal information from the planners, and so forth. Much of that kind of economic behavior may be accounted for by the structure of prices, rules, and incentives. But there is a residual portion that remains unexplained, in the sense that even with perfect prices, rules, and incentives, certain of those activities would continue to occur. We propose to explain this behavior by reference to a fourth structural property, which may be called the organizational structure of the economic system.

By the organizational structure of a system we have in mind the units that comprise the system and the ways in which they relate to one another. A socialist (or any) economy may be organized in many different ways. There may or may not be a central planning board, and if there is, it may be assigned many different kinds of functions. There may or may not be organizational units called ministries, and if there are, they may also have many different kinds of functions. There may or may not be money and banks, and if there are, there are many ways in which the money supply may be regulated. In fact, in the history of the Soviet economy, many such organizational variations have been tried at one time or another.

It is a general assumption in the study of social systems that their performance varies with the way in which the systems are organized. We do not always know precisely how the outcomes may be expected to vary with variations in organizational structure, but that is very often the objective sought in the pursuit of knowledge. In the experimental study of small groups, for example, there are reasonably predictable ways in which the performance of groups (in solving some problem, for instance) will differ, according to whether the communications among the members are organized according to one plan or another. The performance of groups can be made to vary by varying properties other than their organizational structure: one can vary the sex or age of the players, or the nature of the problem requiring solution, or the incentives for solving the problem. The organization of the system is only one of the structural properties that affect performance.

While the empirical literature on the Soviet economy has dealt at great length with problems that are fundamentally organizational in character, there have been very few efforts at providing a theoretical framework for formalizing the organizational structure. David Granick proposed the first organizational model we are aware of, and Benjamin Ward's *The Socialist Economy* is the first monograph-length contribution to a formal organizational study of socialist economic systems. [13] We present no formal organizational model here, but in distinguishing the strictly organizational influences on innovation from those accountable for by the other structural properties, we hope to have made some contribution toward the development of an understanding of organizational problems.

One must emphasize again that the structure of a system's organization is independent of the system's other structural properties. One may abolish ministries and replace them with regional councils, without changing the price structure in any way. Or one could change the incentive structure without changing the organizational structure. Any change in any structural property, however, may be expected to change the outcomes of economic activity, and, we hope to show, in a predictable way. One can combine any organizational structure with any incentive structure in the design of an economic system, much as one can combine any number of eggs with any amount of flour in baking a cake. Some recipes yield inedible cakes, however, and some combinations of structural properties yield unworkable economic systems—with zero or very low outcomes. The art of social design, like that of engineering design, requires an understanding of the system structure, so that the structural elements chosen may be expected to yield satisfactory outcomes. Our formal knowledge of social structure is so much less sure than our knowledge of engineering structure that we must stand in awe of the task set for themselves by the designers of the Soviet economy. And if we find extensive defects in the design, they should be viewed in the light of the boldness of the task.

The Central Role of the Enterprise

One of the reasons that the study of decision making in the Soviet economy has not articulated with the corresponding study in capitalist economies is that the locus of decision making has been thought to be different in the two systems. In the capitalist economy the study of how economic decisions are made centers on the individual enterprise. The theory of the firm and the theory of markets (including demand) exhaust the explanation of the allocation of resources, at least in the pure laissez-faire economy. But in a Soviet-type economy an understanding of enterprise-level decision making may appear to contribute very little to the explanation of the allocation of resources, at least in the pure centrally planned economy. The major allocation decisions are made by the central government, and while enterprise-level decisions may affect the final allocation in some small ways, they are not a major part of the explanation. It is for this reason that theoretical work on centrally planned economies deals mainly with central decision making; with the efficiency of the balancing methods used by Soviet planners to obtain consistent input-output targets, for example, and with the methods of calculating economic returns to investment that are used in the central planning agencies. There have been a number of efforts to formalize enterprise-level decision making, sometimes cast in the same mathematical language that is used for capitalist enterprises; Lagrangian constrained maximization techniques, for example, and linear programming techniques.[14] Such analyses have offered some imaginative explanations of the observed behavior of Soviet enterprises, but they are rarely productive of significant propositions about the economic system. They are rather elaborate efforts to explain curious forms of economic behavior which, however, appear not to count for much in the overall allocation of resources in that economy. It would seem that there is little place for a theory of the firm in the analysis of the Soviet economy, and no place for a theory of central planning in the analysis of a market economy. This asymmetry has been one of the obstacles to the development of a comparative economics of capitalism and socialism.

The approach adopted here is a departure in that it places the enterprise at the center of the decision-making process in the Soviet economy, and therefore coordinate with the place of the enterprise in the capitalist economy. The allocation of resources is determined jointly by enterprises and the central planning apparatus, parallel to the joint behavior of enterprises and markets in the capitalist economy. This elevation of the role of the enterprise requires some justification. First, the location of the center of decision making in the central planning apparatus has never provided a fully satisfactory explanation of how resources actually do get allocated in the Soviet economy. The great mass of familiar evidence about managerial maneuverability within and around the planned magnitudes is a perpetual denial of the view that when one has explained what Moscow decides, one has explained it all. In rejecting that approach, then, we are rejecting an explanation that has never been fully satisfactory, and has always to be accompanied by a qualification of unknown magnitude—"except that enterprises may not respond in the planned way." The behavior of Soviet enterprises is not a mass of "random noise," however. It follows systematic rules, as we shall show, and ought not be regarded merely as a set of disturbances in a pattern of allocation basically determined by the central plan. More parts of the puzzle fall into place if we view the outcomes of Soviet economic processes as the result of the joint behavior of central planners and enterprises than if we regard the enterprise as simply carrying out the instructions of the planners "with certain exceptions."

Second, the instructions or "commands" issued to the enterprise by the central planners are not strictly exogenous to the enterprise's own decision-making behavior. There are many known ways in which enterprises themselves influence the instructions that are later handed down to them by the central planners. We know, for example, that enterprises respond to the "ratchet" principle of planning in such fashion as to influence the level of the targets that will eventually be assigned to them by the central planners.[15] But more important, a fundamental component of the planning process is the drawing up of draft plans by the enterprises, on the basis of a set of broad directives, or "control figures," issued by the central planners. The draft plans are then coordinated by the central planners and returned as final instructions to the enterprises. But the decisions made by the central planners are heavily influenced by the proposals made by the enterprises in the draft plans. If an enterprise, for example, decides to reduce costs by substituting material B for material A, it presents the decision tentatively in its draft plan. Ordinarily the central planners will accept the enterprise's decision, and the final plan will contain an instruction to undertake the recommended substitution. If the central planners resist the recommendation (either because they regard it as a poor decision; or because the total demand for material B exceeds the supply in the summary of the draft plans, and some enterprises must be denied the increase in its use they applied for), the enterprise may fight for it nonetheless, for we know that the process of hammering out final plans involves a great deal of bargaining.[16] In the end, the final official targets—the instructions—may not differ greatly from those originally decided upon by the enterprise and presented in its draft plan. There is no way of knowing how extensive enterprise influence is in this respect, but it appears that a great deal of central decision making turns out to be enterprise-level decision making; the enterprise is commanded to do what it had originally decided to do. This does not apply, of course, to such macroeconomic magnitudes as the overall rate of investment or its allocation among major sectors (although they too are affected by enterprise activity), but it does apply to a large range of year-to-year decisions on resource allocation. Hence, the structural elements that influence enterprise decision making explain more than simply the variations around the targets issued from above; they explain also a substantial proportion of those very targets. And for the same reason, the designers of a centrally planned economy, who must be expected to concentrate their efforts on the design of the central-planning decision-making process, must be careful not to neglect the decision-making process of enterprises. Defects in the latter process will have a substantial influence on the quality of the centrally made plans.

Third, the concern of this study is not economic decision making in general but a particular decision—the decision to innovate. One may conjecture that in a matter like innovation, the role of enterprise-level decision making may be relatively more important than in the normal static allocation decisions of management. It will be argued later, for example, that the slower the rate of technological change, the greater the effectiveness of central allocation; and in a world with no technological change, the central planners could eventually make every decision, leaving none at all to be made by enterprises. But the greater the rate of technological change, the less the capacity of central planners either to promote it or to plan it, and the greater the extent to which innovation is governed by the incentives, prices, and other structural properties of the system that govern the decisions of enterprises. There-fore, since innovation is the outcome that is the center of interest in this study, the case for taking enterprise decision making as the point of departure is somewhat stronger than if our concern were with the general allocation of resources.

Finally, the models that have been fashioned by Western analysts to explain the operation of the Soviet economy were designed in the early postwar period. The patterns of decision making they sought to explain were based on data collected largely from prewar Soviet sources. Among the countless ways in which the Soviet economy of the seventies differs from that of the thirties is that of sheer size. In the first year of the first five-year plan the Soviet industrial sector consisted of some 10 thousand enterprises, employing about 4 million workers and 137 thousand engineers and technicians, with a total fixed capital stock of about 3.3 billion rubles (at 1955 prices). Toward the end of the sixth five-year plan (1969), the number of workers in industry had increased sevenfold, the number of engineers and technicians twenty-sevenfold, and the stock of capital is officially estimated to have grown more than sixtyfold. The number of individual state industrial enterprises reached a peak of 212,000 by 1954, but subsequent mergers brought the number down to about 50,000 in 1969.[17]

It is reasonable to expect that as the scale of a centralized system grows the effective control by the center over the units decreases. One may imagine a number of enterprises so small that the outcomes are totally determined by the decisions of the center. As the number of enterprises increases, some small portion of the decisions begin to be made by (or increasingly influenced by) the enterprises, but the outcomes are still largely explained by the decision of the center. As the number of enterprises continues to grow, the portion of the outcomes explained by central decisions continues to diminish, and the portion explained by enterprise decisions increases. Indeed, somewhere further along in the process of growth a point may be reached at which the portion of the outcomes due to enterprise decision making may exceed that due to direct central decision making. From that point on a model designed to explain centralized decision making may be less useful for the explanation of economic outcomes than one designed to explain the decisions of both central planners and enterprises.

When one reads the monographic literature on Soviet industry based on the evidence of the thirties, such as David Granick's *Management of* the *Industrial Firm in the USSR*, one gets the impression that at that time "Moscow" had a fairly intimate knowledge of the operations of their enterprises.[18] The industrial ministers maintained close contact with their major enterprises, and the heads of their chief administrations supervised the others closely. But by the fifties the center's knowledge of what their enterprise managers were actually doing was greatly reduced. Evidence of the concern over this creeping decentralization was the 1957 reorganization of the whole system of economic administration. The Moscow-based industrial ministers were abolished, and their functions transferred to some hundred-odd newly formed regional economic councils. The reorganization reflected the view that effective central control over the economy had grown weaker over time, and the shift to regional economic councils was an attempt to reassert that control.[19] The attempt appears to have been unsuccessful, and in 1965 the regional council system was abolished and the older ministry system restored. But the problem that motivated the 1957 reorganization has not vanished and has probably grown more severe as the scale of the economy has continued to expand.

Hence, in seeking to explain the process of resource allocation in the early period, the notion of the centralized "command economy," as it was named by Gregory Grossman, provided a successful explanatory model.[20] But we may have now approached the time when that model explains less about how the system really operates than one designed to explain the joint behavior of planners and enterprises. We shall not attempt here to construct a formal model of that kind. But our study of the effects of enterprise decision making on innovation may be a contribution toward such a model.

Summary: The Structural Hypothesis

The argument of this section may be expressed in the form of a hypothesis: given the cultural and historical traditions, the technical characteristics, and the policies of government, the outcomes of any economy are fully explained in terms of four fundamental properties of economic structure: prices, decision rules, incentives, and organization. In statistical terms, the hypothesis states that the variability among the economic outcomes of various possible states of a given economic system, or of various economic systems, that is not explained by nonstructural differences, is fully explained by the four structural variables. The hypothesis has been expressed in its strongest terms not in the belief that it could be sustained in that form but in order that its form stand

forth clearly. Loosely speaking, the hypothesis is that these four structural properties explain most of what it is that one wants to explain in seeking to understand how different kinds of economic arrangements work. It is an expression of what is believed to be "important," or what one ought to look for, in seeking an explanation of such economic behavior as innovation.

In the opening remarks of this section, it was noted that if it were a capitalist economy with which this study were concerned, one would know what structural property to look for in explaining innovative behavior—namely, the structure of markets; but that in examining a socialist economy, one does not quite know what to look for. The structural hypothesis presumes to provide the answer. It specifies the structural properties to examine in explaining behavior, in both socialist and capitalist economies. In the latter case one would still turn to market structure if the objective of the analysis were to understand that economy alone. But for the purposes of comparing capitalist economies with others, market structure will not do. One requires some more fundamental structural elements that are not specific to the capitalist economic arrangements. The four structural properties are proposed as precisely those elements. The "market structure" of a capitalist economy may be regarded as a name given to certain historically-specific forms of the same general structural properties; monopoly, for example, is an economic arrangement in which the decision rule is "produce that output at which marginal cost equals marginal revenue"; the price exceeds marginal cost by a specifiable amount; the incentive is profit; and the organizational structure is one in which the enterprise is a single seller in a market with many buyers. The enterprise in a centrally planned economy differs from this only in that it is characterized by different specific forms of each of the same structural properties. Thus the hypothesis proposes a set of universal elements in terms of which economic systems may be readily compared. Because these four properties are thought to be of universal applicability, it may be hoped that the analysis of the Soviet economy to follow will not be regarded as specific to the structure of a Soviet-type of economy but as a contribution to the understanding of economic systems in general.

The study proposes to show that the innovation decision in the USSR is fairly completely accounted for in terms of these four structural properties of the economic system. But how can one prove a proposition of this sort? And by what kind of evidence can it be supported?

There are indeed certain problems in verifying propositions of this kind in the case of the Soviet economy that require some discussion in this introductory chapter.

1.3. The Quantitative Study of the Soviet Economy

One can be said to "understand" a system when one has a theory about it. The basis of a theory is the specification of those factors or variables that account for the outcome one wishes to explain or predict. The preceding section provides the basis for a theory of the innovative performance of the Soviet economy. It states that to explain the rate of innovation in the USSR, one must look at four properties of the structure of the economy: its prices, decision rules, incentives, and organization.

The basis of a theory tells us only that some outcome is affected by a certain set of factors, but it does not yet tell us precisely how the explanatory factors affect the outcome. A proper theory consists of a set of propositions, testable it is hoped, specifying precisely how the outcome may be expected to vary under various conditions or values of the explanatory factors. A number of such propositions are developed in the text. They take the form, for example, of the assertion that the higher the prices of new products relative to those of established products, the greater the rate of innovation of new products; or the greater the material incentive for producing new products relative to established products, the greater the rate of product innovation will be.

Up to this point the strategy of research on the Soviet economy takes the same form as that of economic research in any society. But it is in the attempt to test behavioral propositions that one faces a serious obstacle in the case of the Soviet economy that does not arise in the case of many other societies. Ordinarily one would seek to test behavioral propositions by gathering statistical data in order to see whether one can infer from the data the existence of the postulated relationship among the variables. In the best of cases one can estimate the values of the parameters that relate the variables, and those values can be employed with other data for predicting the behavior of the variables. The data are ordinarily published by government or trade associations or research organizations. If the data are not available in the form needed for the research, the analyst generates them himself if he can find the funds. If he requires data on the innovation experience of enterprises, he may circulate a questionnaire and often succeeds in collecting the data in the form in which he needs them.

The unfortunate fact is that the data needed for undertaking serious quantitative research on Soviet enterprises are generally lacking. The Soviet government publishes a variety of quantitative data of a macroeconomic nature: on the national income and its main components, on the production levels of a great variety of commodities, on foreign trade, on financial flows of various kinds. The data permit certain kinds of macroeconomic quantitative study of the Soviet economy; one can study aggregate production functions, and one can develop national income accounts with some degree of disaggregation among the main components and sectors of origin. But virtually no data are available that can be used for quantitative microeconomic study of the economy. One finds occasional reports of surveys of the experience of enterprises, and scattered data on individual enterprise performance. But it is impossible to assemble data with which to test propositions of a microeconomic nature. If one wished to test propositions on the effect of enterprise size on the rate of innovation, or on the effect of various incentive schemes on innovation, one cannot expect to do so on the basis of quantitative data on the experience of individual enterprises.

If it were a more open society, the analyst could circulate questionnaires among enterprises and reasonably hope to enlist their cooperation in providing the data needed to test propositions on managerial behavior. The student of the Soviet economy looks with envy at the depth of analysis achieved in such work as that of Edwin Mansfield on the United States economy and C. F. Carter and B. R. Williams on the British, both based on data collected by surveys of enterprises.[21] The collection of survey data in the USSR is obviously impossible for the outside analyst, although Soviet researchers apparently are able and do collect certain data of this kind. But there is another reason why the quantitative testing of propositions is much more difficult in the microeconomic analysis of the Soviet economy. The reason is that the organization of enterprises is established by the state, and when a certain organizational arrangement is decided upon it tends to be applied to all enterprises. The managerial organization of enterprises tends to be the same everywhere, with slight exceptions to take account of special conditions in individual industries. The incentive systems tend also to be the same. But to test hypotheses on behavior, one requires a certain scatter of points so that one can compare, for example, enterprises with one type of managerial structure with those of another, or one type of incentive system with another. Because of the uniformity of organizational properties even if the data were available, satisfactory tests of behavioral propositions would often be impossible to conduct.

Hence the analyst who insists on quantitative microeconomic research must ply his trade somewhere other than on the study of the Soviet economy. But if one's objective is to understand the Soviet economy, one must be content with something less than the kind of data he would require if he were working on the economy of another country. In particular, the kinds of propositions we shall develop here must be tested by standards that fall short of those one would employ in studying the economy of a more open society. The tests must depend upon such evidence as the published accounts of the decision-making process by officials of Soviet enterprises and by economists and others who have greater access than foreigners to the experience of their own country. The evidence is generally qualitative, occasionally supported by scattered quantitative data that must be regarded as illustrative rather than sufficiently systematic to support genuine quantitative tests of propositions. One must rely further on the logic of the propositions in the light of the qualitative evidence—whether they "make sense," or what historians and jurists refer to as the "weight of evidence." These are not proofs as we would use the term if one were fortunate enough to be able to apply statistical and econometric tests. But they are the best that can be done.

1.4. Outline of the Argument

The first structural property with which the study begins is the structure of organization. Chapter 2 describes the organizational units that comprise the economic system, with particular attention to those that are most directly involved in the innovation process. The other chapters of Part I study the effects of that organizational structure upon the enterprise's decision to innovate. The effects of organizational structure are transmitted to enterprises through both the supply of its inputs and the demand for its output. Chapter 3 examines the effects of organization structure on the enterprise's supply of materials and equipment, Chapter 4 deals with the supply of research and development services, Chapter 5 with the supply of labor, and Chapter 6 with the supply of financial resources. The question asked in each chapter is: What is the effect on the enterprise's decision to innovate, of the ways in which the Soviet economy organizes the supply of these inputs to its enterprises? Chapter 7 concludes Part I with the corresponding question regarding the demand for the enterprise's output: the effect on innovation of the ways in which the economy organizes the selling, or distribution, of the enterprise's output. Throughout this part it is assumed that prices, incentives, and decision rules are given.[22]

Part II deals with the influence of the price structure on the innovation decision. The general problem, discussed in Chapter 8, is that the profit rates on new products tend to be lower than those on older products. The source of the problem is to be found in part in the cost behavior of new products, which is discussed in Chapter 9. Chapters 10 and 11 examine various special pricing methods that have been introduced to take account of the unique cost behavior of new products. Product improvement, an important form of innovation, presents certain pricing problems of its own, which are taken up in Chapter 12. This part concludes with the effects of the methods of price administration, as distinct from the principles of pricing, on the innovation decision.

Given the structure of organization and prices, managers follow certain rules in choosing among alternative production programs. The rules of choice and the incentive structure from which they are derived are the subject of Part III. Chapter 14 discusses the incentives and rules that govern decision making in general. Certain special incentives established to encourage the decision to innovate are examined in Chapter 15. Chapter 16 evaluates the general effect of the structure of incentives on the innovation decision. The concluding chapter summarizes the strengths and weaknesses of the economic structure and offers some observations on the prospects for accelerating the rate of innovation.

Notes

1. "Social innovations" of that kind, however, may have the effect of increasing the rate of technological innovation. In the present study, such social arrangements are our independent variables, while technological progress is the dependent variable. The objective is to study the influence of social arrangements on the rate of technological progress.
2. Improved or new services such as faster and safer transportation will be regarded as instances of technological progress only if they are the product of improved technology such as aircraft.
3. Joseph Schumpeter, *The Theory of Capital Development* (Cambridge: Harvard University Press, 1936).
4. The usual English translation is "introduction," as in the expression "introduction of new technology into the economy."
5. P. L. Kapitsa, *Teoriia, eksperiment, praktika (Theory, Experiment, and Practice)* (Moscow: "Znanie," 1966), p. 7.
6. Cited in Alexander Korol, *Soviet Research and Development: Its Organization, Personnel, and Funds* (Cambridge: The MIT Press, 1965), p. 5.
7. Abram Bergson, *The Economics of Soviet Planning* (New Haven: Yale University Press, 1964), Chap. 1.

8. The expression "structure of the economy" is very broad and may refer to any of a great number of structural properties. Those listed earlier may be called "technical" structural properties. The "technical" structure of the economy may be distinguished from its "social" structure, the latter referring to the social arrangements for producing and distributing goods and services. In this study the expression "structure of the economy" will refer to its social structure.

9. Holland Hunter, "Optimum Tautness in Developmental Planning," *Economic Development and Cultural Change*, Vol. 9:4, July 1961, pp. 561-572.

10. E. Zaleski, J. A. Kozlowski, H. Wienert, R. W. Davies, M. J. Berry, and R. Amman, *Science Policy in the USSR* (Paris: OECD, 1969).

11. The problem of integrating incentives and decision rules does not arise in the classical capitalist economy in which the decision maker is an autonomous owner entrepreneur. His incentive is profit, and he has no reason to follow any rules other than those that maximize his profit. Incentives and decision rules are therefore automatically integrated. In the Soviet economy, however, as in the modern capitalist corporation, enterprise decisions are made by hired managers. The "owners" must inform the managers about the decision rules they are to follow, and an incentive system must be designed that will motivate the managers to follow those rules. In any artificially designed social system there is ample room for error, and one ought not expect a perfect articulation of the structural elements.

12. See, for example, Joseph S. Berliner, *Factory and Manager in the USSR* (Cambridge: Harvard University Press, 1957); David Granick, *Management of the Industrial Firm in the USSR* (New York: Columbia University Press, 1954); Janos Kornai, *Overcentralization in Economic Administration* (London: Oxford University Press, 1959).

13. David Granick, "An Organizational Model of Soviet Industrial Planning," *Journal of Political Economy*, Vol. 67, April 1959, pp. 109-130; also *Soviet Metal-Fabricating and Economic Development* (Madison: University of Wisconsin Press, 1967), Chap. 7; Benjamin Ward, *The Socialist Economy: A Study of Organizational Alternatives* (New York: Random House, 1967).

14. Edward Ames, *Soviet Economic Processes* (Homewood, Ill.: Irwin, 1965).

15. If an enterprise overfulfills a plan target in a given period, the central planners often raise the required target for the next period to the level attained in the given period. This has been called the "ratchet" principle (Berliner, *Factory and Manager*, pp. 78-79). Managers, aware of this practice, tend therefore to avoid overfulfilling plan targets by too large an amount. In this way, the enterprise can influence the level of the target assigned to it for next period.

16. Berliner, ibid., pp. 224-230.

17. TsSU, *Strana sovetov za 50 let (The Land of the Soviets After Fifty Years)* (Moscow: Statistika, 1967), pp. 34, 36, 62; TsSU, *Narodnoe khoziaistvo SSSR v 1969 godu* (The USSR National Economy in 1969) (Moscow: Statistika 1970), pp. 45, 165, 497; TsSU, *Narodnoe khoziaistvo SSR* (The USSR National Economy) (Moscow: Gosstatizdat, 1956), p. 42.

18. David Granick, *Management of the Industrial Firm in the USSR* (New York: Columbia University Press, 1954).

19. Another objective of the reorganization was to remove the dysfunctional effects of ministerial "empire building" and of the departmental barriers that had been erected among ministries.

20. Gregory Grossman, "Notes for a Theory of the Command Economy," *Soviet Studies*, Vol. 15, October 1963, pp. 101-123.

21. Edwin Mansfield, *Industrial Research and Technological Innovation* (New York: Norton, 1968); C. F. Carter and B. R. Williams, *Industry and Technical Progress* (London: Oxford University Press, 1957).

22. In the analysis of each structural property it is assumed that the others are given. That assumption weakens the generality of the conclusions, for the structural properties are probably not linearly independent. That is to say, the effect of a given organizational structure on the

decision to innovate is not independent of the kind of incentive structure or price structure with which it is conjoined. The effects of interdependence are noted and discussed at various places in the text; for example, Sec. 4.3 (The Problem of Monopoly) and Sec. 7.3 (The New Sales Rule).

Part I

The Structure of Organization

Chapter 2

The Structure of Economic Organization

Thousands of Soviet managers make thousands of decisions every day. Among the decisions are the choice of materials to use, the size of inventories to maintain, the kinds of equipment to order, the scheduling of production operations, the planning of regular repair and maintenance operations, the order in which goods are to be shipped to different customers, the payment of taxes, the arrangement of bank credits, the decision to sue a supplier for breach of a delivery contract, the contents of a report demanded by the local Party secretary, the distribution of bonus funds among workers, the products to be included in the production program of next year's plan.

Within this vast array of decisions, there is one that is the subject of our study. That is the decision to introduce a new product or a new manufacturing or technological process. The innovation decision competes with the thousands of other decisions that have to be made. With limitations of time and resources, a decision to innovate means that some other problems will be less well attended to, some other activities will be forgone, and some resources shifted from other potential uses.

Sometimes the manager has no choice. He may be obliged simply to act on an order. But generally he has a range of choice. The decision not to innovate is usually available as an alternative to innovating. He can often continue for a long time to produce his established line of products in the familiar old way. Or he can decide to introduce a new product or change over to a promising new process.

The decision to innovate or not, like all the decisions managers must constantly make, is heavily influenced by the structure of the economic system. Given one set of structural arrangements, a thousand managers may introduce a hundred innovations a year. Given another set, they may introduce none. The frequency with which the decision to innovate is made depends on the four properties of the economic structure that we have identified: its prices, decision rules, incentives, and organization. The subject of this part is the influence of organization.

The organizational structure of a system refers to the units that comprise the system and the ways in which they relate to one another. The notion may be illustrated by an example from a field of social research that has been singularly successful in studying the relationship between social structure and performance. That is the experimental study of small groups. In the studies conducted by Alex Bavelas and his associates, for example, a series of experimental five-man groups of students was assigned a common task.[1] One subset of groups was assigned an "autocratic" structure in which one member could communicate with the other four, but the other four could communicate only with him. A second group was organized as a "ring"; each member could communicate only with those on either side of him. Other groups were organized according to other communication patterns. The performance of the groups differed systematically with respect to such measures as number of errors, morale, and the appearance of leadership. The groups consisted of the same kinds of people, with the same incentives and the same "decision rules." They differed only with respect to a single variable, organizational structure, which in this case happened to be the structure of communications. It was the variations in organizational structure that explained the variations in performance.

It is a long way from the laboratory to the real world, and our knowledge is still too primitive to enable us to transfer principles learned in experimental situations to the real world. And we may never really be able to do so. "No experiment," someone said, "can ever duplicate a Socrates being nagged by a Xanthippe." But if we possess no tested principles with which to explain the real-world consequences of particular organizational structures, we can ignore those consequences only at our peril. In fact, some of the most interesting problems of innovation in the Soviet economy appear to be related precisely to the organizational structure of the economy, which is why we have chosen to open the study with that particular property of economic structure.

To study the organizational structure of a social system is to study who does what to whom and with what consequences. In this chapter we identify the who and the whom—the structural units of the economic system—and describe the transactions among them that constitute the economic process.

2.1. The Units of Economic Organization

Four types of organizational units play the crucial roles in the innovation process. They are enterprises, ministries, research and development institutes, and various government agencies. We shall present in this chapter a brief description of each type of unit and the principal kinds of transactions that occur among them. Only those institutions will be identified that play a role in the innovative process and are to be discussed in the body of our study. The description will also be limited to the information required by the argument to follow; readers who wish more information on the system of economic organization and research and development are referred to the works cited in the notes.

Prescript on a New Organizational Unit: The Corporation

After this chapter was written, the Soviet government and Party adopted a resolution in April 1973 entitled "On Certain Measures for the Further Improvement of Industrial Management."[2] The resolution promulgates the establishment of a new type of industrial organization called a "production association," to be formed by the merger of a number of enterprises. The name of the new organization is best rendered in English as a "corporation," for in intent and design it is rather like a large multicompany corporation in a capitalist economy.

Although the corporation is a merger of several preexisting enterprises, it is itself an enterprise in the Soviet legal sense of having its own bank account and financing its expenditures out of its own revenues. Hence it is still the case that the four basic types of organizational units in the innovation process are, as stated above, enterprises, ministries, R & D institutes, and other government agencies. The numbers, sizes, and relationships among these units, however, will differ in various ways after the merger movement is completed from the relationships set forth below.

The resolution orders the ministries to complete the process of establishing the corporations by the end of 1975. It will take the experience of several more years before sufficient evidence is available for analyzing and evaluating the effects of the corporation reform. Even at that time, the significance of the reform could not be assessed except in the light of the organizational structure it replaced.

The evidence on which this study is based derives from the structure of the Soviet economy prevailing through 1973, and to a diminishing extent during 1974-1975 when the decree was in process of implementation. The descriptions of economic institutions in this and later chapters have therefore been left essentially as they had been written, before the promulgation of the decree. At appropriate places, however, the changes mandated by the decree have been noted, and on occasion some speculation has been offered on the likely consequences, particularly in the concluding chapter.

Among the major objectives of the corporation reform is the acceleration of technological progress by eliminating some of the obstacles to innovation analyzed in this book. Our general conclusion is that it will succeed in some limited respects but that many of the major considerations that enter into the decision to innovate are not affected by the reform. If that conclusion is correct, then most of what is said later about the behavior of "enterprises" could be said about the "corporations" of the future. The names of the players will have changed, as it were, but the way the innovation game is played will be fundamentally the same.

The Enterprise

The basic organizational unit of the economic system is the enterprise (*predpriiatie*).[3] The enterprise consists of a group of people and a collection of physical assets for conducting the work of production. At the head is a director who bears the primary responsibility for the enterprise's performance. He is assisted by a chief engineer who is his principal deputy, and by a middle-level managerial staff who conduct the work of the various functional and production departments. The heads of the production departments (foundry, assembly shops, machine shops), or "shop chiefs," are in charge of the general production operations; when an innovation is introduced, it is they who must carry it out. The functional departments are those responsible for accounting, finance, purchasing, sales, personnel, wages, planning, quality control, and so forth. The names are familiar, and indeed an American corporation official would find much that is familiar in the managerial organization of the Soviet enterprise.

In an enterprise undertaking an innovation, every department may find itself involved in one way or another. The planning department sees to it that the innovation is included in the plan, the purchasing department contracts for the delivery of materials and equipment, the finance department negotiates the bank loans or whatever source of finance had been planned, and of course the production officials prepare their shops for introducing the new product or process. But while all departments may be involved as part of their normal work, there are some departments that are more centrally concerned with innovation.

The design department is responsible for product improvement and development.[4] It produces the drawings and blueprints for a new product or a new production installation. It may be a special order job, in which a machine or other product is built to the specifications of a customer.

Or it may be the design of an improved or a new product that the enterprise intends to introduce into regular production. When the design work is contracted out to an outside organization, the design department represents the enterprise in the negotiations.

The technological department works out the process for producing the new product that has emerged from the design department.[5] They are responsible for determining the layout of the machines, choosing the best production techniques, and determining which components of the new product should be produced within the plant and which should be bought from or subcontracted to other enterprises. They work, of course, in consultation with other departments; they may recommend to the design department changes in the original design on the basis of production considerations, and they collaborate with the planning department in calculating the costs of alternative production techniques or in choosing between in-house production or subcontracting the production of components.

The bureau of innovations and inventions[6] is charged with the encouragement of inventive and production-improving activity among the workers and engineers in the enterprises. It provides small-scale facilities for inventors to putter around in and for testing and making mock-ups of their ideas. The bureau also maintains a register of production improvements and inventions that have been certified as accepted, and it arranges for the inventor to receive the monetary honorarium to which he is entitled.

Until recently, enterprises rarely had formal departments for research and development. Such R & D as was done within enterprises was carried out informally in one of the three departments described earlier. In recent years, however, many enterprises have been authorized to organize "scientific research laboratories." About 33,000 such laboratories were reported to have been in existence in 1967.[7] Presumably they are small, appropriate to the more parochial requirements of the enterprises. In a few cases, very large enterprises have been permitted to create full blown R & D institutes. The first and most celebrated of these is the "Scientific-Research, Design, and Technological Institute of Heavy Machine Building," which belongs to the famous Urals Machine-building Plant.[8]

The typical Soviet enterprise is quite large compared with those of other countries. In 1963 only 15 percent of all Soviet industrial enterprises employed fewer than 50 workers. In the United States and Japan the corresponding figures were 85 percent and 95 percent. Of all Soviet industrial enterprises, 24 percent employed over 500 workers, compared to 1.4 percent in the United States and 0.3 percent in Japan.[9] Dr. Kvasha of the Institute of Economics, who developed the data for the USSR, has argued that there are organizational advantages to small-scale establishments and has urged that more of them be organized in the USSR. The Soviet tendency, however, has been in the opposite direction. In recent years, there have been a number of experiments with new forms of organization which further increase the size of the enterprise. One such organizational form is known as the *firm.*[10] Firms are enterprises formed by the merger of a number of smaller enterprises; generally enterprises in similar lines of production. The new corporations of the future, however, will consist of more and larger enterprises, scattered over a larger expanse of territory, and combining both vertical and horizontal principles of integration. The size structure of Soviet (corporate) enterprise will therefore diverge even more widely from that of other countries.

Government Agencies

If the enterprise is the lowest-level production unit of the economy, the highest unit is a group of organizations that may be collectively designated as government agencies.[11] The work of governing the economic activity of the fifty-thousand-odd industrial enterprises is conducted by such organizations as the Central Committee of the Communist Party and its executive organ, the Politburo; and the national Parliament (Supreme Soviet) and its executive organ, the Presidium of the Council of Ministers. To conduct the massive work of government, the Politburo and the Council of Ministers have organized a variety of organizations such as the State Planning Committee and a series of specialized State Committees.

The State Committee on Science and Technology (Gostekhnika) bears the chief responsibility for the coordination of R & D work throughout the economy. It is the chief adviser to the central government on national technological policy, the heart of which is the distribution of R & D funds among the various promising lines of development. It may create new scientific establishments, it supervises the execution of major research projects, and it oversees the process of getting them into the final stages of production.[12]

The USSR Academy of Sciences consists of about 600 members who bear the responsibility for supervising the greater part of the scientific research work of the country. Its executive body is a Presidium of about 30 members. The Academy's jurisdiction includes about 200 scientific establishments employing about 30,000 scientists. The Academy's research work is concentrated in the natural and social sciences and is oriented primarily toward basic rather than applied research. Through its division of Technical Services, however, the Academy conducts ongoing analysis of the practical application of the work being done in its institutes. It is obliged to collaborate with enterprises and submit proposals to the State Committee on Science and Technology regarding applied research and development leading to innovations.[13]

The State Planning Committee (Gosplan) is the central government's chief agency for conducting the work of general economic planning. Part of that work consists of the planning of R & D and of innovation. That work is conducted in the Committee's Department for the Comprehensive Planning of the Introduction of New Technology into the National Economy.[14] In drawing up those plans, the Committee relies heavily on the recommendations of the State Committee on Science and Technology, but the responsibility for decisions apparently lies with the Planning Committee.

The State Committee for Inventions and Discoveries is the government's agency for administering the patents system. It receives patent applications from individuals and research institutes and determines the size of the honoraria for the inventors. It administers the network of patents bureaus located in the ministries and in many research institutes.[15]

These are the central government agencies with which the innovating enterprise is most likely to have to deal. But many other agencies are involved in some portion of the innovation process as part of their regular work. The Ministry of Finance, the State Bank (*Gosbank*), and the Bank for Construction (*Stroibank*) provide the grants, credits, and subsidies available to the innovating enterprise under the provisions of a variety of statutes.[16] The State Committee on Supply (*Gossnab*), which supervises the interenterprise flow of materials and equipment, bears the responsibility for providing for the special and often unforeseeable needs of innovators. The enterprise planning a major innovation that requires a substantial volume of construction work may be obliged to negotiate with the office of the State Committee on Construction (*Gosstroi*). In the production of new products for export or the installation of new imported equipment or production under license from a foreign country, the Ministry of Foreign Trade, the State Committee on Foreign Economic Relations, or the All-Union Chamber of Commerce may be involved.[17] In one way or another, most of the agencies of central government and their offices may have to be negotiated with at some point in the enterprise's innovative activity.

Ministries

One may imagine a socialist economic structure in which the central government assumes responsibility for the direct supervision of each of the 50,000 enterprises. This may be the case if the central government limits to a very small number the kinds of instructions it issues to the enterprises; for example, if the central government does little more than announce the legal prices at which all goods must be sold. But if the economic arrangements adopted require fairly detailed instructions to be given to the enterprises, the appropriate organizational structure requires some administrative intermediaries between the central government and the enterprises. It would be too great a task for the center to try to supervise directly each of the enterprises under the Soviet system of central planning. Hence, the third structural unit, the ministry, is interposed between the central (and republic) governments and the enterprises.

There are four types of industrial ministries in the USSR:

USSR ministries

1. USSR all-union ministries (such as the USSR All-Union Ministry of the Chemical and Petroleum Machinery Industry).
2. USSR union-republic ministries (such as the USSR Union-Republic Ministry of the Meat and Dairy Products Industry).

Republic ministries

3. Republic union-republic ministries (such as the RSFSR[18] Ministry of the Meat and Dairy Products Industry).
4. Republic ministries (such as the RSFSR Ministry of Local Industry).

In 1969 there were 32 USSR industrial ministries; 20 were designated all-union ministries and 12 were union-republic ministries.[19] The USSR all-union ministries are responsible primarily for the engineering and electronic enterprises of the country; the governments of the republics in which they are situated have no authority over them. The two types of union-republic ministries are responsible primarily for enterprises in light industry and mining and metallurgy. If there are only a few enterprises of this kind located on the territory of one of the union republics, they are directly under the jurisdiction of the USSR union-republic ministry of that industry. But if there is a sizable number of enterprises in the republic, the republic government may be empowered to administer them; it does so through a ministry of its own that bears the same designation as the corresponding USSR ministry. For example, the meat and dairy products enterprises located in the RSFSR are under the jurisdiction of the RSFSR Union-Republic Ministry of Meat and Dairy Products Industry. The latter ministry is responsible directly to the RSFSR Council of Ministers, but the USSR ministry of that name enjoys certain kinds of authority over it. All other enterprises are under the sole jurisdiction of one of the republic ministries. The larger of these enterprises are administered directly by a republic ministry such as the Ukrainian Ministry of the Fuel Industry. The smaller of them are administered by agencies of the local (regional, city, and district) governments, which are in turn supervised by the republic's Ministry of Local Industry.[20]

Ministers are appointed by the government and are ex officio members of the USSR or republic Council of Ministers. The Ministry's work is conducted by its major divisions known as "administrations" or "chief administrations." Traditionally there have been two types of administrations, branch and functional, corresponding roughly to line and staff offices. The branch administrations were in charge of all the enterprises in one branch of the ministry's industry; for example, the Administration for Precision Machine Tool Production of the USSR Ministry of the Machinery and Instrument Industry. When the corporation merger reform is completed, however, the branch administrations are to be discontinued. Some will be dissolved and others transformed into the management body of a new corporation. The corporations will negotiate directly with the ministry rather than through the intermediation of the former branch administration. The ministers, however, continue to be responsible for the work of the corporate enterprises and will have to delegate some of that responsibility to someone in some new office or department. It is not yet known how that will be arranged, but that new department may well have the same kind of responsibility, though narrower in scope, than the defunct branch administration.

The functional administrations conduct the general "staff" work of the ministry, and are not affected by the corporation reform. The Technical Administration is the office chiefly responsible for the management of innovation on a ministrywide basis. It coordinates the innovation plans of the ministry and its enterprises and oversees the progress of their innovation activity on behalf of the minister. It also supervises the work of the ministry's research and development organizations and oversees the transfer of responsibility for new products and processes from the R & D organizations to the branch administrations and their enterprises.[21] Other functional administrations deal with finance, economic planning, purchasing, selling, and so forth, for the entire ministry.

Finally, the ministries have a number of other departments and offices dealing with various technical matters. In matters regarding innovation, the chief of such bodies is the scientific and technical council. The minister chairs the council, and the members consist of prominent scientists and engineers, outstanding workers, inventors, and representatives of various government and Party organizations. The council is the minister's chief adviser on the technological policy of the industry. It provides the technical expertise for evaluating the proposals that come before it from enterprises and R & D establishments, and for deciding among alternative lines of technological development. Much of its work is conducted through permanent bureaus or ad hoc committees that study specific problems. When its recommendations are accepted by the minister, and approved when necessary by the State Committee on Science and Technology, it becomes the responsibility of the ministry's Technical Administration to see that they are carried out.

The ministry is the enterprise's "home office." In the past, the director's "boss" was the head of the branch administration, whose own boss was the minister himself. The corporation director's boss will be the man whom the minister sets in charge of the corporation; it is doubtful that the ministers themselves will attempt to supervise the many thousands of corporations from their private offices. These ministry officials hire and fire the directors, determine the size of their bonuses, and influence the progress of their careers. The minister in turn is responsible to the top agencies of government—the Presidium of the USSR (or republic) Council of Ministers and the Politburo of the Communist Party. His own career depends on the performance of the segment of industry that he administers on behalf of the government.

Research, Development, and Design Organizations
The three structural units discussed thus far would be adequate for a general description of the system of economic organization. For our special interest in innovation, a fourth unit must be separately identi-

fied—the research and development organization. Some R & D work has always been done within the enterprises themselves, particularly in the larger ones. But most of it has been done in a complex network of organizations that are independent of the industrial enterprises. The corporation reform will shift the balance toward more in-house R & D, since many of the formerly independent R & D organizations are to be merged into a research-based corporation.

Three types of R & D organizations need to be distinguished. The first is the research and development institute proper.[22] The typical institute specializes in applied research in a specified technological area, which is often contained in the full title of the institute. Examples are the Central Scientific-Research Institute of Technology and Machinebuilding, the All-Union Petroleum and Natural Gas Scientific Research Institute, the Scientific Research Institute on Automation of Production Processes in the Chemical and Nonferrous Metals Industry. The larger institutes like the first named above contain facilities and personnel for the whole development chain, including research laboratories, design offices, testing and experimental facilities, and even small plants for prototype construction and for equipment manufacture. The smaller institutes often depend on other organizations for design and drafting work, pilot operations, and prototype construction. The institutes that are part of the Academy of Sciences network concentrate on basic research and have only occasional dealings with enterprises. Applied research and development is conducted principally in the institutes that are operated by the ministries, and increasingly in the laboratories of the higher educational institutions. It is these that produce the main flow of new product and process designs, some portion of which eventually finds its way into the operations of enterprises. In 1969 there were about 1,700 research institutes of all kinds in the USSR, excluding those of the Academy of Sciences system.[23]

The second type of R & D establishment is the engineering-design organization.[24] In Soviet practice, some specialize in the design of products, and some in the design of production processes. The former is called a design (*konstruktorskii*) bureau and the latter a "project-making" (*proektnyi*) institute. We shall refer to them separately as product-design and production-engineering organizations, and collectively as engineering-design organizations.[25] Their job generally begins when development work has been completed; that is, when the new product or process has been developed to the point where it is thought ready for commercial application. The engineering-design organizations then work out the details of materials, grades, sizes, shapes, and other technical and aesthetic specifications of the final product; and the precise machinery, assembly, quality control, and other production arrangements for manufacturing it. They provide the working drawings, blueprints, specifications, and other technical documents needed by the plant engineers for putting the product or process into operation. Preproduction testing may be done either by the engineering-design organization or the enterprise. Much engineering-design work is done by the larger research institutes in the course of development work, and most enterprises also possess a department of engineering design. The engineering-design organizations also often do some further product development in the course of their own work.

There were about 1,000 engineering-design organizations in the USSR in 1964.[26] The quality of their work is of crucial importance for the success of the enterprise's innovative activity.

The third type of establishment is the construction-engineering organization.[27] They design new factories and construction projects, including the manufacturing and technological processes to be used. They make the recommendations, and often the decisions, on such crucial matters as the location of the plant, the kind of equipment to be used, the degree of automation, the scale of production. They produce the blueprints used by the construction contracting enterprises that build the plant. Since a substantial portion of all new products and processes are introduced in newly built capital facilities, they are a vital part of the innovation process. There were about 1,400 construction-engineering (and surveying) organizations in 1970.[28]

The Party

The four organizational units just discussed are the leading players in the innovation game. It is the relationships among them with which this study will be chiefly concerned in analyzing the effects of organizational structure on innovation. But no institutional sector of Soviet society can be adequately understood without attending to the role of the Communist Party. The Party hovers like a shadow over the shoulder of every social unit in the USSR. Within every enterprise, ministry, and R & D institute, there are units of the Party consisting of the workers in those organizations who happen also to be members of the Party. In each of the hundred-and-thirty-odd provinces of the country (and in all the cities and districts of the provinces) there is a committee of the

Party, the secretary of which is responsible for all Party affairs in that province. This vast network of Party units is welded into a single organization that constitutes the political leadership of the country.[29]

The fundamental decisions of national policy are made by the Central Committee of the Party and implemented by the government's Council of Ministers. Major decrees are issued by either, or sometimes jointly by both. As the top agency of government, it is the responsibility of the Council of Ministers to see that the decrees and policies are carried out. And it is the task of the Party organizations at all levels to assist, oversee, supervise, and in a variety of ways to ensure that the Party policies are being implemented fully and enthusiastically at all levels.

One of the major responsibilities of the Party organizations is to maintain the pressure on enterprises to innovate. "No action earns a Party organ such fulsome praise in the press as its intervention to force a cautious innovator to introduce an invention or new work-technique. It is no accident that the conflict between an energetic Party secretary and a conservative manager over the question of technical innovation is one of the most recurrent themes in the Soviet novel on contemporary industry."[30] One of the developers of a major Soviet innovation, the turbodrill, reports that after a series of failures and reverses, the project encountered great hostility and skepticism on the part of the oil industry officials. It was only the strong Party support they received that enabled them to proceed.[31]

As one might guess, Party officials do not always act as they are supposed to in theory. There are certain pressures upon them to "look the other way" at enterprises that may not be performing very well, and there are contrary pressures that push the Party from time to time into such close supervision of the enterprise as to constitute interference with the proper responsibility of management. But overall the Party does constitute a source of general pressure upon the economic units, among them enterprises, to innovate. The enterprise that fails to do so may expect, among the many unpleasant consequences, to be called before the Party and made to explain and to promise to do better next time.

We shall allude to the influence of Party activity from time to time, but it will not be central to the discussion. Like the other social parameters of our study, the Party affects the outcomes of the economic structure, but the relationship between structure and outcome may be studied independently of the Party's role.

2.2. Economic Planning

The transactions among the organizational units are regulated by the method of national economic planning. There is a vast literature on the Soviet planning system, but only its main features need to be discussed here.[32] The focus of discussion will be the enterprise plan.

General Economic Planning

The plan-making process takes place in two stages. Stage one begins with the issuance of "control figures" by the USSR State Planning Committee to the USSR ministries and to the republic councils of ministers.[33] The control figures establish for each ministry the magnitudes toward which they should aim next year in such matters as rates of production, capital investment, labor force, and so forth. The ministry then assigns control figures to each of its enterprises, which set to work drafting detailed plans designed to meet the targets in their control figures. During the months of July through September, the ministry receives the flow of draft plans from their enterprises and conducts intensive negotiations with both its enterprise and with the State Planning Committee.[34] This is the period during which the Planning Committee strives to balance the planned production with the planned uses of the major industrial materials and equipment.[35] Ministries and enterprises strive at the same time to assure that the final targets assigned to them are realistic; and where possible to maintain a "safety factor" for unanticipated interruptions in production.[36] Eventually the ministries are obliged to accept a final set of plan targets that are officially approved by the Council of Ministers. These approved ministry targets are the basis of the official ministry plans for the forthcoming plan year. The consolidated ministry plans constitute the official National Economic Plan.

Once the ministry is locked into its final plan targets, it concludes the negotiations with its enterprises. The ministry approves a final set of plan targets for each enterprise, which become the basis of the official enterprise plan for the forthcoming year. Nine general indicators constitute the portion of the enterprise plan targets that must be officially approved by the ministry; among them are gross sales volume, gross profit, rate of profit, total wages, and so forth. One of the nine is a list of projects for the introduction of new technology.[37]

The official approval by the ministry of the nine indicators concludes the first stage of the planning process. The second stage begins around September and consists of the elaboration of a detailed enterprise plan designed to lay out the forthcoming year's work. Specific assignments are made to each of the enterprise production shops and administrative departments. The full enterprise plan must be registered with the ministry, but the ministry may hold the enterprise to account only for the nine officially approved indicators. How the enterprise sets about fulfilling and overfulfilling its plan is no business of the ministry—at least in principle.

The standard forms for an enterprise plan provide for 10 main sections and 43 subsections. The main sections are designated by such titles as Production and Sales Plan, Capital Construction Plan, Materials and Equipment Supply Plan, Financial Plan, Cost of Production Plan. The section that incorporates the enterprise's innovation obligations for the year is called the Plan for Raising Production Efficiency, or sometimes simply the New Technology Plan.[38]

The National Economic Plan and the plans of ministries and enterprises constitute an image—ideally a perfectly integrated image—of the national economic process as it is expected to unfold in the course of the entire year. It is only an image, however, and to be transformed into reality it must be converted into concrete actions. The actions take the form of orders to the shop officials by the planning department to produce according to planned schedules; securing the allocation certificates that entitle the enterprise to purchase the centrally planned materials and equipment authorized in the plan; placing orders for those requirements with the supplying enterprise and negotiating delivery schedules and payment terms; arranging for the purchase of other nonplanned materials and equipment; arranging for the sale of one's own products and for the associated transportation services; negotiating with the Ministry of Finance for the state budget subsidies provided for in the plan, and so on. The process of planmaking, massive as it is, is only a small part of the business of managing industry.

Needless to say, one can hardly expect this vast network of plans to be perfectly integrated. Nor can one expect that every enterprise will manage to fulfill every plan target. Hence provision is made for altering plans in the course of the plan year. The consequences of plan imperfections and plan changes will command a good deal of attention in the analysis of enterprise innovative behavior.

The Planning of Innovation

The agencies involved in general economic planning, from the planning departments of the fifty thousand industrial enterprises up to the USSR

State Planning Committee constitute a formidable apparatus. This general planning apparatus, however, is merely the tip of the iceberg. The State Planning Committee is so "overwhelmed by orders"[39] that despite its abundant resources it could not possibly possess the data and expertise required for each of the many parts of the plan that it is obliged to coordinate. For the planning of labor and wages it must rely on the expertise of the specialized State Committee on Labor and Wages, which conducts its own extensive program of data gathering, analysis, forecasting, and planning work. Similarly, it must rely on the financial planning done in great detail by the Ministry of Finance and the State Bank, and on the foreign trade planning done by the State Committee on Foreign Economic Relations and the Ministry of Foreign Trade. In like fashion, the innovation plans that emerge from the general planning process described above are based on an extensive body of ongoing technological analysis and economic planning. It takes place in the State Committee on Science and Technology and the Academy of Sciences network at the top; in the ministries' technical departments and scientific and technical councils; and in the various engineering departments of the enterprises.

The process of general economic planning has a long history and a voluminous literature on the subject has accumulated. In contrast, the planning of R & D and innovation is of postwar origin. Not until 1949 did the National Economic Plans contain a section on the introduction of new technology.[40] In degree of precision and coordination, technological planning still lags far behind that attained in general planning. The reasons are to be found in the inherently greater difficulty of technological planning. Because of the greater degree of uncertainty, it is much more difficult to construct time schedules for R & D work, to foresee the materials and equipment needs far in advance, to anticipate the date on which an innovation may be expected to commence production and to estimate the future changes in the productivity of the innovation. Hence, while formal technological planning is an ongoing and extensive activity, it is not yet closely integrated with the other portions of the general plan. "Plans consist, in fact, of a simple addition of research targets,"[41] is the summary judgment of E. Zaleski on the basis of his extensive study of the subject.

The time scheduling of technological planning conforms roughly to that of general planning. The control figures issued by the State Planning Committee to the ministries contain certain innovation assignments. These are generally innovations of major importance and size, and reflect the high-level decisions on technological policy previously adopted by the State Planning Committee and the State Committee on Science and Technology. The ministry in turn distributes these assignments to specific enterprises in the control figures it issues to them. In addition the ministry includes in the control figures certain innovation tasks not specified by the State Planning Committee but which are part of the planned technological development of the ministry.

When the enterprise receives the control figures, the innovation assignments are turned over to the appropriate departments for elaboration. In many cases an ad hoc Enterprise Innovation Commission is established, chaired by the director or the chief engineer, and including the heads of the major administrative departments, representatives of the trade union and Party, and prominent workers and technical personnel.[42] The commission studies the innovation assignments in the control figures and determines whether they can be carried out and which officials and production shops should be given the tasks. In addition to the innovations specified in the control figures, the commission receives proposals from all the departments and decides which should be undertaken. When the list of planned innovations is established, it is submitted to the various functional departments for integration into the overall enterprise plan; to the planning department for the cost and profit calculations; to the purchasing department for the determination of the materials and equipment requirements; to the finance department to determine the feasibility of financing all the measures and for preparing the applications for bank credits or state budget grants. The analysis by the departments may signify that the preliminary list of projects is not feasible, and the commission may need to revise it. In principle, when the work is done the innovation section of the enterprise draft plan is fully articulated with the other sections and meets all the innovation assignments specified in the control figures. If it proves impossible to meet all the latter, the director must be prepared to do battle with the ministry, armed with the documentation provided by the work of this committee.

In addition to the enterprise draft plans pouring into the ministry in the course of the summer are the draft plans submitted by all the R & D and engineering-design organizations of the ministry. Their draft plans, also based on control figures previously issued to them, consist of lists of the projects on which they propose to work, with estimates of dates of completion, materials and equipment requirements, cost and productivity estimates, and financial requirements. Among the planning tasks of the ministry is the coordination of the R & D requirements in the enterprise draft plans, with the work plans of the R & D organizations. If an enterprise has accepted an assignment to commence work in November on a new product model, the ministry must assure that the R & D organization's plan provides for the completion of development work on that model by March, and the engineering-design organization's plan provides sufficient resources to have the blueprints ready by November.

The consolidated draft plan of the ministry identifies separately each of the projects specified in its control figures; that is, the projects of national importance that will later appear in the National Economic Plan. All other innovations of ministrywide or enterprise-level importance are included only in summary form. The ministry draft plan is submitted to the State Planning Committee, and a copy of that section that deals with R & D and innovation is submitted to the State Committee on Science and Technology.

A parallel stream of draft plans flows upward through the Academy of Sciences network of research institutes. The task of adjusting and coordinating these draft plans takes place at the highest level of government. In general we may expect that the vast set of draft plans requires extensive adjustment. They may as a group require a greater volume of resources than have been allocated for science and R & D, and some proposed projects may have to be dropped or reduced in scope. Or some high-priority project may have been insufficiently provided for, and some ministry may be obliged to take on an additional task it had not anticipated in its draft. Other adjustments need to be made for purposes of coordination, particularly across ministry lines. The Ministry of the Chemicals Industry may insist that it is unable to proceed with the development of a major new process until the research people in the Ministry of the Ferrous Metals Industry come up with a new alloy that can withstand the temperatures. The draft plans of the latter may then have to be changed. For these reasons the ministries may end up with a final set of planned innovation tasks very different from those provided for in their draft plans.

Very little is known about how such decisions are made at these highest levels. The State Planning Committee, the State Committee on Science and Technology, and the Academy of Sciences are obliged to consult with each other on matters of common jurisdiction, but it is to be expected that conflicts will occur because of differences in outlook and areas of responsibility. It is likely that unresolved conflicts are settled ultimately by decision of the Presidium of the Council of Ministers and the Politburo of the Communist Party. The document that these agencies agree upon becomes the National Economic Plan for the forthcoming year. One major section of that plan is the "State Plan of Scientific Research Work and the Introduction of the Achievements of Science and Technology into the USSR National Economy."

The rest of the process of technological planning is similar to stage two of general planning. The State Planning Committee issues final plan targets to the ministries, which the latter in turn distribute among their enterprises. In general these targets are different from those upon which the enterprise draft plan had been prepared. The enterprise must now set about revising its draft plan so as to conform to the final plan targets. A new reduced plan target for total wages may make it impossible to proceed with an innovation they originally hoped to undertake. The ministry may require them to begin next year to introduce a new product they had hoped to put off until the following year. A new automated production line that they had unsuccessfully applied for in the preceding year may now have been approved, and appears as an item in one of their control figures.

The final enterprise plans must provide for all the innovations assigned in the control figures, and in addition for all others the enterprise plans to undertake. Appropriate provision must be made in all other sections of the plan for new or specially skilled labor, for materials and equipment, for construction contracting, for sources of finance, and so forth. When this has been done, the list of those projects that were specified in the control figures—that is, those of national and of ministry-wide importance—is submitted to the ministry for final approval; for that list is one of the nine indicators requiring such approval. The rest of the plan requires only the director's signature to become official.

This sketch of the innovation planning process has concentrated on the organizational features. It has indicated the kinds of decisions that need to be made at various planning levels but not the basis on which they are actually made. Enterprise-level decision making on innovation will occupy most of this study. It will not deal, however, with the vast area of national technological policy, which has been investigated in other studies.[43]

2.3. The Origin of Innovations

The Soviet published sources are a rich body of descriptive material on many aspects of the innovation process. In the spirit of "criticism and self-criticism," enterprise executives, journalists, economists, and officials of all sorts publish a great deal of material pointing to problems in the innovative process and recommending solutions. Materials of this kind, which constitute the bulk of the documentation in this study, provide the outside analyst with a sense of how decisions are made and the considerations that enter into them.[44] But the sources are poor in materials that deal with the whole innovation process on the microeconomic level. It is rarely possible, for example, to trace an individual innovation through from the original idea to its final introduction in any detail. It is difficult, therefore, to describe here the course of a typical innovation and document it at each point in its progress. We can, however, provide a rough impression, based on the sources, of the role of the various organizational units in originating innovations and in influencing their progress.

Government Agencies

Of all the agencies of the central government, the State Committee on Science and Technology is the one most likely to originate innovations. But the originating of innovations is not the primary responsibility of the Committee. Its principal function is to select from among innovation proposals initiated elsewhere, to decide which are to be proposed to the State Planning Committee for inclusion in the National Economic Plan, and to oversee the process whereby major innovations are brought from the laboratory through the various stages until the final implementation. It is best thought of as encouraging innovative activity in the other structural units, and guiding the main lines of innovative activity that originate elsewhere and are implemented elsewhere. Thus the Committee maintains a steady pressure on the entire system to generate new processes and products and to keep them moving swiftly through their various stages until their final implementation. If there is resistance to innovation among other organizational units, that resistance is precisely to the pressures produced by the obligation of this high agency of government to promote innovation.

The State Planning Committee has the obligation of fitting the innovation plans of the ministries into the national plan in such fashion that the resources planned to be devoted to innovational activity (a large component of which is the national investment program) are matched by the material, labor, financial, and other resources available. It must also assure that the benefits from the year's innovation plans, in the form of lower production costs and increased output, are fully accounted for in the plan; that is, if an expansion of some new product is accepted, provision must be made for the use of this product by users. The administration of this interenterprise flow of commodities is not the function of the State Planning Committee but of the State Committee on Supply. It is the Planning Committee, however, that ultimately makes the decision and presents it to the Council of Ministers for approval.

The Planning Committee has no primary responsibility for initiating innovation. But once the decision to proceed with an innovation is taken and made final by incorporation in the plan, then the Committee bears a clear responsibility for exerting pressure on the organization charged with the implementation, such as ministries and enterprises. For it was long ago established that the State Planning Committee is obliged not merely to construct "paper plans" but to maintain an ongoing effort to assure that the plans are fulfilled. In the complicated job of balancing the plan, the Committee is constantly seeking ways of stretching the planned production of individual commodities to match the planned requirements for them. Innovations are a sort of *deus ex machina* for accomplishing this end. A ministry may be compelled to speed up the development work on a new industrial material so that it can be put into production in time to make up for a threatened shortfall in supply. In another ministry the installation of a new automatic machining line may be the device counted on to relieve a labor shortage. The fabric of the national plan is held together by planned innovations of these kinds, and if the R & D institutes and enterprises fail to meet their time schedules, the fabric tends to come apart at those points, with further repercussions on the ability of other enterprises to fulfill their plans. Hence the success of innovative activity is of vital importance to the work of the State Planning Committee.[45] If planned innovations are falling behind schedule, the ministry is likely to be called in by the Planning Committee and asked to explain. And the ministry in turn is likely to demand an explanation from the culpable enterprise, and perhaps to take a variety of measures to assist the enterprise in speeding up its work. Thus the Planning Committee too, although primarily responsible for planning, maintains a steady pressure on the entire system to keep the flow of innovational activity at the planned level. Ideally, it should be impossible for an innovation to "get lost" by accident or by the deliberate action of a reluctant enterprise, for either the State Planning Committee or the State Committee on Science and Technology should discover the lag quickly and demand action.

The activity of the State Planning Committee is not limited to the construction and overseeing of the plan, but also to the administration of changes in the plan that may become necessary in the course of the year. For from long experience it has become the practice to think of the annual plan not as something that is fixed once and forever but that is constantly revised in the course of the year to take account of unplanned developments. These may be due to a harvest that is better or worse than anticipated; to changes in world trade conditions that may require revision of the foreign trade plans; and above all to the fact that a certain proportion of enterprises fail to fulfill portions of their plans, so that the plans of others who depend on their performance must also be changed. Hence enterprises may find themselves under pressure from the State Planning Committee in the course of the year not only to maintain their planned rates of production and innovation but also unexpectedly to add to their plans the assignment of commencing the production of some product that had not been originally scheduled. From some sources it appears that the order may come directly from the planning system, although it is more likely to be transmitted initially to the ministry and then by the latter to the enterprise. In either case, this pressure for innovation comes from the State Planning Committee.

Ministries

Innovations may also originate in the ministries. Many of the ministries' departments consist of men with experience and knowledge of the industry technology, and with the responsibility to search for and propose innovations. This work is centered in the technical department of the ministry. But innovations may also originate in the various engineering departments of the ministry's branch administrations. It is these engineers who would evaluate an innovation tried out in one of the administration's enterprises, and if it is successful, it would be their responsibility to see that it is adopted by their other enterprises. The ministry's scientific and technical council may also originate innovations, for its members are men of broad experience and expertise, and they can view the ministry's entire technological profile from an excellent vantage point. But like the State Committee on Science and Technology, the ministry is more likely to receive innovation proposals from its own enterprises and R & D organizations, and to select among them and oversee the various stages of the process. It also exerts a general pressure on others to innovate, but is not itself a primary source of innovation proposals.

The obligations of ministries with respect to innovation have been laid out in some detail in the new statute that reintroduced the ministry system in 1967. According to the statute, the ministries are obliged to review constantly the technological level of their enterprises, to oversee the progress of innovative activity from the original idea to its final introduction, to promote the introduction of new products and the removal of obsolete products from production, to supervise the creation of new technical standards, and so forth.[46] On matters of sufficient importance to occupy the State Committee on Science and Technology, the ministry works with that organization and is in a sense the transmission belt of innovative pressure from the government down to enterprises. But the ministry is also an independent source of pressure upon enterprises and upon R & D institutes, operating under its general directives to promote innovation. Even if there were no State Committee on Science and Technology, the ministry would press for innovation to the extent that that was required of it by the Council of Ministers. The reason may be direct instruction to encourage innovation, in which case the ministry will wish to be able to report to the Council that its enterprises had scored signal successes in innovating. Or it may be derived from other criteria whereby the work of the ministry is evaluated by the Council of Ministers and the Party. The ministry is required to assume a certain obligation to reduce production costs in its enterprises by a certain percentage, and this may be translated by the minister's technical staff into orders to enterprises to introduce innovations capable of producing higher rates of output. It is in this sense that the industrial ministries are a major source of the pressure on enterprises for innovation.

The ministry bears the responsibility for converting the general decisions of the government agencies into specific directives to individual enterprises. In the case of innovations of major importance, the government may designate directly the enterprise to introduce the innovation. But usually the ministry is given a general order and distributes that order among the enterprises that will carry it out. The ministry, for example, may be obliged to expand the production of some new product next year by a certain percentage; it is then the ministry's responsibility to assign the production tasks to its enterprises. The ministry is held to account for the performance of this task by the Council of Ministers, by the State Planning Committee, and by the State Committee on Science and Technology. Hence the ministry is the direct point of pressure upon enterprises to carry through the innovative program of the government. If an enterprise lags, it is most often the ministry that will call it directly to account; although in the case of very large or high priority projects, the enterprise may be required to account directly to the highest agencies of government.

Research and Development Organizations

It is in the other two types of organizational unit that most innovations originate. The R & D organizations have a primary responsibility for initiating innovations. A new idea may be the outgrowth of their own past R & D work; or it may be suggested to them by research reports of the pure science institutions of the Academy of Sciences; or it may be culled from the general technical literature, both domestic or foreign, to which they subscribe. The exploratory R & D work is done by the organization itself. If it is a minor product improvement, they may proceed with the work on their own authority by including it in the annual plan. They may then require no more than the confirmation of the ministry to proceed with the work when the plan is approved. If it is a proposal of some magnitude, the matter may have to be presented to the ministry's scientific and technical council. The ministry may then authorize the R & D institute to proceed according to the draft plan. Or the ministry may reject the proposal, perhaps in favor of a different line of development being promoted elsewhere. In evaluating these proposals, the scientific and technical council is obliged to consider the general policy of technical development adopted within the ministry or decreed by the State Committee on Science and Technology. For example, a proposal for a new type of boiler to operate on a petroleum fuel may be rejected or modified in view of a general policy to promote the production and development of gas as a fuel.

Thus some portion of the work of an R & D institute consists of innovations originating in its own staff. The rest consists of work that had originated elsewhere and had been assigned to the institute as its project. It may have originated in the pure research done in one of the institutes of the Academy of Sciences. The scientists may have conceived of a possible application of some piece of their own research and presented it to.the State Committee on Science and Technology or to the appropriate ministry. If those agencies found merit in the idea, even if only to take it through the first stage of applied research to explore its potential, then it may be assigned to an R & D institute. The institute will be obliged to include the project in its annual plan and will negotiate with the ministry over the financial and material resources and the time schedule for completing the work. Or the idea may originate in an enterprise, and may then be proposed to the R & D institute; or if it is a substantial innovation, it may go first to the ministry's scientific and technical council, or even up to the State Committee on Science and Technology. If approved, the work is then assigned to an R & D institute.

The Enterprise

Finally, a substantial portion of all innovations originates in enterprises. An improvement in the production process may be worked out in the normal line of work of the technological department. A product improvement or a new product may emerge from the work of the design department or the research laboratory; or by individuals on the basis of work supported by the bureau of inventions. The idea may be original with the enterprise, growing out of its efforts to cope with design or production problems. Or it may consist simply of the adoption, with perhaps slight modification, of an innovation successfully employed by other enterprises. In a self-motivated innovation of this kind, if it is of small proportions, it may simply be included in the innovation section of its draft plan, requiring only the formal approval of the ministry. If it is an innovation of larger proportions, it may have first to be presented to the ministry's scientific and technical council; or to the State Committee on Science and Technology if it is of major proportions. When the required approval is obtained, the project is confirmed in the plan, and the enterprise may proceed.

It often happens that an idea may originate in an enterprise, but the enterprise may lack the facilities or expertise to conduct the required research, development, testing, and design work. If it is a small innovation, the enterprise may negotiate with an R & D institute and enter into a contractual arrangement for the required work to be done on the basis of a negotiated price. If it is of larger proportions, the ministry may take over the administration of the successive stages and assign it to the R & D and design organizations. When the work is completed, the task of putting it into production may be assigned to the enterprise that originated it, and perhaps to other enterprises in the ministry.

Because the major R & D facilities are independent of the enterprises, it is likely that enterprise-initiated innovation is of smaller scale and of a lower level of technological sophistication. Much of it probably takes the form of product improvement or of minor changes in the basic production technology. There may therefore be some tendency, both by Soviet and non-Soviet analysts, to undervalue its actual and potential contribution. It is surely less glamorous than the shiny new models and dramatic technological advances that emerge from the R & D institutes. But from the experience of capitalist economies, the cumulative effect of small technological advances based on the operating experience of enterprises can be very large indeed. In the U.S. cotton textile industry it has been estimated that improvements in detail but not in basic methods contributed a potential 50 percent increase in labor productivity between 1910 and 1936. The introduction in 1925 of mechanical methods for manufacturing electric light bulbs was a major innovation. But in the following six years, an accumulation of small improvements were of a magnitude equivalent to a fivefold increase in labor productivity.[47] In his close study of the petroleum refining industry, John Enos estimated the productivity gains of four major process innovations over the processes they supplanted and then measured the further productivity gains from the improvements subsequently made in the innovations. His conclusion is that "There appear to be greater reductions in factor inputs, per unit of output, when a process is improved than when it is supplanted by a better one."[48]

Innovation in the form of product and process improvement is done in the USSR in both R & D institutes and enterprises. It is the enterprise engineers, however, who work closely with the technology, and who are most likely to be sensitive to improvement possibilities. The large potential gains depend on their efforts and interest. Hence the effect of the economic structure on enterprise-initiated innovation is a major factor in the innovative performance of the economy.

The initiation of innovation is a function that the enterprise shares with the R & D institute and, to some extent, with the other organizational units. There is a second function, however, that is unique to enterprises. That is the function of implementing innovations that originate elsewhere. For no innovation is consummated anywhere unless some enterprise put it into operation.

The innovations assigned to enterprises are generally those that originate in R & D institutes. The major ones are processed through the offices of the State Committee on Science and Technology and are included in the innovation section of the National Economic Plan. Implementation is assigned to the ministries that, in turn, assign them to enterprises. In 1965, it was estimated that 20 to 30 percent of all work on new technology was included in the national plans.[49] Of the remainder, some portion consists of innovations processed at the ministry level and assigned to enterprises for implementation. The other portion, which must be substantial, consists of enterprise-initiated innovations that appear only in enterprise plans.

The national-level and ministry-level innovations that are assigned to enterprises for implementation are usually included in the control figures issued by the ministry and eventually form part of the enterprise plan. In such cases, provision can be made for the labor, materials, equipment, R & D services, financial and other requirements for carrying them out. In other cases, however, innovation orders are issued by the ministry in the course of the year. These are more difficult to handle, for they constitute an additional obligation to those assumed in the original plan, and it is more difficult to arrange for the resource requirements. We may expect, however, that innovation assignments are not simply dropped upon enterprises without their foreknowledge, but some discussion and negotiation with the ministry precedes the actual issuance of the formal order.

When one thinks of the innovation process in a centrally planned economy, it is innovations of this kind one has primarily in mind. In the command-economy model, for example, the primary innovation function of enterprises is to implement the innovations commanded from above. The explanation of the rate and direction of innovation is then derived from the principles and practices of central planning of R & D and investment policy. A great deal is lost, however, if the contribution of enterprises is thought to be limited to the passive implementation of innovations initiated and planned elsewhere. For even with respect to centrally planned innovations, the outcomes are heavily influenced by enterprise decision making.

The most obvious enterprise influence is in the degree of effort put into the implementation of assigned innovations. Given one type of economic structure—that is, organization, prices, rules, and incentives—enterprises will seize eagerly upon innovation assignments and perhaps even compete for them. Effort and resources will be shifted away from other enterprise activities and thrown into the speedy and efficient fulfillment of the innovations ordered from above. Given another economic structure, however, and enterprises may shun innovation assignments like the plague. Nor is there any doubting the capability of an imaginative management to do this. There are ways known to master bureaucrats all over the world of avoiding, delaying, altering, reconsidering, and generally frustrating the intentions of higher agencies; and always supported by incontestably good explanations of why something cannot be done. Between these two extremes—enthusiastic implementation and deliberate avoidance—lies a very great range of responses. Given the flow of centralized innovation orders from ministries to enterprises, the resulting rate of innovation may be very low or very high. The explanation of variations in the rate of innovation within that range is to be found in the effects of economic structure on the enterprise innovation decision.

It is not only in the passive function of implementation, however, that enterprise behavior influences the course of centrally planned innovations. The quality of centrally planned innovation depends also on enterprise initiative. Because of their intimacy with the technology under operating conditions, enterprise production personnel are a major potential source of ideas for innovations. If encouraged by the social structure, their proposals on new product and process design could add significantly to the stock of ideas available to the central decision-making bodies. The agenda of the State Committee on Science and Technology and of the ministries' technical and economic councils would bulge with proposals initiated by thousands of enterprises clamoring for authorization to introduce them. The active participation of enterprises in the evaluation of innovations on the agenda of the higher agencies can also influence the quality of central decision making. Undoubtedly in the USSR today some portion of the innovations enterprises are ordered by ministries to implement derive from proposals that the enterprises themselves decided to submit to the ministries.[50] To that extent the rate of centrally planned innovation is itself a function of enterprise-level decision making reflecting the structure of the economy.

The implementation process itself is affected by the initiative manifested in the enterprises. Because of the uncertainty that characterizes the innovation process, the designs of new products and processes that emerge from the drawing boards of the engineering design organizations require subsequent correction. Some of the deficiencies are immediately apparent to the enterprise engineers, and some become evident during the testing and start-up periods. If changes are difficult to make because of the organizational structure, if they are costly to the enterprise because of the price structure, if they conflict with the official decision rules, or if the changes offer no personal rewards—or perhaps negative rewards—to the enterprise personnel, the innovation will be implemented precisely as the blueprints require, with the consequence of a low level of productivity. If, on the contrary, the economic structure created a vital enterprise interest in the productivity of the assigned innovation, the enterprise personnel will battle with the ministry and the R & D people for improvements on the design. In this regard too, the outcomes of the centralized innovation process depend on enterprise-level decision making.

There is, however, one area of centrally planned innovation that is not affected by enterprise-level decision making, and it is a significant exception. This is the case of the construction of new enterprises. A substantial volume of innovation is embodied in newly constructed enterprises. In such cases the innovator may be the ministry that proposed the new plant to the high agencies of government and received authorization to proceed. Or it may be the construction engineering organization assigned the job of designing the project. The latter bears the responsibility for choosing among the available technological alternatives. If they judge a new process nearing completion of development work to be superior to the established technology, they will design it into the new plant. But if they are skeptical of the claims of the R & D institute, they may choose the older technology, for they will not wish to be responsible for an unsuccessful innovation. In the case of minor portions of the new plant's technology, the choices made by the construction engineering organization are likely to be decisive, but for the basic production technology the final decision to innovate or not is likely to be made in the ministry or at a higher level.

In any event, in the case of new enterprises the innovation decisions are all made before a management group for the new enterprise comes into existence. The enterprise management is not organized until after the decision to construct has been taken, the innovation decisions have been made, and the actual construction is well under way. It is only during the construction period that the management group for the new enterprise is recruited, and the new group does not assume authority or responsibility until the facilities are commissioned. The enterprise as an organizational unit plays no role in that portion of centralized innovation that is embodied in new enterprises.

Summarizing, enterprises account for many of the small innovations and product and process improvements that in the aggregate have a substantial potential impact on the rate of innovation. With the exception of new enterprises, the rate of innovation that emerges from the central planning process may also depend significantly on the behavior of enterprises. Hence the effect of economic structure on enterprise decision making is a major factor in the explanation of the rate of innovation.

Notes

1. Alex Bavelas, "Communications Patterns in Task-Oriented Groups," in Daniel Lerner and Harold D. Lasswell, eds., *The Policy Sciences* (Stanford: Stanford University Press, 1951), pp. 193-202.

2. *Pravda*, April 3, 1973, pp. 1-2. Translated in *The Current Digest of the Soviet Press*, Vol. 25:14 (May 2, 1973), pp. 1-4.

3. For a more extended treatment of the enterprise, see Joseph S. Berliner, *Factory and Manager in the USSR* (Cambridge: Harvard University Press, 1957); David Granick, *Management of the Industrial Firm in the USSR: A Study in Soviet Economic Planning* (New York: Columbia University Press, 1954); Barry Richman, *Soviet Management* (Englewood Cliffs, N.J.: Prentice-Hall, 1965).

4. Officially designated the Department of the Chief Designer (*Otdel glavnogo knostruktora*). In small enterprises it may be called a Special Design Bureau (*Spetsialnyii konstruktorskii buro*, or *SKB*). The adjective "special" serves to distinguish it from a Design Bureau, which normally refers to an independent organization that does the design work for the ministry and sometimes does contract design work for enterprises.

5. Officially, the Department of the Chief Technologist (*Otdel glavnogo tekhnologa*).

6. *Buro ratsionalizatsii i izobretenii* (BRIZ), or literally, the Bureau of Rationalization-Measures and Inventions. The term "Rationalization-Measures" is a Russian cognate of the word "rationalizing" as applied to the improving of the organization of labor and production through systematic analysis. The use of the cognate term reflects the extensive influence on the Soviet economy of "Taylorism," the method of time-and-motion study developed by the American efficiency expert, Frederick Taylor, for increasing the efficiency of work organization. We render the term as "production improvements" here.

7. *Ekonomicheskaia gazeta*, 1967, No. 31, p. 3.

8. Ibid., 1967, No. 38, p. 5.

9. Ia. Kvasha, "Kontsentratsiia proizvodstva i melkaya promyshlennost" (Production Concentration and Small-Scale Industry), *Voprosy ekonomiki*, 1967, No. 5, p. 27.

10. The Russian *firma* is the cognate of the English word "firm."

11. For a detailed discussion of the agencies chiefly responsible for technology, see E. Zaleski, J. P. Kozlowski, H. Wienert, R. W. Davis, M. J. Berry, and R. Amman, *Science Policy in the USSR* (Paris: OECD, 1969), Part I (by E. Zaleski).

12. Ibid., pp. 49-59.

13. Ibid., pp. 207-226 (article by H. Wienert).

14. Ibid., p. 396.

15. Ibid., p. 396.

16. Ibid., pp. 120-124.

17. Samuel Pisar, *Coexistence and Commerce* (New York: McGraw-Hill, 1970), pp. 141-160.

18. Russian Soviet Federated Socialist Republic, the largest of the fifteen republics that comprise the Soviet Union.

19. *Khoziaistvannaia reforma v USSR* (Economic Reform in the USSR) (Moscow: *Pravda,* 1969) (published as a 1969 Supplement to the newspaper *Ekonomicheskaia Gazeta*), pp. 12-13.

20. A. N. Efimov, *Sovetskaia industriia* (Soviet Industry) (Moscow: *Ekonomika,* 1967), pp. 208-215.

21. Zaleski et al., *Science Policy in the USSR*, p. 404.

22. A small but growing volume of R & D work is also carried out by the institutions of higher education, financed both by state budget grants and by contracts with enterprises and ministries. In 1968 the volume of R & D outlays by higher education institutions was estimated by Nimitz at about 390 million rubles, or 5 percent of all R & D outlays. Nancy Nimitz, *The Structure of Soviet Outlays on R & D in 1960 and 1968*, Rand Report R-1207-DDRE, Santa Monica, June 1974. A Soviet source reports the volume to have been 661 million rubles in 1972, indicating a considerable increase, although the figures may not be quite comparable. K. I. Taksir, *Sushchnost' i formy soedineniia nauki s proizvodstvom pri sotsializme* (The Essence and Forms of the Union of Science and Production Under Socialism) (Moscow: Vysshaia Shkola, 1974), p. 49.

23. TsSU. *Narodnoe khoziaistvo SSSR v 1969 godu* (USSR National Economy in 1969) (Moscow: Statistika, 1970), pp. 694, 698.

24. The work of the engineering design and construction engineering organization has been studied in a Ph.D. thesis by Marvin R. Jackson, Jr., *Soviet Project and Design Organization: Technological Decision-Making in a Command Economy*, University of California at Berkeley, 1967 (unpublished).

25. Some organizations do both product design and production engineering (*proektno-konstruktorskie instituty*).

26. Zaleski et al., *Science Policy in the USSR*, p. 407.

27. There are many different kinds of construction-engineering organizations with different specializations. See Zaleski et al., *Science Policy in the USSR*, p. 407 (article by R. Amman et al.).

28. TsSU, *Narodnoe khoziaistvo SSSR v 1969 godu*, p. 517.

29. On the role of the Party in industry, see Jerry F. Hough, *The Soviet Prefects* (Cambridge: Harvard University Press, 1969), Chaps. 4 and 5; J. S. Berliner, *Factory and Manager in the USSR*, Chap. 15.

30. Hough, *The Soviet Prefects*, pp. 119-120.

31. Robert W. Campbell, *The Economics of Soviet Oil and Gas* (Baltimore: The Johns Hopkins Press, 1968), pp. 109-110.

32. See Abram Bergson, *The Economics of Soviet Planning* (New Haven: Yale University Press, 1964), esp. Chap. 7; Alec Nove, *The Soviet Economy* (New York: Praeger, 1966), revised edition, Chap. 2; P. J. D. Wiles, *The Political Economy of Communism* (Cambridge: Harvard University Press, 1962), Part II.

33. In the case of the five-year plans the control figures are called "directives." Our discussion will deal only with the annual plans, which are the plans under which enterprises actually operate.

34. The time schedule for plan making is discussed in "Tekhpromfinplan v novykh usloviakh" (The Enterprise Plan Under the New Conditions), a supplement to *Ekonomicheskaia gazeta*, 1967, No. 22, p. 1.

35. On the techniques and problems of material balancing, see Herbert S. Levine, "The Centralized Planning of Supply in Soviet Industry," U.S. Congress, Joint Economic Committee, *Comparisons of the United States and Soviet Economies* (Washington: Government Printing Office, 1959), pp. 151-176.

36. The bargaining process in plan making is discussed in Berliner, *Factory and Manager*, Chaps. 6, 7, and 8.

37. *Khoziaistvennaia reforma v SSSR*, p. 23.

38. *"Tekhpromfinplan v novykh usloviakh,"* p. 21.

39. A. Birman, "The Talent of an Economist," translated in *The Current Digest of the Soviet Press* (19:13), April 19, 1967, p. 13.

40. Zaleski et al., *Science Policy in the USSR*, p. 75.

41. Ibid., p. 71.

42. *Planovoe khoziaistvo*, 1966, No. 12, p. 79.

43. Zaleski et al., *Science Policy in the USSR*; Jackson, *Project and Design Organizations*; Gregory Grossman, "Information and Innovation in the Soviet Economy", *American Economic Review* 56:2 (May 1966), pp. 118-129.

44. The materials are quite candid and may give an exaggerated impression of the difficulties. On the other hand, the press is censored, and is not given to understating the achievements of Soviet socialism. There is no simple formula that the outside analyst can follow in striving for a balanced judgment. If one had access to the society and could interview officials and conduct survey research, he would stand on surer ground. Lacking that, one must rely instead on experience, good sense, and the maximum of dispassion that one can muster.

45. Granick identifies the central planners and the consuming industries as the chief sources of demand for product innovation. David Granick, *Soviet Metal-Fabrication and Economic Development* (Madison: University of Wisconsin Press, 1967), pp. 232-238.

46. *Ekonomicheskaia gazeta*, 1967, No. 34, pp. 7-8.

47. W. E. G. Salter, *Productivity and Technical Change* (Cambridge: Cambridge University Press, 1966), p. 5 fn.

48. John L. Enos, "Invention and Innovation in the Petroleum Refining Industry," in National Bureau of Economic Research, *The Rate and Direction of Inventive Activity: Economic and Social Factors* (Princeton: Princeton University Press, 1962), p. 319.

49. *Ekonomicheskaia gazeta*, 1966, No. 2, p. 30. The estimate is based presumably on total expenditures on new technology.

50. This is in addition, of course, to enterprise-level innovation that does not require ministry approval.

Chapter 3

The Supply of Inputs: Materials and Equipment

The success of a production operation depends on a sure and steady supply of physical inputs: fuels, materials, components, tools, equipment. Interruption in the inflow of inputs may lead to interruption in the outflow of output, and uncertainty over supply leads to expensive inventory accumulation to minimize interruptions. One of the central tasks of management is to ensure the inflow of materials in the required quantities and qualities and at the proper times.

An act of innovation is a change in the production process. If it is to succeed, it requires a corresponding change in the pattern of inflow of inputs. It may require new materials with which the producer is unfamiliar. It may require new sources of supply and the establishment of commercial relations with new producing units with whom the innovator is unacquainted. The new supplier may have different modes of operation and may be unfamiliar with the procedures and needs of his new customer. For these reasons, the changes in the flow of inputs entail an element of risk for the innovator, and he must be prepared to devote some effort to the reorganization of his system of supply.

One may therefore expect that the attitude of a would-be innovator will depend upon his anticipation of the success with which he can reorganize his system of supply. The greater his confidence in his capacity to ensure his new materials supply, the greater his willingness to undertake a proposed innovation. Or more generally, given the structure of prices, decision rules, and incentives, the decision to innovate will depend upon the capacity of the organizational structure to ensure the supply of material resources.

It has long been known that the weakness of the system of interenterprise supply has been a major shortcoming of Soviet economic organization.[1] Many economic reforms of the postwar period have been designed precisely to improve the supply system. Despite those efforts, outside observers continue to report that "the most salient fact of economic life for the Soviet manager has been the inadequate provision of resources necessary to fulfill the enterprise plan."[2]

It is ironic that of all the ways in which the real Soviet socialist economy might have diverged from the theoretical ideal, the supply system should have proved to be one of the most troublesome. For a major advantage of socialism over capitalism is often thought to be its capacity to introduce a rational structure of interenterprise relations, in contrast to the "anarchy" of the marketplace. It would be an error, however, to attribute the problems of the Soviet supply system to the socialist basis of property ownership. A sufficient explanation may be found in the prevailing state of disequilibrium that characterizes interenterprise transactions in the Soviet Union. The disequilibrium is due in part to economic policy, particularly to the policy of excessively taut planning.[3] It is also due in part to the structure of the economic arrangements, in particular to the imperfections in the methods of pricing and in centralized economic planning. With a different set of policies and structural properties, the socialist economy may well be able to eliminate the perpetual disequilibria that give rise to the uncertainties in supply.

That the fault is in the state of disequilibrium rather than in the socialist basis of property ownership may be seen in the experience of market economies. When the state of their markets is in extensive disequilibrium, as often happens in periods of war and reconstruction, the state of supply is characterized by the same kinds of uncertainty as normally bedevil the Soviet economy. Under those conditions, moreover, business executives often engage in forms of behavior very similar to those of Soviet managers.[4] With respect to the innovation decision, uncertainty over supply affects the capitalist business executive in much the same way as it affects the Soviet manager. In their study of innovation in the postwar British economy, for example, Carter and Williams stress the extent to which the success of an innovation depends on the reliability of outside sources of supply.[5] They cite the failure of a certain innovation involving the automatic production of radio circuits due to faults in the electrical components purchased from other firms. More generally, they report that difficulties in the procurement of supplies were among the most numerous complaints by innovative firms, and they find that one of the indicators of a technically progressive firm is its "ingenuity in getting round material and equipment shortages." Steel was in particularly short supply, and the effect of that shortage on innovative behavior is strongly reminiscent of Soviet experience:

There were five references to difficulty in getting particular qualities, and twenty-seven to slowness of delivery. The "delivery" problem has far-reaching effects. Not only does it affect the rapidity with which new plant and equipment can be built, delaying projects for six months or more; it also in some cases involves duplication of drawing work, since companies that have prepared plans on the basis of the supposed current availability of steel may find that by the time they are able to execute these plans the supposed position has altered, and the plans have to be amended. . . . The steel shortage can have an important cumulative effect when it delays first a pilot-plant and then a full-scale plant.[6]

British experience thus provides some further evidence for the general proposition that the innovation decision depends on the reliability of the system of supply. In particular, an economy of shortages and controls tends to discourage innovation. The difference between British and Soviet experience is that shortages and controls have been transitory in Great Britain but have been a prevailing long-term feature of Soviet economic organization.

3.1. The Organization of Supply

In a market economy, when an enterprise succeeds in purchasing a commodity it requires, it is because some other enterprise had earlier decided to produce and sell it. The commodity may have been produced to order on the basis of a contract previously entered into. Or it may have been produced on the basis of forecasts of demand. In either case the interenterprise flow of commodities depends solely on the decisions of enterprises. There is no other agency responsible for assuring that the supply of individual commodities will be equal to the demand for them.

In the centrally planned Soviet economy a great deal of effort is devoted to the planning of interenterprise supply by structural units other than enterprises. For most industrial commodities in general, and for all major ones, the sale of a product by one enterprise to another is preceded by a great deal of planning work performed by units other than the two enterprises. The planning of the interenterprise flow of commodities is one of the major components of the overall process of national economic planning.

The Documents of Commodity Controls

In a fully monetized economy, money is a generalized claim on real resources. Anyone who has the money can expect to buy what he requires if he is willing to pay the price. The Soviet economy is not fully monetized in that sense. Money is necessary in order to claim resources, but it is not sufficient. Like the U.S. economy in wartime, one needs a document in addition to the money. It may be called a documonetary economy.

The interenterprise flow of commodities is preceded, in fact, by a massive flow of documents. Five documents are of crucial importance. They are controlled commodity lists, statements of requirements, physical balances, distribution plans, and allocation certificates.

The controlled commodity lists (nomenklatura). The basis of supply planning is a set of official controlled commodity lists. The number of such lists has varied from time to time, and from year to year the commodities placed on one or another list are changed. There are now six groups of controlled commodity lists. The planning of supply differs according to the type of list to which a commodity is assigned. The major characteristics of each list are summarized in Table 3.1. We do not know what proportion of total industrial output is covered by those 16,000 commodities, but they include all industrial materials, fuels, and equipment of any significance. The only industrial commodities that appear to be excluded are those produced locally for local use, which may be purchased by what is called decentralized procurement.

Table 3.1. Controlled Commodity Lists, 1968

List Number	Description of List		Agency Responsible for Balances and Distribution Plans	Agency Responsible for Final Approval	Number of Commodities
	Funded or Planned	Centralized or Decentralized			
1	Funded	Centralized	State Planning Committee	USSR Council of Ministers	400*
2	Planned	Centralized	State Planning Committee	State Planning Committee	1,569
3	Planned	Centralized	State Committee on Supply	State Committee on Supply	103
4	Planned	Centralized	All-Union Supply Administrations	State Committee on Supply	3,198
5	Planned	Decentralized	Territorial Supply Administrations	Territorial Supply Administrations	9,228
6	Planned	Decentralized	Ministry (Chief Administration on Supply)	Ministries	1,814
TOTAL					16,312

*Given in the source as 350-400. Source: N. V. Ivanov, E. Iu. Lokshin, and G. M. Demichev, *Ekonomika i planirovanie material'no-tekhnicheskogo snabzheniia v promyshlennosti* (The Economics and Planning of Supply in Industry) (Moscow: *Ekonomika*, 1969), pp. 333-340.

The statement of requirements (zaiavka). For every controlled commodity that an enterprise requires, it must submit a statement of requirements to the supply planning agencies at the time it submits its draft plan. It is on the basis of the consolidated statements of requirements of enterprises that the supply planning agencies calculate the total need for each controlled commodity for production purposes. As one may expect from the nature of the situation, the prudent manager strives to protect his enterprise by padding his statements of requirements a bit, a practice of which the supply planners are fully aware. The tale has been often told and need not be repeated here.[7] The main point is that the filling out of the statements of requirements is a vital function of the enterprise, and its success depends heavily on how well the purchasing department performs that task.

The physical balances (material'nye balansy). The central task of the supply planning agencies is to balance the planned use of each controlled commodity against the planned availability. Since the total planned availability of many commodities, on the basis of the draft enterprise plans, is less than the total planned use, the basic task of the supply planners is to bring availability and use into balance. This is done in a variety of ways, such as obliging some producers to produce more than they proposed in their draft plans, and requiring some users to accept less than they applied for in their statements of requirements. The "forcing" of balance is one of the principal reasons that enterprises often find their supplies of resources to be too small to support the production targets they are obliged to assume.[8]

The distribution plan (plan raspredeleniia). The physical balance of a controlled commodity is not "addressed" to specific organizations. The drawing up of addressed distribution plans is the second principal function of the supply planning agencies. The distribution plan of a controlled commodity matches specific producers with specific users. In the case of the highest priority list (List 1 in Table 3.1), the distribution plans are addressed to ministries. The Ministry of the Chemicals Industry, for example, is obliged to ship specified quantities of sulfuric acid to the Ministry of the Iron and Steel Industry, to the Ministry of Construction Machinery, and so forth. The chemicals ministry then parcels the aggregate target out among its enterprises, and the iron and steel ministry parcels out the allocations of sulfuric acid to its enterprises. The matching of individual producing and using enterprises is done by the supply planning agencies in collaboration with the ministries. In the case of lower-priority commodities (List 5) the distribution plans are addressed directly to enterprises.

The allocation certificate (nariad). The distribution plans, like all economic plans, are a blueprint, or a vision, of the forthcoming year's economic activity. A fifth set of documents is required to transform the vision into an operating force. An allocation certificate is a legal entitlement to purchase the stated quantity of a controlled commodity. The producer of a controlled commodity is forbidden by law to sell to a purchaser who does not possess an allocation certificate. The purchaser is still obliged to pay for the goods, but the sale may not be consummated unless the purchaser has an allocation certificate. It is the legal force of this kind of document that distinguishes a monetary from a documonetary economy.

Allocation certificates are issued to all users by the supply planning agencies on the basis of their distribution plans. At the same time, the supply agencies issue shipping orders (*nariad-zakaz*) to the ministries or enterprises listed as producers in the distribution plans. The allocation certificates and shipping orders enable producers and customers to identify each other and then to draw up legal contracts specifying shipping schedules, technical details, and terms of payment.

The allocation certificate is the most vital document in the economic life of the enterprise. No commodity of any importance can be legally purchased without it. In recent years some progress has been made in expanding the range of commodities that may be freely purchased—without an allocation certificate—but it is still a limited range.[9] It is still fundamentally a documonetary economy, and the allocation certificate is its central document.

The Supply Planning Agencies

Three groups of agencies have been assigned responsibility for planning the distribution of controlled commodities. They are the State Planning Committee, the State Committee on Supply, and the ministries.

The State Planning Committee (Gosplan). The State Planning Committee plans the distribution of commodities judged to be of major importance in the national economy. The most important of these, which are designated "funded" commodities (List 1), are included in the National Economic Plan.[10] The organizations entitled by the distribution plans to receive funded commodities are called "allocation centers" (*fondoderzhateli*).[11] The allocation centers are chiefly industrial ministries, agencies of the State Committee on Supply, and the republic governments. Designation as an official allocation center is a source of considerable power, for that organization controls the subsequent distribution among enterprises of the most vital commodities.[12]

Funded commodities are those that have one or more of the following four characteristics: they are of major national importance and massproduced (coal, gasoline, diesel fuel, rolled steel, steel pipe, major chemicals, major types of machinery equipment); they are in short supply relative to the demand; major imported commodities; and new products to be rapidly introduced into the economy.

The balances and distribution plans for funded commodities must receive the approval of the Council of Ministers. In addition, there is a range of commodities that the Planning Committee is authorized to plan on its own account (List 2 in Table 3.1). The balances and distribution plans of these commodities are drawn up by the Committee's product divisions and are approved officially by the Committee chairmen.

There were about 2,000 commodities on the two lists controlled by the Planning Committee in 1968, about 400 of which were funded commodities. The number of funded commodities has varied greatly in the postwar period, from a high of 2,100 in 1953 to a low of 135 in 1959.[13] The total number planned by the Planning Committee itself, however, has been fairly stable in recent years, in the neighborhood of 2,000.

The State Committee on Supply (Gossnab). The second agency authorized to plan the supply of a large range of commodities is the State Committee on Supply. The Committee's organization consists of three groups of divisions. One group consists of 20 all-union supply administrations (*soiuzglavsnabsbyty*), which are responsible on a nationwide basis for the distribution of a range of commodities indicated by their titles; the All-Union Chief Chemicals Supply Administration, for example. The second group consists of 56 territorial supply administrations, such as the Kharkov Supply Administration. The all-union supply administrations deal only with documents, with the processing of statements of requirements and allocation certificates. The territorial administrations deal with documents too, but are responsible also for the actual handling of the commodities (*realizatsiia*). They operate a network of about 1,500[14] local supply offices (*kontory*), depots (*bazy*), warehouses (*sklady*), and stores (*magaziny*). The third group of divisions consists of eleven all-union construction supply administrations (*soiuzglavkomplekty*) that handle the supply of materials and equipment to construction projects in various industries.

The State Committee on Supply is responsible for the supply planning of all commodities listed in the official production plans of the ministries other than those planned by the State Planning Committee (Lists 3, 4, and 5).[15] It is also responsible for the physical distribution of some portion of the commodities planned by the State Planning Committee.[16] The agencies of the Committee planned the distribution of over 12,000 commodities in 1968, on the three controlled commodity lists for which they were responsible. The largest number, about 9,000, were controlled by the territorial supply administrations. They consisted of the commodities of lesser importance and scarcity, as well as those produced and used primarily within a single territorial district. The State Committee network handled over 60 percent of the total sales of producer goods in the country.[17]

The Ministries. Under the ministry system that prevailed before 1957,[18] the ministries were responsible for the supply planning of all the products now included in the four lower commodity lists in Table 3.1. Commodity lists 3, 4, and 5 have now been taken from them, leaving them some 1,800 commodities on list 6.[19] These consist of commodities that are produced and used primarily by the enterprises of a single ministry as well as other commodities of a low level of priority that are nevertheless thought to require controlled distribution.

The ministries retain nevertheless a great deal of power over the interenterprise flow of commodities, even over those on the first five control lists the planning of which is conducted by the State Committees. The law makes it quite clear that it is the ministries, and not the State Committees, that are responsible for the supply of materials and equipment to their enterprises.[20] With respect to the commodities planned by the State Planning Committee, the ministry provides and therefore controls the information available to that Committee on the production capacity and input requirements of its enterprises. The success of the enterprises therefore depends on the skill with which the ministry's chief supply administration (*glavsnab*) "defends" the draft production plan and statements of requirements.[21] The ministry also possesses a great deal of decision-making authority, both with respect to the inputs required by their enterprises, and the distribution of the output of their enterprises. On the input side, the commodities controlled by the Planning Committee are addressed to the ministries, who are the legal fund holders. The ministry therefore has the power to decide how the funded commodities assigned to them are to be distributed among their enterprises. On the output side, the Planning Committee's distribution plans govern the shipment of commodities produced by one ministry to the enterprises of another. But the specific shipping instructions are given by the producer's ministry to its own enterprises. With tight production schedules, the ministry has the power and the interest to assure that the supply needs of its own enterprises are attended to first. Hence a producing enterprise, originally instructed by its ministry to ship an order to an enterprise in another ministry, may receive a last-minute instruction to cancel that order and ship instead to another enterprise that happens to belong to the same ministry. Ministries have long been chastized for the sort of "departmentalism," but the pressures under which they operate are often impossible to resist.

The State Committee on Supply controls its major commodities (Lists 3 and 4, Table 3.1) in exactly the same way as the State Planning Committee controls its commodities; that is, by means of balances and distribution plans.[22] Since these distribution plans are also addressed to the ministries, they have the same power to control the flow of inputs into and outputs from their enterprises. That the ministries make full use of that power is suggested by the somewhat plaintive remark of the Deputy Chairman of the State Committee on Supply, "The relations between the ministries and the all-union supply administrations are not yet sufficiently clear."[23] A history of frequent organizational changes in the supply agencies reflects the bureaucratic struggle for the power to control the distribution of these commodities.

In the case of commodities on control List 5, the ministry appears to have very little power. For these commodities, all enterprises in a territory, regardless of the ministry to which they belong, must apply to the territorial supply administration. That administration draws up the balances and distribution plans, which are addressed directly to enterprises. A ministry has no direct power to help one of its enterprises obtain a supplementary allotment of these commodities, although a telephone call from Moscow surely helps. The ministry does, however, retain its power over the distribution of those commodities in this group that happen to be produced by its own enterprises. If an enterprise receives an order to ship a certain quantity of the product to some other enterprise, the ministry may countermand that order in its own interests. Someone may be hauled into court and fined as a result, which happens quite often, but the ministry is still the enterprise's boss and its orders are overriding.

3.2. Effectiveness of the Supply System

The system of interenterprise supply set forth in Section 3.1 is that which, with frequent modifications, has governed the flow of resources for the past four decades. It has been effective, in the sense that it sustained the economy through its periods of rapid industrialization, war and reconstruction, and postwar growth. But it has also been inefficient in many respects, leading to extensive hoarding, waste, and misuse of resources. At the least it has been unreliable, and uncertainty over supply has long been the major problem facing industrial managers. A variety of reasons has been set forth to explain why the supply system is characterized by such great unreliability in the flow of intermediate products among enterprises. Following the major American authority on the subject, we may distinguish four principal sources of weakness in the procedures.[24]

First, the methods whereby the supply planners strive to bring the planned use of each commodity into equality with the planned availability generally lead to illusory, or "paper" balances. The equality of planned use and availability is often attained by "forcing" the targets of producers upward and of users downward. In the event, the forced targets are often underfulfilled, and there is simply not enough of the commodity available for all those who received allocation certificates for it. The plan itself is therefore destined for underfulfillment even though it gives the appearance of balance at the time it is officially confirmed.

Second, the process of plan construction consumes a great deal of time, and the time schedules for preparing the documents have not always been met. Enterprises then find themselves working for as many as two or three months at the beginning of the year on guesses as to what their output plans will be, and without the allocations of the materials they require.

Third, supply plans have not always been coordinated with output and financial plans. A major reason for this lack of coordination has been the practice by ministries, out of necessity, of changing enterprise output targets at various times and sometimes frequently in the course of the year. Changes in output targets are not always accompanied by the appropriate changes in supply plans. As a result, enterprises have found themselves with useless surpluses of supplies needed for the original plan but not for the revised plan, and with pressing shortages of supplies needed for the revised but not for the original.

Fourth, for the highest priority commodities, the producing and consuming units in the balancing process are not enterprises but ministries. Many of the difficulties arise in the process of specifying which using enterprises will receive what quantities of each ministry's total allocation of each good, and which producing enterprise will be charged with the production and shipment of which portion of each ministry's total production target of each good. The difficulties may be traced to the complexity and high degree of centralization of this specification process and to a preoccupation with the efficiency of the producers at the expense of the convenience of users.

For the reasons set forth, the balances and distribution plans do not constitute a perfectly coordinated set. Further problems arise in the course of implementation of the plans. Soon after the plan year begins, disproportions begin to arise, and both the supply planners and the ministries begin changing enterprise plans. They "change sellers without the consent of the buyers, they pull a product out of production without first preparing for its production elsewhere, they change both output plans and production schedules," writes a critic.[25] Plan changes are referred to so often in the press that one wonders if many enterprises end the year with the same plan with which they started.

Whatever the sources of the supply problem, the fact of the unreliability of the flow of resources is the chief cause of the well-known practices whereby managers strive to defend their enterprises against the threat of underfulfilling their plan targets.[26] Managers, for example, strive to build a "safety factor" into both their production and supply plans. They strive to have output targets assigned to them which are less than they believe they can produce, and to order more supplies and equipment than they need.

Shortages of supplies also account for various output practices frowned on by the central government. Among the reasons why enterprises often produce an assortment of products different from that planned is that the resources are not available for producing the planned assortment; one produces what he can with the available resources, even if the resulting assortment does not correspond to the plan. Similarly, the prevailing problem of low-quality output is due in part to two aspects of the supply problem: on the one hand, poor-quality materials, or the attempt to spread limited resources too thinly, leads to low quality; and on the other, the general unreliability of supply makes it clear to producers that hungry purchasers will not quibble about quality. To ensure the flow of resources to their enterprises, management has found it necessary to resort to the extensive use of personal influence and inducements, bordering on and sometimes including bribery. A quasi-legal profession of "expediters" has emerged, composed of men with the special contacts and talents needed to minimize the interruption in the flow of resources.

These practices have all developed within the basic structure of economic organization. One may note, finally, that the very structure of industry has been distorted in response to the unreliability of the supply system, as reflected in the practice of "universalism," as it is called. Enterprises have tended to build up their own in-house capacity to produce the principal materials and equipment needed for their basic line of production. In the machinery industry, 71 percent of all enterprises produce their own castings and 84 percent produce their own forgings.[27] Ninety percent of all spare parts are produced to order in the machine shops of the equipment users, rather than mass-produced by the equipment producers.[28] As a result, about 70 percent of the total national stock of machine tools is widely dispersed among the small machine shops of the equipment users rather than being concentrated in the machinery-production industry.[29] In his study of the Soviet metalworking industry, David Granick has demonstrated that the chief cause of this universalism is the effort by management to protect its sources of supply.[30] The reasons are not at all mysterious and are fully understood by Soviet observers. "The logic is simple," is the summary comment by a correspondent in the Party's industrial newspaper. "The fewer connections with other enterprises, the fewer the headaches. From my own shops I'll always get what I need; but if you are tied to others, you're forever in arbitration courts. The chief point is why take the risk? For after all, the additional costs are all accounted for and written into the plan."[31]

3.3. Uncertainty over Supply and the Innovation Decision

The unreliability of the supply system is a fact with which all managers must deal, whether they are innovators or not. If its consequences were the same for all decisions, it would be neutral in the choice among alternatives. In fact, however, its consequences are more severe for innovators than for noninnovators. Hence, if on all other grounds a manager were indifferent in a choice between innovating or not, the effect of the supply problem is to bias the decision in the direction of noninnovating.

The point is that the avoidance of innovation is a device for minimizing uncertainty over supply. In the course of time the noninnovator becomes increasingly familiar with the technical characteristics of the materials he uses and learns to cope with variations in the quality of the materials delivered by his suppliers. He learns which suppliers are more reliable in their delivery schedules and which are less. He establishes channels of communication and influence with the many officials in his ministry and in the central government agencies who have the power to issue the allocation certificates for the many materials on which he depends. His agents also establish relations with the marketing officials in his supplier enterprises, for the mere possession of an allocation certificate is no guarantee that the shipper will be able and willing to ship on time. He manages to stock, legally or illegally, working supplies of the materials that experience has shown to be the least reliable in supply. He is still bedeviled by difficulties, but as long as there are no major changes in his product line and production processes, he may hope to keep them to a minimum.

Consider now the director contemplating a major innovation, either on the initiative of the enterprise or by order of the ministry. He may require a new type of material or component, the technical characteristics of which are unfamiliar to his engineers. He may be assigned new suppliers, perhaps in remote parts of the country, whose reliability in quality or scheduling is completely unknown. He may have to cultivate a new group of officials in the ministry and the agencies of central government. Long-established relations with the State Planning Committee men in the metals division are now of no help, and new ones must be established with the men in the plastics division. The greater the scale of the proposed innovation, the greater the magnitude of the supply problems to be anticipated. And the greater the unreliability of the system of supply, the greater the resistance to innovation.

The act of innovation not only reduces the capacity of the enterprise to protect its supply of materials and equipment, it also generates a set of specific supply problems that do not arise or are of less significance for the noninnovating enterprise. One general cause of the supply problem, for example, is that formal estimates of supply requirements are made far in advance of the time that the supplies will actually be used. The year's supplies are based on a draft plan drawn up during the summer of the preceding year. Hence, the deliveries an enterprise receives in December of one year are based on the statements of requirements submitted a year and a half earlier. The task of forecasting requirements is difficult enough for the enterprise with an unchanging line of production. But in R & D one "doesn't fully know what he will need tomorrow, let alone next month or next quarter or next year," writes Dr. Sominskii.[32] The same is true of technological innovation. In the redesign of a recently installed new manufacturing process, the enterprise may require an instrument or piece of equipment that had not been anticipated a year earlier when the statements of requirements were submitted. Since no statement of requirement had been submitted, the enterprise has no allocation certificate for that commodity. And without an allocation certificate it is impossible to purchase it legally, especially if it is on a high-priority list such as the funded commodity control list. It is the perpetual hunt for materials and equipment without allocation certificates for them, writes an innovating director, that delays for years the start-up time of new processes or products.[33]

Not only is the problem of supply forecasting more difficult for the innovator, but the consequences of supply problems are more serious. Interruption in the flow of supplies in an ongoing production operation may lead to lower rates of output and perhaps underfulfillment of the production and sales targets. But when similar difficulties lead to delays in the installation and start-up of a new production facility, output is zero for the duration of the delay. "For want of a nail" is a parable that looms large in the calculations of any director contemplating a major innovation, for each knows of experiences like that of the Dneprodzerzhinsk Chemical Combine in which a major construction project was held up because of the delayed delivery of 47 tons of stainless steel and a few tons of polyethylene pipe.[34] It is because of such delays that in industries with an advancing technology, innovators may find themselves trapped with a new production facility that is obsolescent before start-up operations are completed and full-capacity production attained.[35]

If innovative activity were not competitive with the rest of the enterprise's production obligations, the risks would be smaller. In practice, however, work on innovation cannot be insulated from the basic production activity. If the enterprise is under pressure to complete an innovation that has been held up because of supply difficulties, it may be "compelled to use its own internal resources for that purpose, which is harmful for the fulfillment of the current production program."[36] Even this alternative is not always available, however, "for the production of new experimental machinery and equipment requires, as a rule, different materials from those that are used in established lines of production (in shape, size, brand, chemical and physical properties)."[37]

A further difficulty arises from the fact that innovators often require special-order jobs or relatively small quantities of various commodities. Suppliers regard these orders as a nuisance and as an interference with their own central production tasks. The size of the orders, moreover, is often smaller than the minimum quantities that suppliers are required to ship directly to customers by the "transit" method. Innovators, therefore, must arrange their purchases by the "warehouse" method; that is, through the network of local sales offices and supply depots. These sources are generally poorly stocked; they obtain their own stocks from the inventories of the large manufacturers who, in turn, treat production for stock as of a very low order of importance compared to their production for large-scale direct delivery under the transit method. To protect themselves, innovating firms sometimes inflate their orders to a size large enough to qualify for a direct "transit" shipment from the manufacturer, "which, naturally, is harmful both to the enterprise and to the state."[38] In general, managers report that the organizations that run the supply system are oriented entirely toward current production and are of little help to an enterprise building a prototype model or testing new processes.[39]

The general property of the problem is that the innovator places his enterprise in a position of increased dependence on other economic units which, under circumstances of unreliability of supply, is the courting of possible disaster. The literature abounds with cases of innovations held up because of inadequate or delayed product development or production in other enterprises and industries. Thus, a series of tobacco plants were designed and built in anticipation of the availability of a new type of instrument. The builder counted on a 1961 order of the State Committee on Automation and Machine-building to the instrument producer to have the instrument in production by 1964. Six plants were almost fully completed by mid-1967, at which time the builder was officially informed that the instruments were not yet in production.[40] Again, the "Russian Diesel" Plant was under orders of the central government to increase the horsepower of their engines. In the course of several years of development work they made a number of significant advances that, however, required certain new metals for chrome piston rings and diamond-honed bushings as well as certain new oil additives. But the research institutes in the metallurgical and petroleum industries were slow in tackling those problems, for the reason (we may infer) that they were chiefly occupied with R & D work more central to the concerns of their own administrative hierarchies.[41]

The effect of supply problems on innovation depends, of course, on the scale of the innovation. Innovations that require extensive construction work appear to pose the greatest problems. Dr. L. Gatovskii, the former Director of the Institute of Economics, has repeatedly expressed concern about the state of supply planning in the construction sector. The reasons for the more serious problems of materials supply in construction work are not unrelated to the uncertainty that characterizes all innovation. Cost estimation in construction work is notoriously unreliable under any conditions—Gatovskii reports that final costs generally exceed estimated costs by 50 to 100 percent. Among the reasons is the fact that construction work often takes a long time, during which conditions change; and construction projects are usually unique, each one presenting its special sources of uncertainty. At any rate, since materials supply plans for construction projects are based on the original cost estimates, the builders may find themselves with approved projects but insufficient materials.[42]

Supply difficulties tend to undermine efforts by the central government to encourage innovation by various structural improvements. In recent years, the bureaucratic burden of undertaking small-scale investments has been eased for enterprises by authorizing the State Bank to grant loans for such purposes. But while this measure of decentralization provides innovating firms with both the authority and the financing for, say, the automation of a process or the installation of a technologically advanced piece of equipment, it does nothing to ease the problem of obtaining materials and equipment. Hence enterprises like the First-of-May Machinery Plant ceased using State Bank credits for its efforts at introducing new technology.[43] The Bank itself, concerned about the default of its loans, appears to have undermined the measure further by requiring enterprises to demonstrate in advance that they have an assured and sufficient supply of raw materials to enable them to employ the new equipment at full capacity.[44] Similarly, the 1965 reform provides enterprises with an additional source of decentralized financing of technological development in the so-called Production Development Fund, which is formed out of enterprise profits. Here too the meritorious intent of the measure has been frustrated by the repeated experience of enterprises that despite the availability of financing, the required equipment or materials are often not available.[45]

The difficulties due to the unreliability of a particular supplier are compounded by the fact that supplying enterprises may be changed without consultation with the customer. The Belgorod Boiler Plant, for example, received its shipments of seamless pipe from a Dnepropetrovsk plant in the first quarter of 1967, from the Urals in the second, and from Nikopol in the third.[46] This "plague" of frequent changes in suppliers complicates the task of scheduling deliveries and raises engineering difficulties when technical properties are not perfectly homogeneous among the various suppliers. On the other hand, customers who are dissatisfied with a particular supplier find it difficult to change to another. A certain large enterprise wished to stop dealing with a container producer in a remote part of the country whose shipments were always tardy and whose products the enterprise "did not really need" anyhow. They searched around and finally located a better supplier with whom a friendly preliminary agreement was duly reached. But the formal negotiations between the two organizations dragged on month after month.[47] The organizational structure makes it difficult for innovators to control their sources of supply by selecting and cultivating suppliers on whom they might hope to rely.

To provide greater stability of supply to innovating enterprises, the planning agencies earmark certain quantities of centrally allocated commodities for specified projects involving new technology. This special treatment is a mark of recognition that reliability of supply affects the innovation decision. But its influence appears to be lost in the overall supply system. For one thing, the special allocations apply only to large-scale work on new technology, which is estimated to cover only 20 to 30 percent of all work on innovation.[48] Second, the original earmarking tends to disappear in the course of the vast flow of paperwork that precedes the flow of commodities. The central supply planning agency designates certain supplies for use only on the new technology projects, but the documents that eventually find their way into the hands of the actual producers and users do not stipulate whether a particular shipment is to be used for innovation work or general production. Hence shipments originally earmarked for the special supply of innovations simply take their turn along with all the others on the production and shipping schedules of the producers.[49]

People whose jobs or interests are focused on the problem of technological progress continue to press for special treatment, for ways of insulating innovative activity from the uncertainties that characterize the general supply system. But special treatment of this kind is not a promising solution. For one thing, it would add one more dimension of complexity to the process of supply planning and administration, which is already abundantly complex. A second and more interesting objection appears to have been anticipated by some proponents of the measure. They urge that when supplies earmarked for innovation are assigned higher priority or sold without allocation certificates, users must be required to use them for no other purpose.[50] The Soviet reader will understand instantly the point of this caution. For if it becomes the general practice that any enterprise can obtain controlled commodities without allocation certificates and can secure priority treatment for its orders simply by declaring that they are to be used for some intended innovation, managers will surely begin to flood suppliers with such orders. The "simulation" of conformity to a bureaucratic regulation is a long-established practice of Soviet management in many spheres of enterprise activity, and it would require no great ingenuity to invent ways of qualifying for special treatment under a regulation of this sort.[51]

But the more general difficulty with proposals of this kind is that they increase the range of ad hoc and arbitrary decision making in the flow of resources. Innovation is only one, though certainly a major one, of the many economic activities that suffer from uncertainty in resource availability. Certain persons, by virtue of their positions or interests, become protagonists of the cause of innovation and urge that exceptions be made. Others do the same for other economic activities that in their view require promotion; the production of spare parts, for example, or the petrochemical industry, or export industries, or the production of consumer goods from waste products, or the repair and maintenance of equipment, or the conservation of nonferrous metals, and certainly the aerospace and military industries. The groups that promote these activities are the equivalent of the interest groups in capitalist economies that urge special legislation in behalf of their activities, from tariff protection to highway beautification. In the Soviet context, such special-interest groups often urge that exceptions be made in the matter of supply.[52] When the source of supply difficulties is of a short-run nature, the case for exceptional treatment may be strong. But when the source of the difficulty inheres in the basic structural properties and policies of the system, the use of remedies by exception serves only to add complexity and arbitrariness to the flow of resources and to lend further encouragement to practices of evasion and simulation.

The alternative to special treatment is to employ general measures for reducing the level of uncertainty in the overall system of supply. Some recent measures of that kind are discussed in the next Section 3.4. We may note in anticipation, however, that it is not simply the uncertainty of the state of supply that discourages innovators. Men who are otherwise prepared to undertake something new generally expect to live with uncertainty. One might guess, indeed, that the innovative temperament rather relishes uncertainty, even though one prefers less to more of it. It may therefore be less a matter of the presence of uncertainty than of lack of authority and power to cope with it. To state the case in the form of a proposition, given the degree of uncertainty generated by the structure of economic organization, the greater the authority or power of the manager to deal with it, the greater his willingness to innovate. Perhaps the major lesson to be learned from the following account is the sense of powerlessness a director must feel in trying to cope with the task of ensuring the flow of supplies for his basic production program, let alone innovation. The author, Director of the October Revolution Chemical Plant, has, incidentally, a Ph.D. degree in economics:

With a touch of fantasy, let us imagine this picture: in the coordinating center of the State Committee on Supply, with the assistance of a special automated system that gathers, processes, and transmits information, they determined the following facts: some very important construction projects have been left without zinc white, because the All-Union Chief Chemicals Supply Administration issued them an allocation certificate for zinc white from our chemical plant in Rostov, but at the same time the All-Union Chief Non-Ferrous Metals Supply Administration withdrew from our plant the zinc from which the aforementioned zinc white is made. . . . This simple bit of information should come to the attention of the Deputy Chairman of the State Committee, Comrade Lebedev. He would then quickly take appropriate measures, for both supply administrations are responsible to him.

But how do matters actually stand now? The officials of the Chemicals Supply Administration know perfectly well that our plant can't manufacture mineral pigments without zinc. They ought to go to Comrade Lebedev who evidently by error had given the order to withdraw the allocation of zinc from our plant. But instead of that, the administration bombards the enterprise with telegrams to ship the zinc white. In the Non-Ferrous Metals Supply Administration they also understand that zinc white cannot be made out of "nothing," but there too no one wants to approach Comrade Lebedev.

And so our enterprise people travel from Rostov to Moscow, go from one supply administration to the other, clarify the obvious, but with no apparent success. Eventually the year draws to an end, and in both supply administrations they breathe easier. The matter has been removed from the agenda, so to speak. But how do people feel at the enterprise, where our equipment stood idle, and on the construction projects that never received the zinc white they need? . . .

Or take this example. At the end of December we were informed that we were to receive an allocation of seed oil for the first quarter of 1967 (the oil is used for manufacturing pharmaceuticals). We got in touch with the supplying enterprise and learned that there is no oil to be had because last year there had been a failure of the apricot crop. Meanwhile the supply agencies have already issued allocation certificates to the medical institutions for pharmaceuticals that we will be unable to manufacture. Now dozens of respectable institutions are seeking ways out of the situation. But clearly it won't be found soon.[53]

3.4. Structural Reforms in the Supply System

The system of commodity controls was established in the early nineteen-thirties, at the inception of the five-year plans. While the principle of planned distribution has remained unchanged, the organizational structures for administering the system have frequently changed. The most recent major changes were introduced as part of the 1965 Economic Reform. The Reform was a serious effort to improve the operation of the economy in general, and parts of it were directed specifically to the problem of supply. The two principal changes that affect the supply system are the establishment of the State Committee on Supply and the introduction of wholesale trade. The final section deals with the tautness of planning, which is the source of many of the problems of supply.

The State Committee on Supply

When the ministry system of enterprise administration was restored in 1965, a number of measures were taken to eliminate some of the major deficiencies of the pre-1957 ministry system. Many of those deficiencies were due to the ministries' control over the supply system. Each ministry controlled the supply of all the commodities produced by its enterprises that were not controlled by the State Planning Committee.

The ministries tended to use their powers to favor the supply needs of their own enterprises. As a result, enterprises often encountered special difficulties in obtaining supplies controlled by other ministries. One of the consequences was the aforementioned tendency toward "universalism," or "autarky," by enterprises and ministries. Another was excessively long hauls; under ministry instructions, enterprises often received goods from suppliers in their own ministry located halfway across the country, since nearby producers of the same goods could not be counted on if they were part of a different ministry.[54]

The State Committee on Supply was established along with the new ministries in 1965 in order to eliminate those deficiencies. The Committee was assigned responsibility for the distribution of some 12,000 commodities (Lists 3, 4, and 5 in Table 3.1) that had been controlled by the ministries before 1957. Since the Committee has no interest in favoring one ministry over another, that source of maldistribution of supplies no longer exists.

This solution, however, involves a certain increase in the degree of centralization of the commodity control system. The 3,000 commodities on Lists 3 and 4 have been moved a step upward from the ministries to the new State Committee on Supply. They are now controlled at the central government level, like the commodities controlled by the State Planning Committee, which is two decision-making levels away from the enterprise. The two State Committees constitute two separate and parallel administrative hierarchies that perform identical supply planning functions for different groups of commodities. Hence the ministry now has two masters instead of one. In organizing the supply of commodities for its enterprises, the ministry must now conduct two separate sets of negotiations with the two State Committees. To the extent that the deficiencies in the supply system are due to excessive centralization in decision making, therefore, the new organizational structure may have compounded some of the problems. The supply problem described by the Director of the October Revolution Chemical Plant in his negotiations with the new all-union supply administrations (from Note 53) is typical of the decades-old difficulties of centralized supply planning. In the past, however, that type of problem was localized in the State Planning Committee. Now it has been extended to the offices of the State Committee on Supply.

The other 9,000 commodities are controlled not in the central offices of the State Committee but in their territorial supply administrations

(List 5). This change is often regarded as a form of decentralization, from the Moscow-based ministries to the regionally based supply administrations. It is indeed an increase in decentralization in the geographical sense. That is, if the measure of decentralization is the mean distance that people and papers are obliged to travel, the establishment of the territorial administrations has increased decentralization. But in the day of telephones and jet aircraft, geography is not the most significant aspect of decentralization. From the point of view of organizational structure, the appropriate measure is not physical distance but levels of decision-making authority. From this point of view, the establishment of the territorial supply administrations involves no change in degree of decentralization of supply planning. The balances and distribution plans that were formerly prepared one level above the enterprise by the ministries are now prepared one level above the enterprise by the territorial administrations.[55] Therefore, in evaluating the change in the locus of control over these 9,000 commodities from ministries to territorial administrations, the significant consequences flow not from any change in degree of decentralization but from the change in the organizational structure of decision making. The question is this: Suppose that for organizational reasons the 50,000 industrial enterprises are to be partitioned into groups and the administration of their economic activity is to be conducted at one level above the enterprises, ought the enterprises to be partitioned by the principle of physical proximity or by the principle of technological affinity? The present organizational structure has adopted the principle of technological affinity for general planning and administration but the principle of physical proximity for supply planning.[56]

Two kinds of benefits may be claimed for the new organizational structure. First, in allocating controlled commodities among users and matching producers with users, the territorial administrations have no organizational interest in favoring certain enterprises in their territories over others. Supply planning decisions for these 9,000 commodities should therefore be less subject to ministerial-organizational bias.

Second, the territorial administrations now have full control over the physical distribution of all commodities shipped by the warehousing method; not only the 9,000 they plan directly but also those on all the controlled commodity lists. This should eliminate the gross multiplication of local supply facilities that characterized the pre-1957 ministry system. At that time each industrial town contained a large number of local supply offices operated by the chief supply administrations (*glavs-naby*) of the ministries. One might find dozens of local offices stocking the same kinds of commodities but each selling only to enterprises of their own ministries. One read often of a commodity, desperately needed by an enterprise, that was abundantly stocked in one supply depot but not available at all in a neighboring one. But because the enterprise was in the "wrong" ministry, it was not able to purchase the commodity. Again, this sort of multiplication of facilities and inflexibility in supply has been eliminated under the new system.

Against these substantial benefits, however, there are certain disadvantages to be noted. The eight-year-long experience with the regional economic councils provides abundant evidence that territorial organizational units can develop an organizational bias as strong as that of ministerial units.[57] The chief of a territorial supply administration has no interest in discriminating among enterprises within his territory, but he does have an interest in discriminating between enterprises in "his" territory and those in others. The success of his administration is measured by the effectiveness of the supply operations in his territory, and complaints from enterprises in remote parts of the country are of less consequence than those coming from influential directors in his own territory. Hence a territorial administration in control of a stock of a scarce commodity is less likely to ship it abroad to another territory than to preserve it for local use.

In establishing the territorial principle of supply, therefore, the Soviet leaders exchanged a technological bias for a geographical bias in the interenterprise flow of commodities. The question is, which bias leads to a more costly distortion in the commodity flow from what may be regarded as an optimal flow? An a priori answer is difficult to give, but evidence and logic suggests that geographical bias may be more costly. Part of the reason is the quality of information available to the decision makers in the two instances. The supply officials in a single ministry deal with a relatively homogeneous group of enterprises with similar technological and economic characteristics. The officials in a territorial supply administration deal with a heterogeneous group of enterprises, with greatly differing technological characteristics. The former are therefore better able to make an optimal choice in allocating a scarce commodity among competing users. Indeed, it was precisely in order to overcome this lack of expertise that the regional economic councils gradually built up huge technical and planning staffs, until each possessed its own global State Planning Committee in miniature. On a somewhat smaller scale, one may foresee that the territorial supply administrations, out of sheer necessity, will gradually expand their technical staffs in order to cope with the supply problems of the entire "little economy" of the territory.

Empirical evidence on the relative efficiency of territorial partitioning and technological partitioning is difficult to assemble. But there is abundant evidence that the long-standing problems of supply continue to arise under the territorial administrations, in their classic form. One enterprise reports its difficulty in submitting its statement of requirements to the territorial wholesale administration in Voronezh:

They are then sent to the ministry; and from there, the statements of requirements are sent back to Voronezh, often with a delay, so that the allocation of materials has already been distributed and the enterprise is left without any.

Another enterprise, in Kursk, used large quantities of corrugated packing board and owned a machine for corrugating flat board. But the territorial supply administration ordered the flat board to be shipped first to Griazi, to be corrugated there. The reason, they said, was to provide work for a corrugating machine in an enterprise in Griazi that was not loaded to capacity. The corrugated board was then reshipped back to Kursk.[58] It is clear that the system does not yet offer an enterprise the opportunity to purchase whatever materials it needs in the light of its own assessment of its requirements.

Summarizing, the establishment of the State Committee on Supply increased the degree of centralization of supply planning for 3,000 high-priority commodities (relative to the pre-1957 ministry system). It maintained the preexisting degree of centralization for 9,000 less-important commodities, but it replaced the technological principle of organization of supply planning by the territorial principle, which changes the direction of bias in supply planning in what may be a more costly way. The chief benefit from the reform may be found not in the organization of supply planning but in the organization of the physical flow of commodities, which is now conducted by the territorial administrations.

Wholesale Trade

A centrally planned economy can adopt a variety of organizational methods for distributing commodities. As discussed in this chapter, the method of commodity controls, which has been in use in the USSR for four decades for the distribution of producers' goods, may be called direct distribution.[59] In this method every ton of coal produced has the name tag of its future user attached to it, as it were.[60] There is a certain common sense in the use of this method, for under the balancing technique of planning, the output plans of enterprises are based in part on the declared input needs of other enterprises. Since the information on user needs is already available, one may as well use it for distributing the output. The purpose of the commodity distribution plans, in fact, is precisely to identify, for the producer, the intended user of each ton or yard of his output.

Sensible as it may be, direct distribution is not the only organizational structure that may be conjoined with the central planning of outputs. At the other extreme, the central planners may fix the output plans of enterprises as at present, concentrating their efforts on assuring that the total availability of each commodity will be equal to the total use. But when that has been assured by output planning, no further central effort is made to match individual producers and users. They can be left to search out each other, either directly or through a specialized intermediary—a middleman. When a middleman is used, this method of distributing commodities is known as trade (*torgovliia*) distribution. Wholesale trade may not seem like the "natural" method for a centrally planned economy, but it is clearly an alternative arrangement to direct distribution.

In fact, the trade method has long been used for the distribution of consumer goods. But direct distribution has always been the cornerstone of the distribution of producer goods. It is indeed so intimate a part of Soviet economic organization that it is difficult to conceive of the Soviet economy operating with a different distribution system. It was therefore a signal event when the program of the 1965 Economic Reforms contained a provision for the introduction of wholesale trade in producers' goods.

It should be noted at the outset that wholesale trade is not intended to replace economic planning. Both direct distribution and wholesale trade are regarded as alternative methods of planned distribution of commodities. The argument is presented in the following authoritative, if somewhat obscure, statement:

Excessive centralization in the distribution of output, which played a positive role in the development of the national economy, has now begun to exert a negative influence on the efficiency of production and supply. . . . The problem is this: with the continued strengthening of the role of state planning, and with optimal balancing of material resources and needs for the whole national economy, we must create the conditions required for the transition from centralized direct distribution (*fondirovanie*) to the planned distribution of producers' goods by means of wholesale trade.[61]

The territorial supply administrations have been assigned the responsibility for organizing the system of wholesale trade. The range of commodities that may be sold at wholesale is determined by the State Committee on Supply. On May 1 the Committee publishes a wholesale commodity list (*nomenklatura*), identifying the goods that may be wholesaled in the forthcoming year. The list changes from year to year, and may include commodities that appeared the preceding year on a controlled commodity list. The territorial supply administrations place orders for these commodities and receive purchase authorizations (*limity*) entitling them to receive delivery.[62] The wholesaled commodities may be purchased by enterprises from the supply organizations at any time; this is an advantage, for, unlike the controlled commodities, no statements of requirements need be drawn up at the time the draft enterprise plan is prepared. Large purchases are shipped by the transit method; the supply organization receives the purchaser's order and then arranges for the direct shipment of the goods from the producer to the purchaser. Small purchases are made by the warehousing method, from the local wholesale stores, depots, and warehouses. It is anticipated indeed that in the future, all R & D organizations will purchase all their materials and equipment through the wholesale trade network.[63]

Wholesale trade may lead to a massive improvement in the capacity of enterprises to ensure their flow of supplies. For the first time in Soviet economic history since 1930, an enterprise confronted by the lack of some materials or tools or components need not be trapped by its failure to have anticipated the need a year in advance. It is no longer obliged to apply to its chief branch administration in Moscow or to dispatch its agents to the All-Union Chief Non-Ferrous Metals Supply Administration in Moscow for an allocation order for zinc. It need only place an order with the local wholesaling organization downtown and expect the required commodity to be delivered with despatch. The reduction in uncertainty over supply would be of even greater value to the innovator than to the noninnovator and would increase the rate of innovation.

At the present time, however, wholesale trade is of interest more as a theoretical notion than as a significant fact. The total sales of all wholesale stores was expected to reach almost 2 billion rubles in 1971. The total national sales of producer goods in 1970, by contrast, was about 230 billion rubles.[64] The literature also treats it largely as something for the bright future. "In the future," wrote the Deputy Chairman of the State Committee on Supply in 1971, "the wholesale commodity list will be broadened."[65] A major text on the supply system devotes only 8 pages to it, out of a total of 354 pages.[66] The modest nature of the program is also reflected in the kinds of commodities that appear on the wholesale commodity list:

cutting and measuring instruments, various metal products and appliances, electric motors, storage batteries, compressors, chemicals, rubber goods, automobile tires, building materials, photographic and radio equipment, textiles, industrial clothing, shoes, electrical products, and so forth. Some kinds of products, obtained by decentralized purchase from local industry, are sold only in the wholesale stores.

It is clear that major industrial products are not available at wholesale. Moreover, the "basic" form of wholesale trade is not the transit shipment, which consists of large orders, but the small purchases made in the wholesale stores.[67] An enterprise may purchase a few tires for the director's automobile at wholesale, but a trucking enterprise is not likely to be able to satisfy its requirements in that way.

Even with respect to the commodities available for wholesale purchase, there appear to be certain significant restrictions. The ideal of wholesale trade is the notion of free sale. In the often-quoted words of the Chairman of the State Committee, enterprises "should be able to buy what they need, how much they need, and when they need it," without having to prepare extensive documentation.[68] There are, however, two major categories of wholesale trade, called limited and non-limited, and the free sale of goods applies only to the latter.[69] Limited trade applies to wholesaled commodities that are in temporary short supply. The document used to ration such goods is called a "limit certificate" which is issued by the wholesale organization.[70] To obtain a limit certificate for a particular good, the purchaser must still fill out a statement of requirements, but the process and documentation are apparently much less burdensome than that required to obtain an allocation certificate for controlled commodities.[71] Nevertheless, the category of limited wholesale trade signifies that some proportion of the wholesaled commodities is not yet available for free sale, and the enterprise that counts on obtaining a limited good may discover that the number of limit certificates is exhausted and the good is not available for purchase. Precise figures are not available, but limited trade is described as the predominant form of wholesale trade.[72]

The minor form is nonlimited wholesale trade. The textbook states:

This form does not require the preparation of complicated documentation, and the materials required by the purchaser may be bought at any time on the basis of a statement of requirements, either by picking the material up in the store, or entirely without the system of statements of requirements, allocation certificates, and allocation shipping orders (*raznariadki*).[73]

Evidently nonlimited wholesale trade also sometimes requires more than simply placing an order and picking up the goods.

The scale of wholesale trade may be further judged by the fact that in mid-1971 there were only 700 wholesale stores in the country,[74] serving 142,000 customers.[75] From the critical comments on them by users (which may be somewhat self-serving), one gets the impression that neither the store personnel nor their stocks are of very high quality. At a 1967 national conference on wholesale trade, for example, the director of a new local wholesale store gave some "inspired" data on the turnover of his store. A reporter of *Ekonomicheskaia Gazeta* subsequently visited the store and found that in fact it was stocked primarily with housewares—buckets, brooms, pots, and pans. Some hand tools were available, but they were too small and of too poor quality for industrial use.[76] From such bits of evidence, one must be cautious not to exaggerate the extent to which the new wholesale network has actually eased the past unreliability of the system of supply. It is, moreover, not yet clear how much authority the wholesalers have in satisfying unplanned needs for goods. Their stocks, for example, are to be normed. This means that they are required to keep their stocks of individual goods within certain limits which, presumably, will be established for them from above.[77] The imposition of such norms reflects a less-than-total confidence in the wholesalers' ability and motivation to manage their inventories and business economically.

On the basis of the evidence, the system of wholesale trade is still too small a part of the interenterprise flow of commodities to affect significantly the reliability of the overall system. Its proponents expect it to expand in the future, but a number of conditions are laid down; planning must first be improved, a better pricing system must first be devised, and so forth. The key condition, however, is that commodities may be transferred from a controlled commodity list to the wholesale list only when "the demand by the national economy for those types of products is basically satisfied."[78] The question of the "tautness" of planning, however, affects not only the status of wholesale trade, but the performance of the total system of supply, and merits a separate discussion.

The Reduction of Tautness

Soviet administrative officials appear to hold the view that the unsatisfied demand for producers' goods is a property of the stage of economic development. The productive forces of the economy, it is held, are not yet large enough to satisfy the national demand. There is little economic sense in this position. The long-standing disequilibrium between supply and demand is the result of both economic policy and economic structure. Both are within the competence of the government to change, and they may be changed in ways that would eliminate the disequilibrium overnight.

Among the structural causes of the general disequilibrium between supply and demand is the structure of prices. The notion of excess demand has meaning only with respect to a certain price. Barring some short-run inelasticities, a set of prices can always be found that will bring the demand for all producers' goods into equality with the planned supply. A change in the price structure alone could thus create the condition that is said to be required for a full transition to wholesale trade.

Had the Soviet leaders wished to eliminate the disequilibria between supply and demand, they could have done so long ago. That they had not done so was a decision of economic policy. The plan has always been regarded not solely as a technical device for controlling resource allocation but also as a device for mobilizing productive energies. If plan targets are too easily fulfilled, managers and workers would be inclined to exert less productive effort than they are capable of. To maximize the volume of productive effort, therefore, it is necessary to maintain taut plans. Output targets must be high enough to be unattainable without great exertion, and input plans must be tight enough to compel enterprises to economize on resources. The test of tautness, indeed, is the extent of plan fulfillment. If all enterprises always fulfilled plans, it would clearly indicate that the central planners were placing insufficient pressure on enterprises. Some degree of underfulfillment is also a disciplining device. Like a little bit of unemployment in capitalism, plan underfulfillment under Soviet socialism helps sustain the work ethic.

There are clearly certain economic benefits from a policy of tautness.[79] Our concern here, however, is not the wisdom of the policy but its consequences for the supply system. The policy of taut planning is the major cause of the high level of uncertainty over supply. The same organizational structure would operate with much less irregularity and unreliability if the policy of tautness were changed.

There are a few indications that suggest a possibility of some relaxation in tautness in the future. One is the growing recognition of the point in literature. Perhaps its most prominent proponents are the economists in the Institute of Mathematical Economics, under the directorship of Academician Federenko. Their point of departure is that recognition of the inevitable "stochastical," or unpredictable, element in economic planning calls for a greater use of inventories of reserve stocks than in the past, when planning was thought to be more deterministic and controllable. They argue that these reserves should not be concentrated at a particular level in the organizational structure but distributed at various levels. The appropriate principle for the distribution of reserves is that each level—enterprise, ministry, and central government—should possess a volume and structure of reserves sufficient to enable it to handle disturbances without having to transmit the effects of such disturbances upward. Enterprises, for example, should possess sufficient reserves to cushion the effect of unanticipated needs by their production units, without having to appeal to the ministry. The ministry should possess sufficient reserves to offset unanticipated disturbances that affect some of its enterprises, without having to appeal to the State Committee on Supply. The test of the adequacy of the reserves held at any level is the stability of their levels; if some units' reserves begin to "dry up," that would be a sign that the structure and volume of reserves at that level need to be adjusted.[80] Recognition of the need for an adequate volume and distribution of reserves is a step toward the reduction in tautness.

A second development is that not only theoreticians but also some administrators appear to be well disposed toward the reduction of tautness. Most interesting in this respect is the account by Chairman Dymshits of the State Committee on Supply, of the derationing of gasoline and diesel oil. These two products have always been regarded as in extremely short supply and therefore subject to strict centralized allocation. In the spirit of reform, it was decided to question whether they are indeed in short supply by an experiment in the province of Voronezh. Public notice was given that allocation certificates would no longer be required, and that fuel depots and filling stations would "sell on demand, without requiring statements of requirements, and there will be no fines on those who do not accept supplies allocated to them."[81]

One can fairly imagine the officials waiting with bated breath in fear of a mad rush by purchasers to buy up the limited supply. In fact, nothing of the sort happened. The author reports—one can almost hear the sigh of relief—that demand rose no more rapidly than elsewhere. The success of the experiment led to the extension of the practice to some other provinces, and to certain other products like building materials, some chemicals, and plumbing supplies.[82] The limited sale of some controlled commodities without requiring allocation certificates is now regarded as a form of wholesale trade. But like wholesale trade in general, the free sale of controlled commodities is still very limited. Five years after it was first tried out in Voronezh it is still referred to as an "experiment."[83]

The Voronezh gasoline experiment cautions the analyst that the existence of commodity controls does not constitute evidence of tautness in the supply system. One can imagine a state in which allocation certificates are required for all commodities, but at the given price structure supply is equal to demand for all commodities. Managers would eventually learn that all required commodities were available for purchase, and uncertainty over supply would decline to a negligible level. The requirement of an allocation certificate would constitute a bit of a nuisance, and inventory levels may be somewhat higher than in the absence of controls. But otherwise managerial decisions would be no different than they would be in the absence of controls.[84]

For the same reason, the absence of controls does not constitute evidence that tautness has been eliminated. The wholesale stores may offer a certain range of commodities for free sale at established prices, but if their stocks are low relative to the demand managers will quickly learn that the source of supply is unreliable. The level of uncertainty will rise, and managers will resume precautionary hoarding and the other practices for ensuring the flow of supplies.

The test of a change in the degree of tautness must therefore be found in the behavior of managers. Some evidence is available on inventory levels. In the period 1961-1965, the growth rate of inventories in industry exceeded the growth rate of output. Since then, we are told, this tendency "has not only been eliminated but the average turnover rate of inventories has been reduced by five days."[85] These data must be taken with some caution, however. The Economic Reform has probably transferred some inventories from industry to the agencies of the State Committee on Supply, which would cause a decrease in the measured rate of inventory turnover in industry. Moreover, one would wish to know how the reduction in industrial inventories was accomplished. If it was the consequence of pressure on enterprises from higher organizations, one may be sure of two things: that the degree of underreporting of inventories by enterprises has increased, and that the level of uncertainty over supply has risen.

In summary, the structural reforms in the supply system do not signify that the degree of tautness has been reduced. The Voronezh experiment and the beginning of wholesale trade have demonstrated that for some commodities the degree of disequilibrium has not been substantial and controls were not necessary, but the elimination of controls in those cases does not mean that tautness has been reduced. The decline in inventories may indicate some reduction in the level of managerial uncertainty over supply, but the evidence is not decisive. We may conclude that if any reduction in tautness has occurred it has not been of massive proportions. In the absence of a major change in national economic policy, the changes in the organizational structure of the supply system have not substantially reduced the level of managerial uncertainty over the supply of materials and equipment. The degree of bias against innovation flowing from that structural cause has therefore not changed in any significant way.

Notes

1. Joseph S. Berliner, *Factory and Manager in the USSR* (Cambridge: Harvard University Press, 1957), Chaps. 7, 11, 12; David Granick, *Management of the Industrial Firm in the USSR* (New York: Columbia University Press, 1954), Chap. 8.

2. Barry Richman, *Soviet Management* (Englewood Cliffs, N.J.: Prentice-Hall, 1965), p. 108.

3. Holland Hunter, "Optimal Tautness in Developmental Planning," *Economic Development and Cultural Change* Vol. 9:4, (July 1961), pp. 561-572.

4. Joseph S. Berliner, "Managerial Incentives and Decisionmaking: A Comparison of the United States and the Soviet Union," U.S. Congress Joint Economic Committee, *Comparisons of the United States and Soviet Economies* (Washington: Government Printing Office, 1959), pp. 349-376.

5. C. F. Carter and B. R. Williams, *Industry and Technical Progress* (London: Oxford University Press, 1957), pp. 77, 112, 183.

6. Ibid., p. 112. They also report the rise of such Soviet-type practices as enterprise "autarky" (uncertainty over the supply of machine tools led a number of firms to establish their own machine-tool production facilities); and the use of *tolkatchi* (supply expediters—"engineers repeatedly visiting suppliers' factories, impressing their management and operatives with the urgency of their order. ...."), pp. 113-114.

7. See Note 1.

8. Herbert S. Levine, "The Centralized Planning of Supply in Soviet Industry," U.S. Congress, Joint Economic Committee, *Comparisons of the United States and Soviet Economies* (Washington: Government Printing Office, 1959), pp. 151-176; J. M. Montias, "Planning with Material Balances in Soviet-Type Economies," *American Economic Review*, No. 49 (December 1959), pp. 963-985.

9. Even the products of local industry, that are not included on any of the six commodity control lists, require the possession of an allocation certificate. The purchaser must submit a statement of requirements to the planning department of the local government in order to receive an allocation certificate. The certificate must be presented to the producing enterprise before the purchase can be made. It is only in wholesale trade that allocation certificates are not required for some commodities (see Section 3.4). N.V. Ivanov, E. Iu. Lokshin, and F. M. Demichev, *Ekonomika i planirovanie material'no-tekhnicheskogo snabzhenie promyshlennosti* (The Economics and Planning of Supply in Industry), (Moscow: *Economika*, 1969), p. 205. This section draws heavily on that source, which was published for use as a textbook in academic departments of economics.

10. Ivanov et al., *Ekonomika i planirovanie*, p. 340.

11. Literally, "fund-holders." The term "fund" is often applied to allocations of commodities on other commodity control lists; that is, a ministry may receive a "fund" of a commodity controlled by the State Committee on Supply, which is not a "funded" commodity. The double usage makes for some confusion, although the sense is usually clear from the context.

12. For many funded commodities there are two sets of balances and distribution plans drawn up, one for current production and one for capital construction use. For some there is a third or fourth set: for agricultural use, or for scientific research use. Ivanov et al., *Ekonomika i planirovanie*, p. 341.

13. Ibid., p. 337.

14. A. I. Baskin, N. V. Belkin, V. S. Korotchenko, V. M. Lagutkin, Iu. F. Mosiakov, V. T. Naumik, V. I. Odessa, and A. A. Iakoli, *Sovershenstvovat' material'no-tekhnicheskoe snabzhenie* (Improve the Supply System) (Moscow: *Znanie*, 1969), p. 316.

15. Ivanov et al., *Ekonomika i planirovanie*, p. 281.

16. All controlled commodities are distributed either by the "transit" method or the "warehouse" method. The transit method is direct shipment by the producer to the customer, and is used for large shipments, generally in carload lots. Smaller purchases are made from the warehouses of the local supply offices of the State Committee on Supply, which receive carload shipments from producers and sell in smaller lots to planned users. These local supply offices handle the distribution of all controlled commodities that are allocated by the warehouse method, including those controlled by the State Planning Committee and by the ministries.

17. Baskin et al., *Sovershenstvovat'*, p. 3. In addition to the State Planning Committee and the State Committee on Supply, there are various other organizations responsible for particular commodity groups, such as petroleum products, agricultural supply, and so forth. See Baskin et al., p. 17.

18. Between 1957 and 1965 industry was administered by territorial economic councils rather than by industry-based ministries.

19. The ministries have also lost their physical control over the interenterprise flow of commodities. The network of local supply depots and warehouses that were owned and operated by the pre-1957 ministries are now the property of the territorial supply administrations.

20. Baskin et al., *Sovershenstvovat'*, p. 15.
21. Ivanov et al., *Ekonomika i planirovanie*, p. 249.
22. Baskin et al., *Sovershenstvovat'*, p. 44.
23. V. Lagutkin, in *Izvestiia Akademii Nauk SSSR-Seriia Ekonomicheskaia*, 1971, No. 1, p. 32.
24. Levine, "The Centralized Planning of Supply."
25. V. Lagutkin, in *Economicheskaia gazeta*, 1971, No. 36, p. 13. Attitudes toward plan changes depend on whether one is a changer or a changee. In another part of the same article, Mr. Lagutkin, Deputy Chairman of the State Committee on Supply, commends the alertness of one of his own All-Union Metals Supply Administrations. In 1970 that organization managed to place orders with enterprises for an additional 22.3 million tons of certain metals that were in short supply, by cutting down on their planned production of less critical metals. To the enterprises affected, those plan changes must appear as irresponsible interference with the rhythm of production leading to a decline in efficiency and a worsening of the enterprise's performance record.
26. These practices are documented in Berliner, *Factory and Manager*, Chaps. 6-12.
27. *Ekonomicheskaia gazeta*, 1967, No. 29, p. 28.
28. Ibid., 1966, No. 52, p. 14.
29. *Planovoe khoziaistvo*, 1966, No. 4, pp. 31-32.
30. David Granick, *Soviet Metal-Fabricating and Economic Development* (Madison: University of Wisconsin Press, 1967), pp. 144-147.
31. *Ekonomicheskaia gazeta*, 1967, No. 31, p. 12.
32. Ibid., No. 10, p. 8.
33. Ibid., No. 34, p. 10.
34. "There are many such examples," writes A. Etmekdzhiian, in *Planovoe khoziaistvo*, 1966, No. 12, p. 5.
35. Dr. L. Gatovskii, in *Voprosy ekonomiki*, 1965, No. 12, p. 12.
36. *Ekonomicheskaia gazeta*, 1966, No. 2, p. 30.
37. *Planovoe khoziaistvo*, 1966, No. 10, pp. 84-85. See also *Voprosy ekonomiki*, 1966, No. 6, pp. 137-138.
38. *Planovoe khoziaistvo*, 1966, No. 10, pp. 84-85.
39. *Ekonomicheskaia gazeta*, 1967, No. 34, p. 10.
40. Ibid., 1968, No. 10, p. 19.
41. Ibid., 1967, No. 11, p. 11. See also *Planovoe khoziaistvo*, 1966, No. 2, p. 4.
42. L. Gatovskii, "Ekonomicheskaia nauka i nekotorye problemy tekhnicheskogo progressa" (The Science of Economics and Some Problems of Technical Progress), *Voprosy ekonomiki*, 1965, No. 12, pp. 13-14. See also the report of the research conducted by the Siberian Division of the Institute of Economics, in ibid., 1966, No. 4, 146.
43. *Voprosy ekonomiki*, 1966, No. 1, p. 115.
44. G. D. Anisimov and I. A. Vakhlamov, eds., *Material'noe stimulirovanie vnedreniia novoi tekhniki: spravochnik* (Handbook of Material Incentives for Innovation) (Moscow: Ekonomika, 1966), p. 84.
45. *Voprosy ekonomiki*, 1967, No. 3, p. 36.
46. *Ekonomicheskaia gazeta*, 1967, No. 52, p. 12.
47. V. Kantorovich, in *Literaturnaia gazeta*, December 24, 1966, p. 2. Translated in *Current Digest of the Soviet Press*, Vol. 19:3 (February 8, 1967), pp. 4 ff.
48. G. Anisimov, in *Ekonomicheskaia gazeta*, 1966, No. 2, p. 30.
49. *Planovoe khoziaistvo*, 1966, No. 10, pp. 84-85. See also *Voprosy ekonomiki*, 1966, No. 6, pp. 137-138.
50. Kaplan and Soifer in *Planovoe khoziaistvo*, 1966, No. 10, p. 85.
51. For a discussion of the practices of "simulation," see Berliner, *Factory and Manager*, Chap. 8.

52. In capitalist economies, during periods of supply restrictions generally associated with war and reconstruction, special-interest pleading also focuses on the materials allocation system. See Berliner, "Managerial Incentives and Decisionmaking," pp. 372-376.

53. *Ekonomicheskaia gazeta*, 1967, No. 10, p. 11.

54. Nove, *The Soviet Economy*, pp. 67-69.

55. If the offices of the territorial administrations were all physically transferred to Moscow, but they continued to exercise the same functions from a distance, there would be an increase in geographical centralization but no change in decision-making centralization. Similarly, if the ministries' offices were spread out all over the country, there would be a geographical decentralization but no change in decision-making centralization.

56. The ill-fated change from ministries to regional economic councils introduced by Mr. Khrushchev in 1957 was a change from the technological to the geographical principle for both general administration and supply planning. By the definition employed earlier, there was no change in the degree of centralization of decision making.

57. The evidence of even longer standing, going back to the behavior of local governmental units since the beginning of the central planning period. See Berliner, *Factory and Manager*, pp. 279-282.

58. *Ekonomicheskaia gazeta*, 1967, No. 52, p. 11.

59. The Russian expression is *material'no-tekhnicheskoe snabzhenie*, literally, "material-technical supply."

60. As well as the particular use for which it is destined; basic production, construction work, repair, and maintenance use.

61. Ivanov et al., *Ekonomika i planirovanie*, p. 319.

62. *Ekonomicheskaia gazeta*, 1967, No. 11, p. 31; Ivanov et al., *Ekonomika i planirovanie*, p. 321.

63. V. Lagutkin, in *Ekonomicheskaia gazeta*, 1971, No. 36, p. 13.

64. V. Lagutkin, in *Izvestiia Akademii Nauk SSSR-Seriia Ekonomicheskaia*, 1971, No. 1, pp. 28, 32.

65. V. Lagutkin, in *Ekonomicheskaia gazeta*, 1971, No. 36, p. 13.

66. Ivanov et al., *Ekonomika i planirovanie*, pp. 319-327.

67. Ibid., p. 324.

68. Mr. V. Dymshits, in *Ekonomicheskaia gazeta*, 1967, No. 18, p. 7.

69. There is a third category called commission trade. Enterprises with excess supplies of materials or equipment may sell them to the wholesale organization, who later resell them; or the wholesaler may act as a middleman, seeking a purchaser for the excess supplies.

70. The Russian word is simply a "limit."

71. Moreover the holder of a limit certificate is not obliged to purchase the good on a certain date, or at all, if his needs should change. The holder of an allocation certificate, however, is obliged to accept delivery of the specified goods, on penalty of a legal action for breach of contract. Ivanov et al., *Ekonomika i planirovanie*, p. 321.

72. Ibid., p. 326.

73. Ibid., pp. 321-322.

74. These stores conduct only small-scale wholesale trade. A certain volume of wholesale trade is conducted by the transit method rather than over the counters of the stores.

75. *Ekonomicheskaia gazeta*, 1971, No. 36, p. 13. This includes not only industrial enterprises but enterprises in many other sectors: transportation, trade, health, education, housing, and so forth.

76. Ibid., 1967, No. 52, p. 12.

77. Ibid., No. 11, p. 31.

78. Deputy Chairman of the State Committee on Supply V. Lagutkin, in ibid., 1971, No. 36, p. 13.

79. Holland Hunter, "Optimum Tautness in Developmental Planning," *Economic Development and Cultural Change* 9:4, (July 1961), pp. 565-567.

80. N. Federenko, in *Planovoe khoziaistvo*, 1967, No. 4, p. 12.

81. V. Dymshits, in *Ekonomicheskaia gazeta*, 1967, No. 18, pp. 7-8.

82. *Ekonomicheskaia gazeta*, 1968, No. 4, p. 25.

83. V. Lagutkin, in *Izvestiia Akademii Nauk SSSR-Seriia Ekonomicheskaia*, 1971, No. 1, p. 33.

84. In districts in which some controlled commodities are sold at wholesale, it has been found that the sales levels do not exceed those in districts where allocation certificates are still required; in the case of some products they are even lower. V. Lagutkin in *Izvestiia Akademii Nauk SSSR-Seriia Ekonomicheskaia*, 1971, No. 1, p. 33.

85. V. Lagutkin, in *Ekonomicheskaia gazeta*, 1971, No. 36, p. 13. The turnover rate is the ratio of the average size of inventories to the total annual output.

Chapter 4

The Supply of Inputs: Research and Development Services

When Soviet writers refer to the subject of supply they have in mind the interenterprise flow of such physical commodities as materials, fuels, and equipment (*material'no-tekhnicheskoe snabzhenie*). There is no general term for the supply of services, nor is there any central agency of government responsible for the supply of services in the way that the State Committee on Supply is responsible for the supply of physical commodities. The production activity of enterprises, however, is no less dependent on the supply of various kinds of services than on the supply of physical inputs. For innovating enterprises in particular, the services of research and development are a crucial input. In an inquiry into the relationship between organizational structure and innovation, therefore, one must ask about the supply of services the same questions asked about the supply of commodities in the previous chapter; namely, how the innovation decision is affected by the ways in which the enterprise's supply of those services is organized.

An innovation is, among other things, an idea. It is possible to imagine a world in which all new production ideas are conceived, developed, and put into practice within enterprises, and none flow among enterprises. In such a world, the structure of the organization of economic units would have little influence on the rate of innovation as far as the flow of R & D services is concerned. But it would surely not be a very innovative world. It would, moreover, be a world in which the bicycle was constantly reinvented, as Mr. Khrushchev used to complain. In the real economy, new ideas generated in individual units are largely based on prior developments elsewhere, and they spread in turn to other units of the system. A given structure of economic organization may therefore be expected to support or restrain the rate of innovation according to the success with which it facilitates the social intercourse in ideas.

One main channel of the flow of ideas is in the concrete form of new products. The innovator-producer transmits the idea to the user in the form of a new kind of material or a new piece of equipment or apparatus, and the innovator-user incorporates it into his own technology. The preceding chapter's discussion of the supply system has dealt with the flow of ideas that are embodied in material commodities. But a substantial flow of ideas is not embodied in this way. An innovator-user may require instruction on the installation and operation of the new equipment. An innovator-producer may require the services of research, development, and design experts in bringing a new idea into the production stage. The system of materials supply does not provide for the supply of such vital services.

4.1. The Research and Development Organizations

In any economy, the production of new technological knowledge may be organized in a variety of ways. It may be produced in the manufacturing enterprises themselves, which incorporate their new knowledge into their own products that are then sold to users. Or it may be produced in nonmanufacturing units that specialize in knowledge production, such as universities or research organizations, which then transfer their results, by sale or by grant, to the enterprises for subsequent incorporation into products or processes.

In the capitalist economies the predominant organizational form is the first kind, or so-called in-house R & D. In explaining the organizational structure of capitalist institutions, it is often useful to seek the cause in the profit-maximizing objectives of enterprises operating under specified market conditions. Yale Brozen has argued, for example, that the reason for the predominance of in-house R & D is to be found in the fact that the producer of new knowledge must usually work closely with the users in order to "debug" the new process or product. In the course of the debugging, valuable "second-stage knowledge" is generated, which is usually not patentable. In order to realize the profits of this second-stage knowledge, firms find it expedient to control the knowledge generated at both, the R & D stage and the stage of application. This they do by incorporating knowledge production and its practical application in a single firm.[1] The structure of the knowledge-production industry thus reflects the individual decisions of many firms, each responding to conditions created by the combined actions of others.

In the Soviet economy, the structure of economic organization, like that of resource allocation in general, is not to be explained as the result of a general, marketlike socioeconomic process. That structure is the result of an administrative decision, taken, to be sure, with certain economizing objectives in mind but not influenced in turn by the actions of competing organizational units. The decision, taken early in Soviet history, was to locate the knowledge-production process primarily in units that are independent of the enterprises that introduce the new knowledge into production.

There are no compelling reasons for the Soviet leaders to have selected an organizational structure similar to that which emerged in the capitalist economic process. For one thing, all knowledge is public in a socialist society; the publicity of knowledge is in fact one of the major advantages a socialist economy may be thought to have over a capitalist economy in the promotion of technological advance. Hence the reason that Brozen adduces for the capitalist structure of knowledge production has no force under socialism. The diffusion of knowledge might indeed slow down if firms were permitted to maintain a proprietary ownership of the special knowledge they gain in the course of introducing new products and processes. In fact, Soviet managers are required to publicize to other firms the knowledge gained in this way. Innovating firms often send missions of their own engineers and technicians around the country, at their own expense, to demonstrate to others how they accomplished their innovation and what they learned from their experience. The Novolipetsk Steel Plant, which pioneered in the introduction of continuous casting of steel, even established a school for people from other enterprises. The plant was for many years the destination of a "pilgrimage" by visitors not only from the USSR but from other socialist countries and from capitalist business firms as well.[2] Hence to the extent that the advantage of in-house R & D is that it promotes the proprietary rights over knowledge by capitalist firms, that structure does not commend itself for the organization of the Soviet economy.

On the other hand, the publicity of knowledge in the USSR does not argue for a structure of independent R & D units either. There is no particular reason why it should be more difficult to enforce a publicity requirement on producing enterprises than on independent R & D organizations. Moreover, the possibility of planning technological progress under socialism in a way that is not possible under capitalism provides no basis for a choice between the two structural forms. R & D within state-owned producing enterprises could be planned as effectively as the work of state-owned R & D organizations. The decision to locate R & D primarily in units that are independent of enterprises was probably made on the rough judgment that, in purely organizational terms, it was a superior structural form.[3]

It is not possible to argue a priori that that judgment was a poor one. There is a great deal of evidence, however, that the structural form chosen leads to serious difficulties in the supply of the R & D services needed for innovation in the enterprise. The explanation of many of these difficulties is to be found not exclusively in organizational structure but also in the related structures of prices, rules, and incentives. It does seem, however, that given the latter structural properties, the organizational form chosen has retarded the rate of innovation.

The Quality of R & D Work

The fortunes of the innovating enterprise depend upon the quality of the services delivered by the R & D establishments. In the best of cases the development work will have been brought to full completion, the product or process subjected to adequate preproduction testing, the plans and blueprints carefully executed and delivered well within prearranged time schedules, the productivity estimates carefully prepared, and expert technical assistance readily available during the crucial production start-up period. If these are the expectations with which enterprises confront the innovation decision, that decision will be taken with relative frequency. To the extent that enterprises expect those conditions not to prevail, the rate of innovation will be lower.

The literature provides abundant evidence of general dissatisfaction with the work of the R & D organizations. We read often about the excessively bureaucratic organization of the R & D institutes and of the large quantity of "insignificant, unproductive and duplicative work" carried on.[4] Almost two-thirds of all research institutes and higher education institutions have never submitted an application for a Certificate of Invention.[5] The All-Union Aluminum-Magnesium Institute, we read, worked on 130 separate projects in 1964, and submitted 28 final reports (*otchet*). But no one knew how successful the work was or how great its potential benefit to the economy. Moreover, the institute had no plan for following the projects up or seeing that they were introduced into production.[6]

The consequence of the inefficient operation of many R & D organizations is the high cost of preinnovation R & D work. Part of that cost is borne by the State, but part is borne by the client enterprise and therefore depresses the net economic benefits to be expected from innovation. In the Saratov region, an analysis was undertaken of 45,000 changes that had to be made by enterprises in the blueprints and drawings prepared by the design organizations. Sixty-five percent were found to be the result of simple carelessness, such as arithmetic errors.[7] In other cases inadequate testing obliged innovating enterprises to make changes in design after production had begun, which drove up the cost of production, lengthened the start-up period, and reduced the return to the innovation.[8] The Piston Plant in Kharkov installed two new automated production lines that had been designed and built by an R & D organization under a contract. The cost of the innovation was 51,500 rubles for each line. Alongside the new lines operated two continuous-flow lines that were not automated and that had been built by the enterprise itself at a cost of 6,000 rubles each. "Thus the cost of the continuous-flow lines was one-eighth that of the automated lines, they used half as much operating labor, and their output per shift was significantly greater."[9]

In this instance, there is no indication that the technical quality of the work performed by the R & D organization was poor. It was the high cost of the R & D services that caused the innovation to yield the disappointing return. Other evidence points to the fact that technical quality is also often unsatisfactory. For example, an inquiry into the work of a special design bureau for grinding equipment disclosed that the bureau regularly fulfilled its plan of projects completed during 1958-1964. But of the 57 projects reported as completed, 13 were later junked as useless and 20 were later returned by the customers to the manufacturer because of structural defects.[10] In four cases, test models and whole test production runs were written off because of design defects. In the seven years of the study, not one of the models developed by the 450-man design bureau got to the final stage of job-lot production.[11] In the light of such experiences, one may expect that an enterprise contemplating an innovation would be somewhat deterred by his anticipations of the quality of work likely to be supplied to it by an outside R & D organization.

Organizational Sources of Quality Problems

The evidence that a great deal of R & D work is of poor quality provides no basis for ascribing the cause entirely to the organizational structure of economic arrangements. Part of the cause is in decisions of economic policy. Some Soviet critics have argued, for example, that in the allocation of resources for R & D, an insufficient proportion is devoted to development work compared to that devoted to research. Inadequate testing of new models before the designs are delivered to the enterprise is one manifestation of this policy.[12] Other causes may be found in the nonorganizational structural arrangements—prices, decision-rules, and incentives—to be discussed in later chapters. But part of the explanation is due to strictly organizational matters: in this case, primarily the separation of the R & D establishments from the enterprises that ultimately introduce the innovations.

For one thing, the long lead times may often be traced to the difficulties of moving the innovation among the various organizations that are separately responsible for the several stages of the overall process. Most R & D institutes, for example, do not contain facilities for engineering design. Hence, when such an institute completes its final report on a completed piece of development work,

There begins a search for production engineering services (*proektirovshchiki*). . . . The production engineering organization will accept the job only after the R & D work has been fully completed. It must then be officially approved, which requires it to go through a long chain of commissions of experts and agreements. The production engineering work takes two or three years. Then after another series of commissions of experts, they have to find a product design (*konstruktorskii*) bureau to prepare the blueprints; and then an enterprise that will agree to produce a prototype model. Months and years pass in this way.[13]

It was for such reasons, reports the critic, that the Petrochemicals Research Institute took 15 years to complete the whole process of bringing aldehyde production by the oxygen-synthesis method from the research stage into final production. The enthusiasm of the R & D people must suffer in the face of these complexities introduced by the dissociation of R & D from the other stages in the innovation chain.

Organizational complexities multiply when the innovation requires the construction of an entirely new enterprise. In that case an efficient innovation-planning arrangement requires the coordination of work along the broad front of the growing technology in such fashion as to take advantage of the complementaries among the new plants. Yet we read that the engineering design organizations in individual branches "don't know and often are not interested" in what other branches are planning to build in a district. One of the consequences is that each plant is built so as to comprise a "closed cycle" of production, with extensive duplication of steam boiler installations, water supply systems, and so forth.[14] With regard to the incorporation of new technology into the plants, a design engineer writes that the time schedules prepared by construction-project planners are often worked out by people who do not take full account of the time needed for equipment design and testing work. The consequent rush to meet impossible time schedules causes poor quality of equipment design and the inadequate testing of new designs and installations.[15] We read further of enormous expenditures on construction-project design work, quite disproportionate to the value of the new construction work actually planned.[16]

The transfer of an innovation from one organization to the next in the process is often the occasion for a general review and evaluation. One gets the impression that a vast amount of time-consuming consultation and advising is absorbed in these interorganizational reviews. One critic urges that at least the size of the numerous scientific and technical commissions be reduced from their present size of 50 to 60, and sometimes 100, to 15 to 20. He raises the "perpetual question" of how to reduce the number of meetings and suggests that at the least R & D people refrain from the practice of inviting eminent scientists to their commissions for the sake of the greater "scientific weight" they lend to a project, rather than for their active participation.[17] All this has, of course, a familiar ring in non-Soviet ears as well. More peculiarly Soviet is the emphasis placed on the large number of organizations and commissions of experts whose approval or agreement must be obtained at various stages of the work. In the process of coordinating the work on a single project, 15 to 20 different agencies may have to be consulted. In the R & D institutes of Novosibirsk, the process of securing official approval from all the agencies that must be consulted accounted for 40 to 70 percent of the total time required at various stages of the work.[18]

The effort devoted to gathering signatures of approval is due partly to statutory requirements and partly to the instructions issued by the several administrative agencies that bear some responsibility for the progress of the innovation. But it also serves as a device for limiting each organization's responsibility for its own stage of the work and for reducing one's vulnerability in the event of difficulties encountered in later stages.

Because of the sharp organizational divisions, technical work done at one stage may be insufficiently coordinated with that to be done in later stages. Design bureaus working on a new machine, for example, "often do not know at what enterprises it will be used."[19] The enterprise may therefore find itself saddled with an innovation ill-suited to its own technological requirements. Managerial complaints dwell not only on the poor quality of R & D services but also on their inability to hold the R & D people responsible. The helplessness felt by enterprises—their inability to control their supply of R & D services— is reflected in this somewhat heated statement by a chief engineer:

In working with [research and design] organizations we are constantly confronted with instances of wrong technical decisions, recommendations, and technical documentation. As a rule, this only becomes clear in the course of testing, or even in the course of starting up small-lot production runs. However, we can bring no actions against these organizations, for their plans have long ago been fulfilled and their bonuses paid out. *In our opinion, institute personnel should be made to pay for their mistakes* [italics in the original]. For our designers, technologists, and planners receive bonuses on the basis of the performance of our whole enterprise, and when we have to pay fines for late shipments or for poor quality goods, this reduces the pay of each member of our collective.[20]

This chief engineer's complaint echoed the sentiments of many others, and in 1967 a governmental decree made the R & D institutes liable, for the first time, to fines and other penalties for the delivery of poor-quality work.[21] The prospect of partial compensation does not greatly increase the manager's eagerness to innovate if he has reason to anticipate the many kinds of troubles that await him because of poor-quality R & D services. Concentration on an established line of production is always an alternative to innovation.

4.2. Other Sources of Research and Development Services

The R & D organizations are the chief source of supply of R & D services to enterprises. They are not the only source however. A certain quantity of R & D work is conducted by enterprises themselves and not obtained in a transaction with other organizational units. In addition, individual persons contribute to the supply of R & D through inventions and improvements in both products and production processes.

In-house Research and Development

Although in-house R & D is not the typical organizational form, most Soviet enterprises possess some facilities for work on innovation. In small enterprises the work may be done in the regular engineering departments, in the department of the chief designer if it is product development and improvement, or in the department of the chief technologist if the work involves the enterprise's manufacturing processes. But the main function of these departments is engineering support of the current production program, not innovation.

Larger enterprises may possess staffs and facilities specialized for work on new products and processes. They are designated "laboratories" for general R & D work and "special design bureaus" for engineering design work. For example, enterprises that produce to special order, such as some machinery and equipment manufacturers, have special design bureaus or departments for drawing up the plans and blueprints for special-order jobs. They usually concentrate on the design of the enterprise's products, and rarely on the equipment that comprises the manufacturing technology.[22] They are sometimes assigned the task of designing an entirely new piece of equipment to be built by the plant for its own use. But if it is a complex piece of machinery developed elsewhere, the design work is likely to be done by outside designers.

The distinctive organizational advantage of an in-house R & D facility is that it reduces the enterprise's dependence upon other organizational units. Management need be less concerned that the innovation might fail for reasons outside of its own control. For that reason, the State has promoted the expansion of in-house R & D facilities in the past decade. The forms of that expansion have varied, depending upon the kind of industry and the size of the enterprises.

Extensiveness of enterprise in-house R & D. Some very large enterprises have been authorized to establish full-scale R & D facilities. The great Urals Machinery Plant, for example, now possesses a facility that has the status of an R & D Institute, although it is under the authority of the enterprise management rather than the ministry.[23] Relatively few enterprises, however, have been assigned full-scale R & D institutes. In most cases the expansion has taken the form of additional factory laboratories, design bureaus, testing facilities and so forth. Precise data are not available on the proportions of R & D work conducted by enterprises. In 1965, the number of factory laboratories was reported to be about 26,000 and the number of enterprise bureaus and departments about 13,000.[24] One can infer little from these numbers, however, about the volume or value of genuine R & D they produce. Most are of small scale, and much of their work consists of minor operations such as product improvement and quality control. In discussions of genuine R & D, the number of enterprises engaged in such work is listed as "over 1,800."[25]

In order to assess the relative importance of in-house R & D, the authors of the OECD study surveyed the journal *Factory Laboratory* and found that only 5.5 percent of the articles originated in factories. Factories accounted for about 14 percent of the certificates of authorship issued to organizations.[26] The indications are that in-house R & D is by no means insignificant, but it is a minor component of the whole. **Reluctance to undertake in-house R & D.** The decision to increase the volume of R & D facilities was supported by certain evidence that enterprises possessing their own design bureaus and laboratories tend to be readier to innovate and more successful in innovation.[27] On the basis of other evidence, however, one may wonder whether the direction of causation is not the other way around. Enterprises are not simply passive agents in such matters. Those under an innovative management tend to press for and to receive more extensive R & D facilities, but others tend to avoid them. Mr. Khrushchev once chastized the management of the celebrated Shchekino Chemicals Combine for precisely such an action. The enterprise had contracted with a Dutch firm to build a new chemicals production plant for them. The director remarked to Khrushchev that he had bought all the production equipment but had economized by not buying the plant laboratory that was part of the original design. "Do you understand what that means?" exploded Khrushchev in a speech. "They have bought everything but the eyes, for without the plant laboratory one cannot watch over the process to control the quality and purity of the product."[28]

One of the reasons that some enterprises seem to avoid possessing their own R & D facilities may be inferred from the critical observations in the literature about the quality of the research people who take the jobs in industry rather than in the independent institutes. The latter offer much greater prestige, better working conditions for research-oriented personnel, and higher salaries. Hence we read that while many enterprises do have some high-quality research personnel in their design bureaus and research laboratories, "including some Ph.D.'s," the number of such people in enterprise research organizations is insignificant.[29] The Electrosila Combine regularly lost its best research people to the independent R & D organizations because the latter were able to offer higher salaries.[30] Conceivably a higher relative salary for research people in industry might increase the productivity of in-house R & D and thus modify managerial attitudes.[31]

The fault, however, may lie not in such matters as salary but in certain problems of internal management of R & D. That manufacturers should complain about the services supplied by the independent R & D organizations is understandable. But that similar strains should exist within enterprises is more puzzling. "It is well known," we read, "how much harm is done to production people by some development engineers' (*razrabotchiki*) habit of forgetting about the products they have created as soon as all the documents of acceptance have been signed."[32] One must expect conflicts of interest of this kind in any organization, socialist or capitalist. But if management were seriously committed to innovation, it surely has the power to impress upon its in-house R & D people a concern with the end result of their work rather than a concern that ends with their stage of it.

Another reason for avoiding in-house R & D facilities is the result of a certain peculiarity in labor accounting. The labor productivity indicator is calculated on the basis of the number of employees classified as "industrial and production personnel." If the enterprise establishes a new engineering design bureau, its staff falls within that category and labor productivity appears to decline. Hence there is a certain "formalistic" reluctance to establish such bureaus, even in large enterprises.[33] At a conference on the subject, Director Kostyna of the "Bol'shevik" Plant reported that many directors with whom he had talked objected to having special design bureaus attached to their enterprises because they reduce the labor-productivity indicator. "But this is self-deluding!" cried Director Kostyna. The stenographic account of the conference reports cries from the floor of "Right!"[34]

A third reason for avoiding in-house R & D was given by the officials of a Moscow machine-tool plant. They objected to having to pay the newly introduced capital charge of 6 percent per annum on the facilities of their design bureau, which was a large one. Their designers, to be sure, produced drawings and blueprints for new equipment for the enterprise's own use, but the documents were later made available without charge to other interested enterprises and organizations. Hence, the bureau was, in effect, working free for other enterprises, while the Moscow plant paid the capital charge. The officials demanded that the bureau should either be placed on an independent business-accounting basis or the enterprise should be relieved of the capital charges on the bureau's facilities.[35]

Resistance to in-house research facilities has evidently had some effect, since we read that in many instances the Departments of the Chief Designer (OGK-*otdel glavnogo konstruktora*) have been separated from their enterprises and converted into independent design organizations.[36] All this is rather puzzling in light of the general tendency toward "universalism"—the extensive vertical integration alluded to earlier. The resistance to R & D facilities is the only case we know of in which enterprises appear not to wish to strengthen their control over a source of supply by incorporating it in their own enterprise. The evidence suggests that the reason for this un-Soviet attitude toward R & D may be the low degree of importance assigned by management to innovation. If the supply of R & D services were thought to be as important as, say, the supply of spare parts or metal castings, enterprises would surely wish to control the former by in-house activity, as they in fact do in the case of the latter.

Individual Inventors

The world of business, unlike politics and the military, does not generally produce romantic types. Yet there is one type that has captured the public imagination. There is a kind of romance surrounding the exploits of the lone inventor working long nights in his basement laboratory and triumphantly producing inventions that revolutionize the world. Little TV dramas are written on the lives of the Bells, Edisons, and Marconis.

The lone inventor is so intimate a part of the history of innovation in the capitalist world that one must ask whether the socialist system has managed to generate such persons or some socialist equivalent. If it has not, one might well conclude that an important factor in promoting innovation has been forgone. The point must not be pressed too far, however, for while individual invention was the major source of supply of new technological ideas in the past, the Soviet economy came upon the scene at a time when corporate invention began to compete with individual invention as an effective source of supply of new technological ideas in capitalist countries. And corporate invention is a kind of activity that a socialist economy might be expected to manage well.

Individual invention does still account for a substantial portion of the generation of new ideas in capitalism. Professor Jewkes and his associates credit individual inventors with about two-fifths of all patents issued in the twentieth century in the United States and Great Britain, a figure that corresponds broadly to the findings of other investigators.[37] Jacob Schmookler found that over half of all inventions are made by persons holding full-time occupations who work on inventions in their spare time, and about half of all inventions patented were issued to people who had less than a college education.[38] The large corporate invention establishments themselves benefit greatly from individual invention. Willard Mueller found that of 25 important product and process innovations introduced by DuPont, 10 were based on the inventions of

DuPont scientists and engineers; the other 15 were purchased from outside inventors, including individual inventors.[39] The Union Carbide Corporation creates new companies to develop and promote new products brought to their attention by individual entrepreneurs. These individual entrepreneurs own part of the stock and manage the companies with a free hand, using some of the services provided by the corporation, such as development and legal services. Half of these ventures have been based on outside innovations.[40]

Carter and Williams, who studied innovation in Great Britain, warn us against the old romantic notion of the typical invention as "an improved mouse-trap, capable of being produced and marketed by an inventor from a shed at the end of his garden."[41] The evidence is nevertheless compelling that the spare-time inventive activity of men with modest educational attainments continues to provide a significant supply of new ideas for innovation.

The Soviet industrial pantheon contains its share of towering figures who distinguished themselves by their innovativeness and their organizational drive. One of the most celebrated is the aircraft designer A. Yakovlev, who was responsible for the famous YAK line of aircraft. Another is the eminent Academician B. E. Paton, founder of the Institute of Welding named in his honor. Most men of inventive or innovative talent, however, develop their careers within the network of established organizations. They hold positions in enterprises or in R & D institutes, and they contribute their innovative talents as part of their professional obligations. The jobs of most working people, however, do not require inventive talent and generally leave little time for it. Among those millions there are many with the potential for contributing to technological progress. The state has not been unmindful of this potential resource and has sought in many ways to mobilize and direct it toward the promotion of technological advance.

A number of organizations are concerned with the organization and support of "mass participation" in inventive and innovative activity.[42] Trade unions and party organizations regard it as part of their normal agenda. Two other national associations are concerned primarily with innovative activity, the Central Directorate of Scientific-Technical Societies, and the All-Union Society of Inventors and Innovators. The membership of the latter associations are organized in local units, in factories and districts, known as Scientific-Technical Societies and Councils of Innovators. This network of organizations is responsible for a mass of voluntary extracurricular activity associated with innovation. An enterprise trade-union organization, for example, may undertake a review of the layout of experimental facilities or of the enterprise's record in fulfilling its new technology plan. The Council of Innovators in an industrial city may operate a program of studying the literature on recent innovations and calling them to the attention of those local enterprises that might benefit from adopting them.

To support the work of individual inventors and innovators, most enterprises contain a unit known as the Bureau of Innovations and Inventions.[43] The bureau's function is to provide facilities for inventors to carry on small-scale tinkering and experimentation and to assist them in carrying promising innovations through to completion. The bureau also assists them in registering officially their inventions and innovations, so that they may qualify for rewards. The work carried on with the assistance of these bureaus accounts for the greater part of the 4 million registered inventions and production-improvement proposals submitted annually. Those figures must be accepted with some caution, since Soviet commentators often express doubt about the standards by which a proposal is officially recorded as a genuine invention or process innovation. Enterprises are also under some gentle pressure to produce statistics showing a proper enthusiasm for the support of this inventive activity. Moreover, in tallying up the results, every proposal counts as one, whether it is a modest reorganization of the work flow in a small enterprise or a major product improvement in a large enterprise. Some proportion, however, consists of innovations substantial enough to be awarded "certificates of authorship" (patents). It is not possible to determine precisely the proportion of all certificates of authorship awarded to individuals, but it is clear, in the words of the OECD study, that they make a "considerable contribution."[44]

The work of individual inventors, organized in the mass-participation movement, augments the supply of new technological ideas generated within the society. The question is, however, whether the organizational obstacles to the passage from invention to innovation encountered in the case of the R & D institutes are less formidable in the case of individual invention. Since most of the inventions originating from this source are relatively small scale, this is likely to be the case. The additional development and refinement they may require before they can be put into production can usually be done by the enterprise's own engineering staff. The more ambitious the invention, however, the greater the likelihood that the process of innovation will require negotiation with other organizations. In particular, if it requires extensive development, design, and testing, the enterprise will have to negotiate with one or more R & D organizations for their services. In such cases individual invention confronts the same organizational obstacles in the passage from invention to innovation as do inventions originating in R & D organizations and enterprises.

4.3. Organizational Reforms

A number of reforms have been introduced for the specific purpose of improving the quality of the R & D services supplied to enterprises. While the structure of organization is a major source of the problem, it is not the only source, and some of the reforms are aimed at other facets of the problem. A 1955 decree, for example, was designed to raise the quality of R & D personnel. The decree required that "as a rule" young graduates of technical institutes should be assigned to work directly in production after graduation and should be permitted to go on to graduate study or to accept employment in R & D organizations only after having had some practical experience.[45] A second set of measures has enlarged the volume of R & D work conducted by the teaching institutions of the higher education system. The objective was both to increase the supply of R & D services to the economy, and to improve the quality of higher technical education.[46]

Other reforms are directed not at the quality of personnel but at the technical quality of R & D work. A considerable literature has developed on methods of improving the efficiency of R & D work.[47] A great deal of attention has been devoted to the application of the "Saratov system" to development and design work. The Saratov system is the Soviet equivalent of the quality-control technique known in the United States as the "zero-defects system."[48] As used in production control, the system consists of the payment of special bonuses to workers in proportion to the volume of their output that passes quality inspection "on the first presentation." Output that is rejected, or that requires reworking before passing a second inspection, earns no bonus. As applied to the work of R & D organizations, the bonus payments are proportional to the number of drawings and blueprints that are perfect "on the first presentation" to the enterprises, that is, require no changes during the process of putting the innovations into production.

Improvements in the quality of the people and the techniques employed in R & D work may be expected to improve the quality of the R & D services supplied to enterprises. They do not, however, confront directly the organizational obstacles to innovation discussed above. They are not directed at what Dr. Gatovsky has called the need to create "a normal economic mechanism for integrating R & D institute and the enterprises."[49] For even with the best-trained R & D personnel, armed with the most advanced techniques, the supply of R & D services to enterprises may be greatly facilitated or greatly impeded, depending on the organizational mechanisms. Organizational structure is the subject of another group of reforms.

Dissolution of the Regional Economic Councils

When the industrial ministries were abolished in 1957, their R & D organizations were distributed among a variety of agencies. Most were transferred to the new Regional Economic Councils in whose territory they happened to be located. Many of the largest and most important ones, however, were transferred to various central government organs such as the State Planning Committee and the several State Committees that were hastily organized at the time. The redistribution of the R & D organizations revealed for the first time the degree of overlap and noncoordination that had grown up under the old ministry system. The State Committee on Automation and Machinebuilding, for example, was given jurisdiction over a large number of R & D institutes that had been working in its field under various ministries. Chairman Kostousov reported that in preparation for drafting the 1961 plan of work for the Committee's R & D organizations a study was made of the proposed plans of over 2,000 scientific research and production-engineering institutes. As a result of the study, 1,860 of the originally planned projects were canceled, "900 of them duplicated one another, and 500 had been previously carried out by other institutions."[50]

It is clear that whatever central planning of R & D was conducted before 1957, it was not very effectively translated into the operating plans of the ministry R & D network. Some better coordination was probably attained among those major institutes subsequently regrouped under the State Planning Committee and the new State Committees. But most of the R & D organizations were transferred to the Regional Councils, and it appears that in their case the degree of duplicative work increased greatly, and the quality fell sharply. For these institutions, which formerly concentrated on a limited range of technology, were now obliged to concern themselves with the R & D work of the great variety of different industries under the jurisdiction of their new bosses, the Regional Economic Councils. The latter, moreover, found it necessary to create new institutes to serve their needs. Consequently the total number of R & D organizations, which had remained fairly stable before 1957 at about 2,800, rose to 3,800 by 1961, "most of the increase being directly attributable to the [Regional Economic] Councils." Moreover, under the ministries a variety of R & D complexes had been formed that consisted, for example, of parent institutes, branches, testing and experimental facilities, and enterprises. After 1957, those complexes were often dissolved; a leading institute in Moscow, for example, might lose one of its major branches to one Regional Council and its experimental plant to another.[51] Soviet analysts, noting the subsequent decline in the quality of R & D work, ascribe it to the extensive duplication and overlap in R & D work going on in different regions. Among the many examples later discovered, the Yaroslav Motor Plant and the Kharkov "Hammer and Sickle" Plant produced virtually identical tractor models, apparently in ignorance of each other's R & D work.[52]

The decline in the Soviet growth rate is generally dated from about 1958, and one of the main indicators of the decline is the rise in the capital/output ratio. Much of our evidence on the slow increase in the productivity of new technology, and in many cases of the absolutely lower productivity of new technology compared with that it replaced, comes from this period. There is a strong presumption that the shift from the industrial ministry to the territorial council helped precipitate the subsequent decline. If so, the restoration of the industrial ministry form of organization in 1965 may be expected in time to raise the quality of work of the R & D organizations. Some of the difficulties in the supply of R & D services were in this sense a transitory factor.

Contractual R & D

The industrial R & D organization traditionally receives all its instructions from its ministry. One portion of the organization's work consists of self-initiated projects initially proposed by the organization itself in its draft plan and subsequently approved formally by the ministry in the course of the planning process. The other portion consists of projects assigned by the ministry. If the lead time is long enough, an assigned project may be included in the organization's work plan. If time is short and the project urgent, the organization could be instructed simply to set to work on it immediately, either in addition to its regular planned tasks or in place of one of them.

The enterprise has no formal way of inserting itself directly into this administrative relationship between R & D organization and ministry. When an R & D project is completed, it is the ministry that decides which enterprise will be required to put it into production, and the order is issued by the ministry to that enterprise. If the enterprise requires some R & D work to be done, it has to apply to the ministry, and if the application is successful, the ministry orders an R & D organization to undertake the work. In practice, these relationships are accompanied by extensive informal consultation and negotiations, so that matters often run more smoothly than one may imagine on the basis of the starkly formal procedures. Often enough, however, the organizational dissociation of the innovating enterprise from its supplier of R & D services generates the obstacles to innovation discussed above.

One line of reform has been a series of related measures designed to give enterprises somewhat greater control over the supply of the services delivered by the R & D organizations. One such measure is a change in the economic status of the R & D organizations from the "state-budget-financed" to the "business accounting" form of organizational unit. The second is the increase in the proportion of the revenues of R & D organizations derived from contracts with enterprises.

Business accountability of R & D organizations. Budget-financed organizations are those that are treated in the same manner as government bureaus. Their operating expenses, like those of the State Planning Committee or the Ministry of Education, are financed almost entirely by direct appropriations from the state budget. If they have any sources of revenue other than budget grants, those revenues are simply turned over to the state budget. Business-accounting organizations, on the other hand, are expected to finance their operating expenses out of the revenues they earn from the sale of goods and services to other economic units.[53] If their receipts exceed their expenses, they turn only a portion of the profit over to the state budget. If their receipts do not cover their expenses, they may receive a subsidy from the state budget to cover the difference.[54]

Soviet administration theory holds that business accounting is a superior device for the control of organizations that produce goods or services for specific users. Because budget-financed organizations are not dependent on "customers" for revenues to cover their expenses, they tend to be less concerned about the quality of the goods or services they produce, and since the "government" pays the bill, they are under less pressure to economize on expenses. Organizations operating on a business-accounting basis, however, may find themselves in financial difficulty if customers refuse to pay because of the poor quality of the goods or services provided or because production inefficiency runs their costs above the planned levels. Business accounting is therefore the standard organizational form for Soviet enterprises. Budget financing is reserved for organizations that, like most government agencies, do not serve specific groups of customers or for other reasons ought not be expected to cover their expenses by the sale of their goods or services.

The industrial R & D organizations have traditionally operated on a budget-financed basis. Like a planning department or a chief administration of a ministry, the R & D organizations were part of the ministry's budget. Only the ministry officials needed to be satisfied with the quality and efficiency of the organizations' work. If they were, the budget appropriation would come through year after year, with no more than the usual bureaucratic wrangling about plans and budgets. Because of their budgetary independence, the R & D organizations suffered little from enterprise dissatisfaction with the quality of their work.

In 1962 the industrial R & D organizations were cut loose from their comfortable financial berth by a major decree of the government.[55] They were transferred en masse from a budget-financed to a business-accounting basis. Their revenues were to come increasingly from contract work negotiated with client organizations, particularly enterprises. The new dependence of the R & D organizations on contract research gave enterprises for the first time the opportunity to exert direct pressure on them, and thus to possess somewhat greater control over the supply of their R & D services.

Contract research. The introduction of contract R & D appears to have eased some of the problems faced by innovating enterprises. They can now negotiate directly with the R & D establishments instead of having to apply to the ministry to issue the appropriate orders. The technical specifications can be drawn up with greater attention to the enterprise's own needs and time schedules. They can monitor the progress of the work more closely. Innovation opportunities can be taken up with greater assurance that, as R & D needs arise, the enterprise can more quickly get the work done by contracting it out. Having a hold on the purse strings, the enterprise can insist on a closer compliance with specifications and timing. A larger portion of the work of the R & D organizations is aimed directly at subsequent innovation, since enterprises are not likely to devote their own financial resources to work from which they do not expect a satisfactory return. Hence the proportion of R & D expenditure leading to eventual innovation is likely to be greater.

The flexibility introduced by the contracting system has also contributed in part to the rise of the "research complex" as an innovation-promoting organizational device. A research complex is a cluster of research institutes specialized in different fields and working closely with neighboring enterprises. The variety of specializations facilitates the interdisciplinary cooperation often required in applied work, and the close association with neighboring industrial enterprises makes for greater ease in prototype construction, testing, and innovation. The most ambitious research complex is the one that has grown up in the Academic City of Novosibirsk, which is taking on some of the characteristics of the research-based industrial clusters around Boston, Palo Alto, and Houston. "The policy of the Soviet government in 'encircling' Novosibirsk with industrial enterprises clearly indicates that this kind of interaction between R & D and industry is envisaged."[56] The success of such ventures requires a large measure of informality and flexibility in the relations among the enterprises and R & D organizations which would be impossible to achieve if they were all obliged to operate strictly within their own ministerial confines. Contracting provides greater opportunities for the establishment of such productive economic relationships.

Limitations of contract research. Perhaps the chief benefit from the introduction of contracting is the elimination of one superfluous administrative link—the ministry—in the innovation process. The contracting system, however, has not eliminated all the problems facing the innovating enterprise in managing the supply of R & D services delivered by independent R & D organizations. For one thing, many kinds of R & D continue to be supported primarily by budget grants: large-scale and fundamental research, projects with a long payoff period, projects that require intensive interdisciplinary coordination, projects with significant externalities that benefit many enterprises but are insufficiently profitable for any one of them, and so forth. Hence the bulk of the income of R & D organizations continues to come from direct budget grants rather than from contracts. Precise data are not available, but it appears that over half of the expenditures of ministry R & D institutes continues to come from budget grants. Contract research by the institutes of the Academy of Services and by the institutions of higher education has increased, but it is still the minor portion of their income.[57]

Certain improvements have been made in the administration of budget-financed research. In the Ministry of the Electrical Equipment Industry, for example, "formerly, funds for scientific research were allocated to the institute in a lump sum; now they are paid out only in accordance with work completed on a particular project, or by individual stages of work."[58] The use of individual earmarked grants instead of the old method of general subsidization has also been growing. It introduces what the OECD analysts call a "contract element" even in budget-financed research.[59] Since the institutes are now on a business-accounting basis, they must perform on each of the projects supported by the earmarked grants in the same manner as on their contracted projects, in order to maintain their inflow of revenues to cover outlays. The ministry's monitoring agencies therefore possess a greater measure of control over the institute's work.

In budget-financed research, however, the R & D organization still works for the ministry rather than the enterprise, and when the project is finally assigned to an enterprise for application, the latter has as little control as ever over the quality of the work. Since the major portion of the incomes of the R & D organizations still come from budget grants, the leverage that the contract system gives to enterprises is limited.[60] It is perhaps for that reason that even so prominent an enterprise as the Zaporozhe Transformer Plant found that the "design organizations as a rule do not accept enterprise orders willingly, and when they do accept them, those orders are the last to be worked on."[61] Not all R & D organizations are in so favorable a position, however. Some find that the volume of contract research in their order book falls short of their planned target. They are then obliged to scramble about for additional contracts, and they enter into contracts for straight production work that has no R & D content and is sometimes far from their line of specialization.[62] While the R & D people complain about this aspect of contract financing, however, it is clearly to the advantage of innovating enterprises to have some degree of excess capacity in the R & D network.

The attractiveness of contract research to the enterprise is somewhat weakened by the limited responsibility borne by the R & D organization. The original standard contract contained a clause stipulating that "a negative result does not free the client from paying the cost of the work." The contractor may have to pay a small penalty for failing to meet the contracted time schedules, but the responsibility for the success of the innovation rests ultimately on the client enterprise.[63] A series of decrees in 1967 and 1968 sought to place greater financial responsibility on the contractor.[64] The R & D organizations are obliged to make changes subsequently required in their original work at their own expense. If they exceed the time limit for making the changes, they are subject to a penalty of 4 percent of the total cost.[65] This tightening of standard contract terms works to the advantage of the enterprise, although it must involve some increase in the volume of arbitration and litigation.

Less progress has been made on the more important matter of writing performances guarantees into the standard contract. Such guarantees, based on the calculated economic return to the innovation, have been urged for some time, but they are not yet part of the standard contract. The subject of the contract is still defined only in terms of a research objective (*tema*). In our view the contractual relations between research organizations and industry must be changed. The subject of the contract should be defined not only by the research objective, but also by a guaranteed return to the enterprise from introducing the new product or process.[66]

It is generally recognized, however—somewhat ruefully—that the techniques for calculating the "economic effectiveness" of R & D work, and of innovation in general, are still too imperfect for use in legal documents.[67] The knife, moreover, cuts both ways; an unsuccessful innovation may be due not to the poor quality of the R & D work but to the incompetence of the client in installing and operating the new equipment or producing the new product. Performance guarantees would place a large additional burden on the crowded dockets of the arbitration courts if they were obliged to adjudicate disputes on the relative shares of responsibility for unsuccessful innovation.

The contracting system provides the innovator with greater flexibility in managing his supply of R & D services. There is a limit, however, to the flexibility that can be attained in the context of central economic planning. Contract negotiations normally take place during the first half of the year. The plans of the R & D organizations, however, are officially approved early in the year and generally provide no unused capacity for taking on new research tasks for the rest of that year. The contractors therefore, "establish very long time periods for carrying out the work, especially in the case of research included in their plans on the initiative of enterprises."[68] Hence, while contracting has established itself as a useful technique under certain circumstances, the search continues for better techniques of coordinating R & D work and innovation. In some cases, after a period of trial, contracting has been abandoned and replaced by new forms of centralized administration. In the Ministry of the Electrical Equipment Industry, for example, contracts between enterprises and research institutes within the ministry have been replaced by what may be called "purchase orders."[69] These orders are based on a new form of detailed project planning in which all stages of a planned innovation, from initial research to final introduction, are planned throughout. The mutual obligations of institute and enterprise are spelled out in sufficient detail that contracts are no longer thought to be necessary for regulating the flow of R & D sources among the organizational units within the ministry.[70]

Conclusion. In evaluating the contribution of contracting, it is well to recall that it is not a novel technique in Soviet economic organization. It is a standard practice in the organization of the supply of materials and equipment. What is novel is its use in the organization of the supply of R & D services. Under the earlier structure of organization, the problem faced by the innovating enterprise in managing its supply of R & D services was somewhat more pressing than those involved in the supply of ordinary goods and services. The introduction of contracting removed some of those special problems. But contracting has not eliminated the uncertainty that plagues the enterprise in the management of its supply of materials and equipment. It might therefore occasion no surprise that it has not proved to be more successful in regard to the supply of R & D services.

While the practice of drawing up purchase and sale contracts has certain advantages in the administration of the planned distribution of goods and services, there are limits to its effectiveness. The use of the same word—"contract"—in different types of economic systems does not signify that it performs identical functions in different systems. The advantage that a contract confers on a client depends on the sanctions that are brought to bear on the contractor if the terms of the contract are not met. In a capitalist economy, those sanctions are potentially quite strong; at the extreme they may involve loss of business and heavy financial penalties affecting large personal fortunes. Such penalties are a powerful disciplining device and therefore give the client rather strong assurances that the terms of the contract will be fulfilled. In the context of the Soviet economy, however, the sanctions that can be imposed in a contractual relationship are not significantly stronger than those employed in noncontractual administrative relationships. If an R & D organization performs poorly on a job it was ordered to perform for one enterprise by the ministry, it will suffer the sanctions of underfulfillment of plan, loss of management's bonuses perhaps, and possibly the replacement of some officials. If that same poor work were performed under an enterprise contract instead of a ministry order, the sanctions would not be significantly more severe. One might not expect, therefore, that in the Soviet context the use of contracts instead of administrative orders would lead to a major change in the enterprise's control over its supply of R & D services.

What is required is some device that would oblige producers to attend more closely to the needs of users, not only with respect to R & D services but to goods and services in general. Contractual arrangements do not get at the heart of the problems. The reform to be discussed next may be closer to the mark.

Competition

The notion of "socialist competition" is not a new one in the Soviet lexicon.[71] It refers to a practice in which a group of enterprises agrees to compete in striving to overfulfill their output plan targets, or some other indicator such as labor productivity. The organization of a socialist competition provides the occasion for the mobilization of effort and enthusiasm by management, trade union, and party organization. Scores are kept on the bulletin boards of the enterprises, meetings are arranged to discuss ways of forging ahead, and efforts are made to keep up the spirit of the game and to harness it to the production effort. The winner receives a money prize put up by the ministry and is treated to a generous dose of publicity. The reward money is distributed among the officials and workers according to a prearranged formula.

It is difficult to judge whether the effort that goes into the organizing of a socialist competition and the money rewards to the winners are justified by the returns in increased output. Soviet empirical research does not normally raise questions of this kind. In any case the term "competition," like the term "contract," does not have the same meaning in the Soviet economy as it does in a capitalist economy. A better term would be "contest." For the outcome of a socialist contest does not affect the interenterprise flow of resources. The losing enterprises suffer no loss of business or revenue. Customers enjoy no direct benefit from socialist competition among the producers of their inputs, although there are indirect benefits to the extent that production may be increased and quality improved.

The problem of monopoly. A rather more substantial meaning is intended as the term "competition" is applied to R & D work. That meaning is set forth in a remarkable article by Academician Trapeznikov. The eminent scientist rejects the notion that in a planned economy duplication of effort is always to be avoided and that only one organization is required to conduct all the R & D work in a given field. In science and technology, as in art, there is no single way. What is required is a "competition of scientific and technical ideas" advanced by different groups of men. For in the absence of such competition,

if scientific and technological monopoly takes shape, the result is a stagnation of ideas. The customer can only say to the design organization, "Please, do at least slightly better." And the monopolistic design organization will answer, "We can do no better; if you don't like it, do it yourself!" And the enterprise will have to content itself with this answer.[72]

In calling a spade a spade, Trapeznikov forced his colleagues to face up to a central issue in the structure of Soviet economic organization. Soviet producers often do act like monopolists, in the sense that they are able to promote the interests of their own enterprises without having to take account of possible reactions by customers or by other producers of the same goods or services. If the customers do not like it, they can do it themselves.

The consequences of monopoly may be seen in an incident involving the Central Scientific-Research Institute of the Paper Industry. On instruction from the ministry the Institute conducted an evaluation of the technical quality of the machinery produced by the Gatchinsk-Roshal' Plant. The evaluation classified 22 of the plant's 24 models as "good." As it turned out, however, the Institute itself had designed most of those models. But the plant officials, who had been dissatisfied with the designs, argued that most of them were far behind the best models currently in use, and they protested the evaluation. The Institute was then required to reevaluate the designs, and eventually acknowledged that not 22 but only 9 could be classified as "good." One can appreciate the critics' desire to provide at least enough competition in R & D to enable authorized persons to obtain a less self-interested critique of technological performance.[73]

Trapeznikov ascribes the monopolistic behavior of the R & D organizations to the presence of a monopolistic structure, a comment that sounds reasonable enough. His solution is to eliminate the monopolistic structural elements in the system by establishing at least two suppliers for the good or service, in this case, for the services of R & D work of all kinds. He argues that the existence of several institutes in a field will not necessarily increase the cost of R & D, because the quality of work will improve. The cost of design work is usually 2 to 3 percent of total construction costs, and the cost of drafting is less than 0.5 percent. Hence, if the best version of two competition entries reduces construction costs by no more than 10 percent, the additional expenditures are worthwhile.[74]

Western experience lends some support to the proposal for the establishment of parallel R & D organizations. Where competition exists, an innovation by one firm confronts competitors with the choice of adopting it or developing their own version. The successful Houdry process of catalytic cracking of petroleum, for example, which was innovated by Socony-Mobil and Sun Oil, confronted Standard Oil (New Jersey) with such a choice. They deliberately decided to try "to invent around" the Houdry patents and within six years succeeded in developing the new and more effective fluid catalytic cracking process.[75] Similarly, Reynolds Aluminum undertook to develop a specialized bauxite ore vessel that Alcoa, "after continued and constant study," had rejected as too expensive. Reynolds proceeded with the project, nevertheless, and the ship that was finally produced saved an estimated one-third of the cost of shipping with conventional equipment. Alcoa subsequently ordered two of the new carriers for itself.[76]

In a capitalist economy parallel R & D, stimulated by competition and patent protection, probably augments the rate of technological progress. To some extent, however, that result is due to an increase in the volume of expenditures on R & D. If Alcoa's monopoly of the aluminum industry had not been dissolved, the specialized ore carrier may not have been built, but the funds that Reynolds subsequently spent on development may have been devoted to other uses. The contribution of competition was to improve technology by allocating a greater volume of resources to R & D.[77]

For this reason, the capitalist experience is not relevant in all respects to a socialist centrally planned economy. In the Soviet economy the volume of resources allocated to R & D is centrally determined, and the issue is rather whether the given volume of resources should be allocated among a large number of different projects or among a smaller number of similar projects each of which is pursued in two or more parallel research efforts. On this issue too, Western experience suggests that parallel R & D has an advantage over single projects. In the development of the atom bomb, for example, five approaches were considered, and the one that was thought to be the least likely to yield results proved in fact to be the one that was finally selected.[78] Experience has been supported by a body of theory which shows that, given the uncertainty inherent in R & D work, parallel and independent effort often proves to be the most efficient strategy.[79] Since this evidence is based more on the universal properties of the R & D process than on its specifically capitalist features, one may expect it to apply to socialism as well.

It is not surprising that the concept of parallel R & D effort should not have developed in the Soviet context. The Soviet philosophical outlook has a strong rationalist element. The system of central planning draws support from the belief that if one plans rationally what each unit should do, and if each unit would indeed do it, one's problems would be readily solved. It is not an inappropriate approach for a world of unchanging knowledge. In such a world there will be little sense in introducing parallel effort and competition among units. The value of such techniques is more likely to occur to persons used to a world in which uncertainty and change are regarded as the normal order of things. Under such conditions one is more likely to believe that two heads may be better than one.

Competition and duplication of effort are most likely to be found in social structures with no central organizing authority. They do not come naturally to planners. Competition and duplication are regarded as elements of irrationality appropriate only to an unplanned society. Uncertainty is something to be minimized and duplication something to be eliminated. Hence, if duplicate effort and competition prove to have some virtue in promoting innovation, this virtue is more likely to arise by accident in an unplanned system than by design in a planned system.

For these reasons, the Trapeznikov proposal must be regarded as exceptionally bold and imaginative. It may have received some impetus, however, from the growing acknowledgment that the Soviet economy is not in fáct as rational as the ideal model would suggest, and that uncertainty abounds. It may also reflect the growing influence of scientists and researchers, in whose work uncertainty is of the very essence. Those whose lives are devoted to the creation of new knowledge are hardly likely to proceed from the assumption of a given state of knowledge. This is the point of Dr. Zhamin's statement, "It is not accidental that many scientists persistently propose that parallel research be carried out on important problems on an equal basis, and that competitive development work of an applied nature be carried out."[80]

It should also be noted that R & D work is not universally characterized by monopoly, as Trapeznikov seems to imply. One reads of fairly intense competition at times. For example, the Novolipetsk Steel Plant, which was the first to innovate the continuous steel-casting process, had developed what is called the "block" construction method, laid out in vertical form. A representative of the Urals Metallurgical Construction-Project Planning Institute (*Uralgipromez*), attending a special training school at the Novolipetsk plant, urged the adoption of the technique developed by his institute, which used a "linear" instead of a "block" construction method and was laid out in a radial rather than a vertical form. He argued vigorously that this design would reduce both capital and operating costs. That point of view was contested by the Central Metallurgical Construction-Project Planning Institute (*Tsentralnoe Gipromez*) which had developed the Novolipetsk process. "Who is right?" asks the reporter. "Each one presents the strong points of 'his' proposal, but is silent about the 'darker' sides."[81] It is clear that these two R & D establishments working in the same field are engaged in parallel development of the same process and have a keen personal investment in their "own" solutions. We do not know how extensive such nonmonopolistic structures are, however, and must rely on inference from the statements of Trapeznikov, Zhamin, and others that monopolistic structures are the normal state of affairs.

Their view is not inconsistent with the evidence presented above of widespread duplication in the work of R & D organizations. Most of that duplication results from inadequate planning of R & D work within ministries and from the imperfect knowledge available to R & D organizations about work being done elsewhere. A considerable number of R & D organizations work on hydraulic-drive assemblies, and the industry produces 776 models of single-stage hydraulic power drives, 643 models of hydraulic equipment, 330 models of pumps, 78 models of hydraulic panels, and so forth. Because the work is poorly coordinated, the parts are generally not interchangeable.[82] Duplication in such cases is costly and does not provide the compensating benefits of openly competitive and parallel efforts. Different organizations pursue similar approaches to identical ends in ignorance of each other's work, instead of pursuing different approaches to the same end by "inventing around" each other. Wasteful effort of that kind accounts for the fact, for example, that in the postwar years the proportion of duplicated inventions in coal combine machinery rose from 40 percent to 85 percent.[83] But more important, when similar R & D organizations belong to different ministries, they are not equally accessible to all enterprises seeking some development work. The fact that there are five R & D organizations in Leningrad conducting research on high-frequency installations[84] does not mean that any one Leningrad enterprise has access to the services of all five. It may have access only to that one which belongs to its own ministry and which has an effective monopoly over the supply of R & D services to that ministry's enterprises. One might describe this as the worst of all possible worlds: extensive duplication of R & D work without the advantages of competitive and parallel investigations.

The proposal to require that there be two or more R & D establishments in all fields is an effort to eliminate monopolistic behavior by eliminating monopolistic organizational structure. It is reasonable to expect that the structure may indeed be the cause, or one of the causes, of the unsatisfactory behavior. The competition over steel-casting technology by the two institutes described earlier suggests that the presence of more than one establishment in a field may advance the quality of development work. On reflection, however, there may well be other system properties that may continue to generate monopolistic behavior even in the absence of a monopolistic structure. It is not at all certain in the Soviet context that two or more R & D institutes will serve a group of customer enterprises with any greater attentiveness than the monopolistic institute described by Trapeznikov. Under conditions of excess demand, for example, they may behave like typical Soviet suppliers of material goods, on the knowledge that "the customer will take anything."[85] Or again, the procedures by which their performance is evaluated may direct their behavior toward the satisfaction of criteria set for them by their ministries; under conditions of imperfect planning and administration, those criteria often lead to gross inattention to the requirements of their customers.

We thus return again to the caution that the efficiency of an organizational structure is not independent of such other structural properties as rules and incentives. The elimination of monopolistic structures by establishing two or more R & D suppliers in all fields will not automatically lead to effective competition among them in the absence of appropriate rules and incentives. To enforce competitive behavior, Trapeznikov proposes further that projects not be simply "assigned" to the R & D establishments but that they be required to "bid" for them. He cites as a model procedure one that has been used for some time in the design of monuments and special architectural projects. Design organizations are invited to submit entries in a competition for the job and the best entry wins the assignment.[86] The aircraft industry has also developed on the basis of competition among such celebrated designers as Antonov, Tupelov, and Yakovlev.[87]

Limitations on the scope of competition. Proposals for the wider use of competition have been in the air for some time.[88] It was given official sanction most recently in the 1968 decree on the improvement of R & D. That decree recommended that measures be taken "for the large-scale development of competition in the field of science and technology, and for the fending off of monopoly in the solution of major scientific and technical problems." It authorized ministries and other agencies of government "when necessary, to assign research tasks, and also product-engineering, design, and technological development projects, to several organizations pursuing different approaches." In that way it will be possible to select the most promising approaches at an early stage of the research program.[89]

The 1968 decree envisions no radical move in the direction of genuine competition. It deals solely with the use of parallel research efforts as a technique of R & D administration. The technique is to be employed "when necessary" in the case of the "most important" scientific and technical problems. It is to be applied only to the earliest stages of work on a new line of R & D. Once the decision has been made on which of the several approaches is the most promising, the "competition of ideas" ends and further development work follows the normal course of R & D planning.

The decree applies only to R & D work "commissioned by the ministry"; it does not apply to work required by enterprises that would continue to be conducted under direct contractual arrangements. Since the ministry is the client, it is the ministry officials whom the R & D organizations will strive to satisfy. There is therefore no assurance that the final product or process design will meet the technical requirements or the demand conditions of the enterprise that will ultimately have to innovate the product or process. If the enterprise has reason to doubt that the R & D institute can supply the services satisfactorily, it will continue to drag its feet. The alternative is to grant to the enterprise rather than the ministry the choice of the R & D organization with which it is to work. If the enterprise were the client, rather than the ministry, and if the competition among R & D organizations enabled the enterprise to select its own supplier of R & D services, the enterprise would enjoy much greater control over the innovation process. A genuine transfer of authority from ministry to enterprise would reduce the scope of central planning, however. Perhaps for that reason, the notion of competition has not been pressed that far.

The proponents of genuine competition among R & D organizations had more in mind than simply the use of the parallel research technique. In the official recommendations of the 1965 conference in new technology, the R & D organizations were to be invited to bid for contracts on the basis of the specifications announced in the proposals. In order to create a vital interest in successful bidding, the budgets of the institutes were to be based primarily on the size of the contracts won in the competitions, rather than on the size of their staffs.[90] If collusion could be prevented, the proposal might well improve the quality of the work, especially if past performance enters in the choice of the R & D institute that wins the contract. The decree, however, provides for no organizational changes that would go as far as that. The promotion of parallel research does not involve the replacement of administration by competition. It involves rather the replacement of a poorer administrative technique by a better.

Conclusion. The term "competition," like the term "contract," has a meaning when applied to a capitalist economy that is very different when applied to a centrally planned economy. The disciplining quality of competition, where it prevails in a capitalist economy, derives from the fate that befalls the least successful enterprises. The owners and managers of capitalist enterprises that consistently fail to compete successfully suffer a loss of personal wealth and income. Eventually the firms may be taken over by new owners and managers or they may be liquidated and their assets sold to other firms. The market for supplying the service will be taken over by new entrants or by the expansion of output by the more successful suppliers. If competition is to be effective in Soviet industry, some equivalent rewards must be found for the more successful institutes and some equivalent sanctions for the less. Under the parallel-research arrangement the management of a successful R & D organization will benefit from larger personal incomes and promotion opportunities, but success does not enable it to expand its staff and its operations.[91] Since the successful organization does not expand, the ministry must continue to turn to the less successful for that portion of its R & D requirements that the more successful cannot handle. Nor does the weak R & D organization need to fear the entry of vigorous new firms against which it could not compete. Competition as it is proposed for the USSR therefore brings no threat of "loss of business" to the unsuccessful competitors. Lower personal incomes may be earned in the weaker organizations, and management may be replaced more often, but those sanctions are applied to weaker firms and R & D organizations generally and are not changed by the practice of parallel research.

The 1968 decree does devote a paragraph to these matters. Ministries are instructed to conduct a comprehensive evaluation of all R & D organizations at least once every three years. On the basis of that evaluation, decisions are to be made about their future development[92] and about the payment of special monetary bonuses. Organizations that have performed poorly may be assigned to different lines of R & D work, and in some cases their management may be strengthened or they may be liquidated.[93] What is envisioned, however, is a tightening of administrative supervision over the R & D organizations. The fate of the institute depends on the case it can present to the visiting committee and not on the relentless workings of a competitive structure of organization.

There are some gains of an administrative nature to be expected from the kind of competition incorporated in the limited use of parallel research. It can help the ministry identify the least-productive organizations and make it easier to replace poor management by better. As in the case of contracts, however, competition introduced into the Soviet organizational structure cannot be expected to produce those benefits it (sometimes) produces in capitalist economies. The "monopoly" that Academician Trapeznikov laments is not a matter of organizational structure *simpliciter*. It is more than the difference between a single supplier of a service and several. It derives from a kind of protection enjoyed by every Soviet organizational unit because it is a creature of the state and ultimately an agent of the state. The enterprise as producer benefits from this protection. But the same enterprise as customer suffers from the protection enjoyed by another enterprise as producer. The mounting attack on monopoly and the form of competition introduced to eliminate it offer the enterprise little hope of a general improvement in its supply of its R & D services.

Research-Based Corporations

The distinctive features of central planning are not to be found in the ways in which the internal affairs of enterprises and other production units are managed. They lie rather in the ways in which the relations among enterprises are organized. The process of introducing an innovation within an enterprise is no˙ fundamentally different in a centrally planned and in a market economy. Such differences as do arise flow primarily from differences in the organization of the interenterprise flow of goods and services.

There are two paths to reform. One is to improve the organizational structure of the centrally planned economy, by developing better ways of coordinating the flow of goods and services among the units in the system. That is the objective of contractual R & D and competition among R & D organizations. The other is to change the organizational structure itself, by converting an interenterprise transaction into an intraenterprise transaction. In that way a problem that is troublesome for the central planners is simply removed from the jurisdiction of central planning and transformed into a function of internal enterprise management, where it can presumably be handled more effectively. The most significant reform embodying this approach is the establishment of the new type of multiplant enterprise called a "production association."[94]

Multiplant enterprises are a standard feature of Soviet industrial organization. The general term for such an enterprise is an *ob' edinenie*, or association. One of the oldest forms is the vertically integrated "combine" (*kombinat*), which is widely used in the metallurgical and chemical industries. Another is the traditional form of horizontally integrated association called a "trust" (*trest*), which is often used to combine a number of small plants into a single enterprise in such industries as woodworking and garment manufacturing.

When the ministry form of economic organization was abolished in 1957, the new Regional Economic Councils had to administer large numbers of small local enterprises formerly under the jurisdiction of the national ministries. To simplify the administrative problem, a new wave of mergers was launched. The new type of association was known as a "firm" (*firma*). The typical firm consisted of about four small enterprises, and while the merger movement met some of the administrative needs of the local Regional Economic Councils, most firms were later regarded as too small to support the objectives of the 1965 Economic Reform.[95] The merger movement, moreover, was heavily concentrated in light and consumer goods industries, where most of the small enterprises were to be found.[96] The chief goal of the firm as an organizational form, however, was not the promotion of technological progress but administrative efficiency.

Upon the return to the ministry form of industrial administration in 1965, the government sought to assure that the new ministries would not be beset by the problems that led to their abolition in 1957. One of those problems was the excessive involvement by the old ministries in the details of enterprise operation, a practice characterized as "petty tutelage." The organizational device chosen to cope with this problem was a new type of association of enterprises known as the "branch production association," or as we have called it, the "corporation."[97] Corporations differ from the "firms" organized in the preceding five years in a variety of ways. For one thing, they are larger. Since the firm-type of association merged on the average only three or four small enterprises, they were thought therefore not to be large enough to carry out those planning and administrative activities that were to be transferred to them from the ministries. Second, the corporation is not simply a form of horizontal integration. It may include enterprises that provide goods and services for each other. Third, and most important for this study, the corporation is intended not simply to improve organizational efficiency but has come to be regarded as a major device for promoting innovation.

The corporate merger movement before 1973. The period following the 1965 Economic Reform was one of extensive experimentation in new forms of corporate organization. The experience of the new corporations was studied closely as the government sought to balance the advantages and disadvantages of the various emerging forms and to decide what the national policy should be. In April 1973 the decision was taken. The resolution of Party and Government entitled "On Certain Measures for the Further Improvement of Industrial Management" declared that the production association was to become the basic form of industrial organization thereafter.[98] The ministries were instructed to start work on plans for the general merger of their enterprises into corporate associations and to devote the next two years to carrying the reorganization out.

Since the reorganization has not yet been completed at the time of this writing (September 1975), it is not possible to present an evaluation of the new system.[99] Moreover it will require the passage of several years before enough experience has accumulated to support an evaluation. The present section will therefore deal primarily with the merger movement in the years between the Economic Reform and the April 1973 Resolution. The discussion will conclude with some observations on the Resolution and its aftermath.

The corporate merger movement developed after the Economic Reform with governmental encouragement but without central direction. Ministries were free to decide on the appropriate structure and internal organization of each merger. This was a new departure in the history of Soviet industrial organization, for the normal practice is the publication of a standard set of tables of organization, to which all organizations are obliged to conform. The rare freedom to develop one's own organizational form has led an unusually rich variety of types of corporation.[100]

Corporations differ, first, with respect to territorial scale of operation. Some are mergers of all the nation's enterprises in a certain subbranch of industry. Such "all-union" corporations sometimes replace one or more of the ministry's administrative units known as the branch chief administrations (*glavki*). In some cases, as in the Ministry of the Instrument Production Industry, all the branch chief administrations have been abolished, or rather converted into corporate-form enterprises.[101] Other corporations are mergers of enterprises in a single republic or in a single city or region. A second set of differences among corporations may be found in the relations between corporate management and the constituent enterprises. In some cases the enterprises lose their legal independence, in others they retain it, and still others are of a mixed type. They differ, third, in the range of output. In some, one large enterprise, usually designated the "head" enterprise, produces a single final product, while the others supply it with components. In others the enterprises produce a variety of final products. They differ, fourth, with respect to the branch of the economy and the kinds of organization included in the corporation. Some consist strictly of industrial production enterprises (*proizvodstvenno-promyshlennye ob' edinenii*),· some combine industrial and agricultural enterprises (*pro-myshlenno-agrarnye ob' edinenii*), and some industrial and trade enterprises (*promyshlenno-torgovye ob' edinenii*).

They differ, finally, with respect to their innovation objectives. Dr. K. I. Taksir of the Institute of Economics distinguishes three types of corporations: production associations, research-based associations, and innovation associations.[102] Production associations are primarily responsible for the production of commodities, and the R & D facilities are provided for the purpose of supporting product improvement and new product development and production. Research-based associations are primarily responsible for research, development work, and innovation, and only secondarily for production. They possess production facilities in order to test and perfect their innovations under actual production conditions, but once they have brought their innovations to the point of successful batch production it is intended that the mass production of the new items will be taken up by the production associations. Innovation associations are modeled after the American "spin-off company."[103] Their objective is to take up ideas developed elsewhere—including the military and space sectors—and to develop them further into products and processes to be introduced by other enterprises and associations. Thus, while the promotion of innovation is a major objective of the corporate merger movement, different types of corporations are intended to contribute to it in different ways.

The formation of corporations may be regarded as an extension of the effort to increase the in-house R & D facilities of enterprises, as discussed earlier. That effort was limited, however, by the size of the typical enterprise. Only the giants have been large enough to contain full-scale R & D facilities. Most enterprises could not manage more than a small laboratory, testing facility, or design operation. A significant shift from independent to in-house R & D required an increase in the scale of enterprise. One of the chief objectives of the corporate merger movement was precisely to increase the scale of enterprise for the purpose of transferring a major proportion of all R & D from the jurisdiction of ministries to that of enterprises.[104]

For such giant enterprises as the Electrosila Combine in Leningrad and the Urals Machinery Plant, conversion to a research-based corporation required only the transfer to their jurisdiction of a major R & D facility that had been previously independent.[105] No new production facilities were required, and very few changes needed to be made in enterprise management. Most of the new corporations, however, were formed by merger of a group of independent organizations. The celebrated Sigma Association of Lithuania, which is widely regarded as a model of a research-based corporation, was formed by merger of seven enterprises, two specialized design bureaus, and a production-engineering establishment.[106] The Association produces electronic computers, calculators, control instruments, and automation equipment. Corporate management is headed by a general director who is supported by a staff with corporate responsibilities for engineering, finance, planning, and so forth. Corporate policy is set by a Directors' Council, consisting of the directors of the member enterprises and R & D organizations, the general director, and his chief deputies.

In its relations with the ministry, the Sigma Association enjoys the same authority as a chief administration. All plan targets are negotiated between the ministry and the corporate management; the assignment of those targets among the enterprises is an internal affair of the corporation. Various of the functions formerly carried out by the individual units are now fully or partially centralized in the corporate management. All selling operations, for example, and all "external relations" are a corporate responsibility. The use of the various special funds that the enterprises formerly managed separately, including depreciation funds, is now partially controlled by corporate management.[107] The member enterprises and R & D organization now concentrate on carrying out the production tasks assigned to them by the corporate management.

While all the new research-based corporations have followed in broad outline the organization of Sigma, in practice a great variety of different organizational forms has emerged. The precise membership of the Directors' Council has varied, and sometimes representatives of various government agencies like the local planning organizations and the State Bank attended the meetings. In some cases action by the Council required a simple majority vote, in others a two-thirds vote. The decisions of the Council were mandatory in some corporations and merely advisory in others.[108] The precise distribution of functions between corporate and enterprise management also varied greatly. In some the member enterprises maintained their own direct relations with the Ministry of Finance: paid their taxes directly, for example. In others all financial relations with state organizations were managed by the corporation. Sometimes enterprises retained full control over the special funds available for incentives, depreciation, small-scale investment, and so forth. In other cases they were partially or fully turned over to the corporate management for centralized allocation.[109]

Most corporations were responsible directly to the ministry. No branch chief administration intervened; they were in fact coordinate in authority with the chief administrations that continued to administer the noncorporate enterprises. They differed from the traditional chief administrations, however, in the fact that they operated on a business-accounting rather than on a budget-financed basis. Not only the member enterprises but the corporation itself maintained individual profit-and-loss accounts. Each was expected to cover its expenses out of its revenues, which were derived from various charges levied on the member enterprises. The revenues covered not only the salaries and expenses of the corporate offices but also those operations that were centrally managed such as labor training, sales and marketing, and so forth.

The corporation is expected to provide a number of benefits to the economy.[110] It will improve planning and administration in the ministries, for the latter have now many fewer discrete units to be supervised directly.[111] It will effect a more rational pattern of production specialization among enterprises than ministries were able to accomplish.[112] Other benefits flow from the centralization of certain functions such as investment planning, sales and purchasing, maintenance, and so forth. But its major contribution is to improve the quality and the rate of innovation. This is to come about chiefly because of the improvement in the supply of R & D services to the corporation, which should reduce managerial resistance to innovation. For management now comes to the R & D organization not like a petitioner hat in hand but as a boss. Moreover the quality of R & D work may be expected to improve, further encouraging the decision to innovate. The long delays in moving an innovation through a variety of separate organizations need no longer occur. All the required facilities are under a single management—laboratories, design offices, testing, and experimental shops in the factories, and the production units themselves. The tendency for R & D people to "lose interest" in an innovation once it leaves their hands is likely to diminish, since the corporate management has a vital interest in seeing the work through to completion. The research program of the R & D organizations are likely to be geared more directly to eventual application, for unlike the government officials in the ministry, the corporate management has to "meet a payroll," so to speak. Management is less likely to support R & D work that might dazzle a ministry bureaucrat but offers little return in terms of hard economic calculation.

The research-based corporation is designed primarily to improve the supply of R & D services within the ministry. Equally serious, however, have been the problems of coordinating R & D work between ministries.[113] If an innovation in one ministry requires some R & D work that is normally carried out by the institutes in a different branch of industry, the structure of organization makes it particularly difficult to get that work done. The research-based corporation has the potential for facilitating innovation in such cases. It depends on whether corporate management will be given sufficient authority to undertake R & D work that is not normally part of its own line of research when that work cannot be satisfactorily supplied from outside by contract. If the corporation's R & D establishment is constrained to work within a limited sphere of technology, however, this considerable potential gain will be forgone.

Turning from the anticipated benefits of the corporation to those observed in practice, reliable data are difficult to find. Most of the evidence takes the form of accounts of the performance of individual or groups of corporations. The enterprises of the Rhythm Association increased their volume of experimental and design work fourfold following their merger into a corporation, and the return to their innovations more than doubled in three years.[114] When the first group of Leningrad corporations was founded, only 41 percent of their output was regarded as equivalent in quality to the best foreign and domestic models. By 1970 that proportion had risen to almost 80 percent, and 300 of their products had been honored with a "seal of quality."[115] Similar accounts can be found of other corporations and cities. Aggregate data, however, are not available, nor are there published studies that seek to determine the portion of such improvements that can be ascribed to the change in organizational form alone. Perhaps the prudent judgment is that some significant gains have been scored in a number of cases and that the corporation is on balance a more effective organizational form for the promotion of innovation.

Problems of corporate organization. Detailed data on the number of corporations are not available but those that have been published provide a broad picture of the pace of the merger movement. In 1965 there were 570 associations in existence embracing about 2,000 enterprises. These were mostly "firms" organized under the Regional Economic

Councils. By mid-1969 the number had fallen to 510, reflecting the dismantling of some of them when the ministry system was reestablished.[116] After this slow start following the Economic Reform, the rate of merger picked up. On the eve of the 1973 Resolution the number had doubled to about 1,000, accounting for about 12 percent of all industrial output.[117] In the two years following the Resolution the number doubled again, and in mid-1975 the output of associations accounted for about 25 percent of industrial output.[118] The merger movement has thus been proceeding steadily, but the pace is somewhat slower than appears to have been the intent of the 1973 Resolution. Evidently the ministers and managers are moving cautiously in the formation of new corporations, in part because of the accumulation of a variety of problems that have emerged in the course of the merger movement.

There was, first, the problem that arises in all major reorganizations everywhere—resistance on the part of those whose power and position are diminished. As one commentator put it, "The question boiled down to: who should administer the enterprises, the corporation or the ministry's chief administration?"[119]

The issue first arose after the 1965 Economic Reform, when some newly reestablished chief administrations launched an "attack" on the "firms" that had been established by the Regional Economic Councils prior to their abolition. The five enterprises of the Sverdlov-Leningrad Machine Tool Association, for example, fell within the jurisdiction of five different chief administrations of the new Ministry of the Machine Tool Industry, and the chief administrations fought to have the association dismantled and the enterprises turned over to them.[120] In the first few years following the 1965 Economic Reform, some firms were stripped of some of their enterprises, and others were dismantled and their enterprises turned over to the chief administrations.[121] Some of the associations that had been dismantled appear to have followed the "conglomerate merger" pattern popular in the United States at the time. Instead of specialization, which was one of the objectives of the corporate movement, they became excessively diversified.

The practice of converting entire chief administrations into corporations also came under fire. It led, in some cases, to excessive territorial dispersion, and to the creation of what was called "monopolization" of an entire subbranch of industry.[122] Chief administrations thereafter grew more cautious before rushing into the corporate form. The Chief

Administration for Pipe Steel, for example, after an extensive study of the experience of others, decided that its enterprises were too large and too dispersed to warrant merger into a corporation.[123]

Apart from purely power considerations, other problems arose that were difficult to resolve. One set of problems concerned the relations of corporation to ministry. The corporation, like the individual enterprise, is a creature of the ministry, and its independence is limited by the authority of the ministry. In the Sigma Association, the corporate management determined the work program of its R & D organizations, but the ministry insisted on establishing both the technical and the economic criteria, or indicators, for evaluating their performance. "Often," wrote the chief engineer, "the two conflict with each other. Therefore the time schedule on development work is artificially held back." The ministry also established the size of the corporate staff and its budget. But the ministry, wrote the General Director, "does not see everything all the time," and he urged that more authority be given to his own Directors' Council.[124] The corporation appeared to enjoy no greater autonomy in its relations to the ministry than the individual enterprise in its relations to the ministry's chief administration.

The justification of the corporate form, however, is not in its greater authority vis-à-vis the ministry, but in its greater flexibility in managing the relations among its member units. Here too, however, a number of problems have arisen, primarily in connection with the role of the Directors' Council.

A central question in the organization of mergers is the distribution of authority between corporate management and the management of the member enterprises and R & D organizations. The organizational obstacle to innovation that the corporate form is intended to remove is the conflicting interests of R & D organizations and enterprises. The corporation is a device for establishing a higher locus of authority in which local interests would be submerged in the general interest. The appropriate administrative arrangement, it would seem, is to abolish the independent authority of the directors of the merged enterprises and R & D organizations, and to transfer it to corporate management. This has not been done. We can only speculate on the reasons. Perhaps it was the combined opposition of the hundreds of influential directors who would have lost greatly in power; their resistance could have greatly slowed down the corporate movement. Perhaps there was a concern over the power that would be concentrated in the corporate management. Whatever the reasons, in the formation of corporations most of the merged enterprises and R & D organizations retained their independent legal status and their directors continued to enjoy a great deal of their previous authority. The organizational expression of that arrangement was the new administrative body, the Directors' Council.[125]

For decades the enshrined principle of industrial administration was "personal management" (*edinonachalie*). According to that principle the director bears full responsibility for the performance of his enterprises, and he alone has the right to set policy and issue orders to his staff. He must, of course, secure the ministry's approval of his policies, but if the ministry is dissatisfied with some aspect of enterprise performance, they have no right to go "over the head" of the director and issue other orders to the enterprise personnel. The ministry must either persuade or order the director to take the appropriate steps. If they remain dissatisfied, they may fire the director, but they may not issue orders to the staff.

The Directors' Council was a departure from the principle of personal management. It was usually represented as "a combination of the principles of personal and collegial management,"[126] and a "further development of the Leninist principle of democratic socialism in the management of the economy."[127] It was nevertheless a breach in the personal authority long associated with the office of enterprise director. The potential for conflict is reminiscent of that which prevailed up to and during the First Five-Year Plan, when ministry, Party, and trade union vied for authority with enterprise management. It was in order to put an end to that conflict that the principle of personal management was introduced.[128] In the case of the new corporation, the basis of conflict is inherent in the kinds of decisions that have to be made by corporate management. Some of the conflicts involve the distribution of funds between the corporation and the enterprises. In those corporations in which the management of the head enterprise serves as the corporate management as well, the question has arisen of the proportion of its expenses that can be ascribed to its corporate duties and should therefore be charged to the other enterprises. If those expenses are charged against the head enterprise's own costs of production, its performance will appear to be poor and its management will suffer in reputation and bonus awards.[129] The larger the proportions of investment, depreciation, and incentive funds that are centrally allocated by the corporate management, the smaller the proportion left to enterprise management.

Any reallocation of resources within the corporation taken for the corporate benefit may upset the production schedules of some enterprises. If an R & D unit has completed a development project ahead of schedule and an enterprise is ordered to drop one line of production and start work on the innovation, that enterprise may find its own profit position impaired.

The published accounts do not give the impression that the diffusion of authority is in fact a significant source of conflict, but hints of it have appeared. In the Moscow Clothing Association corporate management "began frequently, with insufficient reason, to change the production plans of enterprises, divisions, and shops. The Directors' Council studied the question and decided that changes in plans should only be made in exceptional circumstances." The Council evidently served to protect the special interests of the member enterprises against the broader objectives of the corporate management. It is perhaps for that reason that the "management of some corporations undervalue the importance of this new democratic organ of administration." Corporate management seeks to maintain the Directors' Council in an "advisory" capacity and orders its members to carry out day-to-day tasks that should be done by the managerial staff; in many cases complex questions affecting the interests of all the member enterprises and organizations are decided under the old principle of personal management (*edinolichno*). Corporate management sometimes bypasses the Council and sets up special commissions to advise on important issues, and dallies for a long time before carrying out the Council's recommendations.[130]

As a consultative organ, the Directors' Council had a certain value. It also served as a source of pressure upon a particular director who, in pursuit of the interests of his own enterprise, may wish to pursue a policy that would be seriously injurious to the common interest. With respect to innovation, the member enterprises would not long agree to the continued support, at their own expense, of an R & D organization that produces very few results or supplies shoddy work. If the fates of all are affected by the reluctance of one enterprise to pursue a major innovation for which all have been tooled up, that enterprise can be called to account.

The other side of the coin, however, is that when the Directors' Council dominates the corporate management, the mutuality of interests may make it difficult to bring pressure to bear on the weaker members. One of the long-standing characteristics of informal Soviet managerial behavior is the web of "mutual involvement," a relationship in which the members of an organization tacitly support each other against a common threat from outside. [131] Each enterprise has some skeletons in its closet and is not disposed to cause trouble for the others. The Directors' Council gives sufficient power to the individual directors that only in extreme cases are they likely to be called to account. The corporation may therefore become a crutch for the support of its weaker members, a situation that would undermine its capacity to promote innovation. The experience of capitalist corporations may be illuminating in this respect. In technologically progressive U.S. industries like electronics, the major corporations often include semiconductor manufacturing companies as well as companies that use semiconductors in the manufacture of electric equipment and components. A study of the industry reports, however, that this "family relationship" does not give the semiconductor plants a "captive market in supplying the other companies." [132] The equipment manufacturing companies are not obliged to purchase semiconductors from within the corporation, and they frequently receive better service from outside vendors. In the Soviet corporation, however, the Directors' Council is not likely to applaud competition of this kind among its members. Hence, suppliers within the corporation will enjoy a captive market among the user enterprises. However, the noncorporate organizational structure also provides sellers with virtually captive markets, so that the corporate reform is not a step backward in this respect. The point is that in the context of Soviet economic organization, the corporate form ought not be expected to have the same innovation-promoting effect as the capitalist corporate form.

As long as the central government refrained from establishing a national policy on the status and structure of corporations, the merger movement was beset by controversies like that over the Directors' Council. The positive effect, however, was that ministries had a wide latitude of choice in deciding where corporate mergers would be most effective and what organizational structures would be most suitable in each case. The 1973 Resolution put an end both to the controversies and to the range of diversity of organizational forms.

The 1973 Resolution. There was one significant benefit of the corporate merger movement that was not intended. It was pointed out above that a considerable variety of organizational forms have been used in the formation of corporations. This is a new departure in Soviet organizational practice.[133] Ordinarily the structure of Soviet organizations is established by the government. Standard tables of organization are officially drawn up, often in the form of decrees or statutes. The tables of organization in each industry generally allow for some variations, based primarily on the size of the enterprise. But for an enterprise of a given size, the organizational structure must normally conform to that set forth in the official table. Enterprise management is thus deprived of the authority to determine for itself such matters as what departments and divisions it is to have and how large they are to be.

In capitalist enterprises, the authority to design and to change the organizational structure is an important prerogative of management. In their study of British industry, Carter and Williams noted that a major innovation often changes the kinds of demands made on the existing departments and personnel. Certain departments become more important, others less, and in some cases new ones need to be organized. Hence, the authority of management to change the organizational structure is a vital element in the success of the innovation.[134]

There is no reason to think that the Soviet enterprise is different from the capitalist in this respect. Therefore, the traditional standardization of enterprise structure may be regarded as a further obstacle to innovation. For that reason the variety of forms that the new corporations have taken has provided a degree of flexibility in organizational structure that should encourage innovation. This new authority of ministry and management over corporate organizational structure was perhaps as significant a contribution to innovation as the availability of in-house R & D facilities. The appropriateness of allowing such diversity of organizational forms, however, became itself a subject of controversy. A pluralism of organizational forms seems to clash, in some people's view with the orderliness that should characterize a planned economy. Perhaps it smacks too much of the "anarchy of the market." At any rate, more and more voices called for a statute to standardize the corporations' organizational structure.[135] Some corporate general directors have recognized the value of diversity in organizational forms and have vigorously opposed the efforts to introduce "a unified 'universal' structure for corporations. Such efforts seem to us to be not only pointless but also harmful. Every corporation is a unique production organism, reflecting its own internal characteristics and laws."[136] In the end, however, the counsels of diversity and decentralization lost out, and the voices of uniformity and centralized national policy prevailed. The

1973 Resolution resolved the disputes by withdrawing the ministries' power to decide which enterprises should be merged with what R & D organizations and which should not. The corporation was thereafter to become the basic form of industrial organization everywhere. Moreover, the diversity of organizational forms was to be reduced by the promulgation of a statute detailing the lawful organizational forms.

The Resolution directed the ministries to merge all their enterprises into corporations. Two kinds of corporations are to be established: one called a production association and the other an industrial association. Production associations "shall be made up of factories, plants, and research, design, technological, and other production units." Some production associations are to be administered directly by their ministry, in what is called a two-level system of management. The other production associations are to form part of the second type of corporation, the industrial association. An industrial association "is a single production and economic complex made up of production associations, combines, industrial enterprises, research, design, and technological organizations and other enterprises and organizations." Where industrial associations are established, a three-level system of management prevails, consisting of the ministry at the top, the industrial association in the middle, and the production association at the bottom. The ministry will thus be directly responsible for corporations of both kinds: industrial associations in the three-level system and production associations under the two-level system. The ministry is to abolish its former branch administrations. It is likely, however, that some other ministry offices will have to be established to supervise the new corporations. In the transition years 1974-1975, the corporations are to possess all the powers previously assigned to enterprises, although some may be delegated to the member enterprises. The ministry may also assign to the corporations some of the powers formerly held by the branch administrations. The resolution is vague on the distribution of authority between the industrial associations and their member production associations and enterprises. That question was to be settled by the promulgation of a new legal statute detailing the rights and obligations at all levels of the new system.

In March 1974 that statute was issued by the USSR Council of Ministers under the title "Statute on the Production Association."[137] The production association is declared to be the basic organizational unit[138] in industry, replacing the enterprise, that formerly occupied that role.

The distribution of authority between the merged units and the corporate management was decisively resolved in favor of the latter; the member enterprises and R & D organizations cease to be legal persons. The administrative structure is declared to be based on a "correct union of personal management and collegiality," but in practice the former dominates, for the corporate director is given the power to hire and fire the directors of the member units. The explosive issue of the role of the Directors' Council was resolved in the same way. The name of the body is to be changed to the Association Council, and in cases of disagreement between the Council and the general director the latter's decision prevails. There is no longer any question about who is boss. In all significant respects the position of the corporation's general director vis-à-vis the member enterprises and their directors is identical to the traditional position of enterprise director vis-à-vis the enterprise divisions and their heads.[139]

In considering the contribution of the corporations to the promotion of innovation, it should be noted that not all production associations are intended to incorporate R & D facilities, but only those "in the branches of industry that play the decisive role in the promotion of technological progress." In other branches production associations are formed primarily for their general organizational advantages, but they need not contain R & D facilities if the supply of R & D services is adequately provided by the independent R & D institutes and design bureaus of the ministry.[140] Moreover, not all the production associations that have been established are powerful and progressive organizations like Sigma, or Elektrosila. Since the corporate merger movement has now taken on the dimensions of a "campaign," a certain amount of "formalism" has been encountered. Some of the associations are quite small, consisting of only three or four enterprises; in 14 percent of the associations total employment is only about 500 persons.[141] Hence many of the production associations are not expected to make major contributions to innovation. In those large associations that do contain major R & D facilities, however, the significance of the corporation reform is that corporate management now has full control over those R & D facilities within their organizations. A substantial volume of R & D work has been transformed from out-of-house to in-house, which may be expected to mitigate some of the former organizational impediments in the supply of R & D services. One may therefore expect the rate of innovation to rise and its quality to improve. It will take a few years' experience under the new system before the extent of the improvement can be gauged. The early evidence suggests, however, that the merger movement continues to encounter certain difficulties.

The 1973 Resolution, for example, appears to have intended that virtually all industrial enterprises would be merged into corporations by the end of 1975. A mid-1975 report, however, forecasts that by the end of that year only about 25 percent of all enterprises will have been merged.[142] The moderate pace suggests that the ministries are proceeding with those corporate mergers that promise significant gains but are resisting in those cases where little benefit is expected. If that is indeed the correct interpretation, then ministry resistance is a salutary restraint on the traditional pressures for indiscriminate uniformity. On the other hand, the ministries appear to be reluctant to transfer to corporate management all the authority intended by the Resolution. "It is no secret," writes Professor A. M. Birman, "that ministries transmit to associations, which in turn transmit to their enterprises, many more directives than the reform envisages."[143] Similarly the general director of the V. I. Lenin Production and Technical Association in L'vov complains that "even such a purely internal affair of the association as the creation of an inventory of tools is planned by the ministry."[144] Moreover corporate management is not always able to exert the full measure of control over their enterprises envisaged by the reform. In mid-1974 "approximately 60 percent of the production units that are members of associations now in operation have not given up their independence. This means that many production associations are only formally listed as such but in fact remain combinations of isolated factories and plants."[145] In the Kuznetsk Basin Electric Motor Plant, General Director Yudin served both as director of the plant and director of the R & D institute. But even in that double capacity he was unable to enforce a community of interest in innovation. "The interests of the enterprise and those of the institute do not by any means coincide completely either. The researchers and designers want their developments to be introduced into production more rapidly, but the plant personnel have no objective incentive to begin producing new items." In evaluating the prospects of the reform Director Yudin's conclusion suggests appropriate caution: "It is our experience that the formal coordination of institutes and enterprises is not enough to ensure an organic merger of science and industry, and a radical acceleration in scientific and technical progress."[146]

The problem is not entirely one of effective control by corporate management. One reason for the traditional dissociation of R & D from production was the premonition that if production managers had full control over the R & D facilities the researchers would be under pressure to concentrate too heavily on short-run production problems at the expense of longer-run R & D work. Skeptics about the corporate merger movement also warned against that danger. The evidence now suggests that something of the sort is indeed happening. "Experience shows," writes Dr. Taksir, "that in practice there are cases in which some institutes that have been merged into production associations have lost their capacity to carry out significant research, since the production officials compel them to carry out various assignments associated with current production."[147] Thus the strengthening of corporate management's control over the merged units does not assure the promotion of technical advance; on the contrary, unless the concerns of writers like Dr. Taksir are addressed, the effect of the corporate reform may be to reduce the productivity of the nation's R & D facilities.

The March 1974 Statute refers only to production associations. It says nothing about the other major type of corporation—the research-based association. The function of the latter in the promotion of innovation is somewhat different from that of the production associations. Unlike the production associations, that are predominantly producing organizations, research-based associations are intended primarily to carry out R & D work on new products and processes.[148] Unlike the independent R & D institutes, however, they contain production facilities for carrying out full production runs on their innovations. Ideally, when a new product has been brought successfully through its first production runs by a research-based association, the large-scale production of the item will then be taken up by the production associations. The number of research-based associations is relatively small. In September 1974 there were about a hundred in the country, and the number is expected to rise eventually to only about 250.[149] Despite their small number, a core of well-functioning research-based corporations can exert a strong leverage on the rate of innovation. In the cryogenic engineering industry, for example, about 90 percent of all machinery and equipment produced is based on designs developed in the industry's research-based corporations.[150]

While the general purpose of the research-based corporation is clear, there is considerable controversy over the details. Some hold that they should be obliged to maintain batch production of the items they develop, and even undertake mass production, over a long period of time. Others argue that they should turn out only the first industrial batches and then go on to other development work. Within the associations the pressure to shift effort from R & D to production is supported by the fact that monetary rewards depend in large part on the volume of output. "The situation is reaching a point at which at the end of the month some associations frequently dismantle experimental models of new articles and use their assemblies and parts to fulfill the plan for the so-called basic program." The personnel of research-based associations also earn smaller incomes than those in production associations, for they are not "compensated for the losses they incur in creating models of new equipment."[151] The problem of "formalism" has also invaded the formation of research-based corporations. The association "Fire Prevention Technology" is classified as a research-based association, but it possesses no genuine research institute and was formed simply by merger of two enterprises and a design bureau. The "Spark of Lenin" Plant is the major storage battery factory of the "Source" Association, which is a research-based corporation. Of the factory's total output, however, 96.7 percent is straight production and only 1 percent consists of work performed on behalf of the association's R & D institute.[152] Moreover, many of the classic problems of ministry-enterprise relations are reappearing in the relations of ministry to research-based corporations. It is with a *déjà-vu* feeling that one reads, a decade after the Economic Reform, that the research-based association Metallurgical Equipment Research Institute (*VNIImetmash*) receives an output target for experimental equipment from the ministry that is expressed in "tons of equipment." The association's producing enterprise is therefore motivated to concentrate on the production of the heaviest and least complicated models.[153]

The problems encountered in the course of the merger movement serve as a reminder that the effectiveness of an organizational change in a system depends not only on the nature of that change but also on the other structural properties of the system like incentives, decision rules, and prices. In purely organizational terms the merger of enterprises and R & D facilities may be expected to advance the rate of innovation. But much of the benefit will be lost in the absence of corresponding changes in incentives and other structures.

Because of the accumulating accounts of the problems encountered by the research-based corporations, the clamor is growing for the promulgation of another "normative document"; that is, a national statute on the organization of research-based associations. Undoubtedly such a statute will eventually be issued, similar to the 1974 statute on the production association. Perhaps in a centrally planned economy such uniform statutes are necessary, or at least inevitable. They do, however, constrict the range of organizational forms that may be used. The compulsion for uniformity deprives responsible officials of the opportunity to exercise their imagination in designing fluid organizational forms to match the unique properties of different products, processes, and personnel. In none of the enterprise's activity is organizational flexibility as important as in innovative activity. Hence, while the merger of enterprises and R & D facilities may be expected to promote the innovativeness of Soviet industry, some of that benefit will be lost by the imposition of standardized organizational forms.

Notes

1. See Yale Brozen, "R and D Differences Among Industries," in Richard A. Tybout, ed., *Economics of Research and Development* (Columbus: Ohio State University Press, 1965), pp. 83-100. Brozen offers additional reasons in the patent and antitrust laws. He notes that there are exceptions to the practice of in-house R & D, such as the companies that sell their inventions and ideas to user firms. Individuals and small firms that cannot afford the high costs of development also often sell their ideas to larger firms.
2. *Ekonomicheskaia gazeta*, 1967, No. 10, p. 12.
3. Two organizational considerations may have been involved. First, socialists have always regarded the duplication of productive facilities (like R & D) by capitalist enterprises as a form of waste, that socialism ought to be able to avoid. Second, there may have been a premonition that enterprise managers would concentrate so heavily on current production as to neglect innovational activity. For both reasons the appropriate organizational form was a single large specialized R & D center for each industry, rather than many smaller duplicative facilities in the separate enterprises, responsible to enterprise management.
4. *Ekonomicheskaia gazeta*, 1966, No. 2, p. 31. The writer reports that a governmental review of the work of the institutes in 1963-1964 led to the dropping of 16 million rubles worth of projects under way. Alexander Korol reports that 20 percent of all scientific research personnel in the institutes are supervisory and three-quarters of all Ph.D.s in the institutes are in supervisory positions. *Soviet Research and Development: Its Organization, Personnel, and Funds* (Cambridge: The MIT Press, 1965), pp. 117-119.
5. *Ekonomicheskaia gazeta*, 1967, No. 4, p. 14, by the Chairman of the State Committee on Inventions. He concludes that either their work is of very poor quality, or they don't care enough to defend the State's interests by formal registration of their inventions. Some organizations keep submitting applications that are denied; every application for a Certificate of Invention submitted by the State Institute on Project Planning of Glass Factories has been turned down.
6. Ibid., 1966, No. 2, p. 32.
7. Ibid., 1967, No. 51, p. 24.
8. Ibid., No. 23, p. 28.

9. *Planovoe khoziaistvo*, 1967, No. 2, pp. 83-84. The author, N. Tiamshanksii, goes on to report that a third automated line is in the process of installation. His criticism is directed not only at the poor work of the R & D organization but at the purchaser for squandering funds allocated to it by the government for scientific research work. His point is that there is no control over the effectiveness with which these earmarked funds are used by the enterprise. However, he does note that the enterprises' production costs have risen because of the innovation. Since production costs do affect the indicators by which enterprises are evaluated, one wonders why the enterprise did not resist the innovation for this reason.

10. The manufacturers who innovated the new designs, however, bore the cost of the work, not the design bureaus.

11. *Ekonomicheskaia gazeta*, 1966, No. 2, p. 32.

12. E. Zaleski, J. P. Kozlowski, H. Wienert, R. W. Davies, M. J. Berry, and R. Amman, *Science Policy in the USSR* (Paris: OECD, 1969), p. 388.

13. *Ekonomicheskaia gazeta*, 1966, No. 2, p. 32.

14. Ibid., 1967, No. 9, p. 27.

15. Ibid., No. 21, p. 19. The writer notes that the incentive system requires designers to submit their work within the scheduled time limit in order to qualify for bonus. He argues that we cannot plan creative work so "closely" without the quality suffering.

16. Ibid., No. 38, p. 31. Similar data are given for the Ministry of Building Materials. The author ascribes this construction-project planning "fever" to the Ministry's desire to have as much new construction incorporated in their plan as possible. One wonders if the reason is not simply to provide work for the large number of existing construction-project planning organizations.

17. Ibid., No. 24, p. 7. In a single year, reports the author, the institutes of the USSR Academy of Sciences alone invited about 18,000 scientists to their meetings and conferences from other parts of the country. This, of course, does not include the much more extensive network of commissions and meetings of government agencies and of the ministry institutes.

18. Marvin R. Jackson, *Soviet Project and Design Organizations: Technological Decision-Making in a Command Economy*, Ph.D. dissertation, University of California, Berkeley, 1967, p. 280.

19. Zaleski et al., *Science Policy in the USSR*, p. 429.

20. *Ekonomicheskaia gazeta*, 1967, No. 32, p. 13.

21. Ibid., No. 46, p. 4.

22. In capitalist economies also most in-house R & D is carried out on the enterprise's products. Improvements in an enterprise's manufacturing processes are generally based on the R & D work of the equipment manufacturer rather than of the user. Hence one firm's process innovation is usually based on some other firm's product innovation. For this reason, an explanation of the factors determining product innovation contains much of the explanation of process innovation.

23. Ibid., No. 31, p. 3. See also Zaleski et al., *Science Policy in the USSR*, p. 449. The authors of the OECD study refer to enterprises possessing major R & D facilities as "factory centers."

24. TsSU, *Narodnoe khoziaistvo SSSR v 1965 godu* (USSR National Economy in 1965) (Moscow: *Statistika*, 1966), p. 67.

25. Zaleski et al., *Science Policy in the USSR.*, p. 410.

26. Ibid., pp. 413-414.

27. *Ekonomicheskaia gazeta*, 1966, No. 2, p. 32; 1967, No. 11, p. 11.

28. N. S. Khrushchev, *Stroitel'stvo kommunisma v SSSR* (Building Communism in the USSR) (Moscow: *Izd. Polit. Lit.*, Vol. 8, 1964), p. 457.

29. *Ekonomicheskaia gazeta*, 1967, No. 31, p. 3.

30. Ibid., 1966, No. 47, p. 16.

31. Salary scales are set by the state. Management is therefore not able to bid for an outstanding research person on the basis of their evaluation of what he may be worth to the enterprise. If management had the authority to determine salaries, the distribution of talent between the

universities and institutes on the one hand and industry on the other would surely change in favor of industry. That result is likely to be favorable for innovation.

32. *Ekonomicheskaia gazeta*, 1967, No. 48, p. 20.

33. Ibid., No. 11, p. 11.

34. Ibid., No. 37, p. 14.

35. *Planovoe khoziaistvo*, 1966, No. 10, p. 39.

36. *Ekonomicheskaia gazeta*, 1967, No. 11, p. 11.

37. John Jewkes, D. Sawers, and R. Stillerman, *The Sources of Invention*, (New York: St. Martin's Press, 1959), p. 108; Richard R. Nelson, "The Economics of Invention: A Survey of the Literature," *Journal of Business*, Vol. 23, No. 32, April 1959, pp. 111-112.

38. Jacob Schmookler, "Inventors Past and Present," *Review of Economics and Statistics*, Vol. 39, No. 39, August 1957, pp. 321-333.

39. Willard Mueller, "Major Product and Process Innovations, 1920-1950," *The Rate and Direction of Inventive Activity: Economic and Social Factors* (Princeton: National Bureau of Economic Research (NBER), 1962), p. 342. Also J. Jewkes, *Sources of Invention*, p. 185.

40. Robert Charpie, "The Business End of Technology Transfer," *Technology Transfer and Innovation* (Washington: U.S. National Science Foundation, 1966), pp. 48-51.

41. C. F. Carter and B. R. Williams, *Industry and Technical Progress*, (London: Oxford University Press, 1957), p. 122.

42. Zaleski et al., *Science Policy in the USSR*, pp. 441-444; Emily C. Brown, *Soviet Trade Unions and Labor Relations*, (Cambridge: Harvard University Press, 1966), Chap. 9.

43. *Buro Ratsionalizatsii i Izobretenni (BRIZ)*. The term *ratsionalizatsii* (literally, "rationalizations") refers to minor improvements in the manufacturing process, such as a rearrangement of the work flow or a new production jig or tooling-up device.

44. Zaleski et al., *Science Policy in the USSR*, p. 415.

45. Korol, *Soviet Research and Development*, p. 340.

46. Zaleski et al., *Science Policy in the USSR*, pp. 431-432. The measures grew out of a teaching-versus-research debate similar to that which periodically erupts in American universities. The traditional Soviet practice concentrated research in the specialized scientific and R & D institutes; the professors in the higher educational institutions engaged almost exclusively in teaching. The critics of this sharp separation between teaching and research argued that teachers quickly fall behind the state of advancing knowledge if they are not engaged in research. Therefore the graduating students are poorly prepared when they take up positions in the research institutes. The new measures have led to a reduction in teaching loads and an obligation on professors to conduct research work in the released time.

47. *Ekonomicheskaia gazeta* pp. 399-401, 458-464.

48. Robert W. Campbell, "Management Spillovers from Soviet Space and Military Programmes," *Soviet Studies*, Vol. 23, No. 4, April 1972, pp. 590-594.

49. Ibid., 1966, No. 2, p. 27.

50. Korol, *Soviet Research and Development*, pp. 179-180.

51. Ibid., p. 33.

52. L. M. Gatovskii, ed., *Plan, khozraschet, stimuly* (The Plan, Business Accounting, and Incentives) (Moscow: *Ekonomika*, 1966), p. 97.

53. The Soviet word for business accounting is *khoziaistvennyi raschet*, generally contracted to *khozraschet*.

54. Suppose the postal service had an annual operating expense budget of 10 million rubles and received 8 million rubles from the sale of postage stamps. If it operated on a budget-financing basis, the state budget would record the 8 million rubles as government receipts and the 10 million rubles as government expenditures. If it operated on a business accounting basis, however, the state budget would record only 2 million rubles as a government expenditure for a subsidy to the postal service.

55. Zaleski et al., *Science Policy in the USSR*, pp. 465-473.

56. Ibid., pp. 450-452.

57. Ibid., p. 467. This is to be expected since a larger proportion of their work consists of theoretical and pure research, which enterprises cannot be expected to finance.

58. L. K. Fatiukha and E. A. Livshits, *Ekonomicheskoe stimulirovanie osvoeniia i vnedreniia novoi tekhniki* (Economic Incentives for Innovation) (Moscow: *Ekonomica*, 1971), p. 18.

59. Zaleski et al., *Science Policy in the USSR*, pp. 469-472.

60. Some institutes, however, earn a major portion of their revenues from contract research, amounting to 70 to 75 percent in some cases. Ibid., p. 467.

61. Fatiukha and Livshits, *Ekonomicheskoe stimulirovanie*, p. 20.

62. *Ekonomicheskaia gazeta*, 1966, No. 2, p. 31. R & D people have complained that the contract system requires them to spend valuable time seeking contract funds and persuading enterprises of the value of their projects. The OECD analysts offer the perceptive comment that such complaints "unwittingly admit some of the advantages stemming from these arrangements." Zaleski et al., *Science Policy in the USSR*, p. 469.

63. Zaleski et al., *Science Policy in the USSR*, p. 468.

64. *Planovoe khoziaistvo*, 1972, No. 2, pp. 99-100.

65. *Ekonomicheskaia gazeta*, 1967, No. 46, p. 4.

66. *Planovoe khoziaistvo*, 1972, No. 2, pp. 100-101. The author describes a case where performance guarantees have been used successfully.

67. *Ekonomicheskaia gazeta*, 1967, No. 30, p. 30.

68. *Planovoe khoziaistvo*, 1972, No. 2, p. 100.

69. The Russian term is *zakaz-nariad*.

70. Fatiukha and Livshits, *Ekonomicheskoe stimulirovanie*, pp. 7-8.

71. See Brown, *Soviet Trade Unions*, pp. 256-266, for a description of socialist competition.

72. *Pravda*, January 18, 1967, pp. 2-3.

73. *Ekonomicheskaia gazeta*, 1967, No. 7, p. 11.

74. *Pravda*, January 18, 1967, pp. 2-3.

75. John L. Enos, "Invention and Innovation in the Petroleum Refining Industry," NBER, *The Rate and Direction of Inventive Activity: Economic and Social Factors*, pp. 302-304. (See Note 39.)

76. Merton J. Peck, "Inventions in the Postwar American Aluminum Industry," in NBER, *Rate and Direction of Inventive Activity*, pp. 295-296.

77. Nor is it self-evident that the benefits of competition-induced technological progress must exceed the costs. To the costs of the successful projects must be added the costs of all the unsuccessful ones that might not have been undertaken if all production secrets, both patented and not, were made public. On the other hand, the existence of secrecy does promote competitive R & D which often yields large technological advances, and which might not have been undertaken if the previously developed technology were not secret.

78. R. Nelson, "Economics of Invention," p. 117.

79. Richard R. Nelson, "Introduction," in NBER, *Rate and Direction of Inventive Activity*, pp. 9-10.

80. *Ekonomicheskaia gazeta*, 1968, No. 4, p. 18.

81. Ibid., 1967, No. 10, p. 13.

82. Ibid., 1968, No. 8, p. 19.

83. Ibid., 1967, No. 18, p. 18.

84. Ibid., 1966, No. 2, p. 32.

85. Berliner, *Factory and Manager in the USSR*, pp. 149-152.

86. *Pravda*, January 18, 1967, pp. 2-3.

87. Zaleski et al., *Science Policy in the USSR*, p. 455.

88. See Korol, *Soviet Research and Development*, p. 338; *Ekonomicheskaia gazeta*, 1966, No. 2, p. 32.

89. *Pravda*, October 23, 1968, p. 1.

90. *Pravda*, January 18, 1967, pp. 2-3. *Ekonomicheskaia gazeta*, 1966, No. 2, p. 32.

91. It is possible that more successful R & D organizations and enterprises expand more rapidly than less successful. This would be interesting to know, but data are not available. The point, however, is that the rate of growth of an organizational unit is not autonomously determined by its own personnel but by the ministry or other government agency that has jurisdiction over it.

92. The notion may be that successful organizations should be permitted to expand.

93. *Pravda*, October 23, 1968, p. 2.

94. The Russian term is *proizvodstvennoe ob'edinenie*.

95. *Voprosy ekonomiki*, 1967, No. 9, pp. 47-48.

96. V. M. Lagutkin, ed., *Proizvodstvennye ob'edineniia: problemy i perspektivy* (Production Associations: Problems and Perspectives) (Moscow: Mysl', 1971), p. 42.

97. The term 'corporation" is a very rough translation. The Soviet association is not characterized by such properties of the capitalist corporation as limited liability. What is intended by the term is to convey the sense of large-scale multiplant operations and economic power, as in the expression "corporate capitalism."

98. *Pravda*, April 3, 1973, pp. 1-2. Translated in *The Current Digest of the Soviet Press*, Vol. 25:14 (May 2, 1973), pp. 1-4.

99. For a preliminary evaluation of the corporation reform, based on the experience of the earlier "firms," see Alice C. Gorlin, "The Soviet Economic Associations," *Soviet Studies*, Vol. 26:1 (January 1974), pp. 3-27.

100. For a description of the various types that have arisen, see V. M. Lagutkin, *Proizvodstvennye ob'edineniia*, pp. 91-100 and passim. The discussion to follow leans heavily on that book.

101. *Planovoe khoziaistvo*, 1971, No. 11, pp. 12-13.

102. K. I. Taksir, *Sushchnost' i formy soedineniia nauki s proizvodstvom pri sotsializme* (Essence and Forms of Unification of Science and Production Under Socialism) (Moscow: *Vysshaia Shkola*, 1974), pp. 32-36.

103. Ibid., pp. 92-94. Innovation associations are not widely discussed in the sources and do not appear to be as important as the former two types.

104. The statement applies only to the research-based corporations. The corporate movement in general has the broader objective of reducing the quantity of enterprise planning and administration conducted by the government through its ministries.

105. Zaleski et al., *Science Policy in the USSR*, p. 449.

106. *Ekonomicheskaia gazeta*, 1967, No. 23, pp. 8-11; *Voprosy ekonomiki*, 1967, No. 9, p. 51.

107. Ten percent of all the moneys that the enterprises are entitled to deposit in their Material Incentive Funds are turned over to the corporate management for centralized distribution. Fifty percent of the Production Development Funds are similarly centralized. *Ekonomicheskaia gazeta*, 1967, No. 23, p. 8. For an explanation of these funds, see Section 6.3.

108. Lagutkin, *Proizvodstvennye ob'edineniia*, pp. 204-213.

109. Ibid., pp. 227-234.

110. For a discussion of the advantages of the corporate form, see ibid., pp. 84-85, and *Voprosy ekonomiki*, 1967, No. 9, pp. 50-51.

111. *Ekonomicheskaia gazeta*, 1967, No. 35, p. 9; Gatovskii, ed., *Plan*, p. 106.

112. For examples, see Lagutkin, *Proizvodstvennye ob'edineniia*, pp. 121-122; *Planovoe khoziaistvo*, 1967, No. 12, pp. 81-82; *Voprosy ekonomiki*, 1968, No. 4, pp. 82-83.

113. Zaleski et al., *Science Policy in the USSR*, pp. 432-433.

114. *Planovoe khoziaistvo*, 1972, No. 6, p. 153.

115. Lagutkin, *Proizvodstvennye ob'edineniia*, p. 109.

116. Ibid., pp. 42-45. The source is somewhat confusing and these data may not be correct. The 1969 total of 510 is described as referring to "production associations (firms)." It is therefore

not clear whether that number refers only to the pre-1965 firm-type of association, or whether it includes the post-1965 corporations.

117. Taksir, *Sushchnost' i formy*, p. 63.
118. *Pravda*, July 26, 1975. Translated in *The Current Digest of the Soviet Press*, Vol. 27:29 (August 13, 1975), p. 1.
119. *Voprosy ekonomiki*, 1968, No. 4, p. 84.
120. Ibid.
121. *Ekonomicheskaia gazeta*, 1968, No. 7, p. 10. In some cases the firms were dismantled for good reasons. The firms had been organized for the administrative convenience of the territorial Regional Economic Councils, and the mergers sometimes represented more the effect of geographical propinquity than that of economic affinity. The consequence was a tendency toward excessive diversification. Those firms were properly dismantled in the post reform move for a more rational pattern of specialization. See *Voprosy ekonomiki*, 1968, No. 4, pp. 84-85.
122. *Voprosy ekonomiki*, 1967, No. 9, p. 51.
123. *Ekonomicheskaia gazeta*, 1968, No. 10, p. 11.
124. Ibid., 1967, No. 23, p. 9.
125. The Soviet corporate Directors' Council should not be confused with the Workers' Council of the Yugoslav "self-managed" enterprise. There is no talk of seating workers' representatives on the Directors' Council.
126. *Ekonomicheskaia gazeta*, 1967, No. 23, p. 8.
127. Ibid., 1967, No. 23, p. 9.
128. Gregory Bienstock, S. M. Schwartz, and A. Yugow, *Management in Russian Industry and Agriculture* (New York: Oxford University Press, 1944), pp. 8-16.
129. Lagutkin, *Proizvodstvennye ob'edineniia*, p. 241.
130. Ibid., pp. 206-210.
131. Berliner, *Factory and Manager in the USSR*, pp. 243-247.
132. A. D. Little, *Patterns and Problems of Technical Innovation in American Industry*, Report to the National Science Foundation, U.S. Department of Commerce (PB 181573), (Washington, D.C.: September 1963), p. 146.
133. The "firms" were also given considerable freedom in deciding upon their own organizational structure. Robert Campbell ("Management Spillovers," p. 602) has noted that the diffusion of reliability methods has also been left to the informal activities of volunteer groups, "though that is hard to understand when [the Soviets] are usually such zealots for formal organization." Perhaps there was a trend toward increased decentralization of organizational forms at that time.
134. Carter and Williams, *Industry and Technical Progress*, p. 65.
135. Lagutkin, *Proizvodstvennye ob'edineniia*, p. 90; *Planovoe khoziaistvo*, 1972, No. 6, p. 152.
136. *Ekonomicheskaia gazeta*, 1968, No. 7, p. 10.
137. Published as a supplement to *Ekonomicheskaia gazeta*, 1974, No. 18.
138. *osnovnym (pervichnym) zvenom promyshlennosti*.
139. Exceptions may be made in specified cases. For example, member enterprises situated some distance from the corporation's home office may maintain their own bank accounts.
140. Taksir, *Sushchnost' i formy*, p. 69.
141. *Pravda*, May 23, 1975, p. 1. Translated in *The Current Digest of the Soviet Press*, Vol. 27:21 (June 18, 1975), p. 20. Also Taksir, *Sushchnost' i formy*, p. 89.
142. See note 118 above.
143. *The Current Digest of the Soviet Press*, Vol. 27:29 (August 13, 1975), p. 4.
144. *Pravda*, December 23, 1974, p. 2. Translated in *The Current Digest of the Soviet Press*, Vol. 26:51 (January 15, 1975), p. 19.
145. *Pravda*, May 31, 1974, p. 3. Translated in *The Current Digest of the Soviet Press*, Vol. 26:22 (June 26, 1974), p. 4.

146. *Pravda*, January 5, 1975. Translated in *The Current Digest of the Soviet Press*, Vol. 27:1 (January 29, 1975), p. 21.

147. Taksir, *Sushchnost' i formy*, p. 79.

148. Research-based corporations are also expected to concentrate on R & D work that is "new in principle"; that is, genuine inventions and other work on the leading edge of applied science. Ibid., p. 106.

149. *Pravda*, September 18, 1974. Translated in *The Current Digest of the Soviet Press*, Vol. 26:38 (October 16, 1974), p. 6.

150. Taksir, *Sushchnost' i formy*, p. 126.

151. *Pravda*, September 18, 1974. Translated in *The Current Digest of the Soviet Press*, Vol. 26:38 (October 16, 1974), p. 6.

152. Taksir, *Sushchnost' i formy*, pp. 113-115.

153. Ibid., p. 140.

Chapter 5

The Supply of Inputs: Labor Services

In capitalist countries, the labor market affects the innovation process in two ways. Reduction of labor costs is one of the incentives for innovation, and labor resistance to displacement by technological progress is one of the obstacles to labor-saving innovation. The relationship of labor to technological change is a major subject of discussion and research.

The Soviet literature has in the past dealt almost exclusively with the positive effects of technological progress on labor. Technological progress was regarded as a major source of rising labor productivity and therefore as the basis of the future growth of real wages. Since the closing down of the employment agencies following the official declaration in 1930 that unemployment had been totally liquidated,[1] the subject of unemployment was rarely discussed. Similarly, little attention has been given to the possibility that labor-saving innovation may be discouraged by a concern over technological unemployment.

All this has changed in recent years with the increased attention to the subject of technological progress. And with the wider public discussion, we now have a somewhat better understanding of the relationship between the organization of the labor supply and the rate of innovation.

5.1. Organization of the Labor Supply

One may imagine an organizational structure in which labor services are allocated in the same centrally planned fashion as goods and other services. In such a system workers would register for employment with a labor-planning agency, and that agency would then assign individual workers to enterprises on the basis of the labor requirements implicit in the enterprise plan.

For a variety of reasons the Soviets have adopted a different organizational structure in the case of labor. Unlike materials, equipment, and other productive services, labor services are allocated by a decentralized, marketlike process. Wage levels are differentiated in order to attract workers into these regions, industries, occupations, and grades where the demand for them has been generated by the national economic plan. But no central agency directs specific workers to specific enterprises. Workers are expected to find their own employment, and enterprises to recruit their own workers on the basis of the labor requirements implicit in their production plans. A variety of recruitment techniques is used. Some enterprises hold "open door days" for graduating students. Notices of openings are posted on factory gates and on bulletin boards in town, and radio and newspaper advertisements are used to provide information on jobs available.[2]

The central planning apparatus does influence the structure of the labor force seeking employment in many ways. Forecasts of the demand for labor, based on the long-term national planning goals, are used in the planning of the education system. A planned expansion of the chemicals industry, for example, is accompanied by an increase in the number of students accepted in the chemical engineering programs of the technical schools and higher education establishments. Hence when the future new chemicals plants begin operation, they will find trained young people seeking jobs in their enterprises. Government agencies also arrange certain massive flows of labor, such as the flow of labor from the farms to the cities, and the recruitment of labor for the development of new industries in the East, and for the Virgin Lands of Kazakhstan. The setting of wage and salary scales is also a function performed by the government. These centralized activities, however, serve primarily the purpose of influencing the supply of labor so that labor will be available in those regions and occupations that correspond to the demand implicit in the national production plans. Normally the task of recruiting workers is assigned to the enterprises.

This organizational structure for the allocation of labor services was designed not with the innovation decision in mind but for the general purpose of managing the productive activities of enterprises. It may be expected nevertheless to have certain consequences for the innovation decision.

5.2. Innovation and the Supply of Labor

Before the 1965 Economic Reform, the organization of the labor supply posed a problem for the innovating enterprise similar to that presented in the supply of materials. The enterprise plan contained a section in which the planned labor supply was specified in rather great detail. Once the plan was approved, the enterprise was bound to employ no more workers in each occupation and skill level than was specified in the plan. Management was not free, therefore, subsequently to substitute a few skilled high-wage workers for a larger number of less-skilled, low-wage workers, or to change the planned distribution of workers by occupation.

Since management does participate in the making of the plan, they do have some opportunity to obtain a planned distribution of labor consistent with their needs. Their influence is limited, however, by the ministry's notion of what a proper distribution should be. If an enterprise should propose a distribution of labor radically different from that of other enterprises in the same industry, it would encounter some difficulty getting that plan approved. But more significant for innovation is the fact that the labor plan, like the material supply plan, is drawn up in the middle of one year, and governs the enterprise's labor supply up to the end of the next year. The utilization of labor in December 1970 is based upon an estimate made in June 1969. Even in the absence of technological change, forecasts over this length of time are likely often to prove wrong. But in an innovating enterprise, the forecast is more likely than not to be wrong. If the enterprise has undertaken to install a complex new process with which it is entirely unfamiliar, and which will require several years before the "bugs" are removed, it can rarely be sure what the final required composition of labor for that process will turn out to be. The labor plan therefore placed a greater burden on the innovating enterprise than on the non-innovating because of the uncertainty involved in the innovation process.

One of the provisions of the 1965 Economic Reform is the reduction in the number of obligatory targets and quotas contained on the enterprise plan. With respect to labor, all the old quotas have been eliminated except one—the total amount of wages that may be paid out. Gone are the old restrictions on the total number of workers and on their distribution by category. The plan still contains forecasts of the number of workers and their distribution by specialty and skill, but these are merely estimates and are no longer binding. If the occasion should require it, management is free to hire workers of any specialty and skill as long as the total planned wage bill is not exceeded.

In practice there appear to be some limits to the quantity of labor that management is free to hire. In regions experiencing a labor shortage, enterprise requests for additional labor are sometimes scrutinized carefully by the recently reestablished local employment agencies and are often turned down.[3] Despite such informal restrictions, the abolition of the official labor targets in the enterprise plan has removed what had been a nuisance to all managers but a particularly troublesome one to innovators. It increases the innovator's power to respond to unanticipated needs and thus to reduce the risks due to the uncertainty associated with innovation. It may be expected, to that extent, to reduce managerial resistance to innovation.

The reform removed one constraint on management's authority to adjust its labor force in response to technological change. However, the hiring and deployment of labor is not the only kind of authority needed for the successful management of the labor supply in an innovating enterprise. Perhaps more important is the authority to dismiss the labor that may be made redundant by innovation. The dismissal of labor has become a central issue in the effort to accelerate the rate of innovation.

5.3. Technological Unemployment

The potential return to a labor-saving innovation consists of the net savings on the wages of the displaced labor. In some cases a portion of the displaced labor may be profitably transferred to other employment within the same plant, particularly in enterprises whose output is expanding. In general, however, in order to secure the full potential return to a labor-saving innovation, some portion of the displaced labor may have to be dismissed. Managerial reluctance to dismiss displaced labor is cited in the literature as a major factor in the failure of the society to achieve the full potential returns from innovation.

"Research studies show," writes the eminent labor economist E. Manevich, "that the displaced workers very rarely transfer to new jobs in other enterprises." The evidence cited consists of studies of the experience of individual enterprises. In the First Moscow Watch Plant, for example, 48 percent of the workers displaced by technological change were reassigned to jobs within the same shop, and 20 percent were reassigned to jobs in other shops and departments of the same plant. Similar data are available for other enterprises. In many cases, over a period of years enterprises have introduced a series of technological improvements and labor-saving innovations, but employment not only fails to decline but actually increases from year to year.[4]

Upon reflection, the evidence of the kind presented by Manevich and others does not conclusively demonstrate that management is reluctant to dismiss displaced workers. The reassignment of displaced workers to new jobs within the plant may reflect sober economic calculation. Normal attrition due to retirement, illness, and so forth does provide a continual flow of new job openings within innovating enterprises. The expansion of output also provides new openings in many enterprises. It may well be less costly for the enterprise to retrain its own experienced displaced labor for these new jobs than to recruit and train new workers. For this reason alone one would expect a certain volume of displaced labor to be retained within their enterprises.

Furthermore, it is clear that an appreciable volume of labor is in fact dismissed as a result of technological change. In the aforementioned watch plant, 32 percent of the displaced labor was dismissed. In the Gomel Agricultural Machinery Plant, during the period 1958-1964, 41 percent of the lathe operators displaced by technological improvements were dismissed, 35 percent of the assembly shop workers, and about half of the workers in auxiliary operations such as repair and materials handling.[5]

Hence the published data are not inconsistent with the possibility that there may be no reluctance at all to dismiss workers but that a substantial volume of reassignment occurs on strictly economic grounds. To establish the fact one would need to have access to the accounts of enterprises and to form an independent judgment about whether the volume of reassignment exceeds that which would be expected on economic grounds alone. For lack of such data one is obliged to rely upon the uniform judgment of Soviet analysts that enterprises do indeed dismiss many fewer workers than is economically justifiable.

Analysis of the problem shows that the dismissal of workers has not occurred on a scale corresponding to the present stage of the industrial-technical revolution and to the development of social production. The explanation is to be found in a series of objective and subjective causes and deficiencies, many of which can be eliminated in the process of carrying out the economic reform.[6]

Two groups of reasons are most often cited that have their origin in organizational structure. One consists of the legal and moral obstacles against the dismissal of workers in a workers' state. The other is the practice of labor hoarding by enterprises.

5.4. Legal and Moral Obstacles to Dismissal of Labor

The ethic of socialism may be understood to require that no worker should ever be dismissed as a result of technological progress. But few would hold to so pure an interpretation, the implementation of which would obviously be very costly to the society. The more reasonable interpretation is that no individual worker should suffer as a result of technological progress. That interpretation would oblige the society to incur whatever cost may be required to minimize the psychic and financial losses to workers displaced by technological progress. Soviet labor policy has been closer to the latter interpretation than to the former. But in the implementation of that policy the organizational devices actually employed seem to have been derived from the former interpretation, for those devices consist of a set of strong limitations on the authority of enterprises to dismiss workers.

One may imagine three extreme organizational approaches to the problem of the reemployment of workers displaced by labor-saving innovation. One approach would place the burden entirely upon the released workers. A second would place it entirely upon the society. A third would place it upon the enterprise. In practice, the burden is likely to be shared in varying degree by all three. The rate of innovation, however, is likely to be most sensitive to the magnitude of the burden placed on the enterprise. If, in the extreme, the system of labor allocation were so organized that the dismissal of a worker were costless to the enterprise, both financially and morally, the rate of innovation would be relatively high. If, on the other hand, the cost to the enterprise of dismissing a displaced worker were very high—amounting, in the limit, to a categorical prohibition against dismissal—the rate of labor-saving innovation would be correspondingly lower.

Legal Restraints

Management's right to dismiss workers under certain circumstances was written into the Labor Code of 1922. Among those circumstances is "complete or partial liquidation of an enterprise, or a cutback in production." Although the clause does not refer to labor-saving innovation as such, it is the legal basis on which labor displaced by technological change may be dismissed.[7] But the enterprise that sets about aggressively to pare down its labor force in response to technical change faces a number of obstacles.

There is, first, the widely held feeling that it is simply not right for a worker to be deprived of his job in a socialist society. The moral repugnance against technological unemployment may indeed have grown in recent years with the increased public discussion of the social implications of technological progress. It had long been held, and probably widely believed, that in a socialist society the machine can pose none of that threat to labor that constitutes one of the most damning "contradictions" of capitalism. It may well be the case that "workers do not in general resist technological change," as a noted Western scholar has concluded.[8] But while the assertion may be valid "in general," recent sociological research in the USSR calls attention to a considerable uneasiness. "You will hardly find a worker or a foreman who is indifferent about, say, a new semiautomated production line in his shop," writes a Soviet political economist. "He is somewhat fearful about whether he will be able to master the new machine, and he reacts at first with extreme wariness and uncertainty."[9] Labor-saving innovation must lead, moreover, to some displacement of labor, and even if no period of unemployment is involved the transfer of labor cannot be accomplished without personal stress: "having to leave the workgroup to which he has become accustomed, a change in occupation and the obsolescence of his acquired skills and experience, a change in his normal tenor of life associated with having to leave his home for another region or republic."[10]

This growing public acknowledgment that even socialist machines create personal hardships for displaced workers must give support to the moral pressures against the dismissal of labor. There is a "moral principle that people need to have work, not only for the money involved," a Soviet labor economist told Emily Clark Brown, [and so] "it is not easy to fire people."[11] Even an enterprise that makes a determined effort to retrain and reassign some displaced workers may be chastized for having dismissed the others. The Gomel Agricultural Machinery Plant, for example, operated a school of its own that trained over 700 workers a year. Nevertheless, writes a labor economist, they dismissed 41 percent of the lathe operators who had been displaced in the machine shop, and 35 percent of the operators in an assembly shop. The implication is that management must have exerted something less than its maximum effort in retraining displaced workers.[12]

There is, second, a set of laws enacted for the protection of labor. One such law is a 1928 statute that places upon enterprise management the responsibility to arrange for the reemployment, or "labor placement" (*trudoustroistvo*) of all workers dismissed as a result of a reduction in staff. Management is obliged to try to arrange for reassignment to new jobs within the same shop or department if possible, and if not there, then elsewhere within the enterprise. "The absence of a job within the enterprise or institution to which the displaced workers can be reassigned," states a 1967 commentary on that statute, "does not release management from the obligation of taking measures to provide new employment in other enterprises and institutions in the same area."[13] Management's obligation in this respect is policed not only by the local trade union but also by other public bodies. The State Bank, for example, is obliged to assure that suitable alternative employment has been found for displaced workers before they grant a loan for an innovation involving automation.[14] Hence the decision to dismiss a group of displaced workers obliges management to undertake a series of new costs and negotiations in order to discharge its responsibilities under the law.

The dismissal of workers has always been regarded as a serious matter, and management has been obliged to consult the trade union over its dismissal orders. A 1958 law that greatly strengthened the power of the trade union in general, however, provided that management could not dismiss a worker without the agreement of the trade union.[15] The change from "consultation" to "agreement" shifted a great deal of power from management to the trade union. Management must satisfy the factory trade-union committee that there are valid reasons for a proposed reduction of staff of a given size, and that in designating the workers to be dismissed such priorities as seniority have been respected. The committee must also be satisfied that management has made every reasonable effort to find new jobs within the factory.[16] In the opinion of a Western student of the subject, "Thus control over dismissals lay entirely in union hands."[17] Dismissal of workers therefore raises the prospect of unpleasant encounters with the trade union. In extreme cases, a worker's claim that he had been dismissed illegally may involve management in criminal litigation, and Western scholars hold the view "that the Soviet courts in general guard zealously the rights of workers in the labor cases that come before them."[18] Shortly after the 1965 Economic Reform, for example, the Moscow Public Prosecutor criticized managers who took advantage of their new powers in order to dismiss workers illegally. He reminded them that under the Criminal Code such offenses are punishable by dismissal or up to a year's corrective labor.[19]

There is no doubt that management chafes under the legal restrictions against dismissal. Even in cases involving such matters as drunkenness and incompetence, workers are not easily fired. "I think," writes a chief engineer, "that it would be desirable to expand the authority of directors and trade unions in the matter of firing inveterate spoilage producers. We are in favor of special rewards to workers, engineers and foremen who produce high-quality output. But we cannot agree with the labor code that makes it impossible to fire a negligent worker even for repeated spoilage."[20] If it is so difficult to fire workers under such conditions, it must clearly be even more difficult in the case of faithful and competent workers made redundant through no fault of their own but as a result of technological progress.

Labor Market Conditions

It may appear that the absence of general unemployment would serve to reduce managerial and trade-union concern over the fate of dismissed workers. To some extent it probably does; certainly in comparison to market economies that experience periodic mass unemployment. There are nevertheless various conditions in the labor market that reinforce the moral pressure against the dismissal of labor, despite the general level of full employment.

First, while the general level of unemployment is low, there have been growing problems of pockets of unemployment in various industries, regions, and categories of labor. The problem appears to be particularly serious in smaller cities and towns. Among the reasons is the reported concentration of capital investment in the larger cities, which limits the local reemployment possibilities in the smaller cities. In 1959-1965, 60 to 90 percent of all capital investments went to the republic and regional capital cities, which rarely accounted for more than 30 percent of the total urban population of their respective territories. Hence an innovating enterprise in a smaller city faces the prospect of requiring its dismissed workers to leave their homes in order to find new employment. A further factor, in the opinion of that analyst, was the "economically unjustified" curtailment of small-scale industry—producer cooperatives, local industry, and private small enterprise—which might have helped absorb labor displaced by larger-scale technologically progressive industry. Finally, technological progress often leads to changes in the sex distribution of employment. The introduction of semiautomated equipment is usually accompanied by an increase in female employment. But in the changeover to fully automated equipment, female workers are often replaced by male. Hence the sex distribution of workers dismissed because of technological change does not always correspond to the sex distribution of the local demand for labor.[21]

The second problem is that, precisely because of the absence of general unemployment, the state has devoted little effort and few resources in providing the kinds of public assistance normally available to the unemployed. In particular, there is no program of general unemployment compensation, and very little organized effort to help displaced workers find new jobs.

The dismissed worker is entitled either to two weeks notice or to a severance payment of up to two weeks' wages.[22] A number of economists have urged a general program of unemployment compensation for displaced workers, but no move in that direction appears to be contemplated.[23] Stipends are awarded to workers fortunate enough to be enrolled in manpower retraining programs, but until recently there was no large-scale general retraining program. The few programs that have existed were established for specific groups of workers, generally as ad hoc solutions to particular problems. To promote the conversion of railroads from steam to electric power a program was introduced to retrain displaced steam locomotive engineers to qualify as electric locomotive engineers. During the year of retraining the workers receive a wage of roughly half that of an employed steam locomotive engineer.[24] Another special program for the retraining of managerial personnel dismissed as a result of management reorganization provides for the continuation of their salaries for a period not to exceed three months.[25] Many enterprises have also established training programs suited to their specific labor needs. Only by qualifying for one of these programs can the dismissed worker receive an income in a period between jobs.

The national network of labor exchanges was abolished in the 1930s, following the high level of demand for labor ushered in by the First Five-Year Plan. Thereafter the unemployed worker found little organized assistance in securing a new job. In case of dismissal because of technological displacement, he received the assistance of the personnel department of his former employer. Also some local governments established labor exchanges, but by the mid-sixties fewer than 30 percent of dismissed workers found new jobs with the assistance of employment offices.[26]

Since 1967, however, the problem has been relieved by a renewed effort to plan and organize the process of labor recruitment. By decree of the government a set of State Committees on Labor Utilization was organized, one in each republic. The functions of the new state committees include the development of programs for labor retraining, for the relocation of dismissed workers in other enterprises, for organizing the migration of workers to regions experiencing labor shortages, and for providing a better information flow on available jobs.[27] The establishment of these new organizations should make it easier for enterprises to carry out their obligation of finding new employment for their own dismissed workers. Dr. Manevich has proposed that, because of their presence, "there is an increasing necessity to free enterprise management entirely of the responsibility of arranging for the reemployment of dismissed workers," and turn it over to the state committees.[28] Management would certainly welcome such a change, but trade-union opposition is likely to be great. The programs of the new state committees reduce the effort management must make to arrange for reemployment, but management continues to bear the primary responsibility.

5.5. Hoarding of Labor

The legal and moral considerations restrain management from dismissing displaced labor even if it were otherwise to their advantage to dismiss them. Even in the absence of those restraints, however, there is a further consideration that motivates management to refrain from dismissing displaced labor wholesale. The organization of the labor supply fosters conditions that induce the prudent manager to hoard surplus labor.

The hoarding of labor is a practice of very long standing in the Soviet economy.[29] Enterprise management, having in view the difficulties and uncertainties associated with the recruitment of labor, prefers to have a supply of workers in reserve in the event a need for them should arise. Such needs may arise, for example, when the ministry issues new production assignments to the enterprise that had not been provided for in the plan. In such cases the management that had prudently retained a "safety factor" in its labor force is in a better position than one that had reduced its labor force. The hoarded labor is utilized in a variety of ways: in construction work within the factory; in providing the labor force for new production facilities in an expanding enterprise; for peak-load labor requirements during the end-of-month rush known as "storming";[30] for supplying labor to nearby farms during peak-load harvest requirements; and for building housing for enterprise personnel.[31]

The retention of surplus labor may also account for what is sometimes regarded as excessive enterprise expenditures on the retraining of workers. Over 22 percent of all Soviet workers are trained in a new occupation or in higher skill levels within their own enterprises each year. Some workers, "with no particular productive purpose, turn up several times in different enterprises in training programs. The rate of in-plant retraining is considerably greater than that of most industrial countries, and in the opinion of some Soviet specialists, could be considerably reduced without any perceptible loss.[32]

The practice of hoarding labor cannot be ascribed solely to organization structure. Part of the explanation is to be found in such other system properties as the structure of incentives and decision rules. The most proximate cause is not a matter of economic structure at all but of economic policy, chiefly the policy of "taut planning" that generates the condition of "over-full employment."[33] Since the organizational structure of the labor supply enables workers to change jobs relatively easily, excessive labor mobility continues to be a source of concern.[34] Enterprise management confronts the twin problem of a steady loss of workers leaving for better jobs and the absence of a substantial pool of unemployed on which they can draw to fill both recurrent and unanticipated needs. In the absence of strong incentives to economize on labor, the hoarding of labor is the prudent policy.

One of the aims of the Economic Reform was to discourage the hoarding of labor by the aforementioned elimination of labor force quotas in the enterprise plan. The rationale was that the employment quota limited management's ability to cope with unanticipated events that might on occasion require a larger labor force than the quota provided for. They therefore sought as high a quota as they could negotiate, and deliberately sought to maintain employment at that level in order that the quota not be reduced. Elimination of the quota, it was thought, would assure management that they could always hire the additional labor they may require in unforeseen circumstances and would therefore eliminate the advantage of labor hoarding. However, the reform seems not to have had the intended effect. A correspondent of the labor newspaper *Trud* describes the present state of affairs as follows:

Consider the typical enterprise, with all its cares and troubles and daily problems. Today perhaps twenty workers are absent because of colds. Tomorrow a brigade has to be sent off to help out on a collective farm Some supplier had been late in his deliveries and they have to make up for lost time. . . . Naturally it is easier to maneuver if one has surplus labor. Every manager knows that in the next six months someone will retire, someone will have to go to school, someone will find another job. So why worry? Simply hire additional labor in advance. And if it should suddenly turn out that it was a bit overdone, that they had overshot their plan, they can always justify it by claiming an "overplan increase in production"; they "shed a few tears" in the ministry, and they will be helped out the first time.[35]

Perhaps the abolition of the labor quota has reduced the extent of labor hoarding—no aggregate data are available from which one may judge. But it is clear that the practice has not been eliminated and continues to be a source of concern. Many reasons may be advanced. For one thing, it was not the labor quota alone but the condition of a general labor shortage that motivated labor hoarding, and that condition has not changed. Second, it appears from the quoted article that despite the official abolition of the labor quota, the enterprise still has to account to the ministry for its employment policies. As in the case of other aspects of the Economic Reform, authority relations that were to have been transformed by formal organizational changes have managed to persist on an informal level.

The practice of hoarding reduces the benefits to the economy from labor-saving innovation because the released labor is not made available for reallocation to more productive uses. Paradoxically, however, the value to the enterprise of a labor reserve may be a stimulus to innovation. The noninnovating enterprise is obliged to maintain its labor reserve by recruitment on the labor market, generally replacing its annual labor attrition and turnover with young and inexperienced workers. Labor-saving innovation, however, provides the enterprise with a constant flow of released labor from its own workshops. The best and most reliable of them can be retained as a reserve, and the poorer and less reliable workers can be dismissed. Moreover since the deliberate maintenance of surplus labor may cause the enterprise to fall afoul of government and party inspectors, the enterprise must be prudent in the ways in which it secures that surplus. The noninnovating enterprise must continually recruit new workers on the labor market, thus opening itself up to the scrutiny of the new labor exchange inspectors and inquisitive correspondents like the one quoted in Note 35. The retention of labor displaced by technological innovation, however, enables the enterprise to maintain its labor reserve without having to recruit openly, and hence with less risk of exposure. Consequently, the practice of labor hoarding may encourage labor-saving innovation, even though it does not encourage the release of displaced labor for more productive employment.

5.6. Conclusion

A substantial proportion of workers displaced by technological innovation is retained by their own enterprises. Some portion of the displaced labor is retained for sound economic reasons, but most Soviet analysts agree that the proportion retained is excessive. Among the reasons is management's reluctance to dismiss workers in the face of the legal and moral pressures against taking such action in a workers' state.

Such pressures do indeed exist. It is doubtful, however, that they are a serious obstacle to innovation. For one thing, they do not enter at all into product-innovation decisions, which involve no displacement of labor. Second, a certain proportion of process-innovation is capital saving and involves little or no displacement of labor. It is only with respect to labor-saving processes that inhibitions against dismissal of labor may deter innovation. Even in those cases, the inhibitions apply to the act of dismissal and not to the displacement of labor. If the displaced labor is reassigned to employment within the enterprise, there would be little opposition to the introduction of the innovation. To be sure, if the displaced workers must be kept on the enterprise payroll, the prospective profit from the innovation is reduced or may be negative, a result that would tend to discourage innovation. Most Soviet analysts do not focus on this aspect of the problem, however. The thrust of the criticism is not that the legal and moral pressures retard the rate of innovation as such. It is rather that management's reluctance to dismiss displaced labor reduces the social benefit from labor-saving innovation.

On this issue as well one may question whether legal and moral pressures are the major element in the explanation of the low rate of dismissal of displaced workers. The fact that substantial numbers of workers are indeed dismissed suggests that legal and moral pressures are no obstacle when it is to management's interest to dismiss them. Nor are labor market conditions such that management need be greatly concerned about the fates of dismissed workers. Dismissed workers do face a period of unemployment between jobs, but the evidence indicates that it is normally quite brief. A survey of new employees in 4 factories in Gorky reported that 15 percent had been unemployed for 1 or 2 days, 33 percent for 3 to 9 days, 15 percent for 10 to 19 days, 16 percent for 20 to 29 days, and 12 percent for more than a month. A survey in Sverdlovsk found that workers who had quit jobs voluntarily found new jobs on an average of 23 days. Workers dismissed by a Moscow transport enterprise spent an average of over a month seeking new jobs.[36] These data refer to the mid-sixties. With the subsequent reestablishment of the labor exchanges, the average unemployment period has very likely been further reduced. The agency in the city of Kaluga claims, for example, that it has succeeded in reducing the average period between jobs from 24 to 13 days.[37] Under such conditions the absence of unemployment compensation does not cause excessive hardship on most displaced workers.

Hence the organization of the supply of labor services poses no significant problems for the innovating enterprise; certainly nothing on the order of the problems in the supply of materials and of R & D services. The society does lose some of the gains of technological progress because enterprises find it to their advantage to hoard surplus labor. The cause, however, is to be found not primarily in the labor protective laws or in moral pressures, nor in the organization of the labor supply, nor in any defects in the innovation process as such. It is to be found rather in those properties of economic structure and policy that have long motivated management to hoard labor.

One of those other properties is the incentive structure. It will later be shown that the incentive structure, unlike the organizational structure discussed here, has a considerable influence on the rate of dismissal of displaced workers. New incentive structures, like that in the famous Shchekino experiment, are likely to have a greater effect than new organizational structures.[38]

Notes

1. Robert Conquest, ed., *Industrial Workers in the USSR* (New York: Praeger, 1967), pp. 21-22.
2. Emily Clark Brown, *Soviet Trade Unions and Labor Relations* (Cambridge: Harvard University Press, 1966), p. 27.
3. *Trud*, January 29, 1972, p. 2.
4. *Voprosy ekonomiki*, 1969, No. 10, pp. 34-35.
5. Ibid., 1966, No. 8, p. 35.
6. Ibid., 1969, No. 10, p. 35.
7. Mary McAuley, *Labor Disputes in Soviet Russia 1957-1965* (London: Oxford University Press, 1969), pp. 211, 218-224.
8. Brown, *Soviet Trade Unions*, p. 269.
9. *Ekonomicheskaia gazeta*, 1967, No. 46, p. 30.
10. *Voprosy ekonomiki*, 1969, No. 10, p. 38.
11. Brown, *Soviet Trade Unions*, p. 15.
12. *Voprosy ekonomiki*, 1966, No. 8, p. 35.
13. Ibid., 1969, No. 10, p. 36.
14. G. D. Anisimov and I. A. Vakhlamov, eds., *Material'noe stimulirovanie vnedreniia novoi tekhniki: spravochnik* (Handbook of Material Incentives for Innovation) (Moscow: *Ekonomika*, 1966), p. 84.
15. McAuley, *Labor Disputes in Soviet Russia*, p. 85.

16. Brown, *Soviet Trade Unions*, p. 199.

17. Ibid., p. 121.

18. Harold J. Berman, *Justice in Russia* (Cambridge, Mass.: Harvard University Press, 1950), p. 265.

19. Conquest, *Industrial Workers in the USSR*, p. 37.

20. *Ekonomicheskaia gazeta*, 1967, No. 33, p. 13.

21. *Voprosy ekonomiki*, 1966, No. 8, pp. 35-36.

22. Conquest, *Industrial Workers in the USSR*, pp. 34-35.

23. *Voprosy ekonomiki*, 1969, No. 10, p. 38; 1971, No. 2, p. 46.

24. *Ekonomicheskaia gazeta*, 1966, No. 2, p. 29.

25. *Voprosy ekonomiki*, 1971, No. 2, pp. 46-47.

26. Ibid., 1966, No. 8, pp. 36-37.

27. U.S. Congress, Joint Economic Committee, *Soviet Economic Performance: 1966-1967* (Washington: Government Printing Office, 1968), p. 64.

28. *Voprosy ekonomiki*, 1969, No. 10, p. 36.

29. Joseph S. Berliner, *Factory and Manager in the USSR* (Cambridge: Harvard University Press, 1957), pp. 178-181.

30. Joseph S. Berliner, "A Problem in Soviet Business Administration," *Administrative Science Quarterly*, Vol. 1, No. 1, June 1956, pp. 86-101.

31. *Voprosy ekonomiki*, 1969, No. 10, p. 35.

32. Ibid., 1971, No. 2, pp. 47-48.

33. Holland Hunter, "Optimal Tautness in Developmental Planning," *Economic Development and Cultural Change*, Vol. 9, No. 4, Part I, July 1961, pp. 561-572.

34. *Voprosy ekonomiki*, 1971, No. 2, pp. 47-48.

35. *Trud*, January 29, 1972, p. 2.

36. Conquest, *Industrial Workers in the USSR*, p. 36. These figures tell only part of the tale, however, for they report only the experience of workers who had succeeded in finding new jobs. A survey of workers still unemployed is likely to reveal longer periods of unemployment because it would include more workers with poorer employment prospects because of age, education level, skill, and so forth.

37. *Trud*, February 2, 1972, p. 2.

38. In 1967 the Shchekino Chemical Combine was authorized to experiment with a new incentive system in which the wages saved by the dismissal of redundant workers are distributed among the remaining employed workers. The Shchekino system has encountered considerable resistance, and in 1972 it had been used in only 300 enterprises. Murray Feshbach and Stephen Rapawy, "Labor Constraints in the Five-Year Plan," U.S. Congress, Joint Economic Committee, *Soviet Economic Prospects for the Seventies* (Washington: Government Printing Office, June 27, 1973), pp. 551-553.

Chapter 6

The Supply of Financial Resources

The availability of financial resources is not as central a concern in innovation decisions in the Soviet economy as it is in market economies. Command over money is equivalent to the command over real resources in a market economy. In the Soviet "documonetary" economy command over real resources comes in the first instance from the plan. If the enterprise's claim to real resources is first confirmed in the plan, provision is then made for the financial resources required to purchase the authorized goods and services.

Nevertheless proper financial management is a requisite for the conduct of the enterprise's affairs. The chief reason is that prices, decision rules, and incentives are all expressed in financial terms. Inattention to financial matters may therefore cause the enterprise to make the wrong decision, to produce a poor performance record, and to be penalized by low personal incomes. Those issues will be treated later in the discussion of the nonorganizational structural properties of the economic system. Apart from those matters, however, proper financial management is also required to secure the real resources needed for the conduct of economic activities. Even when the enterprise is authorized by plan to secure certain goods and services, if it has managed its financial affairs badly it may be unable to purchase them. Hence while financial considerations may not dominate in decision making, they do enter in all enterprise decisions, including the decision to innovate. To that extent the effect of organizational structure on the supply of financial resources affects the rate of innovation. If the methods of supplying enterprises with financial resources are such that the act of innovation leads to financial stress, management will be hesitant about innovating. If, however, the supply of financial resources is so organized that the act of innovation is neutral or improves the enterprise's financial position, the innovation decision will be encouraged.

All enterprises require funds for such purposes as the purchase of inputs, the payment of wages and salaries, the payment of tax obligations and interest on bank loans, the replacement of capital equipment, and so forth. The innovating enterprise requires funds for all these normal purposes, but in addition it requires funds for certain purposes peculiar to the act of innovation. First, it may require additional funds to finance the acquisition of R & D services. Second, innovation generally requires investment in equipment and sometimes in plant, for which financing must be found. Third, the start-up of new production facilities usually involves high production expenses for a certain period of time. Unless provision is made to finance those start-up costs, the enterprise may have to deflect some of its own funds away from other intended uses in order to see the innovation through to completion. Our task is to evaluate the organizational structure of the system that supplies enterprises with the financial resources for these three purposes.

6.1. Financing R & D

The largest share of all R & D requires no enterprise financing at all. The funds are provided by the state budget and by the ministries, and they support most of the work of the R & D institutions. The remainder is financed by enterprises. It consists of the in-house R & D of enterprises and of the work performed by the R & D organizations under contract to enterprises.

Centrally Financed R & D

Total expenditures on science have grown rapidly in recent years, from 2.4 billion rubles in 1958 to over 15 billion rubles in 1973.[1] About 55 to 60 percent of the total consists of annual appropriations from the USSR state budget.[2] The budgetary appropriations are made to the state agencies responsible for the work of the R & D establishments: the Academies of Sciences, the Ministry of Secondary and Higher Education, The State Committee on Science and Technology, and the industrial ministries. They provide the principal financial support of the work of the R & D institutes. In 1969, for example, the state budget financed 72 percent of the expenditures of the R & D institutes of the Ministry of the Chemical Industry and 56 percent in the Ministry of Electric Power and Electrification.[3]

In addition to the funds provided by the state budget, the ministries possess certain funds for financing R & D, the chief of which is an account called the Special Fund for Financing Scientific Research.[4] This fund is financed by a charge levied on the ministry's enterprises, equal to some small percentage of their total costs of production, generally from one to three percent. Enterprises include this payment to their ministry in their cost of production, so that the cost falls on their customers.[5] Data are not available on the proportion of total R & D financed from these ministry Special Funds.

The Special Fund for Financing Scientific Research is used by the ministry to finance major R & D work within its branch of industry, and sometimes for interbranch collaborative work. Some of the funds are used for the direct support of the ministry's R & D institutes, supplementing the state budget funds. Another part is used for financing contract research, an arrangement that affects the finances of enterprises. The ministry may award a contract to an enterprise for some design and testing work, for example, which is a source of enterprise revenue.[6] Or it may make a grant of funds to an enterprise to finance contract R & D by an independent R & D organization.

Except for this latter type of grant, budget- and ministry-financed R & D involves no financial expenditures by enterprises. The innovating enterprise is therefore the beneficiary of a great deal of R & D work for which it is not obliged to pay at all. When it undertakes to introduce a new automation method developed by an R & D institute, the R & D work incorporated in that method has generally been financed by the ministry. If it is a new product developed by an institute of the Academy of Sciences, the work has been financed by the Academy.

The effect of central financing of R & D is that a major input required for innovation is available to the user at a price of zero. That pricing policy lends strong encouragement to innovation. Moreover, economic theory provides support for a policy of free distribution of technological knowledge, in both capitalist and socialist economies.[7] This beneficial pricing effect is offset, however, by certain incentive problems. Centrally financed R & D takes the form primarily of direct grants to the R & D institutes. The negative effects of grant support on the quality of R & D work, which were discussed in Chapter 4, were the principal reason for the contract-research reform.

Our present concern, however, is not with price structure or incentive structure but with organizational structure. As a method of organizing the supply of financial resources, centrally financed R & D has the virtue of relieving the enterprise entirely of the need to acquire and expend funds for the purchase of that vital input into innovation. The act of innovation poses no new problems, as far as the supply of financial resources is concerned, that are not encountered by the noninnovating firm. From the strictly organizational point of view, the central financing of R & D is neutral in its effect on the enterprise innovation decision.

Enterprise-financed R & D

Enterprises require a supply of financial resources for two kinds of R & D work. One is the support of in-house R & D. The other is for the financing of contract research.

In-house R & D work is financed primarily by the enterprise itself out of the revenues earned from the sale of its output. The expenditures for R & D are charged against current cost of production, under the category of "general administrative expenses." This cost item includes "experimental and testing work, maintenance of enterprise laboratories, expenses associated with invention, and product and process improvement."[8]

In some cases, the enterprise's R & D facilities take on contract work performed for outside organizations. It may be another enterprise that requires certain R & D work for which the given enterprise happens to have specialized equipment or personnel. Or an R & D organization may wish to have some work done, or a prototype model built. Or the ministry may commission the enterprise to undertake an R & D project. In such cases the contract provides additional revenues to the enterprise.

The financing of the on-going R & D work of enterprises poses no particular problems. Since the expenses are regarded as part of the general costs of production, the financial plan provides for the recovery of those expenses out of revenues. This mode of financing encourages innovation, since the enterprise has no less motivation to use these resources efficiently than it has to use any of its productive resources efficiently.

If the innovating enterprise requires R & D work to be performed that is beyond its capability, it must secure the services of an independent R & D establishment. In the past, this required that the ministry order the R & D establishment to assume the task. Financial arrangements were then made between the ministry and the R & D establishment and no enterprise finance was involved at all. Since the contract-research reform, the enterprise must now find the financial resources to pay for the R & D work done under contract.

A number of sources of funds are available to the enterprise.[9] If the innovation has been initiated by the ministry, the funds may be appropriated from the ministry's Special Fund for Financing Scientific Research. The enterprise may also apply for a grant from that Fund for financing an R & D contract on a self-initiated innovation. Second, the enterprise may use some of its own resources for financing a contract, charging the expenses to its cost of production. Third, funds earmarked primarily for capital investment may be used to some extent for financing R & D; State Bank credits, for example, and the enterprise's Production Development Fund.[10]

Data are not available on the volume of enterprise-financed R & D work, or on the relative proportions of the various sources of funds. Most analysts, however, regard the supply of funds as plentiful. The organization of the supply of financial resources for R & D appears to pose no problems for the innovating enterprise.

6.2. Financing Centralized Capital Investment

If the innovation process is defined to include the diffusion of new products and processes through the economy, virtually all capital investment is a part of that process. A new enterprise built by the ministry to produce a new product is part of the diffusion process of that product innovation. Since the enterprise will incorporate recent advances in technology and recent improvements in materials, it promotes the diffusion of process innovation. The least innovative of managers confronts at some time the necessity of replacing worn out plant and equipment. He may prefer to replace it with new plant and equipment physically identical to the old, in order to minimize risk and avoid the effort of retraining labor and reorganizing the production process. He is nevertheless generally obliged to employ modern technology, perhaps because the older is no longer produced, or cost considerations are overwhelming or the ministry would chastize him otherwise. Hence capital investment in general is a part of the innovation process even when innovation is not the primary objective of the investment.

In the planning of capital investment a distinction has long been made between centralized and decentralized investment.[11] The distinction is based on the source of financing. Centralized capital investment is that financed by some combination of enterprise retained earnings, depreciation reserves, state budget grants, and loans from the Construction Bank. Decentralized investment is that financed out of certain special funds set aside for enterprise use, and by State Bank credits earmarked for special purposes including innovation. Enterprise centralized investment must be approved by the ministry, and the largest projects must be approved by the USSR or republic Councils of Ministers as well. Decentralized investment, however, does not require ministry approval.

Centralized investment, which accounts for about 80 percent of total capital investment[12] and includes all large projects, is the subject of this section.

All construction of new enterprises is centrally financed. Centralized investment in existing enterprises may be initiated in the ministry or in the enterprise. In the latter case the enterprise must present a complete set of blueprints, technical specifications, and cost estimates for ministry approval. If the project is accepted, it is included in the enterprise draft plan for the forthcoming year. In the process of developing the national investment plan, enterprises and ministries may be obliged by the State Planning Committee to drop some projects proposed in their draft plans or to undertake others that they had not proposed; or some projects may be scheduled for earlier completion than originally proposed and others for later completion. On conclusion of the plan-making process, therefore, the enterprise may be obliged to accept a plan providing for some investment project it had not intended to undertake, or it may have failed to gain approval for some project it had proposed in its draft plan.

Sources of Finance

Funds for financing centralized investment come either from industry's own financial resources or from resources provided by the state's financial institutions. Industry's own resources consist of the profits of enterprises and from their depreciation accounts. State financial resources take the form of grants from the state budget, or credits extended by the Construction Bank.

Retained earnings. The uses that the enterprise may make of its gross profit are fairly strictly regulated. Certain portions of the profit are set aside in various special funds that the enterprise may use for specified purposes such as incentive bonuses. Other portions are used to pay various obligations to the State, such as the profits tax and the capital charge. Any profit that remains after these deductions and payments is designated as the "free balance." Normally the free balance is simply turned back to the State budget. If the enterprise is authorized to undertake an investment project, however, it is permitted to retain the free balance, or part of it, to be used for financing the project.

Depreciation reserves. All enterprises set aside a certain portion of their revenues as a depreciation reserve. One portion is earmarked for repair and maintenance work and must be used for that purpose. The rest is earmarked for investment in the replacement of capital. In many enterprises not currently undertaking large investment programs, the annual depreciation funds collected exceed the amount earmarked for the financing of capital replacement. That excess is turned over to the ministry, which uses those funds for financing the centralized capital investments of other enterprises. Hence the innovating enterprise may finance its investments not only from its own current depreciation funds but also from those of other enterprises redistributed to it through its ministry.

Nonrepayable budget grants. If the planned centralized investment projects exceed the sum of the enterprise's free balance and depreciation reserve, the remainder is financed by the state budget. The traditional mode of financing is a direct nonrepayable grant. The funds so allocated are administered for the Ministry of Finance by the Construction Bank. The Construction Bank establishes an account from which the enterprise may draw funds to pay for each stage of the construction or installation work as it is completed. The Bank controls the use of the funds by requiring proof that each stage of the work has been completed before authorizing payment.

The use of nonrepayable grants came under mounting criticism in the early 1960s. The chief criticism was that enterprises and ministries treat such grants as costless gifts. They therefore have no incentive to economize on them. No economic consideration restrains them from applying for authorization to undertake centralized investment projects, since if authorization is granted the funds are made available by the state at no cost. Hence the task of selecting among the investment proposals of all ministries falls entirely on the state planning bodies. They can have no confidence that the proposals that come before them have been subjected to a prior screening based on the cost-minimizing efforts of ministries and enterprises. Moreover, once the investments are approved and the budget grant made, the enterprise or ministry has little interest in exerting pressure on the construction contractor to keep costs down. Excessive nagging of a contractor by a client enterprise may cause the former to lose interest in that project and shift his attention to the project of a less disagreeable enterprise. Since the funds are the "government's" and not one's own, there is no benefit to the enterprise from economizing on construction costs.[13]

In the spirit of 1965 Economic Reform, a financing method was sought which would create an interest in the enterprise in weighing carefully their applications for new investment projects and economizing on construction costs. The new method was the use of long-term credits rather than nonrepayable grants for financing centralized investment.

The Credit-Financing Reform

The use of credits for financing capital investment is not a totally new departure. It has been used for financing decentralized investments, to be discussed in Section 6.3. What is new is the extension of credit financing to centralized investment.

The enterprise must still look first to its free balance and depreciation reserves for the financing of an authorized investment project. It is only with respect to any additional financing that the credit reform applies. Nor does it apply to all centralized investment but only to certain specified kinds. First, it applies to all investment that is classified as "expansion and reconstruction" of existing enterprises. Hence it covers all centralized investments in connection with the innovation activities of existing enterprises. Second, it applies to the construction of all new enterprises in which the rate of return exceeds 20 percent.[14]

Since new enterprises are constructed by the ministries, this provision does not affect the innovation decisions of existing enterprises. Budget-grant financing continues to be employed in the construction of new enterprises with an anticipated rate of return below 20 percent, in all investment undertaken by enterprises that earn no planned profit but receive an annual government subsidy, and in such "nonproduction" investments as housing and public facilities.

The credit is repaid out of two sources of enterprise funds: profits and depreciation charges. The month following the official commissioning of the new project, the enterprise begins paying over to the Construction Bank that portion of its depreciation charges on the new facility earmarked for capital replacement. In the quarter following the end of the officially defined start-up period, the enterprise begins paying over the free balance of the profit earned on the new facilities. These two streams of payments continue to be made until the credit is fully repaid. During the repayment period the enterprise is freed from the obligation of paying the annual capital charge on the new facility. Interest must be paid, however, from the time the credit is opened until it is fully repaid. The interest rate is 0.5 percent per annum when the repayments are made on schedule. If the loan is not repaid by the scheduled date, however, the interest rate rises to 1.5 percent. As an inducement to minimize construction periods, the interest rate is reduced if the construction work is completed ahead of schedule.[15]

How is the innovation decision affected by the fact that outside financing of centralized investment may now have to take the form of a repayable credit rather than a nonrepayable grant? The answer depends in part on the amount of financing involved.

In strictly quantitative terms, the change from grant to credit financing has not been of major dimensions. First, grants are still authorized for the financing of several kinds of new investment, particularly for the construction of new enterprises that yield a rate of return less than 20 percent. More significant, however, is the preference of ministries and enterprises for using their own funds rather than applying for credits. Financing out of one's own funds has the obvious advantage of avoiding the need to pay the interest charge and to repay the loan. The motivation is sufficiently strong that some ministries ignore the regulations and finance directly some projects for which credit financing is supposed to be used; for example, projects with rates of return exceeding 20 percent.[16] Dependence on credit financing is also weakened by the abundant retained earnings and depreciation funds amassed by enterprises and ministries. In 1968, 94 percent of all capital investments eligible for credit financing were financed out of enterprise and ministry funds, and only the remaining 6 percent by Construction Bank credits. In the case of investments classified as "expansion of existing enterprises" credits accounted for only 3.4 percent. Since these investments are those most closely associated with enterprise innovative activities, it is evident that the innovation decisions of enterprises must have been very little affected by the reform. It affects chiefly the construction of new enterprises. Of the total of such investments, only 10 percent was financed by the ministries' own resources in 1968, and the balance by long-term credits.[17]

In those instances where credits have replaced grants, it is difficult to find reasons for expecting significant changes in the decision to innovate. The chief gain expected from the reform is that management will be more circumspect in its investment planning because it has to pay interest and repay the loan. The argument would have some force if the funds now used for loan repayment would otherwise have remained with the enterprise for its own use. That is not the case, however.

The problem is that the organizational structure of the supply of financial resources does not give the enterprise the opportunity to accumulate any funds in excess of those earmarked for special planned purposes such as their incentive bonuses. Any profit earned in excess of the specified uses constitutes the free balance and cannot be retained by the enterprise. If the free balance of profit is not authorized for use in the financing of capital investments, "then the enterprises are obliged to turn those funds over to the budget, and cannot retain them for their own use. This preserves the parasitic attitude of enterprises in submitting requests for capital investments."[18]

It is therefore a matter of indifference to the enterprises whether the free balance is turned over to the state budget, as in grant financing, or whether it is turned over to the Construction Bank in repayment of a credit. In contemplating an investment project the mode of financing has no influence on the decision. The investment is financed by "government money" as surely in the case of credits as in the case of grants.

Similar considerations apply to the effect of the interest charge on credit finance. For one thing the interest rate is extremely low, and critics have urged that it be "somewhat increased."[19] In addition, the interest is simply charged to the cost of goods produced by the new facility. In the absence of the interest charge, the calculated enterprise profit would be larger but the larger free balance would again simply disappear into the State budget.[20]

It may be thought that under credit financing the Construction Bank can maintain closer control on the State's behalf over the technical quality of the investment project and the cost estimates. But the same bank is also the State's agent in the administration of budget grants for investment financing. Under grant financing also the bank is obliged to study the technical and economic documentation of investment projects and to maintain some degree of supervision over the course of the work. There is no reason to expect that it can perform that function more effectively simply because the funds it administers are supplied to enterprises as loans rather than grants.

Conclusion

Thus the organization of the supply of financial resources appears to be neutral in its effect on the innovation decision. If the innovation requires that a centralized investment project be undertaken, the dominating concern is to get it approved by the ministry, the Construction Bank, and the central planners for inclusion in the enterprise plan. That approval is gained on the basis of the technical documentation and the economic justification presented. Once it is approved, however, the financial resources are supplied in the manner described. An investment project so approved cannot fail to be undertaken for lack of financial resources.

While financial considerations do not limit the capability of the innovating enterprise to undertake a centralized investment project, they may pose a problem in the process of carrying the project through to

completion. This may occur if the construction contractor is inefficient, or if the technical documentation provided by the engineering
design organizations is unworkable and requires costly changes. The
funds allocated for the project may then not cover the actual costs and
the enterprise may run out of funds for carrying the project through. It
is in such cases that the principles of "business accounting" and "control by the ruble" perform their functions. It is the financial consequences of mismanagement that bring the matter to the attention of
the ministry and the banks who can then require that corrective action
be taken. In the absence of a system of financial controls, mismanagement could continue for long periods before the agencies of the State
became aware of it. This indeed is the principal function of the financial system in Soviet industry. The financial system is not organized for
the purpose of allocating real resources; that is performed by the planning system. The financial system's function is to provide the authorities with a set of signals for determining how well the planned allocation of resources is managed.

With respect to the management of innovation, the methods of organizing the supply of financial resources serves the State's purpose in sig-
naling the presence of mismanagement. That effect is offset somewhat,
however, by management's practice of building a "safety factor" into
its financial plans.[21] Indeed, that practice is the direct consequence of
the Soviet system of economic controls, including financial controls. In
anticipation of the possible financial difficulties that may result from
problems of supply or production, management seeks to provide in the
plan for a larger supply of financial resources than they expect to require. Since the degree of risk and uncertainty is greater in the case of
innovation than in repetitive production activities, we may expect that
the safety factor is correspondingly greater. It is more prudent to submit an inflated cost estimate and later show a saving of financial resources, than to submit a realistic cost estimate and later face the need
to apply for additional funds.

6.3. Financing Decentralized Capital Investment
It has long been recognized that there are certain serious problems in
the planning and management of centralized investment. The development and design work is often far advanced before it is known which
enterprise will be selected to introduce the innovation. Even when the
enterprise has been selected, the ministry and R & D people do not

have as detailed a knowledge of the enterprise's technological characteristics and capabilities as the enterprise's own personnel do. Moreover,
something is lost if the innovation process does not fully tap the initiative of enterprise personnel. Centralized investment, writes a critic, does
not

promote the enterprise's interest in the most rational use of its resources. Often, they receive equipment that they do not need. Furthermore, the enterprise's opportunities to develop and improve their production system depend basically on the decisions of the higher organizations, and only to a lesser degree on the concrete results of their own
work—on their profits or losses.[22]

The purpose of decentralized investment is to encourage enterprise
initiative in investment and innovation. A decentralized investment is
one that the enterprise is authorized to undertake under certain conditions without requiring the prior approval of the agencies of central
planning. The chief condition is that the enterprise manage to obtain
financial resources. Hence the command over financial resources is in
this case intended to be sufficient to command real resources.

About 20 percent of all capital investment is classified as decentralized.[23] It consists of two major forms. One form is financed by the
enterprise's own resources, out of an account called the Production
Development Fund. The other is financed by credits made available by
the State Bank.

Production Development Fund

As early as 1936 the decision was taken to permit enterprises to retain
some of their profits, to be used for certain purposes which they were
thought to desire. The original statute provided that enterprises were
allowed to retain 2 percent of their planned profit and 50 percent of
their profit in excess of the planned amount. The retained profit was
deposited in a special account called the Director's Fund, later the Enterprise Fund. The statute specified the proportions of the fund to be
used for various stipulated purposes such as enterprise amenities (workers' clubs, nurseries) and incentive bonuses. Two of the authorized uses
were "supplementary capital investments" and "supplementary production improvements and technical propaganda."[24] They were "supplementary" in the sense that they were in addition to any such expenditures provided for in the official enterprise plan. Within very broad limits, the use of the funds was fully discretionary.

The size of the Enterprise Fund was tied to profit in order that it might serve as an incentive for cost-reducing process innovation. Subsequent changes were introduced to stimulate product innovation as well. In 1961, for example, the percentages of planned profit that could be retained in the Enterprise Fund were changed in the machine-building industry from a flat 4 percent to a discriminating scale; 10 percent of the profit on what were defined as "new" products could be retained, while only 4 percent of the profit on "old" products could be retained. In 1964, the practice of discrimination was extended to enterprises in the chemical, petroleum, petrochemical, metals, building materials, and other industries.[25]

The Enterprise Fund was designed to serve both as an incentive for innovation and as a source of funds for financing innovation. The incentive effect will be discussed in Chapter 14; our present concern is with the supply of financial resources. The fund did in fact provide the enterprise with its only opportunity to invest without requiring the permission of any higher authorities, and it also provided the resources for financing that investment. The volume of funds involved, however, was so small as to be of little practical significance. In 1964, for example, total outlays from the Enterprise Funds of industrial enterprises amounted to 827 million rubles. Most of that was spent for bonuses, enterprise housing, and a variety of other authorized purposes. Only 120 million rubles were spent on such innovation-related activities as product improvement and the installation of new equipment and processes. In that year, total capital investment in industry amounted to 17 billion rubles.[26] It is clear that none but the most modest forms of innovation could be financed from this source.

One of the major features of the 1965 Economic Reform was a substantial expansion in the volume of profit that enterprises were authorized to retain for various specified uses. The Enterprise Fund was discontinued, and in its place three new "incentive funds" were established. First is the Bonus Incentive Fund, out of which individual incentive bonuses may be paid. The second is the Social Expenditures Fund, for financing clubhouses, vacations, nurseries, residential construction, and so forth. The third is the Production Development Fund.

The statute specifies four uses to which the enterprise's Production Development Fund may be put.[27] The primary use is to finance the introduction of new technological processes, the modernization of older equipment, and the replacement of obsolete equipment by new. Second, the fund may be used to repay State Bank loans taken out for additional financing of new equipment. Third, it may be used for improvements in the "organization of production and the use of labor," a very broad category that would seem to cover any cost-reducing and product-improvement measures. Fourth, the fund may finance other capital expenditures such as construction and installation costs, but only when these costs are incurred in connection with the purchase of new equipment or the expansion of production, housing, and warehousing space. The fund may not be used to finance new construction that is unrelated to the purchase and installation of new equipment.

A rather complex set of regulations governs the quantity of funds that the enterprise may transfer into its Production Development Fund account. The funds come from three sources. First, a certain percentage of the depreciation allowances that are earmarked for capital replacement may be transferred to the fund. The percentage is fixed for the enterprise by the ministry, and ranges from 8 to 68 percent. In the past, all these funds were used for financing centralized investment.

Second, the proceeds from the sale of used equipment or new equipment that is not needed may be transferred to the fund, less the costs of putting the equipment in order and arranging the sale. In the past the proceeds from such sales were simply turned over to the Construction Bank, so that the enterprises had very little incentive to take the trouble to resell idle equipment.[28]

The third source of cash for the Production Development Fund is a certain proportion of the profit of the enterprise. No simple formula like a specified percentage of profit has been employed. Instead, a rather complicated formula is used to determine the amount of profit that may be transferred to the Production Development Fund. The formula is[29]

$$D = K[(k_s \cdot S) + (k_p \cdot P)] \tag{6.1}$$

where
D is the amount of profit that may be retained in the Production Development Fund,
K is the average annual value of the enterprise's stock of fixed capital,
S is the percentage rate of increase in sales revenue,
P is the rate of profit on capital,
k_s is a "normative," or coefficient, to be applied to S,
k_p is a "normative" or coefficient, to be applied to P.

For example, suppose an enterprise is assigned coefficient values of $k_s = 0.017$ and $k_p = 0.0125$.[30] And suppose that in the course of the year it has increased its sales revenue S 10 percent over the preceding year, its rate of profit P is 25 percent, and the average annual value of its capital stock K is 20 million rubles. Then its sales performance entitles it to retain a volume of profit equal to 0.17 percent (that is, 0.017×10) of its capital, and its profit-rate performance entitles it to retain a volume of profit equal to 0.3125 percent (that is, 0.0125×25) of its capital. Together the two "indicators" of performance entitle it to retain a volume of profit equal to 0.4825 percent (that is, 0.17 plus 0.3125) of its capital stock of 20 million rubles, or 96,500 rubles.

If we may regard the manager as seeking to maximize the size of his Production Development Fund, the formula serves as a decision rule for selecting the optimal level of sales, profit, and capital stock. For the present, however, our concern is not with the structure of decision rules but with the structure of organization. The formula defines one of the ways in which the supply of financial resources for innovation is organized. Our concern is with the effect of the organizational structure of financial flows on the innovative decisions of enterprises.

Capital investment financed from Production Development Funds accounted in 1970 for about 9 percent of total capital investment in industry.[31] This is considerably short of the long-run goal of 20 percent,[32] but very much larger than the negligible amount financed from the former Enterprise Fund. One cannot judge from such aggregate data, however, how this change in organization of the supply of finances has affected the innovation decisions of enterprises, because the total volume of investment is fixed by the State. If the Production Development Fund has increased the willingness of enterprises to invest in innovation, that increase would express itself in a greater demand for late-model machinery and equipment, both to replace obsolete models and to substitute for other inputs such as labor, fuels, and materials. In a market economy, an increase in demand would generate an increase in the production of machinery and equipment, which would be registered in the statistics of output. But in the Soviet economy, an increase in the production of machinery and equipment may occur in the absence of any change in enterprise attitudes toward innovation. The increase may represent merely the State's decision to raise the rate of investment by constructing more new enterprises and expanding the capacity of older ones. Even a rise in the observed replacement rate beyond what could be accounted for on the basis of the age structure of the capital stock would not be sufficient evidence of a rise in the enterprise's desire to innovate; it may reflect merely new replacement instructions from the State to enterprises. On the other hand, an increased desire to innovate by enterprises would generate no increase in the production of machinery and equipment if the State chose not to permit an increase in the rate of investment. Therefore the increase in the proportion of investment that is decentrally financed is no evidence that innovative behavior has changed. The investment behavior of enterprises may be no different since the establishment of the Production Development Fund than before. Only the sources of financing may have changed.

A hint that the Production Development Fund has not drastically changed enterprise innovative behavior is provided by the reports that the funds are not fully spent. This used also to be true of the Enterprise Fund. In 1960, for example, the famous Likhachev Auto Plant was authorized to spend 20 percent of its Enterprise Fund for investment in new technology, but it managed to spend only 7 percent.[33] Similar reports now appear regarding the Production Development Fund. In 1970 total expenditures from the funds amounted to 3,341 million rubles, but at the year's end 889 million rubles that had been deposited in the funds remained unspent.[34] This is all the more puzzling since enterprises are not permitted to carry over unspent balances to the following year, a stipulation that constitutes a strong incentive for managers to spend the funds if they possibly can.[35] Moreover there are a number of additional inducements for enterprises to prefer Production Development Fund financing over other forms. Investments financed from this fund are not recorded as part of the enterprise's capital assets for two years. Hence during that period their recorded rate of profit is correspondingly increased. In addition they are not required to pay the capital charge on those investments.[36] One would therefore expect enterprises to spend these funds as rapidly as they accumulate. Perhaps it is the pressure to use unspent funds that explains the reports of misappropriation of Production Development Funds for unauthorized uses.[37] In Ukrainian industry, for example, 8.5 percent of Production Development Funds were used for local road construction and maintenance.[38]

There is further evidence that this decentralization in financing has not been accompanied by a decentralization in decision making. The quantity of profit that an enterprise may deposit in its Production Development Fund depends on the coefficients that are applied to its rate of profit and its increase in sales (see Equation 6.1). Those coefficients are established in advance by the ministry, within limits set by the Ministry of Finance. In establishing the coefficients, the ministry first determines the volume of funds that the enterprise requires in order to finance its planned decentralized investment and to repay bank loans. When that sum is determined, the coefficients are then set at such a level that, when applied in Equation 6.1, the authorized size of the Production Development Fund will be precisely equal to that sum.[39] Hence the primary function of the fund is to finance activities, the size of which had previously been provided for in the plan. It is not as if the size of the fund determines the level of investment that the enterprise can undertake. It is rather the other way around; it is the size of the planned decentralized investment that determines the planned size of the Fund.

The coefficients, once established, are supposed to remain unchanged for some period of time. Hence the enterprise that raises its profit rate and increases sales revenues beyond the planned levels may deposit larger-than-planned amounts in its fund. Those additional amounts may be used to finance investment not originally provided for in the plan. It is only with respect to such additional amounts that the availability of funds may be said to determine the volume of decentralized investment that the enterprise may undertake. But for the most part, the size of the Fund is derivative from the size of previously planned expenditures.

Since the size of the fund depends primarily on the planned expenditures, it is not surprising that the ministry looks closely over the enterprise's shoulder when those expenditures are decided upon. The fund was intended to enable the enterprise to make "independent [decisions] not requiring the agreement of higher authorities."[40] The Director of the Kriukovskii Carbuilding Plant, however, complains that he is handicapped in using his Production Development Fund because "at the beginning of the year the enterprise as a rule does not know which projects the ministry will include in that year's plan, or even the total volume of capital investments."[41] It is clear that in this ministry at least, the enterprise's independence is limited by what the ministry permits it to do, whenever the ministry gets around to giving that permission. Innovation decisions appear to be made in the same way as before the Reform; the only difference is in the financial flows. Before the Reform, the enterprise's profit and depreciation allowances were taxed away, and then returned to it as a budget grant to pay for the authorized investment project. Now, a portion of the profit and depreciation allowances is left with the enterprise in its Production Development Fund to pay directly for the authorized investment. The middleman that has been eliminated is not the ministry but the State budget.

Genuine independence in decision making is further limited by the system of "control by the ruble." The Production Development Fund, like all the enterprise's funds, consists of an account in the State Bank, which has the responsibility for monitoring all expenditures from enterprise funds. This form of control impinges even on those areas of decision making where enterprises are supposed to enjoy some independence. The following is the statement by a chief engineer to a newspaper correspondent:

Yes, the amounts are small. But try to spend freely even those sums which we do have in our Production Development Fund. Here the bank comes forward in its role as a fervent controller. First, at the beginning of the year they demand a complete estimate of our intended expenditures from the Fund. And God forbid that it should ever be changed! But what if, in the course of our work, we decided to buy not that machine tool but another? Or say a piece of equipment turned up that was not provided for in the estimate? . . . We have to begin reworking the estimate, resubmitting it for approval to by various agencies, and so on. . . .[42]

The Production Development Fund does entitle the enterprise to one privilege not formerly available. Before the Reform, all enterprises wishing to invest in innovation were on an equal footing in pressing their cases before the ministry. The fact that an enterprise earned a large profit gave its proposals no greater weight than those of a poorer enterprise. The latter, indeed, may have been preferred by the ministry officials, who wished to improve the general performance of the ministry. Now, however, the successful enterprise with a large Production Development Fund has a stronger claim, because the ministry is under some obligation to authorize a volume of expenditures on innovation equal to the size of the enterprise's Production Development Fund. In this sense, the Production Development Fund has given the successful enterprise somewhat greater leverage in pressing for its innovation proposals.

But this financial advantage is offset by certain disadvantages in the procurement of materials and equipment. The Kriukovskii Plant faces the same supply problem in using its Production Development Fund as all enterprises face in their current production activities:

Thus, the technical documents for the forthcoming year's plan are delivered to us by the engineering-design organization throughout the present year right up to September 1. But an enterprise has to submit its statements of requirements for materials and equipment to the supply organizations by April 1. Hence, instead of filling out the requisitions, we "invent" them. As a result, we pile up stocks of equipment and materials we don't need, while we face shortages of the resources we need."[43]

The Kriukovskii Plant managed at least to get its requirements included in the centralized materials supply planning system. More serious are the supply problems of enterprises whose decentralized investments in innovation are not included in the national plan. This appears to be the case of most projects financed by Production Development Funds. Dr. A. Kurskii points out that the equipment and materials needed for work financed by the Production Development Funds "are not provided for in the supply plans. Therefore, under the present supply system, even if the plan for using the funds is drawn up well in advance, it remains highly provisional."[44] The problem is particularly acute if the project requires construction work that is to be contracted out. The enterprise often finds that the construction contractors are fully booked up with orders for work on centrally planned construction projects. Hence, the holders of decentralized financial resources in their Production Development Funds are unable to find contractors to complete their projects.[45]

A further obstacle is the prohibition against using the fund for the construction of new production facilities. The purpose of the prohibition is to slow down the troublesome increase in the volume of uncompleted construction.[46] Managers had long ago developed the fine art of blackmailing the higher authorities for additional investment grants by starting new projects that they did not have the resources to complete and then demanding additional funds in order to reduce the volume of uncompleted construction. In the absence of this prohibition, the Production Development Fund would provide managers with a greatly enlarged volume of financial resources for starting up large new projects that would take a long time to complete.

The prohibition, however, has prevented enterprises from using all their Production Development Funds even for the allowable purposes. The Automatic Heating Control Equipment Plant in Moscow was built a long time ago, and certain of its oldest buildings need to be demolished and replaced by new ones to house the modern production equipment planned for purchase. But since the plant cannot receive permission to finance the new construction work from the Production Development Fund, reports the director, they cannot purchase the new equipment, and they are, therefore, unable to spend their entire Production Development Fund.[47]

The problem of unspent balances in the Production Development Funds reflects the relative powerlessness of financial resources to command real resources. A number of remedies have been advanced. Some urge a greater expansion of wholesale trade as a system of distribution. Others propose that construction contracting enterprises be required to maintain some reserve capacity, beyond the volume of work they perform on centrally planned projects. Then "enterprises would not have to hunt for contractors, but contractors would instead have to seek out customers" to keep their production capacity fully booked with orders.[48] Changes of this sort are indeed necessary if the purpose of the Production Development Fund is to be realized. As presently constituted the fund provides a source of decentralized financing of a certain volume of investment in innovation that formerly was centrally financed. In the absence of a corresponding decentralization in decision making, however, the change in the organization of financing does not appear to have had a significant influence on the innovative behavior of enterprises.

State Bank Credits

In the 1930s, the only source of financing decentralized investment was the Enterprise Fund. Just before World War II a new source of supply of financial resources was organized. The State Bank was authorized to lend funds to enterprises for what was called "small-scale mechanization." The volume of credit-financed decentralized investment in innovation grew slowly until 1954, when it began to expand more rapidly. Between 1959 and 1970, it rose from 358.8 million rubles to 861 million rubles.[49] Despite the rapid growth, credit-financed innovation remained a relatively small part of the total. As a share of total capital investment, State-Bank-financed investment accounted for only 1.5 percent to 2 percent by the mid-sixties. The percentage varied greatly by industry, however. In some branches of light and food industry, it had reached 20 percent of total capital investment.[50]

State Bank loans are extended primarily for cost-reducing process innovations such as the mechanization of production installations and the replacement of obsolete equipment. To apply for a loan, an enterprise must present to the bank a detailed explanation of the technical and economic data on the innovation, including a calculation of the anticipated return and the payoff period. The normal interest rate charged is 2 percent per annum payable quarterly, but the rate rises to 5 percent on balances unpaid at the expiration date of the loan. The maximum period of loans was gradually extended over the years, and reached six years by 1965.[51] Since the introduction of the Production Development Fund, bank loans must be repaid with the money in that fund. The enterprise must exhaust the resources in its Production Development Fund before it can qualify for a loan.[52]

Proponents of credit financing of decentralized investment in innovation, who understandably include many bankers, present a variety of advantages that this form of financing holds over others. The principal advantage claimed is that the bank does a particularly good job of studying the technical and economic documents in the loan applications, so that the volume of funds wasted on unprofitable innovations is minimized. Thus it is reported that in a sample of 2,775 credit-financed innovations during 1955 to 1963, 87.2 percent were sufficiently productive to have been fully repaid within the loan period. Only 4.9 percent yielded no net positive returns, while 82.1 percent had a payoff period of two years or less; 24.8 percent had payoff periods larger than anticipated, but only 70 percent of those ran over three years.[53] Because of the close control, "cases of irrational investment in new technology, when financed by State Bank credits, are very rare."[54]

The claim may be a bit misleading. The fact that loans are repaid on time is a source of satisfaction to the bankers, but it does not necessarily signify that the innovations were successful. We read, for example, that enterprises that receive loans on the basis of overoptimistic calculations, often have to meet their repayment schedules out of their working capital and retained profit.[55] The bankers would regard these loans as successful because repayments were made on time, but the enterprise may have fallen into financial difficulties because of an unsuccessful attempt at innovation. More significant is the fact that the bank manages to maintain its good record of repayment by financing only those innovations that yield the largest and quickest returns. It skims the cream off each year's innovations, leaving other sources of funds to finance the rest. If the bank were the only source of finance, with its present requirements very little innovation might occur. On the other hand, if the bank relaxed its lending requirements to a level at which the total current planned supply of investment funds would be loaned out, its repayment record would likely be much less successful than it is at present.

The proponents of credit financing urge the continued expansion of bank lending relative to other sources of financing investment in innovation. Their influence was undoubtedly a factor in the introduction of credit financing of centralized investment as well, through the Construction Bank. Dr. Anisimov of the Institute of Economics, a specialist on the economics of innovation, looks forward to a day when most investment in innovation will be financed by bank loans. Budget grants will be a "privileged form" of investment, available only to certain enterprises for specific social purposes.[56] To accomplish this, the relative attractiveness of credit financing to borrowers must be increased, relative to budget financing. This could be done by measures both to restrict budget financing and to increase the demand for bank loans. In recent years, the major measure to reduce the relative attractiveness of budget financing was the introduction in 1965 of a charge on all the capital possessed by an enterprise. Before the capital charge was introduced, there was little incentive for an enterprise to finance an innovation by a bank loan on which interest had to be paid if it could obtain a free budget grant instead. Since the introduction of the capital charge, budget-financed capital is no longer free. A number of additional changes were introduced in 1967. The State Bank may now extend several separate loans to an enterprise for different innovations; in the past, only one loan was permitted at any time. It may lend for the purpose of financing the project-planning and cost-estimating outlays, regardless of whether this work is done within the enterprise or contracted out; presumably in the past these expenditures could not be financed on credit. Loans may now be granted for any form of innovation—not only for investments to increase consumer goods production, as in the past.[57] Proposals for further liberalization of credit financing continue to be promoted by those who wish to see this method extended.[58]

Proponents of bank-financed investment argue that such investment is subject to better control than investment financed by direct grants.[59] This may, if true, be an advantage from the point of view of the State. The very strictness of bank control, however, is one of the factors that discourages enterprises from seeking bank credits. We read, for example, that local bank officers are so restricted by the regulations governing loans that they are unable to respond "flexibly" to enterprise needs.[60] The bank is also very stiff about loans not repaid on time. The interest rate automatically rises to 5 percent, and further credit is completely cut off, even if only two or three months more work are needed to complete the project.[61] Thus, an innovation financed by the bank can lead to problems if it is not immediately successful. The requirement that loans be repaid out of the Production Development Fund, rather than out of the net profit of the innovation financed by the loan, was intended to make borrowing more attractive. In some cases, however, it has had the opposite effect; the size of the Production Development Fund of an enterprise may not be sufficient to cover its repayment and interest obligations to the bank.[62] Such enterprises have to dip into their other funds that may again be a source of financial difficulties.

Finally, investment financed by State Bank credits, like that financed from the Production Development Fund, suffers special handicaps in the supply of materials and equipment. Those problems are peculiar to decentralized investment. An enterprise's centralized investment is also part of the state supply plan, but when innovation is financed from decentralized sources the central planning system makes no formal provision for the real resources to be made available. Hence, even when financial resources are available, bank-financed innovation may fail simply for the lack of real resources.[63]

State Bank financing of decentralized investment continues to be regarded as "disadvantageous" by enterprises. They continue to prefer such other sources of finance as budget grants, retained earnings, and their own Production Development Funds, and turn to bank credits only if all other possible sources are exhausted.[64] The most optimistic proponents anticipate that bank financing will eventually account for about 20 percent of total capital investments in industry.[65] Given the attitudes of enterprises, however, it is not likely that the volume will increase much beyond the 1 or 2 percent attained in the mid-sixties, unless other sources of finance are deliberately reduced in amount.

The effect of credit financing of decentralized investment in innovation may be evaluated in both quantitative and qualitative terms. Has the availability of bank credits increased the total volume of decentralized investment? The answer depends on what alternative sources of finance were available. If credit financing were simply abolished and no other financial resources substituted for it, the volume of decentralized investment would obviously decline by that amount. But if the same quantity of funds were made available by budget grants or by an increase in the size of the Production Development Funds, the volume of decentralized investment is not likely to be changed at all. It might in fact be larger because of the greater attractiveness of those forms of finance. In any event, the volume of decentralized investment is not determined by the quantity of financing but by the quantity of real resources available for that purpose. Insufficient provision for financing may cause the volume of investment to be less than it might otherwise be. But an increased supply of financial resources cannot produce a greater volume of investment than can be sustained by the planned supply of real resources.

Given the volume of real resources allocated for decentralized investment, the question is whether they are better utilized when financed by bank credits or by Production Development Funds. Proponents of credit finance argue that that method imposes an economic discipline on enterprises. The obligation to repay the loans with interest obliges management to search for more profitable innovation and to select the cost-minimizing variants. The argument is probably valid, for although there is some ministry supervision over the use of the Production Development Fund, it is probably less carefully evaluated than the applications for bank credits.

This potential advantage of bank financing is subverted, however, by the existence of the Production Development Fund. The enterprise can simply finance its least productive innovations out of its own Production Development Fund and use bank credits only for those that can pass the scrutiny of the bank officials. Hence bank financing does not necessarily raise the general quality of decentralized innovation. It may simply siphon off the better ones, leaving the poorer to be financed by the Production Development Fund. It follows that the establishment of the Production Development Fund was an error. Given the planned volume of resources allocated for decentralized investment in innovation, the quality of that innovative activity may have been higher if the financial resources were supplied solely through the banking system, operating as a sort of capital market.

This conclusion applies only to decentralized investment. In the case of centralized investment, we have argued above that the innovation decision is influenced very little by the organization of the supply of financial resources through budget grants or bank credits. In centralized investment, however, the investment projects are selected in advance and the real resources allocated to them in the plan. No inducement is required to assure that the resources will be used for the planned purposes. Investment activity is determined by the plan and is not affected by the structure of financial organization. In decentralized investment, however, the real resources may be made available by the plan, but enterprise initiative plays a major role in determining whether and how they will be used. One may therefore expect that the innovation decision will be more sensitive to the structural properties of the economic system.

6.4. Financing Product Innovation

The financial arrangements discussed thus far have dealt primarily with the promotion of process innovation rather than product innovation. This emphasis on process innovation in our account is not accidental. It reflects the relative degree of attention that the governors of the economy have in fact given to the two kinds of innovation. The main thrust of economic policy has always been in the direction of cost reduction. Next to the rapid growth of output, cost reduction has had the highest priority in the design of the structure of the economic organization. It is perhaps for this reason that the first measures to cope with the financial obstacles to innovation dealt with cost-reducing process innovation. The prewar measures discussed earlier—the Enterprise Fund and the State Bank credits—provided decentralized financing for the users of new production equipment and processes. No special attention was paid to the financial problems of the producers of new equipment and products.

Neglect of Product Innovation

This one-sided approach to the innovation process is rather puzzling. After all, one man's process is another man's product. Someone must produce a new material or machine before someone else can adopt it in his own production process. Moreover, in a centrally planned socialist economy one would expect that the adoption of new products would pose much less of a problem than their production. If producers introduced new models and products and discontinued older ones at an optimal rate, there ought to be no particular problem in distributing the new models and products among users. The great potential advantage of the centrally planned economy over the market economy is that, in the former, it is the state of supply that limits production. In the latter, it is the state of demand. To promote innovation in a market economy system one would concentrate on stimulating the demand for new products to encourage an increase in the supply. But in a centrally planned system, one would concentrate on stimulating the supply of new products, leaving it to the planners to distribute them among the users.

The Soviet leaders rejected this line of reasoning at the inception of the great burst of industrialization in the early 1930s. The advanced technology available then was overwhelmingly of foreign origin, embodied in physical machinery and equipment and imported at great cost.[66] As a relatively backward country, the USSR had no influence at all over the rate at which new products appeared on the market; that depended entirely on the structure and policies of the advanced capitalist countries. The governors of the Soviet economy could buy only what they needed as each wave of new machinery and equipment products appeared in the capitalist markets and strive to ensure that they were installed and operating as quickly and efficiently as possible. It was under this set of circumstances that the structure of the Soviet economy was formed.

The one-sided preoccupation with the demand for and utilization of new technology made excellent sense as long as the supply—the rate at which new products appeared—was entirely beyond the influence of the Soviet governors. By the late 1930s, however, the policy regarding imports had changed. Domestic production of new products was substituted for imports. With this change, the rate at which new products appeared was no longer beyond the influence of Soviet policies and practices. On the contrary, it now depended very much on the structure of the Soviet economy and the policies of its governors. A poor structure or policy could conceivably reduce the supply of new products to the Soviet economy to very low levels, and indeed to zero.

One might guess that the structure of economic organization would have been altered in order to give a new impetus to the supply of new products. But it was not. The basic structure remained the same, and such modifications as were introduced continued to operate on the demand rather than the supply side. Reforms in the structure of financial flows, as we have shown, were designed to stimulate the adoption of new products and processes, via the Enterprise Fund and State Bank credits. The supply of new products received no special encouragement.

Other reasons may be adduced for the relative neglect of the supply side of innovation. The policy of high rates of investment relegated con-sumer-goods production to a secondary status. Its growth rate was smaller, wages and salary rates were lower, the quality of personnel was correspondingly poorer, and expenditures for R & D were smaller. Given the low rate of growth of personal disposable real income, no great encouragement was given to the innovation of new industrial con-sumer products. It would be wrong to evaluate Soviet innovative capac-ity by its poor performance in consumer-product innovation. It is not that they could not do it; they never really tried.

A policy of neglect of product innovation in a major sector of the economy may have had a similar, if unintended, effect on other sectors. In capitalist economies, consumer products are a dominating sector of innovative activity, with extensive "backward linkages" into the materi-als and machinery industries. One can hardly imagine a policy to re-press innovation in consumer products that would not have a strong repressive effect on innovation in industrial products as well. In fact, where the structure of particular industries does inhibit innovation, such as the machine-tool and building-construction industries, innova-tion is also retarded in the industries from which they buy and to which they sell.[67]

This is not to say that a "dual economy" is not possible. The specula-tion is rather that product innovation in Soviet industry may have been negatively affected by its deliberate repression in one of its large sec-tors—the consumer-goods industries.

Finally, the rate of product innovation was limited by a technological policy that favored a small number of basic models of a given type of product and long periods of time between model changes. The advan-tages of this policy were several. Fewer models permit longer produc-tion runs for each, with attending economies of scale. Infrequent model changes enable costs to fall continuously, in contrast to the periodic jumps in start-up costs when new models are introduced with greater frequency. Perhaps a further advantage of this policy was that it placed fewer strains on the organizational and labor-training skills of the rela-tively inexperienced managerial force.

The policy had certain noteworthy disadvantages, however. The fewer the number of models, the less specialized they are in particular produc-tion uses, and the higher the costs of the goods produced with their use. If there were but a single all-purpose tractor for all manner of agricul-tural, construction, and logging uses, the tractor would be relatively inefficient in all those uses. But if there were three models designed for the three special uses, each would be substantially more efficient. And if there were several submodels of agricultural tractors specialized for different regions and jobs, agricultural production costs would be still lower.

Moreover, if a tractor model has been in production for several years, technological advances over that period permit a new model to be produced with higher performance characteristics. With each passing year, those characteristics improve. At some date, the (possibly) higher cost of producing the new model instead of the older will be more than offset by the lower costs of operating the new tractor. To continue producing the old model after that date would be wasteful of resources.

There exists, in other words, some optimal number of model types and some optimal production duration for a model. It is wasteful both to exceed and to fall short of those optima. Critics claim that the structure of a modern capitalist economy leads to nonoptimal results, in the form of an excessive number of models of a given type and excessively frequent model changes. In the Soviet case, it is often thought that the results are also nonoptimal, but for the opposite reasons.

Financing Production Start-up Costs[68]

Whatever the reasons for the neglect of product innovation, it was not until the late 1950s that the matter commanded the special attention of the system's governors. The nature of the problem had long been discussed by economists in connection with the innovation task known as *osvoenie*. For lack of a standard English term, *osvoenie* is usually translated literally as the "mastery" or the "assimilation" of new technology. The concept normally refers to product innovation rather than process innovation.[69] It refers to that part of the overall innovation chain that begins after the applied-research and basic development work is completed and an enterprise begins putting the new product into production. It ends when the new installation has attained its design capacity and production costs have fallen to the planned level. We shall use the term "production start-up" as a rough rendering of the meaning of *osvoenie*.

Production start-up involves a series of costs not incurred by the producer of an established product. Two stages of start-up are usually distinguished. The first, or "production-preparation" stage (*podgotovka proizvodstva*), is the period before the first production run begins, during which extensive expenditures are made for such purposes as design work, prototype construction, sometimes the purchase and acquisition of new equipment, and testing. Most of the attention of analysts, however, has been given to the second, or "break-in" stage, which follows the first production run.[70] Production costs tend to be high at the start of break-in as unforeseen design and production problems arise and need to be corrected, workers need to develop new skills, and the scale of production is small. Costs subsequently fall rapidly and eventually reach a stable level. How an enterprise reacts to this predictable cost behavior depends on the structure of prices and incentives, which will be discussed presently. But it also depends on the structure of organization, in this case, on the organization of the flow of financial resources.

Before 1960, all start-up costs were eventually to be recovered by the innovator in the revenues from the sale of the new product. Generally start-up expenses were capitalized and included in the calculated cost of producing the product. The price of the product was then set sufficiently high to enable the enterprise to recover the start-up costs out of future sales revenues. This method of financing created certain problems for the innovator, for while start-up expenses are included in the product price, months or years may elapse before the first production runs are made, and an even longer period is required to recover them fully out of accumulated revenues from sales. In the absence of other sources of finance during that period, start-up expenses must be financed out of the enterprise's working capital or by resort to bank credits. The problem is compounded by the uncertainty associated with innovational activity, and the unanticipated expenses that frequently upset financial plans. For these reasons the act of product innovation may run the enterprise into financial difficulties. An organizational structure for the supply of financial resources through the pricing mechanism alone is therefore an impediment to product innovation.

The New Products Fund[71]

In response to the mounting evidence of producer resistance to product innovation, a new mode of financing was introduced. In June 1959 the Central Committee of the Party recommended the creation of a special centralized[72] fund to finance start-up costs.[73] The Party recommendation was incorporated in a government decree in 1960.[74] Initially the measure was confined to the machinery and metalworking industries, but subsequent legislation extended it to such other producer-goods industries as chemicals, petroleum, petrochemicals, and paper. More recently, similar funds appear to have been made available for some consumer-goods industries. [75] The centralized financing of product innovation is still not the general practice but operates only in those industries where it is authorized by government order. [76]

The New Products Fund (*Fond osvoeniia novoi tekhniki*) is administered by the ministry. It is formed by contributions from all the ministry's enterprises, in proportion to their total production costs. The proportions vary from industry to industry, ranging from 0.3 percent of total planned cost of production in the metals industries to 3.0 percent in the heavy machinery industries. In 1969 the total of all ministry New Product Funds amounted to over 1 billion rubles a year, accounting for about 16 percent of the total financing of innovation in industry. [77] About half of the total was concentrated in the machinery manufacturing industries. [78]

The enterprise treats its contribution to the fund as part of its total production costs. To qualify for grants from the fund, the enterprise undertaking a product innovation applies to the ministry by presenting a documented case including cost estimates. The ministry then selects those projects that promise the greatest returns, within the limits of the size of the fund. Enterprises that do not qualify must finance their start-up costs as before, on the basis of their own financial resources. [79]

Limitations on the use of the fund. In evaluating the impact of the fund on the financial position of product innovators, a number of limitations on its use must be noted. First, the product must be defined as "new" within the meaning of the regulations. A new product is defined as new if (a) it is the first instance of its production in the USSR, or (b) no more than two years have elapsed since it was first introduced in the USSR. [80] Hence the fund is not intended to finance the full diffusion of a new product but only its diffusion for the two years following its first appearance in the USSR. The ministry publishes an annual list of the products that qualify for grants from the fund.

The second limitation is more substantial. Of the two stages of production start-up, the greater attention has always been paid to the break-in stage. "The largest share of start-up costs are incurred after production has begun, in the first few years following the start of regular production." [81] It is therefore curious that the first legislation on the financing production start-up did not deal with break-in costs at all. Indeed it was expressly forbidden to use the New Products Fund for financing those costs. The fund was strictly reserved for the financing of production-preparation costs. Any expenses incurred after the moment the first production rolled off the line could not be paid for out of the fund. Because of this limitation, many economists feel that the fund tackled the minor part of the problem, leaving the major part unresolved.[82] In response to these criticisms, that restriction has gradually been relaxed. The 1965 Economic Reform authorized the use of the fund for financing part of the break-in costs during the first year of production.[83] In 1971, a further relaxation authorized its use "in some cases" even in the second year of production.[84] Nevertheless the New Products Fund should be regarded primarily as a source of finance for production-preparation expenses. The financing of the high break-in costs continues to be the responsibility of the innovating enterprise, with no substantial assist from the New Products Fund.

Certain other limitations may be noted. The size of the fund is not sufficient to cover all production-preparation costs of all product innovators. The balance of their start-up costs, as before, must be financed out of their own working capital.[85] The fund may be used only by producers of new products; none of it may be used to finance the start-up costs of the adopters who first use the new machine or material in their own production processes.[86] New Products Funds have been authorized only in certain industries and may not be used in others. The fund may be used only to finance new products that enterprises are ordered to innovate by the ministry and are included in the Ministry Plan or the National Economic Plan. Only in exceptional cases may enterprise-initiated product innovation be financed by the fund.[87] The amounts enterprises receive from the fund each month are based on estimates submitted in advance and officially approved. Costs incurred in excess of the estimates may not be reimbursed by the fund but are financed out of working capital.[88] In view of the uncertainty associated with product innovation, this is a considerable limitation.

Administrative problems. While no one questions the desirability of encouraging product innovation, a number of questions have been raised about the appropriateness of the New Products Fund as the administrative device for achieving that end. One line of criticism notes that the fund suffers from the perpetual problems of subsidy financing.[89] When start-up costs are financed by the enterprise itself out of its own working capital, or by repayable bank credits, there is a certain incentive to economize. But when they are subsidized by the New Products Fund, the incentive to economize is reduced; or worse, an incentive is created to inflate cost estimates to justify larger grants.[90] The fund inevitably comes to be used for financing not only the necessary start-up costs but also excessive costs that may be due purely to mismanagement and incompetence.[91] Because of the subsidy element, enterprises always prefer to use the fund rather than apply for bank credits.[92] Some authors have urged that a set of norms be established, to limit the subsidy that the enterprise may claim for each expenditure item.[93] The pressure for tighter controls reflects the hidden costs always associated with subsidy schemes. Since the enterprise cannot be counted on to economize, additional resources must be allocated for the purpose of outside supervision and control.

The administration of the New Products Fund by the ministries has also evoked various expressions of dissatisfaction from enterprises. The official instructions that govern the use to which it may be put are described by one analyst as so vague that the enterprise is never clear just what kinds of costs can be financed and how the subsidized costs affect the price that may be charged.[94] Enterprises are supposed to compete for grants from the fund on the basis of the quality of their proposals. Instead, writes one director, the funds are distributed in a "formalistic" way, on the principle of "a little bit to everybody."[95] The consequence is that most enterprises receive such small grants as to greatly reduce the fund's incentive effect for all. The Kommunard Automotive Plant and the Melitopol Motor Plant spent 6.9 million rubles and 4.5 million rubles on product innovation but received from the fund subsidies of only 580,000 and 159,000 rubles.[96] The director of a highly innovative firm complains of the complexity of the financing arrangements. "The funds are transferred to the Ministry, and then we have to spend a lot of time, and write mountains of paper, in order to get them back." He then voiced a sentiment that must be shared by many directors, not only with respect to the New Products Fund but to their managerial activities in general: "If they trust us . . . to use our own judgment in spending the Material Incentive Fund and the Production Development Fund, why don't they trust us to spend these 114,000 rubles?"[97]

While enterprises chafe under ministry controls over the use of the fund, the controls are not so strict as to prevent enterprises from using it for purposes they deem more important than the legislated purpose. It was estimated that, in 1965, 10.5 percent of the grants from the New Product Funds were used for such unauthorized purposes as increasing the working capital of enterprises; in 1969, the percentage had risen to 13 percent.[98] The Ukrainian Ministry of the Iron and Steel Industry spent 217,000 rubles of the fund for increasing working capital and 2.3 million rubles for road building.[99]

In the administration of the fund one can glimpse some of the factors that contribute to excessive innovation lead times. It takes so long to receive payments from the fund that enterprises "are compelled to divert their own or borrowed funds to the new product."[100] Such delays are perhaps inevitable in bureaucracies of all kinds. More interesting is the effect of the centrally planned organization of the economy. To qualify for a grant, the new product must usually be included in the officially approved annual plan. If the decision to innovate is made after the annual plan is confirmed, "they have to wait eight to ten months or more, when it can be included in the plan for the following year. This situation, in our opinion, conflicts with the principle of rational coordination between central planning and enterprise independence."[101]

Conclusion. In evaluating the effect of the New Products Fund on the product-innovation decision, we may note first that much of it remains unused each year. The proportion of the accumulated funds that is actually paid out to innovating enterprises varies by industry, ranging from 65 percent to 90 percent.[102] Moreover, of the funds paid out a significant proportion is used for purposes other than product innovation. The data suggest that the decision to innovate has not been greatly stimulated by the fund. Part of the explanation may be the limitations on its use and the administrative problems discussed earlier. The chief reason, however, is probably the continued unprofitability of new products relative to older ones. The New Products Fund has reduced the degree of unprofitability, but its quantitative effect cannot have been very large.

Even in cases in which large proportions of innovation costs are financed from the New Products Fund, new products continue to be produced at a loss. The Baku Dry Transformer Plant financed 43 percent of its outlays on new products from the Fund and the Dushabin Armature Plant 51 percent, but in both cases the new products were produced at a loss.[103] The Petrov Petroleum Equipment Plant spent 656,000 rubles on the innovation of four new products but received a grant of only 360,000 rubles from the New Products Fund. The other costs were charged to their general cost of production, reducing the profit rate on the other products.[104]

Hence, while the New Product Fund may have reduced some of the resistance to product innovation, the major source of that resistance has not been removed. Innovation activity continues to be concentrated on process innovation. In 1970, only 7 percent of the innovation plans of enterprises consisted of product-innovation activity. But 60 percent was devoted to the mechanization and automation of production processes.[105] The chief impediments to product innovation are to be found not in organizational structure, however, but in the structure of prices and incentives.

Notes

1. Louvan E. Nolting, *Sources of Financing the Stages of the Research, Development, and Innovation Cycle in the U.S.S.R.*, Foreign Economic Report No. 3 (Washington, D.C.: U.S. Department of Commerce, Bureau of Economic Analysis, September 1973), p. 10. The term "science" as used in Soviet financial reporting does not correspond to the widely used Frascati definition of R & D. It includes the social sciences and the humanities, for example, and excludes R & D expenditures financed from the state budget. The official data therefore provide only a rough approximation of the magnitudes involved in the financing of R & D. See E. Zaleski, J. P. Kozlowski, H. Wienert, R. W. Davies, M. J. Berry, and R. Amman, *Science Policy in the USSR* (Paris: OECD, 1969), pp. 95-124.

2. Nolting, *Sources of Financing*, pp. 19-26. These figures refer to the state budget appropriations for "science." In addition, a certain volume of R & D work is financed by state budget appropriations for other categories such as "defense," "financing the national economy," and "education."

3. Ibid., p. 19.

4. Zaleski et al., *Science Policy in the USSR*, pp. 107-109. Another ministry fund that appears to be coming into wider use is called the Unified Fund for the Development of Science and Technology. See Nolting, *Sources of Financing*, pp. 33-34.

5. The question of whether the ministry fund should be charged against their enterprises' costs of production or treated as a deduction from their profits is a subject of controversy. The Ministry of the Electrical Equipment Industry is experimenting with the practice of forming the fund by deductions from profits. *Planovoe khoziaistvo*, 1971, No. 10, p. 24.

6. S. Rogovtsev, *Finansovoe planirovanie na promyshlennykh predpriiatiiakh* (Financial Planning in Industrial Enterprises) (Moscow: *Finansy*, 1966), p. 27, column 13.

7. Kenneth J. Arrow, "Economic Welfare and the Allocation of Resources for Invention," National Bureau of Economic Research, *The Rate and Direction of Inventive Activity: Economic and Social Factors* (Princeton: Princeton University Press, 1962), pp. 614-619.

8. A. M. Kovalevskii, *Tekhpromfinplan v novykh usloviakh i tipovaia metodika ego razrabotki* (The Enterprise Plan under the New Conditions and the Standard Manual for Preparing It) (Moscow: *Ekonomika*, 1968), p. 206.

9. E. Zaleski et al., *Science Policy in the USSR*, pp. 466-467.

10. See Section 6.3.

11. Kovalevskii, *Tekhpromfinplan*, p. 106.

12. *Voprosy ekonomiki*, 1967, No. 7, p. 41.

13. Similar problems arise in all subsidy financing. See the discussion of the New Products Fund, Sec. 6.4.

14. N. E. Droginskii and V. G. Starodubrovskii, eds., *Osnovy i praktika khoziaistvennoi reformy v SSSR* (The Basis and Practice of the USSR Economic Reform) (Moscow: *Ekonomika*, 1971), p. 400. The requirement is expressed as a "recoupment period" of up to five years. The recoup-

ment period is defined as the ratio of the cost of the investment project to the annual profit. If a project that costs 1 million rubles is expected to yield an annual profit of 200,000 rubles, the recoupment period is five years.

15. Ibid., pp. 402-403.

16. *Finansy SSSR*, 1972, No. 2, p. 48.

17. Droginskii and Starodubrovskii, *Osnovy i praktika*, p. 401.

18. P. G. Bunich, "Finansirovanie vnedreniia novoi tekhniki" (Financing Innovation) in *Sovershenstvovanie planirovaniia i uluchshenie ekonomicheskoi raboty v narodnom khoziaistve* (Perfecting Planning and Improving Economic Activity) (Moscow: *Ekonomika*, 1969), p. 200.

19. Droginskii and Starodubrovskii, *Osnovy i praktika*, p. 404.

20. The rate of profit is a matter of concern as far as the incentive to innovate is involved; but here the issue is not incentives but the supply of financial resources.

21. Joseph S. Berliner, *Factory and Manager in the USSR* (Cambridge: Harvard University Press, 1957), Chaps. 6 and 7.

22. *Planovoe khoziaistvo*, 1967, No. 3, p. 71.

23. *Voprosy ekonomiki*, 1967, No. 7, p. 41.

24. Maurice Dobb, *Soviet Economic Development Since 1917* (New York: International Publishers, 1966), pp. 391-392.

25. G. D. Anisimov and I.A. Vakhlamov, eds., *Material'noe stimulirovanie vnedreniia novoi tekhniki: spravochnik* (Handbook of Material Incentives for Innovation) (Moscow: *Ekonomika*, 1966), pp. 58-59.

26. *Voprosy ekonomiki*, 1966, No. 8, p. 115.

27. The following description relies heavily on *Planovoe khoziaistvo*, 1967, No. 3, pp. 70-74.

28. *Voprosy ekonomiki*, 1966, No. 8, p. 116.

29. *Planovoe khoziaistvo*, 1967, No. 3, pp. 72-73.

30. These coefficients are computed by the ministry for various groups of its enterprises. For an explanation of how they are computed, see ibid., which is the source of the illustrative calculations.

31. In 1970 industry spent 3.34 billion rubles out of the Production Development Fund (TsSU, *Narodnoe khoziaistvo SSSR v 1970 godu*) (The USSR Economy in 1970) (Moscow: *Statistika*, 1971), p. 728. In the Ukraine, 76.8 percent of the expenditures from that fund was used for capital investment (*Finansy SSSR*, 1972, No. 3, p. 24). By assuming the same percentage applies to all industry, the all-industry expenditure for capital investment was 2.57 billion rubles. Total capital investment in industry in 1970 was 29.6 billion rubles (TsSU, *Narodnoe khoziaistvo*, cited above, p. 483). Hence investment financed from the Production Development Fund is about 9 percent of the total.

32. *Voprosy ekonomiki*, 1966, No. 3, p. 19.

33. I. V. Maevskii, *Tekhnicheskii progress i rost proizvoditel'nosti truda* (Technical Progress and the Growth of Labor Productivity) (Moscow: *Ekonomizdat*, 1963), p. 113.

34. TsSU, *Narodnoe khoziaistvo SSSR v 1970 godu* (The USSR Economy in 1970) (Moscow: *Statistika*, 1971), p. 728.

35. *Planovoe khoziaistvo*, 1967, No. 4, pp. 16-17. In that article Dr. Federenko recommends that enterprises be permitted to carry over unspent balances. Another author, however, reports that balances may be carried over (ibid., 1967, No. 2, p. 57). Possibly different rules apply in different ministries.

36. *Ekonomicheskaia gazeta*, 1967, No. 11, p. 12.

37. *Finansy SSSR*, 1971, No. 4, p. 52.

38. Ibid., 1972, No. 2, p. 24.

39. *Planovoe khoziaistvo*, 1967, No. 3, p. 73.

40. Ibid.

41. *Ekonomicheskaia gazeta*, 1966, No. 10, p. 13.

42. Ibid., 1968, No. 10, p. 12.
43. Ibid., p. 13.
44. *Voprosy ekonomiki*, 1967, No. 4, p. 36.
45. Ibid., No. 3, p. 36; *Ekonomicheskaia gazeta*, 1967, No. 37, p. 14.
46. *Planovoe khoziaistvo*, 1967, No. 3, pp. 70-71.
47. Ibid., 1966, No. 5, pp. 72-73.
48. Ibid., 1967, No. 3, p. 74; *Ekonomicheskaia gazeta*, 1967, No. 34, p. 14.
49. Anisimov and Vakhlamov, *Material'noe stimulirovanie*, p. 79; *Narodnoe khoziaistvo SSSR v 1970 godu*, p. 736.
50. Anisimov and Vakhlamov, *Material'noe stimulirovanie*, p. 79.
51. Ibid., pp. 79-83.
52. *Planovoe khoziaistvo*, 1967, No. 3, p. 71.
53. *Voprosy ekonomiki*, 1966, No. 1, p. 116.
54. Ibid., 1964, No. 3, p. 47.
55. Anisimov and Vakhlamov, *Material'noe stimulirovanie*, p. 84.
56. *Ekonomicheskaia gazeta*, 1966, No. 2, p. 30. Also *Voprosy ekonomiki*, 1966, No. 11, p. 6.
57. Ibid., 1967, No. 20, pp. 9-10.
58. Ibid., 1966, No. 2, p. 34.
59. *Voprosy ekonomiki*, 1966, No. 1, p. 114.
60. *Literaturnaia gazeta*, December 24, 1966, p. 2. See also Anisimov and Vakhlamov, *Material'noe stimulirovanie*, p. 84.
61. *Voprosy ekonomiki*, 1966, No. 1, p. 117.
62. *Ekonomicheskaia gazeta*, 1967, No. 57, p. 11.
63. *Voprosy ekonomiki*, 1966, No. 1, p. 115.
64. *Planovoe khoziaistvo*, 1967, No. 3, p. 71.
65. Ibid., 1966, No. 12, p. 20.
66. The technology was also contained in the heads of the many foreign advisers hired to assist in and supervise the installation and operation of the new technology and to help train the labor force. The data on the role of foreign technical assistance may be found in Antony C. Sutton, *Western Technology and Soviet Economic Development, 1917 to 1930* (Stanford: Hoover Institutions, 1968), and same author, *Western Technology and Soviet Economic Development, 1930 to 1945* (Stanford: Hoover Institution, 1971).
67. A. D. Little, *Patterns and Problems of Technical Innovation in American Industry*, Report to the National Science Foundation, U.S. Department of Commerce (PB 181573) (Washington: September 1963), p. 111.
68. This section deals primarily with questions of financing start-up costs. Start-up costs are investigated in greater detail in Section 10.3, in the general discussion of costs of innovation.
69. In the most common usage, *osvoenie* refers to product innovation and *vnedrenie* to process innovation. The distinction is not always maintained in practice, however, and some authors use the terms interchangeably.
70. The term *osvoenie* sometimes refers only to the break-in stage.
71. This section deals only with financial aspects of the New Products Fund. For a discussion of its economic efficiency, see Section 10.4.
72. The fund is not centralized at the level of the national government, which is the usual meaning of the term "centralized." It is the ministry that is the agency for the centralized collection and distribution of the fund among its own enterprises. Perhaps it should be referred to as "semicentralized."
73. G. D. Anisimov, *Printsip material'noi zainteresovannosti v razvitii novoi tekhniki* (The Principle of Material Self-Interest in the Development of New Technology) (Moscow: *Ekonomizdat*, 1962), p. 108. An additional reason for the new fund was to permit new-product prices to be reduced in order to encourage adoption.

74. V. S. Sominskii, *Ekonomika novykh proizvodstv* (The Economics of New Production) (Moscow: *Ekonomika*, 1965), p. 203.

75. P. S. Mstislavskii, M. G. Gabrieli, and Iu. V. Borozdin, *Ekonomicheskoe obosnovanie ptovykh tsen na novuiu promyshlennuiu produktsiu* (The Economic Rationale of Wholesale Prices for New Industrial Production) (Moscow: *Nauka*, 1968), p. 109.

76. Anisimov and Vakhlamov, *Material'noe stimulirovanie* pp. 61-62.

77. *Planovoe khoziaistvo*, 1971, No. 3, p. 37.

78. G. D. Anisimov et al., eds., *Nauchno-tekhnicheskii progress i khoziaistvennaia reforma* (Scientific-Technical Progress and Economic Reform) (Moscow: *Nauka*, 1969), p. 208.

79. Anisimov and Vakhlamov, *Material'noe stimulirovanie*, pp. 63-65.

80. *Planovoe khoziaistvo*, 1971, No. 3, p. 36. In some instances the period is extended. In the chemicals, paper, and petroleum industries the period is three years. *Voprosy ekonomiki*, 1972, No. 6, p. 120.

81. Anisimov et al., *Nauchno-teckhnicheskii progress*, p. 20.

82. *Voprosy ekonomiki*, 1966, No. 4, p. 147.

83. *Finansy SSSR*, 1971, No. 4, p. 51.

84. *Voprosy ekonomiki*, 1972, No. 6, p. 119. The report refers to the second year of *osvoenie*. It is assumed that the term in this case refers to the break-in stage, not to the entire start-up period.

85. *Planovoe khoziaistvo*, 1971, No. 3, p. 36. Recommendations often appear for extending the range of expenditures that may be financed from the fund. One author urges that it be used to finance the payment of premium prices for materials needed to speed up the start-up time (*Planovoe khoziaistvo*, 1966, No. 10, p. 85). Another proposes that it be used for the purchase of equipment needed for start-up, and for training expenses (*Ekonomicheskaia gazeta*, 1966, No. 2, p. 31.

86. *Planovoe khoziaistvo*, 1966, No. 11, p. 28.

87. *Voprosy ekonomiki*, 1972, No. 6, p. 120.

88. A. N. Komin, *Problemy planovogo tsenoobrazovaniia* (Problems of Planned Pricing) (Moscow: *Ekonomika*, 1971), p. 152.

89. The efficiency consequences of subsidization are discussed in Section 9.4.

90. Bunich, "*Finansirovanie*," p. 218.

91. *Ekonomicheskaia gazeta*, 1966, No. 2, p. 31; *Voprosy ekonomiki*, 1966, No. 3, p. 21.

92. Anisimov et al., *Nauchno-tekhnicheskii progress*, p. 219.

93. *Voprosy ekonomiki*, 1972, No. 6, p. 122.

94. *Planovoe khoziaistvo*, 1966, No. 11, p. 28.

95. *Ekonomicheskaia gazeta*, 1967, No. 34, p. 10.

96. *Planovoe khoziaistvo*, 1966, No. 11, p. 28.

97. *Ekonomicheskaia gazeta*, 1967, No. 33, p. 11.

98. *Planovoe khoziaistvo*, 1971, No. 3, p. 37. For earlier years the reported percentages of misappropriated funds are much higher, in the range of 35 to 50 percent. The figures are probably not comparable in coverage. See E. Zaleski et al., *Science Policy in the USSR*, p. 111.

99. *Voprosy ekonomiki*, 1972, No. 6, p. 121. See also Sec. 6.3 regarding misuse of the Production Development Fund. Whatever the purposes of the various funds, the Ukrainians seem to manage to use them for building up their highway system.

100. Anisimov, *Nauchno-tekhnicheskii progress*, p. 214.

101. *Voprosy ekonomiki*, 1972, No. 6, p. 120. Other proposals for the reform of the New Products Fund are reported in E. Zaleski et al., *Science Policy in the USSR*, pp. 112-113.

102. Anisimov, *Nauchno-tekhnicheskii progress*, p. 219.

103. *Planovoe khoziaistvo*, 1971, No. 3, p. 35.

104. Anisimov, *Nauchno-tekhnicheskii progress*, p. 206.

105. *Planovoe khoziaistvo*, 1971, No. 3, p. 37.

Chapter 7

The Demand for New Products

Preceding chapters have dealt with the supply of inputs to the innovating enterprise. To conclude the analysis of organizational structure, we turn now to the demand for the innovator's products.

If the subject of study were a capitalist economy, there would be nothing unusual about a chapter devoted to the influence of demand on the innovation decision. One would have wondered in fact why it had not come earlier. For it is the demand for the new product—or what the innovator hopes will be the demand for his new product—that energizes the innovation process. In most cases it is the growth rate of demand that determines the rate of diffusion of a new product from innovators to users.[1] It is for the purpose of creating and expanding demand that the innovator spends substantial sums on advertising and marketing. One would expect that the rate of innovation under capitalism would depend significantly on the way in which the marketing system is organized to satisfy the demand for new products.

It is far from self-evident that the same should be true of a centrally planned socialist economy. One would expect that the system of planning would eliminate the need for the elaborate marketing operations that capitalism seems to require, or at least to employ. In the absence of competition and of producers' motivation to manipulate the desires of consumers, high-pressure advertising ought to find no place. One might properly expect the satisfaction of demand, especially in the industrial sector, to be a relatively simple matter of seeing that whatever is produced finds its way smoothly to the enterprises for which it was produced in the first place.

A casual glance at the literature might well confirm this view. None of the principal monographic studies of Soviet managerial behavior devote as much as a chapter to the marketing of industrial commodities.[2] Past research, however, has examined enterprise behavior primarily from the static point of view of efficiency of resource allocation. Anyone approaching the Soviet economy with this objective in mind would indeed discover that from the enterprises' standpoint satisfying the demand for one's output posed few problems; all the problems lay on the supply side. But when the perspective shifts from static efficiency to the capacity to generate and diffuse innovation, the relationship between supply-

and-demand factors is very different. The problem of demand emerges as a very much more important element relative to supply. Hence if a chapter on marketing is itself something of an innovation in the study of the Soviet enterprise, it is because the topic of study is innovation.

7.1. Effectiveness of the Sales System

The arrangements for distributing the output of enterprises parallels those for the purchasing of materials described in Chapter 3. When the State Planning Committee has secured the government's approval of its distribution plan for the year, the State Committee on Supply proceeds to administer the planned distribution. At various places through the economy certain organizations are designated as allocation centers (*fondoderzhateli*) for the commodities. An allocation center receives from the State Committee on Supply the authority to decide which enterprises may receive specified amounts of various controlled commodities. Many different organizations may serve as the allocation centers for the output of a particular enterprise. Often the chief sales administration of the enterprise's own ministry may be the allocation center for some or all of the enterprise's output. Or the chief supply administration of a major customer ministry may be the allocation center for all or part of its output. One or more territorial supply administrations may also be designated. In the case of consumer goods various organizations of the trade system may be the allocation centers.

The allocation centers are responsible for informing the producers of their obligation to ship goods and for informing the customers of their right to receive those goods. In principle the full planned output of any enterprise should be equal to the sum of the allocations (*fondy*) distributed among those allocation centers that have the right to assign its output to their customers. The sum of the quantities in the allocation orders flowing into the enterprise's sales department in the course of the year should equal its planned output of controlled commodities.[3] The success with which the enterprise manages its sales program thus depends heavily on the efficient administrative work of its various allocation centers.

One might guess that in a disequilibrium market, what the enterprise loses on its input side it regains on its output side. In a seller's market the enterprise experiences difficulty in supplying itself with inputs, but for the same reason it should have no difficulty selling its output. In a buyer's market, its problem is to find customers for its output, but for the same reason it should have no difficulty obtaining its supplies from other overloaded sellers. Since the Soviet economy exhibits most of the attributes of a seller's market, the selling of one's output has in fact traditionally posed fewer problems than the procuring of one's inputs. The enterprise sales department is very much smaller than its purchasing department, and the substantial effort, both legal and illegal, associated with the procurement process is not matched by efforts at selling output.

Yet it would be a mistake to think that the sales process operates as smoothly as depicted in the formal description of the process, and that it does not generate taxing managerial problems. For the noninnovating manager who produces the same output year after year, these problems are a source of some concern, as we shall show in this section. But for the innovator of new products, the matter of selling output looms as a problem of major proportion, as the next section will argue.

Despite the condition of excess demand, enterprises sometimes encounter in their selling operations the same manifestations of inefficiency experienced in their supply operations. The wholesaling organizations evidently can still cancel orders with impunity. One enterprise was faced with the sudden cancellation of orders for a substantial portion of its output of gas shields. They shifted over to the production of new products, certain types of electrodes, but since they had no orders for them in their portfolio, they barely fulfilled their sales plan that year.[4] The problem that dominates the concern of sellers, however, is described by Director Baranov of the Engels Synthetic Fiber Combine. Our enterprise, he writes, is fulfilling its plan perfectly, in volume and assortment, according to the instructions from our chief administration. "And suddenly, thunder out of the clear sky! The allocation orders we receive for shipping our goods add up to less than we have produced. Where shall we put it all? It lies idle in our warehouse for a long time."[5]

A variety of causes may generate this kind of sales problem. One is the long-established practice of "clearance planning," in which the ministry assigns to its enterprises production targets, the sum of which exceeds the ministry's own target. This practice provides the ministry with a safety factor, so that in case some of its enterprises underfulfill their plans the ministry itself may nevertheless fulfill its plan.[6] If the enterprises all succeed in fulfilling their plans in such cases, the total output may exceed the volume of demand reflected in the allocation orders.

A second cause is the mismatching of supply and demand, an inevitable consequence of a central planning process that seeks to plan in the degree of detail that the Soviet system does. A study of the machine-tool industry noted that about 80 percent of all machined parts are smaller than 100 millimeters in diameter and 500 millimeters in length. But the machine-tool industry produces mostly medium and large-capacity tools, with the result that only 20 percent of the demand for small-sized lathes is satisfied.[7] Similarly, universal lathes with screw-cutting capacity are produced in greater number than is justified by the volume of screw-cutting operations.[8] Under the conditions of excess demand some customers may reluctantly agree to purchase equipment ill-suited to their production requirements, despite the higher production cost that entails. But producers will often find themselves with output produced in accordance with plan instructions, for which the ministry has not been able to find willing customers.

The cause most widely cited, however, is the slowness and inefficiency that often characterizes the management of the complex centralized distribution system.[9] At the beginning of 1967, for example, the central organization responsible for the distribution of automobile tires (All-Union Chief Chemicals Administration—*Soiuzglavkhim*) had not yet determined who were to receive the tire allocations for the year. Hence one tire manufacturer, the Voronezh Tire Plant, found that no allocation centers had yet been designated for the 121,000 tires the plan obliged it to produce in the first quarter. The enterprise appealed to its own chief administration (*Glavshinprom*) and to the State Committee on Supply, after which "customers were found, of course." But still things continued to move slowly. The North Caucasus Territorial Supply Administration was notified by the All-Union Chief Chemicals Administration of whom its tire suppliers would be on February 28, but the actual allocation orders designating the specific purchasers arrived in Voronezh only at the end of April, when the first quarter had already ended. Meanwhile, complained the irate director of the tire plant, his output was piling up, no revenues were flowing in, and he had finally to apply for a special interest-bearing loan from the State Bank to tide his plant over. "In a word, we lost thousands of rubles because of these delays which are the fault of the sales organizations."[10]

In the case of the Volgograd Meatpacking Combine, the allocation center for its output had been designated; it was the Rostov Meat and Fish Trade Center (*Rosmiasorybtorg*) of the Ministry of Trade. But no allocation orders had yet arrived for the combine's output of edible and industrial fats, huge inventories of which were piling up in the ware-houses. The combine officials wrote repeatedly to their ministry, to their regional administration, to the wholesale trade organization (*Ros-miasorybtorg*), and to the regional wholesale supply administration (*Rosglavpishchesnabsbytsyr'e*). "But," writes the deputy director, "not only did we receive no allocation orders; we didn't even receive a reply from anyone. And we have no legal power to sell it ourselves, since the merchandise is centrally allocated."

The special correspondent of the newspaper *Economic Gazette*, who looked into the matter, interviewed the trade people for their side of the story.

"I'm not at all disturbed," he was told by one official. "We take what we are supposed to take according to the amounts allocated to us, and the rest should be stored until the interseason period. But I will look into the situation at the Volgograd Plant, and we'll take some of the fats off their hands"—which they never actually did.

The correspondent also interviewed the enterprise's own chief adminis-tration who thought that the whole problem would be solved if their own ministry were placed in charge of the distribution of fats, instead of the Ministry of Trade. "If we were given the right to distribute fats, we would certainly find ways of selling them, and we would not be paying fines. . . . Without these middlemen, who do nothing to promote sales, things would be very different." Meanwhile, the enterprise had to continue producing fats, and even overfulfilled its plan, while thousands of rubles were going into storage costs and even larger penalties were being paid to the State Bank for having exceeded the legal limit on in-ventories. At the same time, the enterprise's bonus funds were falling, since they were operating under the new management system and their bonuses were based on sales volume.[11]

Why should such problems arise in a centrally planned economy, espe-cially one characterized by a prevailing seller's market? Part of the rea-son is that planning is inevitably less than perfect, for all the reasons described in Chapter 3. The problems of supply planning discussed there give rise to corresponding problems of selling. For example, the fact that statements of requirements are drawn up as early as April for the plan to begin in January of the following year is the source of much of the uncertainty and changeability in supply plans. What it means on the sales side is that some enterprises will be instructed to produce cer-tain output, which will later turn out to have no market because of the changes in their customers' plans.[12] But imperfections in planning are not the sole source of the sales problem. Certain of the difficulties just illustrated are rooted in the structure of economic organization and are likely to occur even with a much improved plan-making system. The structural feature that seems to be most at fault is that the units responsible for assigning the enterprise its output plans are not always responsible for assuring that the output is eventually sold. The output plans of the First and Second Moscow Watch Plants, for example, are based on the statements of requirements submitted early in the plan-making period by their chief customers, the Machinery and Instruments Foreign Trade Company (*Mashpriborintorg*) and the domestic trade organizations. "But these organizations bear no responsibility for assuring that the allocation orders are distributed on time, which is why these watch plants build up inventories of watches far in excess of their quotas."[13]

While it is true that the output targets of enterprises are largely derived from their customers' original statements of requirements, it is not the customers but the enterprise's own ministry that assigns or approves the targets. The Ministry of the Chemicals Industry and the All-Union Chief Chemicals Administration (*Souizglavkhim*) "prescribe the entire assortment of production of their enterprises, but as soon as selling problems arise, they wash their hands of it and leave the producers to shift for themselves."[14] It is for this reason that the Chief of the Planning Department of the famous Likhachev Automobile Plant urges that the central planners, who tell the enterprise what to produce, should also take full responsibility for finding a market for all planned output.[15] And the Director of the Omsk Synthetic Rubber Plant, complaining about the "chronic" sales problem caused by the shortage of allocation orders, demands that ways be found to make the responsible persons pay:

We understand, of course, that in any such matters mistakes can happen. But why must the enterprise people pay for them? Why must our enterprise's deputy directors sit for months in Moscow trying to get our rubber shipped out to the users? This is all incomprehensible, for both the rubber producers and the rubber consumers (the tire factories) are part of the same Ministry of the Petroleum Products and Petrochemical Industry; only their chief administrations are different.[16]

7.2. Sales Problems of Innovators
There are some strands of evidence that the sales problems of Soviet enterprises may have increased in severity in the past decade. In the

marketing of consumer goods it is clear that consumer resistance has become more effective and that enterprises are required to devote more attention to the marketing of consumer goods.[17] We read that even in the machinery-production industries the "absence of orders" has led to the curtailment of production.[18] It is alleged that the "tautness" of plans has been reduced in recent years, which may be expected to reduce the degree of excess demand and make selling less easy. Certain provisions of the 1965 Economic Reform, to be discussed later, may have increased the importance of successful selling activity in the concerns of management. Management is now evaluated on the basis of output actually sold, not simply output produced. In the past, enterprises like the Volgograd Meat-Packing Combine already referred to would not have been greatly concerned over the rising inventories of unsold fats; now, the failure to sell means the loss of income to the plant executives. The Reform also introduced a capital charge that enterprises have to pay on their capital stock, including inventories. Hence sellers' profits, which finance their bonuses, are reduced if their inventories of finished goods rise. The capital charge also applies to the materials inventories of customers who are now more reluctant to accept deliveries of materials or equipment they may not need. "Before the Reform," comments one writer, "the chief problem was shortages. Now surpluses are as bad as shortages. Hence, no one wants to pile up surpluses of supplies, even if they have allocation certificates for them."[19] Sentences like the last are a thoroughly new note on the Soviet economic scene.

If the sale of output has indeed become an increasing source of concern for management, the case we are about to make will have greater force. But even if selling problems were a relatively minor nuisance for Soviet managers, the case may still be made. For the significance of the sales procedures and problems associated with a given structure of economic organization depends on whether one is studying the management of economic affairs in general or the management of innovation in particular. If the focus is the management of given production processes, sales procedures and problems may be regarded as a rather peripheral matter. But if the focus is the management of changes in the production processes, the same sales procedures and problems loom as a major consideration, which we shall now proceed to show.

Resistance to New Products and Processes

"Your business is production," says the Soviet State to its enterprises.

"Don't worry about the distribution of your products—we'll take care of that." This is the bargain struck between managers and planners that underlies the centrally planned economy, although it is considerably modified in practice.

For the producer of an established product it is not a bad arrangement, aside from the effects of bureaucratic fumbling. He is given few resources to devote to selling and little authority over that process, but he has little need for them. Particularly under conditions of excess demand, the orders will flow in and his output will move as rapidly as he can produce it. He can devote all his management virtuosity to production.

For the producer of a new product, however, the same arrangement may be the source of severe difficulties. For there is no established body of users familiar with the product and in need of it in order to meet their own production obligations. Potential adopters must first be found to use it or at least to try it. "If the potential customer is not interested in these products, they will not be sold," warns a Soviet analyst.[20] It is the universal experience of innovators that the interest of potential adopters is not spontaneously kindled by the mere information that a useful new product is now available. Consider the following statement from a study entitled *Industry and Technical Progress:*

The possibility that the production or sales department will not be anxious to apply what is handed on to them as a successful development is least where the development is something that they themselves have asked for. Where they have not themselves felt the lack of the new idea, receptivity will be lower and the departments may even have an interest in opposing the idea. Thus, the innovation might disturb the smooth running of the production department. It may be necessary to disrupt output while new machines are installed, to retrain workers, and introduce new staff specialists. All this will increase the problems of the production managers and it may, where there are radical changes in technique, make the managers doubt their capacity to manage.[21]

The authors of this statement believed themselves to be writing about the obstacles to innovation in British industry, as indeed they were. They could just as well have been quoting the Soviet sources on the same subject. In these respects as well as in many others, the management of innovation in all modern industrial societies has much in common. And one of the commonest properties is resistance to change.

Because of the differences in the social context of productive activity in capitalist and socialist systems, one expects difference in behavior, and most of our attention is devoted to such differences. Less attention has been devoted to the extent to which the nonsocial technological facts of life tend to generate similar kinds of behavior in the two systems. Consider the response to a technological change. In the experience of capitalist economies, the user of a new product or process assumes certain risks. He generally has to redesign his own product and change his production process to accommodate to a new type of material. The early user assumes an even greater risk; a great deal of new knowledge developed at some cost from the experience of early users constitutes an "external economy" and is available free to later users.[22] The same technological problems of early use generate very similar economic problems in the USSR.[23]

In addition to the general sources of user resistance, there are some that are peculiar to the Soviet economy or more intense there. Despite the efforts to compel designers to assign greater weight to demand considerations, user requirements are still not sufficiently incorporated into design decisions.[24] Hence the user frequently finds that the new material or equipment is ill suited to his production needs.[25] Maintenance and support services are seldom provided by producers so that adopters of new equipment are left to their own resources in dealing with production and maintenance problems.[26] Equipment is often sold without the specification of performance indicators so that performance guarantees are not generally available.[27] All the problems of supply discussed in preceding chapters, which are widely discussed in the public press, warn the prospective adopter of the trouble he courts by employing a new material or piece of equipment in his production operation.

User resistance is not the only selling problem that the product innovator confronts. Two new plastics plants in Sverdlovsk and Nizhni-Tagil had managed to find a sufficient market for their products. But their customers ran into technical difficulties in substituting the new plastics for older materials and reduced the size of their orders. Both plants subsequently had to operate at less than capacity.[28] Hence, even if user resistance is overcome the product innovator faces selling problems not encountered by the noninnovator because of the uncertainties of technological change.

User resistance, particularly early use, is to be expected in any economy, although it may be somewhat greater in the Soviet than in capitalist economies. But user resistance can, of course, be overcome. Perhaps the greater difference between the two types of systems is to be found in their techniques for overcoming user resistance, rather than in the intensity and origins of that resistance.

Many of the techniques for overcoming user resistance are incorporated in the structures of prices, rules, and incentives and will be discussed presently. Some, however, are part of the structure of organization, particularly the procedures for the sale of output.

Promotional Selling and User Resistance

The logic of central planning leaves little scope for salesmanship. The task is thought of as one of "distributing" commodities rather than "marketing" them. A structure of economic organization that assigns little importance to selling is not ill adapted to the planning of an unchanging noninnovative economy. If the users are thoroughly familiar with an enterprise's products, and if the planners have learned the technical value of each product in all its possible uses, there is no pressing purpose to be served by promotional selling. Such a world approximates a state of "perfect knowledge," and the level of uncertainty is low. The same structure of economic organization, however, has very serious negative consequences if the objective of the system is to promote innovation. The potential user can no longer be expected to know the technical qualities of a new product or process or the consequences for his own production operations of using it. The planners cannot know all the potential applications of the innovation in all its possible uses; indeed the producer of the innovation does not yet know them himself. The state of "perfect knowledge" vanishes, and the level of uncertainty increases. The producer now encounters a resistance to the sale of his new products that was unknown under the previous regime. If innovation is to be encouraged, a place must be made in the structure of economic organization for the diffusion of the new knowledge and the promotion of the new product in the face of user resistance. In the Soviet case, the neglect of promotional selling has had the effect of discouraging innovation.

The stress placed on sales promotion by capitalist innovators needs no explanation. There are even some who hold that the technological gap between the United States and Western Europe is due not primarily to differences in innovational ability but to the superior promotional marketing by U.S. corporations.[29] In promoting new products capitalist firms take great pains to diffuse among possible users the information they require about the technical properties of their new products. Expensive brochures and catalogues are distributed, and in some industries technically trained sales people are among the highest-paid personnel.[30] In contrast one may cite the information problems of the construction-project planning institutes in the USSR. These are the organizations that decide which new building materials, equipment, instrumentation, and so forth are to be incorporated in new plants. An official of the Alcohol Plant Construction-Project Planning Institute (*Giprospirt*) reports that they are not informed of the instruments available for automated operations. The catalogues of "Automation Instruments and Equipment" are unsatisfactory, and they lack information on many new products. Nor do they possess up-to-date information on changes in product lines (*nomenklatura*) of producers or on items that have been withdrawn from production. This often leads to misunderstanding and misfortune. To cope with all this, many project planning institutes are forced to make daily inquiries of the instrument manufacturers about new developments and about changes in product lines. Many institutes have to produce their own information publications for their internal use.[31]

There is in the USSR a vast State-run apparatus for the dissemination and popularization of technical information.[32] But one wonders whether an information flow so organized can have the directedness, cogency, and timeliness that might be expected in a structure of economic organization in which the innovating enterprises themselves had a passionate interest in assuring that all potential users were fully, and overfully, informed of their new products.

User resistance derives not only from insufficient technical information but also from concern over the risks of innovation and from the uncertainty about the benefits. A major purpose of sales promotion in innovative capitalist firms is to persuade reluctant users to try their product. Personal representation has been found to be highly effective. The British Hosiery and Allied Trades Research Association is an industrial research organization supported by the firms in the industry and by government grants. Its research and development work is concentrated on instruments and devices that could be used in the industry's factories. When the association produced its first successful instrument, it informed the member firms by mail and invited them to express interest on a business reply card. Only 5 percent responded. However, after liaison officers were sent to the firms to explain the properties of the device and to demonstrate it, 85 percent ordered the device.[33] That association, it is to be noted, was not a capitalist firm. Its interest in promoting the adoption of its own work was based, not on large profit expectations, but on the desire for the success of the association and the hope of salary increases, and perhaps on a sense of mission. In this respect the British research association is not unlike a Soviet R & D institute or enterprise. But in the Soviet system, the sale of output is the primary responsibility not of the R & D institute or the enterprise but of the distribution system. This arrangement causes some inconveniences to noninnovators, but it may bring disaster to producers of new products. The Ufa Synthetic Alcohol Plant had built several new shops for the production of polyethylene sheets, and "for a long time they found no customers for their product." The same tale is told of the Kuibyshev Synthetic Alcohol Plant after it had introduced a polyethylene shop, of the Vinnitsa Superphosphate Plant after starting up the production of tripolyphosphate, and so forth.[34] The authors ascribe the low rate of capacity operation of many new plants in such progressive industries as polymer chemicals to "disproportions" in the planning of demand and supply. In the absence of promotional information and selling by producers of new products, one may expect such disproportions to be greater for the more innovative enterprises than for the less innovative.

What the analyst regards as a "disproportion," the enterprise manager sees as the piling up of unsold production. From time to time we read of managers taking matters in hand to protect themselves from the inefficiency of the distribution system by active selling. The Dankov Chemical Plant faced the familiar problem that the volume of inflowing allocation orders failed to cover its full output of organic silicon compounds. The reason in this case was that the demand for this product was limited, and their chief administration (*Souizglavkhim*) had divided the limited number of orders evenly among the four producers in the district. But while the other three enterprises waited passively for additional allocation orders to arrive, the Dankov enterprise "stole into foreign zones" and signed independent contracts with buyers in other districts. The indignant chief administration could not "drag the lawbreakers away from the back porch of the very home of the State Committee on Supply," so they ordered the enterprise to break its contracts, which had not been approved by the Chief Sales Administration in whose preserves the enterprise had "poached."[35]

The ordinary enterprise producing a familiar line of products with long-established customers can find itself in difficulty because it must rely primarily on others to arrange the sale of its output. The potential danger is all the greater for a would-be innovator, the sales of whose product must depend on opening up new sales outlets, developing new uses for it, and overcoming user resistance.

Sales Promotion across Industry Lines

In capitalist economies, where most industrial R & D is in-house, the R & D work tends to be concentrated on the enterprise's products rather than on its production processes, technology, and materials.[36] Advances in the construction industry are based on innovations made by building-materials producers, radio and television manufacturers purchase improved components based on innovations in the products of the electronics industry, and machinery manufacturers introduce innovations in the machinery purchased by shoe manufacturers. Thus most firms are adopters of innovations made by their suppliers and are themselves innovators of the new products sold to their customers.

The concentration on product innovation is a response to the market conditions of a capitalist economy. Enterprises are formed and prosper on the basis of a set of technical skills associated with the production and marketing of a certain product line. These skills extend to the use of their customary materials and equipment, but not normally to the production and sale of those materials and equipment. Hence, when they decide to undertake R & D, the expected gains are usually greater if the R & D is concentrated on those things the enterprise is best equipped to exploit, namely, its products.[37]

This pattern of innovation is both consequence and cause of the prominent role of marketing in the capitalist economy. It is probably an efficient practice, although in certain respects it may not be conducive to an optimal rate and direction of innovation.[38] In any case, R & D work is usually closely integrated with the sales operations of firms. The sales engineers of the primary aluminum producers "are in continuing contact with the end-product manufacturers so that the primary producers can facilitate the adoption of inventions in manufacturing processes."[39] Even a quasi-autonomous R & D organization like Bell Laboratories maintains a Systems Engineering Department whose general function is "continually to explore the needs of the Laboratories' customers—the operating telephone companies—while at the same time keeping closely in touch with the technical possibilities of meeting those needs."[40]

In the Soviet economy most in-house R & D follows the same pattern as that of the capitalist countries. The large proportion of R & D that is conducted in the independent institutes also appears generally to concentrate on the main products of the industry, although there are significant exceptions. Because of the "autarkic" tendencies toward universalism, or vertical integration, the machinery manufacturing ministries sometimes conduct research on metallurgy, and equipment-using industries like coal mining may conduct development work on mining machinery. But in the main, R & D is concentrated on the products of their own ministry and enterprises.

Since selling plays so small a role in the Soviet economy, there must be some other reason why the pattern should be the same as that in the United States. Perhaps technological expertise alone is sufficient to explain it. Tailors may be expected to develop better ways of cutting and sewing cloth, but one would not expect them to develop better scissors or sewing machines. The greater or lesser importance of the selling activity may be of little significance as a cause of this pattern of R & D innovation. But given the pattern, for whatever cause, the undervaluation of the selling activity has an unfortunate consequence for innovation. If R & D were concentrated on one's own materials and processes, the innovator and the adopter would be the same enterprise. Adoption would not then be inhibited by the absence of sales promotion. But since innovation is concentrated on products that must be sold to other enterprises, the undervaluation of selling tends to retard the rate of adoption.

The extent of this retarding effect is increased by the administrative structure of economic organization. In the U.S. economy one of the sources of technological change has been called "innovation by invasion."[41] Certain major advances, particularly in older industries, have taken the form of the invasion of one industry's preserve by another more progressive industry. Major advances in textiles have come from the chemicals industries, numerically controlled machine tools were developed not in the machine-tool but in the aerospace industry. Alcoa decided to enter the metals fabrication industry only because the latter were reluctant to assume the risks of manufacturing aluminum pots and pans.[42]

Innovation by invasion is most likely to occur in an economic structure in which enterprises have easy access to the markets of all others. The Soviet economic structure, however, groups enterprises into a limited number of noncompeting ministries. To assess the effect of this structure, suppose that there were no ministries and that the basic structural units were thousands of autonomous enterprises. Then each innovating enterprise would have equal access to all potential adopters regardless of their industrial or territorial characteristics. Given the level of sales activity, a certain rate of diffusion would occur from product innovators to adopters. But the grouping of enterprises into ministries erects a set of partitions, as it were, among enterprises. Since innovation is concentrated on products, innovating enterprises are generally in different ministries from their potential adopters. Given the same level of sales activity, a slower rate of diffusion may be expected because of the obstacles introduced by the ministerial partitions.

The ministerial structure tends to direct the enterprise's technological and administrative attention inward, in response to the needs and pressures from the ministry. The enterprise director and his staff associate with the officials of the other enterprises of their own ministry, whom they meet at ministry production and technological conferences; with officials of their own ministry's departments and administrations with whom they negotiate; and with the research, development, and design institutes of their own ministry. If customer resistance to the adoption of an innovation is to be overcome, it has to be done primarily through ministry channels. The innovator's ministry must persuade the potential adopter's ministry to pressure the latter's enterprises to adopt the new product. The partitioning effect was no less important in the period when the basis of partitioning was the territory rather than the industry group. The ministerial partitioning is one of the causes of the fact that "the production of new technology is still insufficiently tied in with the needs of the branches of the economy, the corporations and the customer enterprises."[43] For, given the product-based pattern of innovation, innovators and adopters are in different ministries.

Reforms like the creation of corporations represent efforts to accommodate to the requirements of technological progress by changes in organizational structure. They do not, however, meet the problem caused by the undervaluation of the sales-promotion activity in a system in which innovation is product based. The discovery of an optimal principle of partitioning would minimize the obstacles to the diffusion of innovation across administrative boundaries. But it would still not provide for the energy and "advocacy" that a recognized and well-supported sales department, with "a direct interest in rapid acceptance," contributes to the promotion of technological change.[44]

7.3. Reforms

Since the 1965 Reforms were introduced, enterprises appear to have increased their selling efforts. Reports on the subject often deal particularly with the sale of new products. It is possible that the reporting and public discussion of selling may have increased, for tutelary purposes, while the efforts actually exerted by enterprises may not have changed very much. Still, there are reasons to believe that the Reforms may have generated a genuine increase in selling activity.

One is surprised to read about an enterprise like the Precision Electrical Instrument Plant which, before designing their electronic computer F-588, had contacted about 50 organizations in order to gauge their sales prospects over the next 5 years. In preparation for starting on a new product, they interviewed over 100 prospective purchasers.[45] Similarly, we read that the in-house design bureau of the Moscow Automatic Heating Equipment Plant has established a special sales department to study what is referred to as their market for sales (*rynok sbyta*).[46] The director reports that the enterprise now maintains close contact with the design bureaus of their customers, the boiler and turbine plants, in order to keep informed of the technological direction in which their customers' products are moving and of the parameters of the new equipment being developed. They also maintain close contacts with the independent institutes that design the equipment in which their products may be incorporated. They try to keep the institutes informed of the instruments they are developing and plan to have in production in the future. In this way, says Director Kurtynin, "from the moment our new products are put into production, we will have a guaranteed market, and the newly designed equipment will be provided with the newest and most efficient technology."[47]

We described earlier how the Dankov enterprise people, frustrated by the chief administration's failure to provide sufficient allocation orders for their output, tried to market the product for themselves by "poaching" in regions assigned to other allocation centers. They were chastized because the result of their successful sales effort was merely to reduce the sales of other producers of the same product, who were part of the same ministry. A more creative solution was found by a sister enterprise, the Silicon Polymer Plant in Zaporozhe, which sought to avoid the experience of the Dankov people by combining a more active sales operations with an ambitious new-product development program:

"We decided that under such circumstances it was hopeless to wait for allocation orders for our whole output," writes Chief Engineer B. Golovnia. "We took the matter of marketing into our own hands." They discovered that when first started up, the production of organic silicon compounds had been geared to uses in the electronics and metals-casting industries. But those industries had subsequently found cheaper substitutes. Meanwhile new uses had been found for different types of these compounds in construction and housewares. They then undertook the production of permanent exterior paints, drying oils, enamels, resins, and other marketable products. They reorganized their production operations and established a market research department, developed new products, brought in some eminent scientists as consultants, and started "a good advertising campaign." Every year they innovate a dozen or so new types of chemical compounds, for which there are always customers eager to sign delivery contracts.[48]

These instances are new straws in the Soviet wind. If they herald the future forms of Soviet economic organization, they suggest that those forms will sanction a much larger place for sales promotion. This, in turn, is likely to be accompanied by other changes, mostly in the direction of greater decentralization of decision-making authority. For it is in the nature of social systems—or of any arrangements that we call systems—that the decision to make certain choices deprives one of freedom to make certain others. In the production system of an economy, for example, one may be free to decide how much steel is to be produced. But having made that decision, one is much less free in deciding how much iron ore and coke to produce. The second choice is heavily constrained by the steelmaking technology.

The same is true of social systems. In the matter at hand the system's governors have chosen to accelerate the rate of innovation. Having made the decision, they are no longer free to choose any structure of economic organization they wish. The "social technology," one might say, constrains the choice. In particular, they are no longer free to employ those structural forms that have inhibited sales promotion activity as in the past. Enterprises like Precision Electrical Instrument and Silicon Polymer are much less likely to undertake extensive new-product innovation in a structure that deprives them of the power to promote and market their products.

One cannot say with great confidence that selling and innovative activity have increased since the 1965 Reforms; trends of this sort are not easy to establish. Nor can one be sure that the changes that have occurred are the direct consequence of the Reforms. Yet the Reforms are of such kind that they may reasonably be expected to have accelerated selling and innovative activity.

The Territorial Wholesaling System

The establishment of the State Committee on Supply and its network of territorial wholesaling organizations has eased somewhat the problems of the enterprise as customer, in the ways discussed in Chapter 3. It does not appear however, to have changed significantly the position of the enterprise as seller. There are now many more allocation centers for the enterprise's output. In the past, its allocation centers were the ministry's chief sales administration or sometimes the corresponding administration of its major customer-ministry. Now, in addition, any number of territorial wholesale organizations may be designated as allocation centers for its output. Hence, the enterprise's allocation orders arrive from a larger number of different sources.

The greater complexity of the distribution system may be the partial cause of what appears to be the aggravation of that old sales problem— an inflow of allocation orders insufficient to cover the enterprise's output. In a perverse sort of way, this growing problem of insufficient allocation orders appears to have increased the sales efforts of enterprises, precisely because of the increasing undependability of the distribution system. In many of the instances reported in the press, some of which have served as illustrations in this chapter, the problem of insufficient allocation orders is cited as the cause of the enterprise's decision to "take matters in hand." Things do sometimes have to get worse before they get better.

But the point should not be pushed too hard. Other factors besides the confusion in the distribution system may have had a greater influence in promoting selling activity.

Direct Selling

Enterprises like the Automatic Heating Equipment Plant and the Silicon Polymer Plant were engaged in a new marketing technique known as "direct selling" (*priamye sviazy*, literally, "direct ties"). The technique was first developed in a celebrated experiment undertaken a year before the 1965 Economic Reforms in two government enterprises named Bol'shevik (in Moscow) and Maiak (in Gorkii). The experiment was designed to test the effectiveness of a structure in which producers and customers negotiate purchase and sales contracts directly with each other in advance of the planning process. The plans of producers and customers that are subsequently drawn up are thus based on prior agreements among the parties. The new procedure differs from the standard practice, in which enterprises' plans are drawn up solely in consultation with, and often on direct instruction from, their own ministries. This older procedure allows for very little influence of the specific demand of the ultimate customers on the producers' plans. Contract negotiations between producers and customers take place only after each one's identity has been made known to the other in the allocation orders that they subsequently receive. Customers are often obliged to contract for the purchase of goods that had found their way into the producer's plan without their (the customers') prior participation. The system of direct selling was intended, in Soviet parlance, to "establish the principle of mutual material responsibility as the basis of the economic relations among enterprises and to strengthen the role of commercial contract." The experiment was regarded as a qualified success, and in 1965 several hundred consumer-goods enterprises converted to the new procedure of direct selling. The procedure was carried over to many other enterprises after the 1965 Reforms.[49]

The original experiments with direct selling took place in the consumer goods industry in response to mounting dissatisfaction and charges of neglect of consumer wishes. There does appear to have been a substantial improvement in the quality of consumer goods and in the effort to satisfy, and increasingly to influence, consumer tastes. The improvement may be credited in part to the technique of direct selling, although the major credit is probably due not to the technique itself but to the accompanying reforms in rules and incentives which have placed much greater emphasis on sales.

Although first introduced in the marketing of consumer goods, direct selling is strongly recommended for industrial goods as well. Some see it as a major device for increasing the flexibility of the economic system. At all levels from enterprise to central-planning organizations, writes the Deputy President of the RSFSR Planning Commission, there must be a "conditioned reflex" in striving to find and establish technological and commercial contacts with customers."[50] In the marketing of consumer goods, the direct selling technique appears to work fairly well, without placing excessive strain on the central-planning apparatus. The reason is that the consumer is at the "unplanned" end of the production chain. Once the goods are in the consumer's hands, they disappear from the production process, and the central planners bear no responsibility for their further progress through the economy. But the industrial customer is still part of the planned system. A sale of materials to him does not end with him but is converted into goods the further flow of which remains the responsibility of the planners. The planners are less likely to accept the more modest role they would have to play under a system of direct selling.

Direct selling calls for a more active marketing role by the enterprises. If the producer seeks out his own customers in advance of the planning process and contracts with them, the act of planning has, in a sense, already been completed. There is nothing left for the planner to do but passively register the intended sale as part of the future plan. If all plans were to be constructed in this way, the planners would indeed be reduced simply to recorders of faits accomplis. There would no longer be a centrally planned economy in the old sense. But more important, the planners are likely to discover, as they record the intended direct sales and purchases of various goods, that certain mismatches occur. Customer X may not have succeeded in finding a source of supply for some input that is vital for his production plans. The planners cannot afford to allow X's output to fall. They must therefore order producing enterprise A to supply the required products to X. But if A had already contracted to deliver it to Y through a direct selling negotiation, A will be forced to break its contract, and Y may in turn have to break its contracts with others. For such reasons the extension of direct selling to the industrial sectors may be expected to conflict with the institutions of central planning.

There is evidence that such conflicts have already arisen. The Dankov plant referred to earlier, which had sought to find its own customers, was charged with "poaching" in the planned markets of other distribution units and was obliged to break its contracts. That case, however, does not reflect the problems of direct selling properly understood. Direct selling means that contracts are drawn up in advance of plan construction. The Dankov people had gone out for business after the plans had been confirmed, and the planning and distribution units had already assumed a set of obligations under the plan. More revealing is the experience of the Silicon Polymer Plant. That enterprise had set about trying to assess demand and to avoid producing products for which they could not sign sales contracts. But their production plan continued to be "choked up" with such products. The enterprise had to apply repeatedly to the ministry for permission to change their plan to exclude those unsalable products and to make room for other products already contracted for. And everyone knows the endless pleading and negotiation required to get such things done at the ministry. "I even met the chief engineer there myself once," writes the special correspondent of the *Economic Gazette.* "How many times has he had to get his plan readjusted to accord with the contracts he had signed!"[51]

Direct selling has followed a pattern often exhibited in the course of the "campaigns" that generally accompany policy or structural changes in the USSR. An idea is first tried out in a few places and judged successful. The idea is then announced as official policy and instructions filter down to party and public officials to implement it in their enterprises. The press joins the campaign by the frequent reporting of the successes of those who adopted the practice, and officials everywhere climb on the bandwagon to share in the rewards of being regarded as progressive leaders. Increasingly the idea is applied in circumstances in which it is not appropriate. Eventually reports of failures, and sometimes of "simulation" begin to appear, the universality of its application is increasingly questioned, and the campaign quietly disappears from the pages of the press. The practice may be retained in those enterprises in which it has been successful but falls into general disuse elsewhere. In the course of a campaign cycle heavy costs are sometimes incurred because of its hasty and sometimes mindless application in inappropriate conditions. This has been the history of campaigns from the Stakhanovite movement in the thirties to Mr. Khrushchev's corn-growing campaign more recently. It is a fair bet that the current "corporation" movement will follow this pattern.

Direct selling was also originally thought to be applicable to all enterprises, regardless of size. Presently notes of criticism began to appear in the press. Large enterprises in particular complained that they could not deal effectively with the many small firms that began seeking direct sales relationships with them. "It is hard to imagine what would happen," writes one critic, "if over 414,000 industrial enterprises were to begin an independent search for such direct selling arrangements for each of their products—with 11,000 building contracting enterprises. . . ."[52]

We may expect that the scope of direct selling will eventually settle down to a limited range of products and enterprises where it proves to be feasible. Within that range it is likely to promote active marketing by producers of consumers' goods, and this in turn may be expected to encourage innovation. But in the production of industrial goods, direct selling tends to conflict with the central planning and distribution system. The conflicts are likely to be fewer when new products are involved, however, for the central planners have not yet taken over their distribution. For this reason, direct selling may be expected to encourage the innovation of new industrial products. In those enterprises and products where it becomes the established practice, it gives producers, for the first time, the opportunity directly to advertise, promote, and try to sell their new products, instead of having to rely on the uninformed and less-motivated bureaucracy.

The New Sales Rule

The effectiveness of any single structural element of a system depends in part on the other structural elements. A given organizational structure may be highly effective when managers are instructed to follow a certain set of decision-making rules. But if those rules are changed, that same organizational structure may cause the system to perform less effectively.

The 1965 Reforms introduced some major changes in decision-making rules, which will be analyzed in detail in succeeding chapters. One of those changes, however, deals directly with the matter of selling. It is therefore appropriate to conclude this chapter with some observations on the effects of that rule change on the organization of new product sales.

Since the 1930s managers were instructed to follow rules that placed primary emphasis on value of output. That structure of rules was appropriate to the prevailing structure of organization, for the job of the enterprise was to produce, and it was the job of other units to distribute the products.

Since the 1965 Reforms, managers are no longer obliged to concentrate on value of output in making production and other decisions. They are instructed to concentrate instead on two different magnitudes, one of which is sales revenue.[53] Other things being equal, in all cases involving a choice, management is now supposed to select that alternative which yields the largest ruble value of sales. Output produced but not sold during a given period is no longer counted as having satisfied the decision rule.

Under the new rule, the effectiveness of the enterprise selling operations plays a much more important role in the evaluation of its performance. The question is whether the enterprise has been given greater authority over the sale of its products, commensurate with its greater responsibility for sales. The only major organizational change in this direction is the authority to engage in direct selling. For the rest, however, that authority is still of limited scope and significance. The ministry can still compel the enterprise to give up business it has attracted by its own efforts, as in the case of the Dankov Plant; and the manager must still spend countless hours persuading his ministry to authorize the required plan changes, as in the case of the Silicon Polymer Plant. The territorial sales organization may still decide, without explanation, not to accept products that they were obliged to purchase under the plan, forcing the producing enterprise to change over to the production of other items without any assurance that they will be sold.[54] Thus, the enterprise manager is now being evaluated by the performance of an activity that the organizational structure still places largely in other hands.

This imperfect articulation between rules and organization has not rendered the reform useless. At the least, the distribution system is under greater pressure by enterprise managers to expedite the sale of their products. In the past a failure to provide a sufficient volume of allocation orders was only a minor inconvenience; if the goods were produced, the bonuses were paid. The cases discussed earlier reveal the deep concern that enterprises now express when the allocation orders are not received. The greater effort devoted to the analysis of the future demand for their products and to advertising and direct selling springs from the same concern. One reads increasingly of demands by irate directors that some way be found of holding the ministries "materially responsible"—meaning by fines and monetary penalties—when a shortfall in enterprise sales is due to ministry rather than enterprise default.

This greater attention to selling in the concerns of management may be credited in part to the new sales-revenue rule. It does not follow, however, that the new rule will encourage innovators. It may, on the contrary, have the opposite effect. Given the prevalence of user resistance to new products, the product innovator faces a greater risk of unsold output than the producer of an established and tested product. Under the old value-of-output rule unsold output was not heavily penalized in evaluating managerial performance. The new sales-revenue rule, however, penalizes unsold output more heavily than before. Faced with a choice between trying to launch a new product or continue the production of a safe established one, management may be less inclined than before to undertake the innovation. That reluctance could be offset to some extent, if the organizational structure gave management greater authority over sales activity, appropriate to the greater risk created by the new rule. A competent manager, confident in the value of his new product, would have less concern if he were given the resources and the free hand actively to seek out potential customers, to advertise and promote the advantages of his product over competing products, to hire and train sales personnel to explain and demonstrate its virtues, to offer special inducements to first adopters of his product, and so forth. No organizational changes of this magnitude have been made. The 1965 Reform introduced a new decision rule that increases the risk of unsold output without arming the innovator with new organizational authority sufficient to cope with the added risk. If the organization of the sale of products discouraged product innovation before the Reform to some extent, that extent must be greater since the Reform.

Notes

1. Richard R. Nelson, Merton J. Peck, and Edward Kalachek, *Technology, Economic Growth and Public Policy* (Washington: The Brookings Institution, 1967), p. 105. Sometimes it is the supply that limits the rate of diffusion, as in the case of penicillin and the Boeing 707, but in most cases it is demand.

2. But all include one or more chapters on the problems of supply. See Joseph S. Berliner, *Factory and Manager in the USSR*, (Cambridge: Harvard University Press, 1958), Chaps. 6, 11, 12; David Granick, *Management of the Industrial Firm in the U.S.S.R.* (New York: Columbia University Press, 1954), Chap. 8; Barry Richman, *Soviet Management* (Englewood Cliffs, N.J.: Prentice-Hall, 1965), Chap. 6. Marshall Goldman's *Soviet Marketing* (New York: The Free Press, 1963) deals only with consumers goods.

3. In the same way, the sum of the allocation certificates flowing into the enterprise's supply department should equal the planned inputs of each commodity in the course of the year.

4. *Ekonomicheskaia gazeta*, 1967, No. 9. p. 11.

5. Ibid., No. 46, p. 11.

6. Berliner, *Factory and Manager*, pp. 83-85.

7. *Voprosy ekonomiki*, 1967, No. 8. p. 131.

8. *Ekonomicheskaia gazeta*, 1967, No. 23, p. 28. The author, Dr. Khatchaturov, notes that part of the reason is that the structure of the machine-tool park of the developed capitalist countries is often taken as the basis of planning the machine-tool output of the USSR. That planning practice must greatly reduce the returns to investment in machine-tool innovation.

9. Ibid., No. 31, p. 29.

10. Ibid., No. 38, p. 15. The same problem arose again in the second quarter. See also ibid., No. 31, p. 28.

11. Ibid., No. 21, p. 22.

12. Ibid., No. 49, p. 12.

13. *Planovoe khoziaistvo*, 1966, No. 4, p. 84.

14. *Ekonomicheskaia gazeta*, 1967, No. 52, p. 15.

15. *Planovoe khoziaistvo*, 1966, No. 1, p. 15.

16. *Ekonomicheskaia gazeta*, 1967, No. 21, p. 13.

17. Marshall I. Goldman, "The Reluctant Consumer and Economic Fluctuations in the Soviet Union," *Journal of Political Economy*, Vol. 73, August 1965, pp. 366-380.

18. *Ekonomicheskaia gazeta*, 1966, No. 2, p. 28.

19. Ibid., 1967, No. 49, p. 12.

20. *Voprosy ekonomiki*, 1967, No. 12, pp. 43-44.

21. C. F. Carter and B. R. Williams, *Industry and Technical Progress* (London: Oxford University Press, 1957), p. 64.

22. Nelson, Peck, and Kalachek, *Technology*, pp. 96, 198-204. The authors recommend that the General Services Administration of the U.S. government set up an experimental procurement service to buy and test new products, in order to speed up early use of new products in the United States.

23. See Sec. 9.2.

24. "Production plans for new equipment are frequently drawn up without the participation of the users." *Voprosy ekonomiki*, 1972, No. 1, p. 70.

25. Designers are criticized for their complaints about directors who, in the interest of cost economies, compel them to simplify designs and employ "primitive" design features. The dominance of design virtuosity over economy is regarded as one of the causes of the overproduction of complex and advanced machine tools relative to the simpler models that are in wider demand. *Ekonomicheskaia gazeta*, 1967, No. 11, p. 11.

26. Criticism of the absence of servicing support is of long standing. One critic has gone so far as to propose that, to stimulate demand for new coal-mining machinery, the machinery producers should bear full responsibility for the maintenance of the equipment they sell for the entire period of its use. They should bear all of the costs, including the costs of the user's downtime. Ibid., 1968, No. 8, p. 17. The proposal would surely increase demand, but it would just as surely reduce the rate of innovation of new models by producers.

27. It is reported that 75 percent of all types of hydraulic panels and 60 percent of all types of hydraulic pumps are sold without performance indicators and therefore carry no guarantees. Ibid., 1968, No. 8, p. 19.

28. A. G. Kulikov et al., eds., *Ekonomicheskoe problemy uskoreniia tekhnicheskogo progressa v promyshlennosti* (Economic Problems in Accelerating Technical Progress in Industry) (Moscow: Mysl, 1964), p. 31.

29. Dr. Donald Hornig, scientific adviser to President Lyndon Johnson, as reported in the *International Herald Tribune*, July 29, 1967, p. 7.

30. Nelson, Peck, and Kalachek, *Technology*, p. 17. Doubts are sometimes raised about whether the large volume of selling costs are justified, both for the society as a whole and for individual firms. With respect to the latter the authors assert that "the intensive and extensive use of salesmen and advertising certainly suggests that firms believe that communication matters." (P. 104.)

31. *Ekonomicheskaia gazeta*, 1968, No. 10, p. 19.

32. For recent statistics on the volume of publications by the organs of scientific and technical information, see *Pechat' v S.S.S.R. v 1971 godu* (The Soviet Press in 1971) (Moscow: Kniga, 1972), pp. x-xix.

33. Carter and Williams, *Industry and Technical Progress*, p. 71.

34. *Voprosy ekonomiki*, 1966, No. 4, p. 31.

35. *Ekonomicheskaia gazeta*, 1967, No. 49, p. 12.

36. Nelson, Peck, and Kalachek, *Technology*, pp. 31-40. This is particularly the case in science-based technologies like electronics and chemicals.

37. An industry supplied by a craftlike unprogressive industry may find it expedient to undertake R & D on its own materials and processes.

38. Nelson, Peck, and Kalachek, *Technology*, p. 82, discuss some of the disadvantages of the pattern.

39. Merton J. Peck, "Inventions in the Postwar American Aluminum Industry," National Bureau of Economic Research, *The Rate and Direction of Inventive Activity: Economic and Social Factors* (Princeton: Princeton University Press, 1962), p. 281.

40. Thomas A. Marschak, "Strategy and Organization in a System Development Project" in NBER *Rate and Direction of Inventive Activity*, p. 537.

41. Donald A. Schon, *Technology and Change* (New York: Delacorte, 1967), pp. 169-171.

42. Nelson, Peck, and Kalachek, *Technology*, p. 81.

43. *Voprosy ekonomiki*, 1972, No. 1, p. 70.

44. Nelson, Peck, and Kalachek, *Technology*, p. 140. On the role of "advocacy" in promoting diffusion, see pp. 204-209. For some cautions against overzealous advocacy, see the study of the weapons acquisition process in the United States in Paul W. Cherington, Merton J. Peck, and Frederick M. Scherer, "Organization and Research and Development Decision Making Within a Government Department," in NBER, *Rate and Direction of Inventive Activity*, p. 402.

45. *Ekonomicheskaia gazeta*, 1967, No. 48, p. 20.

46. Ibid., No. 26, p. 16. That the market research is being done by the design bureau suggests that the interest in sales is closely connected with new-product development.

47. Ibid., No. 34, p. 10.

48. Ibid., No. 49, p. 12.

49. L. M. Gatovskii et al., eds., *Plan, khozraschet, stimuly* (The Plan, Business Accountability, and Incentives) (Moscow: Ekonomika, 1966), p. 161.

50. *Planovoe khoziaistvo*, 1966, No. 1, p. 12.

51. *Ekonomicheskaia gazeta*, 1967, No. 49, p. 12.

52. *Voprosy ekonomiki*, 1967, No. 9, pp. 44-45.

53. The other is profit. See Chap. 14 for details.

54. *Ekonomicheskaia gazeta*, 1967, No. 9, p. 11.

Part II

The Structure of Prices

Chapter 8

Profitability of New Products

When aviation was in its infancy, each pilot operated his own plane. He used the information provided by his instruments and landed his plane himself. If two planes approached an airport simultaneously, they radioed information to each other, and, following accepted conventions, they landed safely—most of the time.

Planes became more complex, better instruments for generating information were developed, and air traffic increased. It was no longer tolerable for each man to pilot his own plane. It became necessary to introduce a new agent to govern the behavior of pilots. Control towers were instituted. Aviation then faced the ancient problem of government—the forms by which the governors should control the behavior of the governed.

There are two fundamental forms of government. The complex information-generating instruments can be located in the control tower, and the tower can then transmit detailed second-by-second instructions to the pilots of the planes approaching for a landing. Or the tower can transmit the information second by second to the pilots and let the pilots land the planes. In the first form, the tower makes all the decisions, and the pilots merely carry them out. In the second, the pilots make their own decisions and carry them out on the basis of the information flowing from the tower. Combinations of the two fundamental forms are also possible, in which the tower issues some instructions along with the information, and the pilots make their own decisions on matters not covered by the instructions.

The early capitalist economies were social systems without government, largely. Enterprises made their own decisions and usually landed safely, although sometimes there were large crashes. For a variety of well-known reasons, control towers were introduced to govern the behavior of the economic units. Modern political economics has become, in effect, what Abba Lerner has called the "economics of control"—the study of the kinds of information and instructions, and the proportions between the two, by which economic systems should be governed.[1] In practice, the governments of modern capitalist economies issue relatively few instructions and most economic activity remains ungoverned.

Some socialist economies like Yugoslavia have adopted or are leaning toward this type of economic government as practiced in the capitalist world.[2] But for most of them the issue is not primarily the extent to which the economy is to be governed. The very notion of a "planned economy" implies a governed economy. The question is rather whether the governors should issue primarily instructions to the pilots of the economic units, or whether they should issue primarily information and let the pilots make the detailed decisions.

The most important kind of information in economic matters consists of the prices of things. Prices are to the economy as altitude and wind direction are to aviation. They are the crucial component of the information needed by economic agents in deciding which goods to produce and which inputs to use in producing them. In the "centralized" government of a socialist economy, the governors use the price information to decide what should be produced and then instruct the managers to produce it. In the "decentralized" form, the governors transmit to the managers the price information on the basis of which the managers decide what to produce. By the clever manipulation of prices, the governors of a decentralized economy should, in principle, be able to guide the managers into making precisely those production decisions that the governors wish them to make.

In practice, the socialist economic systems are neither purely centralized nor decentralized but range along a continuum between the two extreme types. The Soviet economy is perhaps closer to the centralized type than any other. Were it purely centralized, one would devote no part of this study of enterprise management to the analysis of the price structure. For in that case knowledge of the prices of things would contribute nothing to the understanding of managerial behavior.[3] But since it is incompletely centralized, a certain range of decisions is made by enterprise managers. To the extent that those decisions are influenced by the prices of things, an analysis of the structure of prices is a necessary part of the explanation of innovative behavior.

8.1. Prices and Profits

In the analysis of capitalist economies one takes it for granted that prices do exert a major influence on decision making. The reason is that profit is thought to be the major objective pursued by enterprises, and prices are central to the calculation of the profitability of alternative production decisions. In terms of the structural hypothesis (Section 1.2), the importance of price structure in the explanation of behavior derives from the properties of the other structural elements of the economic system; organization, incentives, and decision rules.

In the analysis of a socialist economy, it cannot simply be taken for granted that prices are in fact a major influence on decision making. As in a capitalist economy, it depends on the properties of the other structural elements. One can design an economy in which the organizational structure is such that the price structure plays no role at all in the enterprise's decisions. This would be the case in a system of total and perfect central planning—"perfect computation" in Peter Wiles's felicitous phrase.[4] Similarly one can imagine a set of decision rules and incentives that would cause prices to be ignored in enterprise production decisions. Soviet cement-block factories at one time were assigned a rule directing them to maximize the tonnage of output, and the incentive structure provided for rewards proportional to tonnage produced. In deciding upon the sizes of blocks to be produced, enterprises ignored relative prices and concentrated on large blocks, with a consequent shortage of small blocks on the market.[5] If such circumstances were general, our analysis of the effect of price structure on innovation would serve no purpose.[6] The question of whether a given price structure would encourage or discourage innovation would be of little interest if no one paid any attention to prices anyhow.

In fact the other structural elements of the Soviet economy are such that enterprise managers do generally take prices into account in economic decisions.[7] Since the nature of the decision rules and incentives has not yet been discussed, the reasons for the important role of prices cannot be set forth at this point. Some brief explanatory comments may be made, however.

One reason flows from the organization of the supply of financial resources to the enterprise. Since money serves as a medium of exchange, enterprises are obliged to pay for the labor they employ and the materials and equipment they use. Their supply of funds comes primarily from the sale of their products to other enterprises. If they ignored the prices of the things they buy and sell, their bank balances would diminish and possibly vanish. The supply of funds may be insufficient for the continued purchase of materials and labor, leading to a decline in production and possibly to a shutdown.

As a medium of exchange, however, money does not have the importance in the Soviet economy that it has in a capitalist economy. If the supply of funds were the only reason for managers to attend to prices, the role of prices would be very modest. Any set of production decisions would be acceptable if, at the given prices, the total revenue from the sale of all the enterprise's products exceeded the total cost of producing them. More important is the role of money as the unit of accounting. Where choices are to be made, the decision rules direct management to select that alternative that yields the largest sales revenue and the highest profit rate.[8] The larger the values of these two magnitudes, the larger the rewards provided by the incentive structure. Both sales revenue and profit rate depend on the prices of the enterprise's products, and the profit rate depends further on the prices of the things the enterprise purchases. Hence the importance of prices in making economic decisions.

8.2. The Pricing of Established Products

The price that is of dominating interest to the industrial enterprise is called the wholesale price. That is the price received for a product sold to other enterprises, and that is the price paid for products bought from other enterprises.[9] Wholesale prices are the basis of the retail prices at which consumer goods are sold to the public. The retail price of a consumer good normally exceeds its wholesale price by the amount of a commodity (or "turnover") tax and a retail markup.

Three fundamental principles predominate in determining the wholesale prices of established industrial products. They are calculated on a cost-plus-profit basis, they are unchanged for extended periods of time, and all enterprises that sell a particular product charge the same price for it.

The Principle of Cost-plus-Profit Pricing

The central principle of price formation is that the price of a commodity should be equal to the average cost of producing it plus a reasonable profit markup for the producing enterprise. This principle is thought to be the proper application of Marx's labor theory of value to the special circumstances of a socialist economy.[10] A lively controversy surrounds the issue of pricing, and in practice a number of departures from it have been sanctioned, notably in the pricing of new products. Cost-plus-profit pricing remains, however, the general basis of the pricing of established products.

Enterprise average cost. The first step in price formation is the calculation of a product's average unit cost of production in every enterprise that produces it. The method of calculating average unit cost in the

Soviet enterprise is generally similar to that used in capitalist enterprises but differs in several respects. One major difference is that interest on the enterprise's capital stock is not accounted for as a cost of production, although depreciation of the capital is treated as a cost. The consequence of the omission of interest from cost calculations is that the prices of products do not fully reflect the cost to the society of the capital stock tied up in the process of producing them. The appropriateness of accounting for interest has been increasingly recognized in economic policy, and an interest charge is now included in calculations of the returns to various forms of investment, including investment in new products and processes.[11] Since the 1965 economic reform, moreover, enterprises are obliged to pay a capital charge to the state out of their profit, which indirectly introduces an interest component into prices.[12] For the purpose of price formation, however, interest is still not considered a component of average cost.

A second feature of Soviet accounting is that the direct costs (mostly wages and materials[13]) attributed to the production of a commodity are not the amounts actually spent but calculations of the amounts that should have been spent by a "normal" enterprise. The calculations are based on a set of official "norms"; if the wage norm is 2 rubles per ton of output, then an enterprise that produced 100 tons of output will consider its direct wage cost to have been 200 rubles, regardless of the amount it actually spent on wages. The justification of this method of determining direct costs is that "*ex-post* accounting of costs reflects various unproductive outlays and other deviations from normal operating conditions," which should not be permitted to influence price setting.[14] The consequence of the exclusion of expenses deemed unproductive is that direct costs attributed to a product understate the actual direct costs. The degree of understatement is increased by another practice; the planned norms themselves are set not on the basis of what is regarded as the normal operating conditions of each enterprise, but on the basis of "the experience of the leading enterprises."[15]

The normative method of calculating direct costs is intended to hold the price level down by eliminating all enterprises' unproductive outlays and by excluding entirely the experience of higher-cost producers. What seems to be intended is a sort of "reverse marginalism"; that is, a set of prices that reflect the cost behavior of the lowest-cost producers rather than the highest-cost producers.

Branch average cost. Average unit costs are different in different enterprises, and the second step in price formation is the determination of a single cost measure. The method employed is to compute an average of the unit average costs of all the enterprises producing the product. That measure is known as the branch average cost.

Some Soviet economists have urged that the wholesale price be based not on the average of the producers' costs but on the costs of the highest-cost producer, thus approximating a marginal-cost pricing system.[16] That method has the familiar advantage of generating prices that reflect marginal opportunity cost. The argument has had no influence on policy, however. On the contrary, when the dispersion is large, an effort is made to exclude extreme and unrepresentative cases. If an enterprise has unusually high costs because its plant and equipment are very old and slated for replacement, or if it has exceptionally low costs due to favorable natural conditions, its cost is not included in the average.[17] On balance, most of the adjustments seem to be made in the case of high-cost producers. This downward adjustment augments the "reverse marginalism" caused by the similar adjustments in the calculation of enterprise average costs.

The profit markup. In the centrally planned economy the regulation of the demand and supply of industrial commodities is accomplished not by prices and markets but by the central plan. Wholesale prices are therefore not intended to serve as equilibrium prices.[18] Their function is not to clear markets but to serve as an instrument of "business accountability" (*khozraschet*); that is, of monetary regulation and control over enterprise activity. To carry out the activities incorporated in the plan, the enterprise's revenues must be sufficient not only to recoup production costs but also to provide funds for various other planned purposes such as increasing working capital and making various incentive payments to personnel. To provide these additional revenues, the wholesale price is formed by adding a profit markup to branch average cost.

The markup is intended to be large enough to provide the volume of profits required by a "normally operating enterprise."[19] In practice that seems to mean that profits should be large enough to enable the well-managed enterprise to cover the incentive funds the enterprise is authorized to retain for its own use, and the capital charge it is obliged to pay to the state budget.[20] In the 1967 general price revision it was estimated that for all industry an average profit rate of 15 percent on capital was needed to provide the required volume of profits.[21] The profit rates established for various industries were:[22]

Electric power	10.6%
Petroleum extraction and processing	14.6%
Coal mining	8.0%
Iron and steel	15.0 to 16.0%
Machinery and metalworking	13.0 to 15.0%
Timber and woodworking	12.6%
Building materials	13.6%

The differentiation of profit rates by branch of industry is determined in part by differences in the size of the capital charge introduced after the 1965 Economic Reform. Every enterprise is now obliged to pay to the state budget each year an amount equal to about 6 percent of the value of its average annual stock of fixed and working capital. The charge is designed to motivate enterprises to economize on their use of capital. It is not regarded as a cost of production, however, but as a payment out of earned profit. Hence, in establishing the planned branch profit rate in the 1967 price revision, provision had to be made for enterprise revenues to be large enough to enable them to pay the capital charges. Industries that use large quantities of capital relative to total production costs require a larger excess of revenues over costs to pay their capital charges than industries that use less capital. The former are therefore assigned larger profit markups than the latter in the pricing of their products. The effect is equivalent to the inclusion of an interest charge in product prices, although that charge formally enters the price not as an element of cost but of profit. The inclusion of the capital charge in prices is a gain in the efficiency of economic decisions.

Another new departure is the designation of profit rates in terms of profit per unit of capital. Before the 1967 price revision profit rates were expressed as percentages of cost of production in all contexts: in planning, in evaluating enterprise performance, and in pricing. The change from profit on cost to profit on capital has greatly complicated the pricing process, for it is not practical to calculate the quantity of capital employed per unit of output of every product in the land. Instead, the practice seems to be to limit the designation of planned profit rates on capital to the lowest level of disaggregation at which a measure of "capital per unit of output" can be reasonably calculated. Once the profit rate on capital is established for the aggregate product group, however, some other profit measure is employed in the actual pricing of the individual products. Depending on the cost structure, that measure may be profit on cost of production, or on value added, or on wage costs, or on some other cost element.[23]

Suppose for example that the cotton textile industry is authorized to earn a planned volume of profit of 1 million rubles, the average stock of capital in the industry is 10 million rubles, and the planned total cost of production of all cotton textiles is 5 million rubles. Then the planned profit rate for the industry will be set at 10 percent on capital. That profit rate on capital is equivalent to a 20 percent profit on cost. Therefore, in pricing the individual products of the industry, a 20 percent markup is added to branch average cost.[24]

Since the profit markup is based on branch average cost, realized profit rates vary among enterprises in the same industry, depending upon their product mix and the divergence of their average unit costs from the branch average. The highest-cost enterprises may indeed realize zero profits or even operate at a loss, requiring a subsidy to keep them solvent. Certain modifications of pricing arrangements, notably the use of zonal and accounting prices discussed later in this section (The Principle of Uniform Prices) reduce the range of profits and eliminate the need for some subsidies. Even after the 1967 price revision, however, about 10 percent of all enterprises require subsidies.[25]

The Principle of Permanent Prices

One of the advantages claimed for the Soviet planned economy is that, unlike the capitalist economy, its prices need not fluctuate with short-run changes in market or cost conditions. Not only need they not fluctuate, but they ought not, because planning would be much more difficult if prices changed during the plan period and from one period to another. The advantage and desirability of stable prices is expressed in the policy of regarding wholesale prices as "permanent" (*postoianyi*).

The notion of permanence does not mean that once set they are never to be changed. It means rather that they are set without limit of time.[26] To accommodate to longer-run changes in cost and market conditions, wholesale prices are changed under certain circumstances. The major circumstance of this kind is when the accumulated effects of past changes in cost and demand conditions have caused the existing cost structure to be excessively out of line with the existing price structure. Under those conditions, the government authorizes a general revision of wholesale prices. In a general price revision, all wholesale prices are reviewed in principle, and many are revised. In the postwar period general price revisions have occurred in 1948, 1952, 1955, and 1967. Only the first and last of these were of massive proportions, however, so that, as one authority notes, "it is well known that before 1966-1967, the prevailing wholesale prices were those established basically in 1948, with some adjustments made in 1952 and 1955."[27]

In the periods between general price revisions, specific groups of prices may be revised from time to time. Such partial revisions may occur when a great many new products have been introduced since the last general price revision, or when a general review of quality standards has taken place. It may also be called for by changes in cost conditions in some industries which cause earned profits to fall far below or above planned profit rates. The existence of earned profit rates in the range of 50% to 100% above the official norms, for example, is taken as evidence of the need for a revision of a group of prices.[28] Actual price revisions are undertaken sparingly, however, because of the interdependence of the general price structure. "A partial price revision may introduce incorrect price ratios in other sectors of the economy or may cause an unjustified rise in profits in some third sector."[29]

Two consequences follow from the principle of permanent wholesale prices. One is that management proceeds on the assumption that the prices of its established products will remain unchanged for the indefinite future. Some of its prices may be caught up in some future general or partial price revision, but one never knows when that will be or which prices will be changed if any. In the case of new products, the enterprise will benefit or suffer for a long time depending on the initial price that management succeeds in negotiating with the price agencies.

The second consequence is that, with changing cost conditions, realized profit rates diverge increasingly from the levels planned at the time prices were set. The data on p. 243 show a relatively small dispersion among the profit rates newly established after the 1967 price revision. Before 1967 the dispersion ranged from 16.7 percent in machinery to −17.0 percent in coal mining. The dispersion in profit rates on individual products, however, was even larger than that of industry averages. In 1964, for example, the realized profit rates on 70 nonferrous metal products were as follows:[30]

Number of Products	Profit Rate (Percentage of cost)
6	over 50
5	30 to 50
32	10 to 29
16	0 to 9
4	−1 to −20
7	below −20

Hence, while the principle of a standard profit markup is applied at the time prices are set, it is an inaccurate description of the structure of Soviet prices at any time. Because of the permanence of prices, relative prices at any time may bear little resemblance to branch average costs.

The Principle of Uniform Prices

The preferred principle is that the price of a product should be the same for all purchasers regardless of their geographical location. Under this principle the catalogue usually quotes the price at the railway station of destination, and the price paid by the purchaser includes transportation and loading costs up to that point.

Three principal kinds of departure from this principle are admitted in practice. The first is the pricing of certain products at the railway station of origin, instead of destination, rather like the FOB pricing widely used in market economies. This departure is used when shipping distances are not large, when transportation costs are a small part of total cost, or when the purchaser normally takes possession at the producer's plant.[31] The prices of these products are uniform for producers rather than purchasers.

The principle of uniformity is also modified in the pricing of certain products with wide variations in production costs that are due primarily to such conditions as quality of natural resources or proximity to markets. In such cases different wholesale prices may be assigned to different regions or production zones. The price in each zone is based on the branch average costs of the producers in that oil field or coal region.[32]

With both uniform and zonal prices, average-cost pricing may cause profit rates among producers to vary greatly for reasons that do not reflect the quality of enterprise performance. The reasons may be differences in natural conditions; even in a single price zone natural resources and distance from markets may vary greatly. Or the reason may be differences in the age and quality of capital equipment or differences in distance from market in the case of station-of-destination pricing.[33] Soviet planners seek to use earned profits as a measure of enterprise performance and therefore strive to eliminate from profit the effects of factors not related to that performance.[34] To that end, in industries where such factors cause wide variations in profit rates special "accounting" prices may be used. The uniform or zonal price is quoted in the price catalogue and is paid by the purchaser to the wholesale supplier. But the wholesaler pays the producer a price that may be greater or less than the catalogue price. It is less than the catalogue price in the case of enterprises enjoying better-than-average production advantages, and greater than the catalogue price in the opposite case.[35]

Where accounting prices are used, as in coal mining, it is the accounting price that serves as the basis of the producer's decision making, while the catalogue price is used in the purchaser's calculations. To the extent that wholesale prices affect decision making, the spread between producer and user prices leads to inefficiency in resource use. Accounting prices are used sparingly, however, for it is often difficult to distinguish that portion of profit (or loss) that is due to external circumstances from that due to the enterprise's own managerial skill, or lack of it. "One must not convert accounting prices into a mechanism for covering up mismanagement and other deficiencies in the activity of one or another enterprise."[36]

8.3. Prices and Standards

An economy that regulates prices socially must also regulate quality socially. This has been the experience not only of centrally planned socialist economies but also of medieval guilds and of capitalist economies that have employed price controls in periods of wartime or inflation. For a price is the price of a thing—a good or a service—and a producer obliged to sell that thing at a regulated price must not be allowed to benefit from a reduction in its quality. Price regulation would collapse without quality regulation.

Quality regulation in the Soviet economy is based on a system of government-approved standards.[37] A standard is a document specifying the principal structural and performance characteristics of a product. The official wholesale price catalogues specify both the prices and standards. An entry might read, "Cotton Cloth, State Standard G 4023, 1.40 rubles per yard." A purchaser can refuse to pay that price for a shipment of cloth that does not meet the quality characteristics specified in that state standard document.

A vast quantity of effort is required to produce the set of state standards and to revise them periodically in accordance with the pace of technological progress. The government organization responsible for the program is the State Standards Committee of the USSR Council of Ministers. Under its general supervision is a network of some 400 laboratories and institutes engaged in standardization work in industry. The State Standards Committee itself operates at least 12 research institutes, 41 experimental enterprises, and several information agencies. Conformity to standards is supervised by the State Quality Inspectorate, which operates a network of testing laboratories in the republics and provinces. They conduct their work by spot checks on individual enterprises and by a program of testing. They also organize ongoing and periodic quality inspections by the ministries, the party organizations, and the trade unions.

The standards system is designed to support price administration, both with respect to established products and new products. In the case of established products, its principal function is to maintain the quality of output. For in the absence of standards quality controls would be impossible to enforce. Neither the officials of the State Quality Inspectorate nor the legal department of a complaining purchaser could press a case effectively against a producer in the absence of a comprehensive description of the product. The pressures on producers are such that, faced with fixed product prices, there is always a gain to be made by shaving on one or more quality characteristics of the product. And given the relative weakness of buyers in the centrally planned economy, the role of the standards and inspection service is all the greater.

In the pricing of new products, the standards system serves an additional function. It provides a machinery for evaluating the economic worth of a new product. Consider the price administrator presented with a request for the approval of a proposed price for a new or improved product. The documentation shows that the product is superior to an older model in one or more technical characteristics; and since the improvements involve additional costs, the requested price is higher than the older one. The improvement, for example, may consist of the preshrinking of the fabric so that the new textile is launderable. In the absence of a standards system, the price administrator could do little more than check the calculations and assign the new price. Such a procedure would be easily subject to abuse. What the price administrator may not know is that the new product differs from the older in certain other respects; it may be reduced in width, or in thread count, or some other characteristics. He may also not know that the particular textile is used primarily in industrial applications in which it is not normally laundered, so that the technical improvement has no economic value.

The standards system is intended to prevent such abuses. The regulations specify all the product characteristics that must be reported before a new standard will be officially registered. A new textile standard, for example, may have to specify width and thread count, along with pretreatment, to qualify for registration. The registration procedure, moreover, is a complex process that provides in its course for a review of the technical and economic value of the new product's characteristics. The price agency is not permitted to approve a new price until the new standard has been registered.[38]

In practice the standards system does undoubtedly provide considerable support for price administration. It is clear, however, that its success is far from complete, a fact that should occasion no surprise in so complex an economy with such resourceful managerial officials. Extensive as the set of official standards is, it cannot be expected to encompass the millions of commodities produced. Nor can it prevail against the many pressures on quality in a price-administered economy. The literature contains numerous accounts of precisely those practices that the standards system is designed to forestall. In the machinery industry, we read, the producer "guided by his own interests, improves those characteristics of a product which are easiest for him to improve; although when taken by themselves, without the accompanying improvement of other characteristics, they constitute no real improvement in the product's quality as far as the user is concerned."[39] The problems of price and quality administration will be considered more fully later.[40]

8.4. Profit Rates on New Products

The architects of the Soviet economy faced the task of designing a pricing system that was consistent with Marxian economic theory and met the requirements of the system of central economic planning. The commodities that are the subject of planning consist overwhelmingly of established products. Some, like the basic metals and fuels, had been produced for a long time; and some, like various machinery products, may have been introduced recently. But at any time, and particularly on the occasion of a general price revision, the world to be dealt with consists of a given set of commodities in search of a set of prices. It was in that context that the principles of uniform, permanent cost-plus-profit pricing were developed.

Though designed for the pricing of established products it was only natural that the same principles should also be applied in the pricing of new products. Some minor adaptations had to be made. Since new products have no cost history, branch average cost cannot be computed on the basis of the cost experience of existing enterprises but must be based on estimates. This is merely a technical matter, however. Having survived the crucible of political orthodoxy, the principles of pricing were quite automatically applied to new products.

Probably few considered that the distinction was worth drawing. Of all the significant ways in which types of commodities are usually distinguished from one another—consumer or producer goods, agricultural or industrial, goods or services, primary or processed, labor intensive or capital intensive, final or intermediate product—the distinction between established and new commodities does not seem to demand primary attention. Of all the consequences of a given pricing principle that merit careful investigation, the consequences for the relative output of established and new commodities would not appear of major significance.

Not only was there little reason to consider the consequences of the pricing principles on innovation, but the ideology of the early years gave little reason to consider that innovation might be a problem at all for the socialist society. With the contradictions of capitalism removed, one might well expect a new and unparalleled flourishing of the creative energies of the people. The new products and processes pouring forth from the socialist laboratories could be priced and allocated in the same planned manner as coal, shoes, and railroad cars.

In the course of time opinion on this matter changed. The rate and quality of innovation was increasingly regarded as unsatisfactory. And evidence mounted that a major part of the problem was the pricing of new products. The evidence most widely presented is that earned profit rates on new products tend to be lower than those on established products. The conclusion is that the difference in profit rates discourages product innovation.

The profitability of new products has been extensively studied by Soviet economists. Unfortunately, none of the studies has been published in great detail, but the results are often presented in writings on the general subject of innovation. Because of the paucity of detail, one cannot always be sure of the precise meaning of the terms. In particular we do not know in all cases how the distinction between new and old products is drawn. In the most common usage a product is classified as new for one or two years after the start-up of normal-scale production.[41] That is assumed to be the definition in the data presented here, unless otherwise specified. The profit rates most likely refer to profit as a ratio of total cost rather than of capital.

Typical of such studies is one conducted in 1965 by the Institute of Economics, which reported the following profit rates on new and old machinery products:[42]

Established Products	Rate of Profit (+) or Loss (−); Percentage of Cost
Tractor DET-250	+43.8
Tractor T-100 M	+23.6
Tractor T-100 GM	+30.6
Tractor DT-20	+27.3
Tractor DT-146	+39.9
Tractor Belorus' MTZ-502	+ 9.0
Engine D-108	+22.0
Thread Grinding Machine 5822	+112.0
Vertical Boring Machine 2a 450	+50.8
Screw Cutting Lathe 1K 62	+12.3
New Products	
Tractor DT 75 C	− 7.3
Tractor T-4	−69.1
Tractor T-40	− 2.8
Tractor T-40 P	− 3.7
Tractor T-40 A	− 7.0
Tractor T-50 B	−11.1
Tractor Belorus' MTZ-52 M	+ 3.7
Tractor Engine D-37 M, D-D7B	− 8.0

A large volume of similar data is available on the experience of individual plants. Of the principal products of the Russian Diesel Plant in 1964, the older ones earned an average profit rate of 15 percent, while the average for the new products was 2.7 percent. At the Leningrad Light Industry Machinery Combine, older products earned profit rates ranging from 26 percent to 70 percent, while new products ranged from a profit rate of 5.5 percent to a loss of 24.4 percent.[43] One finds variations, of course. The Barnaul Artificial Fiber Plant, for example, earned a profit rate of 33.3 percent when it introduced the production of a synthetic textile (*kapron*), while the Chernigov plant suffered a loss of 15.7 percent. Combine No. 18, selling polyethylene at 2,200 rubles per ton, realized a profit rate of 181.3 percent, while the Ufa Synthetic Alcohol Plant, selling polyethylene at the same price, suffered a loss of 16.3 percent.[44] When individual variations are averaged out, however, the pattern of the relative unprofitability of new products generally emerges.

In some studies, instead of the simple distinction between new and old products, a more precise measure is used that specifies the number of years since the product was first introduced into production. One investigator studied profit rates on a group of mineral-concentration machinery products produced in 1963. The results show a monotonic relationship between profitability and number of years in production:[45]

Period of Introduction into Production	Rate of Profit per Unit of Output
Before 1955	+13 %
1956-1960	+11.5%
1961-1963	−1.5%

While the published data generally reveal the relative unprofitability of new products, that finding is not universal. An extensive sample survey was conducted jointly by the Central Statistical Administration and the State Planning Committee in 1962 on the profitability of new industrial chemical products, with the following results:[46]

Number of Years in Production	Profit Rate per Unit of Output	Percentage of Total Output
Less than 1 year	11.4%	21.6
1 to 3 years	9.2%	50.6
Over 3 years	42.8%	27.8
		100.0

The profitability of commodities in production over 3 years was vastly greater than that of newer products. But among the newer products an

inversion occurs. Those in production less than 1 year earned a somewhat larger profit than those 2 and 3 years old. The analysts ascribe this
result to the practice of employing exceptionally high temporary prices
during the first year of production; we shall discuss the use of temporary prices presently. But it is also possible that prices and costs of industrial chemicals may behave somewhat differently from those of
other products. The available data are not sufficient for an independent
judgment.

If new products are indeed generally less profitable than older ones,
one would expect to find differences in the average realized profit rates
of enterprises according to their degree of innovativeness. A second
group of studies approaches the question from this perspective. The
usual method is to classify enterprises according to the percentage of
their total value of output that consists of new products. The following
results were obtained for thirteen engineering enterprises in the Moscow
area around 1965:[47]

Enterprise	Percentage of New Products in Total	Rate of Profit, Percent
"Stankonormal'"	0	51.8
Pneumatic Apparatus Plant	2.2	51.4
"Mossel'mash"	16.3	43.7
Kirov "Dinamo"	19.3	40.7
Kuibyshev Electrical Plant	19.8	26.9
Boring Machine Plant	22.5	66.5
"Kalibr"	26.4	56.8
"Freser"	28.2	18.9
Excavator Plant (Dmitrov)	28.6	18.3
"Komsomolets" (Egor'evsk)	35.5	24.0
Automatic Crane (Balashikha)	42.2	19.8
"Red Prolitariat"	60.3	10.9
Heavy Machine Tool (Kolomna)	62.3	10.7

Larger sample surveys confirm the plant data. A survey of 100 machinery enterprises found an average profit rate of about 30 percent for
those with less than 10 percent of their output consisting of new products; but when the proportion of new products approached 50 percent,
the profit rate fell to 8 to 10 percent.[48] In the aforementioned survey
of producers of industrial chemicals the average profit rate on new

products was 17.4 percent, while the average profit rate on the total output of the enterprises was 19.7 percent. Hence the new products exerted a downward pull on profit rates.[49]

The political leaders have now been persuaded that the relative unprofitability of new products is a major obstacle to product innovation. At the 1965 Party plenum, Mr. Kosygin stated that "prices are also called upon to play a large role in solving the problems of raising the quality of output and attaining proper levels of durability and reliability."[50] At a national conference on technological progress in 1967 the point was made more forcefully: "without a fundamental change in the system of prices and pricing, no positive results can be achieved."[51] In response to these views the pricing of new products has become the subject of voluminous discussion. In a complex and increasing number of respects, new products are now priced differently from the standard method of pricing established products.

The "uncompetitiveness"—as it is sometimes called[52]—of new products is an unintended consequence of the casual application to new products of the principles originally developed for pricing established products. Why, one might ask, should uniform, permanent, cost-plus-profit pricing generate such differences in profit rates between new and old products? The answer is to be found in certain properties of new products that distinguish them from established products. One such property is that the production-cost behavior of new products differs in certain crucial ways from that of older products. Hence cost-based pricing leads to different results in the two cases. The next two chapters deal with the cost behavior of new products and with the effort to take it into account in pricing new products.

Notes

1. Abba P. Lerner, *The Economics of Control* (New York: Macmillan, 1946).

2. Superficial observers sometimes fail to distinguish the form of economic government from the type of society in which it is employed. The use by a socialist society of a form of economic government that is also used in capitalist societies does not make it any less "socialist" than the use of steel mills, which are also used in capitalist countries. This stricture is not to deny that societies are influenced by the kinds of economic government—and steel mills—they employ.

3. Although they would be relevant to an understanding of the governors' economic behavior, and of the instructions they issue to managers, which in turn influences managerial behavior.

4. P. J. D. Wiles, *The Political Economy of Communism* (Cambridge: Harvard University Press, 1962), p. xv and elsewhere.

5. Alec Nove, *The Soviet Economy* (New York: Praeger, 1965), rev. ed., p. 163.

6. The statement refers to money prices. Following Gregory Grossman, one might regard this as

an instance of the use of "physical quasi-prices," in which the weights of the blocks of different sizes serve as the effective prices. See his article "Industrial Prices in the U.S.S.R.," *American Economic Review (Proceedings)*, Vol. 49, No. 2 (May 1959), p. 54.

7. Cases like the cement-block factories reflect the complexity of the structure of decision rules. Profit is one of the factors enterprises are supposed to consider, but there are others as well. See Chap. 14.

8. The relative weights to be given to these two magnitudes are discussed later, Sec. 14.5.

9. The price the manufacturer receives is called the "factory wholesale price." The price at which a customer buys is called the "industry wholesale price." The latter price may exceed the former by certain additional costs not borne by the manufacturer, such as selling and transportation costs and indirect taxes.

10. Howard J. Sherman discusses the Marxian basis of Soviet pricing principles in "Marxist Economics and Soviet Planning," *Soviet Studies*, Vol. 18:2, October 1966, pp. 169-188.

11. Abram Bergson, *The Economics of Soviet Planning* (New Haven: Yale University Press, 1964), Chap. 11.

12. See Sec. 14.5.

13. Robert W. Campbell, *Accounting in Soviet Planning and Management* (Cambridge: Harvard University Press, 1963), Chap. 5.

14. Sh. Ia. Turetskii, ed., *Tseny i tarify* (Prices and Service Charges) (Moscow: *Vysshaia Shkola*, 1969), p. 52.

15. Ibid., p. 53.

16. The proposal received a public airing at a 1966 conference on the subject of optimal planning and price formation. The main paper was read by Academician M. P. Federenko, Director of the Central Mathematical Economics Institute. The rapporteur writes:

Advancing the notion of the optimal price as an automatic regulator of resource allocation, the representatives of mathematical economics would set it in the basis of marginal costs. The overwhelming majority of the economists participating in the discussion spoke decisively against the idea. Thus G. I. Levin demonstrated that a price high enough to guarantee that the worst enterprise would cover their costs and earn a normal profit in addition is not an optimal price but a monopoly price. The general use of such monopoly prices would give most enterprises in the cement industry a profit rate of 200 percent on capital, and the Magnitogorsk plant 316 percent.

Voprosy ekonomiki, 1967, No. 5, p. 154.

17. A. M. Matlin, *Plan, tsena i effektivnost' proizvodstva* (Plan, Price, and Production Efficiency) (Moscow: *Ekonomika*, 1970), p. 80; S. G. Stoliarov, *O tsenakh i tsenoobrazovanii v SSSR* (Prices and Price Formation in the USSR) (Moscow: *Statistika*, 1969), third ed., p. 78.

18. Retail prices of consumer goods roughly correspond to market-clearing prices. This is accomplished by adding a turnover tax to the sum of the wholesale price and retail markup. The turnover tax is generally adjusted so as to reduce demand to a level roughly equal to the supply. In practice, however, retail prices tend often to be somewhat below the market-clearing levels, and in such cases the goods are sold off quickly after their delivery to the shops and are not available again until the next delivery.

19. For an interesting summary of opinions on the meaning of the expression "normally operating enterprise," see K. N. Plotnikov and A. S. Gusarov, *Sovremennye problemy teorii i praktiki tsenoobrazovaniia pri sotsializma* (Current Problems in the Theory and Practice of Pricing under Socialism) (Moscow: *Nauka*, 1971), pp. 189-202.

20. A. N. Komin, *Problemy planovogo tsenoobrazovaniia* (Problems of Planned Price Formation) (Moscow: *Ekonomika*, 1971), p. 62. The general principle is modified in practice to take account of certain ministry and national needs as well.

21. *Kommunist*, 1966, No. 14, p. 41. The planned profit also provided for funds to be used by enterprises to finance a certain portion of the planned capital investments.

22. L. I. Skvortsov, *Tseny i tsenoobrazovanie v SSSR* (Prices and Price Formation in the USSR) (Moscow: *Vysshaia Shkola*, 1972), p. 147.

23. Komin, *Problemy planovogo tsenoobrazovaniia*, pp. 78-81.

24. Again, some differentiation of profit markup among product groups may be authorized.

25. Skvortsov, *Tseny i tsenoobrozovanie*, p. 25.

26. Plotnikov and Gusarov, *Sovremennye problemy teorii*, p. 122.

27. Skvortsov, *Tseny i tsenoobrazovanie*, p. 141.

28. Plotnikov and Gusarov, *Sovremennye problemy teorii*, pp. 476-478.

29. P. S. Mstislavskii, M. G. Gabrieli, and Iu. V. Borozdin, *Ekonomicheskoe obosnovanie optovykh tsen na novuiu promyshlennuiu produktsiiu* (The Economic Basis of Wholesale Pricing of New Industrial Products) (Moscow: *Nauka*, 1968), p. 151.

30. Komin, *Problemy planovogo tsenoobrazovaniia*, p. 119.

31. Turetskii, *Tseny i tarify*, p. 47.

32. Komin, *Problemy planovogo tsenoobrazovaniia*, pp. 55-57. A variant of zonal (*zonal'nyi*) pricing is "belt" (*poiasyni*) pricing. Belt prices are differentiated by zone also, but in addition they are priced at the station of destination and therefore include transport costs. Cement and lumber are belt priced. Komin, pp. 56-57.

33. Stoliarov, *O tsenakh*, p. 22.

34. See the discussion of economic rents, Sec. 11.4.

35. Skvortsov, *Tseny*, p. 26.

36. Ibid.

37. The following discussion relies heavily on M. C. Spechler, *The Economics of Product Quality in Soviet Industry*, Ph.D. thesis, Harvard University, May 1971. See pp. 69-87 for a brief history of the standards system.

38. Plotnikov and Gusarov, *Sovremennye problemy teorii*, p. 395.

39. Ibid., p. 378.

40. Chap. 13.

41. The normal scale of production depends on the type of product. The literature distinguishes mass production from lot-size or batch (*seriinyi*, or "series") production. In the production of machinery, equipment, and instruments, the normal scale of production consists of lots ranging from two units to thousands. Products like refined metals, textiles, and so forth are mass-produced. See David Granick, *Soviet Metal Fabricating and Economic Development: Practice versus Policy* (Madison: University of Wisconsin Press, 1967), p. 86, ftn.

42. L. M. Gatovskii, G. D. Anisimov, G. B. Gertsovich, V. G. Pankrat'ev, and E. N. Slastenko, eds., *Problemy ekonomicheskogo stimulirovaniia nauchno-tekhnicheskogo progressa* (Problems of Economic Incentives for Scientific and Technological Progress) (Moscow: *Nauka*, 1967), p. 38.

43. *Planovoe khoziaistvo*, 1966, No. 6, p. 13.

44. Stoliarov, *O tsenakh*, p. 154.

45. A. M. Matlin, *Tekhnicheskii progress i tseny mashin* (Technical Progress and Machinery Prices) (Moscow: *Ekonomika*, 1966), p. 17.

46. Stoliarov, *O tsenakh*, p. 154.

47. Gatovskii et al., *Problemy ekonomicheskogo stimulirovaniia*, p. 35.

48. *Planovoe khoziaistvo*, 1966, No. 6, p. 14.

49. Stoliarov, *O tsenakh*, p. 153.

50. Quoted in Mstislavskii, Gabrieli, and Borozdin, *Ekonomicheskoe obosnovanie optovykh tsen*, p. 10.

51. *Voprosy ekonomiki*, 1967, No. 9, p. 150.

52. Plotnikov and Gusarov, *Sovremennye problemy teorii*, p. 437.

Chapter 9

Cost Behavior of New Products

Two measures of production cost are of major importance in enterprise decisions. One is the unit average cost of each product, the calculation of which was discussed earlier.[1] The other is the average "full cost of output." The full cost of output is the sum of all the costs incurred by the enterprise on all its products during a period of time. Average full cost is the ratio of the full cost of output to the total value of output, expressed in kopeks per ruble.

Average unit cost is important to the enterprise because it is the basis on which product prices are established, and it therefore affects the enterprise's profit performance. The role of average full cost has changed in the course of time. Before the 1965 Economic Reform the enterprise plan contained an official indicator of the planned percentage reduction in full cost. Failure to meet that cost-reduction target constituted underfulfillment of a significant part of the plan. It created the presumption of poor management, and the enterprise might be penalized by the withholding of bonus payments. In addition, ministries compared the average full costs of enterprises with similar output profiles as a basis of evaluation. A high-cost enterprise was presumed guilty unless proved innocent, and while its cost performance may be satisfactorily explained to the ministry, it nevertheless required explanation. This apparent concern with cost in itself appears not only in administrative matters but in economic analysis as well. The Novosibirsk Leather Shoe Combine introduced six new models into production in 1962, which increased enterprise costs by 52,000 rubles. "This kind of 'new' product conflicts sharply with the requirements of technological progress," writes the analyst.[2] That such judgment can be rendered without consideration of the quality of the new products is a reflection of the independent role of pure cost considerations in the evaluation of enterprise performance.

The Reform eliminated average cost of production from the official plan indicators. Management is therefore no longer held officially to account for its cost performance, although unofficially the high-cost producer still has some explaining to do. This change may have diminished the importance of pure cost considerations in economic decisions. However the Reform also elevated profit into a major indicator of the plan, which has the effect of increasing the importance of cost. Perhaps on balance the role of cost factors in economic decisions has not changed greatly, although the reasons for its importance have changed.

Since cost considerations are a significant element in decision making, management may be expected to find cost-reducing process innovations highly attractive; at least if they have some confidence that the estimated cost reduction will be realized. But product innovations generally involve the enterprise in a series of costly expenditures, and average costs tend to rise. It is a widely held view among Soviet scholars that the high cost of introducing new products is the key to managerial reluctance regarding product innovation. Mr. G. D. Anisimov of the Institute of Economics, a major authority on the subject, writes that:[3]

The problem of compensation for these additional expenses [. . . must be considered] one of the most serious problems in the further improvement of the new system of planning and incentives. One may state without exaggeration that this has become the central problem of the economic mechanism for stimulating technical progress.

We may doubt that this is *the* central problem. Since the concern is primarily profitability, it is not cost alone but the relationship of cost to price that should influence the decision to innovate. However, if all the expenses associated with innovation are not fully accounted for in the process of price setting, then the costs of innovation can be regarded as an obstacle to innovation.

The problem is often expressed in the assertion that production costs of new products tend to be "high." The term "high" appears to have a variety of meanings in that context. First, new-product costs of production tend to be high relative to their planned costs of production. Second, production costs of the first producer of a new product tend to be high relative to those of the second, and the later the order in which a producer introduces the new product into his line, the lower his costs tend to be relative to those who introduced it earlier. Third, the production costs of new products tend to be high relative to those of similar established products in the enterprise product line.

9.1. Planned and Realized Costs

The national production-plan targets incorporate the aspirations of the Soviet leadership for the plan year. Attainment of the targets depends heavily on the accuracy of cost estimates. When realized costs exceed the plan estimates, some of the national targets are unfulfilled. The causes must be sought out, and responsible parties held to account.

Hence, even though cost of production is no longer an official indicator of the enterprise plan, the management that runs over its planned cost can expect to be called to account.

Every production operation invokes some degree of uncertainty, and managers have long since developed techniques for reducing the risk arising from uncertainty. One technique is the long-standing practice of building a "safety factor" into the plan targets.[4] Another is to favor alternatives that involve lesser degrees of uncertainty. In both product and process innovation, however, costs can be foreseen with less certainty than is the case of established products and processes; and the more complex and novel the innovation, the greater the risk of exceeding the planned cost estimates. Hence the costs of new products are regarded as "high" relative to those of established products in the sense that the decision to introduce a new product or process increases the risk of exceeding cost targets.

Scattered data are available on the extent to which cost estimates tend to be off in the case of new products. In a survey of machine-tool manufacturing plants, estimates of new-product costs proved to be understated in 85 percent of the cases. Instances are cited of costs that exceed the estimates by eight times.[5] A writer notes that the estimating guidelines and coefficients used in research and development organizations "tend toward a certain optimism."[6]

Cost-estimating errors are not always on the low side. A design bureau in L'vov estimated a number of jobs at what turned out to be twice their actual cost. Because their realized costs were so far below the estimate they showed the large profit rate of 20 percent on cost that year.[7] Enterprises that have successfully managed to build a safety factor into their estimates also end up with realized costs below estimates. The cost estimate on the new wide-gauge harvester ZhVN-6 was 859 rubles, against 632 rubles of actual cost as calculated after production had begun.[8] Sample studies are not available for judging the relative frequency of cost overestimation and underestimation, but the data give the strong impression that underestimation occurs frequently enough to be a serious concern of innovators.

The phenomenon of "cost-overruns" is not unique to Soviet industry, of course. Marshall and Meckling found, in a study of 22 major items of military equipment produced for the U.S. government, that the mean ratio of actual final cost to the first estimated cost was 6.5, or 4.1 if one major underestimate of a missile is excluded.[9] Nelson, Peck, and

Kalachek, who report similar findings, note that the degree of under-estimation tends to be less in civilian industry, where decisions are made more conservatively.[10] The better record of cost estimation may also reflect the fact that civilian products tend to be produced in larger quantities than military items. But from an organizational point of view, Soviet industry may be more akin to U.S. governmental procurement than to U.S. civilian industry.

A number of the reasons for cost underestimation are also similar in the two economies. F. M. Scherer distinguishes two sources of cost-estimating error in U.S. weapons programs: those due to the purely technical difficulties of forecasting results, and the other to various man-made difficulties in development programs. Technical difficulties, which were thought to account for less than 30 percent of time and cost variances in the U.S. study, are undoubtedly similar in the USSR. But the man-made difficulties are also rather similar; the changes in original plans, shortages of funds, and bureaucratic delays in the U.S. programs would sound very familiar to the Soviet executive.[11] There is one source of error in U.S. programs that one might imagine would be confined to market economies, namely, unanticipated changes in the prices of one's inputs. In Soviet industry most prices tend to be stable for long periods, but the partial price revisions that occur constantly do affect the costs of users. Thus we read that in a group of shoe factories in the USSR, the principal reason that new-product costs exceeded planned costs was changes in materials prices.[12] One reason for cost overruns in the United States that is not likely to be significant in Soviet industry is the practice by U.S. military contractors of submitting "unrealistic cost and time estimates . . . to 'sell' a company's proposals."[13] But with this exception, the cost-estimation problems of product innovators are very similar in the two countries.

In some respects the consequences are not very difficult in the two countries either. Before the 1965 Reform, when production cost was an official plan indicator, a cost overrun was a matter of major importance. Now its consequence is probably not greater than a similar occurrence in a capitalist firm. In both cases, explanations would be demanded and, if the cause is negligence or ineptitude, some responsible officials would be punished in some way ranging from a mere reprimand to a financial penalty or perhaps to dismissal. Uncertainty over costs is a source of resistance to product innovation in both economies, but in the total context of the enterprise's innovation decision its im-

portance is probably not great, compared for example to such considerations as the probable gain from a successful innovation or the probable
loss from failure to innovate.

9.2. Leaders' Costs and Followers' Costs

The decision to innovate entails a greater risk of exceeding cost targets
than the decision not to innovate. But all innovators are not alike in
this respect. If one means by the term "innovator" anyone who introduces something new in his own enterprise, then one must distinguish
innovators according to the order in which they introduce a new product or process. The first enterprise in the USSR—or in the world, for
that matter—to introduce a new product incurs certain costs that the
second one may not need to bear, and the third and later followers may
find their innovation costs to be successively lower. Two reasons may
be given for this difference between leaders' and followers' costs: economies of scale and learning costs.

When a new product is introduced for the first time, its properties and
uses are not widely known, and demand tends to be limited. The first
production installations are therefore designed for a relatively small
output capacity. As time goes on, more adopters become familiar with
the product, new uses for it are found, and the production of older
substitutes declines. As the demand for the new product grows, subsequent plants and installations tend to be designed with larger output
capacity. Most production processes exhibit some degree of increasing
returns to scale; that is, production installations with larger output
capacity operate at lower unit production costs in the range of their
rated capacity. Hence the very first innovator of a new product may
soon find himself operating at a disadvantage relative to those who
come after him. For even if all operated at their rated capacity, his average cost will be higher than that of his followers whose plants incorporate greater economies of scale. One would therefore expect the resistance to innovation to be greater in the case of first producers than of
followers.

In the case of a process innovation, the effect of economies of scale is
smaller because the product itself is changed very little if at all, and the
levels of demand and output are stable. Many process innovations, however, are based on products newly innovated elsewhere. The automation
of an engine-boring process, for example, is based on the installation of
numerically controlled machine tools, which are the product-innova-

tions of the engineering industry. As the demand for the latter products grows, costs and prices may be expected to decline because of economies of scale. The first enterprise to adopt the new automatic tools as a process innovation therefore experiences higher production costs than later adopters.

The first producer would experience this disadvantage of economies of scale even if the state of technological knowledge were constant. Technological knowledge means, in this context, the knowledge required to build the most efficient installations at various scales of output. If technological knowledge grows over time, however, then the first producer is at a disadvantage in yet another respect. For even if all later plants were designed for the same scale of output as the first, their average costs would be lower.

A great deal of valuable knowledge is developed out of the innovative experience of the first producer. The knowledge is gained in the course of time at the cost of errors, waste, spoilage, redesign expenses, and so forth. Some of the knowledge takes the form of techniques—or modes of procedure and types of skills. Some of the knowledge also takes the form of technology—new specialized devices or equipment. Both forms of the knowledge are then available to the follower and enable him to introduce the product with fewer production disruptions and at a lower cost. The accumulation of knowledge continues, and successive followers are for a considerable time able to benefit in this manner from the costly experience of their forerunners.

Whether because of economies of scale or learning costs, Soviet managers do exhibit an aversion against being the first to introduce a new product or process. One sees its influence in statements like this petulant remark of Director Novgorodov of the Moscow Heavy Alloys Combine, who had pioneered in a new process and who bore all the headaches while the followers derived the benefits:

If an enterprise is the first in the industry to undertake a full changeover to new technological equipment, it is in a very unfortunate position, because the first models of new equipment are much more expensive (1.5 to 3 times as much) and also require extensive outlays for setting it up and for design modification. Enterprises that introduce this same equipment later on pay much less for it and earn a much higher rate of profit.[14]

Hence a pricing policy designed to encourage innovation must provide not only for those properties of cost behavior that distinguish innovators from noninnovators generally, like uncertainty about future costs. It must also recognize that even among innovators costs behave differently according to the time sequence of the introduction and diffusion of innovations.

9.3. New-Product Costs and Established-Product Costs

The third sense in which the production costs of new products are said to be "high" is the most significant. There are two parts to the proposition: (1) new products entail a set of costs that are not incurred in the current production of established products; and (2) those costs are not uniformly distributed over time but exhibit distinctive time patterns. These innovation costs are associated with the process of production start-up, which is described in Russian as the "mastery" (*osvoenie*) of new products.[15]

Start-Up Costs

The first stage of production start-up[16] is called the production-preparation stage (*podgotovka proizvodstva*). It begins when the decision to innovate is made and ends with the first production run of the product. The one-time costs incurred during this stage consist of expenditures for product design (*konstruktorskaia rabota*), production engineering (*proektirovanie*), purchase and installation of new equipment, redesigning and reorganizing related production equipment and processes, designing and engineering tools and instruments, recalculating labor and material requirements and quotas, preparing technical documentation, testing new materials and semifabricates used in the new production process, and setting up testing and experimental runs at the production site or at the customer's site.

The second, or break-in, stage of production start-up begins with the first production run and ends when the installation is operating at full capacity and at the planned production cost. Normally the initial design of the product and of the engineering system does not fully anticipate all the technical problems that subsequently arise in practice. The materials or equipment may prove not to have the precise characteristics provided for in the original designs, and the product may have unforeseen structural defects. Other parts of the plant's engineering system (production, materials handling, warehousing) may have to be further modified in accommodation to the new installation. For these reasons both the product and the production-engineering system may have to be redesigned. The volume of spoilage is likely to be high while engineering defects are corrected and while labor is learning to work with the new equipment and materials. Further adjustments are required when the first users of the earliest models discover defects that require further correction.

Between these two principal stages of start-up lies the construction period. Some innovations require little construction work. But when new construction work is required, a new set of start-up costs are incurred; and with extensive construction work they may dominate the innovator's concerns. The construction industry is known to be one of the weaker spots in the Soviet economy. The long construction lead times increase the cost of construction work, but insofar as these costs are included in the planned estimates, they are not a major concern of the client enterprise. The problem arises from the frequency with which projects fail to be completed by the planned date. Such delays drive up construction costs because of the additional wage payments, and because costly or subquality substitutes must sometimes be used to keep construction moving when deliveries have been delayed. Inferior quality of construction adds to the break-in costs in the subsequent stage. The break-in period is extended because of interruptions for the repair or rebuilding of defective elements.

With small construction projects, the work is normally concluded during the production-preparation stage, before production commences. With larger projects, the commissioning of the new facilities is sometimes done in sequential steps. That is, the construction schedule is designed so that some part of the production can be started up early, while construction continues on other portions of the project. In such cases the construction work spans the two stages of start-up. It further drives up break-in costs because the first production runs are usually below the design capacity, and because temporary substitutes must be found for the services of those parts of the project not yet completed.

Declining Unit Costs

It is not only the presence and size of start-up costs that distinguish new products from old but also the time pattern in which those costs are incurred. Production-preparation costs are incurred, of course, before production is begun. They therefore cannot be financed out of the current revenues from the sale of that product, nor can they be charged against the cost of production of a product not yet produced. Hence unless special financial and accounting arrangements are made, the innovator faces a drain on his current revenues and a rise in his reported plant average cost of production.

But the most significant time pattern of start-up costs occurs during the break-in stage. The normal tendency during this period is for costs to decline sharply during the first year or two, then to continue declining at a slower rate until a stable normal cost level is attained. This time pattern of new-product-cost behavior has been widely studied in the USSR. A typical set of research results is presented in Table 9.1.[17]

The specific time rates of cost reduction vary greatly among industries, but the pattern is almost universal. Nor is the pattern peculiar to the innovation process in the Soviet economy. It is a general characteristic of cost behavior in innovation and has been extensively documented in capitalist countries; for military aircraft, for petroleum process equipment, for machine tools. In the latter case, for example, it has been found that "unit costs for machine tools are typically reduced by 20 percent for each doubling of cumulated output. In all these cases improvements over the first few years are significant but far less important in later years.[18]

A variety of factors contribute to the declining-cost pattern.[19] One is the "learning by doing" that increases with the cumulating experience of management and labor in the techniques of producing the new product. Another factor, which has a particular salience in the Soviet economy, is the relation between average cost and rate of output. The data on the time rate of change of cost, like those in Table 9.1, usually do not specify the rates of output for each year of production. Where such data are available, they generally show a negative relationship between average cost and rate of output. For example, the rates of output associated with the unit costs of the instruments reported in Table 9.1 (columns 5 through 8) are as follows:[20]

	Year of Production			
	First	Second	Third	Fourth
Instrument A				
Unit Cost	100	58	38	33
Annual Output	13	60	100	100
Instrument B				
Unit Cost	100	69	62	62
Annual Output	15	100	100	100
Instrument C				
Unit Cost	100	117	101	79
Annual Output	9	7	90	100
Instrument D				
Unit Cost	100	88	79	79
Annual Output	3	78	89	100

Table 9.1. Indexes of Individual Production Costs of Selected Groups of Products

| | Agricultural Machinery | | | |
	Soil Cultivating Machines (1)	Sowing and Planting Machines (2)	Harvesting Machines (3)	Totals (4)
Number of models in sample	79	21	40	140
Production cost by year in production: percentage of first year's cost				
Year 1	100	100	100	100
2	89.5	71.4	76.3	78.6
3	87.5	68.6	58.1	61.8
4	81.6	66.8	56.3	58.9
5	70.0	54.1	51.2	58.2
6	67.1	58.7	49.4	54.0
7	66.7	51.6	47.3	52.0
Average for first 7 years in production; percentage of first year's cost	78.2	65.9	60.8	63.7
Number of years required to reach the average for first 7 years	3.6	4.0	2.8	2.9
Average annual percentage cost reduction: Until average level is reached	9.0	13.0	14.2	18.3
After average has been reached	6.5	11.5	10.8	6.2

Sources: Columns (1)-(4): A. M. Matlin, *Plan, tsena, i effektivnost' proizvodstva* (Plan, Price, and Production Efficiency) (Moscow: *Ekonomika*, 1970), p. 79. Columns (5)-(12): Adapted from V. S. Sominskii, *Ekonomika novykh proizvodzv* (The Economics of New Production) (Moscow: *Ekonomika*, 1965), pp. 198-202.

Changes in scale of output often account for the large variations in earned profit rates on different products. In 1972 the "Electrocarbon" Plant earned profit rates of 52.0 percent and 136.7 percent on its commutator brushes EG-61 and MGS-20:[21]

The reason is that the wholesale price was set in the first year of production start-up, when the items were produced in small lots of 10,000 to 15,000 a year. In the second and third, with the completion of start-up and the shift to mass production, costs declined. Thus in the third year of production, 1.5 million units of brush EG-61 were produced and 1 million units of MGS-20.

Differences in scale also account for some of the interenterprise differences in innovation experience. In the aforementioned start-up of production of polyethylene, Combine No. 18 realized a profit rate of

Technical Instruments				Radio Receivers K	Turbo-generator TVS-30	Steam Generator MAT-99/47	Steam Engine EDT-200
A	B	C	D				
(5)	(6)	(7)	(8)	(9)	(10)	(11)	(12)
–	–	–	–	–	–	–	–
100	100	100	100	100	100	100	100
58	69	117	88	98	94.7	90.5	95.0
38	62	101	79	90	92.9	86.9	88.4
33	62	79	79	87	86.3	84.8	85.6
–	–	–	–	78	–	–	–
–	–	–	–	–	–	–	–
–	–	–	–	–	–	–	–
–	–	–	–	–	–	–	–
–	–	–	–	–	–	–	–
–	–	–	–	–	–	–	–
–	–	–	–	–	–	–	–

181.3 percent while the Ufa Synthetic Alcohol Plant and the Sverd-lovsk Plastics Plant suffered losses of 16.3 percent and 29 percent, respectively. All sold their output at the same price. The chief reason for the difference is that the latter two plants produced only one-fifth to one-seventh of the output of the Combine No. 18.[22] Differences in rate of output are not independent, however, of the technical success of the new production process; the low rates of output in the latter plants were apparently due to engineering and related difficulties in getting the level of production up to the rated capacity. The data are also suspect because they deal with a calendar year rather than a year's period of time; if the latter plants started up production in the last months of the year, while Combine No. 18 started up at the beginning, the reported differences in the year's output would be misleading. It is only the magnitudes that would be affected, however; the direction of the relationship between cost and rate of output would not be changed.

Because of the negative relationship between average cost and rate of output, the longer the break-in period, the larger the start-up costs. Two factors account for this. First, it has been found that the quantity of "learning by doing" is a function of the cumulated total past volume of output. Costs are lower on the 100,000th unit of output than on the 1,000th.[23] Hence, the longer it takes the enterprise to reach its 100,000th unit of output, the higher the level of average production costs each year. Second, assuming that the short-run static cost function has the familiar U-shape, average unit costs are high at rates of production below the designed rate.[24] Hence, even in the absence of "learning by doing," the longer it takes to reach rated output capacity, the higher the level of start-up costs.

Long break-in periods are a prominent feature in the innovation process in the USSR, especially when extensive construction work is involved. The OECD study compiled a list of 37 statements appearing in Soviet sources about lead times, but the range of industries is so wide and the stages of the process covered are so varied that generalization or averaging is impossible.[25] By way of illustration, one report is based on a study of 237 completed projects in the Sverdlovsk region, in the machinery, metallurgical, and chemical industries. The period covered is the total innovation process from the beginning of applied research to the introduction of the product or process into operation. The lead times of the projects completed are

up to 2 years,   10 percent of all the projects
3-4 years,   15 percent of all the projects
5 years,   30 percent of all the projects
6-8 years,   45 percent of all the projects

In reports of other studies, the lead times fall on both sides of the five-year median in the Sverdlovsk sample. One source cites 3 to 5 years as the finding of the "majority of authors." The Urals-4 computer took 5 years. The "Komplex" machine for process control took 6 years. The Central Research Institute for Heavy Engineering reports from 4 to 5 years for new technological processes, and 7 to 8 years for new materials. It follows from these long lead times that new-product costs will be higher there than in economies with shorter break-in periods.

9.4. New-Product Costs and Prices

The distinctive cost behavior of new products has always posed a problem in the application of the standard pricing principles to the pricing of new products. Many of the departures from cost-plus-profit pricing that have been authorized at various times were introduced precisely in order to accommodate to the special properties of new products. The forms of that accommodation have been different in different periods.

Before 1950, the major exception to the general principle of cost-plus-profit pricing was the extensive use of subsidies. The prices of many machinery products and some of their major raw-material inputs were set below cost.[26] Start-up costs were presumably among the cost items financed by the subsidies.

Subsidization is a form of deliberate price discrimination and therefore provides a clue to the conception of technological progress that underlies the policy. Michael Boretsky has pointed out, for example, that subsidies were not uniformly extended to all machinery products on the basis of some general principle like degree of factor augmentation but were concentrated in industries that had been assigned high priority in the development plan. Thus "any metal-cutting machine tool 'embodies' technological progress, but a farm tractor does not."[27] David Granick, in his close study of the metal-fabricating industries, concludes that the use of subsidies reflects "a miscalculation as the location of the main resistance to new products: prime attention is given to overcoming consumer rather than producer resistance."[28] Both of those notions came increasingly under criticism, a situation that contributed to the mounting dissatisfaction with the policy of subsidization. The termination of extensive subsidization, however, led to certain new relationships between new-product costs and prices that had a considerable impact on innovation decisions.

The Termination of Subsidies

In 1949 the first of a series of price revisions was made, for the purpose of eliminating subsidies and restoring uniform cost-plus-profit prices. By 1955 the prices of established products came close to the sum of branch average cost plus a 4 to 5 percent profit markup.[29] The earlier price discrimination in favor of machine tools relative to tractors was ended; except for minor differences in profit markups, both were priced in the same manner. And the earlier emphasis on the customer to the neglect of the producer of new technology was modified. The objective was increasingly formulated as the design of a price policy for new products that would somehow take account of the interests of potential producers of new products as well as potential adopters.

The elimination of subsidies required that start-up costs be included in the prices of new products. The practice that has been adopted is to capitalize them; that is, in calculating start-up cost per unit of output, the denominator consists of the output planned for the first several years of production.[30] The capitalization period varies among industries; in machinery production, we read, it was usually 2 or 3 years. However, the pricing methods motivated enterprises to reduce the capitalization period. For in price setting, the authorized profit markup is expressed as a percentage of average unit cost, and the higher the calculated average cost the larger the profit. Hence we read that the full amount of start-up costs is often charged entirely to the first year's output or even loaded on to the first production runs.[31]

However accounted for, the inclusion of start-up expenses in the new product's cost of production led to a sharp increase in the prices of new products relative to old and accentuated the decline in calculated production costs over time. Cost behavior and price policy thus combined to generate the phenomenon of the relative unprofitability of new products as summarized by A. M. Matlin, a prominent authority on pricing and innovation:

With constant prices, the high production cost of new products leads to a relatively small profit on their sales. Subsequently, the decline in cost leads to an increase in profit. Hence the most profitable products are those that have been in production for a long time. Changes in profit rates, with constant prices, are the consequence of the decline in individual production costs as a result of technological progress. But once having arisen, they become an obstacle to further technological progress in industry. The immediate result of the situation is the low level of profit rates, or even losses, in enterprises with relatively large quantities of new products; and conversely, the relatively high profit rates of enterprises that produce older products. Therefore the introduction of new products may be disadvantageous from the point of view of the enterprises' interests.[32]

The discussion has concentrated on the production of new products. But process innovation is also characterized by declining costs over time. Since new processes often consist of other enterprises' new products, the increase in the relative prices of new products causes them to be less "advantageous" to adopters as well. One often reads of cases like the "Hammer and Sickle" Motor Plant in Kharkov, which introduced a new automatic line for machining cylinder blocks. In the first 2 years of production it lost money. Only in the third year did it make a profit, of 14,000 rubles. And in the next 3 years, its profit rose to 74,000, 120,000, 158,000 rubles.[33] When the prices of new automatic equipment were subsidized, the introduction of new processes was less risky for the innovator.

These consequences of the elimination of subsidies launched a discussion about new-product pricing that has continued ever since. In response to the mounting criticism, a series of changes has been introduced in new-product pricing methods, which now constitute a rather complex affair. Some of these changes have subsequently been introduced in the pricing of established products as well. Because of these changes, the expression "permanent cost-plus-profit prices" has become increasingly inaccurate as a shorthand description of the actual Soviet price structure.

Two main lines of criticism have been directed against the application of the traditional principles in the pricing of new products. One was directed not against the principle of cost-based pricing as such but at the wisdom of including all start-up expenses in the cost, and therefore in the price, of new products. The other was a direct attack on the general principle of permanent cost-plus-profit pricing.

Subsidization of Start-Up Costs: The New Products Fund

With the elimination of subsidies, the high start-up costs of new products strained the finances of product innovators and militated against the decision to innovate. One function of the New Products Fund was to encourage the introduction of new products by relieving the innovator of this concern; this financial aspect of the fund has been discussed earlier.[34] The fund has a second function, however—to stimulate the adoption of new products. The widely held view was that the inclusion of all start-up expenses in the cost of the new product led to such high prices that rapid adoption was discouraged. Part of those costs are now subsidized and are financed by contributions into the fund from all enterprises in the producer's ministry. That portion of start-up costs that is financed by the fund is not included in the producer's full cost of production nor in the average unit cost of the new product, and is therefore not included in the price. It has been estimated that the fund has succeeded in reducing the calculated production costs of new products by 14 to 15 percent in various machinery industries, with corresponding reductions in their wholesale prices.[35]

The partial subsidization of start-up costs does not, of course, reduce the social costs of innovation. It merely transfers the burden of paying the costs from the product innovator to all the other enterprises in the same ministry. Two questions may be asked about the economic consequences of the fund. One is whether the subsidy improves the allocation of effort and other resources between new and older products. The second is whether the subsidy ought to be financed by the other enterprises in the innovator's ministry.

The New Products Fund is not the only form of subsidization of new products. They are already heavily subsidized in the sense that much of the research, development, and design work done in the specialized institutes is specific to individual products and is financed by the state.[36] The New Products Fund merely increases the size of the total social subsidy. More generally, however, there is no greater economic justification for relieving the user of the burden of paying start-up costs than there is in the case of normal production costs like labor, materials, and equipment. Both types of costs represent uses of resources necessary to the production of the commodity. The subsidization of any cost item distorts the allocation of resources; the subsidization of wages, for example, would lead to an increase in demand for wage-intensive products relative to materials-intensive products. Similarly the subsidization of start-up costs distorts choices between products that include such costs and products that do not, in favor of the former.

The question is not whether the subsidization of start-up costs increases the demand for new products relative to older ones. Any subsidization of any cost element would have that effect. The question is rather whether that shift in relative demand serves the interests of the economy. In the absence of externalities, there is no reason why it should. If the net benefit to the purchaser of a new product is less than the full cost of producing it, it ought not be produced at all.

In the absence of the subsidy, only those new products would be introduced whose social benefit exceeds their social cost. With the subsidy those new products would continue to be introduced, but furthermore a certain number of additional new products would also be introduced that would not have been without the subsidy. The net benefit to the economy from the latter group of innovations may be negative. They may have contributed to the decline in the efficiency of investment.

Second, one may question the decision to organize the New Products Fund on a ministry basis rather than on a national basis.[37] First, it increases the rate of innovation in the funded ministries relative to the nonfunded. Hence less-productive innovations in the funded ministries may be introduced while more productive ones in the nonfunded ministries are not introduced. Second, the subsidies are financed by contributions from all the enterprises in the funded ministries. These contributions, which are equivalent to taxes, are charged against general costs of production. Hence all costs and prices of the products of funded ministries are increased relative to the products of nonfunded ministries. While there is a certain administrative convenience in this arrangement, there is no economic rationale for it. For one thing the ministry corresponds only roughly to a product grouping, and many individual commodities are produced by enterprises in different ministries. This introduces an arbitrary difference in the cost conditions of the same commodity produced in a funded and a nonfunded ministry. For another, the general price level in funded ministries is raised relative to prices in nonfunded ministries. If the former were the beneficiaries of any externalities generated by the subsidized product innovations, this change in relative prices would be justified. But no case can be made for the presence of such externalities. Moreover, even if a particular new product does generate externalities, they are not likely to be restricted to the other enterprises in the innovator's ministry but would be more broadly distributed.

If the New Products Fund were organized on a national rather than a ministry basis, both of these sources of distortion would be eliminated. New products could compete for subsidies strictly on the basis of their anticipated productivity, without discrimination by the ministry-designation of the innovating enterprise. And the subsidies would be financed by a general charge against all enterprises' costs, thus eliminating the arbitrary increase in the relative prices of the products of funded ministries.

Because of the limitations on the use of the fund discussed in Section 6.4, it has not had a major impact on the rate of innovation. To the modest extent that it has influenced decisions, it has encouraged innovation. Every year a certain number of new products are introduced and adopted that, in the absence of the fund, might not have been. What we do not know, however, is the net economic benefit from those marginal innovations. Because of the subsidy element some of them may yield a negative return, and the distribution of innovations between funded and nonfunded ministries has been distorted in favor of the former. The New Products Fund was a response to the view that a major obstacle to innovation was the high cost of new products relative to established products. Of the two aspects of cost behavior, however, it tackled the one that was of lesser significance: the one-time production-preparation costs of new products. There remained the more serious aspect: the tendency for new-product costs to decline over time. It was that feature of cost behavior that generated the unfortunate differential in profit rates between new and old products. The more radical break with traditional pricing practices came out of the effort to deal with that problem. It led to the erosion of the fundamental principle of permanent prices. In pricing new products, not permanence but flexibility became the desideratum. Some of the most momentous episodes in the Soviet price experience emerged from the search for appropriate methods of introducing flexibility into new-product pricing.

Notes

1. Sec. 8.2.
2. V. S. Sominskii, *Ekonomika novykh proizvodstv* (The Economics of New Production) (Moscow: *Ekonomika*, 1965), p. 182.
3. *Voprosy ekonomiki*, 1968, No. 11, p. 25.
4. For the role of the safety factor in decision making, see Joseph S. Berliner, *Factory and Manager in the USSR* (Cambridge: Harvard University Press, 1957), Chaps. 6 and 7.
5. M. Boretsky, "Comparative Progress in Technology, Productivity and Economic Efficiency: U.S.S.R. Versus U.S.A.," in U.S. Congress, Joint Economic Committee, *New Directions in the Soviet Economy* (Washington: Government Printing Office, 1966), p. 220.
6. *Planovoe khoziaistvo*, 1966, No. 9, p. 13.
7. *Voprosy ekonomiki*, 1968, No. 1, p. 156.
8. P. S. Mstislavskii, M. G. Gabrieli, and Iu. V. Borozdin, *Ekonomicheskoe obosnovanie optovyk tsen na promyshlennuiu produktsiiu* (The Economic Basis of Wholesale Pricing of New Industrial Products) (Moscow: *Nauka*, 1968), pp. 113-114.
9. A. W. Marshall and W. H. Meckling, "Predictability of the Costs, Time and Success of Development," in National Bureau of Economic Research (NBER), *The Rate and Direction of Inventive Activity: Economic and Social Factors* (Princeton: Princeton University Press, 1962), pp. 467-469.
10. R. Nelson, M. Peck, and E. Kalachek, *Technology, Economic Growth, and Public Policy* (Washington: The Brookings Institution, 1967), pp. 93-94.
11. F. M. Scherer, in NBER, *Rate and Direction of Inventive Activity*, pp. 497-500.
12. Sominskii, *Ekonomika novykh proizvodstv*, p. 188. Another reason was the "substitution of some materials [presumably higher-priced, J.B.] for others."
13. P. W. Cherington, M. J. Peck, and F. M. Scherer, "Organization and Research and Development Decision Making Within a Government Department," in NBER *Rate and Direction of Inventive Activity*, p. 401. Also Marshall and Meckling, "Predictability of the Costs," p. 462.

14. *Ekonomicheskaia gazeta*, 1967, No. 33, p. 11.

15. See Sec. 6.4.

16. For a detailed description of the stages of production start-up, see G. D. Anisimov and I. A. Vakhlamov, eds., *Material'noe stimulirovanie vnedreniia novoi tekhniki* (Handbook of Material Incentives for Innovation) (Moscow: *Ekonomika*, 1966), pp. 60-61.

17. For statistical studies of the relationship, see *Voprosy ekonomiki*, 1967, No. 1, p. 118, and *Planovoe khoziaistvo*, 1969, No. 11, p. 28.

18. Nelson, Peck, and Kalachek, *Technology, Economic Growth, and Public Policy*, pp. 105-106.

19. For a review of the contributing factors see Lester Lave, *Technological Change: Its Conception and Measurement* (Englewood Cliffs, N.J.: Prentice-Hall, 1966), pp. 121-126.

20. Sominskii, *Ekonomika novykh proizvodstv*, p. 198. The data are based on the work of K. Tatevosov, first published in 1939. In the indexes of annual output, the output of the fourth years is taken as 100.

21. *Planovoe khoziaistvo*, 1973, No. 8, p. 55.

22. S. G. Stoliarov, *O tsenakh i tsenoobrazovanii v S.S.S.R.* (Prices and Price Formation in the USSR), 3rd ed. (Moscow: *Statistika*, 1969), p. 154.

23. Lave, *Technological Change*, p. 124.

24. This low-output effect should not be confused with economies of scale. The latter refers to the rate of output at which the capital plant is designed to operate at minimum cost. The declining cost problem discussed here is the consequence of the inability of innovators to bring the actual rate of output up to the designed rate quickly. Hence it would be present even if there were no economies of scale.

25. E. Zaleski, J. P. Kozlowski, H. Wienert, R. W. Davies, M. J. Berry, and R. Amman, *Science Policy in the USSR* (Paris: OECD, 1969), Appendix D, pp. 536-539.

26. The subsidies were largest in the periods 1929-1936 and 1940-1949. In the period 1937-1939 an attempt was made to eliminate subsidies, but it was abandoned during the war. Richard Moorsteen, *Prices and Production of Machinery in the Soviet Union, 1928-1958* (Cambridge: Harvard University Press, 1962), pp. 9-10.

27. Boretsky, *Comparative Progress in Technology*, p. 221.

28. D. Granick, *Soviet Metal-Fabricating and Economic Development: Practice Versus Policy* (Madison: University of Wisconsin Press, 1967), p. 235.

29. Moorsteen, *Prices and Production of Machinery*, p. 10.

30. K. N. Plotnikov and A. S. Gusarov, *Sovremennye problemy teorii i praktiki tsenoobrazovaniia pri sotsializme* (Current Problems in the Theory and Practice of Pricing under Socialism) (Moscow: *Nauka*, 1971), p. 371.

31. Mstislavskii, Gabrieli, and Borozdin, *Ekonomicheskoe obosnovanie optovykh tsen*, p. 110.

32. A. M. Matlin, *Plan, tsena i effektivnost' proizvodstva* (Plan, Price, and Production Efficiency) (Moscow: *Ekonomika*, 1970), pp. 79-80.

33. *Planovoe khoziaistvo*, 1966, No. 11, p. 30.

34. See Sec. 6.4.

35. Mstislavskii, Gabrieli, and Borozdin, *Ekonomicheskoe obosnovanie optovykh tsen*, p. 110.

36. A public-goods case can be made for the subsidization of fundamental research and for certain general forms of applied research that are not yet associated with particular future products. No such case can be made for subsidizing research and development that is clearly directed at a particular future product.

37. The question has been raised by N. P. Federenko in *Planovoe khoziaistvo*, 1967, No. 4, p. 16; and by P. G. Bunich in *Voprosy ekonomiki*, 1967, No. 10, p. 51.

Chapter 10

Flexible Pricing

Read the business press in a capitalist country and you will get the idea that new products are the source of great fortunes. Read the Soviet business press and you will conclude that new products are the source of misfortune.

There are exceptions of course. Everybody knows about the Edsel and Corfam. And in the USSR everyone knows about the great aircraft designer, A. S. Yakovlev, and the illustrious Academician B. E. Paton, the innovator of welding techniques. But the major thrust of the message would be clear. In the capitalist enterprise it is usually the new product that brings in the greater profit. In the Soviet enterprise it is the older product. New products are designated by such terms as "disadvantageous" and "noncompetitive."

The classic cause of the noncompetitiveness of new products is the combination of the principle of permanent pricing and the declining cost behavior of new products. Since little can be done about cost behavior, the remedy must be sought in a modification of the pricing principle. Hence it is not surprising to find that it is the economists primarily concerned with technological change who spearhead the drive for more flexible (*gibkii*) pricing.[1] At one time the typical scholarly article expounded on the advantages of stable prices for the Soviet economy. Today one is more likely to find the problem posed as one of developing the proper combination of stability and flexibility.

The first instance of flexible pricing employed on a broad scale was the use of so-called "temporary" (*vremennye*) prices for new products, particularly during the period 1955 to 1967. For a variety of reasons, temporary prices have been greatly restricted in scope since then. Interest has since shifted to other instruments of flexibility, the most promising of which is called "stepwise pricing."

10.1. Temporary Prices

It was the termination of large-scale subsidization in the early 1950s that led to the introduction of temporary prices. As long as machinery prices were subsidized, the fortunes of innovators were not greatly affected by the declining costs of new products. The permanent price was set below cost, and the producer recouped the difference in the form of a subsidy from the state budget. As cost declined, the size of the subsidy diminished, so that the older product did not yield a significantly higher return to the producer than the new product. The variable subsidy served as an instrument for offsetting the effect of declining cost.

Between 1949 and 1955, several successive price revisions virtually eliminated subsidies in the prices of the established products of the time. By the latter date their new permanent prices were high enough on the average to cover costs plus the normal profit. Since they no longer incurred start-up costs, their average-cost levels were stabilized. Costs could be expected to decline slowly with general technological advance but not precipitously as in the case of new products. Hence, with permanent prices, their future earned profit rates would be stable or would rise very slowly.

However, if permanent prices were assigned also to new products first introduced after 1955, with start-up costs provided for in their prices, then their earned profit rates would rise sharply over time. In a short while the structure of prices and profits so laboriously put together by 1955 would begin to come apart again. It was to forestall this danger that the principle of permanent prices was abandoned in the pricing of new products introduced in the engineering industries after 1955.[2] New machinery, equipment, and instruments were assigned not prices "without limit of time" but temporary, or "dated," prices. The temporary price assigned at the inception of production was to be high enough to cover all start-up costs plus the normal profit rate currently authorized on the established products of the industry. After a certain period of time, when start-up costs had largely vanished and average cost was approaching its long-run normal level, the temporary price was to be dropped and a new and lower price assigned, the latter to be a permanent price of the standard kind. Thus by abandoning the principle of permanent pricing in the case of new products, that principle could be preserved for established products without generating excessively high profit rates.

A temporary price is calculated on the same cost-plus-profit principles that are employed in permanent prices.[3] But because of the special properties of new products, certain modifications have to be made.

First, since the price has to be set before the production of the item has begun, the price is based on an estimate of future costs, rather than on actual cost experience. The possibility of error, unintended or deliberate, is therefore greater.

Second, in the case of a new product, the price cannot be based on "branch average cost," since only one or two enterprises are involved. The cost therefore reflects the production conditions and the efficiency of only one or two enterprises.

Third, the estimated cost includes all start-up costs other than those financed by the New Products Fund. The measure of average cost used in pricing is the cost during the first year of normal-scale production.[4] Hence it includes all the break-in costs incurred during the first year. It also includes a portion of the unsubsidized capitalized production-preparation costs; one-third, for example, of the capitalization period is three years.

The cost estimates are prepared by the innovating enterprise and submitted together with a proposed temporary price to the ministry. After a year or so, when break-in costs are largely eliminated, the enterprise is supposed to prepare a new set of cost estimates and to propose a new lower price based on those estimates. When officially approved, that price becomes the product's permanent price thereafter.

The system of temporary pricing prevailed for about a dozen years. By 1967 it was generally regarded as having failed to accomplish its objective, and its use was greatly curtailed. Among the reasons for its failure was the widespread abuse of the rules governing temporary prices that could not be properly policed. But even in the absence of abuses, it is unlikely that such pricing could have achieved the desired relative profit rates for new and older products.

Abuses of Temporary Prices

While the temporary price safeguarded the product innovator against losses, it provided only the normal rate of profit during the first year of production. The sharp decline in costs in the second year, however, created a strong incentive for management to continue selling at the high temporary price. Moreover, the longer management succeeded in delaying the termination of its temporary price, the stronger the inducement for further delay.

Not only was the inducement present but the opportunity was there as well. The introduction of temporary pricing increased greatly the burden on the price-administration agencies. It meant that every new price had now to be shepherded through the complex pricing process twice: once to secure the temporary price and later to secure the permanent price. A large backlog of work piled up in the price agencies, and their ability to limit the duration of temporary prices diminished. Products continued to sell at their temporary prices long after they should have been reviewed, and they were simply "transformed into permanent prices, in effect."[5] They eventually came close to dominating the price structure, particularly in industries experiencing rapid rates of techno- logical progress. In 1964, 40 percent of the output of mining machinery was sold at temporary prices. In textile machinery the figure was 41 percent, and in forging and pressing equipment, 47 percent. Of total machinery output, 32 percent sold at temporary prices. In some in- dividual enterprises the percentage reached 70 percent and higher.[6] Since temporary prices were not listed in the official wholesale price catalogues, the latter became less and less useful for planning and ac- counting.[7] In 1966 the catalogues listed permanent prices for only 20 to 25 percent of all equipment items, or about half of the value of all equipment output.[8] For the rest, the prospective customer or planner or project-designer could not use the price catalogue but had to call the producing enterprise to find out what the temporary price was.

The regulations required the price-setting process to begin well in ad- vance of the first production run, so that the price would be officially approved in advance of that date. With the growing backlog, the price agencies were increasingly unable to get the price approved in time.[9] In those cases, rather than hold up production, the enterprises sold their output at the not-yet-approved draft price, which was technically il- legal. In a 1962 survey of chemicals enterprises, it was found that 7.6 percent of their new products were selling at illegal prices, set by the enterprises themselves and not approved by the appropriate price agen- cy.[10] In some of those cases, it appears, the enterprises were not simply victims of the administrative backlog but had taken advantage of the weakening of price controls to delay deliberately the process of price approval.

A further consequence of temporary pricing was the violation of the principle of uniform prices. The literature is somewhat vague on the point, but it appears that an enterprise introducing a new product into its own product line had the right to apply for a temporary price even if that same product had already been introduced earlier by one or more other enterprises and, therefore, even if a permanent price for that product had already been established. This seems to be the proper inter- pretation of such observations as the following by Dr. Mstislavskii and his colleagues at the Institute of Economics: "The basing of temporary prices on individual costs of production has led to a diversity of prices for identical kinds of products, and to the distortion of correct relationships between those prices and the prices of other types and brands of products that serve similar uses."[11] Thus the price of machine tool Model 676 produced by the Odessa Machine Tool Plant was 1,600 rubles, but the same model produced by the Irkutsk Machine Tool Plant was priced at 2,200 rubles.[12] One consequence of the growing nonuniformity of prices was the erosion of the standard methods of evaluating and comparing the performances of different enterprises: "Identical pieces of equipment received by different enterprises, or received at different times from the same producer, are carried in the accounts of customers at various prices, which weakens the methods of accountability; it makes it difficult to use such important indicators of performance as output per ruble of fixed capital."[13]

The notion of uniformity of prices is in any case difficult to apply to highly fabricated products such as machinery and equipment. Even with permanent prices, it is not clear that Odessa's model of a certain machine tool is or ought to be identical in every way to Irkutsk's and therefore merits the same price. What seems to have happened, however, is that the introduction of temporary prices opened up the whole pricing system so widely, both to error and abuse, that price variation flowed over its normal bounds.

Total profit on new products depends not only on the duration of temporary wholesale prices but also on the level of those prices. It is therefore not surprising that enterprises padded their cost estimates and "in many cases inflated price levels for new products were permitted."[14] As a result, profit rates on new products often exceeded the standard markup to which they were entitled. In a study of 193 new farm machines selling at temporary prices, it was found that in the first year of production their average realized profit rate was 15.7 percent, instead of the standard profit rate of 3 to 5 percent. In the second year of production, however, their realized profit rates rose to 23.5 percent.[15] Hence the inflation of new-product prices and profit rates did not offset the relative unprofitability of new products. It merely raised the general level of prices and profits on both new and established products, while the newer continued to be "disadvantageous" relative to the older.

Control over cost padding is a general problem in all price-regulated economies. But it is a particularly difficult problem in the case of new products because the price must be set in advance of actual production experience. The current regulation requires that the temporary price be officially approved no later than two months before the first output is shipped.[16] But because of the long time required for securing official approval, the draft price proposed by the enterprise is submitted well in advance of the anticipated date of production, on the basis of estimates of future costs. In the case of established products, the price-control authorities have available cost data for many enterprises and for many years, which provide an independent basis for evaluating an individual enterprise's cost calculations. In the case of new products such data are not available, and the authorities are in a weaker position for controlling cost estimation. As a further control, the regulations provide that major customers must be consulted while the temporary price is under negotiation, but that regulation seems to have been widely ignored. In the face of the difficulty of detecting and controlling abuses, it is not surprising that temporary prices "often served as a source of covering various unproductive expenditures."[17]

Finally, abuses in the pricing of products spilled over into abuses in the production process itself. When an established product was assigned a permanent price, that price was not easily changed thereafter. If it happened to provide for a very low profit, it was a burden for the enterprise. The temporary pricing arrangement, however, offered any enterprise an opportunity to secure a new price on any product that was classified as "new." Enterprises were quick to seize upon this opportunity to escape the bonds of low permanent prices. By making a few small changes in an established product, the enterprise could present it as a "new" product and apply for a temporary price that, one hoped, would return a larger profit than the old permanent price. This kind of falsified product innovation, which reached large proportions under temporary pricing, is extremely difficult to detect and to control administratively. It will be treated in detail in the discussion of price administration in Chapter 13. Because it involved deception not only in data about products but in the products themselves, it may have been the most serious of the abuses of temporary pricing.

To summarize the argument, when the price structure was finally stabilized by 1955, it was hoped that the new price level would remain fairly stable thereafter. As so often has been the case, it was the necessity of providing for technological change that upset the good work. Temporary prices for new products were introduced as a modest device for achieving the flexibility needed to accommodate to the peculiar cost behavior of new products. Properly controlled, they should amount to little more than brief disturbances in the solid mass of stable permanent prices. As it turned out, they grew quite out of hand and became the chief source of the subsequent inflation of wholesale prices.

For a time their inflationary effect was concealed from view because the official index of wholesale prices appeared to show that prices were generally fairly stable, and machinery prices in particular seemed to be declining.[18] That index, however, came increasingly under suspicion, both in the USSR and abroad. Two eminent members of the Institute of Economics, Drs. Ia. V. Kvasha and V. P. Krasovskii, who pioneered in the critique of the index, have shown that it was constructed in such a way that new products were simply excluded, along with certain other sources of upward pressure on prices.[19] Under the impact of the accumulating evidence, few continued to doubt that prices had pushed well above the level set in 1955, and that temporary pricing was the primary source of the breach.

Temporary Prices and Profit Rates

The wide publicity given to the abuses of temporary pricing has created in the public mind the view that new-product prices are "too high." Most analysts of the relationship between pricing and product innovation, however, have concluded that new-product prices are "too low." The apparent conflict has created some confusion in the formulation of a pricing policy to encourage innovation.

Temporary prices have been regarded as too high, first, by critics who believe that all start-up costs should be subsidized and excluded from price. This view generally appears in contexts in which the problem of adoption (*vnedrenie*) and diffusion of new products is dissociated from the problem of the introduction (*osvoenie*) of new products. "With the establishment of temporary prices, start-up costs are paid for by the first adopters, which reduces their interest in the product and leads to unequal conditions of economic accountability in different enterprises."[20] Second, temporary prices have been high in the sense that they have been based on the relatively high production costs of the first year of production. Third, because of the widespread abuses in cost-estimation and pricing procedures, temporary prices have generated actual profit rates well in excess of the normal rate specified in the regulations. And fourth, because of these factors, temporary prices have imparted a marked upward pressure on the wholesale price level, even though that effect was not measured in the official price index.

Although in these several respects temporary prices may be regarded as "too high," none of them deals directly with that price relationship that is central to the product innovation decision: namely, the relationship between the prices and costs of new and older products. During the decade of the general use of temporary prices, the data leave little doubt that older products were generally more profitable than new; all the data on profitability presented earlier (Sec. 8.4) were gathered in that period. In that crucial respect, temporary prices were still "too low."

Temporary pricing did not reverse the unfavorable profit relationship between new and older products. But it modified that relationship somewhat in favor of new products. It provided an occasion for a review of the initial price of a new product after it had been in production some time. The permanent price assigned after the review generally eliminated some of the growing profit that had accumulated during the temporary-price period. This result may be seen in the data gathered in the 1962 survey conducted by the Central Statistical Administration and the State Planning Committee. The study compared the profit rates on new products selling at temporary prices with those on new products selling at permanent prices. The sample consisted of industrial chemical products classified as new by the analysts. The average profit rate for all the new products was 17.4 percent. Those selling at temporary prices, however, enjoyed an average profit rate of 26.1 percent, while those selling at permanent prices realized a profit rate of 14.2 percent.[21]

It is these relatively high profit rates on temporary prices that explain the exception noted earlier in the otherwise uniform relationship between profitability and number of years since production began. The figures are[22]

Number of Years in Production	Profit Rate per Unit of Output
Less than 1 year	11.4%
1 to 3 years	9.2%
Over 3 years	42.8%

Products that had been in production over 3 years earned higher profit rates than those in production for a shorter period. But of the latter, those in production under 1 year earned higher profit rates than those in production 2 or 3 years. The reason is that those in production less than 1 year were all selling at temporary prices, whereas of those in production 2 or 3 years, some had lost their temporary prices and were already selling at reduced permanent prices. Hence the price review helped squeeze some of the growing profit out of new products after their costs had begun to fall. Once the permanent price was assigned, however, profit rates continued to rise again as long as the cost decline continued.

While average profit rates on new products selling at temporary prices are generally higher than those selling at permanent prices, the results for individual product groups are more varied. Table 10.1 presents the results of the 1962 survey for various types of industrial chemical products. Although most of the new products selling at temporary prices (columns 4 and 5) enjoy higher profit rates than those selling at permanent prices (columns 1, 2, and 3), there are numerous exceptions such as insecticides and aniline dyes. To interpret the results one would need more information on the degree of "newness" of the permanent-price products at the time those prices were assigned. If the new insecticides given permanent prices in the 1955 price revision had been in production only 1 year or 2 at that time, then the continued decline in start-up costs over the ensuing years could have driven their realized profit rates up to 64.1 percent by 1962. But if the new rubber products assigned permanent prices in 1955 had been in production for 3 or more years at that time, costs would not have declined substantially after that and their profit rates would have remained at the level of the standard profit markup (4 to 5 percent) employed in the 1955 price revision.

The abuses of pricing regulations had varying effects on relative profit rates. To the extent that enterprises managed to delay indefinitely the conversion of their temporary prices into lower permanent prices, the intent of temporary pricing was frustrated. The profit rates on older products were higher than they would have been had the time periods been better controlled. On the other hand, the profitability of new products relative to old was increased by those abuses that enabled innovators to earn much larger initial profit rates than the normal rate authorized by regulation. Tighter controls might have had a negative effect on the rate of innovation.

Temporary pricing may therefore be credited with some measure of success in promoting innovation. As an instrument of price flexibility, however, it was not sufficiently powerful or discriminating to accom-

Table 10.1. Profit Rates on Selected Groups of New Industrial Chemical Products, 1962 (Profit as a Percentage of Average Unit Cost of Production)

Product Type	Registered in the 1955 Price Catalogue (1)	Approved by the Price Bureau of the State Planning Committee (2)
Products Sold at Permanent Prices		
1. Inorganic chemicals (acids, salts, and so on)	−34.8	−5.1
2. Fertilizers	−16.9	−47.3
3. Insecticides	64.1	1.3
4. Aniline dyes	33.3	19.3
5. Synthetic resins and plastics	21.5	43.3
6. Artificial fibers	33.9	19.4
7. Rubber	−	4.4
8. Carbon black	−51.2	−11.1
9. Rubber products	3.5	18.5
10. Other chemical products	10.5	29.1
11. Woodworking products	45.0	9.3
12. Glass and building products	−58.8	−42.5
13. Machinery products	−13.7	11.9
14. Other products	138.2	1.3

Source: S. G. Stoliarov, *O tsenakh i tsenoobrazovanii v SSSR* (Prices and Price Formation in the USSR) (Moscow: *Statistika*, 1969), p. 155.

Note: The meaning of the last four product groups is not explained by the author. They may refer to nonchemical products (furniture, machinery) produced in auxiliary divisions of the chemicals enterprises surveyed. Or they may refer to nonchemical products of other industries not included in the survey but presented in the table for comparative purposes. The former is the more likely interpretation; it would explain the loss (−13.7 percent) on machinery products sold at 1955 prices. The 1955 price revision generally provided a positive profit rate for machinery products. The loss in this case may reflect the high costs of production of machinery in nonspecialized enterprises.

Products Sold at Temporary Prices			All New Products
Approved by the State Committee on Chemicals (3)	Approved by Government Price Agencies (4)	Approved by the Producing Enterprise (5)	(6)
11.8	63.0	–	−10.8
–	17.6	–	−39.2
–	−23.4	2.3	18.7
–	10.3	22.0	12.7
2.3	43.6	3.9	32.4
–	46.0	22.8	29.9
–	6.2	–	4.5
–	–	−22.6	−29.5
–	12.7	37.3	14.9
46.4	31.6	35.2	27.0
–	6.2	6.3	7.5
14.2	1.3	11.0	−11.7
–	39.4	9.0	30.3
–	29.7	26.8	11.3

plish the whole task. Its benefits were dwarfed by the proliferation of abuses and the weakening of central control over the actual structure in prices. It was increasingly regarded as a major cause of the distortions in price structure that led to the general price revision of 1967.

The Retreat from Temporary Prices

The 1967 price revision eliminated most of the disparities in relative prices and profit rates that had developed in the preceding decade. But it was clear that if temporary pricing continued to be used in the same manner as before, in a short time the carefully ordered price structure of 1967 would begin to come apart again. To preclude that result, it was decided to curtail sharply the use of temporary prices.

A decree of June 30, 1966, announced that temporary prices would be limited thereafter in the machinery, equipment, and instrument industries to products that were "introduced for the first time in the USSR."[23] Enterprises taking up the production of an item that had already been introduced by some other Soviet enterprise could no longer apply for a temporary price but had to sell at the wholesale price (temporary or permanent) set earlier. The normal profit rate was limited to a maximum of a 10-percent markup over average cost. Specific limits were also placed on the periods of time that a temporary price could be used. Depending on the duration of the production cycle, a temporary price can be employed for no longer than 9 to 15 months. Finally, the State Price Committee must register every temporary price assigned to a product over which it has price-setting jurisdiction. Although data are not available for judging the effect that the decree has had on actual pricing practice, it is likely that the use of temporary prices has in fact been curtailed, particularly in the period immediately following the promulgation of the decree. Whether the curtailment can be made to stick is another matter. Numerous signs point to some degree of expansion of temporary pricing following the initial curtailment.

First, the notion of a product "produced for the first time in the USSR" appears to have widened under administrative interpretation. That designation is now held to include all products produced under foreign license and all products that have been awarded a Soviet certificate of invention. But, in addition, all products that are included in the national or ministry new-technology plans can also claim temporary prices. "It is true that this criterion permits ministries to establish temporary prices somewhat freely, since the criterion is to some degree subjective," write Drs. Plotnikov and Gusarov.[24] They recommend that this loophole be tightened in the future, a proposal that the ministries are sure to combat, precisely because the present formulation gives them so broad a hand in using temporary prices.

Second, less than 1 year after the initial decree, a new decree was promulgated (March 21, 1967) widening the list of commodities that could qualify for temporary prices. Chemical products, quality metal products, semiconductors, preformed concrete products, and others are now eligible. In the case of consumer goods, the use of temporary prices has been greatly expanded, for both wholesale and retail prices, as part of an effort to stimulate product improvement. And a special provision authorizes all price agencies to use temporary prices "in cases of necessity" for any products at all over which they have normal price-setting authority.[25]

The success of the effort to limit the period that a temporary price may be used will depend on the effectiveness of price controls. Such efforts had been made in the past. In 1964 the maximum period of duration of temporary prices was set at 3 years, but that limit could not be made to stick.[26] This time, however, the State Price Committee is determined to enforce controls vigorously. It has set the tone by turning down a large number of applications for temporary prices. At various times they have refused to register 30 to 40 percent of the applications on the ground that the products did not qualify as "new" under the stated criteria.[27] The pressure from enterprises for the assignment of temporary prices is still there, and the Committee receives substantial numbers of applications. "Unfortunately, a large percentage of these prices are inflated, and the State Price Committee must therefore refuse to register them," comment Plotnikov and Gusarov.[28] Despite the new determination by the committee, evidence continues to appear that the controls are not entirely successful, either over the period of duration of temporary prices or over the cost estimates and profit markups. Five years after the promulgation of the decree limiting the use of temporary prices, one reads that in recent years:

The use of temporary prices in machinery production has led to the fact that the prices of many new types of machinery and mechanical products remain high for a long time. Consequently many engineering enterprises are able to maintain their profit rates at very high levels (25 to 30 percent).[29]

Such disclosures are strongly reminiscent of the years in which temporary pricing was making a shambles of the price level. Dr. Abraham Becker, an American authority of the subject, after reviewing the evidence of continued violations of pricing regulations, concludes, "These were predictable, since many of the conditions making for price creep continue to hold."[30]

Temporary prices are a device for replacing the principle of permanent prices by the principle of flexibility in the pricing of new products. A decade of experience with the extensive use of temporary prices made it clear, however, that they had grave limitations as a device for achieving flexibility. They continue to play a role in the pricing system, but they are now regarded not as the solution to a problem but as a necessary evil. They are "inevitable. They are essential. But they must be correctly applied."[31] With the reevaluation of the role of temporary prices, however, the goal of flexibility has not been abandoned. Attention has shifted, instead, to other pricing devices for achieving flexibility.

10.2. Other Approaches to Price Flexibility

The general acceptance of price flexibility as a proper objective of Soviet price policy may be credited to the effort to cope with the problems of product innovation. The task is now viewed as one of finding the appropriate balance between flexibility and the hallowed principle of permanent prices. The latter, however, is still regarded as the norm, especially among the more conservative economists. In these quarters, flexibility is accepted somewhat grudgingly, to be used only where no alternative is available for dealing with the new-products problem.

The danger foreseen is that under the slogan of flexibility, prices will be converted into an instrument for regulating supply and demand: "at the basis of such proposals lies a concept that is alien to Marxism—the concept of 'market socialism'—which leads to the hypertrophy of the role of the law of value in the socialist state, and in essence to a rejection of the planning of economic development."[32] To writers who hold this point of view, it follows that only cost considerations and not the state of demand should be taken into account in pricing arrangements. Yet in practice, even these writers are obliged to take demand into account when they confront seriously the problems of innovation. For example, one objective of price flexibility as it applies to new products is to reduce prices on older and obsolescent products so that producers will be induced to drop them or replace them by newer models. A widely discussed concern, however, is that the reduction of those prices will have the effect of making the obsolescent products increasingly profitable for users and will thus increase the demand for them.[33] Such concerns reflect the necessity of taking demand into account, even by writers who would otherwise prefer to base prices solely on cost. Thus new-product pricing problems are one of the back doors through which demand slips into analysis, however firmly the front door of orthodoxy is closed to it.

The fact that a reduction of prices on older products increases the demand for them is a spurious problem. It appears as a problem only in a pricing framework that seeks to eliminate demand as a factor in price formation. Nevertheless such views are influential in pricing policy, and they act as a rear-guard defense against the erosion of the principle of permanent prices by flexible pricing arrangements. One form of such defense is to seek approaches to new-product pricing that do not require price flexibility. For example, a widely discussed method of coping with the profit-differential problem is to levy a fixed payment (*fiksirovannyi platezh*), or obsolescence charge, on older products that are regarded as obsolete and should be withdrawn from production.[34] The permanent wholesale price remains unchanged, so that users are not encouraged to increase their demand for it. But the effective price to producers is decreased by the amount of the obsolescence charge, thus reducing the earned profit and encouraging the elimination of that product from production.

This proposal has a certain ideological attractiveness because it appears to preserve the cherished principle of permanent prices. It does so, however, at the cost of discarding another traditional principle, that of uniformity of prices; for the same product could carry different prices for producers and users. The loss in economic efficiency from nonuniform prices, however, is a heavy cost to pay for the preservation of permanent prices.

Despite such rear-guard actions, the scope of flexible prices continues to expand. Although the use of temporary pricing has been curtailed in the engineering industries, it has since been extended to other industries. More significant, however, is the increased use of partial revisions of permanent wholesale prices. Since the general 1967 revision, partial revisions were made in the prices of internal-combustion machines in 1968 and in various other high-profit items in 1969 and 1970.[35] In 1973 there was an extensive downward revision of machinery prices.[36]

Even the five-year plans now make provision for the revision of specified groups of products.[37] To facilitate more frequent price changes, a new financial arrangement has been introduced, the Price Adjustment Fund.[38] This fund meets certain objections to price flexibility that had exercized planning and finance officials; namely, that price changes introduced after plans had been officially approved tend to upset economic arrangements and to complicate financial controls. The fund is a device for minimizing those disturbances. If a permanent price is reduced, producers are compensated by the fund for the difference between their planned sales revenues based on the old price and their actual revenues that are reduced because of the price reduction. Purchasers of the product, on the other hand, are obliged to surrender to the fund that difference between their planned and actual production costs that is due to the reduction in the prices of purchased inputs.[39]

Changes in official wholesale prices are expensive to administer, however, and are limited to cases in which major and enduring inequities have arisen. For shorter-run and minor price adjustments, a different form of price flexibility is used. An enterprise producing an item that is of higher quality than the standard item listed in the catalogue may apply for a surcharge to be added to the price. Items of lower quality may be penalized by a discount in the official price. In this procedure the wholesale catalogue price itself is not changed, but the selling price differs from it by the amount of the surcharge or discount. This method is now widely used in product-improvement pricing (Chapter 12).

All the forms of price flexibility discussed thus far suffer from one major defect. Enterprise and national plans are drawn up on the basis of the existing wholesale prices. The evaluation of enterprise and ministry performance is based on the extent to which their attainments—output, profits, sales revenue, and so forth—exceed the targets established in the plan. If prices are altered after the plans have been drawn up, enterprise revenues and costs change in unanticipated ways. A well-functioning enterprise may incur losses and a poorly managed enterprise may earn windfall gains. Moreover, both short-run and long-run production decisions made with one set of prices in mind may prove later to be uneconomic under the new prices. It is for these reasons that planners are devoted to permanent prices, despite the many other forms of inefficiency generated by prices that remain rigid when cost and demand conditions are changing.

The Price Adjustment Fund is a device designed to reduce some of the financial consequences of price changes. A more interesting approach is a new instrument of flexibility called stepwise pricing (*stupenchatye tseny*).

Stepwise Pricing[40]

Stepwise pricing is a device for building into new-product pricing the foreknowledge that production costs will decline in time. The idea is that when a new product is introduced it is assigned not a single permanent wholesale price but a set of dated prices. Each price is to prevail for a specified period of time, at the end of which it is replaced by the next price. Each price is lower than the preceding. The whole set of prices, together with their official periods of duration, is published in the price catalogue.

Three stages are distinguished in the history of the product, in each of which somewhat different cost and profit considerations enter.[41] Stage one, or the "incentive" stage, encompasses the period from the inception of production to the end of break-in; that is, to the point at which the rated output capacity is attained and costs approach the long-run stable level. The prices during this stage are high enough to cover both start-up costs and an above-normal profit markup. Stage two, or the "normal-profit" stage, lasts up to the point at which the product has become obsolete and is ready for withdrawal from production. Prices are lower during this stage because costs are at the long-run stable level, and the profit markup is reduced from above-normal to normal. During stage three, the "penalty stage," prices are further reduced by allowing only a lower-than-normal profit markup, or in extreme cases by setting price below production cost.[42]

Stepwise pricing offers solutions to several new-product pricing problems that methods like temporary pricing could not cope with. One is the problem that old products, unlike old soldiers, neither die nor fade away—their profit rates are too high. Protected by a permanent or indefinitely temporary price, they tend to yield a steady or growing profit over time, despite their increasing obsolescence. Stepwise pricing arranges for their euthanasia by providing for a terminal low- or negative-profit stage. More important, however, is that stepwise pricing solves the problem of profit differentials between new and old products without requiring unplanned price changes and without raising the level of uncertainty in planning.

Like all good things, however, stepwise pricing generates new problems of its own. The reduction of uncertainty in planning is not an unmixed advantage. If it is known in advance that the price of a certain product will be reduced on a specified date, that knowledge cannot fail to motivate potential customers to delay their purchases, and perhaps motivate producers to accelerate their rates of output. The more serious limitation, however, is the necessity of forecasting production cost levels years into the future. The decade of experience with temporary prices has demonstrated the difficulty of forecasting the production costs of even the first year of production, as well as the administrative problems of keeping enterprises honest in their forecasts. Current prices based on cost forecasts made years earlier will surely lead to some unintended responses. If costs decline more rapidly than forecast, obsolescent products may continue to earn a substantial profit and will survive the terminal price stage. If costs fail to decline at the rate forecast, perfectly viable products will be withdrawn from production because of low or negative profit rates. Surely, enterprises and ministries will clamor to change prices in such cases. Price changes will be more complicated, however, because not single prices but whole future price sets will be involved.

We have little means of knowing how successful cost forecasting will be. It is true that forecasting is no longer a matter of guesswork without empirical foundation. A great deal of empirical research has been done on the time patterns of cost behavior of new products. New products differ from older ones in varying degrees, and in many cases the differences are small enough to warrant using the cost history of the older product as a basis for forecasting the behavior of the new one. Nor is the likelihood of large forecasting errors in itself a reason to reject stepwise pricing. In the world of practical policy the best of all known techniques is likely to be an imperfect technique; it is superior only in the sense of being less imperfect than others. The losses due to forecasting errors in stepwise pricing must be compared with the losses generated by temporary prices or by partial revisions of permanent prices. Stepwise pricing has not yet been evaluated by Soviet economists from this perspective. It would be a difficult exercise, although in principle amenable to investigation.

Among some research workers, the subject of stepwise pricing is now regarded as "the first order of business."[43] In practical price formation it is being approached with caution. It is not intended for general application, we read, but only in industries where obsolescence is rapid and where there is some reasonable basis for systematic cost forecasting.[44]

The method has already been employed in some cases, but we have no data on the extent of its use. It has been reported that in a large-scale revision of prices of engineering products undertaken in 1973, stepwise prices were to be extensively used. They have already "begun to be widely used in our economy. They are also used in other socialist economies."[45]

And in capitalist countries as well, we might add in conclusion.

Stepwise Pricing and Market-Economy Pricing

The time pattern of new-product prices sought in stepwise pricing is remarkably similar to that observed in capitalist economies. Figure 10.1 represents the price history of a typical new product appearing in the U.S. economy in the postwar period. It is derived from the experience of 24 products as disparate as silicon transistors, ethylene, facial tissues, and free-standing gas ranges. The graph shows the relationship between unit price and unit cost (vertical axis) and the accumulated volume of output (horizontal axis).[46] Since both axes are plotted on a logarithmic scale, a straight line represents a constant proportional relationship between price (or cost) changes and changes in accumulated output. Hence if the price-output graph has a constant (downward) slope of one-fifth, for example, it signifies that for each 10 percent increase in

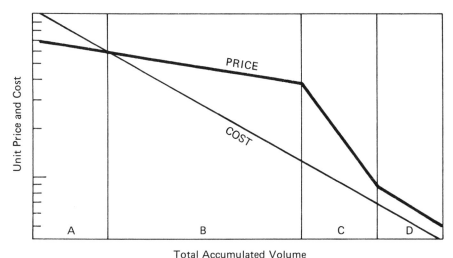

Figure 10.1. Price and cost behavior of new products over time in a market economy.

Source: Boston Consulting Group, Inc., *Perspectives on Experience*, Boston: 1970, p. 21.

accumulated output, price declines by 2 percent.

Four stages may be distinguished in the price and cost behavior of new products. In stage A, unit cost exceeds price and the innovator suffers a loss. Both unit cost and price decline as accumulated output increases, but cost declines more rapidly than price, so that at the end of stage A the product is breaking even. In stage B, cost and price continue their constant (but different) rates of decrease relative to accumulated output, while the profit rate per unit of output rises continuously. At some level of accumulated output the rate of price decline increases, and unit profit rates decline in stage C. Finally, when the product has been on the market for a long time and the accumulated output is very large, the rate of price decline slows down again and approaches the rate of decline of unit costs. Price exceeds unit cost, however, so that the product returns a small unit profit during final stage D.

The reasons for the discontinuities in the price graph are to be found in a variety of economic factors peculiar to a capitalist economy: the structure of the market, pricing strategies, and the stage of the business cycle.[47] Whatever the reasons, the point is that the time pattern of price behavior generated is very similar to that sought in the Soviet technique of stepwise pricing. With that technique, prices decline steadily in a series of steps, at such a rate that the longer the product is in production the lower the rate of profit. Stepwise pricing is thus a device for accomplishing by planning what is accomplished by market forces in a decentralized economy.

The principal difference between stepwise pricing and the market-economy pattern is that stepwise pricing makes no provision for the initial stage A of the market economy in which the innovator suffers a loss.[48] The Soviet innovator is expected to earn a profit from the very first unit produced. Very few innovations achieve that in a market economy. If the innovation decision in a market economy were taken only on the condition that the new product earn an immediate profit, the rate of innovation would be much lower. The initial loss stage serves a certain function in the market economy, however, that has no precise equivalent in the centrally planned economy. The success of the new product depends on the speed with which output can be expanded in order to benefit from economies of scale. That output must be sold, and in the market economy it is the price that determines the amount that can be sold. Hence the reason for the initial loss is the need to attract first adopters and after them the larger market for the growing output.

In an ideal centrally planned economy price does not play that allocative role. But in the Soviet economy it is clear that price does exert a significant influence on resource allocation, and particularly on the resources allocated to innovation. Certainly the governors of the Soviet economy believe that, else we would be at a loss to explain the enormous effort devoted to such devices as stepwise pricing.

At what level then, should the initial prices of new products be set in stepwise pricing? We may assume that there exists some initial price level at which the rate of introduction of new products and the expansion of their output would equal the rate of adoption. If the starting price were set below that level, new products would be introduced at a slower rate than users would be prepared to adopt them. In the opposite case, new products would initially appear at a faster rate than they were sold; surpluses would develop, and the rate of product innovation would decline.

Suppose the architects of stepwise pricing mechanically copied the practice of market economies and set initial prices at levels that involved a loss. The rate of potential adoption would be very high, but the effect on potential producers would be disastrous. For the Soviet enterprise is evaluated on the basis of its short-run performance, and the decision rules are geared to fulfillment of quarterly and annual targets. Hence management would discriminate against new products.[49] The designers of stepwise pricing are therefore correct in requiring that new products earn an immediate profit, given the structure of decision rules.

If the rules were changed in such manner as to assign a greater weight to longer-run profit performance, however, the starting prices of new products could be lowered with no reduction in the rate of product innovation. At the same time the rate of adoption would accelerate. The longer the time horizon provided for by the rules, the lower the initial price could be without reducing the rate of innovation. By varying the time horizon, that initial price could be found at which the rate of introduction of new products would be equal to the rate of adoption.

There is no reason to believe a priori that that initial price level would be below the initial cost level, as it is in market economies, though it may very well be. All that one can say is that as long as the decision rules provide for a short-run time horizon, the initial price must exceed cost. Given the long-run nature of the innovation process, one may conjecture that the greater obstacle to innovation is not the pricing system but the short-run decision rules that make high initial prices necessary. Fiddling with pricing arrangements may contribute less to promoting innovation than giving management 3 or 5 years instead of 1 to prove their worth.

Notes

1. See for example the report on the Conference on Pricing and New Technology, in *Voprosy ekonomiki*, 1967, No. 9, p. 152.

2. A. I. Komin, *Problemy planovogo tsenoobrazovaniia* (Problems of Planned Price Formation) (Moscow: *Ekonomika*, 1971), p. 150.

3. P. S. Mstislavskii, M. G. Gabrieli, and Iu. V. Borozdin, *Ekonomicheskoe obosnovanie optovykh tsen na novuiu promyshlennuiu produktsiiu* (The Economic Basis of Wholesale Pricing of New Industrial Products) (Moscow: *Nauka*, 1968), p. 9.

4. Ibid. Normal-scale production refers to the planned normal rate of output. This might be a job-lot or batch (*seriinyi*) rate of output, or mass production.

5. Komin, *Problemy planovogo tsenoobrazovaniia*, p. 150.

6. Ibid., pp. 117-118.

7. K. N. Plotnikov and A. S. Gusarov, *Sovremennye problemy teorii i praktiki tsenoobrazovaniia pri sotsializme* (Current Problems in the Theory of Pricing under Socialism) (Moscow: *Nauka*, 1971), p. 123.

8. *Planovoe khoziaistvo*, 1966, No. 10. p. 3.

9. Ibid., No. 5, p. 48.

10. S. G. Stoliarov, *O tsenakh i tsenoobrazovanii v SSSR* (Prices and Price Formation in the USSR) (Moscow: *Statistika*, 1969), pp. 151-152.

11. Mstislavskii, Gabrieli, and Borozdin, *Ekonomicheskoe obosnovanie*, p. 9. See also Stoliarov, *O tsenakh*, p. 42; *Planovoe khoziaistvo*, 1966, No. 5, p. 49.

12. R. A. Belousov, ed., *Sovremennaia praktika tsenoobrazovaniia* (Current Pricing Practice) (Moscow: *Ekonomika*, 1965), p. 81.

13. Ibid., p. 80.

14. Stoliarov, *O tsenakh*, p. 24; *Planovoe khoziaistvo*, 1966, No. 5, p. 49.

15. *Voprosy ekonomiki*, 1968, No. 4, p. 77.

16. Plotnikov and Gusarov, *Sovremennye problemy teorii*, p. 125.

17. Mstislavskii, Gabrieli, and Borozdin, *Ekonomicheskoe obosnovanie optovykh tsen*, p. 9.

18. For a careful critique of the official price index, see A. S. Becker, "Ruble Price Levels and Dollar-Ruble Ratio of Soviet Machinery in the 1960's," The RAND Corporation, Report R-1063-DDRE, Santa Monica: January 1973.

19. Ibid., pp. 6-22.

20. Mstislavskii, Gabrieli, and Borozdin, *Ekonomicheskoe obosnovanie optovykh tsen*, p. 108.

21. Stoliarov, *O tsenakh*, pp. 152-153. The profit rates presumably refer to profit as a percentage of cost. In most cases the products selling at permanent prices in 1962 had formerly sold at temporary prices for some period of time. They have therefore probably been in production longer than those products in the sample that were still selling at temporary prices in 1962.

22. Stoliarov, *O tsenakh*, p. 154. See Sec. 8.4.

23. Plotnikov and Gusarov, *Sovremennye problemy teorii*, p. 124-128.

24. Ibid., p. 124.

25. Ibid., pp. 126-127.

26. *Voprosy ekonomiki*, 1968, No. 4, p. 77.

27. Plotnikov and Gusarov, *Sovremennye problemy teorii*, p. 124.

28. Ibid., p. 126.

29. *Planovoe khoziaistvo*, 1971, No. 11, p. 56.
30. Becker, "Ruble Price Levels," p. 16.
31. Plotnikov and Gusarov, *Sovremennye problemy teorii*, p. 123.
32. Ibid., p. 468.
33. Ibid., p. 474; *Ekonomicheskaia gazeta*, 1968, No. 6, p. 11.
34. Plotnikov and Gusarov, *Sovremennye problemy teorii*, p. 474; *Ekonomicheskaia gazeta*, 1967, No. 41, p. 15; *Voprosy ekonomiki*, 1965, No. 12, p. 17.
35. Komin, *Problemy planovogo tsenoobrazovaniia*, p. 185.
36. *Voprosy ekonomiki*, 1973, No. 7, p. 3.
37. Plotnikov and Gusarov, *Sovremennye problemy teorii*, p. 476.
38. *Fond tekushchego regulirovaniia izmeneniia optovykh tsen*; literally, the "fund for the current regulation of changes in wholesale prices."
39. Komin, *Problemy planovogo tsenoobrazovaniia*, pp. 188-192.
40. The following discussion relies primarily on Plotnikov and Gusarov, *Sovremennye problemy teorii*, pp. 469-476.
41. The number of steps in the price set may be greater than three; more than one step may be used for any stage.
42. Plotnikov and Gusarov, *Sovremennye problemy teorii*, pp. 473-474.
43. A. M. Matlin, *Plan, tsena i effektivnost' proizvodstva* (Plan, Price, and Production Efficiency) (Moscow: *Ekonomika*, 1970), p. 196.
44. Komin, *Problemy planovogo tsenoobrazovaniia*, p. 155.
45. Plotnikov and Gusarov, *Sovremennye problemy teorii*, p. 469.
46. The accumulated volume of output is a measure of the total output since the inception of production.
47. See Boston Consulting Group, Inc., *Perspectives on Experience*. Boston: 1970, pp. 12-36.
48. A second difference is that the market-economy pattern in Figure 10.1 has no equivalent to the terminal "penalty" stage of stepwise pricing. The difference is only apparent, however, because most Soviet firms are likely to plan the elimination of a product from their production line before the date on which the penalty price step takes effect.
49. The effect on innovation of the short-run nature of decision rules is noted by David Granick in *Soviet Metal-Fabricating and Economic Development: Practice Versus Policy* (Madison: University of Wisconsin Press, 1967), p. 235.

Chapter 11

Productivity and New-Product Pricing

Flexible pricing was the first major departure from the traditional pricing principles that came about because of the special properties of new products. It was an assault only on the principle of permanence of prices, however. The principle of cost-based pricing remained intact. The second and more significant assault was on the principle of cost-based pricing itself.

Cost-based pricing may be reasonably satisfactory in an economy undergoing very little technological change. In the course of time enterprises and planners would learn to distinguish among industrial products with different relationships between cost and productivity. Suppose aluminum and copper electrical wire were both priced at their average cost of production plus normal profit. Initially, at those prices aluminum wire would be more productive in certain uses and it would replace copper wire in those uses. In other uses copper would replace aluminum wire. In the longer run the planned production of the two products would expand in accordance with demand for them. Since new plants would be technologically identical to older ones, industry average cost would be fairly constant and therefore roughly equal to the marginal cost of production.

As in so many other ways, the structural properties of the economic system adopted by the Soviet leaders look as if it was a stationary state of this kind that they had in mind. As Marxists they did believe that the socialist society need have no special concern about the promotion of technological progress. In the mature capitalist world the rate of technological progress would steadily decline because of the growing contradictions of capitalism. With those contradictions removed, however, the socialist economy would release the creative energies of the masses, and technological advances would proceed at a rate unknown in the past, even in the historically progressive period of capitalism. The socialist planners need not therefore be concerned about the stimulation of innovation. Technological advances would flow abundantly from the laboratories and workshops, and the only task of the planners was to see to their smooth incorporation into the economy.

Perhaps it was this confidence in the natural hospitality of socialism to technological progress that led the architects of the Soviet economy to concentrate on the management of current resource allocation rather than on the active promotion of innovation. Perhaps it was also an undervaluation of the contribution of technological progress to economic growth, a viewpoint that they shared with economists in the capitalist world at the time. It was not until the middle decades of the twentieth century, indeed, that the quantitative importance of technological progress for growth was widely recognized.

Whatever the reasons, they adopted a set of pricing principles that would be reasonably successful in a world without technological change. Cost-based pricing, however, is hostile to technological progress. It is both an obstacle to the promotion of technological progress and an inefficient instrument for resource allocation when technological progress is occurring. The greater the desire for and the rate of technological progress, the more counterproductive that pricing principle is.

The essence of technological progress is the increased productivity of industrial products.[1] The new material or machinery is an advance not because of some change in the cost of producing it but because of a change in the relationship between its cost and its productivity in use. The stationary state tends to a position in which the cost of producing an industrial product is equal to the value of its marginal product or to the gain from using it in production. If a ton of coal costs 10 rubles to produce and there were some uses in which an additional ton of coal could increase output by 15 rubles, then the planners would schedule an increase in coal production. Coal production would continue to expand until all 15-ruble uses were satisfied, then all 14-ruble, then all 13-ruble uses; and so forth until the rate of coal production is great enough to satisfy all users who can produce more than 10 rubles of output with a ton of it.[2] Similarly, if there were any users whose output would decline by less than 10 rubles if they received 1 ton of coal less, their shipments of coal would be curtailed by the planners and delivered to other enterprises who could use it to produce more than 10 rubles of additional output. In this manner all products would eventually find their way to those uses in which the value of their marginal product was equal to their cost of production.

Consider now the effect of the appearance of a new product that costs 20 rubles to produce. In its most productive use—as far as that is yet known—a ton of it can increase output by 100 rubles. In other uses it can increase output by 50, or 30, or 20. In yet other uses it can increase output by only 15 or 10 rubles. To make the best possible use of the new product, the planner would wish to make sure that it is employed initially only in those uses in which its marginal productivity is highest. Since it takes years to expand the rate of production, there will be a long period in which the value of its marginal product exceeds its cost of production. And the more new products that appear on the market, the greater the proportion of all products the marginal productivity of which exceeds cost. In such a world, a price structure that reflects only the relative costs of two products and ignores their relative productivity is a source of a great deal of mischief.

11.1. Problems of Cost-Based Pricing
In the evaluation of Soviet economic planning, the methods of pricing are generally regarded as one of the sources of inefficiency.[3] The analysis normally deals with the pricing of established products. If one examines the effect of cost-based pricing not on established products but on new products, certain additional difficulties arise.[4]

In the first place, the traditional notion of "branch average cost" loses much of its usefulness when applied to new products. The notion was first introduced as a practical application of the Marxian concept of "socially necessary expenditures," at a time when basic industrial materials and mass-produced products dominated industry. But with increasing product differentiation and enterprise specialization, particularly in the engineering industries, "the definition of branch average cost has become more complicated. Often a certain type of product is produced in only one or two enterprises. In that case one is dealing in effect with individual production cost, which depends on the technical level and production organization of that enterprise."[5] When a product is produced in a number of enterprises, the averaging of their costs reduces the influence of individual enterprise peculiarities on the cost-plus-profit price. But if the cost base is that of a single enterprise, as is usually the case with new products, cost-plus-profit pricing may merely compel the user to subsidize the inefficiency of the producer.[6]

Second, in the choice between introducing a new product or continuing the production of an older one, cost-based pricing offers no criterion of decision making. If two partially substitutable products happen to have equal unit costs of production, but the newer one is many times more productive than the older, the profit position of the innovating enterprise will be no different from that of the noninnovative producer. It is possible to provide for higher profit markups for new products, which is what has finally been done. But that is equivalent to the abandonment of strict cost-based pricing, for relative prices would then depend not only on relative costs but on "something else" as well—presumably productivity. It is also possible to reward successful innovation by means other than profit; that is indeed done by methods to be set forth in the discussion of incentives to follow. The governors of the system have been seeking to reduce the use of so-called "administrative measures," however, and to replace them with "economic levers," one of the chief of which is profit. Strict cost-based pricing, however, precludes the use of economic levers in promoting innovation.

Third, if the enterprise has nevertheless chosen to introduce a new product, cost-based pricing provides no guide to the choice among the various forms that a new product might take. It "does not take account of the degree of innovativeness or of the economic benefit (*effektivnost'*) of the new product. The minimal profit rate is automatically added on to the cost of production; the producer therefore has no interest in maximizing the economic benefit of the new product."[7]

Fourth, in the foregoing choices—between innovating and not innovating, and between different forms of innovation—cost-based pricing is simply neutral. With respect to another choice, however, cost-based pricing is positively harmful. An efficient pricing method should lead the enterprise to choose the least-cost method of production. If the price is set on the basis of a standard percentage profit markup on cost, however, profit per unit will fall. If the demand for the new product increased sharply because of the lower price, it is possible that total profit may nevertheless increase. Under Soviet conditions, however, enterprises normally produce close to capacity, and the total output of the new product, like that of the older, is limited by the existing production capacity. Hence the innovation of the new product at lower cost is likely to reduce both unit profit and total profit. The opposite side of the coin is that the enterprise gains by innovating more costly products, or by simply simulating the innovation. Because the notion of "branch average cost" has no significance in this case, detection of such practices is more difficult. The only deterrent to such misdirected innovation is the possibility that sales may decline by a larger percentage than the unit profit has increased, so that total profit may decline. But since marketing is not the principal responsibility of the enterprise, this is not a great deterrent to cost-increasing product innovation. Moreover, cost-based prices are generally below market-clearing levels, so that the demand for most products can be expected to exceed the supply.

Fifth, because of the producer's indifference to the productivity of his new product and his preference for higher-cost innovations, cost-based pricing leads to the introduction of new products that are uneconomic to users. "Unfortunately prices of machinery often increase so much more rapidly than their productivity that it becomes absolutely inefficient to use them. The adoption of such machines yields nothing but losses and a decline in output per unit of capital. For example, in the changeover from machine tool model 372 B to model 3B 722, productivity increased 1.8 times, but the price more than quadrupled."[8] Users also suffer from the practice of simulated product innovation that drives prices up without corresponding increases in productivity. And since new-product prices are based on the costs of individual producers, users are confronted with nonuniform prices for identical products. As reported earlier, the wholesale price of machine tool model 676 produced by the Odessa Machine Tool Plant was 1,600 rubles, and the same model produced by the Irkutsk Machine Tool Plant was 2,200 rubles.[9] With nonuniform prices, users are motivated to avoid placing orders with the supplier designated by the plan and to search instead for lower-price suppliers.[10] These consequences of cost-based pricing help explain the widespread resistance to the adoption of new products and to process innovation. Cost-based pricing gave innovation a bad name.

Finally, cost-based prices do not serve to allocate a new product to its most productive uses. All potential adopters will bid for it if the value it can add to their output exceeds the price they need to pay for it. But in general the new product has different degrees of productivity in different uses. The rationing of the limited supply must therefore be done by the central planners. The problem is not different in principle from that of the central allocation of established products. The planner's knowledge of the properties of established products increases with time, however, while in the case of new products their knowledge always lags behind that of the producers and users. Hence the degree of misallocation is greater. Some highly productive uses of the new product will therefore go unmet, while some less-productive uses will be satisfied. It is difficult, indeed, to avoid instances in which some of the new product is allocated to users for whom the net productivity is less than the price. The more frequent such experiences, the greater the resistance to the adoption of new products by users.

These counterproductive consequences of cost-based pricing on innovation have long been understood by many Soviet economists. The path to reform was blocked, however, by the political commitment to the pricing of products at their "socially necessary expenditures," which has been interpreted to mean their costs of production. The notion that a new machine or material may have a social value, or productivity, greatly in excess of the cost of producing it could not easily be incorporated into that formula.

The opening wedge was provided by the advance of economic theory in a different though related field. The 1950s witnessed an extended debate on the question of how choices should be made among alternative investment projects. The objective was to develop a rational basis for selecting that alternative which would yield the largest economic benefit in the long run. The heart of the problem was the design of a method of measuring the economic value to the society of the future production or cost saving expected from each of the alternative projects. The debate established and popularized the notion that two investment projects might involve the same cost, but one may be very much more "effective," or efficient, or productive than the other. The use of the concept of productivity in investment choice was legitimized by its official acceptance first by the Academy of Sciences and eventually by the Soviet government itself.[11]

The debate established firmly the notion that economic value was not reflected solely in cost of production but that two entities having the same cost of production might differ widely in their economic value. Once established, it was but a short step to the transplantation of that notion to other fields of economic analysis. It provided the thrust for the displacement of cost-based pricing in the case of new products.

The approach adopted is a direct application to new products of the new method sanctioned for choosing among investment alternatives. Suppose it has been decided to construct a high-tension electric power transmission line. The basic variant of the design provides for light, small-gauge cables. That design involves a certain initial capital cost and a certain stream of future output in the form of power transmitted. A second variant consists of heavier and larger-gauge cables. The initial capital cost is higher, but because the power loss is smaller the stream of future outputs is greater. The choice depends on whether the increased productivity of the second variant is worth the additional capital cost. The increased productivity of the second variant is called its "relative effectiveness." It is measured by the discounted present value of the stream of increments in future output.

The 1950s witnessed a growing literature on the applicability of this method to new product pricing. The approach was to compare the productivity, or "effectiveness," of a new machine or material with that of an established product for which it can substitute in production. The established substitute is called the "analogue." The increased productivity of the new product is measured by the discounted present value of the stream of future increments in output that would result from using the new product instead of its analogue. In pricing the new product, account must be taken not only of the cost of producing it but also of its productivity relative to that of its analogue.

After some initial experimentation, authorization was granted in the early 1960s for the inclusion of productivity in new-product pricing in the engineering and metalworking industries.[12] It was subsequently made mandatory for the whole economy by a decree of the Supreme National Economic Council on August 25, 1964. The decree required that the wholesale price of a new product be set so as "to conform to the prices of those established products that are similar to it in design and function, taking account of its higher productivity and also of the other technical and economic advantages that it offers to the user (improved quality of output, reduction in operating costs, and improving labor conditions.)"[13]

While the 1964 decree applied specifically to new-product pricing, it helped legitimize the abandonment of cost-based pricing more broadly. In the general price revision of 1967, for example, an extensive effort was made to achieve consistency in the relative prices of established substitute products, notably in the pricing of various types of fuels, chemicals, and ferralloys. Their prices were determined "by taking account not only of their costs of production but also of their productivity (*effektivnost'*) in use."[14] We do not know how extensively productivity considerations are employed in the case of established products. But in the case of new products it is now supposed to be general.

Although the 1964 decree mandated the inclusion of productivity considerations in new product pricing, it did not specify the method by which that should be done. The method was subsequently laid out by the State Price Committee on May 27, 1965, in a fundamental document called the "Basic Statutes of the Manual for Determining Wholesale Prices of New Industrial Products Taking Account of their Technical and Economic Parameters."[15] The Basic Statutes set forth the theoretical principles and practical methods of calculation recommended by the committee for use in pricing manuals. An intense discussion ensued on the committee's recommendations. Four years later, in 1969, the committee issued an official guide to pricing methods entitled "Manual For Determining Wholesale Prices on New Industrial Products."[16] On the basis of the procedures set forth in that manual, the ministries publish their own detailed manuals (*metodiki*) specifying the price-setting methods to be employed for the products of their industries. The methods examined next are those now set forth in the official manuals.

The official procedure distinguishes three types of new products. The first consists of products that are partial substitutes for some older established product or analogue; like a new coal-cutting machine that has different structural properties and performs somewhat different functions than older models. The second consists of products that constitute part of a parametric group; for example, truck tires with a range of degrees of durability, braking power, and other characteristics. On both these types of new products, productivity as well as cost is taken into account in pricing, but in a somewhat different manner in each case. Most of this chapter deals with analogue pricing and parametric pricing, both of which employ methods similar to those used in the West in the construction of "hedonic price indexes."[17] The third type of new product identified in the official procedure is a genuine invention, for which no analogue exists. The pricing of this type of product will be discussed in the concluding section, along with the pricing of unique products built to special order.

11.2. Analogue Pricing

The basis of analogue pricing is the calculation of the economic "effectiveness" (*effektivnost'*) of the new product. In this context the term is similar to the English expression "economic benefit," as in "benefit-cost analysis."[18] The economic benefit of a new product is the value of the gain to the economy from the replacement of the older analogue by the newer product. In price determination the benefit is measured in rubles per unit output of the new product.[19]

Economic benefit is measured by first calculating two limiting prices. The upper-limit price, sometimes called simply the "limit price,"[20] is the price at which the user would find the new product to be "exactly as advantageous" as the older one; that is, the user would be on the margin of indifference between using the new and the old product. The lower-limit price is the price at which the producer of the new product would be on the margin of indifference between producing the new or the old product. The difference between the upper- and lower-limit prices is defined as the measure of the per unit economic benefit from the introduction of the new product. The wholesale price is then set somewhere in the range between the upper- and lower-limit prices in such manner as to provide an "equitable" sharing of the economic benefit between the user and the producer.

The Lower-Limit Price

The lower-limit price is roughly the same as the old-fashioned cost-plus-profit price. The formula employed is[21]

$$P_L = C + \pi_k K, \tag{1}$$

where C is the average unit cost of production, π_k is the profit rate on capital, and K is the capital stock employed per unit of output of the new product.

The lower-limit price differs from the older cost-based price in several ways. Average unit cost C is estimated for the second year after start-up rather than the first year.[22] And the profit rate π_k need not be equal to the normal rate but may be somewhat higher as in inducement to the producer.[23] The basic formula expresses the profit rate as a percentage of capital, in the postreform manner.

In multiproduct plants, however, it is usually not possible to identify the portion of the capital stock that is used for the production of the new product. In that event the formula to be used is

$$P_L = C(1 + \pi_c), \tag{2}$$

where π_c is the rate of profit expressed in the old manner as a fraction of cost of production.[24]

A further modification is required in industries in which there are large variations in the ratio of value added to total cost of production.[25] Suppose two enterprises had the same total costs, but in the first 90 percent consisted of purchases from other enterprises and in the other only 10 percent. The balance consists primarily of wages in both cases. If the profit markup were based on total cost, they would earn the same total profit per unit. But relative to the size of their labor force, the profit earned by the first would greatly exceed the profit earned by the second. The first would therefore be in a much more favorable financial position and is likely to earn larger bonuses for workers and management. This arrangement would also create an incentive for enterprises to choose more costly materials and to substitute purchases from outside for internal fabrication when possible. Past experience has taught the lesson that such disparities can lead to uneconomic behavior. Hence in such industries the formula to be used for the lower limit price is

$$P_L = C + (C - M) \pi_c, \tag{3}$$

where M is the value of purchases (materials, fuel, components, semifabricates, and so on) from other enterprises. The size of the profit markup is therefore proportional to value added, primarily wages, and there is no profit disadvantage for labor-intensive enterprises.

The Upper-Limit Price
It is in the concept of an upper-limit price that analogue pricing constitutes a major departure in pricing policy. It marks the official recognition of the fact that the social value of a commodity may exceed the socially necessary expenditures required for its production. In the past the objective was to set relative prices as close as possible to relative costs of production. In analogue pricing, however, cost of production merely marks the lower limit below which the wholesale price must not be set. But it obviously cannot exceed cost of production by an indefinite amount. There must be some upper limit above which the wholesale price should not be set. That limit, it is now held, depends on the "value in use," or the productivity, broadly speaking, of the product. Hence relative prices no longer reflect relative costs alone but relative productivity as well.

The significance of the official endorsement of the upper-limit price can be appreciated only in the context of the political history of Soviet economics. The opposing arguments were ominous. It is "a deviation from Marxist teaching on the essence of value and price," wrote the critic M. M. Levitanus. "A major cause of the deviation of prices from values," wrote V.A. Pervushin, "is the wide use today of the practice of planning the prices of interchangeable or similar products (substitutes) on the basis of their use value."[26] The conservative opposition was not able to prevent the introduction of productivity elements into pricing practice, but they were able to limit severely the extent of its use, as will be shown below.

In determining the upper-limit price, the productivity of the new product is calculated not absolutely but relative to that of the established product regarded as its analogue.[27] In the manner of a hedonic price index, one first identifies those technical and economic characteristics that distinguish the new product from its analogue. Then one calculates for each of those characteristics, the economic benefit from the higher performance of the new product relative to the analogue. The sum of the net economic benefits of the new product's characteristics, on a per unit basis, is added to the price of the analogue to yield the upper-limit price of the new product.[28] Hence at any wholesale price below the upper-limit price, the user would gain something by buying the new product instead of the old. If the wholesale price were set equal to the upper-limit price, the full value of the economic superiority of the new product would be captured by its producer and none would be left for the user.

Two types of economic benefits of new products are distinguished. One is that the use of the new product—say it is a machine—may enable the adopter to produce his own output at lower cost than he incurs with the old machine. We may call these user-cost benefits. Second, even if his unit production costs are unchanged, the adopter may benefit from certain properties of the new machine itself, such as greater durability or greater annual output capacity. We may call these user-output benefits. These two types of benefits are expressed in the general formula for the upper-limit price[29]

$$P_u = P_o a + b,\qquad(4)$$

where a is coefficient measuring the increased value of the new machine to the user on account of its user-output benefits alone. That is, even if his own production costs were unchanged, the increased durability and production capacity of the new machine may be worth up to 2.3 times ($a = 2.3$) the price of the older machine (P_o). Then the maximum number of rubles he would pay for the new machine is $P_o a$. If in addition the new machine enabled him to reduce his own production costs, the new machine is worth even more than $P_o a$. In Formula 4, b is the additional number of rubles the machine is worth to him because of its user-cost benefits. The principal task of price formation is the calculation of the values of a and b.

The pricing manuals contain a variety of formulas for computing the value of a.[30] If the new machine has a larger annual production capacity than the older, then $a = O_N/O_O$, where O_N and O_O are the annual output that can be produced by the new and old machines.[31] That is, if the new machine produces three times as much per year as the old one, other things equal, the upper-limit price is three times the price of the older machine.

If the new machine is more durable than the older, the economic benefit of the greater durability is calculated as

$$a = \frac{(1/T_O) + E}{(1/T_N) + E},$$

(5)

where T_O and T_N are the lengths of the useful life (in years) of the old and new products, and E is the time-discount factor assigned to the industry.[32] Thus, if the useful life of the new machine is twice that of the analogue, then P_u is something less than twice P_O.[33]

The procedure for calculating the value of b is taken directly from the method of choosing among investment alternatives. Suppose the total cost of the annual output produced by means of the new machine is less than the total cost of producing that same output by means of the old machine, by an amount equal to 100 rubles. If the machine has a useful life of 4 years, the total saving over its lifetime is 400 rubles. Since future cost savings are discounted, the new machine is worth something less than 400 rubles more than the old machine. The new machine, however, may require some additional capital investments, in the form of construction and installation costs or the purchase of some pieces of auxiliary equipment. These additional capital costs must be subtracted from the total savings in current production costs.[34] The formula that measures the sum of current- and capital-cost savings is

$$b = \frac{C_O - C_N}{(1 / T_N) + E} \pm \Delta K,$$

(6)

where C_O is the annual current cost of producing the output of the new machine by means of the old machine, C_N is the annual current cost of the same output by means of the new machine,[35] and ΔK is the difference between the supplementary capital investments required for the new and old machines.

Combining the three forms of the economic benefit from the replacement of the old machine by the new, the formula for the upper-limit price is[36]

$$P_u = \left[P_O \cdot \frac{O_N}{O_O} \cdot \frac{(1/T_O) + E}{(1/T_N) + E} \right] + \left[\frac{C_O - C_N}{(1/T_N) + E} \pm \Delta K \right]. \quad (7)$$

Formula 7 measures the economic benefit of only three characteristics: productivity, durability, and user cost savings. There may be many additional properties in which the new product is superior, or in some case inferior, to the older. Working conditions may be pleasanter or safer, the output produced by the new machine may be of higher quality, the new machine may generate external economies in other divisions of the enterprise, and so forth. In industries undergoing rapid technological change, the upper-limit price must be discounted by an obsolescence factor.[37] The ministry manuals lay out the detailed methods of calculation. The greater the number and kind of variables that are included, however, the greater the range of subjectivism. Since the producer has an interest in submitting as high an upper-limit price as possible, one may expect a certain amount of exaggeration. Some control is provided by the regulation that "the technical and economic parameters used in the formulas for computing the upper-limit price are determined on the basis of test results on the new product, which must be verified by the purchaser."[38] The more complex the formula, however, the greater the difficulty of genuine control over the producer's claims for his new product.

11.3. The Optimal Price

The lower- and upper-limit prices demarcate the range within which the wholesale price is to be set. But they leave unresolved the crucial question of where within the range it should be set. The 1965 Basic Statutes offered only the vaguest guidance, in the form of the general statement that account should be taken "of the rates of technological progress in the relevant branches of industry, which are reflected in the form of a reduction in producers' cost levels, and also in the degree of satisfaction of the need for the given type of product."[39] The details of how the final price is to be set were left to the authors of the manuals published in the separate branches of industry.

In the discussions of the ensuing years a great many theoretical approaches were advanced. The practical planners who wrote the ministry manuals, however, could not wait for definitive solutions. Various rules of thumb were introduced, mostly involving arbitrary but reasonable judgments, but some based on what are described as "fantastic" formulas.[40] Out of the great variety of points of view there emerged two rules that have been incorporated in later revisions of the pricing manuals. They enjoy a somewhat uneasy coexistence for they lead to different results. One may be called the equity rule and the other the market-clearing rule.

The Equity Rule

In the history of the controversy over cost-based pricing of new products, one strand of criticism emphasized the inequity of that method. All the benefit of technological advance is reaped by the user of new products. He pays for the new machine no more than it costs to produce it, but his own profits are greatly increased. The producer of the new machine, on the other hand, earns at best no more profit than he would have earned had he continued producing the old machine instead of the new. More often than not, the introduction of new products reduces his profits, as we have seen.

The equity argument has both a moral and an instrumental element. It is thought to be simply unfair that the innovator, who takes so much of the risk and expends so much effort, should benefit so little from his contribution to technological progress. But it is also an unfortunate arrangement for the economy as a whole, for the uneven sharing of the fruits of technological progress has a negative effect on the rate and quality of product innovation. The provision of supplementary bonuses and other incentives for successful innovation is all to the good. But such "administrative methods" should not be undercut by faulty "economic measures" such as price and profit policy.

The proponents of this point of view see the source of the pricing problem in terms of the Marxian category of a "contradiction" between the interests of producers and users. The contradiction must be recognized and resolved by setting new-product prices in a way that takes the interests of both producers and users into account in an "equitable" (*ravnopravnyi*) manner.[41] The slogan has sufficient appeal that it increasingly finds its way into the speeches of political leaders. Premier

A. N. Kosygin lectured the delegates at the Twenty-fourth Party Congress in 1971 on the necessity for new product prices that were "advantageous both to the producer and the user."[42] It would be an error to regard such a pronouncement as a mere platitude. It is a pointed criticism of the principle of cost-based pricing, in which the producer just covers costs and the user captures the full benefit of technological advance. It is also an advance over the one-sided promotion of either the user's or the producer's interests that has often characterized the discussion of pricing policy and still crops up from time to time. During the 1967 price revision, for example, "some economists proposed setting prices [on new products] as low as possible, justifying this by the necessity of stimulating the widespread use of new technology. . . . The economists who took the opposite position believed that the prices of new technology were already unreasonably low, and they had to be raised sharply to encourage the producers."[43] The equity rule directs economists to reject such one-sided pleading and to think of the interests of users and producers as related parts of a single problem.

It is a long step, however, from the pronouncement of the need to take both users' and producers' interest into account to the translation of that view into pricing practice. Analogue pricing has provided some assistance in taking that step, in the quantitative concept of the "economic benefit" from an innovation. The economic benefit from a new product is defined as the difference between its lower- and upper-limit prices. Equity is now described in terms of the "sharing of the economic benefit" between the producer and the user. This is an advance in the sense that there is now a specific number of rubles under discussion. If the lower- and upper-limit prices are 60 and 80 rubles, then there are precisely 20 rubles to be shared in determining the wholesale price.

Beyond that, however, there has been no breakthrough in determining what an equitable sharing should be. Instead a number of rules of thumb have been advanced in the price-setting manuals, which appear to be rather arbitrary. The conventional approach identifies three different sets of circumstances. The first is a case in which the upper-limit price is equal to or less than the lower-limit price.[44] In that case the economic benefit is zero or negative, and the new product should not be produced at all.

The second is a case in which the upper-limit price exceeds the lower-limit price by no more than 10 percent. With an economic benefit so small, it is recommended that the wholesale price be set at the level of the lower-limit price; that is, at the standard cost-plus-profit level, including start-up costs.

Third, if the upper-limit price exceeds the lower-limit price by more than 10 percent, the economic benefit should be divided in such manner that the producer receives 30 to 50 percent of it and the purchaser the rest. Suppose, for example, that the upper- and lower-limit prices of a new machine are 150 and 100 rubles. Then the wholesale price should be set somewhere between 115 and 125 rubles.

No economic rationale is provided for the distributions recommended in the second and third cases. They do probably satisfy a general sense of equity, however. That sense of equity may well be part of the reason for the resistance to the competing rule for distributing the economic benefit, the market-clearing rule.

The Market-Clearing Rule

When cost-based pricing was an unchallengeable principle, one took something of a risk to propose that demand considerations should enter in the pricing of industrial products. With that principle dislodged by the problems of new-product pricing, many economists took the opportunity to propose a role for demand. Hence analogue pricing may be credited with a second major departure in Soviet pricing policy. Just as productivity entered price formation through the notion of an upper-limit price, so demand has entered in the form of the market-clearing rule.

The Scientific Council on Price Formation of the Academy of Sciences formally proposed in 1966 that the relationship between demand and supply should determine the point between the two limiting prices at which the wholesale price should be set.[45] If the planned output of the new product is expected to exceed the demand for it, the wholesale price should be equal to the lower-limit price. Since the lower-limit price includes the bonuses to be paid to the producing firm for the innovation, even at that minimal price the producer has an incentive to introduce the new product. But if the demand cannot be fully satisfied at that price, it should be raised to a level high enough to assure that it will be purchased only by those enterprises which can make the best use of it. Finally, if the supply not only of the new product but also of the older analogue products is limited relative to demand, then the price of the new product should be raised to the level of the upper-limit price.

The proponents of the market-clearing rule share with those of the equity rule the view that both producers and users—or supply and demand—must be taken account of in price formation. But they reject the formulation of the problem in terms of equity. Any given price will result in a certain distribution of the economic benefit between producers and users. But the appropriateness of that price should not be judged by whether it resolves the contradiction between their interests equitably. It should be judged rather by its contribution to the interests of the society as a whole. One should search for an optimal price defined in terms of the social interest rather than the relative interests of users and producers. The social interest requires that new products, like resources generally, should be allocated to those uses in which their productivity is greatest. Hence demand must play a role in the determination of the price.

The market-clearing rule offers optimality rather than equity as the basis of new-product pricing. It thus marks the long distance that Soviet economic thought has traveled since Stalin's day when dialectics rather than optimality served as the official framework for public discussion.[46] With the unfettering of economic thought, the concept of optimization has become widely acceptable and somewhat less widely accepted. Once the door is opened to optimization, it is difficult to keep out the related concept of marginalism. Though much less acceptable politically than optimization, marginalism also plays a growing part in the development of modern Soviet economic thought. The analogue pricing problem has provided an ideal context for arguing the merits of marginalist pricing. K. Gofman and N. Petrakov, for example, base their defense of the market-clearing rule in pricing new products on the assumption of diminishing marginal productivity. Their argument merits a lengthy quotation:

The 'Basic Statutes' are based on the assumption that if, say, 1,000 units of a new product are produced, the benefit derived from each successive unit from 1 to 1,000 will be the same. . . . [However] we find that the economic benefit from the increasing output of new products declines discontinuously, as the demand in the higher-productivity uses is satisfied. The volume of production of new products during the start-up period and in the first few years of full production is, as a rule, insufficient to satisfy the full demand in all possible spheres of application; that is, the product is in short supply. If we divide the period during which it is in short supply into several intervals (years, quarters, and so on), then to each interval there will correspond a certain sphere of application whose demand for the new product can be only partially satisfied at the given rate of output of the new product, that is, the so-called marginal sphere of application. The benefit from the use of the new product in this sphere will at the same time measure the economic gain from an incremental increase in output in that planning period. It follows that if the price of the new product in that planning period includes both the cost of production of that product and a sum equal to the economic gain from an incremental increase in output (that is, the selling price is equal to the marginal [or the upper-limit] price in the marginal sphere of application),[47] then both state's and enterprises' interests will coincide in the introduction of new technology. Indeed a price determined in this manner (1) will yield a higher profit rate for the producer (the price will exceed discounted production costs by the amount of the economic benefit in the marginal sphere of use), (2) will create an economic incentive for users to substitute the new product for the old in all spheres in which its use is more productive than in the marginal sphere, (3) will cause the new and the old product to be equally advantageous in the marginal sphere, and (4) will make it disadvantageous to use the new product in those spheres where its use would be premature because of the short supply. In this way, the artificial problem of distributing the economic benefit between producer and user will vanish, and an incentive will exist not only for the introduction of new technology 'in general,' but for the use of new technology first in those applications where it yields the greatest national economic benefit.[48]

In a market economy, market-clearing prices may be an unwise policy for new products under certain conditions; for example, when costs decline sharply with output, and the growth of output is limited by demand.[49] Under Soviet conditions, however, the growth rate of output may be determined in advance, taking account of declining costs and the expected rate of shift of the demand curve. The market-clearing price in any period is therefore the point on the current-demand curve corresponding to the preplanned rate of output. If the planned growth rate of output is optimal, then the market-clearing price so defined is also optimal.

The market-clearing rule is now officially endorsed as a legitimate basis for setting the wholesale price. "In the case of products that are in short supply, the wholesale price may be set close to the upper-limit price for a time, until output is expanded."[50] The regulations are not explicit, however, on the question of when the equity rule or the market-clearing rule should be applied. They state only that demand "should be taken into account" in determining the price. In practice, market-clearing pricing "is currently used only for products that are in extremely short supply, and there are great difficulties in applying it."[51] Despite its strong theoretical support, its future lies ahead, as the saying goes.

11.4. Problems of Analogue Pricing

By admitting productivity and demand into pricing practice, analogue pricing marks a significant advance over cost-plus-profit pricing. It is a complicated method, however, and many problems have arisen that have yet to be resolved. For one thing analogue pricing greatly compounds the difficulties of large-scale price administration. Since the lower-limit price is roughly the same as the traditional cost-plus-profit price, the computation involves all the past problems of cost-based pricing: uncertainty about future costs, controls against exaggeration of cost estimates, and so forth. The one additional problem is a certain vagueness about which profit measure to use: profit as a percentage of capital, or cost, or value added. Where the regulations are as vague as that, enterprises are likely to employ those interpretations that suit their own interests in higher prices.

It is the addition of the upper-limit price, however, that adds a whole new range of pricing problems. Many of them center on the choice of the established product to be used as the analogue in the price calculations.

Choice of the Analogue

The upper-limit price is based not on the absolute performance of the new product but on its performance relative to that of the analogue. Hence the poorer the quality of the product chosen as the analogue, the higher the upper-limit will be. The regulations have sought to plug this possible loophole. If a number of established products can be regarded as analogues of the new product, that one must be selected that has the highest technical and economic characteristics. If the analogue has different degrees of productivity in different uses, one must select that use in which it is most widely employed. If the price of the analogue happens to be a temporary price, or if for any other reason its current earned profit rate is above the industry's normal rate, then in the calculation of the upper-limit price it must be adjusted downward to reflect the normal rate.[52]

While such rules help narrow the range of managerial discretion in the choice of the product to serve as the analogue, a broad latitude still remains. If the analogue product is used in a number of enterprises its performance characteristics are likely to differ from one to the other.

Moreover, it is difficult to set general rules on which and how many characteristics are to be included in the comparison of the new product with the analogue.[53] The sophisticated innovator can be expected to select the analogue and performance characteristics with discrimination, in such manner as to demonstrate a very large technological and economic advance over the analogue.

Proper administrative control over the upper-limit price requires a great deal more knowledge on the part of the administrators than is required for cost-based pricing alone. It is doubtful that the overworked price officials have that expertise. One may therefore expect a greater range of decisions in which enterprises can serve their own interests with impunity. Scattered accounts indicate that enterprises and R & D institutes do indeed manage to select as analogues products with such low-performance characteristics that their new product can be shown to incorporate a relatively large technological advance. In the absence of adequate control, analogue pricing poses a greater danger of inflation of new-product prices than temporary prices.

Limitations on Profit Rates

Cost-based pricing, when consistently employed, restricts the range of earned profit rates within relatively narrow limits. The declining cost behavior of new products widens the spread of profit rates between new and established products, but techniques like stepwise pricing can hold that spread in check. Analogue pricing, however, opens the door to very large variations in profit rates.

Consider an innovation that incorporates a large technological advance, so that its lower- and upper-limit prices are 100 rubles and 300 rubles. Under old-fashioned cost-based pricing, its wholesale price would be the lower-limit price of 100 rubles, consisting perhaps of the production cost of 91 rubles and a profit markup of 10 percent, or 9 rubles. The profit rate under analogue pricing depends on whether the equity rule or the market clearing rule is used. Since it is a highly productive innovation, demand will be high relative to initial supply. Under the equity rule, it is likely to command a price at the 50-percent end of the allowable 30 to 50 percent of the economic benefit. Its wholesale price will therefore be 200 rubles, and its earned profit rate on cost will be in excess of 100 percent.[54] If the market-clearing rule is used, the wholesale price may set anywhere up to the upper-limit price, with a possible profit rate in excess of 200 percent.

While such individual profit rates have not been unknown in the past, they were the result of error, or falsification, or oversight, but not of deliberate policy. Under analogue pricing, however, they would be perfectly lawful. There would be virtually no limit on the range of variation of profit rates on individual products.

That degree of variability in profit rates is regarded as intolerable in the Soviet economy, for a variety of reasons. Innovative enterprises would be so well provided with their own financial resources that the state would lose all financial control over their operations. Enterprises are bound to "stagnate" if they earn high profits under unjustifiably easy conditions.[55] To the extent that personal incomes are related to profits, the income distribution would widen to a degree that may be ideologically offensive. Wide variations in profit rates among products reflect unacceptable deviations of prices from "socially necessary labor outlays." They also virtually guarantee that enterprise behavior will not follow the lines laid out in the plan. They create an irrepressible inducement to ignore the planned assortment of output and to deflect resources away from the production of "disadvantageous" items to the more "advantageous."[56]

In response to these concerns, a major limitation has been placed on the method of analogue pricing. The wholesale price may be set no higher than a level at which the earned profit is 50 percent higher than the normal profit rate for the branch of industry.[57] In the illustration given earlier, the profit rate cannot exceed 15 percent on cost, so that the wholesale price cannot exceed 105 rubles.

In the case of very minor innovations yielding a small economic benefit, the limitation is of no significance. For innovations of any appreciable magnitude, however, the limitation virtually nullifies the intent of analogue pricing. There is no significant "sharing of the economic benefit" if the wholesale price is kept so low. Nor does the measure actually succeed in reducing the flow of excess profit into the bank accounts of enterprises. It merely diverts it from the producers of new products to the users. It is unlikely that a price set as low as that can perform the allocating function of assuring that the scarce new product will be employed in its most productive uses. Nor can a profit rate so limited create the desired inducement for product innovation. The published accounts of the travails of product innovators since the introduction of analogue pricing differ little from those of an earlier period. The Siberian Heavy Electrical Machinery Plant, for example, produced a new model of a generator that was an improvement over its older model in a great many respects. It reduced the annual operating costs of the user by over two-thirds, and its own production cost was 15 percent lower than that of the older model. With such a large economic benefit, if the analogue pricing method were strictly applied, the innovator would have earned a very large profit. Because of the limitation on profit rates, however, the price allowed for only a 10-percent markup over cost. Hence by dropping the older model and producing the new one instead, the innovator's total profit fell by almost 100,000 rubles a year, and his sales revenue declined by 300,000 rubles. The profit limitation has undone all that analogue pricing was designed to accomplish.[58]

The decision to limit the application of analogue pricing in this manner is instructive for an understanding of the forces that shape economic policy. If the volume of innovation profits is thought to be higher than that needed to elicit the maximum innovative effort, the excess could be recaptured by means of variable profit taxes. Excessive personal incomes could be reduced by changing the structure of monetary rewards or by revising personal income tax policy. The misallocation of enterprise resources from planned uses to more "advantageous" uses can be minimized by the use of various types of fixed charges or commodity taxes on high-profit products. As one protagonist observes, the difference between a market-clearing wholesale price and the lower-limit price "should be regarded not as profit but as a tax designed to prevent the employment of the new product in inefficient uses, which should be transferred to the state budget in the same manner as the turnover tax."[59]

Instruments of these sorts would be difficult to administer, but they would permit the advantages of analogue pricing to be preserved without having to accept the undesired consequences. It was decided nevertheless to clap the ceiling on profit rates. That decision reflects a certain traditional attitude toward profits that has long exerted a major influence on economic policy. The attitude is one of deep and abiding hostility to unearned incomes, or "economic rents." Its most concrete form is a pervasive effort to prevent enterprises from earning a profit on any activity or for any reason that is not due to its own good work. If the price of the coke it purchases is reduced, the steel mill must somehow not receive credit or rewards for the subsequent increase in its profit.[60] If one lumbering enterprise is closer to its market than another so that its transport costs are lower, it must not be permitted to earn a higher profit for that reason. A modern new factory produces at lower cost than a prewar one; whatever portion of its higher income that is due to its superior equipment must not be allowed to find its way into its profit. Accounting and administrative officials go to great lengths both to purge profits of their unearned components and to assure that their earned components are recognized.[61]

There is much to be said for that attitude, on grounds of both equity and efficiency. The trouble is that the hostility toward unearned profit differentials has been extended to profit differentials in general. The well-managed enterprise is one that earns the normal profit, or perhaps slightly above. But a large profit generates the suspicion that an enterprise has not been fully candid about its source. One sees abundant evidence of this in the accounts of how enterprises are evaluated. The chairman of the State Planning Committee, for example, took note of a large group of enterprises that had overfilled their profit plan by 50 percent in one year and by 70 percent in the next. Those facts were sufficient proof to the chairman that the enterprises had deliberately "saved up reserves" in order to assure overfulfillment of their plan targets.[62] In another case the chairman of the State Price Committee argued that even over-plan profits earned from the substitution of a lower-price material for a higher priced one should not be left at the disposal of the enterprise. In such cases the additional profit must be taxed away "as quickly as possible, or else it will have a negative effect on the industry's technological policy."[63] If that substitution reduces the quality of the final product, the chairman's recommendation may be a correct policy, but if it does not, the excess profit might be left with the enterprise as an earned reward. In the Soviet context, however, overplan profit is as likely to be the result of some violation of regulations as of clever management.

Abba Lerner once remarked that the difference between communists and capitalists is that communists think it is a sin to make a profit while capitalists think it is a sin to make a loss. In those terms analogue pricing reflects a noncommunist attitude toward profits and economic rents. Its thrust is to reward accomplishment rather than to deny reward to nonaccomplishment. It looks on profit differentials as a way of providing earned incomes, rather than a source of unearned incomes. In the defense of analogue pricing one can see the Schumpeterian concept of profit in the process of rediscovery:[64]

It must be emphasized that the additional profit, called upon to motivate the introduction and diffusion of new and more advanced products, is justified only as a temporary measure. As the output of the new product grows and the demand for it is increasingly satisfied, its profitability should decline and eventually vanish.

The two attitudes toward profit may be associated with the partisans of what are loosely called the liberals and the conservatives in economic policy. The present state of analogue pricing can be interpreted as an uneasy compromise between the two groups. The liberals managed to persuade the authorities that it was a necessary measure for the promotion of technological progress. But the agreement of the conservatives was secured on the condition that the limit on profit differentials be included. The liberals won the skirmish, but the conservatives walked off with the prize. As long as the profit limitation prevails, analogue pricing remains an idea whose real time has not yet come.

11.5. Parametric Pricing

Analogue pricing is used for a new product that is designed to replace an established one eventually. Its technical parameters are therefore presumed to constitute a net technological advance over those of the analogue. Analogue pricing is a method for assigning an economic value to each of the relevant parameters.

Many new products are designed not in order to incorporate technical advances of this kind but rather to fill out or extend a product line. Suppose a certain line of machine tools consists of four models that are virtually identical except for their output capacity; they are rated at 100, 200, 400, and 500 units of output per day. It has been determined that there is a market for a new model outside the present range—say 45 units—or for a new 300-unit model, lying within the present range. In such cases there is no "analogue" in the sense of an older product that can serve as a basis for evaluating the degree of technological advance in the new product. Not only is there no need to base the price on a direct calculation of the new product's economic benefit, but such a price might be "out of line" with the prices of the other products in the group. "It is quite natural, for example, that the price of a 300-unit machine tool should be higher than that of a 200-unit tool, and below that of a 400."[65]

In general, new products of this kind differ from the established models in more than one parameter. They may differ in weight, speed, reliability, durability, and so forth. The products that form the group are known as a "parametric series." A number of methods are set forth in the manuals for pricing additions to a parametric series. One is the "aggregation method." This is used for products that consist predominantly of components and parts for which wholesale prices already exist. The price is formed simply by adding the prices of the components plus the costs of assembling them. This method has been used for pricing products like control boards, instrument panels, guidance stations, and various types of farm machinery.[66] In other cases a point-evaluation method is used, particularly with smaller product improvements and consumer goods.[67] Most widely used, however, is the method of statistical regression. As in the construction of hedonic indexes, the systematic relationship (*zakonomernost'*) between the prices of the established products and their technical parameters is determined by regressing the former on the latter. The regression equation then serves as the formula for pricing the new product into the line. For a certain group of tractors, for example, the following linear regression equation was computed:[68]

$$P = 0.07 + 0.009N + \frac{0.05}{G}, \tag{8}$$

where P is the price in thousands of rubles, N is the horsepower, and G is the weight in tons. A new tractor of any horsepower and weight will be priced according to this formula.

Parametric pricing is now used not only for new products but for revising permanent prices as well. In the 1967 general price revision it was widely used for pricing product groups with a large range of sizes, such as drill bits and broaching tools. About 250,000 individual instrument prices were calculated in this way, or about 70 percent of all instrument prices. Parametric pricing by the regression method is peculiarly well suited for electronic data processing and is therefore of great service during the hectic periods of price revisions. Parametric pricing during the 1967 price revision is reported to have been the first instance of the use of a computer in producing an official price catalogue.[69]

Parametric pricing will help eliminate some of the sources of disorder in the price structure in the past. Strict cost-based pricing, we have seen, can lead to gross inconsistencies in relative prices. A new-product price may be grossly out of line with others in its parametric series if it happens to be produced first in a very high cost or very low cost enterprise or if the producer has padded his cost estimates. In the absence of a systematic method of comparing the technical parameters of new and old products, such errors are difficult to prevent or detect. Parametric pricing, by requiring such comparisons, should improve matters. It has the further advantage of not requiring any cost data.[70] The applicability of the electronic computer to the method should also increase the efficiency of the periodic revisions of established prices.

The effect of parametric pricing on technological progress depends on how flexibly it is applied. It is supposed to be used only for additions to a parametric series that embody no technological advance over the established models. But in a world of changing technology new models often incorporate some advances made since the established models were first produced. The 200-unit machine tool may have been designed 10 years ago and the 400-unit model 5 years ago. It is difficult to imagine that a new 300-unit model designed today would not differ from the earlier models in some characteristics other than capacity. A strict application of parametric pricing in this case would build into the new product's price the relationships of price to performance and cost that prevailed in the past and may now be obsolete. Hence parametric pricing should be reserved for products that not only are part of a parametric series but also incorporate no technological advance. If they are technologically advanced, they should be priced by the analogue method.

The relative ease of computation of parametric prices and the applicability of the electronic computer increase the likelihood that they may be used to excess. We shall have no way of knowing except to look for the judgment of Soviet analysts. The only quantitative statement available is that in 1968 the number of new machinery prices determined by parametric pricing was seven times the number determined by analogue pricing.[71] It is possible that ease of computation may weigh more strongly that appropriateness in the preference for parametric pricing over analogue pricing.

Finally, even in cases in which the established and new models in the parametric series are technologically homogeneous, there remains the problem of start-up costs. Start-up costs are much smaller in the absence of technological change, but any production start-up involves some additional costs. Assume that the prices of the established models are based on cost plus normal profit and that start-up expenses no longer appear in their production costs. If a new model is priced on the basis of the regression equation of established models, it will make no provision for the producer to recover his start-up costs. From all that has been said about pricing and innovation, there can be no doubt that enterprises will resist the introduction of new models under this pricing technique.

This discrimination against new models could be reduced by modifying parametric pricing to permit the use of market-clearing prices in such cases. The original decision to produce a new model must have been based on the presence of some discontinuity or complementarity in the production operations of the users. Suppose, for example that a new tool bit has been invented that greatly reduces the quantity of heat generated during the cutting operation. Users of the tool no longer require a cooling oil with a capacity of 600°; they can use a lower-grade oil with a capacity of 500°. The next-lower grade currently in production, however, is 400°. Presumably the decision to start up production of 500° oil is based on the calculation that there is a net economic benefit from the introduction of the new grade. Hence a market-clearing price could be found that would be low enough to attract users and high enough to cover the costs of producers and provide an additional profit incentive. But a strict application of parameter pricing would yield a price lower than that and therefore discourage the innovation.

Soviet economists have not ignored the difficulties of both analogue and parametric pricing. There is a general awareness of the fact that most new products that fill out a parametric series also incorporate some technological advance.[72] The growing technical literature suggests various methods of handling such cases, and one may expect pricing techniques to continue to improve with experience and research. Many of these problems of new-product pricing are not unique to the Soviet economy but must be dealt with by firms in market economies. In the present state of Soviet economic science there is no reason why the Soviet solutions should be less successful than those of market economy enterprises.

There is one type of pricing problem, however, that must be faced by Soviet economists for which there is no equivalent in the market economy. Parametric pricing establishes the increase in price that a manufacturer can obtain per unit increase in each of the performance parameters. In Equation 8, for example, a 10 percent increase in the power of a 30-horsepower, ¼-ton tractor would increase the price by 25 percent; a 10-percent reduction in its weight would increase the price by 29 percent. Since the pricing formula ignores costs, the producing enterprise can influence its own profit by a judicious choice of the parameters built into the new model. The implications of that power in the hands of producers are well understood:

We know that the producer can influence the quality of the product overall as well as its individual characteristics like power, durability, reliability, construction, and so on. That influence is reflected in prices that are based on technical and economic parameters. But we know something else also. The user requires a certain level of quality and, therefore, certain values of the individual characteristics. These should be taken into account in pricing. On the other hand the producer may overdesign the product with respect to those parameters that are most advantageous for him to increase, from the profit point of view, without regard to the needs of the economy.[73]

Hence, in addition to the general complexity of new product pricing in an advanced economy, the Soviets must cope with those additional sources of distortion that are due to state regulation of prices.

11.6. Pricing Other Types of New Products

Analogue and parametric pricing are applied only to new products that can be reasonably compared to one or more established products. There are two kinds of new products, however, for which comparable established products do not exist. One consists of products that are described in Russian as new "in principle" (*printsipial'no novye izdeliia*). We shall refer to them as "original" products. These are new products that incorporate large technological advances, often based on new scientific discoveries. The examples usually given are the great inventions like the airplane, the electric light, the radio, the transistor, and so forth.[74] The second group consists of products built to special order, like a large special-purpose hydroelectric turbine or an automated assembly line in a particular plant.

Both of these types of products continue to be priced on the old cost-plus-profit principle. There are some differences, however, in the methods of pricing and the profit markups allowed.

Original Products

The examples given in the sources as illustrations of original products suggest that a very small number of products are involved. It is not every day, after all, that the airplane or the radio is invented. From the descriptions appearing in the literature, however, it is clear that a rather broader class of products is involved. They are described as products that are "new in principle," or that "satisfy a new need," or that are "produced for the first time in the USSR." The latter formulation was adopted officially in the 1966 decree that restricted the use of temporary prices to products "produced for the first time in the USSR."[75]

Whatever the intent of the government in issuing the decree, the practice depends on how the price administrators interpret it. Two of the categories developed by the administrators were well within the meaning of the decree: all products produced under foreign license and all products that had been awarded a Soviet certificate of invention. But the third category opened the gate widely: any product that is listed in the national or any of the ministry new-technology plans is now regarded also as "produced for the first time in the USSR." Since the new-technology plan is regarded as evidence of the ministry's devotion to innovation, they are bound to stretch a point in classifying innovations as original so that they can pad the plan a bit.

The reason for retaining the use of temporary prices in the case of original products is the same as that which led to their introduction in new-product pricing in the first place. The justification is somewhat stronger in the case of original new products, however, than for all new products, for uncertainty about future costs is relatively greater. Moreover, the rate of cost decline is probably greater precisely because the technology is newer. It is therefore all the more desirable to make provision for reviewing the price after production has been under way for some time. The chief question is whether the price administrators can confine the use of temporary prices to genuinely original products and prevent the abuses that have flourished in the past.

The reason for continuing the use of cost-based prices for original products is more obscure. Presumably it is because the productivity-pricing formulas are based on a comparison of the new product with an established one, either an analogue or a parametric series. Since original new products have no analogues, the formulas cannot be applied. In practice, however, many of the products in this class must surely have appropriate analogues, particularly those that are classified as original products because they are listed in the national or ministry new technology plans. The ministries in particular have an interest in listing a large number of new products in their new technology plans, not only because it entitles them to temporary prices but also because it strengthens their reputation for innovativeness. Moreover, the methods of calculating relative economic benefits can and have been used for calculating absolute economic benefits. They are used, in fact, at various stages of the research and development process for deciding whether to advance a proposed innovation from one stage to another.[76] Those methods could be used, if only roughly, for estimating the benefits of even a genuinely original innovation.

Equally puzzling is the decision to set the profit markup equal to the average normal profit rate for the enterprise.[77] It was precisely the anti-innovation consequences of that pricing arrangement that led to its elimination in the case of analogue and parametric products. The one concession is that the maximum allowable profit rate has been raised from 5 to 10 percent.[78] Given the present levels of earned profit rates, 10 percent is a less restrictive limitation. But the old problem remains: most enterprises enjoy average profit rates in excess of 10 percent, so that the innovation of original products continues to be "disadvantageous." The negative effects of the profit limitation are somewhat offset by the fact that these are major innovations, on which the attention of state, party, and ministry organizations are focused. It is therefore more difficult for enterprises to discriminate against them than in the case of less-prominent innovations. Nevertheless, the expected economic benefit from original new products is probably fairly large on the average. In the spirit of the new productivity-pricing methods, one would expect that these products would be priced in a manner that would make them more attractive to innovators than the 10-percent limit allows.

Special-Order Products

Special-order products are not innovations at all in the usual sense. They are unique objects, often consisting of an assembly of component units of standard technology, like a power plant, or a specialized machine tool, or an automated processing and assembly line. They are an important form of diffusion of innovations, however, for the component units often consist of recent innovations.

Since they are unique, the notion of "average unit cost" cannot be applied. The price is based instead on the estimated cost of production, as contracted in advance by producer and customer. In the past the profit markup was set on the same basis as new products generally, at the normal profit rate for the industry, usually about 5 percent.[79] The arrangement was more unsatisfactory in this case, however, than in product innovation generally. First, innovations have been unprofitable because most enterprises earned higher average profit rates than the normal rate allowed on new or special-order products. In the case of genuine new products, however, the innovator could look forward to a rising profit rate as cost declined over time. But special-order products are one of a kind and offer no prospect of a brighter future. Hence enterprises were exceedingly reluctant to accept special-order contracts. Second, as in all cost-plus-pricing arrangements, there are strong upward pressures on costs: "The producer of the new equipment is guaranteed against losses, but the situation of the customer remains uncertain until the job is fully completed; furthermore, by the time the customer discovers that he has received expensive and low-efficiency equipment, it is too late to take any corrective measures."[80] Not only is there no inducement for the producer to minimize costs, but there is the usual gain from increasing cost because the profit markup is a percentage addition to cost. Third, the administration of special-order pricing is particularly cumbersome. A special-order price is negotiated by the producer and customer, but the process of securing approval is the same as that required for new-product prices generally. The Siberian Heavy Electrical Equipment Plant has to deal with nine other organizations before a price is officially approved.[81] This is work enough for the price of a product that will be produced for many years thereafter. But when the same procedure must be followed for every one-of-a-kind order, it constitutes a very heavy administrative load, particularly for the engineering enterprises most of whose output consists of special orders.

The only measure taken to reduce the reluctance of producers to accept special orders is an increase in the allowable profit markup. The markup is still supposed to be equal to the producer's average planned profit rate on total output, but it may not be less than 10 percent or more than 20 percent.[82] This is something of an improvement. Enterprises earning profits in excess of 20 percent still find special orders unprofitable, but they are relatively less disadvantageous than they were under the old 5-percent markup.

Despite the disadvantages to the producer, the volume of output produced to special order is evidently substantial, although data are not available on the precise magnitude. A major portion of it is produced by the engineering industries, much of whose normal work consists of unique jobs like a steel rolling mill or a special-purpose turbine. Such enterprises do not have the alternative of discouraging or resisting special orders since the fulfillment of their plans depends on them. In other cases enterprises are under direct instruction to undertake certain special orders, which cannot be lightly avoided. The raising of the limit on the lawful profit rate to 20 percent has also reduced the financial penalty on special orders. But perhaps the major offset to the disadvantages of special orders is the relative ease with which the pricing regulations and controls can be evaded.

Special-order products are at one end of a continuum of industrial products. At the other end are the mass-produced homogeneous products of the primary and processing industries. Those products—coal, rolled steel, sulfuric acid—are dear to a central planner's heart, for they are easiest to plan and their costs and prices are easy to control. In the middle of the range are the fabricated products of manufacturing industry—trucks and lathes and costume jewelry. They are something of a nuisance for they are less homogeneous, production runs are smaller, and pricing, planning, and control are more difficult. But the greatest headaches are at the special-order end, where each product is unique. With standardized products there are numerous enterprises whose production costs can serve as a check on those of any one. But with special-order products, the conditions of every job are different, and each difference in conditions is a justifiable reason for a difference in cost. Hence the control of each job requires a review of all the documentation of that job ab initio. "One must also note that verification of the producer's calculations is extremely difficult, and errors can be detected only by a careful review of the documentation."[83] By the time the review is completed, both producer and customer have long since moved on to other things.

Because of these well-known difficulties of control, the reluctance to accept special orders has been modified by the fact that, despite the limitations on the profit that may be lawfully earned, many enterprises manage to earn profits well in excess of the limits. Special orders increasingly appear as the area in which the most startling abuses of regulations are disclosed. "We cannot permit enterprises to strive to fulfill and overfulfill their profit plans because of inflated prices on special-order jobs," writes Chairman V. Sitnin of the State Price Committee. "One can hardly regard the Shchelkovo Pump Plant as highly efficient on the basis of the fact that the profit it earns on special orders amounts to 75 percent on cost. And it is really quite intolerable when some enterprises, under the guise of special orders, set arbitrary prices even for products that are listed in the official price catalogues."[84] Other accounts refer to reports of enterprises that earn profit rates of "50, 100 percent, and even more" on special orders.[85]

The case of special-order products reminds us that the study of the principles of pricing alone provides only a limited insight into enterprise behavior. The principle of cost-based pricing does tend to discourage enterprises from accepting special orders, just as it discouraged innovation before the introduction of analogue and parameter pricing. It is not only the principles, however, but the way in which the principles are administered, that influence the enterprise's decisions.

The Extent of Cost-Based Pricing

Original and special-order products are now the last bastion of cost-based pricing of new products. One would like very much to know what proportion of all new products fall into these two classes. Unfortunately no firm data are available at all on the volume of output produced on special order. In the case of original products, we have only the estimate of one authority, A. M. Matlin, that about one-twelfth to one-tenth of development work makes use of "new inventions."[86] That estimate, which presumably refers to the value of development work, evidently does not include products that are classified as original simply because they appear in the new technology plans. Adding those to Matlin's estimate we might guess that original products account for a fifth to a quarter of the value of all product innovations. The value of all special-order products may be roughly of the same order of magnitude. Hence something like a half of all new products are still priced on a cost-plus-profit basis.

The category of original products appears to be used increasingly not only for genuinely novel innovations but for some for which analogues do exist. There is a puzzle here, since analogue pricing permits a higher than normal profit rate, while original new products are still priced at the normal rate. It would seem that any new product that could conceivably be classified either as an analogue product or an original new product would be represented as the former by the producer. However, under analogue pricing, the productivity of the new product must be compared with that of the analogue. If in fact the new product does not incorporate any significant advance, or if it is a poorer product than the older one, there are risks in submitting it for analogue pricing. It may be wiser to have it registered, if possible, in the ministry's new technology plan. In that case it will be classified as an original product and, without too much investigation of its productivity, will receive a safe cost-plus-normal-profit temporary price.

All this is conjecture, of course, but it offers a possible explanation of the apparent resurgence of temporary prices. If it is correct, it means that analogue pricing is used primarily for the more-productive innovations, and temporary prices are increasingly resorted to for less-productive innovations. The raising of the maximum profit rate on special-order products to 20 percent was a response to producers' reluctance to accept such orders. It may have been an overresponse, however. As Mr. Sitnin remarked in the statement quoted, some enterprises now find it expedient to classify as special orders products for which established prices exist. In particular, the 20-percent maximum profit rate on special orders is more attractive than the 10-percent maximum on temporary prices. Hence "there has recently been observed a tendency to use special-order prices (with a profit rate up to 20 percent) when the opportunity arises, instead of temporary prices (with a profit rate up to 10 percent)."[87] Such shifts in enterprise behavior testify to the remarkable responsiveness of management to changes in the "terms on which alternatives are offered," which is the meaning of prices as Oskar Lange taught us to think about them.[88] To arrest the abuse of special-order prices, detailed rules have been spelled out specifying the conditions under which a product may be classified as a special order. For example, if standards already exist for the full-scale manufacture of a certain product, and if a customer needs only a few changes, it is not to be classified as a special-order product; it is to be sold at the official wholesale price, with a surcharge based on the costs of making these changes.[89] Needless to say, such refinements are exceedingly difficult to administer, and with compliant customers producers need no great ingenuity to write up an order for a large piece of equipment in such a way as to qualify as a special order.

Analogue and parameter pricing are an advance over cost-based pricing in two ways. First, they encourage genuine innovation by offering a higher profit return. And second, they discourage spurious or low-grade innovation by the explicit attention paid to productivity in the process of price determination. In practice, genuine innovation has been encouraged to some extent. But the discouragement of inefficient innovation has been attenuated by the continued existence of the two areas of cost-based pricing. The category of original products offers an escape valve for the producer of a spurious innovation or of a poorly designed or badly manufactured new product. And special-order products offer an opportunity for increasing profit rates, without having to bear the risks of innovation. The apparent expansion of these two remaining forms of cost-based pricing reflects in part the opportunities they offer hard-pressed noninnovative enterprises to improve their record of achievement.

Notes

1. This discussion does not apply to technological progress that takes the form of new end products like domestic refrigerators or jet fighter-bombers.

2. This assumes constant returns to scale. With decreasing returns, the cost of producing additional tons of coal would rise also as output is expanded.

3. See the summary evaluation by Abram Bergson in *The Economics of Soviet Planning* (New Haven: Yale University Press, 1964), Chap. 8.

4. Martin Spechler has examined the effect of average cost pricing on product quality, in *The Economics of Product Quality in Soviet Industry*, Ph.D. Thesis, Department of Economics, Harvard University, May 1971. Pp. 117-128.

5. A. N. Komin, *Problemy planovogo tsenoobrazovaniia* (Problems of Planned Price Formation) (Moscow: *Ekonomika*, 1971), p. 162.

6. R. A. Belousov, ed., *Sovremennaia praktika tsenoobrazovaniia* (Current Pricing Practice) (Moscow: *Ekonomika*, 1965), p. 80.

7. P. S. Mstislavskii, M. G. Gabrieli, and Iu. V. Borozdin, *Ekonomicheskoe obosnovanie optovykh tsen na novuiu promyshlennuiu produktsiu* (The Economic Basis of Wholesale Pricing of New Industrial Products) (Moscow: *Nauka*, 1968), pp. 9-10. The point is made in criticism of temporary prices, but it applies to cost-based pricing generally. Indeed, the decade of temporary pricing was used by some critics as a basis for launching a general assault on cost-based pricing.

8. Belousov, *Sovremennaia praktika tsenoobrazovaniia*, p. 81. Illustrations of price increases in excess of productivity increases abound in the sources. See also Mstislavskii, Gabrieli, and Borozdin, *Ekonomicheskoe obosnovanie optovykh tsen*, p. 32; *Voprosy ekonomiki*, 1966, No. 11, p. 16, and 1967, No. 8, p. 127.

9. Belousov, *Sovremennaia praktika tsenoobrazovaniia*, p. 81.

10. M. I. Goldman, *Soviet Marketing: Distribution in a Controlled Economy* (New York: The Free Press, 1963), p. 99.

11. The classic study of the history of investment-choice theory is Gregory Grossman, "Scarce Capital and Soviet Doctrine," *Quarterly Journal of Economics*, Vol. 67, No. 3 (August 1953), pp. 311-343. See also Bergson, *Economics of Soviet Planning*, Chap. 11.

12. Belousov, *Sovremennaia praktika tsenoobrazovaniia*, p. 44. The source reports that the method was not widely employed at first, despite the authorization.

13. G. D. Anisimov and I. A. Vakhlamov, eds., *Material'noe stimulirovanie vnedreniia novoi tekhniki-spravochnik* (Handbook of Material Incentives for Innovation) (Moscow: *Ekonomika*, 1966), p. 67.

14. Komin, *Problemy planovogo tsenoobrazovaniia*, p. 122.

15. *Osnovnye polozheniia metodiki opredeleniia optovykh tsen na novye vidy promyshlennoi produktsii s uchetom ikh tekhniko-ekonomicheskikh parametrov*. See *Material'noe stimulirovanie*, p. 68.

16. *Ekonomicheskaia gazeta*, 1969, No. 31, p. 11; Komin, *Problemy planovogo tsenoobrazovaniia*, p. 156.

17. See Zvi Griliches, ed., *Price Indexes and Quality Change* (Cambridge: Harvard University Press, 1971).

18. In various contexts *effectivnost'* may have the meaning of an economic return as in investment planning; or productivity in the case of a machine; or efficiency, when referring to a pattern of resource allocation.

19. The following discussion draws heavily on the article "Prices of New Products" in *Ekonomicheskaia gazeta*, 1969, No. 31, p. 11, by N. Orlov and I. Balabanov, two officials of the State Price Committee, describing the new pricing manual.

20. The term "limit" price is also used to designate the provisional target price used for orientation purposes during the research and development stage. For a discussion of the provisional target price, see Mstislavskii, Gabrieli, and Borozdin, *Ekonomicheskoe obosnovanie optovykh tsen*, pp. 50-75.

21. The formulas in this section are discussed in K. N. Plotnikov and A. S. Gusarov, *Sovremennye problemy teorii i praktiki tsenoobrazovaniia pri sotsializme* (Current Problems in the Theory and Practice of Pricing Under Socialism) (Moscow: *Nauka*, 1971), pp. 363-370.

22. *Ekonomicheskaia gazeta*, 1969, No. 31, p. 11.

23. Mstislavskii, Gabrieli, and Borozdin, *Ekonomicheskoe obosnovanie optovykh tsen*, p. 104.

24. Since the Economic Reform, the official normal profit rate assigned to industries is the profit rate on capital. The profit rate on cost π_c implied by the assigned profit rate on capital π_k is given by the formula $\pi_c = \pi_k K/C$, where K is the total capital stock of the branch (or product group) and C is the total annual cost of production of the planned output.

25. Value added is that portion of enterprise production costs that is not due to purchases from other enterprises. It consists primarily of wages and depreciation.

26. Quoted in Plotnikov and Gusarov, *Sovremennye problemy teorii*, p. 251.

27. In some contexts, economic benefit is calculated in absolute rather than relative terms. For a discussion of the method, see Spechler, *Economics of Product Quality*, pp. 87-99.

28. In some cases, the new product may perform more poorly than the analogue with respect to one or more characteristics.

29. *Voprosy ekonomiki*, 1966, No. 9, p. 119.

30. For a detailed discussion of the calculation of the upper-limit price, see Spechler, *Economics of Product Quality*, pp. 151-160.

31. Plotnikov and Gusarov, *Sovremennye problemy teorii*, pp. 366-367.

32. Ibid. The time-discount factor is a coefficient, expressed as a decimal fraction, that is applied to future costs and benefits. If the coefficient is 0.10, then a quantity of output worth 100 rubles, if available this year, would be worth only 90 rubles (100 × .90) if it were not available until next year, 81 rubles (100 × .90 × .90) if it were not available until 2 years hence, and so forth.

33. Suppose T_O = 3 years, T_N = 6 years, and E = .10. Then a = (.33 + .10) ÷ (.17 + .10) = 1.6.

34. If the new machine requires a smaller supplementary capital investment than the older one, the amount of the difference is added to the current-cost savings.

35. Depreciation is not included in the calculation of C_O or C_N.

36. Plotnikov and Gusarov, *Sovremennye problemy teorii*, pp. 366-368.

37. The treatment of obsolescence is discussed in *Planovoe khoziaistvo*, 1972, No. 5, pp. 82-85.

38. Plotnikov and Gusarov, *Sovremennye problemy teorii*, p. 368.

39. *Voprosy ekonomiki*, 1967, No. 5, p. 33.

40. Ibid. In the draft of one manual it was proposed that the final price be calculated by the coefficient d, defined by the formula $d = \dfrac{1}{(1 + a + b)^T}$, where a is the rate of growth of labor productivity in the producer's industry, b is the rate of growth (or improvement) of the technical and economic parameters of the new product, and T is the useful life of the new product.

Write the critics, "Obviously, adding the percentage growth rate of output per worker in the engineering industry to the percentage increase in the size of an excavator bucket has about the same economic content as multiplying tons of coal by tons of grain." The incident is not to be taken as typical of the quality of price-administration personnel, but it does reflect a real problem of price administration. The more complex and sophisticated the approved pricing methods, the more they strain the capacities of the rank-and-file officials who carry out the work of setting prices.

41. *Planovoe khoziaistvo*, 1973, No. 8, p. 7.

42. *XXIV s'ezd kommunisticheskoi partii sovetskogo soiuza: stenograficheskii otchet* (Twenty-fourth Congress of the Communist Party of the Soviet Union: Stenographic Report) (Moscow: *Politizdat*, 1971), p. 49.

43. Komin, *Problemy planovogo tsenoobrazovaniia*, p. 123.

44. Strictly speaking, in this and the following rules one takes the difference between the upper-limit price and the "lower-limit price plus start-up costs." Although start-up costs are not included in the lower-limit price, they are accounted for in this manner in determining the wholesale price. *Ekonomicheskaia gazeta*, 1969, No. 31, p. 11.

45. *Voprosy ekonomiki*, 1966, No. 9, pp. 121-122.

46. The relationship of dialectics to optimality is discussed by the present author in A. Bergson and J. Berliner, "Economic Aspects of the Party Program," *The ASTE Bulletin*, Vol. 4:2 (Winter 1962), pp. 34-37.

47. The authors repeat in a footnote that the marginal sphere of application is the last sphere of application in order of use; it is the sphere in which the product is used with the minimal economic gain. They note that their recommendation is in direct contradiction to that of the "Basic Statutes," which states that if the planned output of the new product is insufficient to satisfy the total demand the price should be set "for that sphere in which the new product can be utilized with the greatest economic benefit."

48. *Voprosy ekonomiki*, 1967, No. 5, pp. 34-35.

49. Spechler, *Economics of Product Quality*, p. 55.

50. *Ekonomicheskaia gazeta*, 1969, No. 31, p. 11.

51. *Planovoe khoziaistvo*, 1973, No. 8, p. 57.

52. Plotnikov and Gusarov, *Sovremennye problemy teorii*, p. 365; Mstislavskii, Gabrieli, and Borozdin, *Ekonomicheskoe obosnovanie optovykh tsen*, pp. 34-36; Anisimov and Vakhlamov, *Material'noe stimulirovanie*, p. 68.

53. Mstislavskii, Gabrieli, and Borozdin, *Ekonomicheskoe obosnovanie optovykh tsen*, pp. 24-25.

54. The economic benefit is the difference between the upper- and lower-limit price, or 200 rubles. Fifty percent of that, or 100 rubles, is added to the lower limit price, for a wholesale price of 200 rubles. If the cost is 91 rubles, the profit markup is 109 divided by 91, or 120 percent.

55. Plotnikov and Gusarov, *Sovremennye problemy teorii*, p. 445.

56. Ibid., pp. 372, 445.

57. *Ekonomicheskaia gazeta*, 1969, No. 31, p. 11; Plotnikov and Gusarov, *Sovremennye problemy teorii*, p. 372.

58. *Planovoe khoziaistvo*, 1969, No. 10, p. 56.

59. *Voprosy ekonomiki*, 1966, No. 9, p. 122.

60. Komin, *Problemy planovogo tsenoobrazovaniia*, pp. 188-195, describes the elaborate accounting and administrative machinery of the Price Adjustment Fund. Its purpose is to assure that no enterprise suffers or benefits from price changes made by the planners.

61. See, for example, Plotnikov and Gusarov, *Sovremennye problemy teorii*, p. 346.

62. *Planovoe khoziaistvo*, 1968, No. 7, p. 21.

63. *Ekonomicheskaia gazeta*, 1968, No. 6, p. 11.

64. Anisimov and Vakhlamov, *Material'noe stimulirovanie*, p. 70.
65. Plotnikov and Gusarov, *Sovremennye problemy teorii*, pp. 360-361.
66. Ibid., p. 64.
67. See Sec. 12.1.
68. Mstislavskii, Gabrieli, and Borozdin, *Ekonomicheskoe obosnovanie optovykh tsen*, p. 134. In computing the orientation price during the research and development stage, an alternative to the regression method is the "method of rational functions." In this method an equation relating the new product's price to its technical parameters is developed on theoretical grounds rather than on the empirical basis of statistical analysis. See ibid., pp. 76-77.
69. S. G. Stoliarov, *O tsenakh i tsenoobrazovanii v SSSR* (Prices and Price Formation in the USSR), 3rd ed. (Moscow: *Statistika*, 1969), p. 69.
70. Plotnikov and Gusarov, *Sovremennye problemy teorii*, p. 420. The regression technique is also used for studying the relationship of cost variations to variations in performance characteristics, and to cost-control generally. See Komin, *Problemy planovogo tsenoobrazovaniia*, p. 162.
71. Plotnikov and Gusarov, *Sovremennye problemy teorii*, p. 363.
72. Ibid.
73. Ibid., p. 422.
74. Anisimov and Vakhlamov, *Material'noe stimulirovanie*, p. 71.
75. ". . . *izdeliia vpervye osvaivaiutsia v SSSR* . . ." Plotnikov and Gusarov, *Sovremennye problemy teorii*, p. 124.
76. Spechler, *Economics of Product Quality*, pp. 89-92.
77. Mstislavskii, Gabrieli, and Borozdin, *Ekonomicheskoe obosnovanie optovykh tsen*, p. 21.
78. Ibid. The 5-percent limit was established in 1958. Spechler, *Economics of Product Quality*, p. 149.
79. Belousov, *Sovremennaia praktika*, p. 79.
80. Ibid., pp. 79-80.
81. *Izvestiia*, August 15, 1968, p. 3. See also Sec. 13.1.
82. Plotnikov and Gusarov, *Sovremennye problemy teorii*, p. 131.
83. Belousov, *Sovremennaia praktika*, p. 80. The construction industry is often regarded as one of the weakest sectors of the Soviet economy. One reason is that most construction work is, in a sense, produced to special order and is therefore subject to the same difficulties of control as special orders in manufacturing industry.
84. *Ekonomicheskaia gazeta*, 1968, No. 6, p. 11.
85. Komin, *Problemy planovogo tsenoobrazovaniia*, p. 26.
86. A. M. Matlin, *Tekhnicheskii progress i tseny mashin* (Technical Progress and Machinery Prices) (Moscow: *Ekonomika*, 1966), p. 5.
87. Plotnikov and Gusarov, *Sovremennye problemy teorii*, p. 434.
88. That meaning of prices was originally formulated by P. H. Wicksteed. It was popularized by Oskar Lange in his classic study of the role of price under socialism. O. Lange and F. M. Taylor, *On the Economic Theory of Socialism*, edited by B. E. Lippincott (Minneapolis: University of Minnesota Press, 1952), p. 60.
89. Plotnikov and Gusarov, *Sovremennye problemy teorii*, pp. 130-131.

Chapter 12

Pricing Product Improvements

The simplest form of technological innovation is the improvement of established products. Since product improvement advances by small and scarcely noticed steps, the process commands less public attention than the dramatic appearance of decidedly new products. But in market economies, "most development efforts represent only small advances in the state of the arts."[1] Moreover the cumulative effect of product improvement on technological advance is enormous. One need only think of the first models of automobiles or television sets to appreciate its contribution to the technological level at any time.

No sharp line can be drawn between new product innovation and product improvement. But like poverty and unlike pregnancy, imprecision about margins is irrelevant in human action. Makers of social policy must concentrate on the different colors of the social spectrum, leaving it to scientists and lawyers to mark the dividing lines.

The importance of the distinction between new products and product improvements derives from the differences in the social processes by which these two forms of innovation come about. The former generally require larger quantities of resources, both material and intellectual, and are therefore more often generated by persons and groups not directly involved in production. The closer a unit is to the production process itself, on the other hand, the more likely that its contribution to technical progress will take the form of improvements, in both the product and its production process. An economic structure that ignores the distinction may introduce an unintended bias in the relative effort expended on innovation and improvement. A well-known example is a certain property of the Soviet incentive structure that at one time provided rewards that were disproportionately favorable to small technological advances. The consequence was a clustering of research and development effort on improvements, to the detriment of larger-scale advances.[2]

Both product improvements and new products represent advances in what is popularly called the "quality" of goods. When used in this way, however, the term "quality" is generally reserved for improvements. A minor technological advance is regarded as an improvement in the quality of an established product; a major advance is regarded not as a quality improvement but as a new product. The most common usage of the term "quality," however, refers not to product improvement as an act of innovation but to the quality assortment of output. That is the sense of the term in the widely discussed "quality problem" of Soviet industry.

The so-called quality problem takes two forms: products are produced that are below the established quality standards; or if the product is of a type that is classified by grade (that is, there are several official levels of technical standards), firms produce excessive quantities of low-grade standard products.[3] The issue of quality has been analyzed at great length, both in the Soviet sources and in the non-Soviet literature.[4] The sources of the quality problem are the low level of labor skills, particularly in the prewar period; the dominance of output-plan fulfillment as a criterion of managerial performance, which promoted an emphasis on quantity at the expense of quality; and the "tautness" of planning targets, which had the same result; and the prevalence of a seller's market that undermined customers' ability to refuse deliveries of substandard products.

The quality problem is an issue primarily in the analysis of the static properties of the economy. It is therefore not an issue in the analysis of innovation, which deals with the dynamic properties of the economy. That is, one may imagine an economy the technology of which is characterized by an unchanging set of products defined by their technical characteristics. Such a noninnovative economy may succeed in producing an optimal distribution of output in terms of the existing quality standards; or it may generate large quantities of substandard products and excessive quantities of low-grade products. Whether the one or the other outcome is attained depends, among other things, on the various structural properties of the economic system: the structure of organization, prices, decision rules, and incentives. Our concern in this study is a different one, however. It is not with the capacity of the economy to produce an optimal output in terms of existing quality standards but rather to produce products characterized over time by rising quality standards. Innovation, in this sense, is the introduction of products of higher quality that had previously been produced in the economy or in the enterprise. An economy may therefore be highly innovative because of its dynamic properties, but it may also produce excessive quantities of substandard products because of its static properties. Per contra, a noninnovative economy may manage to produce an optimal quality assortment. The analysis of the innovativeness of an economy may shed some incidental light on the static quality problem, but that is a separate concern. The discussion to follow deals with quality primarily in the sense of product improvement as an act of innovation.

12.1. Price Surcharges

Price administration consists of a troika of elements: a product, a standard, and a price. It is the standard that defines "the" product, for which the specified price may be charged. Every price listed in a catalogue refers to a specific product defined by an official standard. No price may be charged for any product not listed in a price catalogue.[5] A product may be sold at a listed price only if it conforms to the specifications in the standard. The troika provides the legal basis of the system of quality control.[6] If a purchaser brings legal action against a shipper because of subquality deliveries, the case is decided by an appeal to the technical specifications contained in the standard.

The system of price and quality regulation was designed primarily to control against price gouging and quality deterioration, practices that normally accompany administered-pricing arrangements. In a world without technological change, it would be an inexpensive system to administer. Technical standards once written would remain for all time, and official prices need never be changed. Technological change, however, involves constant modification of all three elements of the troika, for which suitable arrangement must be made.

There have always existed procedures for introducing new standards and new prices for new products. They were not designed, however, to be used for mere improvements. Product improvement was regarded as a social obligation of the enterprise to be undertaken out of the enterprises' "reserves" and not requiring a change in the price.

The absence of a special pricing arrangement presents no problem in the case of improvements that involved no increase in cost. The specifications in the standard are normally regarded as minima, and the sale at the official price of a product with greater durability or tensile strength than the standard requires is not illegal. If the cost of production is not increased, the innovation brings neither gain nor loss to the producer, and if the cost happens to be lower, his profit will be higher.[7]

Most advances in product performance, however, involve some increase in the producer's cost. It is this type of improvement that was discouraged by the absence of a special pricing arrangement. "What happens to the enterprise when it raises the quality of output, but at a higher cost?" asked Dr. Khatchaturov. "From the national economic standpoint that is entirely efficient, but it may be disadvantageous for the enterprise; for if the price is unchanged, the enterprise will suffer a loss."[8] One path open to the innovator was to contrive to have the improved product defined as "new" and then to invoke the machinery of new-product pricing. That, however, exposed the enterprise to the charge of violating state price discipline; and indeed it was an evasion of the intent of the regulations. It was moreover too complex and time-consuming to be used for every modest improvement. It involved the preparation of the documentation required for the issuance of a new All-Union Standard, the preparation of further documentation justifying the proposed new price, and the shepherding of the documents through the State Standards Committee, the State Price Committee, and the considerable number of other organizations whose agreement must be obtained. This substantial administrative cost and effort are worth incurring for significant innovations. But it was unthinkable that that machinery would be set in motion for every minor improvement. The real choices open to the innovator were to sell the improved product at the old listed price, or to contrive to sell it at an illegally high price, or to avoid trouble by not making the improvement at all.

The first official authorization for a special product-improvement pricing procedure was introduced in the same decree of August 25, 1964, that introduced analogue- and parametric pricing.[9] The decree provided that in the case of quality improvements that increase production costs a new price is not required, but the producer is allowed to add a surcharge to the established price.[10] The use of price surcharges is now the standard method of pricing improvements.

Price surcharges (*nadbavki*) and discounts (*skidki*) have been increasingly used in recent years for a variety of purposes unrelated to innovation.[11] They are used, for example, for pricing products with large seasonal variations in output. They are also used for pricing various types of products that are normally produced in various grades of quality or that require different kinds of special handling or packaging. In these cases, the price catalogue lists the established price for a standard model of the product and then lists the surcharges and discounts that may be applied for each specified grade variation or packaging requirement or season of purchase. In addition to these specific surcharges, most price catalogues identify certain general conditions under which any listed price may be increased or decreased. Three such conditions are typical:[12] (1) if some special work is to be done on the product, upon the order or with the agreement of the purchasers; (2) if the product deviates from the standard, with the permission of the appropriate authorities;[13] and (3) if the product is destined for export and requires additional processing or packing. Such uses of surcharges and discounts have increased the flexibility of the pricing system generally.

In the use of surcharges for pricing improvements, the amount of the surcharge is determined by the same methods as are used in pricing new products. The economic benefit of the improvement may be calculated in a manner similar to analogue pricing, and the benefit is then divided between the producer and user by some rule of thumb: "usually it is divided in the proportion of 3:7 in favor of the user."[14] Or one of the methods of parametric pricing may be used: statistical regression, the aggregation method, or the point-evaluation method. The last is used more often in product-improvement pricing than in new-product pricing, particularly when some of the characteristics are not easily quantifiable. It is widely used for consumer goods, regarding such characteristics as fashion, ease of laundering, and various aesthetic properties. In the point-evaluation method a committee of experts first identifies the product characteristics that are regarded as significant and establishes arbitrary numerical ranking scales for each one, say from zero to ten. They then assign to the product a numerical ranking for each of those characteristics; finally a set of relative weights are applied to the characteristics, and the weighted total score is tallied up. If the total for the improved product is 30 points, for example, and the total for the basic product is 25 points, then the improved product is entitled to a surcharge of 20 percent.[15]

Product improvements are referred to in the Soviet writings as "increases in quality," or "product modernization." They are usually distinguished from new products by such rough descriptions as a "partial improvement without a change in basic characteristics."[16] Producers and price administrators must exercize some judgment in deciding whether to treat an innovation as a new product and assign it a new price or whether to treat it as an improvement of an established product and authorize a surcharge to the old price. Once it is decided that the innovation is to be treated as an improvement, there are two approaches for gaining authorization to levy a surcharge: the "basic price" approach and the State Quality Certification procedure.

The Basic Price Method

The basic price method was introduced primarily for the purpose of simplifying general price administration. It also serves, however, to promote the diffusion of innovations.

For many types of products, the price catalogue specifies a price for only one or several basic models of the product, the characteristics of which are described in the official standards in the usual way. In addition, the catalogue lists a set of quality variations on the basic model and specifies the additions to the basic price that may be charged for each variation. For example, Price Catalogue No. 17-04, Part I, specifies the following surcharges that may be added to the prices of various basic models of pressure gauges:[17]

| | Price Surcharges, in Kopeks | | | | | | |
| | Steel and Plastic Body | | | Aluminum Body | | | |
Supplementary No. Part or Finish	60 mm	100 mm	150-160 mm	100 mm	160 mm	200 mm	250 mm
1. Flanged Rim	–	25	40	25	40	60	80
2. Unbreakable Cover	–	20	40	20	40	60	–
3. Luminescent Face	15	25	40	25	40	–	–
4. Special Treatment for Use with Acid, Acetylene, and so forth	5	10	15	10	15	20	–
5. Addition of Red (Yellow Green), Lines at User's Request	2	2	2	2	2	2	2

In evaluating the effect of base-product pricing on the rate of innovation, one must distinguish the initial introduction of improvements from their diffusion through the economy. With respect to diffusion, the effect is surely favorable. Many of the parameters specified in the catalogue refer not to improvements but to various special-purpose modifications of the basic product; some users may require a flanged rim on the gauge and others not. Some of the modifications, however, consist of recent innovations. A method may have recently been introduced for treating gauges by a process that increases their durability and reliability when used with acids or acetylene. When a price surcharge for that treatment is listed in the catalogue, producers are more likely than in the past to incorporate that advance in some portion of their output since they can now easily recover the additional cost.

The chief limitation of basic pricing for diffusion is that it cannot possibly provide for all known improvements. Basic pricing is not used for all products but only for those with a reasonably small range of variation in fairly standardized characteristics.[18] And even for those products that are base priced, it is not expedient to specify a surcharge for every known variation. If a certain recent innovation happens not to appear among the listed characteristics, the catalogue provides no authorization for producers to add a surcharge. This, however, implies no criticism of the basic pricing method itself; it is a natural limitation of any administered pricing arrangement that it cannot provide for every possible contingency. More troublesome are some of the consequences that may follow from the responsiveness of enterprise behavior to relative prices. The calculation of the large number of individual surcharge rates is an exceedingly complex task for the pricing agencies, and perfect precision is not to be expected. In view of the relative weakness of the influence of demand on production decisions, an error in determining the size of the allowable surcharge may motivate enterprises to produce either all acid-resistant gauges or no acid-resistant gauges, with nothing in between.

While basic pricing has a limited positive effect on diffusion, it has very little influence at all on the initial introduction of improvements. The parameters specified, and the range of their values, reflect the state of technological knowledge at the time the price catalogues are published. Therefore the catalogues can make no provision for even major improvements first introduced after they were published or revised. This limitation is inevitable in the case of improvements that could not have been foreseen at the time prices are set. It could be modified, however, in the case of improvements that consist of extensions of the range of some parameter. Truck tire prices could be set, for example, with surcharges specified for service lives well in excess of the maximum currently attained. The best current performance may be 40,000 miles, but estimates could be made of the economic benefit from future improvements up to 100,000 miles, and appropriate surcharges calculated. Then a tire manufacturer who engineered a method for attaining 50,000 miles would have authorization for a surcharge immediately at hand. This possibility is discussed in the literature, but the manuals generally recommend that it not be done because the uncertainty over the benefits and costs of future improvements would make it hazardous to set surcharge schedules in advance.

The basic price method is designed not only to promote product improvement but also to cope with the static "quality problem." Under pressure to reduce costs and meet output targets, enterprises have often resorted to measures that reduced the quality of products. The most expedient way to do this was to reduce the quality of some product characteristic that was not specified in the standard; to substitute spot welding for the more expensive process of riveting, for example, or a plastic for a metal part in some minor component. The basic price method has helped in the effort to combat quality deterioration because it has made it possible to increase greatly the number of product characteristics that can be specified in the catalogues. The 1967 price revision, for example, increased the number of parameters for surcharges in rolled steel products from 67 to 104. Surcharges have now been specified for such operations as heat treatment, special chemical composition, mechanical qualities, purity and uniformity, finishing, and so forth. The catalogues also specify discounts to be deducted from the prices paid when quality is lower than that in the basic-product standard. The price catalogue for transformers authorizes a surcharge of 250 rubles per unit reduction of no-load loss below the base-model standard, and a discount of 150 rubles for each unit of loss in excess of the standard.[19]

Basic pricing may be expected to improve the general quality performance of Soviet industry, even in the absence of technological change. If the sizes of the surcharges are properly set, producers would suffer no loss in filling orders for higher-quality or special-treatment products. Soviet writers continually stress the advantages of the simplification of pricing procedures under basic pricing. "The producer, using his price catalogue, can determine for himself the wholesale price to be charged as he moves from one variant to another and does not have to apply to the pricing authorities for official confirmation of the price."[20] And the quality discounts increase the likelihood that a penalty will be paid for subquality output. To be sure, a foolproof system of quality control through pricing is not possible. It is infeasible to specify every imaginable parameter of quality. Moreover, even in the past quality deterioration was not confined to unspecified product characteristics but often involved violation of the standards themselves. Basic pricing, however, has helped tighten the fabric of controls.

State Quality Certification

If a product improvement does not qualify for a surcharge authorized in a price catalogue, the enterprise may apply for a seal of quality (*znak*

kachestva). The award of a seal of quality is accompanied by an authorization to add a specified surcharge to the certified product. This qual-
ity-certification procedure has developed in recent years into a major
program for promoting product improvement.

The general rules for quality certification are laid down by the State
Standards Committee, on the basis of which the ministries issue manuals of procedure to be used by their enterprises.[21] While the details
vary from ministry to ministry, the general procedure is the same.[22]
Each year the ministry is required to submit a list of products to be
presented by their enterprises for quality certification. The list includes
all new and improved products. The certification of quality is performed by special ad hoc State Certification Commissions, consisting of
experts representing the producing ministry, the principal customer
ministries, and other interested state agencies. The commissions study
the technical and economic claims made for the product and may conduct independent performance tests. Three quality grades are used:
highest, first, and second quality. To qualify for the highest grade, the
product (a) must be superior to any similar product currently in production, (b) must exceed the existing standards, and (c) must provide a
larger economic benefit to users than the older models.[23] If the product
is certified by the commission as of the highest grade, the producer is
then authorized to stamp the product with an official seal of quality for
a designated period of time ranging from 1 to 3 years. During that period the producer may add a surcharge to the wholesale price of the
product. Upon the termination of the period, the right to use the seal
of quality and to add the surcharge lapses, although the product may be
submitted for recertification at that time, perhaps with some further
improvements.

If the product fails to secure certification as of highest quality, the
commission may certify it as of first quality. This is an honorable grade,
but it does not carry with it the right to use the seal of quality and to
apply a surcharge. Finally, if the new product is designed eventually to
replace older models, the commission may review the latter and certify
some of them as second quality. Some future date may be then established on which the second-quality product should be retired from
production. For output produced after that date, a discount may be
imposed on the wholesale price.

When a product is certified as of highest quality, the State Standards
Committee publishes a new state standard for that product or a revised

version of the old standard; in both cases, the product characteristics or parameters of the new or revised standard are higher than the old; in particular, a longer guarantee period is usually provided for. The committee then announces a date by which all other producers of that type of product are obliged to attain the level of the new or revised standard; the committee is also obliged to maintain a check on the "fulfillment" of the new standards by other enterprises.

The seal of quality may be withdrawn before its official expiration date if the actual output does not meet the specifications claimed at the time of certification. Action for withdrawal may be initiated by the enterprise itself, or by state inspection agencies, or by dissatisfied users. The State Standards Committee and the enterprise's ministry may forbid any further shipments of certified goods found to be defective and may call to account any officials who continue to ship certified output that is below the quality level for which it was certified.

The size of the surcharge is determined in the manner prescribed in the ministry manual for pricing new products, that is, by some method of calculating economic benefit. For small improvements, simple parametric pricing is used, but in some instances the full analogue-pricing method is used, with the calculation of upper- and lower-limit prices.[24] The surcharge is to be set so that the producer receives 30 to 50 percent of the economic benefit. But again, as in new product pricing, there is a ceiling on the volume of profit that may be earned: the additional profit from the surcharge should fall in the range of 50 to 100 percent of the normal profit for the product group.[25] The rules governing the size of discounts on second-quality products are somewhat looser than those on surcharges. In practice they are set so that the earned profit rate may range from zero up to the normal profit rate.[26]

State quality certification is designed to stimulate product improvement by combining "administrative" and "economic" levers. In both respects it has probably helped. The organized process of quality certification requires enterprises to make some regularized effort at quality improvement. The future would not be very bright for a managerial group that continually avoids presenting its products for formal certification, or worse, that does appear for certification but has its offerings regularly turned down by the commissions. The number of applications for certification—2,300 in 1967 to 1968—is not overwhelming, but it is impressive. Moreover the commissions take their job seriously. Many proposals are turned down or are modified because of unstable quality, improper materials, or poor design. Substantial economic benefits are reported from the introduction of certified products.[27] Soviet observers generally agree that product improvement has been encouraged, although it is difficult to evaluate the extent.

Nevertheless there are limitations on the effectiveness of both the certification procedure and the pricing method. On the basis of the history of such "administrative" methods as quality certification, we may expect that they will be conducted with a full share of "formalism" and "simulation." The social machinery for conducting the State quality certification procedure strikes one as extremely cumbersome and time-consuming, both for the enterprise and for the economy as a whole. Extensive documentation must accompany each product submitted for certification, special commissions of experts must meet and study the products and the documentation, and special attention must be paid by supervisory organizations to the quality of output during the validation period of the seal of quality. We have seen no study of the national administrative cost of the system of State quality certification, but it may well be a significant offset to the gains in product improvement.

Among the costs of the procedure is the acquisition of information on the quality of foreign products. To qualify for a seal of quality, a product must be shown to conform to the highest-quality foreign and domestic analogues. But most enterprises do not possess information on the technical specifications of foreign products, and such information as they have is usually not current. Since the competition of foreign products in the domestic market is not a factor with which Soviet producers have to contend, it is not of great moment for them to be informed of foreign technology. The absence of foreign information has been described as a "fundamental difficulty . . . which naturally does not permit an objective evaluation of the contemporary technological level of that product."[28]

The pricing arrangements have succeeded in increasing the profitability of product improvement, compared to the period when no special product-improvement pricing arrangements existed. The extent of the increase is somewhat limited, however. The regulations require that the guarantee period under state certification must be lengthened, and the cost of repairing or servicing defective products returned under the terms of guarantees is borne by the producer and comes out of profit.[29] But perhaps more significant is the ceiling limiting the size of the surcharge to 50 to 100 percent of the normal profit rate. That is, if an improved product would normally be priced at 200 rubles, including 20 rubles of normal profit, then the surcharge should be between 10 and 20 rubles, and the price plus surcharge between 210 and 220 rubles.

With that kind of limitation, the portion of the economic benefit going to the producer will vary inversely with the size of the benefit. The larger the scale of the technological advance, the smaller the relative profit reward to the innovator. Thus, two new models of a certain piece of electrical machinery produced economic benefits calculated at 3,222 rubles and 1,176,965 rubles, respectively. The first was entitled to a price surcharge of 1,250 rubles and the second, to 1,780 rubles. Hence the producer of the first improvement received 38.8 percent of the economic benefit from his rather modest attainment. The producer of the second improvement, which must have been a remarkable technological advance, received only 0.2 percent of the huge economic benefit from his work.[30] The ceiling tips the scales of profit rewards overwhelmingly in favor of small things. Only the most minor improvements succeed in earning as much as 30 percent of the economic benefit. Most producing enterprises are reported to receive 10 to 12 percent of the economic benefit.[31] The inducement to the adopter of the improved product is correspondingly greater. These figures suggest that the problem of diffusion still seems to be the more important in the opinion of the Soviet leaders, while the initial introduction of improvements continues to take second place.

While the system is still described as one of surcharges and discounts, discounts appear to play a very minor role. The size of a discount is supposed to reflect the economic loss from the continued production of the second-quality product, but "no method for calculating the size of the loss has yet been worked out."[32] Since neither the producing enterprise nor its ministry has a burning interest in reducing the profitability of any of their products, the future of price discounts is not very bright. In the absence of discounts or price reductions on older models, the latter continue to be more profitable than improved products even with their surcharges. In the Ministry of Electrical Products in 1970, the overall planned profit rate (on cost) was 24 percent, but the planned profit rate on new products, including all surcharges, was only 14 to 15 percent. "Analysis of the data for a series of enterprises has shown that where older products are more profitable than newer ones, the price surcharges do not accomplish their purpose."[33]

There is one reason often expressed for the reluctance to use discounts that merits closer examination. The reduced price to users "may create favorable conditions for using that product, increasing the demand for it; since it has become obsolete, however, its use is disadvantageous from a national point of view."[34] To retard that possible increase in demand, the recommended practice is to establish different prices for the producer and the customer, a procedure that violates the principle of uniformity of prices. In the heavy machinery industry, for example, discounts are applied to the price the producer receives, but the purchaser continues to pay the full wholesale price.[35] The discount is therefore a commodity tax in effect. In the electrical products industry, on the other hand, discounts are practically not applied at all.[36]

To evaluate this reason for the reluctance to use price discounts, one must ask first why any enterprise would choose to continue producing an older model after its price had been discounted and its profit rate reduced below the normal level. There are always alternatives, like changing over to the production of the new or improved product or producing an entirely different product. Indeed, the very purpose of the discount is to motivate the enterprise to select one of those alternatives. If it nevertheless fails to do so, the reason must be that the next-best alternative would yield even lower profits than the continued production of the older product.[37] The higher authorities must recognize this too, for they could, if they wished, cause that product to be discontinued simply by issuing direct orders rather than by the indirect method of discounting the price. A direct order to stop the production of some product on a certain date might be effective for some more flexible enterprises. But for some it would be disastrous. Lacking the skills or equipment to start up the production of the improved product, production would either grind to a halt, or resources would be wasted in an unsuccessful effort to produce the improved model. For these enterprises, the continued production of the outdated model may contribute more to the economy than any alternative.[38] Both the improved and outdated models would continue in production for what may be an extended period of time.[39]

If the selling price of the older product were unchanged, the demand for it would decline as the output of the improved product expands. At some point the demand would be less than the quantity still being produced. If that output is to find a market, the price must be reduced. It is true that at the lowered price, new uses would be found for the older model that were uneconomic at the earlier price. This seems to be the concern about the use of price discounts. There is no economic basis for it, however. If at the lower price both producers and users benefit from the continued production of the older product, then its benefits must exceed its real costs. To maintain the old price above the market clearing level in order to force the discontinuation of production would have the same negative effect as a general direct order to discontinue production. More would be lost than gained.

The argument just presented is not inconsistent, in its main lines, with Soviet economic analysis of optimal replacement policy. Yet it has not been incorporated into the point of view of officials and practical economists who deal with innovation, as the reluctance to use price discounts demonstrates. Often the resistance to new economic notions can be explained by their inconsistency with Marxian theory. In this case, however, the resistance may lie elsewhere, in what may be called a "technological bias."

12.2. The Technological Bias

In his classic study of the evolution of Soviet investment policy, Gregory Grossman notes the influence of a preference for "relatively more 'advanced' technological solutions—an important notion in the folklore of Soviet industrialization."[40] That notion pervades the literature on innovation in general, but it appears most prominently in the discussion of product improvement. The bias toward the technologically advanced product or process helps explain a variety of policies, among them the reluctance to discount the prices of older models.

The technological bias does not appear in the technical economic literature that deals explicitly with the economic benefits of technological advance. And the new methods like analogue and parameter pricing oblige innovators and price administrators to focus explicitly on economic benefits. Nevertheless, the technological bias persists both in the general literature and in innovation practice. It is supported, in the first place, by the importance assigned to quality in official policy. The Program of the Communist Party declares that "the continuous improvement of the quality of products is an absolute requirement for economic development. The quality of the products of Soviet enterprises must be significantly higher than that of the best capitalist enterprises."[41] Perhaps it is taken as self-evident that the costs and benefits of product improvement must of course be considered. But the exhortation to improve quality is so often unaccompanied by the qualification that quality improvement has become an end in itself in decision making.

The technological bias is also reflected in economists' critique of the dominant role of engineers and designers in the research and product development process. Designers, we read, produce beautiful models that lighten human labor and increase productivity. Their colleagues admire their work and regard it as the epitome of technological attainment. But when the economists study the data, they often conclude that the product is not economic because the outlays in producing it exceed the possible cost reductions that may be attained from its use in production.[42] This difference between the engineering and economic perspective undoubtedly exists in all economies, but the economic control over technological advance may well be stronger in the capitalist business world than in the Soviet planned economy.

One consequence of the technological bias is that performance parameters are pushed beyond the margin that would be dictated by strictly economic calculation. In the base-product pricing method, the allowable price surcharges increase with the value of each parameter; "Ideally," writes a close Western analyst of the subject, "no quality would be unnecessarily high."[43] The price discounts, on the other hand, associate low-performance parameters with poor management, fines, penalties, and damages. "There is a certain connection between quality changes and price, on the basis of which the manager can determine in advance the economic advantages of increases in product quality, and the economic damage from a lowering of product quality."[44] In like fashion, state quality certification is geared to the "improvement in quality," and its whole thrust is toward higher durability, less vibration, reduction in periods between repair, and similar advances in other technologically defined characteristics. The standard of performance to be attained is the "highest worldwide and domestic technology." Hence, "today, in connection with state quality certification, there is a genuine danger of a tendency to strive thoughtlessly to equal the best foreign models, without regard to our domestic needs and resources."[45] The reported instances of excessive performance quality tend to be concentrated in high-priority industries: machine tools too large and complex for their normal uses; excessively durable bearings and motors; superconductors, special fuels, and chemical products of nonoptimally high quality.[46]

Before the introduction of price surcharges the cost increases associated with quality improvement served as a deterrent to the increase in performance parameters, both justified and unjustified. Now the additional costs are covered by the surcharge. There are warnings in the fine print that the economic benefit from a marginal increase in performance should not exceed the marginal cost, and some attention may be paid to that in the case of major innovations. But for the standard product improvements involved in state certification, it is unlikely that a full-blown benefit-cost calculation is made in each case. Thus we read that the Efremov "Red Proletariat" Plant in Moscow produced a new model machine tool 1K62 which increased the period between capital repairs from 5 to 7 years and which afforded a benefit to the user of 164 rubles per year per machine tool. However, the improvement caused a threefold increase in the labor cost of producing the tool.[47] Moreover, as we have seen, since it is the technological more than the economic value of a parameter that counts, enterprises concentrate on the improvement of those characteristics that are "easiest" for them to handle. Hence, as a result of the technological bias the rate of technological advance measured in purely technological terms (if we had such a measure) would exceed the rate measured in economic terms.

A second consequence of the technological bias is that enterprises discriminate against one class of innovations that are of significant potential benefit. These are products with lower performance parameters but which are produced at substantially lower cost. Innovations of that kind are an important component of technological progress in capitalist economies. The typical industrial product is employed in certain uses in which some of its performance parameters are fully exploited but in others they are redundant. A ball bearing, for example, may have a durability range that is appropriate for a certain use, but its maximum speed of operation may be greatly in excess of the speeds employed in that use. A useful innovation may consist of a cheaper bearing with a new design or material that has the same durability but permits the bearing to be used only at lower speeds. The new bearing would displace the older one in those of its uses in which the higher speed was not needed. More important, however, at the lower price the new model may find new uses that were not economic at the price of the older model. One major pattern of diffusing innovations is the opening of new markets for lower-performance models sold at lower prices. The diffusion of computers has followed this pattern, for example. Nor should the technological attainment of this form of innovation be undervalued. The most sophisticated manufacturing technology is often required not for the production of the largest and highest-performance computers with a limited range of use in industry and research but for the mass production of small low-performance computers produced at such low cost that they can be priced for mass markets.

Such innovations do indeed occur in Soviet industry. Because of the technological bias, however, they tend to be made less often than they should be. The would-be innovator must confront admonitions like the following: "One cannot consider a cost reduction as justified if it is accompanied by a lowering of quality. It is intolerable that some Soviet machine tools, with production costs two to three times below those of similar foreign models, are inferior to the latter in reliability and tolerance levels."[48] It would take a most independent-minded manager to come proudly before a state quality certification commission with a new product that is of poorer quality, though produced at very low cost.

The somewhat surprising implication is that the technological bias leads to a higher-than-optimal technological level of Soviet industrial products. Relative to the optimum, too many high-performance product improvements are introduced and too few low-performance. That implication flies in the face of the widely held view that Soviet products are generally of low quality, certainly compared to other industrial nations, and probably also compared to some optimum for the USSR itself.[49] The apparent paradox requires an explanation.

Philosophers tell us, when faced with a paradox, draw a distinction. The appropriate distinction in this case is that between the dynamics of technological advance and the statics of product quality as discussed earlier. It is entirely possible that, of the genuine product improvements made in each period, too many involve advances in performance characteristics and too few consist of low-cost low-performance models. Yet the quality of all the models in production at any time may be poor. Such an economy would, for example, produce too many large-bucket, high-speed excavators that, however, break down under full loads or at high speeds. Hence the technological bias is not inconsistent with poor quality.

In describing the preference for higher technological performance as a "bias," we mean to suggest that it is not a major consideration in the innovation decision. That decision is made primarily on the basis of other considerations, but in choosing among alternatives some additional weight is given to innovations with higher technological characteristics. Those other considerations, however, might be such as to favor low-technology alternatives. In that case there would be no paradox in the joint presence of a technological bias and a pattern of low-technology innovations.

In fact, before the mid-sixties production cost occupied precisely that role among the major considerations in decision making. Cost entered, first, as an element in profitability. But it also entered again, independently of profit.[50] That is, if one alternative enabled the enterprise to reduce its production cost by more than another, management would prefer it even if it yielded a somewhat lower profit. When cost reduction is an independent element in decision making, the consequences for innovation are opposite from those of the technological bias. Instead of pushing performance parameters beyond the optimum, they are kept below the optimum in order to economize on production cost, and instead of discriminating against low-cost, low-performance models, enterprises prefer them.

Since cost reduction was a major consideration in decision making, its consequences dominated in behavior. It led, however, not merely to a preference for lower-performance innovations but to some of the most severe distortions in the innovation process. Since most product improvements require some increase in production cost, the emphasis on cost reduction had a strong retarding effect on innovation. Equally serious was its effect on product quality. "The evaluation of enterprise management is oriented toward the reduction in outlays on production. As a result management . . . strives actively to 'economize' by skimping on finishing operations and by using poorer materials."[51] Efforts to improve product quality foundered in the face of the pressure for cost reduction.

By the mid-sixties, the heavy emphasis on cost reduction was finally recognized as one of the villains in the structure of decision rules. Its dethronement as a major element in decision making began with the new-product pricing decree of August 25, 1964. That decree contained a specific and pointed authorization for enterprises to provide in their plans for an increase in production costs when that increase is associated with a product improvement.[52] In the light of the traditional emphasis on cost reduction, this was a remarkable change in policy. The 1965 Economic Reform finally eliminated production cost entirely as an independent criterion of enterprise performance. It now enters the decision-making process only in the more neutral form of a component of profit.[53]

Before these reforms, the effects of the technological bias were swamped by those of the cost-reduction criterion. With the latter now removed, the pattern of product improvement should reflect more visibly the effects of the technological bias. Underemphasis has been replaced by an overemphasis on technological advance. There is reason to believe, however, that the technological bias may diminish in time as economic analysis continues to inform national policy. The general notion of an optimum, which in earlier days was thought to convey a somewhat anti-Marxian orientation ("There are no fortresses that Bolsheviks cannot storm.") is now a respectable concept. In the literature on innovation, one increasingly finds the desideratum expressed as the optimal level of a technological parameter and less often simply as improvement in quality. In this respect as in others, Soviet thought and practice may benefit from the experience of other socialist countries. The journal of the USSR State Planning Committee, for example, has published an interesting note on the subject by the Hungarian economist, Pal Karpati.[54] Karpati calls attention to the loss inflicted on the economy from the noncompatibility of equipment, in particular from the overproduction of high-performance, high-cost machinery that is put into operation alongside lower-performance equipment that holds down the rate of operation of the whole production assembly. As a result, expensive equipment is used for operations that are far below its rated capacity. He cites surveys of machine-tool utilization in Hungary in which, for example, the preponderance of equipment is used on production work at the lowest size range of its capacity.[55] The result is an overexpenditure on capital, electric power, and so forth. Among the remedies proposed by Karpati is a reform of the pricing procedure. He rejects the view that under socialism, price should be a device simply for recouping outlays and providing for a small profit margin. Price should rather reflect the "influence of the market" and should be "a regulator of production and an incentive for technological progress."

"Technological progress is not an end in itself," he writes. "Experience has shown that a technical improvement in a machine is not always optimal from a production and economic point of view. The presence in many engineering enterprises of universal machines for which there is no need at all is not an achievement of technical progress." There is a large gap between the growing acceptance of this point of view, and its incorporation in pricing and other policies. But that gap is likely to diminish in time.

Notes

1. R. R. Nelson, "The Economics of Invention: A Survey of the Literature," *Journal of Business*, Vol. 32:2 (April 1959), p. 119.
2. See Sec. 15.3.
3. In some cases, excessive quantities of higher-grade products are produced, excessive, that is, in terms of the planned distribution (or "assortment") of production by grade. Such "violations of the assortment plan" are often explained by the peculiarities of the price structure, which motivate enterprises deliberately to produce excessive quantities of high-priced goods in order to fulfill output plan targets. See J. S. Berliner, *Factory and Manager in the USSR* (Cambridge: Harvard University Press, 1957), Chap. 8.
4. See the monographic study by M. Spechler, *The Economics of Product Quality in Soviet Industry*, Ph.D. thesis, Department of Economics, Harvard University, May 1971. Also Berliner, *Factory and Manager*, Chap. 9.
5. Except for products produced to special order and products selling at temporary prices. The latter are not listed in the catalogues, but they are registered with the State Price Committee.
6. On the use of technical methods of quality control in Soviet industry, see R. W. Campbell, "Management Spillovers from Soviet Space and Military Programmes," *Soviet Studies*, Vol. 23:4 (April 1972), pp. 590-602.
7. While innovations produced at lower cost increase profit, in the period when the output rule was the major criterion of performance, such innovations were discouraged. See Sec. 14.3.
8. Akademiia Nauk SSSR, *Planirovanie i ekonomiko-matematicheskie metody* (Planning and Mathematical-Economic Methods): Essays in Honor of V. S. Nemchinov (Moscow: *Nauka*, 1964), p. 72.
9. P. S. Mstislavskii, M. G. Gabrieli, and Iu. V. Borozdin, *Ekonomicheskoe obosnovanie optovykh tsen na novuiu promyshlennuiu produktsiu* (The Economic Basis of Wholesale Pricing of New Industrial Products) (Moscow: *Nauka*, 1968), p. 153. Some earlier experiments with price surcharges and discounts on consumer goods are discussed in Spechler, *Economics of Product Quality*, pp. 144-145.
10. The decree also gave formal permission for the planning of increases in labor intensity and cost of production, if accompanied by an improvement in quality. This provision was a response to the overemphasis on cost reduction at that time, which caused enterprises to shun improvements that caused average cost to increase. Mstislavskii, Gabrieli, and Borozdin, *Ekonomicheskoe obosnovanie optovykh tsen*, p. 153.
11. K. N. Plotnikov and A. S. Gusarov, *Sovremennye problemy teorii i praktiki tsenoobrazovaniia pri sotsializme* (Current Problems in the Theory and Practice of Pricing under Socialism) (Moscow: *Nauka*, 1971), pp. 345-358.
12. Ibid., p. 357.
13. If substandard output is produced without prior permission of the authorities, certain sanctions are imposed. Ibid., p. 356.
14. Ibid., p. 349.
15. Spechler, *Economics of Product Quality*, pp. 103-106; Plotnikov and Gusarov, *Sovremennye problemy teorii*, pp. 418-419.
16. Mstislavskii, Gabrieli, and Borozdin, *Ekonomicheskoe obosnovanie optovykh tsen*, pp. 12, 152.
17. Plotnikov and Gusarov, *Sovremennye problemy teorii*, p. 358.
18. Ibid., p. 347.
19. Ibid., p. 352.

20. Ibid., p. 347.

21. The basic statutes were issued in 1967 (*Ekonomicheskaia gazeta*, 1967, No. 17, pp. 31-33), and a model "Uniform System of Quality Certification for Industrial Products" (EKAPI) was published in 1971 (*Planovoe khoziaistvo*, 1973, No. 8, pp. 10-11). Quality certification is discussed in Spechler, *Economics of Product Quality*, Chap. 5.

22. The following description applies primarily to the Ministry of Heavy Machinery. *Ekonomicheskaia gazeta*, 1973, No. 33, p. 16.

23. Ibid., 1967, No. 17, pp. 31-33.

24. *Planovoe khoziaistvo*, 1973, No. 8, p. 53.

25. *Ekonomicheskaia gazeta*, 1973, No. 33, p. 16. *Planovoe khoziaistvo*, 1973, No. 8, pp. 53-54.

26. *Planovoe khoziaistvo*, 1973, No. 8, p. 11.

27. Spechler, *Economics of Product Quality*, pp. 170-173.

28. *Ekonomicheskaia gazeta*, 1967, No. 43, p. 13; Spechler, *Economics of Product Quality*, pp. 85-86.

29. *Ekonomicheskaia gazeta*, 1967, No. 17, p. 33.

30. *Planovoe khoziaistvo*, 1973, No. 8, p. 54.

31. Ibid., p. 11. In the electrical supplies industry the surcharges amounted to only 4 to 5 percent of the calculated economic benefit (ibid., p. 53).

32. Ibid., p. 11.

33. Ibid., No. 8, pp. 53-54.

34. Plotnikov and Gusarov, *Sovremennye problemy teorii*, p. 438; *Voprosy ekonomiki*, 1966, No. 11, p. 150.

35. *Ekonomicheskaia gazeta*, 1973, No. 33, p. 16.

36. *Planovoe khoziaistvo*, 1973, No. 8, p. 52.

37. Assume for this argument that profit is the only basis of choice among alternatives.

38. Provided that the variable cost of production of the older model is less than the total cost of production of the improved model. If that condition is not satisfied, then production of the older model should be discontinued.

39. Until the original equipment wears out or requires extensive repairs, or until management and labor can be retrained or replaced.

40. G. Grossman, "Scarce Capital and Soviet Doctrine," *Quarterly Journal of Economics*, Vol. 67, No. 3, August 1953, p. 317.

41. Plotnikov and Gusarov, *Sovremennye problemy teorii*, p. 316.

42. A. M. Matlin, *Tekhnicheskii progress i tseny mashin* (Technical Progress and Machinery Prices) (Moscow: Ekonomika, 1966), p. 9.

43. Spechler, *Economics of Product Quality*, p. 143.

44. Plotnikov and Gusarov, *Sovremennye problemy teorii*, pp. 318, 354.

45. Ibid., p. 312.

46. Spechler, *Economics of Product Quality*, pp. 253-254.

47. Plotnikov and Gusarov, *Sovremennye problemy teorii*, p. 311.

48. Mstislavskii, Gabrieli, and Borozdin, *Ekonomicheskoe obosnovanie optovykh tsen*, p. 152.

49. For an analysis of optimum quality of Soviet products, see Spechler, *Economics of Product Quality*, Chap. 2.

50. See Secs. 14.3 and 14.4.

51. *Voprosy ekonomiki*, 1966, No. 11, p. 148. The author notes that supply shortages also contributed.

52. Mstislavskii, Gabrieli, and Borozdin, *Ekonomicheskoe obosnovanie optovykh tsen*, p. 153.

53. While elimination of cost reduction has removed one major source of resistance to innovation, the post-Reform decision rules contain other sources of resistance. See pp. 437-445.

54. *Planovoe khoziaistvo*, 1968, No. 1, pp. 94-96.

55. For similar experiences in the USSR, see Plotnikov and Gusarov, *Sovremennye problemy teorii*, p. 310.

Chapter 13

Price Administration

In the anecdote of the talking horse, the marvel was not in what he said but that he talked at all. In human affairs as well, the significance of an act of behavior is often less in the act than in who did it. It more or less follows that in explaining the behavior of enterprises, the question of who sets prices may be as important as the principles by which they are supposed to be set. The preceding chapters dealt primarily with the principles of pricing. This chapter concludes the study of pricing with an examination of the relationship of price administration to the innovation decision.

Mr. A. N. Komin of the State Planning Committee has given this succinct statement of the basis of price administration: "Every price originates first of all in the enterprise itself; it is then reviewed in the ministry; and after that, finally, in the Price Committee."[1] Since the enterprise initiates the new-product price proposal, it exerts a substantial influence on what the price will eventually turn out to be.[2] The essence of price administration, however, is that, with only minor exceptions, every price must be reviewed and approved by other agencies of government before it may be lawfully charged.

An elaborate structure of state agencies has been established to administer the pricing system.[3] At the summit is the State Price Committee of the USSR Council of Ministers. The committee is the Council of Ministers' chief executive agency for carrying out national policy in the administration of prices. It operates under the general directives issued to it by the Council of Ministers, and it presents the council with its own recommendations for changes in price policy. Among its functions are

to promote a unified price policy at all levels of the economy, to revise prices when necessary in accordance with conditions of production and sales, to achieve uniformity in the prices of substitute products, and to eliminate differences in the prices of similar products . . . to improve the effectiveness of state and public control over the observance of established prices, to improve the price system and the methods of price formation and the calculation of costs of production and distribution.[4]

Where its work affects the areas of responsibility of other agencies of government, it is obliged to enlist their participation, notably the State Planning Committee, the State Standards Committee, the Ministry of Finance, the Central Statistical Administration, and all the agencies and ministries over whose prices it has jurisdiction, including the Ministry of Transportation, the State Committee on Construction, the Ministry of Health, and so forth.

The USSR State Price Committee is responsible for approving the wholesale prices and publishing the price catalogues for all "basic types of industrial and food products," such as coal, petroleum, metal ores, electrical machinery, machine tools, textiles, and so forth. The committee also approves the retail prices of all basic consumer goods. About 80 percent of the output of heavy industry and half of all consumer goods fall within the jurisdiction of the committee.[5]

At the second level of price administration are the state price committees of the union republics. The republic price committees operate under the general instructions and supervision of the USSR State Price Committee; they are responsible jointly to that committee and to the councils of ministers of their respective republics. Within their competence fall all basic producer and consumer goods not priced by the USSR Committee, particularly products that are both produced and used primarily in a single republic. They include food processing, knitting, and leather and shoe machinery; household electrical appliances; and various local building materials and woodworking products. They also have the residual right to approve all prices of products produced by republic-level or local-level enterprises that happen not to be listed in any price catalogues.

At the lowest level of government are the price departments of the provincial governments. They are responsible jointly to the price committees of their republics and to the executive committees of their respective provincial governments. Their authority is limited to products delegated to them by their republic price committees. These include local fuels and building materials and many of the products of local-level enterprises.

Parallel to this governmental apparatus is another extensive network of price offices in the ministries and enterprises. Each ministry contains a price department, and most enterprises do as well. The principal responsibility of these offices is to produce the documentation required by the government price agencies regarding the prices of their major products and to represent the interests of their organizations in price negotiations with the government agencies. They have in addition the right to set final prices on a restricted range of products, without requiring the approval of the government price agencies. This applies primarily to special-order products. The prices of special orders are negotiated by the producer and customer, but they must be approved by their ministries. The only cases in which the enterprise may set a price without requiring the approval of either its ministry or a price agency are "relatively inexpensive" products or services produced on special order and equipment or spare parts produced by an enterprise for its own use.[6]

In the case of established products, the chief responsibility of the price agencies is to conduct the partial and general price revisions. On each such occasion the USSR State Price Committee issues general manuals setting forth the procedures and rules to be followed by the ministries in calculating and submitting their proposed price revisions. On the basis of these general manuals the ministries publish detailed manuals adapted to the special conditions of their own ministries. The calculation of the revised prices is the joint work of the ministries' price departments, the enterprises, and various of the research institutes. The government price agencies receive the proposed price revisions submitted by the ministries, verify them, and give the final stamp of approval, often after extensive negotiation. They then publish the official wholesale price catalogues that govern as of the date of the revision.

Between price revisions, the price agencies are occupied primarily with the pricing of new products. They publish the general instructions and manuals for new-product pricing which serve as the basis of the ministry manuals used by the enterprises. They establish the procedure that must be followed in getting a new price approved. And they give the final approval to all new prices.

Two stages are distinguished in the process of price formation for new products: the development and the plan stages.[7] The development stage starts with the drawing up of the official document known as the "technical assignment" (*technicheskoe zadanie*). This document is the basis on which the design and product engineering organizations undertake the development work on the new product. It contains a full technical description of the product to be developed, including a set of the technical and economic parameters to be attained. The stage ends with the testing of a prototype model of the new product.

The first time a price is assigned to the new product is at the beginning of the development stage, where it is known as the "limit price." It is calculated in a manner similar to that used later in determining the "upper-limit price" in the analogue method of wholesale pricing. That is, it is the highest price at which the future user would find it profitable to buy the new product rather than the older one. The limit price serves to orient the designers and production engineers in their development work. Their task is to develop a product with the given technical characteristics at a cost sufficiently lower than the limit price to warrant putting it into production. Responsibility for establishing the limit price belongs to the organization that issues the technical assignment, which may be the State Committee on Science and Technology, or a ministry, or an enterprise. To reinforce the requirement, design and product-engineering institutes are forbidden to accept an order that does not contain a limit price among the specifications.[8]

The plan stage begins when the new product appears as part of the plan of the innovating enterprise. It is at this stage that the new product is assigned its wholesale price, with which this chapter is primarily concerned. The process begins with the calculation of a draft wholesale price by the innovating enterprise, following the pricing principles set forth in the preceding chapters. Between this draft price and the final approval, however, lies a very complex administrative procedure.

13.1. The Complexity of Price Administration

The number of individual prices used in the Soviet economy approaches 10 million.[9] In the 1967 general price revision, "several million" of those prices were revised. The price catalogues that had to be republished because of the price changes totaled 38,000 pages. In the electrical supplies industry, 12 individual catalogues were issued, totaling about 2,600 pages and containing 50,000 prices. The catalogue for instruments alone covered 360,000 prices.[10] Commenting on the size of the task of price revision, Messrs. Plotnikov and Gusarov remark, "One need only note that if every price catalogue in the country were revised only once every 10 years, then each year we would have to review about 80 catalogues."[11] In the years in which there are no general price revisions, pricing activity is less hectic. In 1968 the USSR State Price Committee registered 95,000 prices, 42,000 of which were for new products.[12] The republic price committees registered another 40,000 prices.

There is nothing distinctive about these numbers, large as they seem. Every modern industrial economy must deal with millions of prices. If one added up the number of prices listed in all the price catalogues of all industrial and commercial firms in an advanced capitalist economy, the total may well be larger. And in both types of economy a vast number of man-hours must be devoted to product pricing. One is puzzled at first to read that in the USSR only "a few hundred people" are employed in all the government price agencies in the country. But most of the day-to-day work on pricing is done in the ministries, institutes, and enterprises, which prepare the documentation and submit the proposed prices to the government agencies. Moreover, during general price revisions the government agencies have to "create from scratch a much larger apparatus." In a partial revision of heavy-industry prices, they drew on the work of people in over 200 research and design organizations and a large number of enterprises.[13] In the 1967 general price revision, 200,000 research and design organizations were drawn into the work.[14] In market economies, there is normally no equivalent government involvement in pricing. But every company devotes some of its manpower to pricing and individual prices vary more frequently in response to market conditions and model changes. There are no data on which to base a judgment on the relative amounts of labor devoted to pricing the two types of economy.

The distinctive characteristic of Soviet price administration, then, is not in the number of prices nor in the effort devoted to pricing. It lies rather in the distribution of the authority over price setting. A considerable number of organizations have the authority and the responsibility to participate at some point in the process of determining the wholesale price of a new product. The experience of capitalist countries with price fixing in wartime is suggestive of the enormous administrative complexity of the task of setting the prices, defining quality standards, and policing the price and the quality of the products. The experience has filled economists with something akin to horror at the thought of ever having to do it again. The USSR, of course, has had a much longer experience with price setting, but they have also undertaken the much more massive task of determining centrally virtually every price in the economy.

There is a sense in which most industrial prices in the capitalist economy are also fixed. The price list of every industrial firm, to say nothing of the catalogues of such mail-order giants as Sears, Roebuck and Company, is the result of the long labors of perhaps tens of thousands of people. But that is where the buck stops, as it were. One can gauge the scope of the Soviet effort by imagining that all the price lists of all companies constituted merely draft proposals submitted to the price-setting agencies of the government, and that the latter were charged with the task of reviewing them, coordinating them, checking the quality standards, approving them, and policing them.

There are two aspects of Soviet price administration that must be distinguished. First, if enterprises were permitted to set their own prices without requiring the approval of any other organization, a certain amount of time and effort would be devoted to the calculation of prices, but much of it would be done informally and some reliance would be placed on the judgment of an experienced staff. If one other organization is responsible for verifying and approving the price, however, it cannot rely on the informal calculations of an enterprise but must require enough information to undertake an independent evaluation. Hence an elaborate set of regulations has been issued requiring an extensive formal documentation of the draft price of every new product. As it appears to Mr. M. Karpunin, chief of planning of the Siberian Electrical Machinery Plant, "there is first the draft price, then the explanatory memorandum, then the most detailed calculations explained line by line, then the table comparing the technical and economic characteristics of the product with its older analogue, then copies of the technical specifications, then copies of the documents on the results of official tests, then a sketch or photograph of the product."[15] This extensive documentation is one source of the complexity of price administration.

Second, while the government price agency is the ultimate arbiter of the price, there are other organizations that must be consulted in the negotiations. One might imagine an administered price system that, in its simplest form, involved only bilateral negotiation. In market economies most special-order contract prices are set that way, in direct negotiation between producer and customer. Government contracting is also primarily bilateral—say between a military procurement agency and an industrial contractor—although another government agency may serve as a financial watchdog. But in Soviet price negotiations a variety of organizations are involved, depending upon the type of product and the kind of price applied for. The following is a description of the procedure by Mr. S. G. Stoliarov, a prominent authority on price statistics:[16]

The process for setting wholesale and retail prices on new products is rather complicated. First the enterprise calculates its outlays for the new product, prepares a statement of its technical characteristics, drafts a price proposal, and submits all the documentation to its ministry along with the blueprints (if possible, also with a prototype model of the product). The ministry is obliged to check the documentation, then secure the agreement of the purchaser to the proposed price, and then give official approval to the price if that lies within its jurisdiction, or else submit the draft price to the Price Committee for its approval. . . .

If the customer agrees to the price, the producer's ministry approves it either as a permanent price or as a temporary price for about one to one-and-a-half years. If the customer does not agree, the question of what the temporary price will be drags on for many months. When the temporary-price period expires (as a rule the time limits are not observed), the whole process is then repeated in getting approval for the permanent price; though with the difference that the documentation must be submitted to the government agency that is authorized to approve that particular permanent price according to the government decrees. In the great majority of cases that agency is the Price Committee of the USSR State Planning Committee, where a mass of materials bearing on the approval of permanent prices piles up, a process that also takes a lot of time. That's the situation regarding the approval of wholesale prices.

Still other organizations may have to be consulted under various conditions: the State Standards Committee if the product involves the approval of new standards or a departure from established standards; the State Committee on Science and Technology if it is a major innovation; the Ministry of Foreign Trade or the State Committee on Foreign Economic Relations if it is an export item; and possibly various research and design institutes. In retail-price setting a major complication is added in the obligatory participation of the Ministry of Finance. The financial organs are involved because of their responsibility for levying the "turnover tax," the commodity tax that is a principal source of the government's revenues. Depending on the product and the industry, the number of agencies drawn into the process may be formidable. Mr. Karpunin of the Siberian Heavy Electrical Machinery Plant presents the following "schema" that had to be followed for pricing each of its new products and special orders: "producer → producer's chief administration → customer → customer's chief administration → planning department of the customer's ministry → customer's deputy minister → producer's chief administration → planning department of the producer's ministry → producer's deputy minister → State Price Committee."[17]

One can only speculate on the reasons that have led to the complexity. Planning Chief Karpunin, in urging a more simplified approach to price formation, writes, "what we want is more trust in enterprises." But it is not simply a matter of government mistrust of enterprises. In the centrally planned economy, each organizational unit is held to account for the administration of some line of state policy, and it demands some control over all decisions taken elsewhere that may affect its own plans and instructions. Moreover, the mistrust is not always directed downward but extends upward as well. There is a widespread tradition of the voluntary seeking of written approval of important decisions by one's senior officials and others, as a sort of protection against incrimination in case the decision later proves to have been a bad one. Even in the absence of formal procedures, the practice of "collecting signatures" tends to widen the network of organizations brought into decision making.

13.2. Consequences of Administrative Complexity

There are three consequences of the complexity of price administration that affect the enterprise's innovation decisions. First, it is a costly process. Second, it takes a long time to secure final approval of a new-product price. And third, the innovation decision is made under conditions of great uncertainty about what the final wholesale price will be.

Administrative Costs and Delays

The cost of administering prices would be minimal if the State Price Committee were the only other agency involved. But it is considerably increased by the involvement of the other organizations. Each of them may enter a demurrer, challenging a cost item here or a design feature there. Most of the cost elements are only estimates anyhow, since the process of securing the price takes place before production begins. Hence the estimates are easy to challenge and difficult to defend. The regulations require that each material and component be listed and its price justified by reference to the appropriate catalogue. If new materials or components are used, however, their prices may not yet be listed in any catalogue, thus requiring elaborate explanation and inviting further challenges. The burden on the enterprise depends on the nature of its production and the frequency with which new prices must be sought. The official of the Siberian plant describes his as one of the "thousands of enterprises specializing in small-lot and special-order products, so that each year the volume of new products amounts to 20 percent of total output or more."[18] For such enterprises the documentation of all new prices required each year, including one-time special orders, is extremely burdensome.

The time required to conduct the documents through each office in the long chain is very long. The Siberian plant estimates that when everything goes well, with no postal delays and no more than the usual waiting time in each office, it takes at least two to three months to gain final approval of the price. But if someone should fall ill or drag his feet, the period can be greatly extended.[19] To gain approval of the retail prices of consumer goods may take 3 to 6 months, and sometimes even longer.[20] In the case of temporary prices the entire procedure must be followed twice, "once for approval of the temporary price, and a second time for the permanent price, which takes over six months and perhaps even more than a year."[21]

Delays in processing new prices are often extended because of snags in the processing of the new technical standards. The latter procedure involves another vast world of administration.[22] In an effort to tighten the enforcement of standards, it was decreed in 1966 that no new-product price may be approved until the technical standards have been approved and registered in the next edition of the All-Union Standards Information Registry.[23] It is a reasonable regulation, since an effective standards system is essential for successful price administration. The consequence, however, is to add a new, and sometimes extensive, detour in the already lengthy journey of the new price through the price-administration chain. For the process of securing approval of standards is no less complex than that of receiving approval of a price. Messrs. Plotnikov and Gusarov have described the process of registering standards for new toys, a relatively simple process because the product is regulated by the republic agencies and does not have to be approved by the national agencies:[24]

Thus, in the Russian republic, models of new toys and their technical specifications are examined by the enterprise's industrial design council;[25] agreement is then sought from the technical department of the Chief Administration for Toy Production of the RSFSR Ministry of Light Industry; it is then examined by the industrial design council of the chief administration. Next the technical documentation and the prototype models of the toys are sent on to the municipal public health center for certification that they are not harmful, after which the models are submitted for approval to the industrial design council of the RSFSR Ministry of Education; and if the toy is produced in Moscow, then approval must also be sought from the Commission on Toys of the Moscow Chief Administration for Retail Trade.

Reports on the time taken for approval of standards run from about three months on upwards; 80 days for a new carburetor, 110 to 427 days for various items of photographic equipment, 108 to 120 days for a radio receiver.[26] Ordinarily the process of registering standards begins before the price-approval process and should be completed earlier. If no hitches occur, only time and labor are involved. But if the standard has not yet been approved by the time the price has found its way to the State Price Committee, the pricing process is stalled until the standard is cleared.

To speed along the process of price negotiation, the authorities are supposed to publish detailed time schedules that the innovator is obliged to follow.[27] If the time schedules are observed, the price should receive final approval at least a month or so before the first unit is ready to be sold. We read, however, that such obligatory schedules are not always published, and that there are no penalties on the organizations that sit on the documents for long periods before sending them on to the next link in the chain. Hence "the output of new products often begins even before any wholesale prices have been set for them."[28] One of the uses made of "pushers"—the discredited but vital occupation of expediting negotiations—is to speed up the progress of the papers along their way.[29] "In practice, last year, for every one of our products that required a temporary or special-order price, approval of the price was obtained by unauthorized travel expenses [for expediters—J.B.] and at the cost of a most agitating pressure. We had to 'push,' because we had to sell our machines," writes the planning chief of the Siberian plant.[30]

It is particularly irksome for an enterprise that had managed to carry an innovation successfully through all its earlier stages to find itself stymied at this last stage of getting its price approved. A Moscow machine-tool plant, for example, undertook to raise the quality of its products to world standards, partly as a result of increased export orders. Its labor and material costs rose, and the enterprise applied for the standard price surcharge for high-quality products. But because of the long delay in the price-setting agency, the enterprise fell behind its tax payment schedule by 450,000 rubles, and it lost its incentive payments. They managed to cover their losses for a while only by increasing the output of other products and reducing their general production costs.[31] Generalizing on this matter of delays, an expert on innovation writes, "In many cases, the time spent by an enterprise in developing a new product is less than the time required for the review and approval of the price at all administrative levels."[32]

Uncertainty

When the forthcoming appearance of a new product is first announced, neither the innovator nor his prospective customers can have confidence that the provisional price will hold when the product is finally delivered. The innovator may find that the profit to which he is entitled by the formal pricing principles, on the basis of which he undertook the innovation, may be whittled down or turn into a loss at the end of the price negotiation process. By that time it is too late to reverse the decision to innovate. The Red Triangle Combine undertook to increase the durability of their rubber tires by 30 to 35 percent, at an increase in their production costs. But the price increase never materialized, and the profit rate on the tires fell from the expected 13 percent to 2.5 percent.[33] The Omsk Synthetic Rubber Plant had counted on higher prices for its higher-quality products following the 1967 price revision. "Alas, we looked into the price catalogues, and in fact they are not there."[34] Or, when the negotiations over the new price are completed, the enterprise may discover that the price has been increased but by too little to justify the higher production costs of the new product, to which the enterprise is now committed. The Yaroslav Tire Plant introduced a new product line that increased durability by 1.5 to 2 times, at a cost increase of 35 to 60 percent. But the approved price increases were only 26 to 37 percent, caused a decline in the enterprise's profit rate, and in the case of some products led to an actual loss.[35]

The customer, on the other hand, may find that the provisional price, which induced him to adopt the new product, turns out to be much lower than the final wholesale price. The problem is particularly serious in the design of new plants, where decisions on the materials and equipment to be used must be made long in advance of the actual purchase. Mr. Podshivalenko, deputy chairman of the Bank for Construction, attributes the persistent underestimation of construction costs to this cause. About half of all machinery and equipment employed in the design of new construction projects consists of new items, the prices of which are not yet included in the official price catalogues used by the designers. Their prices have to be estimated from the prices of analogous items that are included in the price catalogues. When the construction project plans are approved and orders are placed for the machinery and equipment, the builders then discover that the wholesale prices have been set substantially higher than had been estimated.[36] An official of a construction engineering institute, which is charged with the responsibility of incorporating the latest technology into its designs, attended a show in 1965, at which a manufacturer exhibited a model of a new dilatometric regulator that would soon be in production. The manufacturer announced a provisional price of 25 rubles, very close to that of the older model which was to be withdrawn from production because of defective design. But at the end of 1966, the manufacturer was already asking a provisional price that was twelve times as high, and in June 1967, an official but still "provisional" price of 203 rubles was announced.[37] The effect of this uncertainty is to discourage early adoption. It leads also to a faulty choice among alternative technologies, since the machinery selected on the basis of the estimated price may not have been selected had the high wholesale price been known at the time.

The degree of uncertainty appears to be greatest in the case of new consumer goods where two additional influences are brought to bear, the forecasting of consumer demand and the appetite of the government's tax collectors. "Here," writes Mr. Stoliarov,

the enterprise's calculations are not always taken into consideration, and in setting retail prices they begin "from the other end," so to speak; that is, they try to find in the existing price catalogues prices that correspond to the quality and makeup of the new products. At the same time the financial authorities try to set a price that would bring in the largest tax receipts, while the retail trade people worry about excessively high prices for fear that they will not sell. The outcomes vary. In most cases some "compromise" price is worked out, and it may therefore turn out that, after deducting the retail markup and the turnover tax, the producing enterprise is left with a wholesale price that does not cover the costs of production of the new product.[38]

The decision to produce a new or improved consumer good appears to be taken with only the vaguest guess about what the price will turn out to be.

The complexity of price administration is a greater burden for the innovator than for the noninnovator. The latter has little occasion to enter the arena of price negotiation. His prices have all been fixed some time in the past, and only during periods of price revision must he engage with the pricing bureaucracy. The more innovative the enterprise, the more of its energies and resources that must be committed to the work of price negotiation. The administration of prices thus reinforces the resistance to innovation due to the principles of pricing. Because of those principles, if the enterprise follows strictly the pricing rules in the manual, it expects its average profit rate to decline. In addition, because of the complexity of the administrative process it must confront also the costs and delays of price negotiation and the uncertainty about what its price will actually turn out to be.

One possible response is always available: to avoid or delay the commitment to innovate. "In many instances," writes Mr. Stoliarov, "the heads of enterprises do not undertake product improvements because they dread the long time and the mass of trouble involved in getting approval for new technical specifications and prices."[39] While this concern is probably not in itself a major deterrent to innovation, it does add to the weight of the other properties of organizational and price structure that discourage product innovation. The more troublesome response to administrative complexity, however, is the widespread evasion of pricing regulations that it generates.

13.3. Evasion of Regulations

It has long been known that the interests of Soviet enterprises often clash with the intent of the formal procedures. The consequence is a pattern of informal enterprise behavior that ranges from such relatively innocent practices as wining and dining responsible officials to outrightly illegal practices like falsification of reports. These practices pervade all major areas of enterprise activity: output planning, procuring materials and equipment, choosing among alternative output mixes, and preparing financial accounts.[40] It therefore comes as no surprise that price administration is characterized by some degree of evasion as well.

The official description of these activities is "violation of state price discipline." While violations occur in the case of established as well as new products, certain of the practices are more readily applied to new products. We may distinguish four forms that such violations take. First is the simple evasion of administrative regulations, not only by enterprises but by ministries and government agencies as well. Prices that are supposed to be submitted for approval to higher agencies are pushed through without that approval. Provincial price agencies, for example, give their own approval to prices of commodities that fall within the jurisdiction of the republic or national price committees. And enterprise directors contrive to define some of their standard output as special-order products as a pretext for bypassing the pricing agencies and charging a high price.[41]

Second, enterprises manage to obtain prices higher than authorized by the regulations. Some enterprises, we read, "misrepresent . . . their costs of production in the documents submitted to the pricing agencies." In analogue and parameter pricing, the upper-limit price may be increased by exaggerating the new product's performance characteristics or by the judicious choice of a low-quality established product as the analogue. In special-order products, some enterprises manage to secure prices that yield a profit rate of "50 percent, 100 percent, and more," instead of the limit of 20 percent provided in the regulations.[42]

Third, products are sold at higher prices than those in the official catalogues. Sometimes the official prices are simply ignored. "Some enterprises, even when official wholesale prices exist, continue to sell for a long time at higher prices or at prices that have never been approved."[43] In other cases the catalogue prices are misapplied, especially in the use of surcharges and discounts. Enterprises often add a surcharge with no justifiable reason, "for the purpose of increasing profit."[44] Or surcharges to defray loading costs are added when the catalogue price is FOB railroad station of origin and is therefore supposed to include such costs.[45] Price discounts, on the other hand, are not used when they are supposed to be. New products often require materials of higher quality than are readily available from other enterprises. The innovator may therefore have to produce substandard output because his suppliers cannot meet quality standards. In such cases the new product should be sold at a discount. But "by selling lower-quality output at the new prices, they receive an unearned profit."[46]

By the nature of these practices, it is not possible to gauge the frequency of their occurrence in quantitative terms. That they are deeply embedded in the economic structure is evident from the fact that they have endured for decades and have survived a variety of reorganizations of the economy. Reference to them appears often enough in the Soviet sources that we know them to be an ongoing source of concern. As for their effect on innovation, it is possible that it may be beneficial in some ways. The complexities of price administration—cost, delays, and uncertainty—tend to discourage innovation. So do limitations on innovation profits. The possibilities of evasion offer opportunities to bypass some of the administrative complexity and to reap larger rewards for product innovations. Evasion may have some of the properties of a "second-best" solution. If a set of administrative regulations leads to poor results, some looseness in their implementation may make matters better rather than worse.

These ruminations apply to the three kinds of practices set forth earlier. There is a fourth kind, however, which is a very different matter. Variations of it have also occurred under price administration in capitalist countries, but its major forms are distinctively Soviet. It also appears to be much more extensive in the USSR than the other three. And its effect on the innovation record of the economy is pernicious. That practice is the simulation of innovation.

13.4. Excessive Product Differentiation

"We are tied to our prices like a goat to a stake," writes the director of a Moscow retail shop.[47] It is the principle of permanent prices that is the source of the problem. For once a price is fixed, the enterprise is stuck with it for a long time despite changes in production and cost conditions. One of the few ways in which a manager can hope to have his price increased is by contriving to have his product classified as new, a practice that entitles him to a new price. The crux of the administrative problem is the apparently simple question of when is a new product new? In a market economy this is a serious question only for statisticians and economists, who must worry about how to measure technological change.[48] It is a question of no particular salience for the manufacturer. For him the question is whether the commodity will or will not sell at a particular price. The "market will decide" whether it is new or not; and in any case the producers-goods market will be less interested in whether it is new than in its price and performance relative to other products. But in a price-administered economy, socialist or capitalist, the question of whether a product is to be defined as new or not is of crucial importance to the manufacturer, for upon this matter of definition hinges the question of whether he can get a higher price for it or not. The man who must be persuaded that it should count as new is the official in the price-setting agency. Hence a great deal of managerial ingenuity goes into the redesign of products with the minimal number of changes for the specific purpose of getting the product reclassified as new. The eminent economist Sh. Turetskii writes,

Often, under the guise of a new model or commodity, practically the same kind of product is produced with an insignificant (and often not needed) change in the design, the details of its construction, and so forth, but at a higher price. Control over standards, formulas, technical specifications, and everything that determines the social utility and the use value of commodities has clearly weakened in recent years.[49]

The permanence of prices is not in all cases an unwelcome restraint on the producer. How the goat feels about the stake depends on the grass in the neighborhood. Tethered in a new green pasture, he may not notice the stake at all. It is only when the grass runs out that the stake begins to bind. So it is with prices. In the years following the introduction of a new product, costs decline while the price remains constant. One does not mind being tied to that price. At the other extreme are established products the profits on which have been squeezed out in earlier price revisions. If the product has been in production for a long time, its technology is fully shaken down and costs are not expected to decline any further. If the enterprise is a relatively high-cost producer of that product, the fixed price may even exceed cost, and the enterprise may suffer a loss. That is the price that binds.

A genuine innovation or improvement is a way of breaking loose from the stake. Even under the old cost-plus-profit pricing method, the introduction of a new product was the reason for securing a new price that would at least yield the normal profit rate. And in subsequent years as cost declined, the profit rate would rise. Under the new techniques of analogue and parameter pricing, the starting profit rate even exceeds the normal level.

The new-product pricing regulations were written for the purpose of encouraging genuine innovation. But genuine innovation is an act of technical and organizational creativity requiring talents not given to all men. Moreover, it is risky and beset by obstacles. It does not require great imagination, however, for men of lesser talent and daring to bend the regulations to their own benefit. The literature abounds with illustrations of simulated innovation and its costs to the economy:

Following an insignificant improvement in the instrument and the assignment of a new model number, the wholesale price was raised 2.5 times. Prices are also raised without justification on new models of machine electric motors, foundry equipment, and so forth. Each year the Ministry of Transportation overpays its suppliers by an amount equal to half of its allotted capital investment because of the small design and engineering changes constantly being made in its rolling stock.[50]

Artificial product innovation takes many different forms, depending upon the kind of product and the enterprise's technological skills. In one of its forms, for example, the enterprise, "guided by its own interests, improves those product characteristics that are easiest for them to deal with. . . ."[51] Usually the technique involves a small change in the physical form of the product. In other cases it may involve no changes at all but a repackaging of a set of established products into a single unit presented as a new product. The Siberian Agricultural Machinery Plant, for example, applied for a price on its new furrowing and seed-shelling combine, Model LDS-4. "In fact this was not a new machine at all but an aggregate of three established equipment items assembled as a unit." The sum of the wholesale prices of the three components was 460 rubles, and a reasonable estimate of assembling cost was 90 rubles, for a total of 550 rubles. The enterprise, however, submitted a cost estimate of 1,138 rubles in its price application.[52]

The simulation of product innovation is a long-standing practice in Soviet industry and was well known in the prewar period.[53] Quantitative data on this kind of activity are particularly difficult to come by, since, in addition to the normal problems of collecting data on illicit behavior, it requires a judgment on whether a "new" product is genuinely new. It does appear, however, that the extent of the practice expanded greatly following the introduction of temporary pricing in 1955. Designed to encourage genuine innovation, the institution of temporary prices opened the administrative door to a flood of claims for temporary prices on "new" products. In the subsequent criticism of temporary pricing, the encouragement it gave to simulated innovation was regarded as one of its chief defects. It is difficult to judge how the extent of the practice was affected by the curtailment of temporary pricing since 1966. The new pricing principles require that the productivity of new products be considered in price determination. This requirement may filter out the least productive of the simulated innovations that might have gotten through in the past. On the other hand, under temporary pricing only the normal profit rate on cost was allowed, at least officially. The newer pricing methods allow higher profit rates based on productivity advances, and therefore increase the gains from a successfully simulated innovation. They also introduce performance characteristics into pricing, and therefore require more technological information than cost-based prices. Since only the producer possesses that information initially, the power of the producer vis-à-vis the price administration is increased.[54] Most significant, however, is the high priority assigned to innovation in the past decade. The increased pressure on and inducements to enterprises and ministries to innovate may succeed in raising the rate and quantity of genuine innovation. But it will surely increase the volume of simulated innovation as well. In evaluating reform proposals, perceptive analysts now include in their evaluation the possibilities and consequences of simulation. On a certain pricing proposal designed to reduce the profit rate automatically the longer a machine is in production, A. M. Matlin writes: "This may seem like an alluring proposal at first glance. For who can be against higher prices for newer technology? Unfortunately, however, there is no guarantee that a newly introduced machine is better than a machine first produced sometime earlier."[55] The more intense the pressure to innovate, the less the likelihood that the newer will also be the better.

One of the consequences of the kind of competition that characterizes modern capitalist economies is excessive product differentiation. Too many brands and models of individual products are produced at any time, and models change too frequently over time. A planned socialist economy might be expected to come closer to the optimal degree of product differentiation and, by eliminating the wastes of excessive numbers and changes of models, attain a higher level of economic welfare. In the earlier period of Soviet economic history, policy was directed to that end. A limited number of models was produced, by mass-production methods wherever possible.[56] Once a model was in full production and the technology shaken down, it continued to be produced for long periods of time until the accumulated technological advances warranted a major model change. This picture of the Soviet economy may have to be revised for later years in the light of the simulation of innovation. We have no way of comparing the extent of the excessive product differentiation in the two types of economy. But the view that the centrally planned socialist economy avoids this defect of capitalist economic organization cannot be sustained.

Although the sources are different, the costs of excessive product differentiation are similar in the two systems. The resources invested in development and model changeover are withdrawn from other uses in which the social benefit would be greater. In one respect, the costs are greater in the Soviet economy. In addition to the enterprise resources devoted to simulated innovation, there are the costs of centralized price administration. Each new model adds to the paperwork required as the price traverses all the agencies that are required to give their approval. With respect to technical standards alone, as a result of artificial product differentiation, "a huge number of technical specifications has been approved, which has greatly complicated the task of unifying and standardizing products, and in many cases has made it impossible to compare the technical specifications of basically similar goods."[57] The mass of simulated innovations that clog the administrative machinery reduces the effectiveness of supervision and control and, by reducing the risk of detection, lends further encouragement to the practice.

The extensive simulation of innovation complicates the interpretation of Soviet innovation experience. First, it must be kept in mind in evaluating Soviet data on the frequency of product innovation. Some portion of the reported number of new products introduced each year consists of these minimally differentiated products. Second, it exaggerates the officially reported growth rate of real output because of the downward bias it introduces in indices of price changes. The bias is particularly large in the machinery price index. As explained by two prominent Soviet critics, the source of the bias is that the index fails to take account "not only of new products but also of the price changes of many products that are really old models with insignificant modifications that were made chiefly in order to break away from the permanent catalogue prices."[58] The greater the extent of simulated innovation, the greater the degree to which real price increases fail to be expressed in the general index. Hence some portion of the reported annual growth of output consists not of real production but of the higher prices charged.

Third, simulated innovation may account for some portion of the decline in the efficiency of capital experienced since the late fifties. In part it is a matter of pricing. Suppose the prices of capital goods are rising while their productivity is unchanged, in the sense that each new unit of capital yields the same annual increase in output. If the rise in prices is not fully excluded from the price index, the calculated growth rate of capital will exceed that of output and the productivity of new capital will appear to be declining. In addition to this pricing effect, however, there is reason to believe that the increased pressures on enterprises to innovate in the past decade has caused the rate of productivity growth of new capital to decline. The weaker the demand made on enterprises to innovate, the more their effort is devoted to other tasks that they are best equipped to perform. Only those innovations would be introduced that yielded a higher return than other activities. The greater the pressure to innovate, the larger the number of enterprises that try their hand at it without the skills to carry it out well, and the greater the number of innovations that appear with small or negative productivity advances. Both the price-increasing effect and the productivity-decreasing effect contribute to a decline in the observed productivity of new capital. At the least, they offset whatever gains in genuine technological progress that may be credited to the new pricing arrangements and other measures of encouragement to innovation. At the worst, they may have more than offset the gains.

Finally, when the practice of simulated innovation is kept in mind, the traditional pricing principles prove to be less of a source of mischief than the critics allege. The evidence, it will be recalled, consists of data that show profit rates to be much higher on older products than on new. Those high profit rates, however, are the result not only of permanent cost-plus pricing but also of the simulation of innovation. In deciding which of its older products to replace by minimally differentiated new ones, the enterprise does not choose randomly. It drops from production only those that realize profit rates lower than the normal rate, which is the minimum rate the simulated new product is expected to earn; and among them, the products dropped are presumably those yielding the lowest, including negative, profits. This systematic weeding out of low-profit older products contributes in this way to the increase in the average rate of profit on older products. Hence to the extent that the gap in profit rates was an obstacle to innovation, the remedy should have been sought not only in the reform of the pricing principles but also in the elimination of simulated innovation. The latter, however, is not easily done in a system of administered prices. The reason may be seen by considering the techniques of control available to the agencies of price administration.

13.5. Price Controls
One task of price administration is to establish orderly procedures for conducting the business of price determination. If the organizational units can be counted on to conduct their work precisely according to those procedures, that would be the only task. If, however, their interests are such that they may be motivated to evade the procedures, there is a second task for price administration—to establish controls that would minimize departures from official procedures. The greater the

motivations for evasion, the larger the task of control.

Responsibility for controlling price behavior is lodged primarily in the network of price committees and other agencies that conduct the work of price setting. In addition to control by committees, the state has sought to enlist the purchasers of goods as agents of control over the producers of goods.

Control by Committees

Responsibility for the control of enterprise behavior is lodged in a variety of agencies.[59] It is useful to distinguish specific controls from general controls. Specific controls are exercized by agencies charged with responsibility for a particular aspect of enterprise activity. The Ministry of Finance, for example, exercises control specifically over the enterprise's financial affairs, the State Committee on Labor and Wages controls that branch of activity, and so forth. The agencies of general control are responsible for all enterprise operations, including finance, labor and wages, and other matters for which specific controllers also exist. Some of the agencies of general control are part of the enterprise itself; such inbuilt controllers are the enterprise party and trade-union organizations. Others are external to the enterprise, like the ministry, the local government and party organizations, the Ministry of State Control, and the State Bank.

Control over pricing activity follows that pattern. The State Price Committee and the republic and the provincial price committees exercise control specifically over pricing matters. But all the agencies of general control are charged with the responsibility of seeing that the pricing procedures are properly followed, along with all other administrative procedures.

In the light of the broad network of controls, the extensive practice by enterprises of evasive and illegal activities is something of a puzzle. A variety of explanations have been given, two of which apply particularly to pricing practices. One is the limited resources available to the agencies of specific control. The other is the conflict among the various roles assigned to certain of the general control agencies.

In a sense all the price-administration agencies and other organizations that process the applications for new prices serve as agents of control. Part of their job is to evaluate the enterprises' cost estimates and performance claims and to verify that the price calculations follow the principle set forth in the manuals. Under the best of conditions the official sitting in Moscow handling masses of documents for many different kinds of products is hardly a match for the plant engineers and account-ants who know their costs and products intimately. With the limited manpower resources available, however, the pricing officials cannot de-vote to each application the time that a thorough control would re-quire. Moreover, control over enterprises is not the only task of the pricing officials. Their main task is to execute national price policy, to check on consistency of a proposed new price with the general price structure, to maintain the principle of uniformity by assuring that a proposed price is not different from that of an identical product manu-factured elsewhere, and so on.[60] The pricing agencies do have special departments for price inspection, but their staffs are quite small. In any case, "it would be impossible to exercise direct control over all enter-prises even if the entire price-administration apparatus were occupied with the work of control."[61]

The task of direct price control is therefore largely delegated to the ministries, under rules laid down by the State Price Committee. The ministries, however, typify the conflict of interests that weakens many of the agencies of general control. For one thing, when the work load of price setting is excessive, the government pricing agencies often turn much of it over to the ministries, who then become in effect the price-setting agencies. In the 1967 general price revision, over a hundred price catalogues were prepared by ministries of the engineering industries themselves for the products of their own enterprises.[62] An organization can hardly be an objective controller of its own work. More significant, however, is that the ministries themselves are evaluated by their perfor-mance, which depends in turn on the successes reported by their enter-prises. Hence, "nowadays, unfortunately neither the producing enter-prises nor their ministries have an interest in reducing the prices of their products."[63] The commonality of interests derives from the pressure exerted on both ministry and enterprise to take on plan tasks that they may not be able to fulfill. To protect themselves from such pressures, "the ministries, enterprises, and other agencies take up defensive posi-tions in the drafting of plans and try to reduce the level of the plan targets for growth of output and profit."[64] Hence if an enterprise has succeeded in building up a high profit rate on an established product whose production cost has declined greatly, the ministry can hardly be counted on to initiate a price reduction. For, like the enterprise, the ministry "strives to maintain for a long time the high profit rate in its branch of the engineering industry."[65]

Some organizational structures are surely better than others for attaining a particular objective. It is a merit of Soviet society that it is able to change unsatisfactory arrangements, although the frequency and magnitude of changes may be excessive at times. The problems that the periodic organizational changes are intended to remedy, however, may not be amenable to solution by organizational change at all. The best of all feasible arrangements of administrative control may reduce the incidence of evasion of regulations and simulation of innovation. But it would not cut into the heart of the problem.

The crux of the matter is that administered pricing is simply a bad arrangement for controlling prices under conditions of technological change. In the total absence of technological change the identity of individual products, once defined by the pricing officials, never changes. No provision needs therefore to be made for pricing new products. Some established prices need to be revised occasionally in response to changing costs. But since there are no new products, all costs are basically stable, changing slowly only in response to changes in tastes, or resource availability, or foreign trade. Price revisions are therefore relatively rare and easy to control. Administered pricing, like centralized economic planning generally, is entirely suitable to the task in this administrator's dreamworld.

Conditions are very different when technological change is occurring, and particularly when the society's governors wish to accelerate it. The centralized administration of prices becomes a nightmare in such a world. Regulations must now be written for assigning prices to new products. Such regulations require administrators to make frequent decisions on matters that never arise in an unchanging world; how different must one product be from another to qualify as a "new product." If it is a new product, is it also a better one, and if so, how much better; if it is better by different amounts in different uses, how should the overall economic value of its technological superiority be measured; how much will it cost to produce something that has never been produced before? The innovators themselves, who are closest to the new technology, can only roughly guess the answers. It is all the more difficult for the administrators, whose knowledge of the technology always lags behind that of the producers; and the greater the pace of change, the greater the lag. To compound the administrator's problem, the acceptance of applications for prices on new products is an open invitation to all imaginative managers to improve their enterprises' positions.

For stripped of the detail, what administered pricing boils down to is that it is not the buyer but the price administrator against whom the innovator is pitted in the pricing game. A new product is anything the man in the Price Committee can be persuaded to regard as a new product, and its price can be as high as he can be convinced to agree to.[66] No administrative controls can close the door on the opportunities such regulations offer to enterprising managers. Suitable though it is in a world without technological change, centralized price administration cannot cope with the pricing problems of a technologically changing world. And the greater the rate of technological change and the social commitment to advance it, the less the suitability of that arrangement for setting prices.

It is therefore no accident that in recent years more and more Soviet voices are calling for the replacement of "administrative methods by economic methods." What that means is that economic behavior is to be controlled by enterprises pursuing their own interests rather than by direct administrative regulation. In this context, it is the customer pursuing his interests, rather than an administrator, who is to be counted on to control the producer's innovative and pricing behavior. Customers, according to this view, are better controllers than price committees.

Control by Customers

If demand can indeed be made to play a more prominent role in pricing many of the problems that are so intractable to administrative solution would vanish. The peculiar question of whether a "new" product is really new is of little interest to the industrial purchaser. What interests him in any product, new or old, is its price and its usefulness in his own production operations. The administrator presented with a simulated innovation is asked only to sign a document. But a customer is asked actually to buy the thing, which is a very different matter. No administrator can restrain a producer's appetite for a high price as effectively as the sobering discipline of having to sell the product to skeptical, cost-conscious customers. No administrator can match a customer's experience and vitality of interest in assessing the performance claims for a new product to be used in his own production operations.

To enlist this awesome customer power in the service of price control, a variety of methods have been introduced. They may be classified as indirect and direct methods.

Indirect methods are those in which the interests of potential users are represented by agents other than the customers themselves. The replacement of cost-based pricing by productivity-pricing principles is such a method. In cost-based pricing only the producer's interests are taken account of in setting the price.[67] Productivity pricing requires that the value of the new product's performance characteristics be taken into account in pricing. Customers are protected from having to pay a high price for a new product, the cost of which greatly exceeds the older model but the productivity of which is scarcely increased.

Productivity pricing may be expected to weed out a certain number of ineffective innovations that would slip through under cost-based pricing. The trouble with such indirect methods, however, is precisely their indirectness. Price administrators and committees of experts cannot evaluate the productivity and cost savings to be expected from a new material or machine as well as the ultimate users themselves. Even if their general technical competence is equal or higher, they do not have as full a knowledge of the variety of specific applications of the product in different enterprises with different output profiles. The experts on quality certification commissions are usually engineers and scientists of the research and design institutes serving as consultants to the ministries and pricing agencies. In the light of the technological bias that pervades innovation activity, their judgment is inevitably influenced more by the technological features of the product with which they are most conversant than with its economic properties. A commission of experts, intrigued perhaps by the technological ingenuity of a new product, is more likely to certify it as a significant advance than the enterprise engineers who will have to use it and must consider its cost and productivity. Industrial users as a group are likely to place different evaluations on new and improved products than research and development scientists and engineers.

The difficulty is all the greater in the case of consumer goods, where subjective evaluations predominate. In State Quality Certification the experts of the certification commission sit around the table and decide that the shoes of a certain kind should be evaluated on three criteria: durability, styling, and softness of leather. They then rank the new model of a shoe on a five-point scale for each of these qualities on the basis of their judgment, and the price surcharge is set on the basis of the sum of points.[68] Evaluations of this kind are a form of economic government for the consumer but not of and by the consumer. Like market research they very likely increase the social value of what gets produced. But at best they are efforts to second-guess the ultimate customer. The consequences of bad guesses are less serious in the case of consumer goods than in the case of producer goods, however. They are not "distributed" as producer goods are but are placed on sale in a marketlike arrangement. If the experts have guessed badly, the new shoes will simply remain unsold at the established price and will eventually be withdrawn from production. But in the case of producer goods, once a new product has been certified by a state certification commission, it will most certainly continue in production and eventually replace the older model that the experts have decreed to be of lower quality.

Even if the evaluation committees possessed all the knowledge that the customers possess, they cannot be expected to promote the customers' interests with the diligence that the latter would exert on their own behalf. The price administrator has his own work to get on with, and the expert collects his consultant's fee and returns to his regular job. When the negotiations over a new price are completed, that is the end of it for them. If the price is too high in relation to the product's value, they hear little more of it. But the industrial customer may have to live with it. In circumstances in which he is able to choose between a new product and an older one, he would be singularly unimpressed by the fact that some price officials in Moscow certified the new product's price to be fair. "If they think so, then let them buy it," he would surely say or feel.

Indirect methods are fundamentally administrative in nature, although the administrative agents are charged with the responsibility of attending to the customer's interests. The direct methods, however, make the customer himself a party to the innovation process, without the intermediation of a government official. In new-product pricing this is done chiefly by requiring that the customer be consulted and his agreement secured in the course of the price negotiation. If the customer is a single enterprise, as in the case of a special-order product, that enterprise as well as the ministry must be included in the routing list of the documentation. If the product is for general use, the ministry whose enterprises purchase the largest proportion of the output is consulted. The purchasing enterprise or ministry has the opportunity to study the documentation, evaluate the productivity claims in terms of their own production needs, protest them if they are exaggerated, or argue that the proposed price is excessive for the uses to be made of the product.

One would expect that the direct involvement of the customers in the pricing process would put an end to such practices as simulated innovation and overpricing of new products. In fact it does not work out that way, and the reasons are instructive. There is no doubt that customers do indeed participate in the price negotiations. The irritated Mr. Karpunin of the Siberian Heavy Electrical Machinery Plant had to route his pricing proposals through four different offices of his customers and their ministries, a procedure that accounted for much of the complexity and delays in price setting.[69] In the absence of this kind of scrutiny the incidence of evasion would surely be greater than it is. But although the opportunity is available, Mr. Stoliarov reports that "customers as a rule have not made use of their rights to check the calculations during the pricing negotiations on the machinery, equipment, and instruments to be delivered to them, and they don't exercise the controls needed to assure that the established prices are observed."[70]

Part of the explanation of the deficiencies in customer control is the complexity of price administration. Price catalogues are published in small issues, primarily for the use of producers. Hence we read that customers do not have full files of the price catalogues of all their suppliers and have no easy way of checking the official prices of all their purchases.[71] One would guess, however, that if the prices they pay are of vital concern to customers, they would make the effort to double-check their invoices. The larger part of the explanation is that it is often not in the interest of customers to exercise the opportunity to resist high prices. In some cases the customer is simply indifferent to the price he has to pay. Centralized capital investment is often cited as an activity in which this attitude prevails, because once the price of the equipment is set, the financial resources to pay for it are simply made available. If the equipment is overpriced, the appropriation will merely be larger. The major concern of the investing enterprise is to get the project under way quickly and to assure that the appropriated funds are spent on time, not to quibble about price.[72] More troublesome than customer indifference to price, however, are those circumstances that cause the customer to benefit from being charged a higher price:

It is well known that in various branches of the engineering industries there has recently been a covert raising of wholesale prices, manifested in the more rapid increase in the prices than in the quality of output. The agencies responsible for price setting have all the necessary administrative authority, but it is very hard to combat that tendency because nowadays it is not only the producers but also the purchasers who have an economic interest in higher prices. For with higher prices [on the materials and equipment bought from other enterprises–JB] the purchasers' value of output and sales rise; and if the increased prices are reflected "within the authorized time limits" in their financial plans, the purchasers can only welcome it.[73]

The villain in this case is the aforementioned concern to eliminate economic rents, both positive and negative.[74] Just as enterprises are not permitted to benefit from favorable circumstances that do not reflect their own good work, so they are protected from losses due to unfavorable circumstances that are not the consequences of their own poor work. The enterprise as producer is not permitted to retain excess profits earned because of short-run increases in demand for its product; and the enterprise as customer is not obliged to suffer from price increases in its materials and equipment. Sensible as this rule may be for administrative purposes, it has an unfortunate influence on the customer's perception of where his interests lie. If increases in the prices he pays to other enterprises have no effect on his own position, he has no interest in contesting them; and if, as in the situation quoted, his position is actually improved by having to pay higher prices, his usefulness for purposes of price control is completely eroded.

Circumstances do occur in which a purchaser would suffer from an increase in his input prices. The quoted passage refers, for example, to plan changes made "within the authorized time limits."[75] What this means is that the customer must know of a forthcoming price increase sufficiently in advance of the time his plan is approved to be able to make provision for it in his plan. If the price increase comes suddenly in the course of the year, however, it threatens to drive his costs above the planned level, and it is then more difficult to explain it away as due to factors outside of his control. The delivery of subquality or overpriced materials or equipment in the course of the plan period is also threatening to the customer's interests, and the extensive arbitration and litigation over breaches of contract are evidences of the customer's ability and willingness to contest his suppliers on these occasions.[76] It is in such circumstances that the customer's interests do motivate him to combat price increases, and customer control operates as it is supposed to. But while interests are properly marshaled in such cases, there are organizational obstacles to the pursuit of those interests. The most the customer can do is protest a proposed price. It then becomes a matter of who can present the most persuasive case and muster the strongest bureaucratic clout. For the decision is taken by the price committee. If the protest is denied, the customer has little further recourse. In particular, in the short run he cannot refuse to buy the overpriced product, for in the planned economy one simply does not run to competitors for better products and prices; although in the longer run one can contrive to find a better substitute or manufacture the item in one's own plant or ministry. Moreover, since the system normally operates as a seller's market, the alternative to buying an overpriced product is often to buy nothing at all, a course that may be disastrous for one's production operations. Under such conditions one does not easily risk "spoiling one's relations" with an important supplier by disagreeable protests over prices. In planned as in market economies, the effectiveness of customers in the control of prices diminishes when a seller's market prevails.

The limited success of customer control reflects the general problem of economic reform. Since the structural properties of an economic system are interrelated, a reform of one part of the system may fail not because of its own defects but because of difficulties in another part of the system. In this case, an effort has been made to improve the price structure by the perfectly sensible device of strengthening the role of demand in price determination. The results have been unsatisfactory because the other structural properties have not been correspondingly altered. The structure of organization denies the customer the kind of authority he needs in order to resist price evasion by producers. And even if he had the authority, the decision rules and incentives are such that the customer has no interest in exerting the controls desired by the reformers. A serious effort to introduce effective customer control requires a set of coordinated changes in various elements of economic structure.

13.6. A Proposal for Decentralized Price Administration

The question for economic theory is, "By what principles should new-product prices be set?" The question for administrative theory is, "Who should set the prices?" The answer to neither question alone is sufficient to explain the actual structure of prices. Any set of pricing principles can yield a variety of results, depending on who is designated to apply them.

In the search for a price structure that would be more hospitable to innovation, a number of changes have been made in the principles of pricing, which have been examined in the preceding chapters. No major changes have been made, however, in the locus of price-setting authority. The short answer to the question of who sets prices is still the State Price Committee. One wonders why the spirit of reform that managed to invade the principles of pricing has stopped short of tampering with the question of who should set the prices.

It is not that proposals for change have not been forthcoming. They have, and it is useful to conclude with an examination of one such proposal that has been in the air for some time. After the exhausting experience of the 1967 general price revision, Chairman Sitnin of the State Price Committee suggested for consideration that enterprises be given greater authority to set their own prices on new and improved products:

At the same time one cannot but agree that centralized price determination entails an unwieldy volume of calculations and verification and often causes delays in setting prices. Therefore, we have to give thought to finding ways of increasing the authority of enterprises in determining individual prices, while maintaining the mechanism of centralized supervision of pricing. The way that we see of accomplishing this is to calculate economically sound coefficients of costs and profits for individual types of products. With such periodically reviewed coefficients, enterprises would receive the opportunity to set the prices of their new products, without violating state price policy and the established price level.[77]

The proposal to turn the job of product pricing over to the producers is not entirely new. It has been put forth by economists attracted to market-type arrangements; the period of the New Economic Policy in the 1920s is sometimes offered as a model of successful decentralization. It was actually tried experimentally in two garment factories, Bol'shevik and Maiak, in 1964. But when that experiment was extended to other factories, the right to set prices was withdrawn, and it was not authorized in the 1965 Economic Reform.[78] What is new in this case is not the proposal itself but the source from which it comes. Yet it is not surprising to find the government's chief price administrator urging that the government reduce its role in price determination, particularly after the harrowing experience of a general price revision. In market economies also, the officials brought into government to serve as price administrators in wartime are often converted by that experience to a passionate distaste for that way of managing a nation's economic affairs. Mr. Sitnin, however, does not propose removing the government entirely from the price-setting business. He opposes that on both ideological and practical grounds. He wishes not to decentralize pricing but to decentralize price administration. The prices on all established basic products would continue to be set by the government. But his agency would be relieved of the job of having to check and approve the prices of all the new products and improvements that it presently handles.

In considering the kinds of controls over innovating enterprises that would be required under his modest proposal, Mr. Sitnin puts little faith in the use of customers as controllers. We already use that method, he writes elsewhere, in the requirement that the purchaser's agreement must be obtained in new-product pricing. "Experience has shown that agreement often amounts to nothing more than that the producer dictates the prices and the customer is compelled to accept them."[79] Having given up on the economic method, he proposes instead a different administrative method of control. His agency would publish a set of coefficients specifying the normal quantities (*normativy zatrat*) of labor, fuel, and materials to be used in the manufacture of all types of products, and the normal profit rates that may be applied. The innovating enterprises would then set their own new-product prices by applying those coefficients. If the agency does a proper job in calculating the coefficients and keeping them abreast of technological change, and if the innovators honestly apply them in pricing, the desired price structure will emerge without the price agency having to set the actual prices.

Mr. Sitnin's proposal has been on the table for a number of years and has generated some support.[80] No action has been taken on it, however, and the reasons may be guessed from a consideration of its implications.

The proposal is designed to improve the structure of prices by an organizational reform in pricing. Ignoring for the moment the fact that no other elements of economic structure are to be changed, one may doubt that this organizational reform will have the desired effect on the price structure. First, it is difficult to imagine how one would set about determining in advance the normal quantities of steel and glass and copper that may be used per unit of each of all future products. Even if they could be determined, the number of such coefficients would greatly exceed the number of products. Hence both the complexity and the magnitude of the task of determining the normal coefficients would be many times greater than the present task of setting new-product prices directly. The price structure that would emerge from this organizational arrangement is therefore likely to be less satisfactory than the present one. Moreover, in specifying that the price agency would set only the normal cost and profit coefficients, Mr. Sitnin seems to contemplate a return to cost-plus-profit pricing. That pricing principle certainly eases the organizational task; a vastly greater effort would be required to determine centrally the coefficients that would be needed for analogue and parameter pricing. But a return to cost-based pricing would restore those distortions in the structure of prices that led to the abandonment of that pricing principle. For this reason as well, the change in the organizational structure for pricing would cause price structure to deteriorate.

Second, while the organization of pricing is to be changed, no other changes are intended in other parts of the organizational structure: in planning, materials supply, financing, marketing, and so forth. Centralized price determination has a certain consistency with the centralized organization of the enterprise's relations with other organizations. But to decentralize pricing while retaining extensive centralization elsewhere is to increase the incidence of organizational strains. For example with the centralized distribution of commodities, the government accepts the major responsibility for arranging the sale of output. Under that marketing arrangement it is wise for the government to set prices as well. But if the enterprise is given the right to set prices while the government continues to accept responsibility for marketing, the opportunities for price gouging and simulated innovation are increased. In the extreme, the government will have to take care of the sale of whatever the enterprise produces and at whatever price it charges. It is true that the reforms in marketing organization in recent years have shifted some of the responsibility from government to enterprises. However, to the extent that it still shields the producer from most of the burden of marketing, an increase in the producer's pricing power may be expected to increase the incidence of abuse.

Finally, the proposed pricing reform anticipates no changes in what are referred to as the "interests" of enterprises. In the analysis of price, those interests are associated with the pursuit of profit and the consequent pressure for higher prices. Centralized pricing restrains the upward pressure on prices, although it generates extensive practices of evasion. But the proposal to turn pricing over to the producers weakens even that restraint. If the price committee cannot prevent abuses when they set prices directly, they will be even less successful if they retreat to the setting of cost and profit coefficients and let the enterprises use them to set prices. Hence the intent of Mr. Sitnin's reform will be defeated unless accompanied by appropriate changes in the way enterprises define their interests.

But what determines the enterprise's perception of its interests? In the discussion of pricing we have simplified matters considerably by regarding the enterprise as primarily interested in profit. That assumption has been adequate for the explanation of the set of problems clustering on the issues of price structure and innovation behavior. With the discussion of pricing now concluded, it is time to consider the matter of interest more fully.

What Soviet analysts refer to as the enterprise's interests is the product of the last two structural properties of the economic system—decision rules and incentives. Given the organizational structure and price structure, the rate and direction of innovative activity may be expected to vary according to the structure of rules and incentives. It is to those two structural properties that our discussion now turns.

Notes

1. A. N. Komin, *Problemy planovogo tsenoobrazovaniia* (Problems of Planned Price Formation) (Moscow: *Ekonomika*, 1971), p. 23.

2. Strictly speaking it is only the prices of new products that originate in enterprises. During periods of price revisions, changes in the prices of established products may be initiated by the State Price Committee or any of the research institutes or other agencies that assist in the revision.

3. The balance of this section relies primarily on two sources: A. I. Skvortsov, *Tseny i tsenoobrazovanie v SSSR* (Prices and Price Formation in the USSR) (Moscow: *Vysshaia shkola*, 1972), pp. 42-47 and 134-137; and S. G. Stoliarov, *O tsenakh i tsenoobrazovanii v SSSR* (Prices and Price Formation in the USSR) (Moscow: *Statistika*, 1969), pp. 38-41.

4. Stoliarov, *O tsenakh*, p. 39.

5. Komin, *Problemy planovogo tsenoobrazovaniia*, pp. 21-22; Stoliarov, p. 40.

6. K. N. Plotnikov and A. S. Gusarov, *Sovremennye problemy teorii i praktiki tsenoobrazovaniia pri sotsializme* (Current Problems in the Theory and Practice of Pricing Under Socialism) (Moscow: *Nauka*, 1971), p. 132.

7. *Proektnaia i planovaia stadiia.* P. S. Mstislavskii, M. G. Gabrieli, and Iu. V. Borozdin, *Ekonomicheskoe obosnovanie optovykh tsen na novuiu promyshlennuiu produktsiu* (The Economic Basis of Wholesale Pricing of New Industrial Products) (Moscow: *Nauka*, 1968), pp. 15-22 and Appendix 1.

8. *Ekonomicheskaia gazeta*, 1969, No. 31, p. 11.

9. In the mid-sixties the number of prices was reported as 8 to 9 million. R. A. Belousov, ed., *Sovremennaia praktika tsenoobrazovaniia* (Current Pricing Practice) (Moscow: *Ekonomika*, 1965), p. 21.

10. Stoliarov, *O tsenakh*, p. 76.

11. Plotnikov and Gusarov, *Sovremennye problemy teorii*, p. 461.

12. The others consisted of revised prices of established products and prices of imported products. Of the 95,000 prices, 66,000 were prices of domestic civilian products. 28,000 were imported products, and 1,000 were temporary prices. Ibid., p. 130.

13. Belousov, *Sovremennaia praktika*, p. 21.

14. Stoliarov, *O tsenakh*, p. 76.

15. *Izvestiia*, August 15, 1968, p. 3.

16. Stoliarov, *O tsenakh*, p. 46.

17. *Izvestiia*, August 15, 1968, p. 3.

18. Ibid.

19. Ibid.

20. Stoliarov, *O tsenakh*, p. 49.

21. Ibid., p. 151.

22. On the administration of the standards system, see Plotnikov and Gusarov, *Sovremennye problemy teorii*, Chap. 8 and pp. 482-487.

23. *Vsesoiuznyi informatsionnyi fond standartov* (VIFS), which is operated by the State Standards Committee.

24. Plotnikov and Gusarov, *Sovremennye problemy teorii*, p. 394.

25. *Khudozhestvennyi sovet.* Such councils have been organized in an effort to raise the aesthetic level of Soviet products.

26. Plotnikov and Gusarov, *Sovremennye problemy teorii*, p. 393.

27. Ibid., pp. 482-486.

28. *Planovoe khoziaistvo*, 1966, No. 5, p. 48.

29. J. S. Berliner, *Factory and Manager in the USSR* (Cambridge: Harvard University Press, 1957), Chap. 12.

30. *Izvestiia*, August 15, 1968, p. 3.

31. *Planovoe khoziaistvo*, 1966, No. 10, p. 33.

32. Ibid., 1967, No. 12, p. 73.

33. *Ekonomicheskaia gazeta*, 1967, No. 11, p. 11.

34. Ibid., No. 21, p. 13.

35. *Planovoe khoziaistvo*, 1966, No. 11, p. 27.

36. Ibid., No. 10, p. 3.

37. *Ekonomicheskaia gazeta*, 1968, No. 10, p. 19.

38. Stoliarov, *O tsenakh*, pp. 46-47.

39. Ibid., p. 49.

40. Berliner, *Factory and Manager*, Chaps. 6 to 12.

41. Stoliarov, *O tsenakh*, p. 146; Komin, *Problemy planovogo tsenoobrazovaniia* pp. 26-27.

42. Komin, *Problemy planovogo tsenoobrazovaniia*, pp. 26-27.

43. Stoliarov, *O tsenakh*, p. 147.

44. Komin, *Problemy planovogo tsenoobrazovaniia*, p. 27.

45. Stoliarov, *O tsenakh*, p. 147.

46. *Ekonomicheskaia gazeta*, 1968, No. 6, p. 10; Stoliarov, *O tsenakh*, pp. 146-147.

47. *Komsomol'skaia Pravda*, March 12, 1968, p. 2. Quoted in *New York Times*, March 13, 1968.

48. It is no less serious for Soviet statisticians and economists. See later the discussion of the reliability of the Soviet machinery price index.

49. L. M. Gatovskii, A. V. Bachurin, S. P. Pervushin, B. M. Sukharevskii, and G. D. Anisimov, eds., *Plan, khozraschet, stimuly* (The Plan, Accountability, and Incentives) (Moscow: *Ekonomika*, 1966), p. 203.

50. Belousov, *Sovremennaia praktika*, p. 81.

51. Plotnikov and Gusarov, *Sovremennye problemy teorii*, p. 378.

52. Mstislavskii, Gabrieli, and Borozdin, *Ekonomicheskoe obosnovanie optovykh tsen*, p. 113.

53. Berliner, *Factory and Manager*, p. 221.

54. M. Spechler, *The Economics of Product Quality in Soviet Industry*, Ph.D. thesis, Department of Economics, Harvard University, May 1971, p. 63.

55. A. M. Matlin, *Tekhnicheskii progress i tseny mashin* (Technical Progress and Machinery Prices) (Moscow: *Ekonomika*, 1966), p. 19.

56. D. Granick, *Soviet Metal Fabricating and Economic Development: Practice Versus Policy* (Madison: University of Wisconsin Press, 1967), pp. 44-47.

57. Gatovskii et al., *Plan, khozraschet, stimuly*, pp. 143-144.

58. *Voprosy ekonomiki*, 1968, No. 4, p. 77. The reliability of the Soviet machinery price index is studied in A. S. Becker, "Ruble Price Levels and Dollar-Ruble Ratios of Soviet Machinery in the 1960's," The RAND Corporation, Santa Monica, Report R-1063-DDRE, January, 1973.

59. On the structure of general controls over enterprises, see Berliner, *Factory and Manager*, Chaps. 12 to 16.

60. Uniformity is most difficult to maintain in the case of products in the jurisdiction of republican and local price committees. Because of inadequate exchange of information, identical products carry different prices in different areas, particularly on consumer goods. Stoliarov, *O tsenakh*, p. 147.

61. Komin, *Problemy planovogo tsenoobrazovaniia*, p. 27.

62. *Voprosy ekonomiki*, 1968, No. 5, p. 35.

63. Plotnikov and Gusarov, *Sovremennye problemy teorii* p. 429, ftn.

64. Komin, *Problemy planovogo tsenoobrazovaniia*, p. 195.

65. *Voprosy ekonomiki*, 1971, No. 8, p. 56.

66. The condition of excess demand reinforces the upward thrust of prices, but it is not a necessary condition. As long as the organizational structure places the chief responsibility for the distribution of industrial products on the central planning agencies rather than on enterprises, producers need have no concern that their new-product prices may be too high. If a product is in excess supply at a given price, the planners will either reduce the planned output of the product or compel the customers to accept allocations of it. In the case of consumer goods, however, producers' pricing behavior is restrained by excess supply.

67. This is not to say that the customer's interests are not affected by cost-based pricing. He profits greatly if a highly productive innovation is priced at cost, and he suffers if he is obliged to purchase a poor new product priced at cost. Cost-based pricing, however, does not take the customer's interest in productivity into account.

68. The method is illustrated in the official instructions on conducting the certification procedure, in *Ekonomicheskaia gazeta*, 1967, No. 17, p. 32.

69. See Sec. 13.1.

70. Stoliarov, *O tsenakh*, p. 42.

71. *Planovoe khoziaistvo*, 1966, No. 5, p. 49.

72. Stoliarov, *O tsenakh*, p. 46. One would expect that the introduction of the capital charge will generate a greater interest by investors in the prices of the equipment they purchase.

73. *Voprosy ekonomiki*, 1967, No. 5, p. 35.

74. Sec. 11.4.

75. *svoevremenno.*

76. On the role of litigation and arbitration in conflicts over quality, see Spechler, Chap. 6.

77. *Ekonomicheskaia gazeta*, 1968, No. 6, p. 11.

78. H. G. Shaffer, "Industrial Price Policies in the Soviet Union and East Europe: Theory and Practice," Kansas Slavic Papers No. 9, (Lawrence: University of Kansas, 1972), pp. 29-30, ftn. 65.

79. *Voprosy ekonomiki*, 1968, No. 5, p. 36.

80. See for example Komin, *Problemy planovogo tsenoobrazovaniia*, p. 167.

Part

Incentives and Decision Rules

Chapter 14

General Incentives and Decision Rules

All economic decisions are made on the basis of certain principles, or rules. A French businessman follows rules of his own making in deciding whether to adopt a certain new technique or not, or whether to expand or contract his rate of output, and by how much. A Yugoslav bank official follows certain rules in deciding whether to grant a loan request or not. The rules may be highly complex, involving extensive computations, or they may be simple and rough and ready, in which case we refer to them as "rules of thumb."[1]

It is useful to distinguish rules employed for one's own decision-making purposes from those employed for the purpose of controlling the actions of others. Rules of the first kind are instruments of calculation believed to be the best for attaining some objective. Unlike the second kind, they have no directive authority. They are not instructions that one must follow out of the obligations of office but are guides to oneself for best accomplishing what one wishes to accomplish. A businessman seeking to maximize profits, for example, may employ an instrumental rule such as to "produce a level of output equal to the break-even point" or to "produce that level of output at which marginal cost equals marginal revenue." Similarly, a central planning committee charged with the task of drawing up balanced plans must devise certain rules for itself in order to attain that objective. When the demand for a commodity exceeds the supply in the first draft of a national plan, for instance, Soviet planners are guided by the following rule: "whenever possible, it is the sectors of secondary importance . . . which have their allocations cut or are called upon to use substitutes."[2] Rules of this kind are designed and employed as instruments of planning as long as they are thought to lead to the best solutions of the problem of balancing a plan.

One can learn a great deal about an economic system by a study of the instrumental rules employed by those who make economic decisions. This indeed is the basis of the economic analysis of capitalist systems, and it has been similarly employed in the analysis of socialist central planning. In both cases, the objective of the analysis is to study the social consequences of decision-making units acting according to those rules, and the mode of analysis does not differ greatly in its application to the two types of economic system.

It is the second kind of decision rule, however, that is of special interest in the study of socialist economies. These are rules that are imposed by a central authority upon all subordinate units. They are not instrumental rules but directive rules; they direct the subordinate units about how to proceed in deciding among various courses of action. Such rules are employed not only in socialist economies, of course, but in capitalist economies as well—in the relations between the central management of a large firm and its various divisions, for example. The new-products division of a corporation may be assigned the rule to put into development all products that promise a return of at least 20 percent. But in the capitalist economy there is no equivalent to the directives flowing from Soviet central government to all enterprises. It is those directives that govern the flow of economic life, as the market does in capitalist economies. Hence the directive rules are of crucial importance in the analysis of the centrally planned socialist economy, for the quality of the economic results depends heavily on the wisdom with which those rules are designed. In the following, when we refer to rules for decision making, we shall have directive rules primarily in mind.

14.1. The Nature of Directive Rules and Incentives
The relationship between decision rules and economic efficiency developed out of the analysis by Oskar Lange and Abba Lerner of decentralized socialist and controlled-capitalist economies.[3] The Soviet economy, however, is not decentralized in their sense. It is a centrally planned economy in which the major economic decisions are made not by enterprises but by the central planners. One might suppose therefore that the study of directive rules of decision making would contribute little to the understanding of how the economy operates. Indeed in the purest model of a centrally planned economy, the planning commission would make in advance every decision that would need to be made by each production unit in the course of the planning period. Each enterprise would be presented with a plan containing detailed instructions on the quantities of each product to be produced each day, the quantities of labor, materials, and other inputs to be used, the schedules specifying how much of each product is to be shipped by which means of transportation to each of a specified list of customers, and so forth. Under a regime of perfect central planning, the managers of the production units need to make no decisions at all. They are simply executors of the instructions contained in the plan. In such an economy there are

no directive rules; there are only instrumental rules on the basis of which the State makes all the economic decisions for the attainment of its own objectives, which are then transmitted as specific instructions to the managers.

The Soviet economy is not as centralized, of course, as this model of a perfect "command" economy. The State is neither competent, nor does it really wish, to make every decision for every enterprise. It must therefore formulate some rules for the guidance of enterprises that have to make those decisions not made in advance by the State. The form of those rules has had a substantial effect on the operation of the economy and the efficiency with which it functions. It has also had a profound effect on the rate of innovation.

Relationship between Rules and Incentives

The rules answer the question, "What should I do?" Incentives answer the question, "What will I get if I do it?" A set of rules, instrumental or directive, is a necessary part of an economic system. But incentives are not. One may imagine an idealized socialist manager who had no other purpose in life than to follow the rules laid down by the governors—a sort of *Homo Sovieticus.* In that world there would be no need for an explicit incentive structure. The economic system would be complete if it specified only the structure of organization, prices, and rules.

At the other extreme one may imagine the manager to act like a socialist *Homo Economicus.* He asks not what he can do for his country but what his country can do for him. In such a world it is not sufficient to lay down the rules for decision making and expect managers to follow them: the governors must design in addition a set of incentives to harness the ambitions of managers in the service of the economy.

In the early years of the Soviet period there was some hope that the socialist society could count on the spirit of public service as a sufficient motivation for economic activity. With the intense industrialization drive of the thirties, however, that hope was gradually abandoned. In a historic declaration in 1931, Stalin renounced the equalitarian wage ethic that had obliterated "any difference between skilled and unskilled work, between heavy and light work."[4] Following his biting denunciation of "equality mongering," there evolved a new policy in which personal "material incentives"—primarily money incomes—became the major instrument for motivating economic activity. Social rewards have not been ignored. To the extent that a government can shape the hierarchy of prestige by medals, publicity, honors, perquisites, privileges, and awards of various kinds—successful managers earn a fuller measure of such rewards than the less successful. But alongside the social rewards there has developed a complex set of monetary incentives.

The addition of an incentive structure alters somewhat the status of the decision rules. In choosing among alternatives, *Homo Sovieticus* consults the formal rules laid down by the governors. *Homo Economicus*, however, consults first the incentive structure and in effect deduces the rules of choice that are implicit in the incentive structure. We may call these deduced rules the "operating rules." With an ideal incentive structure the operating rules are identical to the formal rules, and the two types of manager would make the same decisions. With an imperfect incentive structure, which one must expect in any real economy, the operating rules may differ from the formal rules, and incentive-oriented managers may make different decisions than do their State-oriented colleagues.

In a general normative study of the Soviet economy, it would be convenient to postulate that managers behave like *Homo Sovieticus* and then study the quality of the formal directive rules. The central question one would like to answer is, "Are the formal rules such as to direct *Homo Sovieticus* to make those choices that the governors would make were they in his place?" For the study of the innovation decision, however, it is the operating rules that are most instructive. The Soviet manager may not correspond to *Homo Economicus* in all respects, but there is little doubt that the incentive system is the dominant consideration in decision making. The governors indeed intend it to be, and they rely heavily on the incentive system to motivate desired forms of behavior. Well-functioning enterprises are expected to earn larger rewards than poorer ones, and to some extent the earning of large rewards is regarded as evidence of good management.[5] Moreover the formal rules are, for the most part, not codified or directly articulated but are communicated through the incentive structure.[6] When the governors decide, for example, that in choosing the product mix managers should give greater weight to total profit and less to gross value of output, that change in the formal rule of choice is communicated by a change in the incentive structure. The order of analysis will therefore consist first of an examination of the incentive structure, then of the operating rules that follow from the incentive structure, and then an evaluation of the consequences of those incentives and rules on the decision to innovate.

The Structure of Incentives

The money income of management consists of a number of distinct elements, the size of each of which is governed by its own regulations. Hence it is appropriate to refer to the "structure" of incentives. One must distinguish first between general and specific incentives. General incentives are the rewards for the conduct of the enterprise's basic business· producing a high level of output, choosing the proper combination of products (the product mix), and economizing on production costs. It was discovered a long time ago that the general incentive structure led to a set of operating rules that motivated enterprises to neglect certain specific kinds of activity that the planners wished them to attend to. To direct attention to those activities, a set of special incentives has been introduced, each providing rewards for the performance of a specific task, such as collecting and processing scrap metal, producing a sufficient quantity of spare parts, and so forth. Both the general and specific incentives affect the innovation decision, although in different ways. The present chapter examines the influence of the general-incentive structure on innovation, and the next deals with the structure of specific incentives.

The general incentive structure for managerial officials evolved during the nineteen thirties. It varied somewhat in form from time to time and from industry to industry; the last major modification occurred in the 1965 Economic Reform. One feature that has endured, however, is a money reward system consisting of both a base salary and a supplementary bonus the size of which varies with enterprise performance.

The salary is the larger part of the money income of officials. Salary scales are established by the ministries, under general policies laid down by the Ministry of Finance and the State Committee on Labor and Wages. They are differentiated by industry, by size of enterprise, and by position within the enterprise. Salary differentiation is the major monetary incentive for general economic activity. Successful performance increases the manager's opportunity for promotion to higher positions within the enterprise or for promotion to larger enterprises leading to higher salaries.

In addition to his salary, the manager is entitled to a variety of bonuses to the extent that his enterprise achieves certain specified results. The most important of these is the bonus that is based for the fulfillment of the basic targets of the plan. The size of this basic bonus is determined by a schedule that indicates the sum that may be paid, according to the degree that one or more specified plan targets has been attained.

It is generally acknowledged that the incentive that is most significant in determining the enterprise's operating rules is the basic bonus. While the salary accounts for the larger proportion of the managerial income, it is a fixed monthly sum. The size of the basic bonus, however, varies from month to month according to enterprise performance, and that performance responds to managerial decisions. Hence to the extent that income motivates behavior, it is to the variable bonus that management will turn as a basis of decision making rather than to the invariant salary. In the longer run, moreover, since the bonus is tied to the general performance of the enterprise, the enterprise that earns large bonuses also compiles a record of superior performance, and its managers may look forward to promotions and higher salaries as well.

By analogy to the role of profit in the market economy, one slips easily into the term "maximization" in discussing the relationship between the bonus and the operating decision rules. It is not a bad formulation if certain qualifications are kept in mind. One is that at various times the planners have made a practice of raising the plan target for the next period if it had been overfulfilled in the preceding period. Aware of this "ratchet" principle employed by the planners, management often chooses to produce less than they can and to be content with a less-than-maximum bonus.[7] One might express this qualification by the formulations employed in the analysis of capitalist economies; by regarding managers as "satisficing" rather than "maximizing" the bonus, or as maximizing the bonus in the long-run rather than in each short-run period. Second, managers often refrain from selecting the alternative that yields the largest bonus if it is glaringly inconsistent with the Party's political or economic priorities, or with the intent of a "campaign" that happens to be under way at the time. This qualification is also similar to those found in market economies; like the monopolist who prefers to "let sleeping dogs lie" and forgoes some marginal profit rather than attract the attention of the bloodhounds in the Anti-Trust Division. One might describe such behavior as "constrained maximization," but in the absence of a mathematical formulation of the constraint there is little analytic gain to compensate for the inelegance of the expression. We shall therefore regard the qualifications as have been duly noted and proceed with the formulation widely used in the analysis of Soviet managerial behavior. As expressed by Dr. J. Zielinski in his study of the

Polish economic reforms, "Socialist managers are essentially bonus maximizers, and their behavior can be explained to a degree comparable to a profit-maximizing assumption of a market economy, in terms of this goal."[8]

14.2. The Classical Incentive Structure

The general managerial incentive structure developed during the thirties and endured for the three decades that may be called the "classical period." The period ended, more or less officially, with the 1965 Economic Reform. The incentive structure consisted of three elements: the salary, the basic bonus, and the Enterprise Fund. Since only the latter two varied with enterprise performance, they may be regarded as the basis of decision rules.

The Basic Bonus

In a planned economy it is eminently reasonable that the incentives should be so ordered as to motivate managers to fulfill their plans. The device developed in the 1930s for achieving that end was the linking of the size of basic bonus to the degree of fulfillment of the plan. The full enterprise plan, however, details a great many different activities. Those activities that can be quantified are expressed in the form of "indicators," like gross value of output, or kilowatts of electric power per unit of output, or output per unit of capital. Since it is impractical to produce a formula relating the size of the bonus to the performance of all the planned activities, it became the practice to select one, or sometimes two, of the most important indicators and to link the size of the bonus directly to the plant performance as measured by that indicator.

For most of Soviet history a single indicator was used—the percentage fulfillment of the planned target of total output. The director and chief engineer, for example, might be entitled to a bonus each month equal to 37 percent of their salary if the month's output target is fulfilled 100 percent, and an additional bonus equal to 4 percent of their salary for each percentage point overfulfillment of the target.[9] The bonuses of lower-level officials are computed in the same way, although the rates are lower. The rates also vary by industry and by size of enterprise.

In designating the output-plan target as the direct bonus indicator, the planners were aware that managers would be motivated to concentrate effort and resources on those activities that yielded the largest increases in output, to the neglect of other parts of the plan. To forestall that result, it became the practice to append to the basic bonus schedule one or more conditions that had to be met before the basic bonus could be paid. The conditions generally take the form of supplementary plan targets. Three plan targets have been most widely used as conditional bonus indicators. The first is the product-mix target. The plan normally lists the quantities of each of the plant's major products that was to be produced. If the enterprise produces less than the planned quantity of any one product, the product-mix condition is regarded as unsatisfied regardless of the degree to which the other product targets are surpassed. The second is the planned percentage reduction of plant average cost of production. The third is the planned rate of profit, or sometimes the volume of profit. If one of the conditional bonus indicators is not met in any period, the basic bonuses are not to be paid regardless of the extent to which the overall output indicator has been overfulfilled.

The use of conditional bonus indicators was not entirely successful. The planners focused attention so heavily on growth of output that in administrative practice the conditional indicators were widely ignored. Managers who reported a respectable degree of overfulfillment of the output target could generally, though not always, expect to receive the basic bonus even if the product-mix target or the cost-reduction indicator were not attained. Moreover, in deducing their decision rules from the incentive structure, management tended to regard the conditional indicators at best as "constraints." One tried to schedule the plant's activities so as just to attain the cost-reduction target; but one would reject any alternative that reduced cost below the target if it also reduced the value of output. Hence value of output dominated all other indicators of enterprise performance in managerial decisions.

The Enterprise Fund

In addition to the salary and basic bonus, the general incentive structure provided for a special fund of money that could be used to finance various benefits to the plant personnel. The size of this Enterprise Fund was determined by the degree of fulfillment of the profit target rather than the output target. If the enterprise fulfilled its quarterly total-profit target by 100 percent, it was authorized to transfer an amount ranging from 1 to 6 percent of its profit into its Enterprise Fund. In addition, if its profit exceeded the plan target, it could transfer 20 to 30 percent of the over-plan profit to the Fund.[10] The precise percentages were assigned by the ministry under regulations laid down by the Ministry of Finance. The moneys in the fund could be devoted to three groups of uses, in proportions specified by the government. These three categories of use are interesting to note because after the 1965 Economic Reform each of them became the basis of a separate fund. About 40 percent of the fund was used for providing additional bonuses to plant personnel, as well as for other payments such as assistance to people in temporary personal financial difficulties. Another 40 percent was used for financing certain enterprise activities such as increasing working capital and financing the purchase of small units of equipment. And about 20 percent was used for various social purposes like building housing for plant personnel, expanding plant recreational facilities, and improving the childrens' summer camp.

The Enterprise Fund shares with the basic bonus the quality of varying with plant performance. But for a variety of reasons it was regarded as distinctly less important than the basic bonus as the motivation in decision making. For one thing the size of the fund was limited—in no quarter could it exceed 5 percent of the total enterprise wage bill. Consequently the size of the management bonuses distributed from the fund was small compared to the basic bonus. On the eve of the Economic Reform the bonuses paid out of all Enterprise Funds amounted to an average of less than 1 ruble per worker per month.[11] Moreover the bonuses from the fund were not determined by a precise schedule. Management and trade-union officials decided each month who would get how much, so that one never knew in advance what the bonus rewards would be for alternative decisions.[12] For these and other reasons, management assigned little weight to the fund bonuses in their operating decisions. This is not to say that the fund was ignored. The opportunity to add to the plant's housing and recreational facilities, to supplement working capital, and to provide even modest bonus supplements to the workers was of some value to management. But in most current operating decisions, it was the effect on the basic bonus that dictated the choice.

14.3. The Classical Decision Rules

It is fair to say that the design of the incentive structure has been one of the most taxing tasks of social engineering undertaken by the governors of the Soviet economy. *Homo Economicus* follows very different rules of choice than *Homo Sovieticus* would, and the incessant tinkering with incentives reflects a hope of finding ways to narrow the divergence.

There exists no official compendium of the normative rules of choice in a Soviet-type economy, of the kind pioneered by Abba Lerner for his model of a controlled economy.[13] Neither does there exist a full statement of the operating rules derived by Soviet managers from the structure of incentives and followed in their economic choices. We shall therefore not seek precision of formulation but rather to capture the sense of the rough rules of thumb that managers appear to employ as guides in decision making. The six rules sketched out now are not to be regarded as a full catalogue of the operating rules of choice, but they do explain a large portion of managerial behavior under the classical incentive structure.

The Rules of Choice

The rewards offered by the classical incentive structure depend on the fulfillment of various plan targets. The level of those targets is therefore of central importance to management. A variety of decisions that have to be made have an effect on the level of the plan targets themselves. The first two rules govern the manner in which that effect is taken into account generally in decision making. The other four rules deal with the specific indicators that enter into decisions.

The target rule. In the classical incentive structure, performance is measured not absolutely but relative to the plan targets. The size of the bonus depends, for example, not on the absolute value of output produced but on the ratio of produced output to the plan-output target. Hence the lower the plan target, the larger the bonus for a given volume of output produced. The operating rule that follows from this feature of the incentive structure directs management to build a "safety factor" into the enterprise plan by seeking to have the various targets set at minimally feasible levels. The rule affects primarily the enterprise's decisions regarding the information submitted to or withheld from the ministry and the government agencies. This rule is the source of those activities referred to in the literature as "striving for reduced plans."

The ratchet rule. This rule is derived from a planning device that has been dubbed the "ratchet" principle.[14] Uncertain about the true performance capability of the enterprise, the planners regard the performance in any period as the revealed minimal level of its capability in the next. Hence the larger the volume of output produced in any one period, the larger the output-plan target is likely to be in the second period, and therefore the smaller the bonus in the second period. The rule that follows from these relationships directs management to define the problem of choice among alternatives as the selection of the optimal, rather than the maximal, degree of overfulfillment of plan targets. If a number of alternatives offer the possibility of overfulfillment of a plan target by 1, 5, 10, or 20 percent, the last is not necessarily to be preferred; the 10- or the 5-percent result may be chosen.[15] There are no precise rules for determining such optima, however, but much of the art of successful management consists of the sense of where to stop.

The two rules just described apply to plan and performance indicators generally. The other rules identify the indicators that are of primary concern in decision making: value of output, product mix, production cost, and profit. Most decisions involve some trade-off among them: one alternative yields a larger value of output than another, but at a higher production cost. These rules may be regarded as the principles used for ranking alternatives in the order of their desirability.

The output rule. This rule follows from that feature of the incentive structure which links the size of the basic bonus to the percentage fulfillment of the gross output target.[16] The rule requires that primary consideration be given to the effect of each of several alternatives on output-plan fulfillment. In practice it means that when production is proceeding at a rate sufficient to fulfill the output target, all enterprise activities are to be scheduled as planned. But if the current rate of output lags behind the rate needed to fulfill the output target, some scheduled activities should be dropped and replaced by others that will contribute more to the fulfillment of the output target. The output rule may be said to dominate the structure of rules, in the sense that the weight assigned to all other considerations (cost, profit) at any time depends on the rate of fulfillment of the gross output target.

It should not be thought that it was only crassly materialistic motivations that projected the output rule into the position of dominance. The thrust of political and administrative exhortation supported the notion that fulfillment of the output plan is the first obligation of the patriotic official. The Soviet constitution itself proclaims the plan to be part of the fundamental law of the land, and this is generally taken to mean the output plan. Hence even *Homo Sovieticus*, to the extent that he sought to discern the formal decision rules from the Party's pronouncements and the ministry's reactions, would conclude that output is the primary basis on which decisions should be made.

The product-mix rule. This rule derives from that portion of the enterprise plan known as the "assortment plan."[17] A decision that has often to be made involves the alternatives in Table 14.1.

Table 14.1. The Product-Mix Rule

	Plan Targets	Alternatives		
		(I)	(II)	(III)
Gross Value of Output	100	103	98	101
Assortment Plan:				
Product A	60	60	60	58
Product B	30	32	30	34
Other Output	10	11	8	9

An alternative like the first is preferred because it provides for overfulfillment of the gross output target and also meets the assortment plan. It is that alternative that is incorporated in the enterprise's production program at the beginning of the month. In the course of the month, however, the enterprise often begins to lag behind its production schedule. The first alternative may no longer be feasible, and a choice must be made between the second and third. In that case the product-mix rule directs management to prefer the third to the second. Fulfilling the output target is more important than meeting all the individual product targets in the assortment plan. It is this rule that generates the practices known as "violation of the assortment plan" or the concentration on "advantageous products" in the "drive after gross output."

The cost rule. The cost target is expressed in the plan as a certain percentage cost reduction; perhaps 6 percent per year, or ½ percent per month. To any product mix and total value of output there corresponds a certain total cost that meets the cost reduction target. In Table 14.2 the planned output is 100, and it would have to be produced at a total cost of 90 rubles to meet the cost reduction target.

The cost rule dictates that in designing the production program each month, alternatives like II and III should be rejected. Alternative I, if it is feasible, should be preferred. With an output of 103, the output plan is overfulfilled; and the total cost (90) is less than the total cost required to meet the cost reduction target for that level of output (92).

Table 14.2. The Cost Rule

	Plan Targets	Alternatives		
		(I)	(II)	(III)
Total Output	100	103	98	102
Total Cost Target	90	92	89	91
Total Cost Achieved		90	86	93

But if alternative I proves to be unattainable, the production program must be rescheduled, with the choice often reducing to alternative II or III. In that choice, "as pointed out by Professor Birman, the decision-making rule was to reach the assigned targets regardless of cost."[18] Alternative III is to be preferred because the output target is fulfilled, although at a cost (93) in excess of the planned cost for that output (91).

Both the product-mix and the cost rules derive from the status of those two targets as conditions of payment of the basic bonus. One may wonder why the rules that management deduces from the bonus structure sometimes direct the selection of alternatives that lead to underfulfillment of those targets. Why choose an alternative that meets the output target but not the cost-reduction target if the bonus will not be paid anyhow? Why is that alternative (III) to be preferred to one in which the output target is underfulfilled but the cost-reduction target fulfilled (II), which would also yield no bonus? One reason for preferring the former is that when the official bonus structure offers no basis of choice, as in this case, management looks elsewhere for its cues. One of those cues is in the ministry's power to authorize payment of the bonus, even when one of the conditions is not met, if the fault is clearly not the enterprise's. The enterprise that regularly overfulfills its output target finds the ministry quite willing to be persuaded that it had no other recourse, in those months in which the product-mix or cost-reduction condition was not met. The dominance of the output rule is thus communicated not only through the formal incentive structure but in such informal ways as well.

The profit rule. The operating rules are too crude to provide a complete ordering of alternatives. They serve as a basis for making some choices but not others. In Table 14.3, for example, if I and II are the only alternatives, the output and cost rules offer no basis of choice:

Table 14.3. The Profit Rule

	Plan Target	Alternatives			
		(I)	(II)	(III)	(IV)
Total Output	100	101	101	106	105
Total Cost Target	90	91	91	93	93
Total Cost Achieved	–	89	88	92	90
Total Profit	10	12	13	14	15

Of the alternatives that meet the cost-reduction target, the cost rule assigns no additional weight to those that yield lower costs than others. But the profit rule does assign additional weight to the higher-profit alternative. Hence the profit rule directs management to prefer alternative II to I.

Under the cost rule, a lower-output alternative is never preferred to a higher-output alternative if both meet the cost-reduction target. But under the profit rule, a lower-profit alternative may be preferred. If III and IV were also feasible alternatives, in the absence of the profit rule, alternative III would be preferred over all the others, subject, of course to the ratchet rule. The profit rule, however, reduces the margin of preference of III over IV, and may indeed cause IV to be chosen over III; especially if under the conditions at the time a 6-percent overfulfillment approaches the limits of the ratchet rule.

Thus the profit rule occupies a different status in the rules structure from that of the production-mix or cost rules. The latter serve merely as constraints. Profit, however, is assigned a positive weight. The source of this special status of profit, relative to cost and product mix is that the latter are merely symbols, whereas profit is a matter of substance—a sum of money. The role of the cost target in the incentive structure is like the role of the score in a ball game. The score determines the winner but is not itself the reward for winning. The reward is the kudo, or the cup, or the cash. In the classical Soviet incentive structure, meeting the cost targets is necessary for a winning score, but the rewards consist of other things, one of which is profit.

Profit is a tangible reward for two reasons. One is that the size of the Enterprise Fund depends upon the profit earned—particularly overplan profit. The second is that the larger the profit, the larger the flow of financial resources that passes through the enterprise's hands. For both reasons the relative profitability of two alternatives is assigned some positive weight in the choice between them. But the same reasons serve to explain the subordination of profitability to output in the decision rules. In the general incentive structure, Enterprise-Fund bonuses are exceedingly small relative to the basic bonus, as we have seen. Second, as we have also seen, the supply of financial resources is of secondary importance in the organizational structure of the economy. Mismanagement of finances can affect adversely the production performance of an otherwise successful enterprise; and the enterprise controlling large financial resources can avoid certain problems that may beset another that operates with smaller bank balances. But these concerns over finance derive from the dominating objective of fulfilling the output plan.

Consequences for Innovation

The consequences of the classical incentives and rules on decision making generally have been studied at length.[19] Two main conclusions may be drawn. First, they can be credited with a large measure of success in mobilizing managerial effort. They motivated management to maintain pressure on the labor force and to strive for the economical use of the most tightly allocated resources. The degree to which the annual national plans have in fact been fulfilled is to a large extent due to the drive by enterprises as producers to supply the products needed by enterprises as customers to fulfill their own plans. Second, however, those same incentives and rules account for a great variety of decisions that entail inefficiency and waste of resources.[20] The objective of economic reform, indeed, has been to devise an incentive structure that would preserve the effort-mobilizing quality of the classical structure, while reducing the divergence between the operating rules of *Homo Economicus* and the formal rules of *Homo Sovieticus.*

Turning to the consequences of the classical rules on the innovation decision in particular, it is useful to treat product innovation and process innovation separately.

Product innovation. Imagine a management council evaluating a proposal to revise the production program to include a new product. What properties must the revised program possess, one might ask, that would motivate management to choose it with enthusiasm? The operating rules provide the guide to the answer. If the revised program yields a larger value of output than the current program, it is clearly to be considered seriously. If in addition it increases the volume of profit, it will almost certainly be chosen. And if it furthermore reduced plant average cost, it would be greeted with joy.

To present the question in this way is perhaps to overdramatize the issue. But it does clarify the basis of the conclusion that the rules of choice derived from the classical incentive structure are profoundly hostile to product innovation. In virtually all respects the consequences of including a new product in a production program cause that program to be rejected under the operating rules of choice.

The principal source of resistance to new products is the dominance of the output rule. Since new products tend to reduce the current rate of output, the rules structure tends to discriminate against alternatives that include product innovation.[21] A variety of factors influences the degree of resistance. First, the tauter the plan targets, the greater the risk of underfulfillment. Hence the target rule offsets the resistance to innovation, to the extent that the enterprise has managed to secure easier plan targets. Second, if the new product has been included in the enterprise plan, the risk is somewhat less than in the case of an innovation introduced in the course of the year. Provision is more likely to be made for the supply of materials and R & D services, and the plan targets may be adjusted in anticipation of the expected decline in output during start-up. Since such preparations cannot be easily made in the course of the year, innovations undertaken after the plan is approved are more threatening.

Third, while the price structure affects primarily decisions made under the profit rule, it also affects decisions made under the output rule.[22] In the latter case, however, it is not the relationship of price to cost that counts. It is rather the relationship of price to the availability of real resources, without respect to their cost. When resources must be shifted from other activities to current production in accordance with the output rule, one must calculate the net change in the value of output caused by the reallocation of that bundle of resources. If the alternative under consideration is the replacement of an established product by a new one in the product mix, the decision turns on whether the new product's price is sufficiently larger than the established product's price to compensate for the lower rate of production of the new product relative to what the rate of production of the established product would have been.

Viewed in this light, the price structure may on occasion encourage innovation, even when the choice is dominated by the output rule. Minor product innovations that do not entail significant interruptions in the production process are encouraged by the output rule if they carry sufficiently higher prices. And innovations that bring large price increases may be undertaken despite the large start-up interruptions. David Granick has explained the high rate of introduction of Western products by Soviet machinery enterprises during the first Five-Year Plan in these terms. In those years the real limitation on the output of that industry was the metal supply. Hence the objective was to generate the highest value of enterprise output with strictly limited metal inputs. As it happened, new products based on foreign advanced models were more highly fabricated than the older domestic models. With cost-based pricing, they therefore carried much higher prices and yielded a higher value of output with the given metal supply. As the years went by, however, the machinery plants operated under a growing number of constraints on their operations in addition to that of the metals supply alone. Hence the rate of product innovation declined.[23] Ordinarily, however, the value of output yielded by the bundle of resources used in an established product is larger than it would be if the resources were shifted to the production of a new product. The decline in output is rarely compensated by the higher price of the new product, even under the new pricing techniques like analogue pricing.

Since new products are produced at high initial costs, one might expect that the cost rule would also discourage product innovation; for plant average cost would rise in the year the new product was introduced. The cost-accounting regulations, however, require that products first introduced in the current year be excluded from the calculation of the percentage reduction in plant average cost.[24] Hence the high first-year start-up costs do not affect decisions made in accordance with the cost rule.

In calculating profit, however, all costs and revenues are included. New products reduce profit on both ends by driving up total costs of production because of start-up expenses and by depressing revenues because of the decline in output. The profit rule therefore supports the dominant output rule in discouraging product innovation. If there were no sources of product innovation other than those generated by the general incentive structure, very few new products indeed would be introduced in Soviet industry.

Process innovation. One of the major functions of the cost condition in the basic bonus regulations is to stimulate process innovation. To that end, the cost condition is expressed not in absolute terms, as so many rubles per unit of output, but in relative terms, as a certain percentage decrease in cost relative to the cost incurred in the preceding period. The obligation to reduce costs, rather than simply to minimize costs, has a significant positive effect on the rate of process innovation. If during the planning period the enterprise were required merely to minimize cost, the noninnovative management that sought out no new ideas or actively discouraged them could propose a cost target no different or even higher than last year's cost. It would be correctly argued that the target is the minimal cost level attainable with known techniques. The enterprise that had certain cost-reducing measures tucked aside as a safety factor, unknown to the ministry, could make a similar case, for it is difficult for the ministry and planners to challenge the enterprise's assertion that a certain cost level is the minimal attainable. But if the obligation is to reduce cost rather than to minimize it, such responses are ruled out by fiat. It is simply unacceptable to propose a cost level for next year that is not below this year's by some respectable percentage. The management that presented such a plan proposal would at the least be sent back to the drawing board and possibly reprimanded or fired. In this manner the annual pressure to reduce costs engaged management in a genuine search for cost-reducing process innovations.

The classical incentive structure contains no element for stimulating product innovation as successfully as the cost rule serves to induce process innovation. Much of the innovation and diffusion of process improvements that occur annually in Soviet industry may be credited to that rule. However, their effectiveness in promoting process innovation is diminished by a variety of factors. The chief of them is the dominance of the output rule in the rules structure, which has certain negative consequences for both the choice among possible innovations and the time rate at which they are put into operation.

The cost rule obliges the enterprise to introduce a certain number of cost-reducing measures each year. But the output rule requires that those measures be selected that carry the least risk of interruption in the rate of production. The consequence is a bias in favor of small and relatively riskless measures, like the acquisition of some new fork-lift trucks or the insulation of heat-transfer apparatus with a newly developed material.[25] Innovations involving a significant change in the basic production process, on the other hand, are given little support in the incentive structure. They carry the risk of underfulfilling the output plan, possibly for a considerable period of time, and even a large potential cost reduction offers no reward sufficient to compensate for the loss of bonuses.

The only kind of major process innovation encouraged by the incentive structure is one that offers the prospect of large savings of real resources which could then be used for overfulfilling the output plan. Most such innovations, however, reduce the per-unit use of only one or two inputs, like labor or some raw material, while the per-unit use of the complementary inputs is either unchanged or increased. Unless the enterprise has some assurance of securing additional allocations of the complementary inputs, then the additional output cannot be produced.

Given the organizational structure of materials supply, it is risky to count on such additional allocations. Moreover, to benefit from a major innovation of this kind, the enterprise would have to introduce it in the course of the year, outside of its regular plan. That would be difficult to manage, particularly if it required any significant unplanned capital expenditure. For if it were included during the plan-making period as part of next year's plan, the output target itself would be increased to reflect the added productive capacity of the improved process. Since the enterprise has little to gain from including such an innovation in its plan and is unlikely to be able to finance it or to procure the complementary inputs outside of its plan, few such innovations are induced by the general incentive structure.

The time rate at which innovations are introduced is also governed by the dominant output rule. In scheduling the work for any period, the alternatives initially chosen are those that promise both the fulfillment of the cost-reduction target and the overfulfillment of the output target. If production proceeds at the rate planned, the initial schedule is maintained. If output begins to lag behind the planned rate, however, then work is rescheduled in a manner that will augment the rate of output. Higher-cost alternatives not included in the original schedule may now be adopted if they will help fulfill the output plan. A new product mix may be chosen which will yield a higher value of output with the available resources, though perhaps at higher cost. End-of-period "storming" drives costs up still further. Hence the output rule leads to a periodicity of innovation activity, with a clustering of process improvements and innovations at the beginning of the month, quarter, and year and a slacking off toward the end.

The profit rule, which uniformly discourages product innovation, has a mixed effect on process innovation. If there were no profit rule, the cost-reduction target would oblige enterprises to incorporate a certain rate of process innovation in their plans. But there would be no stimulus to undertake innovations in the course of the year that were not included in the plan, since the incentive structure requires only that the cost target be fulfilled and offers no additional reward for reducing cost below the target percentage. In this respect the profit rule encourages process innovation by offering that additional reward. However, since process innovations also tend to reduce current rates of output and current revenues, they decrease the volume of profit. Since the decline in output affects revenues very quickly while the decline in cost occurs over the longer run, on balance the profit rule may discourage process innovation.

Other problems have been generated by the form of the cost rule. The generalized command to reduce costs is a rather blunt and indiscriminate instrument for inducing process innovation. Some enterprises are better at that game than others, and the state of the art offers more opportunities for process innovation in some industries than in others. Hence the constant pressure for cost reduction is bound to lead to a certain amount of simulation of process innovation. We also know that "the striving by enterprises and other organizations continuously to reduce cost has in the past often pushed them into lowering the quality of output."[26] Finally, while the cost rule does succeed in pressuring enterprises to include a set of process innovations in their plans, there is nothing in the rules structure to induce them to plan for the maximum feasible number of innovations. On the contrary the target rule directs management, in negotiating the plan, to secure the smallest possible cost-reduction target. Hence the enterprise often has a number of cost-reducing measures in its portfolio that could be introduced next year but are excluded from the plan under the direction of the target rule. The consequent understatement of the cost-reducing potential of the economy is a nuisance for planners, but it would not be a serious matter if the excluded innovations were nevertheless introduced in the course of the year, in addition to the planned innovations. But that is unfortunately restricted by the ratchet rule. To reduce costs too sharply this period is to be saddled with an excessively low cost target next period. The combined effort of the target and ratchet rules is to attenuate the innovation-promoting influence of the cost rule.

These qualifications do not alter the general conclusion that the classical decision rules offer some positive support for process innovation but very little for product innovation. It is of interest to note that Soviet industry is similar in this respect to certain segments of American industry. The distinction is sometimes drawn between market-oriented industries in the United States like garment manufacturing and production-oriented industries like textile mills. Garment firms are attuned primarily to customer's demand, and innovation takes the form of the frequent introduction of new products. The mills, on the other hand, see themselves primarily as producers of cloth, and innovation is thought of as "faster and more efficient production of cloth." They are "committed to present product, to present means of production, to present capital equipment,"[27] a description that characterizes Soviet industry generally. Why some industries in a capitalist economy should be production oriented rather than market oriented need not concern us here. In the Soviet economy, however, production orientation is clearly a direct consequence of the incentive structure and the dominance of the output rule. The point of interest is that, in both types of economy, production orientation channels innovational activity primarily into the adoption of small-scale cost-reducing process innovations.

The time horizon. The incentive structure specifies not only the indicators of performance that determine the rewards. It also specifies the dates on which performance is to be evaluated and rewards determined. The designation of dates has an effect on the innovation decision that is independent of the particular indicators specified.

The incentive structure is designed primarily to support current economic planning and is therefore keyed to the fulfillment of the monthly plan. On the last day of each month, the books are closed, as it were, and the rewards distributed. And next day the slate is wiped clean for the next month's trial. Some portion of the total annual bonuses are based on quarterly and annual results, but the monthly bonus predominates. Hence whatever the indicators that measure performance, it is the change in their values over a very short period of time that determines the size of bonus. An incentive structure so designed is bound to discourage innovation, for new products and processes generally cause performance indicators to decline in the short run.

But monthly plan accounting is not the full explanation. Successful innovations do eventually raise the performance indicators. Even discounting for some present-time preference, managers might be expected to forgo some short-run bonuses for the prospect of much larger bonuses in the future. The graver defect is that those large future bonuses are precluded by the ratchet principle. "After new technology is introduced," writes Dr. Manevich, "higher plan targets are established, and therefore it is harder to fulfill them and to earn bonuses."[28] No large future incomes await the innovator who forgoes short-run bonuses. Hence it is the combined effect of the monthly accounting period and the ratchet principle that explains the short time horizon of decision making.

"Today's five-kopek piece is dearer . . . than tomorrow's ruble," writes the critic A. Birman.[29] Dr. Birman is correct to note the pernicious influence of the short time horizon. But his characterization is wrong.

The problem is precisely that there is no ruble tomorrow. The impact of the short time horizon is greatest in the case of an innovation conceived and introduced during the year and not provided for in the plan. For if it is incorporated in the plan, the ministry may be persuaded to modify somewhat the targets for gross output and cost reduction, and the risk of encountering supply problems is smaller. There is some evidence that managers indeed see matters this way in the reports that innovations conceived during the year tend to be shunted into the "hold" file. There they accumulate until the end of the year, when they can be included in the following year's plans. The delay involved in this bunching of innovations is costly to the economy, particularly in fields of rapidly advancing technology.

The possibility of including innovations in the plan reduces the negative effect of the short time horizon but does not eliminate it. For innovation is inherently uncertain and risky, and the plan targets are rarely adjusted sufficiently to compensate for the risk. One would therefore expect, then, in the choice among innovations to be included in the plan, alternatives that offer large long-run benefits and large short-run losses in output and profit are discriminated against, and those are preferred that offer small long-run benefits but minimal short-run losses in output and profit.

Many of the innovation-inhibiting consequences of the rules structure just discussed arise not from the indicators themselves but from the brevity of the time horizon imposed on decision making. If the profit rule directed managers to consider the long-run profitability of alternative rather than the short run, both the rate of innovation and the long-run return to innovation would be higher. The short time horizon also deprives the cost rule of a certain positive effect it might have in promoting product innovation. The cost-reduction target in the classical incentive structure is derived from the cost behavior of individual products. The current year's unit cost of each product is compared to its unit cost in the preceding year and the percentage of cost reduction calculated. The percentages are then averaged, each one weighted by the proportion of that product in the current year's total value of output. The weighted average is the measure of the enterprise's performance in reducing cost.[30] In the case of products first introduced in the current year, however, the notion of cost reduction cannot be applied. Hence such products are simply ignored in the calculation. The planned percentage of cost reduction applies only to what is called "comparable output," that is, currently produced products that were also in production last year.

Given this feature of cost accounting, the cost rule directs management to regard product innovation with indifference.[31] In the longer run, however, the cost rule would tend to encourage product innovation because of the declining-cost behavior of new products. In the second year of its production, the new product is counted as part of comparable output. Since its unit cost declines sharply between the first and the second year, it improves the calculated overall percentage of cost reduction. Hence the enterprise that regularly introduces new products enjoys a higher annual percentage cost reduction than the noninnovator. Thus while the cost-reduction rule is neutral with respect to product innovation in the short run, it encourages it in the long run. Because of the short time horizon, however, the potential inducement to product innovation has no practical effect in decision making. The product innovator does indeed derive a benefit in the form of the greater ease in meeting cost-reduction targets, but it is rather like an economic rent. One can hardly imagine a manager giving any but the smallest passing weight to this long-run consideration in a choice that raises the possibility of a succession of short-run declines in output.

There is one minor respect in which the short time horizon may encourage innovation. The classical incentive structure is asymmetrical, in the sense that income increases with the percentage overfulfillment of the monthly output plan, but it does not decrease in proportion to underfulfillment. Hence, we read, in months in which it appears that the plan will not be fulfilled, the production program is altered to include a variety of risky activities planned for future periods. Expenditures planned for future months are incurred in the current month, and other costs are loaded on to the current month's accounts.[32] The enterprise thus chooses a program yielding a large shortfall from the current month's targets, but the prospect is enhanced for large bonuses for several succeeding months. The published accounts of such decisions make no mention of innovative activities specifically, but we may deduce that they are not ignored. Because of the asymmetry, the output-restricting and cost-augmenting effects of innovation can be concentrated in a few of the year's months. The loss of income would be less than it would be if the plan were underfulfilled by a small amount in a series of successive months. The effect of these short-term influences on decision making generally is undoubtedly negative on the whole. But the degree of additional freedom they provide may have some offsetting positive effect on the decision to innovate.

A short time horizon is stifling to innovation not only in socialist but in capitalist economies as well. A National Science Foundation survey found that companies concerned, as they put it, with "staying in business" or holding the "market" focused their research programs on short-run problem solving. But companies with a "lower time-discount factor" concentrated their research on the long-run development of new products.[33] A survey of British industry also concluded that "the 'time horizon' is further away, and the 'planning period' is longer in progressive firms."[34] However, the short time horizon is fairly general in Soviet industry because the incentive structure is more or less uniform whereas major sectors of capitalist industry are able to develop longer planning horizons. The perspective of innovative corporations is reflected in an observation by Mr. Robert L. Hershey, a vice-president of DuPont:

We assume that the DuPont Company is going to be in business as far into the future as anybody can see. We assume that we are operating in an organization that has permanence. This puts a very great restriction on some of the decisions we can make. We cannot make a decision just by looking at what results it will bring next week; we must look ahead and see what the probable results will be next year, or in the next ten years."[35]

Soviet enterprises are, of course, no less long-lived than American corporations, so that cannot account for the shorter time horizon of decision making. Before World War II, rapid turnover of Soviet managerial officials contributed to the short planning perspective, but that has also been changed. Managers today expect to remain in their enterprises, and indeed in their present posts, for relatively long periods of time.[36] What had not changed throughout the classical period, however, is the short-term nature of the decision rules imposed by the incentive structure. In his pioneering comparative study of industrial management, David Granick concluded that the incentive structure is a major source of differences in managerial behavior in the USSR and various capitalist countries:

Finally, the vast bulk of bonuses is paid on the basis of monthly and quarterly performance, in contrast to the situation in American and European firms where they are based on annual results. Moreover, they are paid out at once, while managerial bonuses in American firms are usually distributed over the course of several years so that the individual manager's dollar amount of bonuses received does not fluctuate as much as do bonuses earned. The Russian practice leads to substantially greater fluctuation of bonuses than would otherwise occur. Thus, it can be seen that Soviet managerial bonuses, unlike those of American, British and French companies, represent a very powerful force making for suboptimization."[37]

The rejection of the long-run benefits of innovation because of short-run losses in output and profit is a major form of such suboptimization.

14.4. The Prelude to Reform

Many of the defects of the classical incentive structure were known in Stalin's time and were often reported in the published sources. Proposals for modest alterations were occasionally advanced in print and a certain amount of tinkering with the structure occurred from time to time. With the passing of Stalin, however, the volume of critical analysis accelerated. Ministries and enterprises were given greater latitude to experiment with alternative incentive structures and the frequency of change increased. On the eve of the 1965 Economic Reform, many of the features of the classical structure had already been greatly altered. In retrospect one can see in those changes the prelude to the Reform. They merit attention because they illuminate the objectives of the Reform and pave the way for the analysis of its effects.

Of the many directions of change, three are of primary interest for their effect on the innovation decision. The first is the payment of special bonus supplements for enterprises that introduce new products. The other two involve changes in the role of cost considerations in the innovation decision.

New-Product Bonus Supplements

It had long been known that management discriminated against introducing new products because they cause the rate of output to decline. Not until May 1957, however, was an effort made to modify the general incentive structure, which was the source of the resistance. In that month the basic bonus regulations in the engineering industries were revised to offer a special incentive for new products. The revision took the form of a supplement to the basic bonuses of management, in proportion to the percentage of new products in the total output. The original schedule was[38]

Percentage of New Products in Total Value of Output	Percentage Addition to the Basic Bonus
5-10	up to 10
10-20	up to 20
20-30	up to 30
30-40	up to 40
over 40	up to 50

Thus if a managerial official was entitled to a basic bonus of 150 rubles on the basis of the enterprise's output plan fulfillment, and if 25 percent of that output consisted of new products, his basic bonus would be increased by an amount up to 30 percent, or 45 rubles, for a total bonus of up to 195 rubles. The supplement for general enterprise management was based on the overall enterprise results. The supplement for managerial officials of individual production divisions was based on the proportion of new products in the output of their divisions.[39]

The new-product bonus supplement altered the decision rules. It was no longer sufficient to know only the value of output of alternatives in order to choose among them. One must know in addition the percentage of new products in each alternative. If that percentage in one alternative was higher than in another, it might now be preferred even if the value of output is less. Thus the effect of the supplement was to offset the anti-innovation bias of the output.

The principle of a special bonus supplement for new products was deemed a success and gradually applied more broadly. In 1964, it was extended from the engineering industry to a variety of others: chemicals, petroleum, paper, and cellulose, and so forth.[40] It was also extended from the basic bonus to the Enterprise Fund as well. Before 1960, an engineering enterprise could transfer about 1 percent of its planned profit to its Enterprise Fund. Afterward, that percentage was differentiated; 4 percent of the profit on established products and 10 percent of the profit on new products could be transferred to the fund.[41] The general principle was sufficiently established by the time of the 1965 Economic Reform that it was incorporated into the new general-incentive structure.

The new-product supplement is what we have called a special incentive. It is to be distinguished from the general-incentive structure, which is the subject of this chapter. Special incentives will be discussed in the chapter to follow.

Measurement of Cost Reduction

The second change involves the method of measuring the cost performance of the enterprise. In the classical incentive structure the cost condition was expressed in the form of a percentage decrease in the cost of production of "comparable" output. The cost rule therefore directed management to ignore the costs of new products, since they are not part of comparable output.

The confinement of the cost-reduction condition to comparable output came under increasing fire, for two reasons. First was the old problem of determining when a new product is to be classified as new. Evidently enterprises that introduced even major product improvements sometimes failed to get their innovations classified as "new" products. The added costs were therefore not excluded from the calculation of cost reduction, and bonuses were lost because the cost-reduction condition was not met. The Russian Diesel Plant, for example, introduced a number of product improvements that raised the performance characteristics of their engines, for a net benefit calculated at 11 million rubles. But their total production costs were increased by 2 million rubles. Hence their financial position deteriorated, their cost reduction target was defined as "underfulfilled," and they were regarded as a lagging enterprise—"with all the moral and material consequences."[42]

Second, in some industries the proportion of output that enterprises managed to classify as new was very large, amounting to over half of all the output of various engineering industries.[43] The exclusion of this substantial volume of output from the cost condition reduced the effectiveness of the incentive structure as an instrument for focusing effort on cost reduction. Moreover, the allocation of overhead and other costs among products is not easily controlled, and the reported cost of comparable output could be manipulated by charging a variety of expenses to noncomparable output. The high start-up costs of new products was due in part to these consequences of the confinement of cost-reducing performance to comparable output.

In 1958 the form of the cost condition was changed by decree. The dominant measure of cost became "total cost per ruble of output" expressed in kopeks per ruble.[44] Both the cost-reduction plan target and the cost condition in the basic-bonus structure were expressed in that measure. The cost of comparable output continued to be used for various purposes, but it no longer served as the basis of the cost rule.

Under the classical cost measure, as we have seen, managers could ignore the high start-up costs of new products in evaluating a product-innovation proposal. The cost rule therefore encouraged process innovation and was merely neutral with respect to product innovation. Under the new measure, the cost rule continued to encourage process innovation but was no longer neutral with respect to product innovation. In evaluating a product-innovation proposal, its effect on the cost condition must be taken into account, along with its effect on output and profit. That effect, however, no longer depends solely on the cost of the new product; it depends also on its price. Hence enterprise pressures for higher prices, formerly derived only from the output and profit rules, were not supported by the new cost rule. The introduction into the incentive structure of a cost measure in the form of "the reduction in costs per ruble of output compels enterprises to strive for a maximum increase in the prices of new products."[45]

The decision rule derived from the new cost condition directed management to prefer those alternatives with lower cost/price ratios than last period's average. The effect on the rate of product innovation depends on the cost/price ratios of new products relative to those of older products. If they are smaller, the new cost rule encourages product innovation; if they are larger, it discourages product innovation.

The cost/price ratio, however, is nothing other than the rate of profit on cost, in inverse form.[46] The effect of the change in the cost measure is not merely an innocent modification of the cost condition in the incentive structure. It amounts to the abandonment of a pure cost condition and the substitution of a new profit-rate condition in its place. The consequence was to augment the influence of profitability in the innovation decision.

Cost-Based Bonuses
The third change was also designed to direct greater attention to cost reduction. In the classical incentive structure, the planned percentage cost reduction was merely a condition to be met before the bonus could be paid. There was no incentive to reduce cost below the target figure. As early as 1952 the government authorized an experiment to test the consequences of elevating cost reduction from a mere condition in the basic bonus structure, to a determinant of the size of the bonus itself.[47] After some hesitant fits and starts the principle was put into general practice. A decree of July 1, 1959 ordered that all basic bonus regulations be recast to make cost reduction the principle indicator of the size of the basic bonus.[48] The details varied by industry. In coal mining, for example, the bonus amounted to 8 to 15 percent of the

monthly salary for fulfillment of the cost-reduction target, plus an additional 1 to 1.5 percent of the salary for each 0.1 percent overfulfillment of the target. In the textile industry the percentages were 8 to 12 percent for fulfillment and 0.8 to 1.2 percent for overfulfillment. The cost-reduction target was expressed in terms of the new measure—kopeks per ruble of output.[49]

The bonus for fulfillment of the output target was dropped. But in most industries, bonuses continued to be paid for overfulfillment of the output target. The bonus was set in the range of 3 to 5 percent of the monthly salary for each percentage overfulfillment of the output target.[50]

Since this new bonus structure was supplanted a few years later by the 1965 Economic Reform, there is no need to pursue its effect on the operating rules and on the innovation decision. Only one point is of interest, however. The output and cost rules implicit in the classical incentive structure were not equivalent to a profit rule. As we have seen, an alternative that involved an increase in both value of output and average cost was to be rejected if it exceeded the cost condition, even if it increased profit. When the basic bonus varies with cost, however, the implicit rule of choice is similar to a profit rule. For in the centrally planned economy, the opportunity to increase profit by varying output is quite constricted, but there are few restraints on the possibility of increasing profit by reducing cost. Hence the Soviet firm looks primarily to cost reduction when it is motivated to increase profit. When the basic bonus varies not only with cost but also with output, however, the implicit rule is virtually equivalent to a profit rule. It may be called a weighted-profit rule since the bonus regulations provide different rewards for proportional changes in output and cost.[51] Hence decisions made under the new bonus structure were profit-based decisions, although they were formally expressed in terms of cost reduction and output expansion.

During the period that these changes were being introduced, an extensive controversy was under way on the question of whether profitability should be established as the primary basis of managerial decision making. In retrospect it is now evident that that transformation was in fact occurring in practice. The redefinition of the cost condition in units of kopeks per ruble of output and the elevation of cost to a determinant of the size of bonuses were both responses to the growing conviction that managerial choices are somehow distorted unless output and cost received roughly equal attention in decision making. As a consequence of these changes in the incentive structure, profit had already become the dominating element in the rules of choice, in fact if not in name. In selecting profitability to serve thereafter as one of the major bases of enterprise choice, the 1965 Economic Reform thus largely formalized what the search for efficiency had already achieved.

14.5. The Economic Reform

The Reform terminated the sharp division between the dominant output-based bonus and the small profit-based Enterprise Fund that characterized the classical incentive structure. It consisted, in effect, of the abolition of the basic bonus as an independent incentive element and the reconstitution of the Enterprise Fund, greatly enlarged, as the dominant element of the incentive structure.

In the administrative implementation of the Reform, the name "Enterprise Fund" was dropped, perhaps to dissociate the new arrangement from that rather undistinguished institution of the past. The three uses of the old fund—bonuses, social expenditures, and minor investments—were separated into three administratively distinct accounts, called Incentive Funds. They may be called the Bonus Fund, the Social Expenditures Fund, and the Production Development Fund.[52] The last two funds serve as an incentive in the same limited sense as the corresponding parts of the old Enterprise Fund, and we shall discuss them briefly. It is the Bonus Fund, however, that is now the repository of the proved motivating power of the old basic bonus, and it is therefore the primary source of the new decision rules. It is on that fund that the analysis will focus.

The Economic Reform did not put an end to the flux in the incentive structure that characterized the preceding decade. The details have continued to change, and the present-day incentive structure differs substantially from that first announced in 1965. We shall pass over the earlier versions and discuss the incentive structure in use during the Ninth Five-Year Plan (1971-1975).[53]

The Incentive Structure

The bonus rewards of management now come predominantly from the Bonus Fund. The larger that fund, the larger the incomes of management. Hence the regulations governing the size of the fund are the key to the new rules of decision making.[54]

The size of the fund. The Bonus Fund is a special account into which the enterprise may transfer some portion of its earned profit. The transfers are made quarterly, with a final adjustment at the end of the year on the basis of the year's performance. A rather complex procedure has evolved for determining the volume of profit that may be transferred into the Fund.

The size of the fund depends initially on the enterprise's five-year-plan targets. At the time the five-year plan is drafted, each enterprise is assigned a series of plan targets for each of the five years, and also a sum specifying the size of the Bonus Fund if those targets are fulfilled. Hypothetical enterprise K, for example, whose five-year plan was officially approved in 1971, received the following plan figures for 1974:[55]

Value of output, 1974 percent of 1970   136.1%
Gross rate of profit, percent of capital   32 %
Labor productivity, percent of 1970   133.6%
Bonus Fund, thousand rubles   812.4

The second step occurs when the time comes to draw up the actual 1974 annual plan. Enterprise K may propose the same targets as those above, confirmed earlier in its five-year plan. In that case the planned Bonus Fund for the year will be 812,400 rubles. But if they take on larger (or smaller) plan targets, they are entitled to a larger (or smaller) planned fund. The change in the size of the fund is computed on the basis of three coefficients (*normativy*) relating to each of the forgoing three targets. The sales revenue coefficient of Enterprise K for example, is .00512.[56] For each percentage point that the actual 1974 output target exceeds the five-year plan's 1974 target, Enterprise K is entitled to increase its Bonus Fund by an amount equal to .00512 times their total 1970 wage and salary payments. Suppose they assume a 1974 output target of 137.5% of 1970, 1.4 percentage points greater than the five-year-plan target of 136.1% of 1970, and suppose total 1970 wages and salaries had been 6,412,000 rubles. Then the planned 1974 Bonus Fund may be increased by 46,000 rubles (.00512 × 6,412 × 1.4). Similarly, if the profit-rate coefficient is .00310 and the 1974 profit rate is only 31.3%—0.7% less than the five-year-plan target for 1974—the planned 1974 Bonus Fund is reduced by 14,000 rubles (.00312 × 6,412 × 0.7). The productivity coefficient is applied in the same way. The general formula for the planned Bonus Fund in any year may be written as:

$$B = \overline{B} + W_o [k_v (V - \overline{V}) + k_p (P - \overline{P}) + k_l (L - \overline{L})] \qquad (14.1)$$

where

B is the size of the Bonus Fund in the current annual plan (for example, 1974).

$\bar{B}$ is the size of the current year's (1974) Bonus Fund as approved in the enterprise's five-year plan (1971 to 1975).

W_o is the total wage bill in the last year preceding the current five-year plan.

V, P, and L are current year's (1974) actual targets for increase in value of output, for the profit rate, and for the increase in labor productivity.[57]

$\bar{V}$, $\bar{P}$, and $\bar{L}$ are the corresponding five-year-plan targets (established in 1971) for the current year (1974).

k_v, k_p, and k_l are the corresponding coefficients.

The third step is the computation of the size of the final Bonus Fund. The sum actually transferred from the enterprise's profit to the Bonus Fund account exceeds or falls short of the planned size B, depending on the degree of fulfillment of the annual-plan targets. But two of the targets used in the computation are somewhat changed in this step. Instead of the value-of-output target, a sales-revenue target is used. And instead of the gross profit rate, the net profit rate is used, net, that is, of the charge on capital. Finally, the coefficients applied to the targets that have been overfulfilled (or underfulfilled) must be at least 30 percent smaller (or larger) than the coefficients used in the second step. The formula for the final size of the Bonus Fund is

$$B' = B + W_o [a_s k_s (S' - S) + a_p k_p (P'_n - P_n) + a_l k_l (L' - L)]. \quad (14.2)$$

The primed symbols are achieved values and the unprimed are plan values and

where

S is the sales revenue.

P_n is the net rate of profit.

$a\text{'s} = \begin{cases} 0.7 \\ 1.3 \end{cases}$ when the expression in parentheses is $= \begin{cases} > 0 \\ < 0 \end{cases}$.

The other symbols are the same as in the preceding formula.

Adjustments for innovation. Sales revenue, the profit rate, and labor productivity are the principal determinants of the size of the fund. Further variation is authorized, however, for certain activities associated with innovation.

In anticipation of the current Bonus Fund regulations, the ministries were ordered to grade the quality of all their enterprise's products according to the three-level classification used in State Quality Certification. The enterprise five-year plan contains a set of targets for the percentage of each year's output to consist of highest-quality products. In preparing its 1974 annual plan (the second step) the enterprise may undertake to produce a larger percentage of highest-quality output than had been targeted (for 1974) in the five-year plan. The size of the 1974 planned Bonus Fund may then be increased by a certain percentage (predetermined by the ministry) for each percentage point that the 1974 annual target exceeds the five-year-plan target for 1974. In the third step, the Bonus Fund may be increased or decreased, relative to its planned size, according to the degree of success in attaining the planned percentage of highest-quality output.

Second, the ministries have been assigned a reserve Bonus Fund that may be used to offset the negative effects of innovation on general enterprise performance. If an enterprise's output and profit are expected to decline temporarily because of the start-up problems of new products or processes, its Bonus Fund would be diminished accordingly. In that case the ministry may supplement the enterprise Bonus Fund out of its own reserve to make up for the decline.

The size of these innovation adjustments is not governed by precise formulas. The regulations provide only that the procedures and the amounts are to be determined by the ministry in consultation with the enterprise management and trade union.

The uses of the fund. The annual plan specifies the year's targets and the volume of profit to be deposited into the fund if the targets are met. It also specifies the sums to be spent in the course of the year for each of the uses to which the money may be put. The planned distribution of the Bonus Fund is worked out in consultation between management and the trade union, under general state regulations.

The fund is used primarily to finance various supplements to wages and salaries, three of which are the most important. First are the basic bonuses, distributed among individual plant personnel in accordance with the established formulas. These are similar to the basic bonuses of the classical incentive structure. Second are the end-of-year bonuses, paid to all enterprise personnel, on the basis of the overall enterprise performance for the year. Third are various special-achievement bonuses, paid from time to time to persons who made exceptional contributions to the performance of high-priority tasks, particularly in process and product innovation. In addition, some of the funds may be used for bonuses for the winning teams in intraenterprise socialist competitions, for special welfare payments to employees in need of assistance, and for other personal awards.

If the plan targets are overfulfilled, the size of the fund will be larger than planned, and larger bonuses may be paid than originally planned. In the opposite case smaller bonuses will be paid. These adjustments in the planned distribution of the Bonus Fund are made in consultation between management and the trade union.

The Decision Rules

Although a decade has passed since the introduction of the Economic Reform, the current version has been in operation only since 1972.[58] The published sources do not yet provide a sufficient basis for a full statement on the rules of choice that management has deduced. Evidence on managerial behavior in the period 1966 to 1971 is of only limited use, for the current incentive structure is substantially different from the earlier post-Reform versions. The discussion will therefore be limited to some speculation on the ways that the current rules may be expected to differ from those of the classical period.

The profit rule. It is in the role assigned to profit that the current incentive structure differs most sharply from the classical. Profit is now important for two reasons. First, performance with respect to the profit indicator is the principal determinant of the size of the Bonus Fund. The regulations require that about 60 percent of the Bonus Fund be governed by the profit indicator and 40 percent by the sales-revenue indicator. That is, if the profit target is just fulfilled, the Bonus Fund will be at least 60 percent of its planned size regardless of the degree of overfulfillment of the revenue target. In the opposite case, the Bonus Fund will be only 40 percent of its planned size.[59]

Second, the Bonus Fund is financed out of enterprise profit. Hence if total profit declines, the enterprise may end up with a smaller Bonus Fund than it is entitled to, simply because the earned profit is too small to finance it. Moreover, as in the classical period total profit continues to be important to the enterprise for the reasons of the financial organization of the economy discussed earlier. Hence the profit rule now dominates the structure of rules as the output rule did formerly.

The way in which profit enters into decision making is somewhat complicated by the fact that different measures of profit are used in different contexts. Two measures predominate, however: the rate of profit and total profit. In fact, the rules structure may be better described as having not one profit rule but two: a profit-rate rule and a total-profit rule.

In the determination of the size of the Bonus Fund, it is the rate of profit that serves as the indicator. As defined since the Reform, however, the rate of profit is a very different concept from that employed in the classical period. The Reform required the enterprise to pay to the State Treasury a sum equal to about 15 percent of the value of its annual average stock of fixed and working capital. The profit indicator is now net profit; net, that is, of the capital charge, plus certain fixed payments to the state and interest on bank loans.[60] This newly defined net profit is the numerator of the profit rate. The Reform also changed the denominator from total cost of production, which served during the classical period, to the average annual stock of fixed and working capital. Hence the present-day profit-rate rule leads to very different choices from the classical profit-rate rule. The principal difference is that capital-intensive alternatives are ranked much lower than in the past.

The size of the year's Bonus Fund depends on the extent to which the achieved profit rate exceeds or falls short of the planned profit rate. Hence the profit-rate rule directs management to rank alternatives in order of their effect on the rate of profit. But total (net) profit enters into the choice as well, because management is also interested in the absolute volume of profit for the reasons mentioned. Hence in ranking alternatives management follows not only a profit-rate rule but a total-profit rule. The latter directs management to prefer alternatives that yield a larger total profit.

The principal difference between the two rules is the way in which the capital stock enters into the choice. The size of the capital stock affects the net profit in two ways: depreciation is an element in the calculation of production cost; and the capital charge is deducted from total gross profit in the calculation of total net profit. In these two respects, the capital costs of a set of alternatives influences their ranking in the same way under both profit rules. But the profit-rate rule introduces the capital stock into the calculation in a third way, which does not apply to the total-profit rule—as the denominator in the profit rate. Hence if there are two alternatives that yield the same net profit, the total profit rule is neutral in the choice between them, but the profit-rate rule directs the choice of the one with the smaller capital stock.

The sales-revenue rule. The organizational structure of the centrally planned economy assigns the function of distributing output not primarily to the producing enterprises but to the ministries and planning agencies. It was therefore reasonable to design the classical incentive structure so that management would concentrate on producing rather than selling output. The output rule must receive credit for having contributed to the high level of effort expanded in producing output and increasing its volume. One unfortunate consequence, however, was the neglect of the salability of output. Goods were produced "for the warehouse" and were counted toward the fulfillment of the output plan, regardless of whether or when or how they were subsequently sold to other enterprises or to the public. In decisions regarding quality or product mix, the choice was based on the value of output produced and not on the next stage of distribution.

The Reform replaced output by sales revenue in the determination of the size of the Bonus Fund. Hence the incentive structure no longer encourages the production of output delivered to the warehouse but not sold or only sold later at reduced prices. The corresponding rule directs management to evaluate alternatives according to their contribution to revenue rather than to output.[61]

The size of the Bonus Fund depends in part on the sales revenue realized relative to the planned sales revenue. In certain industries, the planned output is all that the planners wish to have produced, and an incentive structure that encouraged overfulfillment of plan would defeat that purpose. In those cases, sales revenue is replaced by total (net) profit in the Bonus Fund formula. The size of the fund is then determined almost entirely on the basis of profit performance; about 60 percent by the rate of profit and most of the remainder by the volume of net profit. We do not know how many enterprises fall into this category, but the number appears not to be very large.

The labor-productivity rule. The earliest versions of the reformed incentive structure included only sales revenue and the profit rate in the Bonus Fund formula. The current version has added labor productivity, defined as the ratio of value of output to employment. If the planned target of labor productivity is surpassed or underfulfilled, the planned Bonus Fund is increased or decreased by a certain amount for each percentage point of variation from the plan target.

In the absence of a labor-productivity rule, output and employment would still be taken account of, for both sales revenue and profit depend on value of output, and employment determines labor cost. What the addition of the productivity rule does is to bias the choice somewhat against labor-intensive alternatives and in favor of material- and capital-intensive alternatives. Labor is double counted, as it were: first in calculating profitability and then in calculating labor productivity. To some extent, the result is an offset to the double counting of the cost of capital, which enters into the calculation of both net profit and the profit rate. Since the three bonus indicators are weighted by different coefficients, the new bonus structure is considerably more complicated than the classical, and both its normative consequences and incentive value are more complex.

The innovation rules. One objective of the pre-Reform modifications of the classical incentive structure was to infuse an implicit concern with innovation into managerial decision making. That objective has carried over into the present incentive structure, in the form of the various adjustments to the size of the planned Bonus Fund. It is useful to distinguish those adjustments that constitute positive incentives from those that are compensatory in form.

The positive incentive is the upward adjustment of the planned Bonus Fund in proportion to the percentage of highest-quality products in the total output. The corresponding rule directs management to consider explicitly the quality distribution of alternative production programs and to rank them in order of quality.

The compensatory adjustments relieve the innovating enterprise of the potential loss in bonuses due to the start-up of new products and processes. If the ministry can be persuaded that a certain planned innovation must, under the best of management, reduce profit and output for some time, the ministry may grant the enterprise a sum of money large enough to compensate for the expected decline in the Bonus Fund. The corresponding compensation rule directs management to make certain adjustments in its ranking of alternative programs. If, under the other rules, one alternative is rejected in favor of another because it yields less profit and revenue, the compensation rule directs that one more question be asked about the alternatives before making the choice: "Do they involve innovation?" If one or both do, then on reevaluation the order of preference may be reversed.

The target and ratchet rules. A major defect of the classical structure was the incentive it generated to seek low plan targets and to avoid overfulfilling them by too large an amount. It was largely to remedy that defect that the three-step system of Bonus Fund determination was invented.

The five-year-plan annual targets set the bench marks for each of the year's current annual plans. If the five-year-plan output target for 1974 was 1 million rubles, then the enterprise that accepts a target of less than a million rubles in its current 1974 plan suffers a diminution of its planned Bonus Fund. If it accepts a larger target, its planned Bonus Fund is increased. The incentive structure now penalizes the enterprise that accepts targets below its potential, and the old target rule no longer prevails in annual planning. Moreover, the coefficients are constructed on the "contract bridge" principle; if the enterprise expects to produce 1.3 million rubles of output, the reward will be larger if it submits a plan target of 1.3 million than if its target is 1.2 million or less.[62]

The target rule still prevails in drafting the five-year-plan, however, for the smaller the targets in that plan, the larger all future annual Bonus Funds will be for given levels of future performance. In fact, precisely because the targets of that plan influence reward levels for so long a period of time, the target rule is likely to operate with greater force than ever before applied in annual planning.[63] Nevertheless, the elimination of the target rule from current planning is a substantial achievement.

Since the planners need no longer be concerned to combat the operation of the target rule in current plan making, there is no reason for them to retain the ratchet principle of target setting. The incentive system can be counted on to induce management to propose the highest targets they can expect to attain, in their best judgment. If the planners see things that way, the enterprise loses nothing by producing as high a level of output and profit as they can, regardless of the plan targets.

We do not yet know, however, if the planners do in fact see things that way. Old habits of operation do not vanish at once, even under changed circumstances. If an enterprise produced an exceptionally large volume of output in one year because of what it regarded as unusual conditions not likely to recur, it might be prudent to propose for next year a target smaller than this year's output. Whether the old pressures generated by taut planning will permit planners and ministries to accept such plan-target decisions by enterprises is not yet clear. But the structure of the new incentive system, at least, no longer supports a ratchet rule in short-run decision making.

Toward the end of the five-year-plan period, however, we may expect the ratchet rule to recur. The targets for the next five-year plan are likely to be influenced by the output and profit levels achieved in the last year or two of the current five-year plan. Since so much rides on the targets set in the next five-year plan, the enterprise will be motivated to hold back on output and cost reduction in the preceding year or two.

In summary, the use of the five-year plan targets as bench marks has eliminated the target and ratchet rules from managerial decision making in the first few years of the five-year period. But the target levels of the five-year plan now assume an importance greater than that of the annual targets of the past. Hence the ratchet rule is likely to reassert itself as the new five-year-plan period approaches, and the target rule may well operate with unusual force in the negotiations over the five-year targets.

Consequences for Innovation

One is impressed above all with the complexity of the new incentive structure. Earlier versions had a degree of simplicity that encouraged efforts to deduce the decision rules by mathematical analysis. The bonus formula could be regarded as a linear function of a very few variables, and the conditions that maximize the value of the function under given constraints could be viewed as the basis of the decision rules.[64] With the present level of complexity, however, as well as the uncertainty over such matters as the size of the innovation adjustments, it is doubtful that the operating rules deduced by management are at all approximated by the logic of constrained maximization. Indeed, it is likely that in evaluating alternatives, managers are now much more uncertain than before about just what incentive rewards may be expected from the choice of one over the other.

If a certain incentive structure leads to optimal choices, an increase in uncertainty over the consequences of alternatives would reduce efficiency. If the incentive structure leads to nonoptimal choices, however, it does not follow that an increase in uncertainty reduces efficiency. For if, in full knowledge of the results, bad choices are made, then uncertainty about the results may cause better choices to be made. Like the theory of the "second best," a little bit of ignorance may sometimes improve matters in an imperfect world.[65]

With respect to innovation, the classical incentive structure made it perfectly clear that established products were to be preferred to new products. If it were less certain that innovation would reduce the rewards, the rate of innovation might have been higher. More generally, it may be conjectured that an increase in uncertainty in an incentive structure leads to an increase in the frequency of choice of those alternatives that are least preferred under that structure. The somewhat perverse conclusion is that the new Soviet incentive structure, by muddying things up more, may have reduced the resistance to innovation.

The current structure differs from the classical not only in level of complexity but in a variety of its specific properties. The discussion will be confined to those that affect the decision to innovate.

Product innovation. The change in the method of measuring the rate of profit has a certain effect on innovation. The cost of the capital required for an innovation is now assigned a greater weight in the innovation decision than in the past; it reduces the numerator of the profit rate by the amount of the capital charge, and it increases the denominator, which is now not total cost but the value of the capital stock. Hence the more capital intensive an innovation, the more likely that it will be rejected, relative to past practice.

Since most innovations require some capital investment, the effect of the new definition of the profit rate is to reduce the rate of innovation, in the sense of the frequency with which new products and processes are introduced. But the net return to investment in innovation may be greater than in the past. For in the absence of a charge for capital the social cost of innovations did not enter fully into the enterprise's calculation. Some portion of pre-Reform investments in new products and processes must therefore have yielded lower returns than would have been secured if the same resources were invested in the expansion of established products and processes.

The feature of Economic Reform that has attracted the greatest attention, however, is not the change in the measure of profit but the augmented role of profit in the incentive structure. The impact of that change on the innovation decision is much less significant than the less-publicized change in the time horizon of decision making.

The role of profit had been increasing for almost a decade before the Reform, although not always by that name. The Reform merely consummated and extended a trend already well under way by establishing profit as the main bonus indicator and as the financial source of bonuses. But nothing was done to extend the time horizon of decision making until the 1971 regulations on the Ninth Five-Year Plan. Hence we have more than a decade's experience during which the role of profit relative to output was greatly augmented, compared to the classical period, but decisions continued to be made on the basis of short-run considerations. Nevertheless, the sources give no indication of a substantial reduction in managerial resistance to product innovation.

Nor should a change have been expected. Given the structure of prices and the cost behavior of new products, a short-run profit rule is no less discouraging to product innovation than the old short-run output rule. Under the output rule new products are "disadvantageous" relative to established products because they depress the rate of output in the short run. Under the profit rule, they are "disadvantageous" because they reduce the short-run rate of profit. Both rules direct management to discriminate against new products, although for different reasons.

The introduction of future annual targets in the Ninth Five-Year Plan was the first major break with the short-run time horizon imposed by the classical incentive structure. Under that structure, the bonuses lost in a succession of months were never recovered. Now they may be. A new product may depress the average rate of profit for some period of time, and in the short run bonuses may decline. But if the innovation is successful, costs will eventually decline, and its profit rate will exceed the average. The enterprise will thereafter be able to accept and fulfill profit-rate targets in excess of those set some years earlier in its five-year plan. Since the coefficients that determine the size of the increases in the planned Bonus Fund are not to be changed during the five-year period, the successful innovation will generate a Bonus Fund substantially larger than that originally set for the year in the five-year plan.

The new operating rules therefore direct management to evaluate alternatives not in terms of their effect on the income of this month and next's but in terms of streams of earnings extending for months or years into the future. Undoubtedly management will discount future bonuses to some extent. Nevertheless, the longer time horizon leads to an ordering of alternatives that is different from that of the classical period. Some alternatives that would have been rejected under the classical rules on the basis of their short-term outcomes will now be preferred when evaluated on the basis of their long-term stream of outcomes. Since the returns to innovation extend over the long term, alternatives involving innovation rank higher under the new rules than under the classical.

The favorable effect of the longer time horizon depends on the elimination of the old target and ratchet rules from the rules structure. The target rule no longer applies in current planning, but it applies fully in the making of the five-year plan. The regulations are not clear on the point, but it does appear that the size of the annual future Bonus Fund as set in the five-year plan is independent of the profit and other targets set in the plan. The former is set on the basis of the planners' judgment of what constitutes an equitable and effective Bonus Fund for a well-managed enterprise of a certain size. That sum is evidently in the range of 10 to 12 percent of total wages and salaries.[66] The targets for the profit rate and the growth of output appear to be set independently of the planned size of the fund. Two enterprises with the same labor force may be assigned Bonus Funds of the same size; but if a large state investment program is planned for one of them, it will be assigned higher output targets than the other. The higher the targets assigned, the larger the profit rate and output that will have to be achieved in each of the next five years in order to secure a Bonus Fund of the planned size. The target rule applies fully under these conditions, and, as argued earlier, so much now rides on the five-year-plan targets that the enterprise must strive mightily to keep them low. Moreover, judging from past experience, as the end of the five-year-plan period approaches, the enterprise is likely to anticipate that its current performance will influence the levels of its targets for the next five years. In that case the ratchet rule will direct that effort to be reduced.

The consequence for innovation is that as the end of the five-year-plan period approaches, it is unwise for enterprises to undertake innovations that will realize increased profit and output only after the new five-year plan begins. If they do, the targets in the next five-year period will be increased and the earnings possibly reduced. It is also unwise to disclose to the ministry and planners the innovations that are being considered for future introduction, for the returns are greater if the five-year-plan targets are not jacked up in anticipation of their introduction.

These considerations apply only to the period approaching the end of a five-year plan. Once a new five-year period has begun, the incentive structure itself no longer generates a target or ratchet rule. The longer time horizon in decision making may therefore be expected to yield a higher rate of innovation than in the past.

Two additional provisions of the current incentive structure serve to increase the attractiveness of product innovation. One is the quality adjustment of the size of the Bonus Fund. Like the augmentation of profit, this is also a carry-over of a change already introduced during the prelude to the Reform. The provision as written appears to be intended to improve the static quality distribution of output rather than to promote product innovation as a form of technological advance. However, most new products are likely to be classified as of highest quality by the ministry and will therefore qualify for the adjustment. The second is the adjustment for losses of bonuses because of the start-up of new products and processes. Both adjustments increase the relative ranking of alternatives involving new products.

The two innovation adjustments also affect the time horizon of decision making. A short time horizon inhibits innovation because of the short-run losses that innovation normally entails. The smaller those losses, the less the resistance to innovation. Hence by compensating enterprises for some of the short-run losses, the innovation adjustments mitigate the anti-innovation effects of a short time horizon.

Finally, in addition to demoting output to a secondary place in the incentive structure, the Reform provided that it be measured not by value of output produced but by value of output sold. The change may be expected to improve the quality of product innovation. In the past a simulated new product counted as output produced, even if its quality was poor and it could not be sold. Under the sales-revenue rule that alternative would rank lower than under the old output rule. On the other hand, given the organization of product marketing, the sales revenue rule is more discouraging to innovation than the output rule. Marketing, as we have seen, is more important in the case of new products than of established products. Moreover it is an activity over which management has little control in the organizational structure of the economy. The size of the bonus of an enterprise that decides to innovate now depends to a greater extent than before on the performance of outside economic units. Hence alternatives involving new products must for this reason rank lower than they did in the past. The change from output to sales revenue may therefore reduce the incidence of spurious innovation but at the cost of a somewhat greater risk associated with genuine innovation.

Process innovation. The major inducement for process innovation in the classical period was the cost-reduction condition. In the present incentive structure cost no longer appears as an independent indicator. Total cost continued to influence decision making, however, as a determinant of net profit. The cost of labor and capital has a further effect on the Bonus Fund through the profit-rate and labor-productivity rules. In all of these respects management is still directed to prefer lower-cost alternatives to higher. Alternatives that involve cost-reducing process innovations therefore continue to rank high under the new bonus indicators. The major deterrent to process innovation in the past was the effect of production start-up on the main bonus indicators. The lengthened time horizon of decision making has reduced that deterrent. A successful innovation may reduce short-run bonuses if the rate of output and the rate of profit decline. But both eventually recover and exceed their earlier levels. Thereafter the stream of additional bonuses more than recovers the short-run losses of bonuses, at least until the next five-year plan begins and new Bonus Fund coefficients are established. In addition, the compensatory adjustments of the fund for losses due to production start-up mitigate one of the classical obstacles to innovation.

The new incentive structure is therefore more hospitable to process innovation than the classical, primarily because of the lengthened time horizon. Some minor qualifications may be noted. First, while lower-cost processes are preferred to higher, the peculiar double counting of labor and capital costs may bias the choice between labor-saving and capital-saving innovations. The bias will depend on the relative sizes of the Bonus Fund coefficients, which are determined in a manner that is arbitrary from the point of view of pure factor costs. For example, enterprises with different capital/output and capital/labor ratios will have different coefficients. They will therefore make different choices among a set of alternatives that have different capital-saving and labor-saving characteristics, although the social cost of labor and capital is the same for both. Second, as in the case of product innovation, the target and ratchet rules are likely to reassert themselves as the end of the five-year-plan period approaches. The result will be a bunching of innovations in the first years of the period and a slowdown toward the end, during which some cost-reducing opportunities are forgone. Labor-saving innovations are the least likely to be introduced in the last year of the five-year period; on the contrary, we may expect the wage bill to be somewhat padded in that year. The reason is that the size of the Bonus Funds in the Ninth Five-Year Plan was set as a fixed percentage of the wage bill in 1970, the last year of the Eighth Plan. The lesson will not be lost on management. The larger the enterprise's wage expenditures in 1975, the larger the planned Bonus Funds that may be secured in the Tenth Plan (1976 to 1980).

These qualifications diminish somewhat the benefit from the new incentive structure. But they do not alter the main conclusion that it is likely to generate a higher rate of process innovation than the classical structure.

The other funds. The analysis has concentrated on only one of the three Incentive Funds—the Bonus Fund. Some remarks on the other two funds are in order.

In the original provisions of the Reform the size of the Social Fund was determined by a formula similar in form but not identical to that governing the Bonus Fund. Hence the rules derived from the two funds differed somewhat. To simplify the administration of the incentive structure, the use of an independent formula for the Social Fund was discontinued. The size of the Social Fund is now set as a fixed percentage of the Bonus Fund. In the Ninth Five-Year-Plan period that percentage was set equal to the percentage relationship of the two funds that prevailed in 1970.[67] Hence the alternative that maximizes the size of the Bonus Fund now also maximizes the size of the Social Fund. The latter therefore has no independent influence on decision making.

The Production Development Fund, however, is organized on somewhat different principles, which were discussed in detail earlier (Sec. 6.3). Like the other two funds, its size varies with sales revenue and with the profit rate. But the corresponding coefficients are applied not to the total wage and salary expenditure, as in the other two funds, but to the average value of the year's capital stock. Moreover, each year's fund depends on the size of the same year's capital stock. Hence the rules derived from the Production Development Fund rank capital-intensive product innovations higher and capital-saving process innovations lower than the rules derived from the other funds. The point is probably not of much consequence, however, for the other two funds are the more potent personal incentives.

Summary. There are two broad features of the classical incentive structure that affected adversely the innovation decision. One was the specific indicators that determined the structure of decision rules. The other was the short time horizon of decision making. Both of these features have been changed since the Reform.

The change in the bonus indicators has had the lesser effect on the innovation decision. Product innovation depresses both the profit rate and the rate of output. Managers operating under the new profit rule are therefore no less inclined to discriminate against new products than those operating under the old output rule. The establishment of sales revenue rather than value of output as a bonus indicator may in fact increase the resistance to product innovation because enterprises have little authority to engage in the promotion and marketing activities that new products require. It may, however, reduce the incidence of spurious innovation. Decisions regarding process innovations are not significantly affected by the new indicators.

The more significant advance concerns the effect of the time horizon on the innovation decision. The short time horizon of the classical incentive structure was an impediment to innovation because of a certain feature of the innovation process, namely, the benefits accrued in the longer run, while losses are incurred in the short run. There are two ways in which this source of resistance to innovation may be reduced. One is to lengthen the time horizon of decision making. The other is to reduce the short-term losses from innovation. Both approaches have been incorporated in the new incentive structure.

The time horizon has been extended by the device of employing five-year-plan targets as stable bench marks for measuring current performance. Since the ratchet principle is no longer applied, successful innovators can expect to gain more in bonuses in the long run than they lose in the short run. The rate of innovation may therefore be expected to rise. The crucial question is whether the longer-run perspective can be established in practice. There is reason to believe that in the later years of each five-year-plan period the target and ratchet rules may reappear and restore the short-run horizon, at least until the new five-year targets are set. It will also require that innovators be permitted actually to reap the large long-run rewards for which short-run losses were earlier incurred. In view of the hostility to economic rents, such a policy will require some unusual self-discipline by the governors of the economy. Since the three-step incentive structure has been in force only a few years, there is insufficient evidence at present for judging the extent to which a longer time horizon has in fact been introduced into decision making. It is disconcerting to read that as late as 1973 "the enterprise incentive system (the Incentive Funds) is based not on the indicators expected to be attained in the long run but on the indicators of current performance, that is, the indicators of this very day."[68]

The second approach, however, diminishes the necessity for a longer time horizon. If the short-run losses from innovation are fully compensated by the ministry, that source of discrimination against new products and processes relative to established ones will vanish. It is probably not intended that the innovation adjustments to the Bonus Fund will fully compensate for the losses. But to whatever extent they do, they raise the relative position of innovations in the ranking of alternatives.

Notes

1. Rules are to be distinguished from regulations. Regulations specify procedures to be followed. Rules specify the criteria for making choices; they are sometimes referred to as "rules of choice."

2. H. S. Levine, "The Centralized Planning of Supply in Soviet Industry," in U.S. Congress, Joint Economic Committee, *Comparisons of the United States and Soviet Economies* (Washington: Government Printing Office, 1959), p. 164.

3. O. Lange and F. M. Taylor, *On the Economic Theory of Socialism*, B. E. Lippincott, ed. (Minneapolis: University of Minnesota Press, 1952), pp. 57-143; A. P. Lerner, *The Economics of Control* (New York: Macmillan, 1946).

4. A. Baykov, *The Development of the Soviet Economic System* (New York: Macmillan, 1947), p. 226.

5. But not rewards that are too large. Because of the hostility to economic rents, very large earnings evoke suspicion that management has benefited from factors other than their good work or that some unlawful practices have been sanctioned.

6. Certain formal rules are precisely stated, like those governing the choice among investment alternatives. The rules supply the mathematical formula to be used in calculating the economic benefit from each alternative, and the decision maker is directed to choose that alternative that maximizes the benefit. See Sec. 15.1.

7. J. S. Berliner, *Factory and Manager in the USSR* (Cambridge: Harvard University Press, 1957), pp. 78-80.

8. J. G. Zielinski, *Economic Reforms in Polish Industry* (London: Oxford University Press, 1973), p. 311. This conclusion is shared by David Granick, a close student of managerial behavior in both socialist and capitalist economies. See his *Managerial Comparisons of Four Developed Countries: France, Britain, United States, and Russia* (Cambridge: MIT Press, 1972), p. 52.

9. See Berliner, *Factory and Manager*, for various bonus rates, pp. 29-32.

10. B. M. Richman, *Soviet Management: With Significant American Comparisons* (Englewood Cliffs: Prentice-Hall, 1965), pp. 144.

11. L. M. Gatovskii, A. V. Bachurin, S. P. Pervushin, B. M. Sukharevskii, and G. D. Anisimov, eds., *Plan, khozraschet, stimuly* (The Plan, Accountability, and Incentives) (Moscow: *Ekonomika*, 1966), p. 65.

12. Berliner, *Factory and Manager*, p. 69.

13. Lerner, *Economics of Control*.

14. Berliner, *Factory and Manager*, pp. 78-80; Zielinski, *Economic Reforms*, p. 122.

15. A second reason for avoiding excessive overfulfillment of a plan target is that it raises the suspicion that management had deliberately sought to keep the plan target far below capacity.

16. Gross value of output is defined as the value of finished output plus the net change in value of goods in process. Different measures of output have been used at various times and in various industries, including physical measures like tons or yards. Managerial choice is remarkably sensitive to the units in which output is expressed in the incentive structure, and much of the incessant tinkering with incentives was designed to find the measure that would induce the optimal choices. See Alec Nove, *The Soviet Economy: An Introduction* (New York: Praeger, 1965), rev. ed., Chap. 6. Our analysis will be confined to gross output since it was the predominant measure during the classical period.

17. The assortment plan appears in Part II of the enterprise plan, called the "Production and Sales Plan." See Sec. 2.2.

18. L. Smolinski, "Soviet Planning: How It Really Began," *Survey*, No. 67 (April 1968), p. 113.

19. Berliner, *Factory and Manager*, Chaps. 3, 4, and passim; Nove, *The Soviet Economy*, Chap. 6; Richman, *Soviet Management*, Chaps. 8 and 9. The most searching analysis of incentive structures in a centrally planned economy is Janucz Zielinski's *Economic Reforms in Polish Industry*, Chap. 6.

20. Zielinski investigates the "mis-incentives" generated by the incentive structure. David Granick approaches the problem as one of "suboptimization," in "Managerial Incentives in the USSR and in Western Firms," *Journal of Comparative Administration*, Vol. 5:2 (August 1973), pp. 169-199.

21. The output rule impedes not only the innovation process but the R & D process as well. For example, the production programs of many experimental plans—plants designed primarily to produce experimental runs of new products for testing and development—include a certain volume of standard production. The latter is included in order to keep the plant operating at full capacity, since the volume of experimental work fluctuates greatly. For these plants as well, the dominant rule appears to be the output rule. As a result we find references to what we might expect: the director of an experimental plant points out that they try to avoid experimental work and new products and prefer to concentrate on their regular production runs that are more "advantageous." Advantageous means that the bonus system supports the dominance of the output rule. *Ekonomicheskaia gazeta*, 1967, No. 22, p. 13.

22. The point does not apply in cases in which the output target is expressed in physical rather than value units.

23. D. Granick, *Soviet Metal-Fabricating and Economic Development: Practice Versus Policy* (Madison: University of Wisconsin Press, 1967), p. 237.

24. See Sec. 14.4.

25. The OECD study comes to the same conclusion. E. Zaleski, J. P. Kozlowski, H. Wienert, R. W. Davies, M. J. Berry, and R. Amann, *Science Policy in the U.S.S.R.* (Paris: OECD, 1969), p. 428.

26. P. S. Mstislavskii, M. G. Gabrieli, and Iu. V. Borozdin, *Ekonomicheskoe obosnovanie optovykh tsen na novuiu promyshlennuiu produktsiu* (The Economic Basis of Wholesale Pricing of New Industrial Products) (Moscow: *Nauka*, 1968), p. 153.

27. A. D. Little, *Patterns and Problems of Technical Innovation in American Industry*, Report to the Natural Science Foundation, U.S. Department of Commerce (PB 181573), (Washington: September 1963), pp. 60-61.

28. *Voprosy ekonomiki*, 1959, No. 1, p. 45.

29. *The Current Digest of the Soviet Press*, Vol. 19:13 (April 19, 1967), p. 14, translated from *Novyi mir*, 1967, No. 1, pp. 167-189.

30. *Ekonomika promyshlennykh predpriiatii: uchebnik* (Textbook on the Economics on Industrial Enterprises) (Moscow: *Gospolitizdat*, 1962), pp. 348-349.

31. Since the absolute cost of new products is ignored in the calculation of the percentage cost reduction, the enterprise has an interest in producing the new product at as high an initial cost as possible. For with cost-based pricing, the higher the cost, the higher are the price and profit. Hence, "not only the sellers but the purchasers of products have an economic interest in higher prices," write K. Gofman and N. Petrakov in *Voprosy ekonomiki*, 1967, No. 5, p. 33.

32. *Voprosy ekonomiki*, 1968, No. 3, p. 132; *Planovoe khoziaistvo*, 1966, No. 1, p. 66.

33. National Science Foundation, *Science and Engineering in American Industry* (Washington: Government Printing Office, 1956), p. 44. Cited in R. R. Nelson, "The Economics of Invention: A Survey of the Literature," *Journal of Business*, Vol. 32:2 (April 1959), p. 124.

34. C. F. Carter and B. R. Williams, *Industry and Technical Progress* (London: Oxford University Press, 1957), pp. 182-183.

35. D. Morse and A. W. Warner, *Technological Innovation and Society* (New York: Columbia University Press, 1966), p. 46.

36. D. Granick, "Managerial Incentives in the U.S.S.R. and in Western Firms," *Journal of Com-*

parative Administration, Vol. 5:2 (August 1973), pp. 186-187. Granick argues that slowing down of managerial mobility has increased short-run suboptimizing behavior because the prospects of promotion in the longer run are reduced.

37. Granick, ibid., p. 194.

38. G. D. Anisimov, *Printsip material'noi zainteresovannosti v razvitii novoi tekhniki* (The Principle of Material Incentives in the Development of New Technology) (Moscow: *Ekonomizdat*, 1962), p. 66.

39. G. D. Anisimov and I. A. Vakhlamov, eds., *Material'noe stimulirovanie vnedreniia novoi tekhniki: spravochnik* (Handbook of Material Incentives for Innovation) (Moscow: *Ekonomika*, 1966), pp. 50-51.

40. Ibid., p. 49.

41. Anisimov, *Printsip*, p. 107.

42. A. G. Kulikov, V. G. Lebedev, N. A. Razumov, and A. P. Cherednichenko, eds., *Ekonomicheskie problemy uskoreniia tekhnicheskogo progressa v promyshlennosti* (Economic Problems of Accelerating Technological Progress in Industry) (Moscow: *Mysl'*, 1964), pp. 147-148.

43. See Sec. 10.1.

44. *Voprosy ekonomiki*, 1959, No. 11, p. 80.

45. A. M. Matlin, *Tekhnicheskii progress i tseny mashin* (Technological Progress and Machinery Prices) (Moscow: *Ekonomika*, 1966), p. 18.

46. The unit profit rate is $(p - c)/c = (p/c) - 1$, and where p is the product price and c is unit cost. Here (p/c) is the inverse of the cost/price ratio (c/p). The fact that the new cost measure was equivalent to a profit measure was noted by Soviet analysts. See *Voprosy ekonomiki*, 1959, No. 11, p. 80.

47. *Voprosy ekonomiki*, 1957, No. 2, pp. 140-145; *Planovoe khoziaistvo*, 1959, No. 8, pp. 47-53.

48. *Voprosy ekonomiki*, 1959, No. 11, p. 82.

49. N. I. Bereznoi and A. I. Zhdanov, *Spravochnik ekonomista i planovika promyshlennogo predpriiatiia* (Handbook for Economists and Planners in Industrial Enterprises) (Moscow: *Ekonomika*, 1964), pp. 686-691. The percentages to which each official was entitled depended on the size of his enterprise and his position.

50. Ibid., p. 693. Most products are to be produced in amounts exceeding the plan targets, if possible. Some products, however, are planned to be produced in precise amounts, and production in excess of those amounts is discouraged. In the case of the latter, output produced in excess of the planned amount is not counted toward the overfulfillment of the enterprise total output target.

51. In a normal (unweighted) profit rule, the bonus for an additional 100 rubles of profit is the same, whether the additional profit is due to an increase in revenue or to decrease in unit cost. In a weighted-profit rule, the size of the bonus for an additional 100 rubles of profit varies according to whether it is attributable to increased output or decreased unit cost.

52. The three Incentive Funds are referred to collectively as *Fondy ekonomicheskogo stimulirovaniia*. Their respective names are *Fond material'nogo pooshchreniia*, *Fond sotsial'no-kul'turnykh meropriiatii*, and *Fond razvitiia proizvodstva*.

53. The principal sources for the discussion are the supplement to *Ekonomicheskaia gazeta*, 1971, No. 22, titled "Calculation of the Normal Coefficients and the Incentive Funds for the Ninth Five Year Plan"; and an article in *Ekonomicheskaia gazeta*, 1972, No. 23, pp. 15-16.

54. The bonuses earned by individual officials are determined by formulas similar to those used in determining the overall size of the fund.

55. The illustration developed here is taken from the supplement to *Ekonomicheskaia gazeta*, 1971, No. 22, p. 12.

56. The method for calculating the size of the coefficients is given in the source of the illustration.

57. The current year's (1974) targets for value of output and labor productivity are expressed

as percentages of the value of output and labor productivity in the last year preceding the current five-year plan (1970), not in the immediately preceding year (1973). The purpose of employing such cumulative targets is to encourage a longer planning horizon.

58. The regulations were worked out in 1971, to be introduced in the 1972 enterprise plans.

59. The 60-40 division is used for calculating the size of the revenue—and profit-rate coefficients (*normativy*). The labor-productivity target is ignored in the calculation.

60. "Net profit" is our rendering of the Russian *balansovaia pribyl'* (literally, "balance-sheet profit").

61. Since it is only in the third step of Bonus Fund determination that the question of salability arises, the use of sales revenue as the indicator is confined to that step. In the first two steps value of output still serves as the indicator.

62. *Voprosy ekonomiki*, 1973, No. 10, p. 4.

63. The point has been noted by Soviet authorities and is a source of concern. An effort is to be made to combat the expected effort by enterprises to secure low plan targets in the Tenth Five-Year Plan. Ibid., pp. 6-7, and ibid., 1974, No. 1, p. 128.

64. For an interesting exercise in the mathematical analysis of the bonus structure, see Bertrand Horowitz, "Accounting Controls and the Soviet Economic Reforms of 1966," American Accounting Association, Studies in Accounting Research No. 4 (Evanston: 1970).

65. R. G. Lipsey and R. K. Lancaster, "The General Theory of Second Best," *Review of Economic Studies*, 1956-1957, Vol. 24 (1): No. 63, pp. 11-32.

66. These are the percentages used in the illustrative calculations presented in the sources cited in Note 53.

67. Supplement to *Ekonomicheskaia gazeta*, 1961, No. 22, p. 11.

68. *Voprosy ekonomiki*, 1973, No. 10, p. 56.

Chapter 15

Special Innovation Incentives and Rules

General incentives direct attention only to the summary characteristics of the behavior they are intended to motivate. In deciding whether to produce A or B, one considers only their contribution to the total value of output or to total profit. One ignores the specific properties of the alternatives; whether they are producer or consumer goods, whether they are to be exported or used domestically, whether they are new or old.

In an ideal economy, the general-incentive structure will motivate management to choose an optimal program of activities with respect to all their specific properties, even though those properties are ignored in decision making. In an imperfect world, however, some activities will be carried to excess and others neglected. Too many motorcycles may be produced and too few spare parts for them. The remedy is sometimes sought by changing the price structure and the organizational structure. But often it is sought by changing the incentive structure, particularly when the neglected activity is rather localized, like spare-parts production. The most common of such remedies is the introduction of a special incentive to motivate increased attention to the neglected activity. Hence, alongside the general-incentive structure, there has evolved an extensive set of special incentives.[1]

In the absence of special incentives, the operating rules direct management to regard the alternatives as sealed "black boxes," with tags attached labeled "total profit" or "value of output." The alternatives are to be ranked on the basis of those general tags alone; one is supposed to ignore any differences in the content of the boxes other than the differences inscribed on those tags. The special incentives oblige management to pry open the boxes to see what else they contain. If one contains more spare parts than another, for example, an additional tag must be appended to the boxes to note that difference. Management is then expected to consider, in the ranking of alternatives, not only the information on the general tags but also that on the tags describing the specific details. A different ranking will result, an outcome that is precisely what the special incentives are designed to achieve.

The special incentives consist of bonuses for the performance of specific activities. There are special bonuses for fulfilling the plan for the production of spare parts, for reclaiming and selling scrap metal and waste, for reducing the volume of spoilage, for economizing on the use of electric power, oil, nonferrous metals and other specified materials in short supply, for producing consumer goods from waste materials, for reducing downtime on repair jobs, for reclaiming used bearings.[2] Some of these bonuses are available in certain industries but not others, and the sizes and terms may vary among enterprises. Among this network of special incentives are several designed specifically to encourage innovation activity. They are the subject of this chapter.

We shall be concerned primarily with monetary awards. It should be noted, however, that a variety of nonmonetary, or "moral," awards have been established to honor inventors and innovations.[3] The most prestigious is the Lenin Prize, awarded annually for outstanding achievements involving fundamental advances in some branch of science or technology. Other awards are the USSR State Prize and various personal prizes awarded by special order of the government and the presidium of the USSR Academy of Sciences. Some of these national prizes carry money rewards and other perquisites. Outstanding inventors and innovators may also receive such honors as the title "Hero of Socialist Labor." The republics as well issue titles called "Honored Republican Inventor."

Among the special monetary rewards for innovation, the most prominent is the Innovation Bonus Fund, to be discussed first. A variety of other bonuses are available for activities associated with innovation. Following a brief description of these others, the discussion will conclude with some observations on the decision rules generated by the special innovation incentives.

15.1. Innovation Bonus Fund

In the earliest days of the Soviet regime, legislation was introduced to protect and encourage invention. The problem was to establish a form of what in effect was a property right, or at least a claim on income, that was not in violation of the principles of a socialist society. The form that developed is known as a "certificate of invention." A certificate of invention differs from a patent in that it does not confer rights of ownership or of control over the use to be made of the invention.[4] As early as December 1918, however, the principle that a certified inventor is entitled to a special monetary reward was incorporated into law.[5] Legislation governing inventions continued to develop throughout

Soviet history, and the rewards for inventors have evolved in line with other Soviet policies regarding technological progress.[6]

The attention devoted to the reward of invention was not paralleled by attention to the later links in the innovation chain. Perhaps the reason is that while invention was regarded as an individual act beyond the requirements of duty and ought therefore to be specially rewarded, the introduction of inventions into production was a normal obligation of a Soviet working person and should require no special reward. Or perhaps it was thought that invention was a creative act that could not be anticipated and planned but that once the inventions appeared the process of adoption and diffusion could be readily planned. Whatever the reason, it was not until after World War II that the promotion of innovation was assigned an independent place in the structure of incentives.

The Origins of the Innovation Bonus

The first major independent incentive for innovation was introduced in 1946, in the form of a bonus for the design and production of experimental models of new technology.[7] It was employed first in the heavy machinery industries, but it was later extended to other branches of machinery production and to the chemical and nonferrous metals industries. The bonus was not available for all innovations but only for those specially designated, particularly for products that substituted for imports. If the innovation was satisfactorily completed, the bonus was paid regardless of whether the enterprise's total output target was fulfilled. The bonus was paid to the innovating enterprise, to be distributed among the personnel directly involved in carrying the innovation through to completion. The size of the enterprise bonus was set in advance, as a percentage of the total wage bill.

The chief weakness of this bonus system was later thought to be the fact that the size of the rewards was in no way dependent on the value, or the productivity, or what later came to be called the "economic effectiveness" of the innovation. The bonus was designed to be large enough to provide what was thought to be a reasonable supplement to the salaries of the personnel involved. One might regard that approach as consistent with what was then thought to be the essence of a "labor theory of value." That is, the value of a new product or process, like the value of any commodity, was equal to the quantity of labor embodied in it. If two groups of engineers expended roughly the same amount of time in producing two new experimental models, then their products were of equivalent "value" and they were entitled to equal compensation. There was no place in the theory, or in the incentive system that incorporated that theory, for the notion that the two products may have very different "values" in some other important sense, or that the rewards to the innovators should be based not on the value of the labor time expended but on the productivity of what they produced. The other characteristic of this early system was that the bonuses were provided only for that portion of the innovation chain that ended with the production of an experimental model. The later portion of the chain that involved bringing the innovation into production was not yet included.

The reforms in the pricing of new products originated, as we have seen, in the debate on the choice among investment alternatives.[8] That same historic debate precipitated the launching of the first effort to forge a special innovation incentive that would reflect the productivity of innovations. In September 1955 a working group in the State Committee on Science and Technology produced a draft of an innovation bonus system that would accomplish that objective. The proposal contained the following schedule:[9]

	Size of Bonus, as a Percentage of the Annual Economic Benefit
For innovations specified in the national economic plan	Up to 25% but not to exceed 5 million rubles
For innovations specified in the ministry plan	Up to 20% but not to exceed 3 million rubles
For innovations of only enterprise-level importance	Up to 10% but not to exceed 1.5 million rubles

The proposal marked a number of breaks with tradition. First, it introduced the principle that a bonus should be paid not only for the preliminary stage of design, production, and testing of the experimental model but for the entire process culminating in production and start-up. Second, the size of the reward was not simply a proportion of wage expenditure but depended on the productivity of the innovation as measured by the concept of "annual economic benefit" (to be discussed presently). The arrangement was therefore roughly equivalent to a profit-sharing plan. Third, and boldest of all, was the size of the reward, amounting to as much as 25 percent of the annual economic benefit up to a limit of 5 million rubles.[10] One may well imagine that bonuses of this size may have had an enormous impact on the manager considering the choice of introducing an innovation or continuing with the old established product or process. But the proposal was not accepted. "Unfortunately," writes the author, "this valuable piece of work was never fully put into practice; due to the objections of the financial organs, the draft of the statute was limited to the machinery industry."[11]

Ministries of Finance are notorious for their conservatism, and the Soviet Ministry of Finance is probably no exception. We are not told exactly what its objections were, but they probably concerned the very large sums that could be paid out to successful innovators. Such sums may have introduced serious problems of financial planning, by plowing large additional amounts of money into the pockets of the consuming public. And they may have introduced a considerable departure from the distribution of income that was held to be ideologically acceptable. Whatever the reasons, the proposal was never introduced in the form and to the extent intended. The bonus decree finally issued by the government in 1956 retained the principle that the size of the reward should be proportional to the productivity of the innovation. But the size of the reward was greatly diminished.

Economic Benefit and the Bonus Fund

The innovation bonus system introduced in 1956 was subsequently amended on a number of occasions, notably in 1964.[12] In its present form it consists of three elements: an Innovation Bonus Fund, a schedule relating the size of the bonus to the economic benefit, and a formula for calculating the size of the economic benefit.

Every enterprise adds to its cost of production an amount varying from 0.2 to 1.0 percent of its total wages. A certain percentage of that sum (25 to 50 percent) is deposited in a separate enterprise account known as the Innovation Bonus Fund.[13] The balance is transferred to the ministry and deposited in a similar ministry account. The moneys in the fund are used to pay bonuses for successful innovations. The enterprise's fund finances bonuses for small-scale measures included in the enterprise plan. The ministry fund finances the bonuses for innovations listed in the ministry and national plans. An important stipulation is that only innovations included in an official plan qualify for bonuses.

The precise percentage of total wages deposited in the fund varies by industry, to reflect the state's priorities. In the machinery and metalworking industries the amount is 1.0 percent, in building materials 0.5 percent, and in light industry 0.3 percent. By special arrangement, the sum is 4 to 8 percent in scientific-research and design organizations. The percentage of the total that may be retained by the enterprise is also differentiated by industry.

The fund thus limits the sum that may be paid out as innovation bonuses to a certain percentage of total wages. Within that limit, the amount paid out to an enterprise or team ("collective") credited with an innovation is calculated according to the following schedule:[14]

Annual Economic Benefit, Thousand Rubles	Collective Innovation Bonus, Percent of Annual Economic Benefit
Under 10	6-25, but not over 2,000 rubles
10-20	5-20, but not over 3,400 rubles
20-50	4-17, but not over 6,000 rubles
50-100	3-12, but not over 10,000 rubles
100-500	2-10, but not over 35,000 rubles
500-2,000	1-7, but not over 80,000 rubles
2,000-5,000	0.7-4, but not over 150,000 rubles
over 5,000	0.5-3, but not over 200,000 rubles

The annual economic benefit that determines the size of the bonus is calculated by means of a formula adapted from the general literature on investment choice.[15] The only economic benefit recognized in the formula is that due to the reduction in production costs. In the case of a process innovation, the benefit is measured directly by the formula:[16]

$$B = [(c_O + Ek_O) - (c_N + Ek_N)] A, \tag{15.1}$$

where

B is the annual economic benefit from replacing the older process by the new one.

k is the average value of the capital employed per unit of output of the given product.

c is the average current cost of production (*sebestoimost'*), including prime costs and depreciation.

Subscripts O and N refer to the older and newer processes, respectively.

E is standard rate of return, or discount rate, officially assigned to the industry.

A is the expected annual output of the given product, in physical units.

When the innovation is not a process but a new product like a machine or a material, the cost-reduction benefit may come from two sources. A new shoemaking machine, for example, may cost less to produce than an older model; and it may also reduce the cost of producing shoes relative to the cost when the older model was used. In the R & D stage an effort is made to evaluate the second source of benefit and to include it in the total expected benefit from the new shoemaking machine. But in the innovation stage the producer of the shoemaking machinery can receive a bonus from the Innovation Bonus Fund only if he has introduced a new process that reduces the cost of producing shoemaking machinery. A new model of a shoemaking machine, however, is not a process innovation but a product innovation and therefore does not qualify for a bonus from the Innovation Bonus Fund. Product innovations are rewarded in other ways. In productivity pricing, for example, the price of the new shoemaking machine will be high enough to enable the product innovator to capture some portion of the cost savings in shoe manufacturing in his profit, and therefore in his basic bonus. The shoe manufacturer, however, presumably can qualify for a bonus from the Innovation Bonus Fund if he introduces the new shoemaking machine into his manufacturing process and thereby reduces the cost of producing shoes.

The innovation bonus to which the enterprise is entitled under the schedule must be paid regardless of whether the output plan is fulfilled or not. The precise amount paid out for each innovation is set by negotiation, within the percentage limits specified in the schedule. The percentages are expressed in the form of a range, to give the authorities the opportunity to vary the size of the reward by such criteria as the importance of the innovation, the degree of technical originality, and so forth. When the size of the "collective innovation bonus"[17] is determined, the sum is distributed among the persons who participated in the innovation. The size of the individual bonuses is set in negotiations involving the trade union, enterprise management, and the ministry.

It should be noticed that the size of the collective innovation bonus has been greatly scaled down from that proposed by the State Committee on Science and Technology in 1955. For the largest innovations the State Committee proposed a bonus up to 25 percent of the annual economic benefit; the schedule now in force sets the percentage in the range of 0.5 to 3 percent. The proposed maximum of 5 million rubles has been reduced to 200,000 rubles. One can only speculate on the extent to which the rate of innovation might have been increased had the State Committee's proposal been adopted.

A profit-sharing arrangement could potentially provide huge incomes for innovators if the rewards were strictly proportional to the economic benefit. The innovation bonus is not designed to be open-ended in that sense. While the size of the rewards is roughly proportional to economic benefit, the incomes that may be earned from innovation are limited in four ways.

First, the size of the Innovation Bonus Fund is limited to a certain percentage of total wages. That limitation provides the Ministry of Finance with some assurance that, regardless of the innovativeness of an industry, total incomes earned will not exceed the planned amount. It is possible that an enterprise Innovation Bonus Fund might be exhausted at midyear by the bonuses paid out according to the schedule. For the balance of that year, no further bonuses could be paid out and successful innovations go unrewarded. This happens often enough to highly innovative enterprises to have become a source of concern; they discover that the bonuses to which they are entitled are not forthcoming or are paid in much smaller amounts, "which causes them to lose confidence."[18] It is for this reason that critics seek more "open-ended" bonus formulas.[19] Most enterprises, however, earn much less in innovation bonuses than is available in the funds. Hence of the total sum made available annually in the Innovation Bonus Funds, only one-third to one-half is actually disbursed to individuals in the course of the year.[20]

The second limitation is that the bonus is not available for all innovations but only for those listed in the annual New Technology Plan. The list of innovations eligible for bonuses from the ministry's Innovation Bonus Fund must be approved by a deputy minister at the same time the enterprise New Technology Plan is approved. The list of innovations eligible for bonuses from the enterprise's own Innovation Bonus Fund must also be approved, but by the head of the chief administration rather than by a top ministry official.[21] The sources are rather vague on the criteria used for determining eligibility. The innovations rewarded from the ministry's fund evidently consist of those regarded as "most important," like those "approaching the best models in the world, in terms of their characteristics." But those eligible for reward from the enterprise's fund may be more modest, including innovations introduced earlier in other enterprises.[22] It is clear that bonuses are limited to some portion of the total number of innovations introduced annually, but the size of that portion is not known.

The third limitation on the size of innovation bonuses is the schedule of bonus payments. The percentages of economic benefit decline sharply as the absolute size of the economic benefit increases. Hence the limit of 200,000 rubles for any single innovation is probably rarely earned.

These three limitations restrict the volume of innovation bonuses that may be paid out to all enterprises. They still allow, however, for the possibility of very large bonuses for some enterprises and for some innovative persons. One highly innovative enterprise, for example, could conceivably walk off with the entire ministry Innovation Bonus Fund, and if that sum were distributed fully among its most innovative personnel, the bonuses per person could be huge. The consequent inequality in income distribution would be quite unacceptable. Hence a fourth limit has been placed on the size of innovation bonus rewards. No person may receive in innovation bonuses in any year an amount in excess of one-half of his base salary in industries like chemicals and engineering, or of one-quarter of his salary in light industry and construction.[23] Since the decision to innovate is made by individuals, this limit on individual innovation bonuses is the most significant of the various limits.[24]

15.2. Other Special Incentives for Innovation

The Innovation Bonus is only one, although the major one, of the special monetary incentives for innovation. Before considering the others, it should be noted that the New Technology Plan itself may serve to some extent as an incentive for innovation, although of a nonmonetary kind.

The New Technology Plan is one of the main sections of the Enterprise Plan. Since plan fulfillment is the "law of the land" and the clear obligation of management, and since careers and promotions depend on the fulfillment of assigned plan tasks, the New Technology Plan is potentially a considerable incentive for innovation. Even if there were no special bonuses, management might be expected to exert some effort to meet the targets of that portion of the plan.

The chief problem is the difficulty of developing a satisfactory general measure of performance. The simplest indicator, which has in fact long been used, is the number of innovations completed. If the enterprise's New Technology Plan consists of 20 individual projects, 18 of which are completed, then the plan is regarded as 90 percent fulfilled. The consequences of such an indicator can be readily foretold. Since the individual measures vary greatly in complexity and scope, enterprises operate "on the principle of the easiest to fulfill."[25] All innovations are equal by this indicator, and there is no incentive to take on difficult assignments or to suggest them to the ministry. The problem was dramatized when it was decided in 1960 to use the New Technology Plan as a device for forcing greater managerial attention to innovation. That was done by a regulation forbidding the payment of the basic bonus if the New Technology Plan was not fulfilled. Among the consequences were, first, the increasing resistance by enterprises to the inclusion in their plans of projects that promised a large return but were risky, "for fear that in case of failure they would get neither their bonuses for the introduction of new technology nor the bonuses for regular production work."[26] Hence the proportion of slack in these plans rose, and the planned level of economic returns fell as enterprises negotiated themselves easier new-technology tasks.[27] Second, the scheduling of innovation projects increasingly followed the practice of "storming." In the 1961 National Economic Plan, 42 percent of the new-technology projects were scheduled for completion in the IV quarter, 27 percent in the third quarter, and only 5.7 percent in the I quarter.[28] By loading most of the innovation work on to the last quarter's plan, enterprises sought to assure that the innovation plans of the first three quarters would be fulfilled and the basic bonus earned, although the last quarter's bonus might have to be sacrificed.

The unfortunate regulation not only failed to promote innovation but distorted innovation planning as well. It was therefore dropped in 1964, and fulfillment of the New Technology Plan is not now a condition for either the general Bonus Fund or the Innovation Bonus Fund.[29] It is still, however, part of the enterprise plan, and management is held to account for it. Those concerned with the planning of technological progress continue to search for some measure of fulfillment that is superior to the simple "number of innovation measures completed." The chief alternative is a measure of economic benefit. For a decade it has been continually urged that all innovations in the plan should be accompanied by a calculation of the expected economic benefit.[30] That is an extremely time-consuming operation, however, and it has proved impossible to implement. Hence we read that "the fundamental indicator used in the reporting of technological development is still the report of the number of measures of new technology introduced."[31] With so crude a measure, little of the potential incentive effect of the New Technology Plan can be realized.

Innovation Start-up Bonuses

The Innovation Bonus is available only to the team—or "collective"—responsible for the development, design, testing, and installation of the facilities associated with an innovation.[32] Once the facilities are installed, the responsibility for the next stage of production start-up falls upon the production personnel. The start-up stage does not qualify for the collective innovation bonus. It is at this stage, however, that the major interruptions of the rhythm of production occur and where the largest losses of basic bonuses may be suffered because of the innovation. The general incentive structure motivates shop personnel to concentrate on the basic output and to regard the completion of start-up operations as of distinctly secondary importance. This disincentive effect of the general incentive structure is one of the causes of the long lead times in innovation.

To compensate for the heavy burden placed on production-shop personnel, a special incentive for start-up has been introduced. The size of the bonus depends on the degree to which the rated capacity of the new product or process has been attained. For example, the schedule for the iron and steel industry is[33]

Percentage of Rated Capacity Attained	Bonus for Each Percentage of Rated Capacity, as a Percentage of the Monthly Wage Fund of Those Currently Engaged in the Start-up Process.
61-80	1-2.5
81-90	2.5-5
91-100	5-8

The bonus does constitute an incentive for the production people to get on with the job of getting the rate of output up to capacity. The schedule provides no incentive to speed up the process, however, except in the sense that the more rapidly the rated capacity is attained the more quickly they are rewarded. But there is no loss of bonuses, only a delay in receiving them. To add an inducement for speed, there is an additional supplement of 15 percent of the wage for attaining the rated capacity ahead of the planned date or for exceeding the rated capacity. The bonuses are to be paid out of the ministry's New Products Fund (Sec. 6.4), in addition to any other subsidies from that fund to which the enterprise may be entitled. The total of the bonuses earned may not exceed 0.5 to 1.5% of the estimated cost of the installation.

Innovation Supplements to the General Bonus Fund

Both the Innovation Bonus and the Start-up Bonus are designed to off-set the reduction in the basic bonus that generally accompanies innovation. However, they fall short of that objective in two respects. First, they are available only to the personnel directly involved in the innovation and start-up processes. This presumably includes most top enterprise management and top management in the shops in which the innovations take place. But those managerial officials and workers who do not qualify for these special bonuses experience a loss because of the decline in general economic performance and the reduction in the basic bonuses. Innovating teams have therefore suffered from the lack of co-operation and, on occasion, from the hostility of other divisions of the enterprise. Second, the collective bonus is available only for innovations listed in the plan. Unplanned innovations are therefore discriminated against.

In the period of the prelude to the 1965 Economic Reform, the problem was recognized in the case of product innovations by the introduction of a special New Product Bonus Supplement (Sec. 14.4). It was set up, however, not as an independent bonus schedule—like the innovation bonus—but as a supplement tacked on to the general-incentive structure. The size of both the basic bonus and the enterprise fund was increased in proportion to the percentage of new products in the total output. Some compensation was therefore available even to those who did not share in the innovation bonuses.

The first manual of instructions on the Economic Reform retained the principle of a new-products supplement. It provided that the size of the Bonus Fund may be increased if the percentage of new products in total output was increased.[34] But for some unaccountable reason, the provision appears to have been dropped in subsequent manuals of instructions. Hence enterprises were deprived of bonus supplements for new products, a decision that came as something of a blow to them. The Moscow Compressor Plant "Borets," for example, bemoaned in print the loss of the 700,000 rubles they earned earlier on the basis of the percentage of new products in their total output.[35] The ministries retained the right to employ new-product supplements if they wished, but it ceased to be mandatory.

The weakening of the special-bonus provision for product innovation was widely criticized in the economics literature.[36] Eventually it was restored, but in somewhat altered form. The general-incentive structure introduced in the Ninth Five-Year Plan period provides that the size of the enterprise Bonus Fund is to be supplemented in proportion to the percentage of "highest-quality output" in the total.[37] Since most new products will presumably be classified as highest-quality by the ministry, it is in effect a new-products supplement. Soviet authorities in fact regard it as referring to the "relative proportion of new products in total output,"[38] although the official regulations refer only to "highest-quality" products,[39] and presumably include established products as well. In addition to this new-products supplement, the regulations also entitle the innovating enterprise to apply to the ministry for supplements to its Bonus Fund if it can show that the fund had declined because of innovation activity. These restored innovation supplements reduce some of the resistance to innovation by enterprise personnel generally, and particularly by those who do not qualify for the Innovation Bonus or the Start-up Bonus.

Other Innovation Bonuses

A variety of other forms of remuneration are available to enterprise personnel for activities associated with innovation.

Bonuses for inventions and improvements.[40] A long-established procedure provides for certain money rewards to persons credited with inventions and improvements. To qualify for an award, the originality of the measure and the priority of the inventor must be certified by a committee of experts, and the measure must be put into production. The size of the award depends on the annual economic benefit, according to Table 15.1.[41]

In the case of inventions, the award is based on the largest annual economic benefit in the first five years following its introduction. The award is paid by the first enterprise or ministry to adopt the measure. If the inventor is certified to be a group, rather than an individual, the award is distributed among its members. The program of awards is administered by the enterprise's Bureau of Innovations and Inventions, under general rules laid down by the USSR State Committee on Inventions and Discoveries.[42] In 1964 the average invention and improvement was credited with an economic benefit of about 650 rubles.[43] On the basis of the payments schedule, the average award was therefore in the neighborhood of 40 to 50 rubles.

These awards are in recognition of the creativity of the invention or

Table 15.1. Awards for Inventions and Improvements

Annual Economic Benefit, Rubles	Award, Percent of Annual Economic Benefit	
	Inventions	Improvements
Less than 100	25%, but not less than 20 rubles	13.75%, but not less than 10 rubles
100-500	10% + 10 rubles	7% + 10 rubles
500-1,000	12% + 25 rubles	5% + 20 rubles
1,000-5,000	10% + 45 rubles	2.75% + 45 rubles
5,000-10,000	6% + 250 rubles	2% + 85 rubles
10,000-25,000	5% + 350 rubles	1.75% + 110 rubles
25,000-50,000	4% + 600 rubles	1.25% + 235 rubles
50,000-100,000	3% + 1,100 rubles	1% + 360 rubles
over 100,000	2% + 2,100 rubles, but not over 20,000 rubles	0.5% + 860 rubles, but not over 5,000 rubles

improvement. They are independent of the Innovation Bonus that may later be paid to those credited with having put the invention or improvement into production.

Bonuses for assistance in introducing inventions and improvements. The process of development, testing, and introduction of an invention into operation requires the cooperation of many persons other than the inventor who receives the award for it. Not until 1963, however, was an effort made to provide a special monetary reward for eliciting that cooperation. It took the form of a new fund known as the Bonus Fund for Assisting in the Introduction of Inventions and Improvements.[44] The enterprise may deposit into that fund an amount equal to 35 percent of the sum paid out as awards to those credited with inventions and improvements introduced in its plant.

The fund is used to distribute bonuses to the people who gave assistance in carrying the invention or improvement into operation. The fund is permanent, in the sense that any balance unexpended by the end of the year may be carried over into the next year. The designation of the persons to receive the assistance bonuses and the size of the awards is worked out in consultations that include management, the Bureau of Inventions, and the trade union. The opinion of the inventors is given considerable weight. However, no person may receive a sum of assistance bonuses in any one quarter that is greater than 50 percent of his quarterly base salary.

A certified invention or improvement need not be listed in the enterprise New Technology Plan, particularly if it is of small proportions. If it is listed, however, it can then qualify for a regular Innovation Bonus. The regulations declare that a person may receive a bonus from either the Innovation Bonus Fund or the Bonus Fund for Assisting in the Introduction of Inventions and Improvements but not from both. As a further limit on the total volume of individual bonuses, no person may receive in any year more than 1,200 rubles from both funds.

Invention competition prizes. To stimulate public interest in inventions and improvements, there is a program of open contests for the best solutions to a technical problem described in the announcement. A highly publicized competition, for example, was one promoted by the chemical industry in 1959, for inventions and innovations in the field. A sum of 1.2 million rubles was allocated as prize money for the winners.[45] We do not know how extensive such competitions are, but we read that "in the enterprises of Moscow Province alone more than a thousand thematic contests are held for the best invention or improvement.[46]

The contests are normally conducted by enterprises but with the permission of the ministry. The funds for the awards generally come from appropriations from the State budget, but enterprises sometimes provide the stake out of their own funds. Contest winners receive monetary awards in the form of bonuses, but we do not know their size.

New-product export bonuses. "The prestige of our country demands that our exported products be of high quality and be delivered at the time agreed upon."[47] Accordingly, a special bonus system was established in 1964 for enterprises producing goods for export.

The bonus applies only to products included on a list issued jointly by the USSR Ministry of Foreign Trade and the USSR State Committee on Foreign Economic Relations. The list covers products that require particularly high standards of production and delivery, irrespective of whether they are new or not. It is very likely, however, that the list includes most new technological products that are exported, for this bonus is usually referred to in the context of rewards for innovation.

The bonus is paid out of another special enterprise fund. The enterprise adds to the price of the product delivered to the foreign trade organization an amount averaging 1 percent of the wholesale price for manufactured products and 0.2 percent for primary products.[48] The fund finances the bonuses paid to the enterprise personnel participating directly in the production and sale of the export product.

In enterprises producing equipment, machinery, and instruments, no official may earn in export bonuses in any quarter an amount in excess of one month's salary. In all other enterprises the maximum is three-quarters of a month's salary. This bonus may be received in addition to any other earned for another purpose.

While Soviet inventors receive certificates of invention rather than patents, the government takes out foreign patents to protect Soviet inventions abroad. It also sells licenses to foreign firms wishing to manufacture products patented by the Soviet government. A special bonus is available for Soviet personnel for the handling of the patenting and licensing arrangements.[49]

15.3. Decision Rules and Incentives

Most of the special innovation incentives are built around the measure of economic benefit. The formula for calculating economic benefit is one of a set of related formulas that are increasingly being employed in decisions when the benefits and costs extend over a period of time. They are used in choices among alternative investment projects, in pricing new products, and in the choice among alternative designs at various stages of research and development. The formulas serve fairly explicitly as rules of choice. The decision makers are supposed to apply the formulas to the various alternatives and to select the one that yields the largest value. The value to be maximized is usually the present value of a stream of future cost savings, discounted at some standard rate of return.

The decisions to which these rules apply have a broad impact on the rate and direction of technological progress and on the rate of economic growth. The quality of the decision rules has therefore occupied the attention of a large number of Soviet economists, and an extensive literature has developed analyzing the formulas in current use and proposing improvements. The evaluation of those rules also occupies a prominent place in Western research on the Soviet economy.

The subject is too vast to be treated here in any detail. Our discussion will deal briefly first with a few selected technical points that bear on the efficiency of the rules implied in the formulas.

The Calculation of Economic Benefit

The formulas currently used at all levels of economic decision making date from the publication in 1960 of a volume by the Academy of Sciences entitled, *Standard Manual for Determining the Economic Returns to Capital Investment and New Technology.*[50] Most ministries, research institutes, and design organizations now possess official manuals recommending or requiring the use of formulas adapted from the 1960 volume to the special conditions of the decisions they normally have to make.[51]

The great advance in the present-day rules over earlier practice is the incorporation of a charge for capital in the calculation of economic benefit.[52] Before the new formulas were employed, to the extent that cost reduction governed the choice among innovations, the operating rule directed management to choose the alternative that yielded the lowest current cost of production (including depreciation), regardless of the quantity of capital it required. The process of technological advance therefore absorbed a certain quantity of capital that could otherwise have been employed in other uses. The new formulas direct management to reject alternatives in which the reduction of current cost has been obtained by means of an excessive use of capital. The innovation process therefore now absorbs capital only to the extent that the capital generates larger benefits than it would yield in other uses.

The standard rate of return employed in the formulas varies by industry and ranges from 0.1 to 0.33.[53] When no standard rate has been assigned, the figure of 0.15 is to be used.[54] Hence the same set of alternative innovations would be ranked differently by the management of different enterprises. The lower rates of return are assigned to industries that are thought to merit special treatment because the returns to current investment are reaped in the very long run or because their rate of technological progress affects the rates of others. The critics point out, however, and the defenders concede, that there are other ways of attaining those goals that do not distort the choices among innovation alternatives, as differentiation of rates of return does.[55] The losses due to the differentiation of rates of return are small, however, compared to the benefits from the incorporation of the charge for capital in the decision-making process.

There are a number of respects, however, in which the rules lead to decisions that are less than optimal, three of which may serve as illustration.[56] The first is the effect of the deficiencies in the general price structure. Both the current and capital costs employed in Formulas 15.1 and 15.2 are based on the official prices of materials and machines. If one alternative uses a large amount of some material the price of which does not fully reflect its relative scarcity, the benefit to the economy from the choice of that alternative will be less than that calculated by the formula. A 1963 survey by the Central Statistical Administration found, for example, that in one-third of all cases in which a plastic part had been substituted for metal the effect was to raise rather than reduce production costs. At the same time the plastic product "was in short supply in uses in which it would have been possible to reduce costs sharply,"[57] In extreme cases efforts are made to compensate for the deficiencies of the price structure—by applying "coefficients of deficitness" to such products, for example.[58] While some egregious errors in choice may be avoided by such methods, they can hardly offset the pervasive effects of the imperfect price structure.

Second, the economic return depends on the scale of output of the new product or of the established product to be produced by the new process.[59] In applying the formula, under the conditions of central planning it is reasonable to charge decision makers to assume "that the rates of output of all goods are already determined by the plan balances, and the issue is only how to satisfy these requirements."[60] At the research and development stage, however, a certain amount of guesswork must be involved in predicting future planned rates of output of established products, and a great deal more in the case of new products that have not yet been put into production. Moreover, the optimal rate of output of any product should itself depend in part on the cost of producing it, while the unit cost depends reciprocally on the rate of output chosen.[61] It is therefore possible that the planners may select in the future a rate of output different from that assumed earlier when the innovation choice was made; had that rate of output been used in the formula serving as the decision rule, however, a different alternative may have been chosen. "Thus," we read, "in introducing automation processes, account is not always taken of the fact that they are economical only for large volumes of output, and most of all for mass production. Quite a few such miscalculations are made in designing engineering processes."[62]

The problem of scale is complicated by the fact that while the R & D people are concerned only with total output, the ministry must decide how the total output is to be distributed among its producing enterprises. The ministries are exhorted by economic theorists to distribute output targets in such a manner as to capture the economies of scale.[63] Given all the pressures on the ministry, however, that result is not often attained, and many enterprises operate some of their equipment at output levels well below the optimal. Hence a new piece of automatic equipment may show a very large annual economic benefit as calculated by means of Formula 15.2, but the benefit may be due not to a genuine technological advance but to the economy of the scale of output assumed in the formula. If the existing equipment were operated on the scale assumed for the new one or redesigned for that scale, it might prove to be more productive than the innovation. Neither the R & D people nor the enterprise personnel have an interest in looking into cases where this may have occurred, but research economists have turned up instances. The newly designed SK-4 Grain Combine replaced the smaller SK-3 because the formula showed it to be more productive. It was later demonstrated, however, that if the total volume of field work planned for the large SK-4's were attained by producing a larger number of the smaller SK-3's instead, the unit cost of producing the SK-3 would have declined by a third. Hence the calculation uncorrected for scale exaggerated the social benefit of the innovation.[64]

Third, a well-designed decision rule should include all costs and benefits in the calculation. In principle one would expect the centrally planned economy to be fairly successful in this respect. There is ample evidence, however, that some costs and benefits are often missed, particularly costs. For example, the rate of return on the conversion of the Magnitogorsk Combine to natural gas was originally calculated as 77 percent (or a recoupment period of 1.3 years). But in the calculation no account was taken of the cost of construction of the main pipeline from Bukhara to the Urals and of the time required for its construction, which was more than three years.[65]

The oversight in this case was very likely due to the organizational structure; the cost of the pipeline was borne by an organizational unit external to the unit planning of the innovation. Efforts are under way to assure that innovations of that magnitude are made at a sufficiently high planning level that none of the costs would be regarded as external. Equally serious, however, are the problems of pure social costs, like those associated with the pollution of air, water, and land. Although the Soviets are to be credited with a number of successful efforts to incorporate social costs and benefits in resource policy, the sad conclusion drawn by Marshall Goldman, the principal student of the subject, is that "based on Soviet experience, there is no reason to believe that state ownership of the means of production will necessarily guarantee the elimination of environmental disruption."[66] It should also be noted that if external costs and benefits tend to be ignored at such high planning levels, the problem must surely be no less severe in enterprise-level decision making than it is in capitalist economies.

These problems, and many others, are widely discussed in the Soviet sources, and there is a lively search for solutions. The technical quality of the rules is likely to continue to improve, but in the practical world ideal rules are never likely to be found nor are they always desirable. Not the least of the reasons is that, as Academician Khatchaturov has wisely pointed out, "One must keep in mind that economic calculations are usually carried out by rank-and-file designers and planning officials, who must be given simple and clear instructions."[67] One has the impression that in capitalist economies the calculations that actually underly innovation decisions are also rather imprecise, however refined the analytic treatises on the subject. In their study of British industry, Carter and Williams found that of 100 firms engaged in real development work, 13 used an explicit financial criterion of about 20 to 33.5 percent per annum. Another 10 used a "turnover concept"—that is, the price increase should be enough to enable them to write off the equipment in "an appropriate number of years." Others used a "big savings" notion, without being very specific. Firms tended to stress that "commercial acumen" cannot be set down in rules, but there had usually been some prior estimates of returns.[68] It all creates a nagging suspicion that in evaluating the rules of choice in any economy, technical problems like the three noted here may be less significant than the motives of the people who use the rules.

Rules and Incentives

If decision makers are genuinely motivated to choose the best solution, they will generally not do too badly. The point is made in the anecdote of the illiterate small businessman who had made a fortune by methods that could not be fathomed by the Business School graduates who studied his firm. When asked the secret of his success, he replied, "I try not to be grasping. If I buy something for one dollar, I sell it for two dollars. One percent profit should be enough for anyone."

Like the businessman, the rank-and-file Soviet managerial official could make rather good decisions even with imperfect rules and imaginative arithmetic, if the motivation were strong enough. The peculiarity of the Soviet incentive structure is that the official rules are looked upon not as ways of achieving a goal but as obstacles to be overcome in achieving a goal. Or otherwise put, the operating rules derived from the incentive structure differ from the formal rules implied in the economic-benefit formulas. Four illustrations will serve.

First, most formulas require that the economic benefit of an innovation be measured not absolutely but relative to some established product or process it is designed to replace. The problem this requirement generates is the same as that which arises in analogue pricing (Sec. 11.4). The innovation decision depends crucially on the product or process chosen by the decision maker as the base or analogue. The manuals direct that of all the established products or processes, one should select as the analogue that which has the highest technological and economic characteristics. However, writes a prominent Soviet critic, "experience shows that the selection of the base models by such principles creates the possibility of demonstrating an economic benefit from any variants at all of a process or a machine, including those known to be uneconomic."[69] One may cite as an instance a project for a new hydrolysis plant, the parameters of which were shown by the designers to be superior to those of the existing Belsk plant by 30 to 40 percent. A review of the calculations showed, however, that by all reasonable absolute measures of performance the proposed new plant was grossly inefficient, though less so than the existing Belsk plant.[70] When an innovation is of such poor design that it cannot be shown to be superior to any existing model, there is still a way out. "To increase the economic benefit [of the innovation], technological processes are often designed using such expensive specialized equipment that they could not stand comparison with even the existing processes."[71] The innovation can then be shown to yield a large economic benefit relative to the new process deliberately designed to be uneconomic.

Second, the innovation bonus schedule is a sliding scale, in which the percentage of the economic benefit paid out as a bonus declines as the absolute size of the economic benefit increases. Hence, "for one innovation with an annual economic benefit of 2 million rubles the maximum bonus is 80,000 rubles; but for 20 innovations with an economic benefit of 100,000 rubles each, the maximum of bonuses is 200,000 rubles, or 2.5 times as large . . ."[72] The operating rule derived from this kind of schedule is that in choosing between two innovation programs with the same total economic benefit, the one with the larger number of small measures is to be preferred. Given the high responsiveness of Soviet managers to the terms in which alternatives are offered it is not surprising to read that choices are indeed made with this rule in mind. In addition to the anecdotal evidence, there happens in this case to be statistical evidence as well. It was found that in the Byelorussian Republic between 1965 and 1969 "the average size of the economic benefit per innovation had a tendency to decline." Of all innovations in the range of 10,000 to 20,000 rubles of economic benefit, the average benefit per innovation declined from 16,540 rubles to 14,150 rubles.[73] A similar decline occurred at all other economic-benefit levels. To the extent that the decline is due to the peculiarities of the bonus schedule, with no other economic justification, the consequence is a decline in the quality of innovation activity.[74] In the same vein, the republics' enterprises responded enthusiastically to the exhortation for increased innovativeness that accompanied the Economic Reform. "In the Byelorussian Republic the number of measures of new technology introduced in 1969 was over twice the number introduced in 1965 . . ."[75] The Byelorussian people are undoubtedly highly innovative, but one is entitled to be somewhat skeptical about the capacity of any society to double its rate of innovation in five years. If "numbers of innovations" is to count as a measure of performance, one can be sure that the appropriate numbers will be forthcoming.

Third, the size of the new-products supplement to the Bonus Fund depends on the number of products that are classified as "new" and listed in the enterprise's New Technology Plan. But "after a new model of some product or other has been created and the first production runs have been made, it is withdrawn from the new technology plan [presumably by the ministry. JB] and thereafter it is counted as part of the regular production plan." The operating rule derived from this feature of the incentive structure is not difficult to guess. Management either drops the product from production if it can or restricts the quantity produced. Hence, "the bonus system provides no incentive to expand the mass production of new products."[76] Perhaps this is one reason that the new Bonus Fund regulations have converted from a "new-product" to a "highest-quality" supplement. If a new product has been removed from the New Technology Plan but continues to be classified as highest quality, it will now continue to contribute to the Bonus Fund. Judging from past experience, however, the problems of controlling the classification process are not very different. "The concepts of newness, of the originality of new materials, of changes in technology and so forth, are defined very imprecisely in the administrative documents. Careless executives take advantage of this, and try to classify all their newly produced goods as of highest quality."[77] The difficulty of control may serve a positive function in this case, however. To the extent that managers succeed in getting their recently introduced products classified as of highest quality, there will be less motivation to drop them from production or curtail their rates of output.

Fourth, the size of the Innovation Bonus Fund, like that of the general Bonus Fund, is proportional to total wages. In both cases, however, that feature of the incentive structure generates a rule that discourages enterprises from choices that reduce wages. "The more innovative the enterprise, the larger the number of workers released from production. Total wages therefore decline and so does size of the bonuses for technological progress."[78] The consequence is a bias against labor-saving innovation, or at the least against the removal of displaced labor from the enterprise payroll.[79]

The incentive problem was judged serious enough in the case of the general Bonus Fund to have led to the addition of labor productivity to the set of Bonus Fund indicators.[80] In the case of the Innovation Bonus Fund, most of the pressure is to substitute profit for wages as the determinant of the size of the fund, and to finance the fund from profit rather than as a charge against cost of production.[81] The electrical products industry is already experimenting with that practice.[82] Again, a profit-based fund would be more neutral in its influence on the innovation decision than a wage-based fund. But profit could conceivably grow virtually without limit in an innovative enterprise, and so therefore might the innovation bonus. Such "open-ended" plans will surely not be greeted warmly by the gentlemen in the Ministry of Finance. The current structure of incentives, both general and specific, reflects the victory of those who have urged the necessity of strong monetary incentives for innovation. But there is an equal and opposite view, also widely held, that the size of those incentives must be strictly limited. The limits on innovation rewards are of crucial significance in the effects of the incentive structure on the innovation decision.

Notes

1. The distinction between general and special incentives is now drawn by Soviet writers. See *Planovoe khoziaistvo*, 1972, No. 11, p. 66.
2. For illustrations of various special incentives, see *Planovoe khoziaistvo*, 1967, No. 10, p. 94, and *Voprosy ekonomiki*, 1968, No. 6, pp. 21-24.
3. G. D. Anisimov and I. A. Vakhlamov, eds., *Material'noe stimulirovanie vnedreniia novoi tekhniki-spravochnik* (Handbook of Material Incentives for Innovation) (Moscow: *Ekonomika*, 1966), p. 19.

4. For a general discussion of certificates of invention, see S. Pisar, *Commerce and Coexistence* (McGraw-Hill: New York, 1970), pp. 325-328.

5. G. D. Anisimov, *Printsip material'noi zainteresovannosti v razvitii novoi tekhniki* (The Principle of Material Incentives in the Development of New Technology) (Moscow: *Ekonomizdat*, 1962), p. 42.

6. See E. Zaleski, J. P. Kozlowski, H. Wienert, R. W. Davies, M. J. Berry, and R. Amman, *Science Policy in the U.S.S.R.* (Paris: OECD, 1969), pp. 474-476.

7. Anisimov, *Printsip*, pp. 53-56.

8. Sec. 11.1.

9. Anisimov, *Printsip*, pp. 58-60.

10. Although 30 percent of the total bonus was to go to the ministry, the balance to be distributed among enterprise personnel could still be very large.

11. Anisimov, *Printsip*, p. 60.

12. Anisimov and Vakhlamov, *Material'noe stimulirovanie*, pp. 100-114. It is also discussed in Zaleski et al., *Science Policy*, pp. 483-485.

13. The full name is the Bonus Fund for the Creation and Introduction of New Technology (*Fond dlia premirovaniia za sozdanie i vnedrenie novoi tekhniki*).

14. *Planovoe khoziaistvo*, 1972, No. 11, p. 67.

15. For a technical discussion of the investment-choice problem, see A. Bergson, *The Economics of Soviet Planning* (New Haven: Yale University Press, 1964), Chap. 11.

16. The formula is adapted from Zaleski et al., *Science Policy*, p. 459.

17. The term "collective bonus" is often used to refer to the total bonus paid to the "collective" or team responsible for the innovation. It is to be distinguished from the individual bonuses distributed to the members of the team.

18. L. M. Gatovskii, A. V. Bachurin, S. P. Pervushin, B. M. Sukharevskii, and G. D. Anisimov, eds., *Plan, khozraschet, stimuly* (The Plan, Accountability, and Incentives) (Moscow: *Ekonomika*, 1966), p. 320; also *Planovoe khoziaistvo*, 1966, No. 6, p. 18.

19. See Gatovskii et al., *Plan*, p. 321, and *Ekonomicheskaia gazeta*, 1966, No. 2, p. 34, for examples.

20. Zaleski et al., *Science Policy*, p. 485.

21. Anisimov and Vakhlamov, *Material'noe stimulirovanie*, p. 29.

22. Ibid., p. 24.

23. Ibid., p. 111.

24. Further limits on individual bonuses are discussed in the next chapter.

25. *Planovoe khoziaistvo*, 1966, No. 11, p. 32.

26. Gatovskii et al., *Plan*, p. 314.

27. The evidence is of the following kind. In Azerbaidzhan in 1960 the New Technology Plan was fulfilled only 68.1 percent, and the economic benefits of the planned tasks totaled 21 million rubles. In 1962, however, the "number of measures" included in the Republic plan increased by 20 percent, and the plan was fulfilled 83.9 percent. But the economic benefits of this "increased" plan were estimated at only 10 million rubles. Similar results were found in various branches of industry. Gatovskii et al., ibid., p. 314.

28. Anisimov, *Printsip*, p. 97.

29. V. S. Sominskii, *Ekonomika novykh proizvodstv* (The Economics of New Production) (Moscow: *Ekonomika*, 1965), p. 206.

30. See for example, Gatovskii et al., *Plan*, p. 238; *Planovoe khoziaistvo*, 1966, No. 11, p. 32.

31. *Voprosy ekonomiki*, 1972, No. 1, p. 71.

32. A minor qualification is that up to 10 percent of the innovation bonus may be paid to people who did not take part directly but who "actively influenced" the process. Sominskii, *Ekonomika*, pp. 205-206.

33. *Ekonomicheskaia gazeta*, 1967, No. 47, p. 17.

34. Anisimov and Vakhlamov, *Material'noe stimulirovanie*, p. 95.

35. *Ekonomicheskaia gazeta*, 1967, No. 32, p. 12.

36. See, for example, *Planovoe khoziaistvo*, 1968, No. 6, p. 32; ibid., No. 8, p. 37.

37. See Sec. 14.5.

38. *Voprosy ekonomiki*, 1973, No. 10, p. 3.

39. *Ekonomicheskaia gazeta*, 1972, No. 23, p. 15.

40. The word "improvements" is a loose translation of the Russian *ratsionalizatorskie predlozhenii* (English cognate: "rationalization measures"). An improvement differs from an invention in the degree of originality. It is described as a "change" in a product or process rather than as a new product or process. See Anisimov and Vakhlamov, *Material'noe stimulirovanie*, p. 13.

41. Anisimov and Vakhlamov, *Material'noe stimulirovanie*, pp. 9, 14. This section is based primarily on this source.

42. See Sec. 2.1.

43. Anisimov and Vakhlamov, *Material'noe stimulirovanie*, p. 6.

44. Ibid., pp. 16-18. The Russian name is *Fond premirovaniia za sodeistvie vnedreniiu izobretenii i ratsionalizatorskie predlozhenii*. This fund is to be distinguished from the Innovation Bonus Fund, which is not tied directly to any certified invention. The fund discussed here is designed specifically to support the program of awards for inventions and improvements.

45. Anisimov, *Printsip*, pp. 102-103.

46. Anisimov and Vakhlamov, *Material'noe stimulirovanie*, pp. 18-19.

47. Ibid., pp. 41-43.

48. Subcontractors who qualify for the bonus add the charge to the price in billing the enterprise that ordered it from them.

49. Anisimov and Vakhlamov, *Material'noe stimulirovanie*, p. 18.

50. *Tipovaia metodika opredeleniia ekonomicheskoi effektivnosti kapital'nykh vlozhenii i novoi tekhniki.* See Bergson, *Economics of Soviet Planning*, pp. 252-255.

51. The manual in current use dates from a 1969 revision. *Voprosy ekonomiki*, 1974, No. 3, p. 27.

52. In Formulas 15.1 and 15.2 the capital charge is incorporated in parameters E and T.

53. *Planovoe khoziaistvo*, 1972, No. 11, p. 68.

54. Zaleski et al., *Science Policy*, p. 459.

55. *Voprosy ekonomiki*, 1967, No. 7, p. 48.

56. For a more extended evaluation of the economic-benefit formula as employed in R & D, see Zaleski et al., *Science Policy*, pp. 458-465.

57. *Voprosy ekonomiki*, 1966, No. 4, p. 30.

58. Bergson, *Economics of Soviet Planning*, p. 263.

59. In Formula 15.1, the scale of output is expressed in parameter A. In 15.2, the values of total cost C and total capital K depend on the assumed rate of output. The output level is therefore implicit rather than explicit, as in Formula 15.1.

60. *Voprosy ekonomiki*, 1967, No. 7, p. 42.

61. The problem of optimal scale is discussed in Bergson, *Economics of Soviet Planning*, pp. 242-243.

62. A. G. Kulikov, V. G. Lebedev, N. A. Razumov, and A. P. Cherednichenko, eds., *Ekonomicheskie problemy uskoreniia tekhnicheskogo progressa v promyshlennosti* (Economic Problems of Accelerating Technological Progress in Industry) (Moscow: *Mysl'*, 1964), p. 240.

63. Akademiia Nauk SSSR, *Planirovanie i ekonomiko-matematicheskie metody* (Planning and Mathematical-Economic Methods) (Essays in Honor of the Seventieth Birthday of V. S. Nemchinov) (Moscow: *Nauka*, 1964), p. 70. Academician Khatchaturov urges the ministries to shut down production lines that operate below rated capacity and concentrate the equipment in a few plants at which it will operate at full capacity.

64. A. M. Matlin, *Tekhnicheskii progress i tseny mashin* (Technological Progress and Machinery Prices) (Moscow: *Ekonomika*, 1966), p. 51.

65. Kulikov et al., *Ekonomicheskie problemy*, p. 190.

66. M. I. Goldman, *The Spoils of Progress: Environmental Pollution in the Soviet Union* (Cambridge: The MIT Press, 1972), p. 7.

67. *Voprosy ekonomiki*, 1967, No. 7, p. 45.

68. C. E. Carter and B. F. Williams, *Industry and Technical Progress* (London: Oxford University Press, 1957), pp. 82-83.

69. Matlin, *Tekhnicheskii progress*, p. 50.

70. *Voprosy ekonomiki*, 1967, No. 3, p. 30.

71. *Planovoe khoziaistvo*, 1966, No. 11, p. 30.

72. Ibid., 1969, No. 2, p. 5.

73. Ibid., 1972, No. 11, p. 68.

74. It should be noted that the bold 1955 proposal by the State Committee on Science and Technology provided that the bonus was to be a fixed percentage of the economic benefit (Sec. 15.1). A fixed percentage would be more neutral in choices among innovations than a sliding scale. But it would have permitted some very large bonuses, probably the reason that the Ministry of Finance vetoed it.

75. *Planovoe khoziaistvo*, 1972, No. 11, p. 68.

76. Ibid., 1969, No. 2, p. 7.

77. Gatovskii et al., *Plan*, pp. 198-199.

78. *Planovoe khoziaistvo*, 1972, No. 11, p. 70.

79. See Secs. 5.4 and 5.5. There are offsets to this bias, of course, in the general incentive structure; the Bonus Fund increases if costs are reduced and profit raised.

80. The new Bonus Fund regulations provide that if labor productivity rises, the size of the fund may be increased (Sec. 14.5). The regulation was introduced as an inducement to enterprises to reduce their labor force.

81. See Gatovskii et al., *Plan*, p. 321; *Ekonomicheskaia gazeta*, 1966, No. 2, pp. 31, 34.

82. *Planovoe khoziaistvo*, 1972, No. 11, pp. 70-71.

Chapter 16

Incentives and Innovation

The outcomes of economic activity depend not on the properties of each element of economic structure separately but upon their joint operation. The structure of organization, separately considered, may generate strong obstacles to innovation. But one may imagine an incentive structure so potent that managers would readily surmount the organizational obstacles and produce a high rate of innovation. Similarly the price structure may play havoc with the general performance record of the enterprise that innovates. But if the independent rewards for innovation were sufficiently large relative to those for general performance, management would ignore those price effects and throw itself into the task of innovation. However, the greater the obstacles to innovation contained in the organizational and price structure, the greater the burden on the incentive structure to promote the rate of innovation sought by the governors of the economic system.

The effectiveness of the incentive structure in promoting innovation depends on the size of the rewards for innovation relative to those for noninnovation. It depends also, however, on how well the incentive structure is administered. With these two questions we conclude the examination of the relationship between the incentive structure and the decision to innovate.

16.1. The Income of Management

Soviet industrial managers are among the highest-paid persons in the country. They are not the highest. It is interesting to note that the director of a major scientific research institute earns a salary that is 50 percent larger than that of the highest-paid industrial executive in the country.[1] The salary differential reflects the relative prestige of the two occupations in the USSR. If the objective is to accelerate technological innovation, one wonders whether the Soviets have got their priorities straight. Running a noisy factory and counting kopeks may not be as elevating an occupation as the search for new subatomic particles. And it is science that opens the pathways for modern technology to follow. It is not Minerva, however, but Vulcan who works the forge. It is a plausible speculation that the society that honors—and pays—its industrialists more than its scientists may achieve a higher rate of technological advance.

It is widely believed that the best young engineers and scientists in the USSR are more attracted to the research institutes than to the factories. Nevertheless the status and income of industrial managers are high enough to have attracted a corps of competent and hard-working men and women.[2] Managerial incomes are higher, relative to the rest of the population, than the egalitarian ethic of socialism might lead one to expect. In his close comparative study of management, David Granick measured the ratio of the money incomes of high-level industrial managers (the lowest earners within the top 1 percent) to the average income of all male manual workers. In the USSR, high-level management receives two to three times as much as the average worker, about the same as in Great Britain. In the United States the figure is three and a half times, and in France it is four to six times. If income taxes were excluded, the difference between the USSR and the capitalist countries would be further narrowed. These comparisons exclude stock options and deferred compensation, however; if they were included, the difference between the USSR and the others would be widened.[3]

The base salaries of Soviet managers are established by the ministries within limits set down by the State Committee on Labor and Wages. The rates differ by industry, by size of enterprise, and by managerial position. A sample of the salary rates that prevailed in the largest enterprises in various industries during the period 1955-1973 is presented in Table 16.1.[4]

In the smaller enterprises of each industry, the salary scales are lower.

Table 16.1. Representative Salary Rates in Various Industries

Industry	Director	Chief Engineer	Senior Engineer	Engineer	Technician
Coal Industry Coal and Slate Mines	400	380	–	115-140	110-135
Ferrous Metallurgy Ore Mining	300-350	270-320	–	–	110-130
Machinery Industry	300-330	260-300	105-135	95-120	70-80
Building Materials Industry	200-220	180-200	100-120	90-110	70-80
Food Industry	180-200	160-180	95-110	80-100	70-80

In the building materials industry, for example, the directors of the smallest enterprises earn about half the salary of the directors of the largest.[5] Most managerial officials receive in addition certain "personal supplements" that are added to his base salary to form the "personal salary." One such supplement is a longevity payment that is proportional to the official's years of service in the industry. In the mid-fifties the longevity supplement alone averaged about 10 percent of the base salary,[6] but its size is reported to have been reduced since then.[7] Since the bonuses appear to be calculated as a percentage of the personal salary, the supplements can augment earnings considerably.[8]

The salary is determined by the manager's position and the size of his enterprise and is not directly affected by the quality of performance. In the longer run, however, the successful managerial official may expect to be promoted within his plant or offered a higher-paying job in a larger enterprise. Salary differentiation must therefore have some influence on decisions regarding innovation. The direction of that influence is not clear, however. The successful implementing of a number of innovations surely increases the chances for personal advancement. A few grand failures, however, may be enough to end the prospect of a bright career. Moreover, the decline in the monthly measures of performance that accompany even innovations that are eventually successful tarnishes the official's reputation with the ministry. One has the impression that the ministry values most the tightly run enterprise that can be counted on to fulfill its plans regularly and does not come running repeatedly with excuses for some failure or other and with pleas for supplementary funds or materials.

Salary differentiation, however, is not designed to serve directly as the basis of decision making:

A system of base salaries, however well it defines the relative incomes of different groups of working people, does not capture all the special features of their relative contribution to the successful performance of the enterprise or shop. The payment of labor on the basis of the salary alone, independently of performance, would introduce elements of wage-leveling and would not promote an increase in the incentive value effect of earnings. Therefore the salary system is supplemented by a system of incentive payments to managerial, engineering, technical, and administrative personnel for increases in the technical and economic indicators of the performance of the enterprise and its subdivisions.[9]

It is the supplements to the salary, then, that are counted on to motivate those choices that affect the performance of the enterprise. The qualitative features of the system of bonus supplements were examined in the preceding chapters. Their quantitative dimensions are discussed now.

The Size of Bonuses

Policy regarding the share of bonuses in managerial income has gone through a number of wide fluctuations. In 1934, early in the industrialization drive, it amounted to only 4.2 percent. With the gathering assault on "equality mongering," it rose to 11 percent by 1940, and under the wartime pressures to elicit the maximum of effort it was permitted to rise to almost 33 percent in 1947. With the return to normalcy, it declined to 12 to 15 percent in the mid-fifties.[10] The years 1956 to 1960 were a period of general reform in the wage structure, one of the main objectives of which was to reduce income equality.[11] The share of bonuses in managerial income consequently dropped from 10.9 percent to a new low of 7.7 percent in 1961.[12]

That sharp deemphasis of bonuses is now regarded in retrospect by Soviet analysts as having been a great error. "It substantially reduced people's material incentives to improve the performance indicators."[13] As the prelude to the Economic Reform advanced, the share began to rise once more and reached 15.7 percent by 1965. Since the introduction of the Reform it has continued to rise, from 21.5 percent in 1966 to 34.5 percent in 1970.[14]

Since the bonus varies directly with performance, the larger the share of bonuses in total income, the greater the inequality of income among enterprises and persons. Hence the periods in which the commitment to equality was strong were years in which the share of bonuses declined. When the pressures for economic growth mounted, however, the commitment to equality diminished and the share of bonuses rose. The recent rise of that share to its highest level in Soviet history may therefore be taken as an index of the intensity of the current dedication to economic growth.

Bonuses are a stronger incentive in decision making today than ever before. It is therefore all the more important to examine the consequences that the total bonuses earned by management have on the decision to innovate. For the quantitative evidence we may look first at the distribution of all enterprise incentive funds expended in industry in 1971 (Table 16.2).

The tabulation reflects the dominant size of the general incentives, and particularly the role of the Bonus Fund, in the structure of incentives.

Table 16.2. Total Expenditures from All Enterprise General and Special Incentive Funds, 1971

	Millions of rubles	Percent
General Incentive Funds	9,568	85.6
Bonus Fund	4,143	37.0
Social Expenditures Fund	1,701	15.3
Production Development Fund	3,724	33.3
Special Incentive Funds	1,616	14.4
Enterprise Funds*	80	0.7
Consumer Goods Production from Waste and Scrap	294	2.6
Socialist Competition Prizes†	197	1.8
Overplan Profit Fund for Housing Construction	30	0.2
Innovation Bonus Fund	165	1.5
Local Industry Development Fund	204	1.8
Other Special Funds	646	5.8
TOTAL	11,184	100

Source: TsSU, *Narodnoe khoziaistvo SSSR 1922-1972gg.* (USSR National Economy 1922-1972), (Moscow: *Statistika*, 1972).

*Some enterprises had not yet changed over to the management system of the Economic Reform and continued to maintain an Enterprise Fund.

†These prizes are funded by the ministries, for competitions among enterprises. Prizes for intraenterprise competitions are paid out of the enterprise's Bonus Fund.

Payments from all special incentives amount to 16 percent of those from the general incentive funds. The Innovation Bonus Fund payments in particular amount to only 4 percent of those from the general Bonus Fund. The relative magnitudes strongly suggest that the primary consideration in decision making is the effect on the Bonus Fund. For the typical enterprise, it would require a very large increase in the Innovation Bonus Fund to compensate for a small decline in the general Bonus Fund.

Table 16.2 does not tell the full story, however. Some of the funds listed are used in whole or in part for purposes other than bonuses; for the construction of enterprise housing, or for production purposes. Nor is there a clue to the content of the "Other Special Funds" category, which is of substantial magnitude and probably includes various special innovation inventives. What we should like to know is the proportion of all bonuses earned that come from various sources. A partial tabulation from scattered data is presented in Table 16.3.

Bonuses and other supplements amount to 16.8 percent of the salaries of all employed; of those classified as "engineering and technical per-

Table 16.3. Bonuses as a Percentage of Salary*

	All Employed	Engineering and Technical Employees
All Bonuses and Awards of which:	**16.8**	**28.0**
Bonuses Charged to the Wage Bill†	8.4	2.7
Bonuses from the General Bonus Fund‡	6.8	20.7
All Other Bonuses of which: §	1.6	4.6
Innovation Bonus Fund	0.34	n.a.
Export Bonuses	0.27	n.a.
Socialist Competition Prizes	0.19	n.a.
Producing Consumer Goods from Wastes	0.13	n.a.
Economizing on Fuels	0.11	n.a.

Source: E. K. Vasil'ev and L. M. Chistiakova, *Effektivnost' oplaty upravlencheskogo truda v promyshlennosti* (Effectiveness of the Payment of Administrative Labor in Industry) (Moscow: *Ekonomika*, 1972), pp. 99, 124.

*The source gives the size of bonuses as percentages of total earnings. In this table they are presented as percentages of salary.

†These are primarily piece-rate bonuses, which are the major supplements earned by manual workers. They are charged against wage costs, unlike the other bonuses, most of which are paid out of special funds. Some personnel classified as engineering and technical employees evidently also receive such bonuses (2.7 percent of earning of all engineering and technical personnel).

‡Including the basic bonuses of nonmanual workers, as well as the end-of-year bonuses awarded from the general Bonus Fund to all personnel.

§The source reports the special bonuses as percentages of "all other bonuses" (p. 99). They are presented here as percentages of base salary.

sonnel, which includes all managerial officials as well as rank-and-file technicians, they amount to 28 percent. Bonuses from the Innovation Bonus Fund, however, are an extremely small supplement to the salaries of all employed (0.34 percent). However, most of the bonuses from that fund are paid to engineering and technical personnel, including management. Unfortunately no data are available on their share of the earnings of engineering and technical personnel. They cannot be very large, however, since "all other bonuses" amount to 4.6 percent of salaries.

We do not know the extent of the dispersion of bonuses around the average, either among enterprises or among subgroups of the large category, "engineering and technical personnel." Scattered data lead one to expect that the dispersion is quite large. One of the fullest of such records, that of the Rostov Agricultural Machinery Plant is presented in Table 16.4. The bonuses are presented as percentages, not of base salary as in Table 16.3 but of personal salary (base salary plus personal supplements).

The Rostov Plant was clearly a well-managed enterprise. In a year in which the bonuses of engineering and technical personnel amounted to 21.5 percent of salaries on the average,[15] the director and department heads of this enterprise supplemented their salaries by 40 to 60 percent. Moreover, it must have been a highly innovative enterprise. Innovation Fund bonuses were of roughly the same size as the basic bonuses. Bonuses for inventions and improvements were also of substantial magnitude. For all of the managerial officials these two sources of bonuses for innovation exceeded the size of the basic bonus. From the size of the export bonuses we may guess that a significant portion of the agricultural machinery produced by the enterprise was sold abroad. Since those bonuses are supposed to be paid only for exported products that are classified as "new" or as of "highest quality," some portion of them may also be derived from product innovation—perhaps half. About a third of the director's bonuses may therefore be credited to the innovation activity of the enterprise, amounting to a supplement of about 20 percent to his base salary.

It does not follow, however, that the net increase in the director's salary on account of innovation was 20 percent. The high degree of effort and resources committed to the new products and processes must have been at the expense of the other ongoing work of the enterprise. From all that has gone before we must expect that the general performance

Table 16.4. Managerial Bonuses in the Rostov Agricultural Machinery Plant, 1966 (Percentage of Salary)*

Position	Basic Bonus (from General Bonus Fund)	Innovation Fund Bonuses	Export Bonuses
Director	9.6	8.0	16.8
Chief Production Engineer	12.2	19.6	6.7
Chief Welding Engineer	14.0	12.8	6.1
Chief Metallurgist	13.7	17.9	5.6
Chief Designer	13.7	12.0	5.6
Chief Mechanical Engineer	13.2	12.0	5.0
Chief of Power Engineering	13.3	9.2	5.2
Head of Production Scheduling Department	12.8	17.8	11.1
Head of Planning Department	14.4	19.2	6.0
Head of Department of Scientific Work Organization	14.1	9.8	4.5

*Source: *Planovoe khoziaistvo*, 1968, No. 1, p. 18.
*The bonuses are percentages of the personal salary, that is, base salary plus personal supplements like longevity.
†Some of these may come from the enterprise's own funds, and some from the ministry's.
‡These are the bonuses discussed in Sec. 15.2.
§One gathers from the literature that the funds for personal assistance are rather like "welfare" or "relief" payments to people in temporary need of help. How these high paid officials managed to cut themselves into that pie is something of a mystery.

Spare-parts Bonus	Socialist Competition Prizes†	Bonuses for Inventions and Improvements‡	One-time Personal Assistance §	Total
7.1	11.0	6.7	3.6	62.8
6.1	6.1	8.4	3.2	62.3
5.9	4.0	4.9	2.1	49.8
5.0	5.0	3.3	–	50.5
4.5	4.7	3.3	7.0	50.8
3.9	3.7	2.2	2.2	41.2
4.3	4.7	2.4	2.1	41.2
6.9	4.3	2.5	–	55.4
6.7	5.1	5.3	5.8	62.5
4.2	4.3	0.8	4.0	41.7

indicators would have been higher had the decisions to innovate not been taken. The general Bonus Fund would therefore have been larger, and perhaps other special bonuses had to be forgone. One can only guess at the sum of other bonuses forgone because of innovation. Since this appears to be a well-managed enterprise, the returns to effort in ongoing production work would be high. The bonuses forgone may therefore have been as much as 5 to 10 percent of the salary. Under these assumptions, the net increase in the director's salary due to innovation was perhaps 10 to 15 percent.

That modest magnitude may be partly explained by the relatively small size of funds available for special innovation bonuses in industry. The Innovation Bonus Funds of all industry, as we have seen, amount to only about 4 percent of the general Bonus Fund (Table 16.2). On the average then, for each ruble of basic bonus, only 4 kopeks are earned from that fund. The incentive effect cannot be judged from the average, however, for many enterprises rarely innovate, and successful innovators may expect to earn much more than that. The Rostov plant, indeed, must be remarkably innovative, for its Innovation Fund bonuses matched those from the general Bonus Fund virtually ruble for ruble.

There is a second reason, however, that the net increase in earnings due to innovation is relatively modest, even for a highly innovative management. That is the practice of establishing upper limits on virtually every part of the incentive structure.

The Limits on Income

The incentive structure is designed to link income to performance. But that link operates only up to a certain level of income, beyond which no further income accrues for superior performance.

The earliest official instructions on the drafting of innovation incentives, issued in 1921, provided that the size of the bonus for each innovation was to be determined separately on the basis of a preestablished schedule. No upper limit was established on the size of any bonus.[16] That principle was not put into practice, however, and in subsequent legislation the general view was that the individual bonuses should not be permitted to increase without limit, even when the size of the bonus is to be proportional to economic benefit. The principal reason for this view is that an excessive increase in bonuses, relative to base salaries, "might undermine the role and significance of the base salary, which is the instrument of state regulation of levels and relative size of the earnings of engineering and technical personnel among sectors of the economy, occupations, and positions."[17] A second reason is certainly a concern with the equity of income distribution. Perhaps a third is the efficiency consideration. Beyond a certain level, additional income may cease to serve the economic purpose of eliciting additional effort. It may constitute merely an economic rent, enriching the recipient without providing additional economic benefit. Whatever the reasons, the appearance of unusually high personal incomes has been taken as evidence of a certain deficiency in the incentive structure, requiring a reform that would eliminate such "excesses"(*izlichestva*).[18]

In accordance with this view, all of the bonus regulations establish limits to the amounts that may be paid out under each of the incentive systems. The total size of the Innovation Bonus Fund, as we have seen, is limited to the enterprises' contributions of 0.2 to 1.0 percent of their total wages. Hence in a year of exceptional innovation performance, bonuses earned under the schedule may exceed the size of the fund, and the volume of bonuses paid out may be limited simply by the exhaustion of the fund. For each innovation, moreover, there are absolute upper limits to the bonus that may be earned by the innovating group, regardless of the economic benefit of the innovation. The general Bonus Fund, however, is not constrained by such a firm ceiling. In principle the size of the fund in any year can rise without limit as the bonus indicators rise. But a conditional constraint is the requirement that the volume of enterprise profit left, after the payment of the capital charges and other obligations, be at least as large as the size of the Bonus Fund to which the enterprise is entitled by the bonus formula. If it is not, then the fund can be no larger than the net profit earned.

All these various limits place ceilings on the total volume of bonuses that may be paid out in any year. However, they do not limit directly the volume of bonuses that may accrue to individuals. It would therefore still be possible for some individuals to earn exceedingly large incomes. The absolute limit on the bonus for any innovation is 200,000 rubles. If a small number of people were responsible for that innovation, their individual bonuses would be huge indeed. If at the same time the enterprise turned in an unusually high record of performance that year, they would collect large basic bonuses in addition, plus whatever special bonuses the enterprise earned.

To foreclose this last possibility of the earning of excessive incomes, a set of limits have been established on the volume of bonuses any person may receive. Since 1959, no individual may earn a basic bonus in excess of some specified percentage of his salary. In most industries, the figure is 40 percent, but in high-priority industries like coal, oil, metallurgy, and chemicals it is 60 percent.[19] The basic bonus of top management, however, is limited to the average percentage of salary earned by all engineering and technical personnel.[20] Since that average is generally below the maximum allowable 40 to 60 percent, the effective limit on top management's bonus is rather less than the maximum.

Originally, it was thought that individual earnings from the special incentives could be controlled by establishing limits on each of them. The Innovation Fund bonuses paid to any person is limited to 25 to 50 percent of the recipient's base salary, depending upon his position and his contribution to the innovation. An additional and more restrictive limit is that the sum of an individual's bonuses from that fund may not exceed 1,200 rubles a year.[21] Similar limits are placed on the export bonus and the other special bonuses. These limits on each of the special bonuses, however, could still build up to a very large sum if a person managed to collect the maximum on a large number of them. In the past, indeed, "many ministries and agencies exerted very weak control over the bonuses of managerial personnel, and there were cases of excesses in the award of bonuses. The bonuses management received from the Bonus Fund often amounted to less than they received from the special bonuses." The consequence was that management concentrated so heavily on the latter that it "weakened their incentive to improve the general indicators of the enterprise's performance."[22] To reverse that result, a blanket limit was set in 1970 on the sum of all special bonuses. "The bonuses of managerial officials from all special bonus regulations may not exceed an amount equal to four months' salary per year."[23] The ministries may extend this limit somewhat in the case of top management, for two types of special bonuses. The sum of innovation bonuses and national Socialist Competition Prizes may amount up to two months' salary per year, in addition to the four months allowed for all other special bonuses. The extension requires the special permission of the ministry and may be given only to directors, deputy directors, and chief engineers.

The establishment of limits on individual bonuses is designed to prevent the erosion of the base salary as an element of income and to maintain the basic bonus as the dominant consideration in decision making. The imposition of the limits, however, raises a serious question about the size of the rewards for innovation relative to those for non-innovation.

Relative Bonuses and the Innovation Decision

The director is not entirely free to select the program of innovative activity of his enterprise. The new products and processes flowing from the R & D institutes are eventually assigned to various enterprises and must be incorporated in their plans. The pressure for rising profit rates and lower costs obliges the enterprise to search for process innovations and to incorporate them at a rate sufficient to meet the targets.

Nevertheless the enterprise's rate of innovation can vary considerably in response to the incentive to innovate. If the incentive is weak, management can minimize the number of innovations the enterprise is ordered to undertake by the ministry. It can mobilize data to prove that it is not the best enterprise for that particular job, that the innovation does not fit its production profile or its capital-stock development plan, or that some other important assigned tasks will suffer. Moreover, even the innovation plans "handed down" by the ministry are "more often than not . . . born at the enterprise." By "slowing down the design bureau's work on long-range models and seeking to cut back their plans," managers can minimize the number of assigned innovation tasks.[24] They can reduce the budget of their Bureau of Inventions and Improvements, staff it with bureaucrats of minimal competence, and generally discourage its work. They can reduce costs by seeking the most riskless process innovations and improvements, preferably those pioneered by other enterprises and perfected elsewhere. Let us call this a noninnovative program of work.

At the other extreme, if the incentive to innovate is strong, management may not only accept the innovation tasks assigned by the ministry but may actively compete for them. They will moreover seek out and develop major new products and processes on their own initiative and introduce them into production at the maximal rate possible with their resources. The Bureau of Inventions and Improvements will receive large appropriations, and active encouragement will be given to the speedy application of the ideas developed there. This may be regarded as a highly innovative program of work.

Suppose a certain well-run enterprise is managed by a very competent director capable of adopting either a noninnovative or a highly innovative program. What we should like to know would be the relative rewards for adopting the one or the other. The orders of magnitude of various possible results are collected in Table 16.5.

Column A lists the outer limit on bonuses of all kinds. The maximum for the basic bonus (40 to 60 percent of salary) plus all special bonuses ("four months' salary") is 73 to 93 percent of salary. This is the normal maximum for all managerial officials. For those directors and other top-management officials whose limit is extended by two more months' salary by special order of the ministry, the maximum would be 90 to 110 percent of salary.

Column B lists the probable size of the bonuses of competent managers of a well-run enterprise that is not particularly innovative. The sum of the bonuses and prizes currently earned by the average managerial and engineering official amounts to about 40 to 50 percent of the base salary.[25] The more competent managers who earn more than the average may therefore supplement their salaries by perhaps 60 to 80 percent (line 4).[26] Their special bonuses (30 percent) may be close to the limits (33 percent), but none of it will consist of innovation bonuses. The basic bonus of 30 to 50 percent accounts for the rest. In the absence of exceptional innovation performance, top management will not be granted the two-months' extension (except possibly for a socialist competition prize).

If that management group adopted the highly innovative program, and if they lost none of the bonuses earned under the noninnovative program, their income may change in the manner depicted in column C. They may be entitled to large special innovation bonuses; but since the limit on all supplementary bonuses is 33 percent, they cannot in fact

Table 16.5. Managerial Bonuses for Innovative and Noninnovative Programs (Percentage of Base Salary)

	Limits	Noninno-vative Program	Innovative Program	
			No Loss of Other Bonuses	Probable Loss of Other Bonuses
	A	B	C	D
1. Basic Bonus	40-60	30-50	30-50	20-40
2. Special Bonuses for Noninnovative Tasks	}33	30	30	25
3. Special Bonuses for Innovation		–	3	5
4. Total	73-93	60-80	63-83	50-70
4. Extension for Some Top Management	17	–	17	10
6. Total	90-110	60-80	80-100	60-80

pick up more than an additional 3 percent. Hence the total rises only to 63 to 83 percent of salary. Top management's bonuses may rise to 80 to 100 percent, however, if they are granted the extension.

Normally, however, a high rate of innovation causes the noninnovation bonuses to decline. The basic bonus may decline to 20 to 40 percent, and the special noninnovation bonuses to 25 percent (column D). The decline of the latter makes it possible to receive a larger sum of special innovation bonuses (5 percent) and still keep within the 33-percent limit for all special bonuses. Hence the bonus for most managers will amount to 50 to 70 percent of salary. If top management receives the extension, it is not likely to be given year after year, nor is it likely to be fully utilized. Hence perhaps 10 percent is a reasonable addition. The total for top management may therefore be 60 to 80 percent of salary.

These rough orders of magnitude place the relative rewards for innovation in a new perspective. The schedule of bonuses from the Innovation Bonus Fund creates the impression of very large potential rewards for innovation, up to a limit of 200,000 rubles. The effect of the limits of individual bonuses, however, is to scale the actual rewards down sharply. The competent director who runs a tight enterprise, maintains labor discipline, concentrates on current production operations, and avoids all but the most modest innovations earns a rather handsome supplement of 60 to 80 percent of salary for himself and his staff (column B). If he took on the risks and burdens of a high rate of innovation and succeeded in walking off with the maximum of every possible bonus, his total would be one-third larger (column C). Under the more reasonable assumption that there is some disruption of current production operations, the innovative program provides an income (column D) that may be no larger or only slightly larger than the noninnovative program.

The incentive structure introduced during the Ninth Five-Year Plan may be interpreted as an effort to shift the relative rewards from those of column D to those of column C, that is, to prevent a decline in the basic bonus as a result of innovation. The measures employed are the quality supplement and the ministry's contribution to enterprises whose other bonus funds have declined because of innovation. We do not yet know whether those measures have succeeded. But even if they do, the orders of magnitude do not strike one as large. The question is whether an excellent manager who can earn the rewards of column B with virtually no innovation will be motivated to undertake an innovative program even for the rewards of column C.

Our guess is that the differential reward for innovation, relative to the reward for competent but noninnovative management, is too small to induce a high rate of innovation, and that the small differential is a major obstacle to innovation. Whatever effect the incentive changes in the Ninth Five-Year Plan have had, they appear not to have been large enough to have made a tangible difference. So, at least, does it appear to close Soviet observers. The case was strongly put by Mr. Z. Sirotkin, Chief Design Engineer of the Byelorussian Motor Vehicle Plant and USSR State Prize Laureate, writing in *Izvestiia* in 1974:[27]

Unfortunately the "mechanism" of the Economic Reform has proved insufficiently effective when applied to the question of putting new equipment into production. After all, for production workers, the manufacture of a new machine means, first of all, new concerns and difficulties. The work rhythm is disrupted, and many new problems appear. Under the existing situation, this causes the performance indicators to decline and the enterprise incentive funds grow smaller. It is for this reason that some plant executives brush aside innovations proposed by science.

... This is especially true if the plant has achieved a stable work rhythm and high-quality output and has all the benefits the Economic Reform provides; as for material incentives to induce changes, there are none.

In a time of general well-being the plant manager would have to be a very farseeing person indeed to feel any concern or anxiety and to undertake the preparatory work for producing a new model of the machine. For in the next few years that promises many difficulties.

If the new incentive structure has extended the time horizon of planning at all, it is still the short run, in Mr. Sirotkin's informed view, that prevails in managerial decisions. Within that time horizon, the well-managed stable enterprise expects its position to decline as a result of innovation.

Would management respond to an increase in the rewards to innovation relative to noninnovation? And if so, how large an increase would be required to attain some desired rate of innovation? Or in more technical terms, how elastic is innovative effort with respect to income? No one can presume to know the answers to these questions, and least of all the outside observer. The writer, however, once had occasion to ask the following question of a number of Soviet economists: "Suppose managers were permitted to earn a fixed percentage of the economic

benefit of their innovations, without limit, so that the successful innovator of several highly productive technological advances might even become a millionaire. Would such an incentive system substantially increase the rate of innovation?"

Most of my Soviet colleagues thought it would; some applauded the
idea with enthusiasm and others more cautiously. One perceptive chap
denied it, however. "You are thinking like a bourgeois," he chided,
"and you do not understand the circumstances of a socialist economy.
What would anyone do with so much money in our country? One can't
invest in the ownership of productive property, as in yours. And one
would soon run out of consumer goods to buy. Large incomes would
do no good at all."

Perhaps he is right. It is remarkable, however, that there is virtually no
discussion of this issue in the published sources.[28] Proposals to remove
or enlarge the limits on the size of various enterprise incentive funds are
made from time to time, but I have seen no proposal to remove the
limits on bonus earnings of individual persons. In recent years it has
become customary to pretest various proposals for reform by experimenting with them in selected enterprises. To my knowledge, no such
experiments have been conducted to see whether innovative effort
would increase in response to increased relative rewards for innovation,
and by how much.

The reasons for the public silence on the question must be largely
ideological. Some who have thought about it may have come to the
same conclusion as my Soviet colleague, that increased differential incomes would not greatly stimulate innovation. Those who may have a
different view would be somewhat reticent to advance it. After all, the
very use of monetary incentives still invokes ideological caution, let
alone the possibility of very large increases in their use. "One must not
lose sight of the fact that greater reliance on the method of material
incentives increases producers' interest in money incomes," one reads
from time to time in the pages of the journal of the State Planning
Committee. "The power of money grows, and on that ground there
may occur deviations from socialist principles of production."[29] Yet if
it should be decided to increase greatly the income possibilities from
innovation, an ideological justification could easily be found. The Soviet principle of income distribution is that rewards should be proportional to one's work or, more broadly, to one's social contribution. It
can readily be shown that the social contribution of innovation is very

large indeed, and it is therefore no violation of the principle to offer correspondingly large incomes to innovators. On the contrary, by that same principle the meager and sometimes negative rewards to innovators may be taken as evidence that innovators are "exploited" in Soviet society. For they alone among Soviet producers earn less than they have contributed.

If it should happen to be true that innovative effort is indeed highly elastic with respect to income, then the present incentive structure is very costly to the Soviet economy. Each year the economy is deprived of many innovations that would have been introduced in response to a modest increase in the relative incomes of innovators. If the elasticity is positive but small, those additional innovations could still be called forth, but it would take much larger relative incomes for innovators to bring them forth. The policy would still serve the governors' objective of promoting economic growth, however. For if it takes 1 million rubles of personal income to produce an innovation that yields an economic benefit of 5 million rubles, then the failure to offer that million deprives the economy of 4 million rubles of value that it could otherwise have had. If innovative effort is highly inelastic with respect to income, however, then the present incentive structure is not the obstacle to innovation that we have judged it to be. In that case, further reform in the relative rewards for innovation would contribute nothing to the promotion of innovation.

Changes in the incentive structure may be precluded as an instrument for promoting innovation, either because of ideological reasons or because innovative effort may be inelastic with respect to income. There are other instruments, however. For the rate of innovation is determined not only by the incentive structure but also by the organizational and price structures. Given the present incentive structure, if the organizational and price structures were purged of some of the obstacles to innovation examined earlier, the rate of innovation would rise. And if innovative effort is at all responsive to income, then suitable reforms in the organizational and price structures will reduce the size of the relative rewards required to generate some desired rate of innovation. Or loosely put, if innovators had fewer headaches in getting supplies and R & D services, and if prices were not so perverse, much more innovation would be forthcoming even with the present narrow differential in the rewards for innovation relative to noninnovation. Because of the political sensitivity of the subject, and perhaps some uncertainty about the elasticity of innovative effort with respect to income, it is likely that the thrust of future reform will be directed at the structures of organization and prices rather than at the structure of incentives.

16.2. Administration of Incentives

The effectiveness of an incentive structure depends not only on the relative size of the rewards for various activities. It depends also on the skill with which the incentive plans are administered. The question is of particular importance in a centrally planned economy like the Soviet because of the heavy component of administration in economic matters. Every economy, to be sure, even the most decentralized, reflects to some degree the effect of administrative decisions. But in the Soviet economy that degree is uncommonly large. Administrative decisions are made, of course, within the bounds of established rules and regulations, but the range of discretion is considerable. Hence the price of a product, as we have shown, is essentially whatever some administrative official has decided it should be. Similarly the size of the earnings of any manager is whatever some other administrator has decided it should be. Hence a crucial element in managerial success is the capacity to influence the process of administrative decision making.

Many of the issues of incentives administration are fairly general and are similar to those of price administration, which were discussed in detail in Chapter 13. They need therefore be noted only briefly here. There is one issue, however, that is peculiar to incentives administration. That is the distribution of incentive funds among enterprise personnel.

General Issues of Incentives Administration

The general incentive structure, we have seen, has grown increasingly complex since the initiation of the Economic Reform. Parallel to the general incentive structure, however, there are in addition the thirty-odd special incentive systems, each of which involves its own requirements of administration and control. Among the latter, the one we have examined most closely, the Innovation Bonus Fund, requires the application of fairly sophisticated techniques of calculating the present value of the costs and benefits of every eligible innovation submitted for a bonus.

Soviet analysts of price administration have published estimates of the volume of effort consumed by that activity, which are reported earlier (Sec. 13.1). We have found no corresponding estimate of the effort involved in administering the incentives system, but it must clearly be substantial. Under the best of circumstances, one must expect some portion of the work to be somewhat slipshod. In fact, much of it is done by people who are not equipped to handle the more complex calculations. For instance, the Ninth Five-Year Plan incentive regulations required every enterprise to plan its Bonus Fund on the basis of its principal performance indicators. The Almalysk Mining Combine's 1975 plan targets consisted of increases (over 1970) of 29 percent in sales revenue, 57 percent in profit, 36 percent in output per man, and a decrease of 6.2 percent in output per ruble of capital. In a stroke of bold simplification, the Combine's clerks computed the arithmetic average of the four percentages—29 percent—and determined that the 1975 Bonus Fund should be 29 percent larger than the 1970 Bonus Fund.[30]

The general Bonus Fund is relatively simple compared to the calculations involved in the Innovation Bonus Fund. The manuals for calculating economic benefit are written by economists, but there appear to be few people with training in economics among those who apply them. The proper calculation of economic benefit is perhaps most crucial in the R & D institutes. Those are the calculations used in choices among alternative product and process designs and in the decision to put a certain innovation into production and to assign it to an enterprise. We read, however, that there are no or very few economists employed in the institutes. When they are employed, their status is unclear, and they are often not consulted until the projects have been long in development and may have proved to be of low quality. The heads of institutes claim that if they could attract economists with high qualifications to work in their organizations they would expand the economic services in their organizations, "But such economists are not easy to find." Hence complex problems like optimal plant location are sometimes made "like a blind man poking around on a map."[31]

In enterprises, calculations of economic benefit are supposed to be made in advance of innovation decisions and they must be made in completing the documents that accompany applications for innovation bonuses. We read, however, that in many enterprises the work is turned over to the bookkeepers.[32] Some advanced enterprises have organized special bureaus of economic analysis within their technical departments for the specific purpose of carrying on the estimation of economic benefits and preparing the innovation plans, but in other enterprises that work is simply divided up among a number of different departments.[33] The Special Design Bureau of the Gomel' Agricultural Machinery Plant is the central organization of the country for the design of equipment used in mechanizing silage production. The bureau had only one economist on the staff of 150 engineers and technicians, and he had no specialized training.[34]

A number of consequences follow from the excessive demands that the complexity of the incentive structure places on the abilities of the people who must administer it. First, it is no surprise that the calculations of economic benefits are often badly made. The purpose and manner of discounting future costs and benefits are not widely understood and are sometimes simply ignored, even in calculations involving large capital investments.[35] Each ministry has its own manual to be used by its enterprises, and in some industries several manuals are used. In the automotive industry the seven different manuals in use recommend different methods. Hence a new machine that showed an economic benefit of 32 million rubles by one calculation showed a loss of 7 million rubles by another.[36] The effect of the complexity of the calculations is compounded by the self-interest of those who make the calculations in showing large benefits. Hence we read that the estimated benefits of innovations included in the state plan turn out later to have been too high by a third to a half.[37] In some cases innovation decisions are made without any prior calculation of economic benefit, and in others the calculations are made only after the work is far along.[38]

Second, the link between the economic benefit of an innovation and the bonus awarded to the innovation group is rather tenuous. One reason is a consequence of the sensible view that the innovating group ought to know in advance the size of the bonus they will receive when the work is completed. This view is incorporated in the administrative regulation that the economic benefit and the associated bonus of each innovation must be communicated to each group at the time the innovation is formally included in the enterprise plan. In order to carry out this regulation, however, the size of the bonus must be based not on the ex-post (*fakticheskii*) calculations of economic benefit realized but on the estimated (*raschetnyi*) benefit—calculated at the time the decision to innovate was taken—"which more often than not is higher than the ex-post calculation."[39] Hence cases sometimes occur in which bonuses are paid out for innovations, the actual benefit from which proves to be "nothing or extremely small. This means that state money has been spent for no purpose, with none of the results it should have brought."[40]

The link between economic benefit and the size of the bonus is further attenuated by the form of the bonus schedule. The schedule is expressed in the form of large intervals; for an annual economic benefit between 2 and 5 million rubles, the bonus may be anywhere between 0.7 and 4 percent of the benefit. Hence there is a large range of administrative discretion. In the Minsk Automotive Plant two innovations were awarded identical bonuses, although the calculated economic effect of one was twice the other.[41] The wide latitude provides a degree of flexibility that may be beneficial if judiciously used, but it also allows for "subjectivity and extraneous factors," to say nothing of influence and abuse. A substantial proportion of innovation bonuses—over a third—are paid without respect to economic benefit at all, primarily for theoretical design and research work for which direct economic benefit cannot be directly calculated. In those cases the bonus to the group is calculated simply as a percentage of the total wages spent in carrying out the work. "The trouble with this method of determining the size of bonuses is that people strive to prolong the duration of their work on new technology."[42]

Finally, because of the sheer volume of time and paperwork, it is inevitable that short cuts are taken on the one hand, and delays are encountered on the other. Despite the regulations, the required calculations are not always made in advance of the commencement of work, and the innovation groups "often do not know what they will receive for completing the task, and have little incentive to complete it within the established time."[43] When the work is completed, the documents for formalizing the bonus application must be filled out. The "Hammer and Sickle" Motor Plant in Kharkov innovated a new process for producing synthetic diamonds. The application for the innovation bonus consisted of 10 separate documents. In addition to the work involved in completing the documents, 24 signatures of approval were required from 13 officials of the enterprise and the local Economic Council. The bonus was awarded a year after the innovation work was completed.[44] The deputy director of a plant in Riga reports that only 20 percent of the bonuses are paid out within 2 months; the rest takes 10 to 11 months before the negotiations with the ministry are completed.[45] Since the pay slips record the sum of bonuses at the time they are paid rather than at the time they are earned, one does not know how much has been received for which innovation, and this year's bonuses reflect last year's innovation performance.[46] Nor do the pay slips always distinguish the innovation bonuses from the other supplements to the month's salary. Hence "at times it is hard to separate them out of the overall earnings, and people have the impression that it is all simply a supplement to wages."[47]

The administration of the incentives structure could be improved in two ways: by reducing its complexity, and by improving the technical skills of the administrators. Improvement from the second source comes automatically and steadily with the general year-to-year increase in levels of education and training. One ought not expect, however, any general reallocation of trained manpower from other activities into incentives administration, as is often called for by authorities whose special concern is incentives. Useful as it might be to improve the quality of incentives administration, trained people are still probably more productive in other uses.

Exhortations appear from time to time for the simplification of the incentive structure. The time has come, said the president of the USSR State Planning Committee, to abolish many of the special incentive systems and to incorporate their objectives into the general Bonus Fund.[48] The greater pressures, however, appear to favor an increase in the number of special incentives. The pressures grow out of efforts to repair all manner of perceived deficiencies by the device of establishing a new special bonus. One writer proposes a new bonus for an enterprise that delivers ahead of schedule special-order products destined for another enterprise that is introducing a new product or process.[49] Another wishes to offer a special bonus to enterprises that finance innovations by applying for bank loans rather than for state investment funds.[50] It is in such piecemeal manner that the present incentive structure grew to number over 30 special bonuses.[51] Moreover, in analyzing the Polish experience, where the number of special bonuses once reached a peak of 50, Dr. Zielinski observes that it is difficult to cancel bonuses once established because each one "represents the income of the management personnel."[52] Short of a radical review of incentive policy, it is difficult to foresee any significant administrative improvement through simplification of the incentive structure.

Personal Distribution of Bonuses

In the classical incentive structure the basic bonus of each official was determined by the schedule relating the size of the bonus to the percentage fulfillment of the enterprises' output target. The Enterprise Fund, however, was a "collective incentive," and some procedure had to be devised for determining how large a bonus each employee was to receive. The distribution was determined in consultations between management and the trade-union officials, with the broad objective of assigning bonuses in proportion to each person's contribution to the enterprise's performance. Those bonuses were so small, however, that the subject did not generate much interest.

The Innovation Bonus Fund was also set up as a collective incentive. The procedure employed was the same as that used for the Enterprise Fund, except that the ministry's approval was generally required, particularly for large bonuses and for the individual bonuses of top management. The question of what principles to employ in distributing the collective bonus among individuals now commanded more attention in the literature. But this bonus was also relatively small compared to the basic bonus and the issue did not generate heat.

The distribution question exploded into a major controversy, however, following the 1965 Economic Reform. The Reform transformed the basic bonus from an individual incentive to a collective incentive—the general Bonus Fund. The issue of who gets how much became a matter of internal enterprise administration which, moreover, now affected a major portion of individual incomes.

The dominant critique of distribution practices is that too large a share of the collective bonuses is paid out to higher-income personnel. In the case of the general Bonus Fund, the critique was leveled against the managerial and technical staff as a whole who were charged with having walked off with an undeservedly large share relative to that left for the workers. And top management in particular was charged with excessive feathering of their own nests. As an illustration of what is regarded as excessive, the deputy director of the Elektrosila Plant in Leningrad received four times the innovation bonus of the chief design engineer.[53] The chief accountant of the A. S. Popov Plant received 50 percent more in innovation bonuses than the technical people who headed up each of the innovation projects.[54]

To put an end to the annual controversy, the government issued a regulation in 1969 providing that thereafter the annual growth rate of the bonuses of the nonmanual staff may not exceed the growth rate of the Bonus Fund itself. The effect was to stabilize the relative shares of manual and nonmanual labor at the level prevailing in 1968.[55] Within the nonmanual group, however, top management continues to walk off with very large shares:[56]

In many enterprises the directors and their deputies, the chief specialists and the department heads receive bonuses not only from the general incentive system but also from the special incentives, while the engineering and technical staff and the workers as a rule receive bonuses from only one or two sources. Hence the size of the bonuses of managerial personnel significantly exceeds those paid to engineers, technicians, foremen, and workers.

A second line of criticism, however, is directed not at the inequality of bonus distribution practices but at excessive equality, particularly in the case of the Innovation Bonus Fund. As a rule, we read, innovation bonuses are distributed mechanically among shops and departments, usually simply by total wages but sometimes in proportion to number of employees;[57] in either case, with no relation to their contributions. The objective is "not to offend anyone."[58] Hence everybody who can be possibly regarded as having participated in or cooperated in the innovation receives some award. The result is a large number of small awards, amounting to as little as 3 to 5 rubles. In the R & D institutes, the bonuses are divided up among the staff with no reference at all to individual performance, to the point that "bonuses have lost any meaning and have become merely regular additions to the pay of the whole staff."[59]

The two lines of criticism are not necessarily contradictory. Enterprises evidently differ widely in their distribution practices and the degree of inequality may vary over a considerable range. It is also possible that within enterprises the most influential managerial and engineering group carry off a very large share, while the balance is distributed widely in small portions so as "not to offend anyone." In the absence of systematic data on bonus distributions throughout industry, it is impossible to tell.

Even if those data were available, however, they would be of little help in forming a judgment about the effectiveness with which the distribution of bonuses is administered. Soviet writings on the subject deal primarily with what may be called the "functional" distribution of innovation bonuses among the stages of the innovation chain. The regulations recommend that 30 to 50 percent of an innovation bonus be allocated to those responsible for the research and design stage, 20 to 35 percent to the preparatory work for production, and 25 to 40 percent for start-up.[60] But little research appears to be done on the personal distribution of rewards.

In corporate innovation generally, Soviet or capitalist, the design of an optimal incentive structure is extraordinarily difficult. If incentives and innovation were simply a matter of individual stimulus and response, it might not be in vain to seek the formula that would predict the rate of innovation to be expected from each incentive structure. But when the innovator is a group, of somewhat amorphous membership, one must determine in addition that portion of the result that may be imputed to each member of the group. Socialist and capitalist executives probably differ little in the wisdom of their judgment in these matters.

There are some distinctive features of the distribution problem in Soviet industry. All administrative authority operates under a single source of control centered in Moscow. While a certain range of variation is permitted in order to accommodate to local circumstances, central control imposes a greater degree of uniformity and constraint than is to be found in more decentralized economies. Second, in the socialist enterprise management operates in something of a fishbowl. The trade-union officials are involved in all bonus distribution matters, and labor's influence has a considerable weight that further limits the extent to which administrative opinion can prevail. Hence the boundaries within which administrative judgment on incentives distribution can be exercised are more restricted, from above and from below, in Soviet industry than elsewhere.

For this reason there may be some loss in the effectiveness of the incentive structure. In a general evaluation of incentives, however, the major problem is to be found not in distribution of the rewards for innovation but in the size of those rewards. An improved method of distributing innovation bonuses would do little to offset the towering consequences of an incentive structure that rewards competent but conservative management abundantly and offers little more for innovation.

Notes

1. M. Yanowitch, "The Soviet Income Revolution," *Slavic Review*, Vol. 22:4 (December 1963), p. 693.

2. J. Berliner, "Managerial Incentives and Decisionmaking: A Comparison of the United States and Soviet Union," in U.S. Joint Economic Committee, *Comparisons of the United States and Soviet Economies* (Washington: Government Printing Office, 1959), pp. 349-376.

3. D. Granick, *Managerial Comparisons of Four Developed Countries: France, Britain, United States, and Russia* (Cambridge: The MIT Press, 1972), pp. 258-264.

4. USSR State Committee on Labor and Wages, *Tarifnye stavki i dolzhnostnye oklady* (Wage Rates and Salaries) (Moscow, 1960), as reported in Andreas Tenson, "Wage and Salary Rates in the Production Sphere of the Soviet Economy," Radio Liberty Dispatch, June 15, 1973, pp. 11-12.

5. E. A. Lutokhina, *Oplata truda inzhinerno-tekhnicheskikh rabotnikov* (Earnings of Engineering and Technical Employees) (Moscow: *Ekonomika*, 1966), p. 40.

6. TsSU, *Promyshlennost' SSSR: statisticheskii sbornik* (USSR Industry: A Statistical Handbook) (Moscow: *Gosstatizdat*, 1957), p. 28.

7. E. K. Vasil'ev and L. M. Chistiakova, *Effektivnost' oplaty upravlencheskogo truda v promyshlennosti* (Effectiveness of the Payment of Administrative Labor in Industry) (Moscow: *Ekonomika*, 1972), p. 27.

8. The bonuses reported here are presented in the source as percentages of the personal salary.

9. Vasil'ev and Chistiakova, *Effektivnost' oplaty*, p. 81.

10. Granick, *Managerial Comparisons*, p. 278.

11. L. J. Kirsch, *Soviet Wages: Changes in Structure and Administration* (Cambridge: The MIT Press, 1972), Appendix B, pp. 180-184.

12. Vasil'ev and Chistiakova, *Effektivnost' oplaty*, p. 83.

13. Ibid.

14. Ibid., p. 87.

15. Ibid.

16. G. D. Anisimov, *Printsip material'noi zainteresovannosti v razvitii novoi tekhniki* (The Principle of Material Incentives in the Development of New Technology) (Moscow: *Ekonomizdat*, 1962), p. 37.

17. *Voprosy ekonomiki*, 1966, No. 6, p. 7; ibid., 1973, No. 10, p. 10.

18. Vasil'ev and Chistiakova, *Effektivnost' oplaty*, p. 100.

19. G. A. Egizarian and L. S. Kheifets, *Problemy material'nogo stimulirovaniia v promyshlennosti* (Problems of Material Incentives in Industry) (Moscow: *Ekonomika*, 1970), p. 144.

20. Vasil'ev and Chistiakova, *Effektivnost' oplaty*, p. 99.

21. Anisimov, *Printsip*, p. 93.

22. Vasil'ev and Chistiakova, *Effektivnost' oplaty*, p. 100.

23. Ibid., p. 100; *Finansy SSSR*, 1972, No. 4, p. 42.

24. *The Current Digest of the Soviet Press*, Vol. 36:12 (April 17, 1974), p. 9; from *Izvestiia*, March 23, 1974, p. 1.

25. In 1970, the bonuses of all engineering and technical personnel amounted to 34.5 percent of salary (Vasil'ev and Chistiakova, *Effektivnost' oplaty*, p. 87). The bonuses of managerial officials are above the average. Hence they may average 40 to 50 percent of salary.

26. The management of the Rostov Agricultural Machinery Plant earned 40 to 60 percent of salary in 1966 (Table 16.3). Between 1966 and 1970 the all-industry average for engineering and technical personnel rose from 21.5 percent to 34.5 percent (ibid.). If the Rostov people have kept pace with the average, they would have earned about 60 to 80 percent in 1970.

27. *Izvestiia*, March 23, 1974, p. 1. The translation is adapted from that in *The Current Digest of the Soviet Press*, Vol. 36:12 (April 17, 1974), p. 9.

28. For examples of oblique references to the issue of limits on incentives, see *Voprosy ekonomiki*, 1966, No. 8, p. 141 (remarks by B. M. Sukharevskii) and p. 146 (remarks by B. Rakitskii).

29. *Planovoe khoziaistvo*, 1968, No. 10, p. 38.

30. Ibid., 1973, No. 3, p. 65.

31. A. G. Kulikov, V. G. Lebedev, N. A. Razumov, and A. P. Cherednichenko, eds., *Ekonomicheskie problemy uskoreniia tekhnicheskogo progressa v promyshlennosti* (Economic Problems of Accelerating Technological Progress in Industry) (Moscow: *Mysl'*, 1964), pp. 241, 246-248.

32. G. D. Anisimov and I. A. Vakhlamov, *Material'noe stimulirovanie vnedreniia novoi tekhniki-spravochnik* (Handbook of Material Incentives for Innovation) (Moscow: *Ekonomika*, 1966), p. 33.

33. *Ekonomicheskaia gazeta*, 1967, No. 48, p. 20.

34. Ibid., 1963, No. 40, p. 12.

35. *Planovoe khoziaistvo*, 1969, No. 1, p. 33.

36. E. Zaleski, J. P. Kozlowski, H. Wienert, R. W. Davies, M. J. Berry, and R. Amman, *Science Policy in the USSR* (Paris: OECD, 1969), p. 461.

37. *Planovoe khoziaistvo*, 1968, No. 6, p. 35.

38. *Voprosy ekonomiki*, 1969, No. 4, p. 71.

39. *Planovoe khoziaistvo*, 1972, No. 11, p. 69.

40. *Voprosy ekonomiki*, 1967, No. 12, p. 12.

41. *Planovoe khoziaistvo*, 1972, No. 11, pp. 68-69.

42. L. M. Gatovskii, A. V. Bachurin, S. D. Pervushin, B. M. Sukharevskii, and G. D. Anisimov, eds. *Plan, khozraschet, stimuly* (The Plan, Accountability, and Incentives) (Moscow: *Ekonomika*, 1966), p. 316.

43. Anisimov and Vakhlamov, *Material'noe stimulirovanie*, p. 28.

44. *Planovoe khoziaistvo*, 1966, No. 11, p. 32; for other examples, see *Ekonomicheskaia gazeta*, 1967, No. 33, p. 11, and *Current Digest of the Soviet Press*, Vol. 21:48 (December 23, 1969), p. 30.

45. *Ekonomicheskaia gazeta*, 1968, No. 4, p. 10.

46. Anisimov and Vakhlamov, *Material'noe stimulirovanie*, p. 54.

47. *Planovoe khoziaistvo*, 1967, No. 8, p. 79.

48. Ibid., 1968, No. 7, p. 23.

49. Ibid., 1966, No. 10, p. 85.

50. Ibid., No. 1, p. 115.

51. Ibid., 1967, No. 7, p. 23.

52. J. G. Zielinski, *Economic Reforms in Polish Industry* (London: Oxford University Press, 1973), pp. 203-204.

53. Zaleski et al., *Science Policy*, pp. 484-485.

54. *Ekonomicheskaia gazeta*, 1968, No. 4, p. 10; see also Anisimov, *Printsip*, p. 64.

55. Kirsch, *Soviet Wages*, pp. 150-157.

56. Vasil'ev and Chistiakova, *Effektivnost' oplaty*, p. 131.

57. *Planovoe khoziaistvo*, 1966, No. 6, p. 17.

58. Ibid., 1967, No. 8, p. 79.

59. Zaleski et al., *Science Policy*, pp. 476-477.

60. *Planovoe khoziaistvo*, 1966, No. 6, p. 16; Anisimov, *Printsip*, pp. 62-65; Zaleski et al., *Science Policy*, p. 460.

Chapter 17

Strengths, Weaknesses, and Prospects

"We must create conditions," remarked Party Secretary Brezhnev, "that will compel enterprises to produce the latest types of output, literally to chase after scientific and technical novelties, and not to shy away from them as the devil shies away from incense."[1]

On the one hand are achievements like the celebrated exploits of space exploration. On the other are the enterprises that shy away from innovation like Mr. Brezhnev's devil. A concluding statement must account for both.

There is a large and intricate literature on the quantitative measurement of the rate of technological progress. The conclusion of the most authoritative of the quantitative comparative studies, those of Abram Bergson, is that technological progress has proceeded at a fairly modest rate in the USSR.[2] That conclusion is broadly consistent with the qualitative evidence on the innovative process in Soviet industry. There are potent forces for the promotion of technological progress, but they are blunted by the pervasive obstacles to innovation that inhere in the economic structure. This summary account will offer some general observations on the factors that promote innovation and those that inhibit it. The findings are summarized in a consideration of the balance of risks and reward that the economic structure presents to the manager contemplating an innovation. The discussion concludes with some reflections on the kinds of structural reforms that might serve to reduce the risks and raise the rewards for innovation.

17.1. The Sources of Innovation

The great Soviet resource for the promotion of innovation is the large corps of scientists and engineers. In 1965 about 400,000 young people graduated from all institutions of higher education.[3] The thrust of technology is reflected in the dominance of engineering institutes, which accounted for 40 percent of the total. About half of all the graduates of the universities took their degrees in the sciences and mathematics, and a quarter of all teachers' college graduates were in those departments.[4]

The cumulative effect of the heavy emphasis on these fields over the decades is the large body of technically trained personnel in the laboratories and factories. In 1965, 1.6 million members of the labor force were classified as engineers, a third of whom were employed in industrial enterprises. But for every engineer in industry, there was another employed in a scientific research establishment or an engineering design organization.[5] Of all persons who hold a Ph.D. degree (*kandidat*), one-quarter are engineers. Engineers are the second largest group of persons holding the senior Soviet degree of Doctor of Science.[6]

The supply of scientific and engineering personnel for innovation is amply supported by the supply of real resources. Between 1958 and 1972 the state budget expenditures for the financing of the entire national economy increased threefold. However, expenditures on science, including applied research and testing-design work, increased sixfold over that period.[7] The supply of resources is not unlimited, of course, and critics have identified several areas in which the promotion of innovation suffers from inadequate facilities, notably for testing and experimental work. Overall, however, the state has supported the commitment to technological progress with a substantial volume of human and material resources.

In addition to the supply of resources, a number of other factors account for the innovative successes of the economy.

Innovation by Order

One may question whether a centrally administered system of innovation can attain the results the Soviet leaders desire. But one cannot doubt that it serves to promote a significant amount of innovation. The research and design institutes are staffed by reasonably competent people who know the technology and to some extent the economics of their industries. They can draw upon their own inventiveness as well as upon the technological developments in other countries for the production of a stream of inventions and of improvements on existing technology. The technical personnel of the ministries are capable of screening the work produced in the institutes and selecting the most promising for implementation. The technical advisers of the central government, concentrated in the Academy of Sciences and State Committee on Science and Technology, are capable of evaluating the recommendations of the ministries and determining the order in which the stream of completed development work should be put into production. The centrally organized innovation plans are transmitted as orders to the enterprises that have been selected by the ministries to introduce the innovations, and they will eventually be introduced.

In the case of established enterprises, this kind of innovation by order encounters a certain amount of resistance as we have set forth earlier, but a substantial portion of new technology is incorporated into new enterprises the management of which has not yet been organized, and the innovation decisions are made prior to the new management coming into existence.[8] It has been forcefully argued that the quality of design and construction of new enterprises suffers when it is supervised by people who will not themselves be responsible for the plant's management. The remedy is to organize the future management group as soon as the decision to build the plant is made, so that they can participate in the decisions at the inception.[9] The managers of plants not yet in existence, however, have no current output targets to defend and are not subject to the anti-innovation pressures that managers of existing enterprises face. Hence the new technology incorporated into new enterprises does not depend on the initiative or cooperation of an invested management, nor does it encounter the resistance found in established enterprises. The proportion of all investment accounted for by new enterprises has declined since the early years of the industrialization drive, but it is still a substantial force for innovation.

Nor is resistance to innovation by order ubiquitous. All machinery and equipment eventually wear out, and even conservative managers may find it expedient to replace it with new technology, on occasion only because the original models are no longer in production but often because of its economic advantages. Moreover there are many circumstances in which management welcomes an order to introduce a particular innovation, for a great many reasons, including the sense of craftsmanship and entrepreneurship of capable men, the possibility that successful innovation may promote the careers of some of the enterprise management, and the system of incentives for innovation. Similar factors play a role in stimulating a certain amount of self-initiated innovation by enterprises. We have shown that the incentive system does encourage innovations of certain kinds, particularly cost-reducing innovations that involve a minimum of risk. The deficiencies in economic structure act to slow down the rate of innovation that might be attained with other structural properties, but a certain volume of innovation by order proceeds regularly from drawing board to adoption.

Priority

The forces promoting innovation vary from sector to sector, reflecting chiefly the priorities of the system's governors. In the sectors that enjoy the highest priority the structural obstacles to innovation are attenuated and higher rates of innovation may be expected. They obtain a larger share of the resources for innovation, their incentive systems are such as to attract the best people, they receive the larger share of the attention of the Party and of the various state agencies, so that innovation by order is more readily accomplished.

At the top of the priority list is military and space technology, in which the Soviets have scored some of their most spectacular successes. Soviet accomplishments in these fields are often alluded to in public discussion as evidence that allegations of endemic Soviet deficiencies in promoting innovation are ill founded, or that the problems are of minor proportions. But Soviet achievements in these fields provide no direct evidence of the innovative quality of the economic structure, for they have in effect been removed from the normal operation of the economic system.

It is useful to distinguish mission-oriented activity from economic activity. In mission-oriented activity the engineering task is defined by a set of technical objectives: to develop a plane with a given speed and payload within an assigned period of time, or to develop a space capsule component with specified reliability and weight characteristics within a given time. The cost of production plays a very minor role in the engineering problem, and within very broad limits the development group is provided with all the resources they declare to be necessary for accomplishing the mission. Their purchasing operations are removed from the normal channels of product distribution, and their scientific and technical personnel are perhaps among the best in the land. They can call on the technical advice of any persons in the research institutes and universities whom they may think useful.

Mission-oriented projects are probably managed in very similar ways in all modern industrial societies when they concern matters of national priority. Hence the relative attainments of nations are determined primarily by the quality of their best engineers and scientists. The best Soviet scientists and engineers are surely the equal of the best of other nations, and, when provided with the opportunity to work in a social context similar to those in other countries, one ought to expect that their achievements will rank with those of the best.

To a certain extent the quality of the society does affect their work; the natural experiment is muddied by the fact that "other things" are not fully equal. Soviet military and space designers and engineers are not able to draw upon their economy for components and materials that meet their requirements as fully as in other industrial nations.[10] They may not have the number and quality of computers available elsewhere or the metals or chemicals with the precise specifications required. The deficiencies may be remedied in part by the special production facilities available to them, which may be used to produce required items to special order. And the design of systems and components may have to be varied to fit the kind of technological support that the economy best provides; heavy booster rockets, for example, may compensate to some extent for deficiencies in miniaturization technique. By such methods the effect of a lesser degree of technical support from the economy is somewhat reduced, but it nevertheless must constitute something of a handicap to Soviet designers and engineers in their competition with those of other countries. But this is all by way of qualification. By and large, mission-oriented projects more or less hold "other things equal," and Soviet successes in space and military technology may be taken as evidence of the high quality of the nation's engineers and scientists.

Economic activity, in contrast to mission-oriented activity, is governed not by technical parameters but by social values.[11] The objective is to attain the maximum of value from a given set of resources, and the economic maximum is rarely equivalent to the technical maximum. The development of an automobile tire that lasts 100,000 miles may be a great technical feat, but if the cost is very high, it may have no economic usefulness at all. The standard by which we measure the goodness of an economic system is its success in valuing products and resources and in guiding the choice among production alternatives toward an optimum in terms of those values; in the structure of prices and decision rules, in other words. Moreover, mission-oriented projects are of small scale, compared with the problem of organizing the economic activity of an entire society. They are small enough so that they can be governed by "administration"; that is, they operate as single enterprises under a single project management. And however complex the tasks of administering a single enterprise however large, they are relatively simple compared to the design of a system for coordinating the activities of thousands of enterprises, that is, an economic system. Hence the problems of organizational structure that we have examined in this study, which are the problems of economic activity, do not arise in mission-oriented activity.

There is therefore no inconsistency in the fact that the Soviets can score great innovation successes in such mission-oriented activity as space and defense, while they face grave difficulties in promoting innovation in economic activity. The point is encapsulated in an incident that is alleged to have occurred at the time the Soviets introduced the first civilian jet aircraft, the TU-104. The story, which may be apocryphal, is that in celebration of the event, the Soviet authorities invited officials of airlines from all over the world to visit Moscow for a demonstration flight. Many other aircraft firms were, at the time, still working on their models but had not yet put them into production. After the flight, which was entirely successful, an official of a foreign aircraft firm was asked his opinion of the plane. "It's a magnificent aircraft," he replied. "I wish we could afford to fly a plane like that in our country." If the development task in other countries were defined by technical characteristics, rather than by such economic considerations as payload, cost of operation, and so forth, it would probably have been accomplished much earlier.

Mission orientation alone might produce a technically advanced product but, like the civilian aircraft, an economically inefficient one. In the case of military production, however, there is a second distinctive feature that imposes a keen cost-consciousness as well. Unlike civilian industry that is shielded from competition by the structure of the economy, the world outside imposes an inescapable element of competition in military production. Nancy Nimitz writes, "the Ministry of Defense has built-in motives for choosing new technology with care, because it does have to reckon with competition, and because its performance—if tested—will be measured by unavoidably real criteria."[12] And since the defense budget is unavoidably limited, the force of competition compels the military to economize—to seek the "more rubble for the ruble."

At the second level of priority are the sectors of modern technology: chemicals, electronics, and the engineering industries. Like military and space, they enjoy special incentives in the form of higher wage and salary rates, and they receive relatively large appropriations for research and development. They are also the subject of occasional "campaigns," in which special attention is lavished on them and special efforts devoted to their development. They are the sectors in which new innovation incentive schemes have generally been first tried out. For these reasons one would expect the rate of innovation to be higher here than in lower-priority industries. But unlike the military and space sectors, these industries are not withdrawn from the main course of economic activity. They are not mission-oriented but economic institutions, and they participate fully in the social intercourse of economic life. In the case of these industries the problems of economic structure operate as anywhere else, modified to some extent by their higher priority.

The benefits that high priority confers on some sectors is purchased at a cost, however, and that is the relative neglect of the low-priority sectors, which are primarily the area of consumer goods. Wages and salaries are lower, they receive smaller appropriations for research and development, and when unanticipated shortages arise these are the sectors that are expected to wait a bit longer. Since the relative priority of different sectors is a matter of state policy, one would err in judging the innovative capability of the Soviet economy from the performance of those sectors. Tourists and casual observers note the poor quality of Soviet consumer goods compared with what one finds in some other socialist and many other nonsocialist countries, and sometimes conclude too quickly that the Soviets cannot manage their technology very well. That conclusion is not warranted from that evidence. Since it is an area that is deemphasized as a matter of deliberate policy, the absence of innovation in that field may be taken rather as evidence of the success of the policy. Were it otherwise, one might judge the Soviet leaders to have lost control over their economy and to have permitted too large a volume of resources and effort to be deflected away from the fields that they judge to be more important. Hence in evaluating the capacity of the Soviet economy to generate innovation, one should consider their turbines and not their passenger automobiles. The fleetness of a nation should not be judged from the races in which it has chosen not to run.

One may wonder, however, whether the low priority of consumer-goods production may not have implications for the rate of innovation in the rest of the economy. It is conceivable that the insulation of a large sector of economic activity from the mainstream of technological progress may have retarding effects on that mainstream. The toleration of low standards of quality and design in a major sector of production may spill over into other sectors, to the extent that there is any movement of people among the sectors, as there surely is. If consumer-goods manufacture, particularly durables, could be an independent locus of innovative activity, some of its innovations and personnel could find their way into other sectors of the economy and generate technological advance there. And if innovators in the producers-goods fields could think of the consumer market as a potentially mass user of their innovations, the stimulus might be rather greater; for it is often the case that a new development finds uses, after it is introduced, that were not in the minds of the innovators, and which convert a possibly marginal innovation into a highly beneficial one. But this happens only when the consumer-goods industry is populated with persons who are on a perpetual search for new ideas and have a substantial personal interest in locating them and putting them to work. The subtle wall that insulates consumer-goods production from the kind of intense improvement mindedness and innovativeness that the Soviet leaders would like to see in other sectors may in these ways hold back the innovativeness of the rest of the economy in some measure. One can only conjecture, but it remains an interesting question whether a society can cut one of its largest sectors off from the major body of innovative effort without some loss in the innovativeness of the other sectors.

The Socialization of Knowledge

Soviet enterprises are all public organizations, and their technological attainments are open and available to all members of society, with the exception of course of information classified for military or political reasons. The public nature of technological knowledge contrasts with the commercial secrecy that is part of the tradition of private property in capitalist countries. Soviet enterprises are obliged not only to make their attainments available to other enterprises that may wish to employ them but also actively to disseminate to other enterprises knowledge gained from their own innovation experience. The State itself subsidizes and promotes the dissemination of technological knowledge through the massive publication services of the All-Union Institute for Scientific and Technical Information.

The socialization of knowledge is generally regarded as one of the strengths of the system in the promotion of technological advance. It probably serves to accelerate the diffusion of new technology. It may also contribute to the rate of growth of new knowledge, since there is no present knowledge that can be lawfully kept as the proprietary secret of some people and not made available to others. However, there are reasons to question whether the benefits are as great as are generally supposed.

For one thing, there are certain restrictions on the free flow of technological information in the USSR. The pervasive secrecy on matters involving defense and internal security has a broadly inhibiting effect on the dissemination of information, by both givers and receivers. Robert Campbell concluded from his study of "spillovers" from the space and military sector into general industry that "it seems to have been very difficult for the Russians to identify innovations in space and military programmes and bring them to the attention of an authority able to cut across the secrecy barrier and to get them transferred."[13] Barriers of that sort are quite understandable. But apart from strictly defense matters, in a world of extensive bureaucratic organization it is inevitable that "departmental jealousy, and what may be called subordinate secrecy (concealing one's true capacities from one's superiors) are practiced widely."[14]

On the other hand, information flows more freely in capitalist economies than is often supposed. One hears allegations that capitalist enterprises sometimes purchase patents for the purpose of preventing other firms from introducing them. But incidents of such suppression are not common, and there are few documented cases. Some innovations are no doubt held up for periods of time in order to maintain the capital position of enterprises. That would delay the rate of innovation, but it is not likely that major innovations could be permanently suppressed. Moreover, of the total quantity of technological information in the society only a small proportion can be kept secret, and then only for limited periods of time in most cases. The technological literature provides publicity to a very large range of technical information. And the exchange of information among scientific and technical personnel at meetings and in the course of professional work, as well as the movement of personnel among enterprises, leads to a fairly wide dissemination of all but the most precious information. It is part of the lore of R & D that the most valuable piece of information regarding a new development is the information that a certain result has been achieved. The knowledge that something has been done reduces greatly the cost to others of figuring out a way of doing the same thing. Knowledge of that kind cannot be kept secret for it becomes public when the product itself is first announced. That knowledge is sufficient to enable other firms to judge whether or not to invest in a license or to undertake their own R & D on the product.

Even when it is possible to maintain certain pieces of knowledge secret for some period of time, it is generally not economic to do. Information on new technology in rapidly advancing fields obsolesces quickly, and it is costly not to use it. Generally it is made available for sale, either by licensing arrangements or by direct purchase. Bell Laboratories, for example, pioneered the development of semiconductors between 1947 and 1952, and sold the knowledge in a rather original manner:

In 1952 Bell held a large meeting attended by about 50 companies and several representatives from each. Here they divulged to these companies their latest proprietary information on the fabrication and design of semiconductor materials and devices. All attendees had paid a $25,000 fee which was to be applied against future royalties on semiconductors. This was the time when many of the companies attending the meeting, as well as others who were not subsequently licensed, decided to get interested in semiconductor research, development, and production in real earnest, and it could well be said that the origin of the semiconductor industry derives from this meeting.[15]

Bell's knowledge-marketing technique was unique, but it does reflect what is probably the dominant view—that hot new technological knowledge is too valuable to be kept secret for very long. Cases of suppression must be regarded as the exception.

Finally, the proprietary nature of technological information may itself generate new knowledge. As noted earlier, Standard Oil (New Jersey) developed the fluid catalytic cracking process only because they decided to try to "invent around" the patents that protected the Houdry process (Sec. 4.3). Had the Houdry process been available at no cost, the subsequent innovation might not have been undertaken; indeed, in the absence of the patent system, the development of the Houdry process might not have received financial backing. The value of proprietary knowledge is to be found not only in the commercial considerations that underlie the patent system, however, but also in the nature of the R & D process. We have noted that in certain kinds of development work it is sometimes thought that if the development group is split into two teams that work independently without communicating with each other, the results are better than if they work as one group (Sec. 4.3). The argument is that the gains from the exploration of different technical solutions may be greater than the losses from the smaller scale of effort.

If one could measure these things, it may well be true that the Soviet R & D man gives and receives information from his colleagues more freely than the R & D man in a capitalist firm. But that conclusion is not at all certain, and in any case the difference is less than is generally supposed. The comparison with capitalist economies is not the central point, however. To evaluate the net contribution of the socialization of knowledge to the promotion of innovation in the USSR, one must imagine an alternative in which certain types of knowledge in the USSR could be lawfully treated as proprietary by those who produced it, for some limited period of time. Our guess is that the alternative would produce a higher rate of innovation than the present policy. But while the evidence is sufficient to question the accepted views, it is hardly strong enough to reject it.

The Borrowing of Foreign Technology

Nations no less than men are not islands unto themselves. All social systems function in an environment, and the historical experience of nations reflects not solely the structure of their society but also the qualities of the environment within which their history unfolds. A favorable environment may cause a poor structure to yield a satisfactory performance, and an excellent structure may produce poor results because of an unfavorable environment. The dominating feature of the social environment in which the economic development of the Soviet Union has taken place is the fact that the world was populated with nations on a higher level of technological development. This is another way of saying that at the time of the Revolution, the USSR was an underdeveloped country, and its policy was to "overtake and surpass" the leading capitalist countries. For an underdeveloped country with this objective, the task is to appropriate the technology available outside as rapidly as possible. The process of development is fundamentally one of borrowing and incorporating the technology developed earlier elsewhere. It is not a purely passive task, of course, for the borrowing must be adaptive; the underdeveloped country has different traditions, different natural resources, different degrees of skills among its people, and different proportions among the factors of production. It cannot therefore mechanically appropriate what is available elsewhere but must adapt it to its own special conditions. But the point remains that the task is primarily one of taking from the store of knowledge already available elsewhere and not of generating new knowledge. A nation that has successfully made the transition from an underdeveloped to a developed country, as have Japan and the USSR, has in fact demonstrated its capacity to borrow and incorporate the technology of others.[16]

Soviet growth has benefited greatly from the borrowing of foreign technology.[17] In the 1920s and early 1930s, the borrowing took the form of extensive imports of foreign goods, particularly machinery and production facilities, as well as the import of technical assistance services. Foreign technicians and engineers came to the USSR in considerable numbers to assist in the installation of new production facilities and to train Soviet personnel in the operation of the plants; and Soviet personnel went abroad to work in foreign plants and study in foreign universities. By the mid-thirties the rate of import of foreign technological equipment slowed down greatly, and the Soviets turned to the domestic manufacture of the major proportion of their equipment. Small orders of foreign equipment continued to be purchased, and some effort was devoted to acquiring single models of foreign technology for the purpose of using them as prototypes for copying the design and producing the objects domestically. Foreign technological knowledge continued to be appropriated also in the form of technical and scientific journals.

The appropriation of foreign technology was undoubtedly a wise policy on the part of the Soviet leaders. It is one of the factors often pointed to as part of the explanation of the rapid rate of industrial growth.[18] For one would expect that, other things being equal, a given quantity of resources devoted to the attainment of a capital stock equivalent to that accumulated earlier by a pioneer in development would attain that goal at a more rapid rate than that required earlier by the pioneer of the development process.[19]

After World War II, the rate of acquisition of advanced technology from the capitalist countries dropped sharply. The drop was due partly to the Western embargo on trade with communist countries, and partly to the autarkic policies of the Stalin period. Since 1970, however, the political détente between the USSR and the United States led to a revival of the process of technology transfer to the USSR. The magnitude that the renewed flow will eventually attain depends heavily on the national policies of the partners, which depend in turn on each side's assessment of the probable benefit to the USSR. If the Soviets judge that benefit to be very small, they will lose interest. The United States may well have second thoughts if they judge it to be very large.

The question lies outside the scope of this study, but our findings have some implications for the answer, which may be set forth. The rate of growth of factor productivity in the USSR, as reported by Abram Bergson, has been well below that of the major capitalist countries at equivalent levels of industrial development.[20] Some portion of the difference may be ascribed to the high rate of technology transfer among capitalist countries through the normal processes of commodity and capital flows. The rate of productivity growth of such countries as France, Germany, and Japan may therefore be regarded as the upper limit to the rate that the USSR might attain.

The international transfer of technology takes place through three media: publications, products, and persons. The USSR has always maintained a massive inflow of foreign technical publications, and no significant increase is to be expected from that source. The benefits from increased technology transfer will have to come from the other two media.

We have argued the case elsewhere that the chief source of the international transfer of technology is not the movement of publications and products but the movement of persons.[21] International scientific meetings are part of the process, as well as study and research by citizens of one country in the universities and laboratories of another. A major contribution in the transfer of technology, however, as distinct from science, is the travel of sales engineers and businessmen in search of both customers for their new products and foreign sources of new technological products and processes. They transfer a great deal of knowledge of the new technology available in their own country, and they acquire information on competing technology available or in development elsewhere. Officials of multinational corporations are particularly active in this process, but national firms in fields of advanced technology participate heavily. The contribution of this vehicle of technology transfer may be gauged by imagining that all international commercial travel was suddenly forbidden. The diffusion of knowledge would continue through the technical publications and trade in products incorporating new technology, but the rate of diffusion would be greatly diminished and the international rate of technological advance would decline perceptibly.

The restrictions on the movement of persons, both ways, across the borders of the USSR is perhaps the major reason that the Soviets are not members of the international high-technology club. The typical Soviet engineer simply does not know what products and processes are used successfully in other countries; what "the competition" is producing, as it were, what ideas or products he could appropriate from abroad, and least of all what ideas are still on the drawing boards or in development abroad. Few Japanese or American sales engineers come to spread their catalogues and inform him of the technical specifications of their new machines, and he has never seen the production or management setup of the best foreign firms.[22] Hence, however extensive the future increase in the inflow of advanced products from abroad, the Soviets cannot benefit from international technology transfer to the extent that the other countries do unless the travel restrictions are greatly reduced. Some controlled increase in foreign travel by politically certified persons may be expected, and some increased accessibility of Soviet enterprises and laboratories to foreign businessmen. But short of a massive political transformation, a significant dropping of the bars is inconceivable.

There remains the technology that is transferred through physical products: new machines, new materials, and new production facilities. Some gain will be secured on this account. The automobile plant built in the USSR by Fiat engineers with Fiat equipment may be expected to produce a superior product at lower cost than a Soviet-built plant. The gains are the greater if the plant is financed on credit. These are similar to the normal gains from trade that benefit all trading nations. For various well-explored reasons relating to such matters as currency inconvertibility and pricing problems, the Soviets tend to derive a smaller net gain from a given volume of trade than do other countries.[23] The gain is likely to be significant nevertheless.

Apart from the gains from trade, the question is, to what extent will the technology incorporated in advanced imported products spill over into the domestic technology? That spillover is an important component of the contribution of technology transfer through trade to the rate of productivity growth of other countries. One form of it is the discipline that the competition of foreign products imposes on domestic industry. The presence of high-quality Japanese pocket calculators at low cost on the American market compels American producers to invest new funds and effort into R & D or to leave the market. The second form is the technological information implicitly contained in the product itself, which may be borrowed and incorporated in one's own products.

The first form of spillover derives primarily from the operation of competitive markets. In the centrally planned economy it is not likely that superior imported products will displace domestic ones on any significant scale. The possibility of incorporating the advanced technical characteristics of imported products into Soviet products is feasible, however. That in fact has long been practiced by Soviet designers, and has been a major vehicle for the borrowing of foreign technology in the past. The success of this method does not depend on large-scale imports of foreign products, however. It requires the purchase of only a few models, which can then be stripped down and analyzed. No détente is required for the Soviets to benefit from this form of borrowing; the tightest embargo is unlikely to prevent the Soviets from acquiring through third or fourth countries the few prototype models needed for technical analysis.

The gains are likely to be less today, however, than they were in the thirties. The reason is the change in the locus of high technology from the mechanical engineering industries to electronics and petrochemicals. The technical advances incorporated in a new truck or lathe are fairly easily extracted from the physical products themselves. As production men say, "the technology is transferred along with the product." But the physical form of an integrated circuit gives no clue to the closely controlled manufacturing technology required to produce it. Only if the manufacturer were willing to disclose the details of the process or to sell or license the production equipment could the Soviets obtain the technology used for producing that product. Some manufacturing technology of that kind will be available to the Soviets at a price. But few capitalist firms are likely to sell their most advanced technology, and least of all their forthcoming advances that are still in development. The direct purchase of foreign manufacturing technology will therefore yield a net benefit to the Soviets, but in the fields of rapid technological advance the stock of such acquired technology is likely to lag behind that of the originating countries.

There is a certain similarity between the mission-oriented sectors of Soviet industry and the economies of the advanced capitalist countries. Both are repositories of high technological attainment and both are, in a sense, "foreign" to the main body of Soviet industry. Both are large potential sources of technology transfer for elevating the levels of Soviet technology. The results of Robert Campbell's investigation of the spillovers from the space and military programs are therefore instructive. Professor Campbell writes:[24]

Finally, whatever weaknesses there may be in the mechanism for identifying managerial innovations, and evaluating them as potentially worth transferring, or in taking measures to diffuse them, the most serious bottleneck in the diffusion process seems to be on the receiving end. Apparently, many managerial weaknesses persist in the general economy not because there is no known technique for handling a problem, but because the incentive system is such that management has no real interest in improving aspects of its performance.

There is some disposition among the governors of the Soviet economy to regard borrowed technology as the deus ex machina. It offers a way of attaining the high rate of technical advance greatly sought, without having to tamper once again with the fundamental economic structure. If Campbell's findings and our own speculations are correct, other than the gains from trade the net benefits from the foreign technology that succeeds in penetrating the economic structure will be very modest. Borrowed technology is no substitute for structural change.[25]

17.2. The Limits on Innovation

The scientific and technical manpower in Soviet industry and the various other sources of innovation account for the rate of technological progress attained by the economy. This study has examined in detail the structural properties of the economy that have limited the rate of technological progress attained. We may conclude with some general observations on the structural obstacles to innovation.

Why Nobody Cares

When an innovation has traversed successfully the long path from conception to general adoption, one can be sure that all along the way there were people for whom it was a matter of great concern whether it succeeded or not. The theme that pervades the Soviet sources is that nobody cares very much about innovation.

In the years 1963 to 1964 a huge effort went into the publication of industry manuals to be used by engineering designers in calculating the returns to investments in new capital projects. In 1966 a survey by the Bank for Construction found that only 15 percent of all projects had actually made the required calculations.[26] The others did not bother. The R & D institutes are busily engaged in the design of new products and processes, but they do not take the trouble to study the technology and production processes of the enterprises that are to use their designs. The latter, for their part, "stand off to the side" when "they should involve themselves actively in the process of creating the new technology."[27] In the design of new production facilities, the choice of the machinery to be used is made by the engineering design organization. "Any equipment at all may be chosen for the enterprise under construction as long as it fits the technological process that has been designed. Any equipment will be paid for as long as it has been included in the officially approved estimate."[28] Nobody cares about the price, neither the design engineers nor the management of the enterprise for whom the facility has been designed.

Analysts of social phenomena divide, by training and perhaps by disposition, into those who view events in structural terms and those who seek explanations in cultural terms. The latter look to the national character of the Russians—the land of Oblomov—or to its historical traditions, or to deeply held attitudes about initiative and authority. Our approach, however, has been to search for the answer in social structure. This is not to deny that there are national differences in attitudes toward work and authority, and that these differences constitute part of the explanation of differences in national attainments. The argument is rather that for any given set of cultural characteristics, behavior varies with the structure of the social arrangements within which people behave. In the case of the USSR in particular, there is little reason to believe that cultural characteristics are so different from those of other advanced industrial nations as to offer a major part of the explanation in differences in performance. The capacities of Soviet engineers and managers to work and create, to assume responsibilities, and to organize people and machines, are not inherently different from those of other nations. We have therefore assumed that, given the appropriate social structure—organization, prices, incentives, decision rules—the economic behavior of Soviet men and women is not likely to be very different from that of other peoples.

The culturological explanation is not confined to foreign observers of the Soviet scene. It is widely held within the USSR itself and has sufficient respectability that it may, in our view, lead the Soviet into paths of reform that will yield little benefit and deflect them from finding their way to more effective solutions. One of its forms is the enthusiasm developed in the USSR in recent years for the introduction of "business schools" and "management training." The problem, it is said, is that our managers must learn to attain the "cultural level" of your American managers.[29] They must learn how to organize, how to manifest initiative, and how to develop those aggressive "businesslike" characteristics that are so impressive in American corporate executives. It is because our managers lack these characteristics that our economy does not perform as well as it might. For there is nothing wrong in the way we run our economy. Those who urge us to decentralize our system fail to realize that central planning is our great strength: just as the centralization of American industry in the hands of a few great monopolies is the real strength of the American economy. What we need is not any major reform in our economic arrangements but the education of our managers in the techniques and style of operation that your best corporate managers exhibit.

This point of view, sketched out from a number of conversations with Soviet scholars, must be highly attractive to those with a deep commitment to the traditional practice of central planning and to the dominant role of the Party. To hold this view is to feel secure in the belief that there is no need for vast reforms that may let loose who knows what economic convulsions and what kinds of political dissolution that may threaten the hegemony of the Party itself. Our system works perfectly well, is the implication of this view; we need only to teach our managers the tricks that the best capitalist managers have learned, and then the fundamental superiority of our socialist system will become manifest.

If the analysis in our study is correct, this view will lead the Soviets into a blind alley. Not entirely blind, of course, because it is likely that certain modern Western managerial techniques would contribute to the improvement of Soviet managerial performance. Such teachable techniques as mathematical inventory control, computerized production scheduling, various kinds of operations research methods, and so forth are likely to contribute some benefit. But they do not get to the heart of the problem, which in our view lies in the structure of the economic system. With the best stock of techniques teachable by the best business school in the world, the Soviet manager obliged to operate in the social structure of the Soviet economy would soon find himself making the same kinds of economic decisions as are widely criticized in the Soviet literature today. If the problem is that nobody cares, the fault is not in the people but in the structure of the system.

Risk and Reward

In each planning period, management has before it a portfolio of possible product and process innovations. A wide range of choices may be made. At one extreme, they may decide to introduce none of them, continuing instead with the established production program. At the other extreme, they may adopt a program of rapid innovation. Or they may choose a program anywhere within that range.

The incentive structure consists of a set of formulas and schedules specifying the bonuses to be awarded for each of a variety of outcomes. Each of the programs among which the manager must choose specifies a set of planned outcomes. Applying the bonus formulas and schedules, one can calculate the incomes that would be earned from the successful implementation of each program.

One of the main findings of this study (Sec. 16.1) is that the competent manager who concentrates on current production operations and minimizes the rate of innovation can earn a substantial supplement to his salary in the form of bonuses. If he succeeds in implementing a program of rapid innovation, however, his income will not be much larger. On the face of it, the structure of incentives may seem to explain why nobody cares about innovation.

That explanation is incomplete, however. Successful innovation does generally offer larger rewards than successful noninnovative management, though perhaps by a modest amount. One has the impression that even in such cases, the decision to innovate is taken less often than the calculus of relative rewards would lead one to expect. Something other than the schedules of incentives enters into decision making and biases choices against the decision to innovate. That factor is risk.

In the analysis of innovation in capitalist economies, a central place is assigned to the role of risk in decision making. Many of the sources of risk derive from the nature of capitalist economic relationships. Because of the privacy of enterprise, decisions must be made in ignorance of other decisions being made elsewhere. Because of the inherent fluctuation in economic activity, resources must be committed today on the basis of tenuous forecasts of tomorrow's business conditions. Soviet socialism, however, has been designed to eliminate these sources of risk. Knowledge is socialized in the regime of public enterprises, and central planning has replaced the anarchy of the market. Hence the Soviet economic literature devotes little explicit attention to the analysis of the role of risk in decision making. The incentive structure specifies the size of the bonus for a 5-percent increase in sales revenue, for an innovation yielding an economic benefit of 10,000 rubles, for a 1-percent decrease in electric power utilization, and so forth. No explicit attention is given, however, to the risk associated with the decision to include each of those tasks in the production program.

If the alternatives confronting the Soviet manager were riskless, the omission would be of no consequence. In fact economic choice does involve risks of various kinds, and alternatives differ in the degree of risk they entail. The evaluation of risk is therefore an inescapable component of decision making.

For bullfighters, mountain climbers, and gamblers, risk bearing, like virtue, is its own reward. The smaller the probability of being able to attain a certain goal, the more attractive is the pursuit of it. Most people, however, both socialist and capitalist, prefer to avoid risk, particularly in the mundane activity of earning a living.[30] Riskier alternatives are chosen only if the rewards are judged to be correspondingly greater.

There are probably more bullfighters among innovators, socialist or capitalist, than among the population at large. But one would hardly design for a whole society an economic structure geared to the disposition of its bullfighters. In choosing among alternative programs of action most people consider not only the relative rewards offered for the successful attainment of each but also the relative probability of earning each reward. Moreover for the general run of economic activity some additional reward must be offered to induce the bearing of risk.

Viewed in terms of reward alone, the incentive structure might seem to offer some modest encouragement to innovation. For the successful innovative program does yield an income somewhat larger than the successful noninnovative program. Viewed in terms of the relationship of reward to risk, however, the incentive structure is highly discriminatory against innovation for all but the most inveterate bullfighters.

Any structural reforms designed to accelerate the rate of innovation must therefore alter the traditional balance of reward and risk. With no change in the incentive structure, that requires a reduction in the risk of the decision to innovate relative to the risk of deciding to forgo innovation. The appropriate alteration of the balance of risk may be accomplished by a structural change designed to increase the degree of enterprise autonomy over its transactions with other enterprises and organizations.

Autonomy.
The structure of the Soviet economy embodies a certain Marxian interpretation of the social nature of technological progress. The historical contribution of capitalism is to build up the productive capabilities of the nation by the application of advancing technology. In the course of time the inherent contradictions of capitalism increasingly brake the pace of technological advance and stagnation ensues. The socialist revolution puts an end to the conditions that stifled technological advance and releases for the first time in history the full creative energies of the masses.

Technology was a central element in the building of the new society. "The Soviets plus Electrification equals Communism" was Lenin's often quoted formula. Nevertheless the active promotion of technological advance was not considered a central objective in the design of the new economic system. The main task was to replace the anarchy of the capitalist marketplace by an orderly process for allocating the nation's resources. If that were sensibly done, technological progress would flourish more or less automatically. Freed from the chains of private property and appropriately provided with resources for invention and innovation, the new socialist men and women will manifest the full potential of human creativity.

Many of the structural features of the economy examined in our study may be traced back to this view of history. The organizational dissociation of R & D from production is a sensible arrangement if one anticipates a full harmony of interests—no "contradictions"—among all working people. Cost-based pricing is a useful pricing principle if one has no concern about its consequences for the relative prices of new and established products; that is, if socialist managers may be expected to make their decisions on broad grounds of social benefit rather than narrow grounds of relative profit. Other than inventors' rewards, no special monetary incentives for innovation were introduced until after World War II, and the decision rules focused attention on those activities that were central to the fulfillment of the current national plan. For it was the plan that replaced the anarchic capitalist market, and with a well-ordered plan inventive and innovative effort would be readily forthcoming.

Had the Soviet economy attained an exemplary rate of technological progress, there would have been no cause to dispute that view of the fundamental harmony between the Soviet version of central planning and the promotion of technological progress. The historical record, however, warrants a reconsideration.

Soviet economic structure grants a wide range of autonomy to enterprise management over its own internal operations. Management has little autonomy, however, over its transactions with other enterprises and organizations; that is the domain of central planning and administration. In a regime of perfect planning, all enterprise decisions would be riskless with respect to external transactions, including the decision to innovate. If supplies of goods and services arrived without fail, management would be quite happy to let the central planners take care of that and other external transactions. If planning is imperfect, however, all decisions involve a degree of risk on account of external transactions. In that case the absence of enterprise autonomy does have certain consequences on decision making, for management is obliged to devise strategies to reduce the degree of risk. Among the many such strategies one of the most familiar is vertical integration—internalizing the production of some of the goods and services that were formerly purchased externally.

If the risk due to imperfect planning fell equally on all alternatives, the absence of autonomy would have no discriminatory effect against the decision to innovate. As we have seen, however, the decision to innovate increases the degree of risk in all external transactions—with suppliers, customers, price administrators, and so forth. The strategy that managers have devised to protect the enterprise from that risk is, unfortunately, the minimization of the rate and extent of change in production processes. If one uses the same inputs year after year, relations with suppliers are stabilized; different inputs, on the other hand, mean new and untried suppliers, or new technical specifications that old suppliers may not be able to attain. The central planners can readily find customers for established and familiar products; untried new products may not move as easily as that. The prices and profitability of established products are known; the prices and profitability of new products will not be known until after the long journey through the bureaus of standardization and price administration.

Hence there is a "contradiction," as Soviet analysts would say, between Soviet central planning and the promotion of technological progress. The contradiction could be resolved in two ways. One is to improve the quality of central planning so that the decision to innovate would not plunge the enterprise into difficulties that are avoided by a decision not to innovate. The other is to grant the enterprise greater autonomy over its transactions with other enterprises and organizations. If the enterprise could easily drop a deficient supplier and turn to another more eager for its business, if it could react quickly to changes in its supply plans as dictated by the needs of product redesign, the perils of innovation would be considerably reduced. The innovator's need for autonomy is greatest with respect to the supply of R & D services; to decide which services to provide in-house and which to contract out; to be able to shape the structure, policies, and personnel of in-house R & D to suit the enterprise's special needs; to be able to shop around for outside technical services and to pay for them on the basis of one's own judgment of their value to the enterprise. Given the caution with which potential adopters view new products and processes, the innovator requires greater autonomy over the disposition of his output. The success of the innovation depends to a considerable degree on the confidence that the producer can inspire in prospective users, particularly first adopters. That course requires promotion, merchandising, advertising, special financing, and servicing and guarantees, none of which are functions that the remote central planners have the competence or the interest in performing.

Greater autonomy over organizational structure would be more effective if it were accompanied by greater autonomy over pricing. Many new products that could be sold at a profit are sold at a loss because of the imposition of uniform price-setting regulations. If enterprises had greater latitude in setting their own prices on such products, innovation would be greatly encouraged; subsidization could still be employed for the others. Equally beneficial would be the reduction in the delays and uncertainty over what the price will eventually turn out to be.

One can interpret the economic reforms of recent years as efforts to extend the scope of enterprise autonomy; within the broad limits of central planning, to be sure. But they have not quite come to grips with the problems of autonomy that are specific to the innovation process. The 1965 Economic Reform, for example, released enterprise management from its former obligation to account for the numbers of employees within each employment category. Only the total wage bill is specified in the plan, and management is now free to hire more people in one category and fewer in another as long as total wages do not exceed the plan target. In this and other ways the Reform restricted the "petty tutelage" that the central organs formerly imposed on enterprises. This new autonomy granted to management, however, extends primarily to the internal operations of enterprises. That is surely helpful, but it is not in internal management that the problems of innovation lie. It is in the enterprise's relations with other enterprises, the suppliers of its goods and services and the customers for its products, that the innovator feels the grip of central planning and administration. It is in the nature of those relations that the structure of a centrally planned economy differs most sharply from that of a market-type economy.

The recent adoption of the corporation form of industrial organization does indeed affect the autonomy of the enterprise over its transactions with other economic units. The method used, however, is the internalization of what were formerly external transactions. It provides a legal sanction for that form of "autarky" that enterprises have always sought informally to protect their operations from the vagaries of supply administration—vertical integration. It transfers certain flows of goods and services out of the domain of central planning into that of internal enterprise administration. All transactions among the new corporate enterprises, however, are governed as before by the central planning apparatus.

The reform does confront directly one major source of the sentiment that "nobody cares" about innovation. In those corporations that are to be research based, a single management group will exercise autonomy over both the research and design work and the implementation of the innovation. That may be expected to improve the quality and augment the rate of innovation. The larger question of autonomy is not touched however. Corporate management appears to have no greater autonomy over their external transactions than did the management of their smaller predecessors. Their prices will continue to be centrally administered as before. To the extent that some portion of the flow of goods and services is now internalized within the corporations, the domain of responsibility of central planning and administration is reduced. Relieved from some portion of the detail with which they formerly had to deal, the central planners are likely to carry out their work more effectively, a procedure which will diminish the resistance to innovation that the lack of autonomy generated in the past. The magnitude of the gain in innovation depends on the degree of improvement in the effectiveness of central planning anticipated from the elimination of detail.

The corporation reform is a device for coping with the problem of autonomy without any major deviation from the traditional Soviet principles of central planning. In a few years the outcome will be known. If the quality of central planning will have improved to the extent hoped for, the question of enterprise autonomy over external transactions will disappear from the agenda. If not, it will surely reappear in the discussion of the next reform.

Socialist Competition and the Invisible Foot

When a society commits itself to one type of economic structure, it forgoes certain advantages that alternative structures possess. It is often possible, however, to gain some of the advantages of another structure by adopting some of its properties. The United States has not relied solely on market processes for generating technological progress but has introduced a considerable element of governmental direction and support, although not to the extent that it may be called "planning." The USSR has also tinkered with ways of broadening the scope of enterprise autonomy, and the extensive black market provides an additional if unlawful element of enterprise control over sources of supply.[31]

There are limits to the extent that one system can incorporate features designed for another without eventually diminishing the effectiveness of its own fundamental structure. The Soviet designer of an economic reform would have of course to keep such limits well in mind. On the other hand there is a lower limit beneath which the degree of autonomy awarded would be merely formal and would offer no genuine increase in enterprise control over its external transactions. The test of the significance of the actual autonomy conferred by a reform is whether or not it gives rise to genuine competition among enterprises.

The term "socialist competition" has been employed to describe the contests in which enterprises strive to achieve the highest scores on some prearranged indicators of performance (Section 14.3). The contests normally focus on a set of production tasks of various kinds, like overfulfilling output targets by the greatest amount. The winning enterprise is entitled to reward its workers by a special distribution of bonuses. The losers lose nothing.

It is not such contests but genuine competition that is likely to emerge from an increase in enterprise autonomy. The reason is that an increase in the security of the enterprise as buyer will entail a decrease in the security of the enterprise as seller. For autonomy to be meaningful to an innovating manager, he must be free to drop an unreliable supplier and be reasonably confident that he can place his order directly with a more reliable one, without having to clear with the central planners. Any organizational structure that confers that degree of autonomy places all enterprises under the threat of a loss of sales and revenue. It may therefore be argued that increased autonomy over supply will not reduce the general level of risk in economic activity. It merely shifts the burden of risk bearing from the enterprise as purchaser to the enterprise as seller. If the increased security over sources of supply is expected to encourage innovation, will not the decreased security over sales and revenue discourage innovation?

We believe that it will not. On the contrary the security that central planning provides to the enterprise as seller has as unfavorable an impact on the risks of innovation as the insecurity of the enterprise as buyer. In a "seller's market" there is no risk in the decision not to innovate. High-cost producers face no threat of loss of sales to competitors who have cut prices on the basis of process innovations. New-product models do not sweep into the markets of producers of outdated models; the central planners do not allow that. If this security regarding sales and revenue is reduced by an increase in enterprise autonomy over sources of supply, that autonomy would be twice blessed as an instrument for promoting innovation. In the current choice between innovating or not innovating, the risk of the first alternative is high, while the second is riskless. Increased autonomy would both reduce the risk of innovating and introduce for the first time an element of risk in the decision not to innovate. In this last respect, the economy would benefit from one of the major sources of innovation in capitalist economies.

Adam Smith taught us to think of competition as an "invisible hand" that guides production into the socially desirable channels. By a curious ideological confluence both Adam Smith and the designers of the Soviet economic structure had in mind the smooth allocation of resources under a basically unchanging technology. Central planning may be regarded simply as a visible form of the same guiding hand that operates invisibly in capitalism. But if Adam Smith had taken as his point of departure not the coordinating mechanism but the innovation mechanism of capitalism, he may well have designated competition not as an invisible hand but as an invisible foot. For the effect of competition on innovation is not only to motivate profit-seeking entrepreneurs to seek yet more profit but to jolt conservative enterprises into the adoption of new technology and the search for improved processes and products. From the point of view of the static efficiency of resource allocation, the evil of monopoly is that it prevents resources from flowing into those lines of production in which their social value would be greatest. But from the point of view of innovation, the evil of monopoly is that it enables producers to enjoy high rates of profit without having to undertake the exacting and risky activities associated with technological change. A world of monopolies, socialist or capitalist, would be a world with very little technological change.

Socialist critics of modern "monopoly capitalism" find it difficult to explain the high rate of innovation in the advanced capitalist countries. The reason, of course, is that they are not at all monopolistic, much as they may like to be. Modern capitalist industry is dominated by large oligopolies, and the will to believe must be very strong indeed to fail to see the evidence of the intense competition for sales among the oligopolies. Corporations are profoundly concerned with their "share of the market," and any innovation that increases one firm's share sends the others scurrying for innovations to recapture their share. In a survey of 204 British innovations, about 40 percent were undertaken for such reasons as, "Obviously, we *had* to do it," reflecting a passive response to market pressures rather than active pursuit of profit.[32] The experience of U.S. industry is that "a firm may dawdle if the result is merely slower growth of profits, but it is likely to be activated when the result is a serious erosion of a previous profit or market share position."[33] Here is the invisible foot applied vigorously to the backside of enterprises that would otherwise have been quite content to go on producing the same products in the same ways, and at a reasonable profit, if they could only be protected from the intrusion of competition.[34]

The experience of modern capitalism may be relevant in this respect to the problem of innovation in Soviet industry. In adopting central planning as the foundation of economic structure, the Soviets sought the benefits of a socialist version of the invisible hand. They lost the benefits of the invisible foot, however. Soviet organizational structure confers on all enterprises a form of monopolistic protection against aggression on their business by other enterprises. That is the lesson of the case of the Dankov enterprise, which was accused of "poaching in foreign territories" when it sought to sell its new products in the markets designated for other suppliers (Section 7.2). Protected in this way by the central planning system, producers are under no pressure to innovate, other than the pressure from their own "home office" in the ministry. The pressure is thus of the kind that the Russians call "administrative measures" rather than "economic measures." The quality of one's products is judged primarily by one's own administrative bosses, who have an interest in declaring them to be excellent. If there were a Ministry of the Automotive Industry in the United States, we would surely still be producing the Edsel, for the planners would have limited the total production of automobiles so that the buyers would have had no alternative. The DuPont Corporation was obliged to drop the production of Corfam after eight years of development and promotional effort and an investment of $108 million.[35] It was undoubtedly an excellent product, and under Soviet conditions the producers would certainly have received a handsome bonus from their ministry. But under competitive conditions the quality of one's product is judged not by one's own superiors but by one's customers, and it would be compared with the quality of other producers' products. If dissatisfied customers have no other place to go, life is easier for both the producer and his ministry. But if the customers have a genuine alternative, the pressure for product improvement is constant and ineluctable. Moreover the quality of new products and processes would improve. Spurious innovation, discussed at length earlier (Section 13.4), would greatly diminish if an autonomous customer rather than a government official were the judge of the quality of a new product.

The investment in the Edsels and the Corfams was in retrospect a social loss, and the simple logic of socialism suggests that a well-organized society ought to be able to avoid these losses that a capitalist society must sustain. The issue, however, turns not on the question of capitalism or socialism but rather on the social evaluation of risk. Both capitalist and socialist societies can minimize the losses of unsuccessful ventures if they are content with a very low rate of technological change. But neither can escape the losses of unsuccessful development projects if they seek a high rate of technological advance. In the Soviet case, the organizational structure that protects producers against losses from both their own unsuccessful innovations and the successful innovations of others is itself a massive obstacle to the promotion of innovation.

Dissolution of enterprises. In considering the kinds of autonomy that may best serve to promote innovation, it would be instructive to study the experience of capitalist economies, some elements of which may be adaptable to Soviet conditions. The Western literature on innovation devotes a great deal of attention to the conditions of entry and exit of firms and products in markets. Technological change is a major cause of the dissolution or bankruptcy of enterprises. Large capitalist corporations no longer operate in the range in which bankruptcy is a serious possibility. Their weaker divisions and plants are subject to dissolution, however, and smaller companies are systematically weeded out by market forces. Some inefficient enterprises survive by public subsidy or by a privileged protection from competition, and some efficient enterprises fall victim to the market power of larger competitors. But rough as the process is, the continuous exit of plants and companies precludes the permanent freezing of resources rendered obsolete by technological change.

The performance of inefficient Soviet enterprises can sometimes be improved by such measures as a change in management, retraining of labor, capital investments, and so forth. In some cases, however, the cost of renovation far exceeds the potential gain, and where the source of the problem is in such conditions as remoteness from markets or the exhaustion of national resources, they cannot be made viable at any cost. In recognition of such considerations, the Soviets have long had a bankruptcy statute on the books, but it is rarely invoked. The most recent effort to provide it with teeth was a decree of 1954 which provided that enterprises in difficulty should be entitled to credits and to special assistance from the ministry. If that did not help, then the enterprise must be declared insolvent and its property sold at auction. But, reports Professor A. Birman, no such cases are known. In practice, enterprises are always saved by shifting their obligations to others. The continued "parisitism" of poorly operating enterprises is a permanent strain on the resources of the society:

The sphere of economic relations requires an economic mechanism that will operate objectively, regardless of the conscientiousness and good will of an official in a given department. This mechanism must be irrevocable and the effects of violating it inexorable. Indeed, economic conditions are needed that would leave an enterprise with only two paths: work well or close down![36]

The socialist economy finds it very difficult to dissolve unsuccessful enterprises. Part of the reason is that it involves the displacement of workers and the loss of seniority, occurrences which seem contrary to what ought to happen in a worker's state. Even when provision is made for the support of the displaced workers and their retraining until they can be placed in other enterprises, the spirit of socialism seems to hold it inappropriate for workers to be "thrown out of jobs" in a socialist state. Perhaps a related reason is that in socialist societies citizens think of their interests primarily in terms of their role as producers, for the very idea of socialism is associated with the notion of the abolition of exploitation of workers. If the primary concern were to maximize the level of welfare of citizen as consumer, then there would be little resistance to displacing and shifting citizens as workers when that were necessary to increase consumer welfare. But when the primary concern is with citizen as worker, then the welfare of workers tends to be purchased at the cost of their welfare as consumers. This attitude is particularly evident in the production of services, such as restaurant and hotel services. One gets the impression that the point of the operation is to assure the protection of the workers' collective, and that the services provided to consumers are an afterthought. The orientation is perhaps supported by the extent to which the worker's life is tied in with the operations of his factory. It provides his housing in most cases, it is the center of his social clubs and sports clubs, it provides the nursery that takes care of his children when they are small and the summer camp they attend when they are older.

Whatever the reasons, the distastefulness of displacing workers is one source of the difficulty of dissolving enterprises in the USSR, as it is also a problem encountered in the technological displacement of labor associated with technological progress (Chapter 5). There are other difficulties, however. The central planning system gives the ministries a proprietary role over their enterprises, and the performance of ministries is judged by the performance of their enterprises. The "failure" of enterprises reflects ill upon the ministers, and the latter are disposed to protect "their" enterprises. Moreover the planning system, by its control over the number of enterprises and the output of each, maintains a certain level of demand for the products of the submarginal enterprise. If enterprises in general were given the right to choose suppliers, however, and if successful suppliers were permitted to expand output to accommodate their increases in orders, and if in addition customers were authorized to create their own sources of supply, then grossly inefficient enterprises would no longer have the protection of an artificially created demand for their inferior goods and services. It is relatively easy for the director of an inefficient enterprise to explain to his own minister why he should be permitted to remain in operation and to produce for the Soviet people. But it is very much more difficult to explain to a frustrated customer why he should continue to buy obsolete products when the customer has the alternative of another source of supply. Hence an expansion of enterprise autonomy over its sources of supply would not only increase the rate of innovation but would also perform the useful function of forcing the liquidation of inefficient enterprises that drain the resources of the nation.

Conditions of entry. Despite the problems, it does not seem excessively difficult to design a reform in which increased autonomy of enterprises would not be frustrated by the immortality of inefficient suppliers. More difficult would be the design of a socialist equivalent of the conditions of entry into capitalist markets. The effort would be worth the while, however, for it is on the side of entry, even more than exit, that the most powerful agents of innovation are to be found. The Western literature devotes considerable attention to the role of newly formed firms in the promotion of innovation. Maclaurin, Bright, and Schlaiffer found that established firms, even when they are relatively progressive, "are usually backward about radically new inventions." The established firms in the communications field, like Bell and General Electric, were not interested in the new invention—radio. The existing aircraft engine firms ignored the new jet engine. It often requires new firms to take up the introduction of a radically new technology.[37] Often the new firms are formed by former employees of established corporations: Texas Instruments and Fairchild were organized by former employees of Bell Laboratories,[38] a number of large computer firms were organized by former employees of IBM, and a number of new firms in Connecticut were started by inventors whose former employees would not finance their inventions.[39] Universities have also been the source of formation of new enterprises: in the Boston area some 200 new companies have been generated by the "people transfer process" from the MIT community.[40] Some corporations like Union Carbide make a practice of introducing innovations by establishing new firms headed by the engineer or scientist who originated or developed the proposal if he appears to have the appropriate entrepreneurial talents as well. The corporation retains a financial interest in the new company and provides financing and technical assistance, but the objective is to turn the entrepreneurial task over to a new and enthusiastic leadership rather than entrust it to the established management.[41]

It is clear that the process of new-company formation has provided a powerful stimulus to innovation. It has increased the general mobility of technical people and businessmen, "broadened the base of knowledge," and helped keep trade secrets from remaining secret indefinitely.[42] But perhaps most important, it has provided outlets for entrepreneurial energies that would have been restricted by having to operate within established organizations.

It might well be possible for the Soviet economy to allow the autonomous formation of new entrepreneurial groups within the general limits of centralized planning. It would be more difficult, however, to conceive a reform that would incorporate a second powerful source of innovation under capitalism: ease of entry into product markets. The success of new products like belted tires and transistorized radios is based on the rapid takeover of the general market for radios and tires. The large entrepreneurial profit is primarily due to the rapid expansion of sales and not to the profit rate per item sold, which is often not very large. Eventually the competitors reenter the market with their own models of the new product, market shares are restabilized, and the innovators' profit returns to the normal level. The killing is made in the few months or years before the market shares are restabilized. A related form of entry is "innovation by invasion," in which the markets of a conservative industry are invaded by the enterprises of an entirely different but progressive industry (Section 7.2). For it is not unusual that the engineering and scientific personnel in a particular industry exhaust the technical possibilities of further advance in that field. Advances may come rather from persons working in an entirely different field with new technical conceptions. Thus the major innovations in textile production have come not from the textile industry but from the chemical products industry (synthetic fibers). The major advance in recent years in machine-tool design was developed not in the machine-tool industry but in the aircraft industry (numerical controls). In order to take the greatest advantage of this characteristic of technological change, organizational structure must be such as to impose no boundaries along industry lines. Producers must be free to consider the whole economy as a potential customer for the products they may develop, and not simply the special markets that they have been accustomed to supply. The central planning system with its ministerial organizational structure drawn on industry lines has tended to erect barriers against invasion. If the same barriers prevail in the case of the future corporations, the possibility of invasion would continue to be remote. Producers would be expected to restrict their horizons and not poach in the markets of others. And perhaps more important, they would be protected against invasion of their markets by others. The invisible foot will continue to be hobbled.

17.3. The Balance of Risk and Reward
The balance of risk may be shifted in favor of the decision to innovate by improvements in the efficiency and reliability of central planning, by reforms that increase enterprise autonomy, and perhaps in other ways that may yet be devised. If the balance of risk is sufficiently improved, the rate of innovation may attain a level deemed satisfactory by the governors of the society. If not, the burden of promoting techno-

logical progress will fall on the balance of rewards.

The rewards for economic activity depend on two sets of factors: the measured outcomes and the incentive structure that specifies the bonuses for each level of each outcome. The relative rewards for innovation could therefore be increased by altering either of those factors. The measured outcomes of innovative activity could be increased by modifying the price structure so as to increase the prices of new products relative to older products. That indeed was the objective of the new pricing principles introduced in the past decade (Chapters 10, 11, and 12). The incentive structure could be changed by increasing the size of the bonus payable for each thousand rubles of net economic benefit due to an innovation. That was the plan of the working group in the State Committee on Science and Technology, which was vetoed by the conservative gentlemen in the Ministry of Finance (Section 15.1). But all such measures would be defeated by that decisive feature of the incentive structure—the upper limit on the incomes that any person may earn (Section 16.1). As long as that limit is maintained, the boldest incentive structures, including a full-blown profit-sharing plan, could not greatly increase the relative personal rewards for innovation.

The removal of that limit, however, would not necessarily increase the rate of innovation. It all depends on the responsiveness of managers to changes in relative monetary rewards. At one end of the range of possibilities, managers might greatly increase the rate of innovation in response to a small increase in the relative rewards for innovation. One would say in that case that innovative effort is highly elastic with respect to income. At the other end, managerial response may be inelastic; very large increases in the income possibilities for innovation would then generate very little additional innovation. Or the elasticity may be somewhere between those extremes.

Soviet economists appear to differ in their judgment on this matter (Section 16.1). A compelling argument is that the promise of large incomes does not have a strong motivating force in a society in which the volume of consumer goods is limited and the private ownership of productive resources is forbidden. Behavior will therefore not be highly responsive to incomes that could accumulate only in savings banks. On the other hand, there is abundant evidence that Soviet managers are highly responsive to income within the present normal range of income variations. Slight changes in the rules defining the outcomes for which bonuses are available often generate massive changes in decision making corresponding to the new rules. The only test we have of responsiveness to incomes larger than the normal range is the economic activity of the black market. The evidence suggests that there is a considerable pool of entrepreneurial talent that is prepared to bear high risks indeed in response to large income opportunities. Perhaps most of those persons are bullfighters by disposition, and therefore not typical of Soviet managers in general. The kinds of risk involved in the normal innovation decision, however, are much less severe than those assumed by the entrepreneurs of the economic underworld. The same level of income opportunities may therefore generate a substantial response in men of more normal disposition.

The size of the rewards required to encourage managers to bear the risks of innovation may well be smaller in socialist societies than in capitalist. For a given level of risk or probability of success, the smaller the loss from failure, the smaller the reward for success required to induce the bearing of the risk. Both Soviet and capitalist managers risk the loss of current income, and perhaps future income, if their career prospects are reduced. But capitalist managers also generally acquire wealth in the form of the securities of their corporations, which diminish in value if innovation is unsuccessful. Since the Soviet manager risks only income, and not both income and wealth, a smaller reward should be required to induce the bearing of a given level of risk. This consideration increases the possibility that the rewards needed to elicit a given innovative effort may not fall outside the range of the ideologically acceptable. The smaller personal risk assumed by the Soviet manager, however, has a certain disadvantage as well. Most of the loss to the society due to unsuccessful innovation is borne by the State, in the form of resources invested with small or negative returns. In the capitalist economy those losses are borne by the corporate owners, including corporate officials, and they therefore enter into the innovation decision. "However," writes Professor Birman, "it cannot be denied that the absence of the risk of bearing material loss, because the means of production are socialized, fosters irresponsibility and sluggishness among many economists."[43] We read from time to time of recommendations that managers be made to bear a larger proportion of the risk—for example, by deductions from their base salaries in case of failure along with bonuses in cases of success.[44] Such incentive reforms could improve the quality of decision making by internalizing more of the social costs of the alternatives in the innovation decision. But if the personal risk of the manager is increased, the size of the reward will have to be correspondingly increased to maintain the rate of innovation.

It should be possible to generate some firmer evidence on which to judge the elasticity of innovative effort with respect to income. The method of social experiment has been widely used in the USSR in recent years to assess the likely outcome of a proposed structural reform. Some enterprises could be assigned experimentally a new incentive structure designed to increase greatly the relative rewards for innovation. The results could provide a more secure, if not decisive, basis for judging the responsiveness of managers.

A finding that innovative effort is highly elastic with respect to income would be ideologically distasteful to the governors of the society. But it would greatly ease the task of accelerating the rate of technological advance. For then a relatively small increase in the income possibilities for innovation would yield a large increase in the rate of innovation. If a small change in the balance of rewards would do the whole job, there would be no need to tamper with the balance of risk. No unpalatable structural reforms like enterprise autonomy and competition need be undertaken.

If it were found that innovative effort is not highly responsive to increases in income, however, the governors would be confronted by some hard choices. It would require very large increases in income possibilities to generate the desired increase in the rate of innovation. It would require also a substantial increase in the planned production of consumer goods and services, of the kind purchased by the upper-income population. The consequent increase in the inequality of income distribution would be awkward at the least and possibly quite unacceptable.

Instead of increasing the income possibilities for innovation, one might consider reducing the income possibilities presently available for non-innovation. The competent manager who concentrated conscientiously on the current plan targets but minimized the rate of innovation would then earn no more than his salary. Bonus supplements could be earned only by including innovation tasks in the production program and fulfilling them. The balance of rewards would then be more favorable to innovation but without driving incomes above the level currently earned by the highest-income receivers. That plan is not likely to be entertained seriously however. It would surely unleash a flood of spurious innovation, but that problem would have to be confronted in any increase in the relative rewards for innovation. The greater objection is that it would demolish the incentive system for what after all is the fundamental requirement of managers in a centrally planned economy— to overfulfill current plan targets. There must be some differential reward for outstanding performance of noninnovative activities.

An inelastic managerial responsiveness to income, then, would foreclose the possibility of accelerating the rate of innovation by changing the balance of rewards. The full burden would fall on the balance of risk. The sorts of changes required in that case are no more palatable than large increases in income inequality. They too involve a retreat from cherished Soviet principles of economic organization.

The elasticity of innovative effort is probably not entirely independent of the balance of risk. In the present economic structure, the elasticity might be thought to be low but still positive; a moderate increase in the income possibilities for innovation would yield a small increase in the rate of innovation. But if the relative risk of innovating were reduced, the elasticity would be higher, and the same increase in income possibilities would yield a larger increase in the rate of innovation. These ruminations suggest that future structural reforms ought to proceed along both lines. Innovation incentives might be increased up to the degree of income inequality that would be ideologically acceptable. And enterprise autonomy over external transactions might be extended to the degree that was politically feasible. That joint approach would yield the largest increase in the rate of innovation attainable by structural reform alone.

At the present time there is little prospect of further structural change. The eggs have been put into two baskets: the corporation reform and the import of foreign technology. If our analysis is correct, they are likely to generate a marginal improvement in the quality and rate of innovation, but they do not confront fully the major structural obstacles to innovation. It will take the passage of some years before their contributions can be assessed. Nine years elapsed between the beginning of the last Economic Reform in 1966 and the planned completion of Corporation Reform in 1975. If the same time span of assessment and decision prevails, we shall know in 1984.

Notes

1. *Pravda*, March 31, 1971. Translated in *The Current Digest of the Soviet Press*, Vol. 23, No. 13 (April 27, 1971), p. 10.

2. Abram Bergson, *Soviet Post-War Economic Development* (Stockholm: Almqvist & Wiksell, 1974), pp. 21, 25.

3. E. Zaleski, J. P. Kozlowski, H. Wienert, R. W. Davies, M. J. Berry, and R. Amman, *Science Policy in the USSR* (Paris: OECD, 1969), p. 141.

4. Ibid., p. 160.

5. Ibid., p. 145.

6. Ibid., p. 161.

7. State budget expenditures for 1958 and 1972 may be found in TsSU, *Narodnoe khoziaistvo SSSR v 1965 godu* (The USSR National Economy in 1965) (Moscow: *Statistika*, 1966), p. 781; and the corresponding volume for 1972, p. 725. Science expenditures are in Louvan E. Nolting, *Sources of Financing the Stages of the Research, Development, and Innovation Cycle in the USSR*, Foreign Economic Report No. 3, U.S. Department of Commerce (Washington, D.C.: Bureau of Economic Analysis, September 1973), p. 10.

8. Gregory Grossman, "Innovation and Information in the Soviet Economy," *American Economic Review*, Vol. 56:2 (May 1966), p. 122.

9. *Voprosy ekonomiki*, 1968, No. 2, pp. 122-123.

10. Nancy Nimitz, *The Structure of Soviet Outlays on R & D in 1960 and 1968*, Rand Report R-1207-DDRE, Santa Monica: June 1974.

11. The difference between the demands of rocketry and atomic energy development, on the one hand, and normal economic processes, on the other, is noted in K. N. Plotnikov and A. S. Gusarov, *Sovremennye problemy teorii i praktiki tsenoobrazovaniia pri sotsializme* (Current Problems in the Theory and Practice of Pricing under Socialism) (Moscow: *Nauka*, 1971), p. 312, ftn.

12. Nimitz, *Structure*, p. 43.

13. Robert W. Campbell, "Management Spillovers from Soviet Space and Military Programs," *Soviet Studies*, Vol. 23:4 (April 1972), p. 607.

14. Grossman, "Innovation and Information," p. 120.

15. A. D. Little, *Patterns and Problems of Technical Innovation in American Industry*, Report to the National Science Foundation, U.S. Department of Commerce (PB181573) (Washington: September 1963), pp. 160-161.

16. The point is sometimes made that in its extensive import of foreign technology and technical assistance the USSR demonstrated its incapacity to generate its own technological advance. This is the thesis of Antony Sutton's *Western Technology and Soviet Economic Development, 1917-1930* (Stanford: The Hoover Institution, 1968). The same evidence, however, lends itself to another interpretation; namely, that the USSR demonstrated its capacity to do what a developing country ought to do—to advance its development by making the maximal use of the opportunity to borrow the technology of more advanced countries. See the author's critique of Sutton's book in *The Journal of Economic Literature*, Vol. 8:3 (September 1970), pp. 844-845.

17. The studies by Sutton, cited in the preceding note, constitute the most extensive documentation of Soviet borrowing of foreign technology.

18. The "advantages of backwardness" are analyzed by Alexander Gerschenkron in *Economic Backwardness in Historical Perspective* (Cambridge: Harvard University Press, 1962), especially pp. 5-30.

19. The differences in the development strategies of pioneers and followers are studied in Joseph S. Berliner, "The Economics of Overtaking and Surpassing," in Henry Rosovsky, ed., *Industrialization in Two Systems: Essays in Honor of Alexander Gerschenkron* (New York: Wiley, 1966), pp. 159-185.

20. Bergson, *Soviet Post-War Economic Development*, p. 16.

21. The discussion to follow summarizes the paper, Joseph S. Berliner, "Some International

Aspects of Soviet Technological Progress," *South Atlantic Quarterly*, Vol. 72:3 (Summer 1973), pp. 340-350.

22. Except for the other technologically advanced socialist countries, particularly the German Democratic Republic and Czechoslovakia. The effect of the postwar Western embargo on the USSR was considerably diminished by the accessibility of the technology of those countries.

23. Franklyn D. Holzman, *Foreign Trade under Central Planning* (Cambridge: Harvard University Press, 1974), especially Part IV.

24. Campbell, "Management Spillovers," p. 607.

25. Nancy Nimitz arrives at this same conclusion on the basis of her study of Soviet military R & D. Nimitz, *Structure*, pp. 58-61.

26. *Voprosy ekonomiki*, 1967, No. 3, p. 24.

27. *Planovoe khoziaistvo*, 1966, No. 3, p. 14.

28. A. M. Matlin, *Tekhnicheskii progress i tseny mashin* (Moscow: *Ekonomika*, 1966), p. 82.

29. The term "cultural" is used here not in its anthropological sense but in the conventional Russian sense, meaning "style," or propriety, or general personal attainment.

30. On the preference of American corporations for low-risk alternatives, see R. Nelson, M. Peck, and E. Kalachek, *Technology, Economic Growth, and Public Policy* (Washington: The Brookings Institution, 1967), pp. 54-55, ftn. 14.

31. The role of illegal activity in enterprise management is discussed in Joseph S. Berliner, *Factory and Manager in the USSR* (Cambridge: Harvard University Press, 1957), Chaps. 11, 12. For more recent material on the subject, see Zev Katz, "Insights from Emigrés and Sociological Studies on the Soviet Economy," U.S. Congress, Joint Economic Committee, *Soviet Economic Prospects for the Seventies* (Washington: Government Printing Office, 1973), pp. 88-94.

32. C. F. Carter and B. R. Williams, *Investment in Innovation* (London: Oxford University Press, 1958), pp. 57-58. It is interesting to note that the larger the number of innovations a firm had introduced, the more they tended to give "active" reasons for innovating.

33. Nelson, Peck, Kalachek, *Technology*, p. 71.

34. We refer here only to this single aspect of competition. There are other aspects that inhibit innovation. See C. F. Carter and B. R. Williams, *Industry and Technical Progress* (London: Oxford University Press, 1959), Chap. 15.

35. *Barron's*, March 22, 1971.

36. *Literaturnaia Gazeta*, 1967, No. 2 (January 11), p. 10. Translated in *Current Digest of the Soviet Press*, Vol. 14:5 (February 22, 1967), p. 11. Professor Birman cannot quite bring himself to support fully the thrust of this strong position. In another article he writes, "In conditions of capitalism 'natural selection' of businessmen is in progress daily and hourly. . . . Entrepreneurs who are inept at maneuvering go down the drain. Some economists think a drain is necessary for us too, or else economic accountability will be a mere formality. We do not share this opinion: in economics, as in pedagogy, more can be achieved through encouragement than through punishment." *Novy mir*, 1967, No. 1. Translated in *Current Digest of the Soviet Press*, Vol. 19:13 (April 19, 1967), p. 16.

37. R. R. Nelson, "The Economics of Invention: A Survey of the Literature," *Journal of Business*, Vol. 32:2 (April 1959), p. 109.

38. A. D. Little, *Patterns and Problems*, p. 174.

39. Nelson, Peck, and Kalachek, *Technology*, p. 71.

40. Richard S. Morse, "The Technological Gap," *Industrial Management Review*, 8:2 (Spring 1967), p. 87.

41. Robert Charpie, Director of Technology, Union Carbide Corporation, in National Science Foundation, *Proceedings of a Conference on Technology Transfer and Innovation* (Washington: Government Printing Office, 1966), pp. 48-49.

42. A. D. Little, *Patterns and Problems*, p. 174.

43. *Novy mir*, 1967, No. 1, translated in *The Current Digest of the Soviet Press*, Vol. 19:13 (April

19, 1967), p. 10. Personal risk is often reduced by decisions that shift the burden to the State. Lenin Prize laureate Dr. M. Nemtsov argues, for example, that excessive resources are expended on the construction of pilot and experimental plants to minimize the risk of failure in production. If a small portion of those resources were used instead for more theoretical work and micromodeling, one could move directly from applied research to production with only a slight increase in risk. (*Ekonomicheskaia gazeta*, 1968, No. 8, p. 20.) The construction of pilot plants secures a small reduction in risk at very high cost. But the risk is personal, while the cost is the State's.

44. *Voprosy ekonomiki*, 1968, No. 3, p. 133.

Anisimov, G. D., *Printsip material'noi zainteresovannosti v razvitii novoi tekhniki* (The Principle of Material Incentives in the Development of New Technology). Moscow: *Ekonomizdat*, 1962.

Anisimov, G. D., and I. A. Vakhlamov (compilers), *Material'noe stimulirovanie vnedreniia novoi tekhniki: Spravochnik* (Material Incentives for Introducing New Technology: A Handbook). Moscow: *Ekonomika*, 1966.

Anisimov, G. D., et al. (eds.), *Nauchno-tekhnicheskii progress i khoziaistvennaia reforma* (Scientific-Technical Progress and Economic Reform). Moscow: *Nauka*, 1969.

Baskin, A. I., et al., *Sovershenstvovat' material'no-tekhnicheskoe snabzhenie* (Improve the Supply System). Moscow: *Znanie*, 1969.

Becker, Abraham S., "The Price Level of Soviet Machinery in the 1960's," *Soviet Studies*, XXVI:3, July 1974, pp. 363-379.

Belousov, R. A. (ed.), *Sovremennaia praktika tsenoobrazovaniia* (Current Pricing Practice). Moscow: *Ekonomika*, 1965.

Bereznoi, N. I., and A. I. Zhdanov (eds.), *Spravochnik ekonomista i planovika promyshlennogo predpriiatiia* (Handbook for Economists and Planners in Industrial Enterprises). Moscow: *Ekonomika*, 1964.

Bergson, Abram, *The Economics of Soviet Planning*. New Haven: Yale University Press, 1964.

_____, *Soviet Post-War Economic Development*. Stockholm: Almqvist & Wiksell, 1974.

Bergson, Abram, and Simon Kuznets (eds.), *Economic Trends in the Soviet Union*. Cambridge: Harvard University Press, 1963.

Berliner, Joseph S., "The Economics of Overtaking and Surpassing," in Henry Rosovsky (ed.), *Industrialization in Two Systems: Essays in Honor of Alexander Gerschenkron*. New York: Wiley, 1966, pp. 159-185.

_____, *Factory and Manager in the USSR*. Cambridge: Harvard University Press, 1957.

_____, "Managerial Incentives and Decisionmaking: A Comparison of the United States and the Soviet Union," in U.S. Congress Joint Economic Committee, *Comparisons of the United States and Soviet Economies.* Washington: Government Printing Office, 1959, pp. 349-376.

_____, "Some International Aspects of Soviet Technological Progress," *South Atlantic Quarterly*, 72:3, Summer 1973, pp. 340-350.

Bienstock, Gregory; S. M. Schwartz; and A. Yugow, *Management in Russian Industry and Agriculture.* New York: Oxford University Press, 1944.

Boretsky, Michael, "Comparative Progress in Technology, Productivity and Economic Efficiency: U.S.S.R. Versus U.S.A.," in U.S. Congress, Joint Economic Committee, *New Directions in the Soviet Economy.* Washington: Government Printing Office, 1966, pp. 133-256.

Boston Consulting Group, Inc., *Perspectives on Experience.* Boston: 1970.

Brown, Emily Clark, *Soviet Trade Unions and Labor Relations.* Cambridge: Harvard University Press, 1966.

Brozen, Yale, "R and D Differences Among Industries," in Richard A. Tybout (ed.), *Economics of Research and Development.* Columbus: Ohio State University Press, 1965.

Campbell, Robert W., *The Economics of Soviet Oil and Gas.* Baltimore: Johns Hopkins University Press, 1968.

_____, "Management Spillovers from Soviet Space and Military Programmes," *Soviet Studies* XXIII:4, April 1972, pp. 590-602.

Carter, C. F., and B. R. Williams, *Industry and Technical Progress.* London: Oxford University Press, 1957.

_____, *Investment in Innovation.* London: Oxford University Press, 1958.

Charpie, Robert, "The Business End of Technology Transfer," in U.S. National Science Foundation, *Technology Transfer and Innovation.* Washington, 1966.

Conquest, Robert (ed.), *Industrial Workers in the USSR.* New York: Praeger, 1967.

Droginskii, N. E., and V. G. Starodubrovskii (eds.), *Osnovy i praktika khoziaistvennoi reformy v SSSR* (The Basis and Practice of the USSR Economic Reform). Moscow: *Ekonomika*, 1971.

Efimov, A. N., *Sovetskaia industriia* (Soviet Industry). Moscow: *Ekonomika*, 1967.

Egizarian, G. A., and L. S. Kheifets, *Problemy material'nogo stimulirovaniia v promyshlennosti* (Problems of Material Incentives in Industry). Moscow: *Ekonomika*, 1970.

Ekonomika promyshlennykh predpriiatii: uchebnik (Textbook on the Economics of Industrial Enterprises). Moscow: *Gospolitizdat*, 1962.

Fatiukha, L. K., and E. A. Livshits, *Ekonomicheskoe stimulirovanie osvoeniia i vnedreniia novoi tekhniki* (Economic Incentives for Innovation). Moscow: *Ekonomika*, 1971.

Federenko, N. P., et al. (eds.), *Planirovanie i ekonomiko-matematicheskie metody* (Planning and Mathematical-Economic Methods). Moscow: *Nauka*, 1964.

Feshbach, Murray, and Stephen Rapawy, "Labor Constraints in the Five-Year Plan," in U.S. Congress, Joint Economic Committee, *Soviet Economic Prospects for the Seventies.* Washington: Government Printing Office, 1973.

Gatovskii, L. M., "Ekonomicheskaia nauka i nekotorye problemy tekhnicheskogo progressa" (The Science of Economics and Some Problems of Technical Progress). *Voprosy ekonomiki*, 1965, No. 12, pp. 13-14.

_____ et al. (eds.), *Plan, khozraschet, stimuly* (The Plan, Business Accounting, and Incentives). Moscow: *Ekonomika*, 1966.

_____ et al. (eds.), *Problemy ekonomicheskogo stimulirovaniia nauchno-tekhnicheskogo progressa* (Problems of Economic Incentives for Scientific and Technological Progress). Moscow: *Nauka*, 1967.

Goldman, Marshall I., *The Spoils of Progress: Environmental Pollution in the Soviet Union.* Cambridge: The MIT Press, 1972.

Gorlin, Alice C., "The Soviet Economic Associations," *Soviet Studies* XXVI:1, January 1974, pp. 3-27.

Granick, David, *Management of the Industrial Firm in the USSR.* New York: Columbia University Press, 1954.

_____, "Management Incentives in the USSR and in Western Firms," *Journal of Comparative Administration* V:2, August 1973, pp. 169-199.

_____ , *Managerial Comparisons of Four Developed Countries: France, Britain, United States, and Russia.* Cambridge: The MIT Press, 1972.

_____ , *Soviet Metal-Fabricating and Economic Development: Practice Versus Policy.* Madison: University of Wisconsin Press, 1967.

Grossman, Gregory, "Industrial Prices in the USSR," *American Eco-*

nomic Review XLIX:2, May 1959, pp. 50-64.

_____, "Information and Innovation in the Soviet Economy," *American Economic Review* LVI:2, May 1966, pp. 118-129.

_____, "Notes for a Theory of the Command Economy," *Soviet Studies* XV:2, October 1963, pp. 103-123.

_____, "Scarce Capital and Soviet Doctrine," *Quarterly Journal of Economics* LXVII:3, August 1953, pp. 311-343.

Hunter, Holland, "Optimum Tautness in Developmental Planning," *Economic Development and Cultural Change*, Vol. 9, July 1961, pp. 561-572.

Ivanov, N. V.; E. Iu. Lokshin; and F. M. Demichev, *Ekonomika i planirovanie material'no-tekhnicheskogo snabzhenia promyshlennosti* (The Economics and Planning of Supply in Industry). Moscow: *Ekonomika*, 1969.

Jackson, Marvin R., *Soviet Project and Design Organizations: Technological Decision-Making in a Command Economy*. Ph.D. dissertation, University of California, Berkeley, 1967.

Jewkes, John; D. Sawers; and R. Stillerman, *The Sources of Invention*. New York: St. Martin's Press, 1958.

Khoziaistvannaia reforma USSR (Economic Reform in the USSR). Moscow: *Pravda*, 1969 (1969 Supplement to *Ekonomicheskaia gazeta*).

Kirsch, Leonard J., *Soviet Wages: Changes in Structure and Administration since 1956*. Cambridge: The MIT Press, 1972.

Komin, A. N., *Problemy planovogo tsenoobrazovaniia* (Problems of Planned Pricing). Moscow: *Ekonomika*, 1971.

Kornai, Janos, *Overcentralization in Economic Administration*. London: Oxford University Press, 1959.

Korol, Alexander G., *Soviet Research and Development: Its Organization, Personnel, and Funds*. Cambridge: The MIT Press, 1965.

Kovalevskii, A. M., *Tekhpromfinplan v novykh usloviakh i tipovaia metodika ego razrabotki* (The Enterprise Plan under the New Conditions and the Standard Manual for Preparing It). Moscow: *Ekonomika*, 1968.

Kulikov, A. G.; V. G. Lebedev; N. A. Razumov; and A. P. Cherdnickenko (eds.), *Ekonomicheskie problemy uskoreniia tekhnicheskogo progressa v promyshlennosti* (Economic Problems of Accelerating Technological Progress in Industry). Moscow: *Mysl'*, 1964.

Lagutkin, V. M. (ed.), *Proizvodstvennye ob'edineniia: problemy i perspektivy* (Production Associations: Problems and Perspectives). Moscow: *Mysl'*, 1971.

Lange, Oskar, and Fred M. Taylor, *On the Economic Theory of Socialism.* Minneapolis: University of Minnesota Press, 1938.

Lerner, Abba P., *The Economics of Control.* New York: Macmillan, 1946.

Levine, Herbert S., "The Centralized Planning of Supply in Soviet Industry," in U.S. Congress, Joint Economic Committee, *Comparisons of the United States and Soviet Economies.* Washington: Government Printing Office, 1959, pp. 151-176.

Little, A. D., Inc., *Patterns and Problems of Technical Innovation in American Industry,* Report to the U.S. National Science Foundation (PB 181573), September 1963.

Lutokhina, E. A., *Oplata truda inzhinerno-tekhnicheskikh rabotnikov* (Earnings of Engineering and Technical Employees). Moscow: *Ekonomika,* 1966.

McAuley, Mary, *Labor Disputes in Soviet Russia 1957-1965.* London: Oxford University Press, 1969.

Maevskii, I. V., *Tekhnicheskii progress i rost proizvoditel'nosti truda* (Technical Progress and the Growth of Labor Productivity). Moscow: *Ekonomizdat,* 1963.

Mansfield, Edwin, *The Economics of Technological Change.* New York: Norton, 1968.

_____ , *Industrial Research and Technological Innovation.* New York: Norton, 1968.

Matlin, A. M. *Plan, tsena i effektivnost' proizvodstva* (Plan, Price, and Production Efficiency). Moscow: *Ekonomika,* 1970.

_____ , *Tekhnicheskii progress i tseny mashin* (Technical Progress and Machinery Prices). Moscow: *Ekonomika,* 1966.

Montias, John M., "Planning with Material Balances in Soviet-Type Economies," *American Economic Review* XLIX:5, December 1959, pp. 963-985.

Moorsteen, Richard, *Prices and Production of Machinery in the Soviet Union, 1928-1958.* Cambridge: Harvard University Press, 1962.

Morse, Dean, and Aaron W. Warner, *Technological Innovation and Society.* New York: Columbia University Press, 1966.

Mstislavskii, P. S.; M. G. Gabrieli; and Iu. V. Borozdin, *Ekonomicheskoe obosnovanie optovykh tsen na novuiu promyshlennuiu produktsiiu* (The Economic Basis of Wholesale Pricing of New Industrial Products). Moscow: *Nauka*, 1968.

National Bureau of Economic Research. *The Rate and Direction of Inventive Activity: Economic and Social Factors*. Princeton: Princeton University Press, 1962.

Nelson, Richard R., "The Economics of Invention: A Survey of the Literature," *Journal of Business* XXXII:2, April 1959, pp. 101-127.

Nelson, Richard R.; Merton J. Peck; and Edward Kalachek, *Technology, Economic Growth, and Public Policy*. Washington: The Brookings Institution, 1967.

Nimitz, Nancy, *The Structure of Soviet Outlays on R & D in 1960 and 1968*. RAND Report R-1207-DDRE. Santa Monica, Calif., 1974.

Nolting, Louvan E., *Sources of Financing the Stages of the Research, Development, and Innovation Cycle in the U.S.S.R.* Foreign-Economic Report No. 3. U.S. Department of Commerce, Bureau of Economic Analysis. Washington, 1973.

Nove, Alec, *The Soviet Economy* (rev. ed.). New York: Praeger, 1965.

Pisar, Samuel, *Coexistence and Commerce*. New York: McGraw-Hill, 1970.

Plotnikov, K. N., and A. S. Gusarov, *Sovremennye problemy teorii i praktiki tsenoobrozovaniia pri sotsializme* (Current Problems in the Theory and Practice of Pricing Under Socialism). Moscow: *Nauka*, 1971.

Richman, Barry, *Soviet Management*. Englewood Cliffs, N.J.: Prentice-Hall, 1965.

Rogovtsev, S., *Finansovoe planirovanie na promyshlennykh predpriiatiiakh* (Financial Planning in Industrial Enterprises). Moscow: *Finansy*, 1966.

Schmookler, Jacob, "Inventors Past and Present," *Review of Economics and Statistics*, Vol. 39, August 1957, pp. 321-331.

Schon, Donald A., *Technology and Change*. New York: Delacorte, 1967.

Sherman, Howard J., "Marxist Economics and Soviet Planning," *Soviet Studies* XVIII:2, October 1966, pp. 169-188.

Skvortsov, L. I., *Tseny i tsenoobrozovanie v SSSR* (Prices and Price Formation in the U.S.S.R.). Moscow: *Vysshaia Shkola*, 1972.

Sominskii, V. S., *Ekonomika novykh proizvodstv* (The Economics of New Production). Moscow: *Ekonomika*, 1965.

Spechler, Martin C., *The Economics of Product Quality in Soviet Industry*. Ph.D. thesis, Harvard University, May 1971.

Stoliarov, S. G. *O tsenakh i tsenoobrazovanii v SSSR* (Prices and Price Formation in the U.S.S.R.) (third ed.). Moscow: *Statistika*, 1969.

Sutton, Antony C., *Western Technology and Soviet Economic Development* (3 vols.). Stanford: Hoover Institution, 1968.

Taksir, K. I., *Sushchnost' i formy soedineniia nauki s proizvodstvom pri sotsializme* (Essence and Forms of the Union of Science and Production Under Socialism). Moscow: *Vysshaia Shkola*, 1974.

"Tekhpromfinplan v novykh usloviakh" (The Enterprise Plan Under the New Conditions), (Anonymous), Supplement to *Ekonomicheskaia gazeta*, 1967, No. 22.

Turetskii, Sh. Ia. (ed.), *Tseny i tarify* (Prices and Service Charges). Moscow: *Vysshaia Shkola*, 1969.

Vasil'ev, E. K., and L. M. Chistiakova, *Effektivnost' oplaty upravlencheskogo truda v promyshlennosti* (Effectiveness of the Payment of Administrative Labor in Industry). Moscow: *Ekonomika*, 1972.

Ward, Benjamin, *The Socialist Economy: A Study of Organizational Alternatives*. New York: Random House, 1967.

Wiles, P. J. D., *The Political Economy of Communism*. Cambridge: Harvard University Press, 1962.

Yanowitch, M., "The Soviet Income Revolution," *Slavic Review* XXII:4, December 1963, pp. 683-697.

Zaleski, E.; J. A. Kozlowski; H. Wienert; R. W. Davies; M. J. Berry; and R. Amman, *Science Policy in the USSR*. Paris: OECD, 1969.

Zielinski, J. G., *Economic Reforms in Polish Industry*. London: Oxford University Press, 1973.

Index

Industry, as focus of study, 2

Inflation, 320

Informal behavior, 167, 373

Innovation: advances careers, 477, 505; "advocacy" of, 223-224; bunching of, 417, 420, 442, 458; and capital investment, 175; capital-saving, 168, 442-443; defined, 3-4; first to introduce, 262; by "invasion," 222-223, 534; labor-saving, 160-161, 167-168; and labor supply, 156-169; lead times, 102, 203, 264, 268, 459; by order, 504-505; and organizational autonomy, 141-142; output declines during, 413-415; planning of, 43-47; rate of, defined, 4-5; resistance to, 3, 372-373, 524; rewards for, relative to noninnovation, 487-489, 521; rules, 435; social, 23 n1; stages of, 103-104, 107; unsuccessful, costs of borne by state, 536; user requirements ignored in, 217; *see also* Bonus Fund, Innovation

Innovation associations, 132

Innovation decision, influence on: of credit-financed investment, 178-179, 195; of economic structure, 7-8; of financial resources, 171; of New Products Fund, 203-204; of operating rules, 402; of other enterprise decisions, 29; of price administration, 368-373; of Production Development Fund, 186-190; of profit, 296, 426; of technological bias, 355-356

Innovation, pressure for: by Party, 41; quality of innovation declines because of, 378-379; spurious innovation stimulated by, 378

Innovation, process, 4, 183, 195, 198, 418; under classical rules, 415-419; cost targets encourage, 258; declining cost in, 270-271; emphasized over product innovation, 204; under Reform rules (1965), 441-443; *see also* New processes

Innovation, product, 4, 183, 198; under classical rules, 413-415; financing of, 195-204; increases costs, 258; less frequent than process innovation, 204; low profit rates discourage, 250; neglected in 1930s, 195-198; under Reform rules (1965), 438-441; and time horizon, 297; *see also* New products

Innovation, small-scale, 53-54; classical rules encouraged, 416; economic value of, 54, 339; excessive rewards for, 339; profit-rate ceiling encourages, 350

Innovation, sources of: borrowed foreign technology, 513-518, innovation by order, 504-505; priority sectors, 505-510; scientific and technical manpower, 503-504, socialization of knowledge, 510-513

Innovation, spurious, 334, 375-380, 418, 573; increases administrative burden, 379; sales-revenue rule discourages, 441; temporary prices stimulated, 377

Innovations: as ideas, 97; number of, as measure of innovativeness, 457-459; postponed until new plan period, 420; productivity of, ignored in pricing, 302-305

Innovations, initiation of: in enterprises, 53-55, 201; in government agencies, 48-50; in ministries, 50-52; in R&D organizations, 52-53

Innovative effort, income elasticity of, 490, 492-493, 535-538

Institute for Scientific and Technical Information, 510

Interest: and capital charge, 243; and cost calculations, 241; on investment credits, 178-180; on State Bank credits, 191-193, 212

Interest groups, 78

Inventions, 328, 333; rewards for, 450-451, 461, 463

Inventories, 90-92, 213-215

Inventors, individual, 108-111

Investment: centralized, 175-181; choice, debate over, 452, 454; decentralized, 181-195

Jewkes, J., 108

Kachalov, N., 3
Kalachek, E., 259
Kapitsa, P. L., 3
Karpati, P., 357
Khatchaturov, T. S., 342, 468
Khrushchev, N. S., 97, 106
Komin, A. N., 361
Kostousov, A., 112
Kosygin, A. N., 254, 315
Krasovskii, V. P., 283
Kurskii, A., 189
Kvasha, Ia. V., 34, 283

Labor: effects of technological progress on, 155; forecasting requirements of, 157; hoarding of, 165-167; and innovation, 156-158, 167; mobility, 166; supply, organiza-